BETA ALPHA PSI, FROM OMEGA TO ZETA OMEGA: THE MAKING OF A COMPREHENSIVE ACCOUNTING FRATERNITY, 1946–1984

Terry K. Sheldahl

Garland Publishing, Inc.
New York and London
1986

For a complete list of Garland's publications in accounting
please see the final pages of this volume.

Acknowledgement is made to the following for photographs reproduced in this book: *Beta Alpha Psi national files*: Exhibit no. 25; McConahey; Alpha Rho Chapter; Smally; Nu Chapter; Sigma Chapter team; Beamer presenting award; Stone and Taylor; Penz in office; Alpha Chapter banner; Daiker and Grady; Niswonger; Dean, Roger, and Olsen; Van Voorhis; Hay and Dixon; Hay, ca. 1960; Odmark and Penz; Golden Anniversary gathering; National Advisory Forum; National Councils; Donley and Moorehead; Accountants of the Year; Southeast Regional Meeting; National Student Meeting; American Accounting Association and Beta Alpha Psi headquarters; Harke; Matthews; National Councils, 1982, 1983; Graduate Case Analysis team. *Theata Chapter*: Exhibit no. 15. *Robert S. Maust*: Exhibit no. 23. *Miami University Archives*: Skelton. *C. Aubrey Smith*: Tierney; Bickham. *University of Arkansas Archives*: Cook; Alpha Iota Chapter. *New York University Archives*: Campfield. *University of California, Berkeley, Archives*: Lambda Chapter. *A. J. Penz*: Penzes and their home. *Arthur Anderson & Co.*: Claire. *Omicron Chapter*: Omicron Student Seminar; J. Mueller with Omicron Chapter; Omicron Chapter alumni members. *Charles W. Taylor*: Taylor. *American Accounting Association*: Hayes and Gonzalez.

Library of Congress Cataloging-in-Publication Data

Sheldahl, Terry K.
Beta Alpha Psi, from Omega to Zeta Omega.

(Accounting thought and practice through the years)
Bibliography: p.
Includes indexes.
1. Beta Alpha Psi—History. 2. Accounting—United States—Societies, etc.—History. I. Title.
II. Series.
HF5601.B443S54 1986 657'.06'073 86-31800
ISBN 0-8240-7855-1

Design by Bonnie Goldsmith

The volumes in this series are printed on acid-free, 250-year-life paper.

Printed in the United States of America.

This monograph is part of the history project sponsored and supported by the National Council of Beta Alpha Psi. Although many members of Beta Alpha Psi reviewed and commented on various drafts of the manuscript, the author is soley responsible for this work.

Project Directors:

Richard W. Metcalf, University of Nebraska-Lincoln, 1983-1985
David E. Tinius, Seattle University, 1985-1987

National Council of Beta Alpha Psi - 1987

Board of Directors:

Joe R. Fritzemeyer, Arizona State University, President
Jan R. Williams, University of Tennessee, President Elect and Director of Publications
William R. Welke, Western Michigan University, Director of Chapter Activites
Donald L. Tang, Portland State University, Director of Administration
Richard J. Murdock, The Ohio State University, Past President
M. Douglas Ivester, The Coca-Cola Company, Chairman Advisory Forum
Karen L. Mackiewicz, Touche Ross & Co., Alumni Representative
Macey S. Winn, Price Waterhouse, Alumni Representative

Councilors:

Robert M. Brown, Virginia Tech
F. Eugene Butts, Appalachian State University
Ted D. Skekel, North Texas State University
Michael R. Lane, Bradley University
William M. Voss, Ohio University
Mary Soulier Ziebell, Seattle University

JAMES M. McCONAHEY, Ca. 1939, year of his election to Grand Council

To the memory of

JAMES M. McCONAHEY (1875-1955), Delta '21,
National President, 1941-47, and Charter
Beta Alpha Psi Historian, 1948-54

LIST OF CHAPTERS

TABLE OF CONTENTS

Part 2. The Moderate Reformist (or Fourth) Era, 1961-70

LIST OF EXHIBITS

PREFACE

This book is a sequel to a history of Beta Alpha Psi's first quarter century that appeared four years ago. Starting with chapter reactivation directly after World War II, it concludes, officially, with the year 1983-84. As with the earlier volume, broad and detailed coverage is structured in terms of distinct "eras" embodying dominant themes, in this case fundamental ones (notably expansion, participation, and reform) that do not end with the emergence of new defining elements. In dating the four periods recognized, one of them still in progress as the study ends, calendar years were used. The references in the title to 1946 and 1984, for example, represent the respective fraternal years 1945-46 and 1983-84, each ending with a late-summer meeting of the Grand or National Council.

With a partial exception in regard to part 1, relating to the years 1946-60, "perennial" fraternal topics approached in the first volume through separate chapters have been integrated within overall treatment of each era. Coverage is oriented basically toward the national fraternity, and the work of the governing Council. All 162 chapters that had been formed as of the summer of 1984, 139 of them (counting a reactivated unit) since the war, are cited at least once, however. By happenstance, several of those references, primarily to groups installed after 1979, are limited to appendix material not included within the index. As the study progresses, increasing attention is given to the relationship between the structure and composition of the National Council and the development of the national program. Coverage of the fifth and sixth eras (as numbered consecutively

from the fraternity's origin), 1971-84, is in good measure organized along those lines.

Inclusion of an index, along with one (more elaborately organized) for volume 1, will assist readers in locating material of particular personal interest. The proper-name indexes complement the topic-oriented tables of contents. As a unified historical narrative, however, the work is not especially suited to use as a reference manual that is consulted mainly for narrowly defined purposes of the moment.

This book documents a vital element in the education of American accountants since 1945. Its potential audience thus extends beyond persons affiliated with Beta Alpha Psi, and those with a special interest in relevant historical fields, to the nation's accounting educators and professional accountants in general. With this thought in mind, every effort has been made to combine reliable scholarship with readable and interesting coverage. Current and future leaders of the fraternity, particularly at the national level, may find this interpretation of nearly four decades of development to be useful in one way or another relative to their own service. Local chapters may wish to make use of some of the material within their programs.

I wish warmly to thank the Board of Directors of Beta Alpha Psi for commissioning this study in 1984, and providing financial support during the two years of preparation. Special thanks are due to Richard Metcalf and David Tinius, for taking leadership roles in initiating the study, and serving as supportive project directors. I am likewise grateful to Thomas Burns, the first project director on the earlier volume, for his contribution as an ex-councilor to the invitation extended me to resume the historical work; and to Garland series editor Richard Brief, for accepting the study for publication, in 1984, at the very beginning of its development,

and for graciously and significantly extending the time limits for completion, as the dimensions of the project became clear. At a broader level, I much appreciate the support of Gary John Previts, who enthusiastically endorsed my embarking on a new Beta Alpha Psi volume at a time that the two of us were discussing a major research collaboration.

This work was enriched immeasurably by material obtained from interviews conducted with twenty-two former national presidents, counting the written responses of Vern Odmark and Harold Royer, and a tape recording submitted by prewar president C. Aubrey Smith. The interviewing was based, in general, on flexible use of the questionnaire presented as appendix 1, or a similar earlier version. A number of the leaders have generously responded to one or (usually) more follow-up inquiries, including Henry Anderson, Wilton Anderson, Thomas Burns, Doris Cook, Leon Hay, Robert Maust, Fred Mueller, James Pattillo, Williard Stone, Vern Vincent, and Robert Wasley. I am especially indebted to Professor Mueller for providing a wealth of vital source material retained from his days as secretary-treasurer.

Although interviews could not be arranged, 1953-54 president S. M. Wedeberg and recent leaders Joyce Dean, Jack Kiger, and Richard Metcalf also provided valuable information. A 1979 visit to the newly opened national office in Sarasota, arranged by interim national administrator Kenneth Matthews, yielded useful material selected for my attention by Secretary-Treasurer Dean, and files that underlie coverage of Mu and Alpha Chapters developed in chapters 4 and 6. Executive Secretary Nancy Harke without fail replied promptly, and fully, to my many requests for information from national headquarters. Nonfaculty councilors Albert Cohen, Nicholas Ecos, Thomas Nessinger, and Andrew Rosman, and National Advisory Forum members Robert Maynard and Robert Pivik, made excellent contributions to the study regarding their own major areas of participation.

The Beta Alpha Psi community in general is indebted to A. J. Penz for developing original essay material edited to form the bulk of chapter 7. Three writeups on his international and post-retirement activities were reluctantly omitted, based on absence of Beta Alpha Psi themes.

Photographs were obtained from, or authorized for use by, many sources besides national fraternal files supplied, in part, by Doris Cook and Vern Odmark. They include Thomas Burns, Thomas Nessinger, Paul Gerhardt, and Bobbe Barnes, from Omicron Chapter, Arthur Andersen & Co., the American Accounting Association, and Theta Chapter; former national presidents Penz, Smith, Maust, and Charles Taylor; and archivists at the Universities of Arkansas and California (Berkeley), Miami University, and New York University. Professor Taylor also provided voluminous files on the 1969 golden-anniversary observance that largely underlie the latter half of chapter 11.

Beyond the photographic realm, many university archivists made important contributions to this book, including but not limited to those from the twenty campuses surveyed in 1985 on the participation of black students within Beta Alpha Psi chapters during the first postwar era. I would borrow at this point an adaptation made by historian Joel Williamson (an authority, coincidentally, on American race relations) from lines attributed to medieval poet Omar Khayyam:

> I wonder often what the archivists buy
> One half so precious as the stuff they absolutely give away.

Several current or former chapter advisors and a number of deans and other academic officials have supplied information requested, as have representatives of the American Accounting Association and the National Association of Accountants. For making possible the extensive coverage provided of the relationship between Beta Alpha Psi and the American Assembly of Collegiate Schools of Business, I am highly indebted to AACSB

officials Milton Blood, James Viehland, and Sharon Barber. Finally, I wish to thank all fraternal alumni, professors, and practicing accountants not already covered who have generously contributed content for this study.

Four persons deserve warm thanks for their very dedicated, and substantial, labors in the production of this volume. My wife Mary Jane typed chapters 1-7 and 9, and Linda Haynie of Savannah typed the balance of the text, excluding chapter 8. The two indexes are based on minor refinements of extremely detailed data collections produced by Deveaux Donley of Jackson, Miss. (vol. 1), and Laura Callahan of Savannah (vol. 2).

Leo Parrish, my dean at Savannah State, enabled me to finish the book earlier than would otherwise have been possible by arranging for me a very flexible schedule during the current fall term. Finally, I want to thank my family for unique contributions without which the study would never have been completed. Mary Jane's patience and (certainly) her gainful employment were vital factors, besides the typing, along with the support of our parents, Mr. and Mrs. Everett Sheldahl of Delaware, Ark. and Mr. and Mrs. John Sullivan of Savannah.

Comments from readers would be welcome.

Terry K. Sheldahl

Savannah State College
Savannah, Georgia
September 30, 1986.

PART 1. THE POSTWAR EXPANSION-IST (OR THIRD) ERA, 1946-60

CHAPTER 1

REACTIVATING THE CHAPTERS, AND "OPENING THE GATES" TO WOMEN AND MINORITIES

The phrase "Postwar Expansionist Era" sums up the major themes within Beta Alpha Psi over a period, 1946-60, of significant growth at a variety of levels. To provide a base for growth, reactivation of twenty-one local chapters was already underway when the Grand Council held its first postwar meeting in September 1946. Regular communication of encouragement and support from the Council contributed to the virtual completion of that process over the following year.

The remainder of the period was "expansionist" in several fundamental ways, as shown in chapters 1-6. First, as discussed presently, the fraternity "opened the gates" of membership to women students by amending its constitution; and to racial and religious minorities, already constitutionally eligible, by taking meaningful initiatives suited to broad social currents.

Second, the chapter roster both grew at a pace previously unknown within Beta Alpha Psi and reached a group of campuses more diversified than earlier sites. Third, such developments combined with nationwide growth in higher education to produce annual membership increases far exceeding prewar levels, inviting enhanced fraternal interest in alumni status.

Marked expansion required expanded means of fraternal control by the Grand Council, serving to promote active local chapters. Fourth, then, the Council introduced a formal "ratings" or "activity" program, and resumed chapter "visitation" at a rate comparable to that of a

flourishing but very brief span just prior to the Depression.

Reactivation was already in progress when a bare quorum of Grand Councilors assembled in Chicago at the beginning of the academic year 1946-47 to resume national operations of Beta Alpha Psi. A useful initiative had been taken the previous spring by one of the two absentees. The Council took a more decisive step by voting for immediate resumption of the fraternal periodical, within whose pages widespread chapter activity would be reported during the year.

Reactivation, 1945-47

Developments Prior to Fall 1946, Taking Note of Elwell's Letter

As related in volume 1, there had been some renewal of chapter operations during the school year 1945-46 and the following summer. Five chapters had initiated 33 men in the fall, more than the number inducted the prior year, and thirteen chapters had averaged more than ten initiates each (for a total of some 140) over the spring and summer. Six groups had added no members for three or more years, however, with the isolated exception of one person in 1943-44. Only Nu Chapter at Colorado submitted an audit report for the year, a situation that Secretary-Treasurer Fayette H. Elwell found "readily understandable" since reactivation had often occurred late in the school year, or over the summer months.

Elwell had written listed faculty advisors across the nation on April 20, 1946, "urging them to reactivate their chapters, so that each one" could "be going at full force not later than" the fall. Although the impact of the letter is not known, during the summer that followed at least four chapters were reactivated or (in the case of Xi at Syracuse) conducted a large initiation. Thirty-eight or 39 members were inducted at Xi Chapter, Sigma at Wisconsin (Elwell's campus), Chi at Oklahoma A. and M., and Gamma at

Northwestern. The last two groups had been wholly inactive for three years. In addition, Omicron Chapter at Ohio State, Rho at Minnesota, and Beta at Oregon evidently initiated 25 members in late spring, and Lambda at Berkeley took in 17 students either then or in early summer.[1]

Reactivation had of course only begun, since initiation of members was scarcely the essence of a professional fraternal program, and six of the twenty-one chapters had not even reached that starting point. It was thus the central topic on the minds of the three men present at the Palmer House in Chicago for the first Grand Council meeting since 1941.

The First Postwar Grand Council Meeting

President James M. McConahey, Secretary-Treasurer Hazen W. Kendrick, and Councilor Thomas M. Dickerson met on September 7, 1946. "[U]navoidably absent" were Past President George E. Bennett and interim secretary-treasurer Elwell, the retiring councilor whose report covering the 44 months beginning December 1, 1942, highlighting his own 39 1/2 months of stewardship, was presented by Kendrick. Wartime president McConahey was presiding over his first meeting; Kendrick was resuming office following military discharge; and Dickerson was attending his first Coucil meeting. The combined group presented only three years of prewar membership on the governing body.

---

[1]Fayette H. Elwell to Grand Council of Beta Alpha Psi (Secretary-Treasurer's Report, [December 1, 1942], to July 31, 1946), August 1, 1946, p. 6, quoted; Grand Council Cashbook, 1931-49, pp. 54, 56; "Letters from Local Chapters," News Letter of Beta Alpha Psi (Newsletter) [2] (November 1946):8, 11; Terry K. Sheldahl, Beta Alpha Psi, from Alpha to Omega: Pursuing a Vision of Professional Education for Accountants, 1919-1945 (New York and London: Garland Publishing, 1982), p. 747; and Xi Chapter, Beta Alpha Psi: 1966 Directory, Syracuse University ([Syracuse, N.Y.: Xi Chapter, 1966]), "Date of Initiation Listing," s.v. "1946 - April, August." Given long, irregualr titles, references to secretary-treasurer reports will be simplified.

The Alpha to Omega tabulation omits the 1946 summer initiations of 14, 7, and 5 members at Xi, Chi, and Gamma Chapters, respectively, and understates by 1 the spring or summer totals at Xi, Theta at Texas, and (perhaps) Sigma. The overall total for the spring and summer was thus 140 or 141.

Considerable discussion of reactivation yielded no new policies, in regard for example to chapter reporting practices. Four low-cost visitations were tentatively planned, including trips to inspect Mu and Upsilon Chapters at New York (NYU) and Florida, both dormant since 1942. Also to be visited were Beta Chapter at Oregon and Gamma at Northwestern, a group whose first initiations in three years, made only twenty days earlier, had probably not as yet been reported. Still wholly inactive, besides Mu and and Epsilon, were Pi Chapter at Western Reserve, Councilor Dickerson's school; Alpha at Illinois, home of early presidents Scovill, Littleton, and Schlatter; Tau at Maryland; and Phi at Louisiana State. Dickerson may have planned to visit NYU in conjunction with his service as a member of the Committee on Accounting Procedure of the American Institute of Accountants, based in New York.

There is no indication that any of the visitations, at least three of which were intended to be made in coordination with independent business, was actually carried out. An action of broader importance to full-scale reactivation was taken as a result of the 1946 meeting, however. Publication of the Beta Alpha Psi Newsletter was resumed immediately, under the editorship of Kendrick.[2] That initiative may have itself have contributed vitally to the excellent progress that would be reported in the periodical over the next year.

Resumption of the Newsletter

Solicitation of chapter news, and publication of the reports, were

---

[2]Thomas M. Dickerson to Author, interview (Charlotte, N.C.), April 18, 1980; Grand Council of Beta Alpha Psi, National Minutes Book, 1922-63 (incomplete), entries for 1939 (p. [5]), 1940 (p. 2), 1941 (p. 4), 1946; "Letters from Local Chapters," Newsletter [2] (November 1946):8; and Sheldahl, Alpha to Omega, p. 747. The apparent absence of visitation in 1946-47 is documented in chapter 6.

ready methods of stimulating more than nominal reactivation. The Newsletter of November 1946 contained notices from ten of the twenty-one chapters, several of them current through the middle of the month listed. In general the remaining chapters reported significant activity in the two Newsletters issued the following spring.

Reports of Fall 1946

Alpha, Mu, Pi, and Phi Chapters were among the nonreporters, as were two groups that had in the spring or summer made their first inductions in three years, Zeta at North Dakota and Sigma at Wisconsin. The most active wartime chapter, Lambda at California at Berkeley, was ironically another unit providing no material for the first postwar issue.

Gamma Chapter reported merely that five members had been initiated at Evanston in August, and (through the accounting department chairman) Upsilon noted only that reactivation was "in full swing," a statement that was a bit premature in light of a report filed later in the year. Regular copy had been provided by eight local groups, as follows:

1. Delta at Washington had resumed operations in April after a lapse of nearly four years. For the balance of the semester, biweekly dinner meetings had been held, featuring papers by active members or outside speakers, and attracting many alumni members. Weekly dinner meetings were underway by early fall, and planning had already started for the traditional spring banquet

2. Theta at Texas had just conducted a barbeque for active members and thirty-four "member elects"

3. Iota at Southern California, reactivated a year earlier, was conducting an active program amidst large accounting enrollments

4. Nu at Colorado was basically inactive pending a December initiation (destined to be delayed a month by a coal shortage that would require an early holiday recess), because only one member had returned in the fall. The chapter president just elected, had transferred to Florida (although he would not be cited in later Upsilon Chapter reports)

5. Omicron at Ohio State was about to initiate more than twenty new members within a banquet setting shared with accounting sorority Lambda

Alpha Sigma, and would be participating actively in anniversary observances by the local accounting department and Institute of Accountancy

6. Tau at Maryland, anticipating resumption of regular monthly meetings the following semester, presented a number of alumni notes, including the loss of a charter member in the Pacific war

7. Chi at Oklahoma A. and M., revived during the summer, planned to hold semi-monthly meetings during the school year. All sixteen active members or pledges, including future Grand Council president Nolan E. Williams, were military veterans. Having accepted emblematic red and black ribbons at a smoker, the eight pledges were carrying out a chapter tradition by "wearing the traditional balance sheets" on campus

8. Omega at Miami University, just reactivated, was expecting to add a number of new members during the year and to conduct semi-monthly meetings.

The reference to the military backgrounds of all Chi Chapter students was particularly in keeping with President McConahey's opening "Greetings." He noted that as veterans flocked to the campuses, active members were likely to be "older and more mature" than their predecessors, being "anxious" to get settled in their chosen profession or business."

Favorable developments within the remaining chapters were reported in Newsletters of March and May, 1947, along with further progress at schools already noted.

Reports of Spring 1947

Gamma and Upsilon Chapters, which had earlier provided minimal information, reported in turn some difficulty in reorganization, despite initiation of 27 members during the year, and formal reactivation in March with induction of 37 students. The March report from Northwestern that election of officers had been delayed foreshadowed problems that would arise the following year. More positively, Tau Chapter was able to report revival during the spring semester, beginning with "[a]n impressive initiation and banquet."

Rho Chapter at Minnesota reported merely the induction of seven members.

Otherwise, the eleven groups not heard from earlier reported at least some measure of non-initiation activity, prospectively in the case of Beta Chapter at Oregon. Of the groups having been dormant for the longest duration, Mu at NYU conducted an extremely active program throughout the academic year; Phi at Louisiana State resumed operations in the fall, prior to hosting guest speakers at several banquet meetings, and Alpha at Illinois did so early in 1947; and Pi at Western Reserve was finally reactivated in late spring. New Members included future Beta Alpha Psi leaders Leon E. Hay, an Illinois undergraduate, and (in the summer) A. J. Penz, an LSU faculty member about to depart for the University of Alabama. Two years earlier, incidentally, Professor Hay's future wife had been a student of "Andy" Penz at Baton Rouge. Bobbye Hay would become a certified public accountant, and much later (1981-83) serve as an accounting instructor at the University of Arkansas.[3]

Overall, the year 1946-47 was extremely successful for Beta Alpha Psi.

Retrospective on the Year 1946-47, Noting Isolated, and Brief, Reactivation Delays

During the year the twenty-one chapters initiated 745 men as active members, more than double any prewar total, and fourteen of them submitted audit reports. Accounting was clearly a popular field of study among

---

[3] "Chapter News Items," Newsletter [2] (March 1947):8-13, (May 1947):10-17, passim in each case; James R. Hasselback, comp., Prentice-Hall Accounting Faculty Directory: 1983 and . . . Directory: 1984 (Englewood Cliffs, N.J.: Prentice-Hall, 1983, 1984), "Alphabetical by School," s.v. "University of Arkansas"; "Letters from the Local Chapters," and Jas. A. McConahey, "The President's Page," Newsletter [2] (November 1946):8-12, 4, quoting pp. 4, 11; A. J. Penz, Resume (University of Alabama), May 1969, as revised [April 1985], p. 2; and Penz to Author, interview (Columbia, S.C.), April 18, 1980. The resume cited was, in its original form, part of the 1968-69 "Golden Anniversary Files" developed by Secretary-Treasurer Charles W. Taylor.

The Chi Chapter pledge tradition would later be adapted by Alpha Iota Chapter at Arkansas, presumably under the influence of Chi alumnus Professor Nolan Williams, "Alpha Iota's Pledge Week," Newsletter 5 (November 1960):316.

the returning veterans who were so strongly represented in the college classrooms. Induction totals ranged from 7 students at Tau and Rho Chapters to 60 at Lambda (Berkeley) to 96 at Theta, the largest yearly influx of members during the Texas chapter's first half-century.

Actually, as reported by Professor John Arch White (soon Councilor White), the vast increase in accounting enrollments at Texas had seriously hindered the effective reactivation of Theta Chapter:

> We have been so overrun with students and extra work here at the University that the staff members have been absolutely unable to devote the proper amount of time to such student's organizations as ours. Another handicap is that the students themselves, being older and professing to be in a great hurry to finish their education, are not inclined to devote very much time to extracurricular activities.

Even so, the huge initiation total (65 at the April ceremony alone) assured a strong base for the following year, as noted by the chapter president in the May Newsletter.

Against this background, Secretary-Treasurer Kendrick reported in August 1947 that all chapters had been reactivated. He went on to note that this had been a considerable achievement, since few if any "old" members had returned to their chapters, and (in line with White's remarks) expanded enrollments had increased the academic workloads of faculty advisors. Under such conditions, the student maturity cited by President McConahey would have been particularly important. Kendrick observed also that "considerable . . . work" still remained "in acquainting the chapters with the routines to be accomplished and their responsibilities," particularly since there had been substantial turnover in chapter officership over the year.

Pronouncement that basic reactivation was complete turned out to be slightly premature, because Gamma Chapter at Northwestern would revert to inactivity in the fall of 1947. Perhaps the earlier difficulty in filling chapter offices was based in part on initiation of senior students. In

any event, Gamma apparently lay dormant until new members were inducted and chapter officers were elected in May of 1948. At Evanston the next fall, however, a "revitalized" chapter of thirty-seven active members was holding "regular" meetings. Plans had tentatively been made for a chapter visitation in late October by past president McConahey, in conjunction with the annual Grand Council meeting (being held in Chicago), but illness had forced the charter Delta Chapter member to remain home in Seattle.

Illness likewise prevented McConahey from visitation in 1948 to two other campuses where fraternal reactivation had moved slowly. Both Beta and Rho Chapters, at Oregon and Minnesota, reportedly had conducted little business in 1947-48 beyond initiation of members, a condition that most likely had existed the preceding year as well.

Despite the personal circumstances that kept Professor McConahey, in his last year of official service, from participating, the Grand Council in 1947-48 began an active program of chapter visitation as one means of exercising reasonable control over the reactivated fraternity.[4] Full coverage is provided in chapter 6.

Expansion of the chapter roster beyond the prewar level would begin in the fall of 1948, when President Thomas M. Dickerson installed the first "double-letter" chapter at Alabama. A constitutional amendment adopted on Dickerson's motion at the very close of his Council tenure would

---

[4]"Chapter News Items," Newsletter [2] (March 1947):9, indented citation, (May 1947):11-12; W. E. Dickerson to James M. McConahey, May 29, July 30, 1948; Grand Council Minutes Book, 1947, pp. 1-[2], 1948, p. 1; H. W. Kendrick, Secretary-Treasurer's Report, 1946-47, pp. 3 (quoted), [11]; "Local Chapter News," Newsletter [2] (November 1948):12, quoted; McConahey to W. E. Dickerson, April 6, August 3, September 5, October 17, 1948; and C. Aubrey Smith, Sixty Years of Accounting Education on the Forty Acres (Austin, Texas: University Stores, 1974), pp. 71-78 (Theta membership, 1924-73).

McConahey's correspondence with secretary-treasurers of the Grand Council, 1947-54, is maintained in a separate national file.

lead in time to marked increase in membership at any particular chapter site. Specifically, it permitted chapters to admit students of either sex.

"Opening the Gates" to Women, at Local Option

From the beginning Beta Alpha Psi had been a men's organization as a matter of fraternal law, although only active membership had always *expressly* been restricted to "male person[s]." At the first Grand Council meeting after the war, in 1946, a letter was discussed that had been received from Miss Jennie M. Palen, Chairman of Public Relations for the American Woman's Society of Certified Public Accountants, founded in 1933. Miss Palen had requested membership in Beta Alpha Psi. Following "careful consideration" of the request, the Council reaffirmed the traditional policy by which the fraternity existed '"for the benefit of male students"'. Since election to membership of any kind was strictly a local chapter function, Palen's gender was only one reason that her wishes could not be honored.

"Several" women requested membership information during the school year 1946-47. The governing body would finally act in 1950, by authorizing the election of women members at local option. Generally, the chapters rather promptly opted for coeducation, including two groups that had previously coexisted within an accounting sorority, and such a pattern would be maintained as the fraternity grew steadily through the 1950s. Four chapters would retain all-male identities well into the fourth era, however, not counting the only earlier unit housed at a men's college. Their holdout against coeducation may not have had material effect upon their initiation levels, because female enrollment in accounting remained very low during the decade.

Adoption of the Constitutional Change

Gathered in Cambridge, Mass. on September 7, 1950, were Councilors

Thomas M. and William E. Dickerson (no relation), Gould Harris, Charles Staehling, and John Arch White. On the second night of the meeting they met with faculty representatives from nine of the twenty-six active chapters, constituting the "Grand Chapter." Because those faculty leaders played an important role in a most basic constitutional change, they should be identified:

1. Jack Daiker, Maryland
2. Williard E. Stone, Pennsylvania
3. W. E. Karrenbrock, UCLA
4. C. F. Reimer, Western Reserve
5. E. I. Fjeld, City College of New York
6. William B. Jencks, Ohio State
7. A. J. Penz, Alabama
8. James S. Lanham, Florida
9. Robert Deriman, Southern California
10. Hermann C. Miller, Ohio State.

Through Professors Harris, Staehling, and White, NYU, Berkeley, and Texas were also represented at the meeting. Miller and Karrenbrock were former presidents of the Grand Council, while Stone, Penz, and Jencks would later in the third era head the fraternity. Like Miller and Jencks, President (William) "Dick" Dickerson was from Ohio State.

The major issue discussed at the Grand Chapter meeting was amendment of the constitution to permit initiation of "girls who are otherwise eligible for membership." All fifteen men present favored such a change, provided that chapters would be allowed to remain exclusively male if they wished. While admission of women members was likely to be welcomed on many campuses, the local option approach prevented a serious objection from groups that might strongly oppose a coeducational requirement.

Upon Thomas Dickerson's motion, the Grand Council the following day, September 9, unanimously approved the change by substituting the word "student" for the words "male person" in article 6, section 1, of the fraternal constitution. This section specifically governed active membership, but the other categories (honorary and faculty) were by implication also made coeducational. The local option element, not specified within the constitution itself or

the supporting bylaws, was provided for by an interpretation rendered by the councilors, as reported to the local chapters.

By acting to advance professional opportunity for women students in accounting, the Grand Council also assured growth in fraternal membership (though for some time hardly of a dramatic scale), and thus improvement in the financial base of Beta Alpha Psi. These practical considerations were no doubt an important element in the broader policy summarized by Tom Dickerson as one of "expansion anywhere" (his emphasis).[5] Since women's colleges have rarely if ever offered studies in accounting, and do not have business schools, there was no thought of extending the fraternity to a new class of institutions.

Led by six chapters holding November initiations, many chapters would act promptly to admit women, establishing a trend that would spread quickly. In two instances an obscure accounting sorority was absorbed within Beta Alpha Psi.

Early Fraternal Coeducation

Eight pioneering chapters, fall 1950-51

Eight chapters admitted women members during the fall term of 1950-51. Included were Alpha Gamma Chapter at the City College of New York (in December) and Pi at Western Reserve (in January), initiating six females each. They were preceded, however, by six other groups.

---

[5]Thomas M. Dickerson to Author, interview, April 19, 1980, quoted (his emphasis); Grand Council Minutes Book, 1946, p. 1 (quoted), 1950, p. 2; H. W. Kendrick, Secretary-Treasurer's Report, 1946-47, p. 3 quoted; and [John Arch White], "Grand Chapter News," Newsletter [3] (November 1950):5-6. A commemorative item on Palen's organization, by E. L. Slocum, is cited in note 12.

Fraternal membership requirements that included being a "male person" were stated in article 3 (III) of the constitution adopted in 1921. Membership coverage was moved to article 5 three years later, and to article 6 in 1927. Sheldahl, Alpha to Omega, pp. 94, 101-102, 107, 117-19, 821.

The first female member of Beta Alpha Psi was inducted by Omega at Miami of Ohio on November 8, 1950. Jeannine Skelton (McKee) was an accountant for an Ohio manufacturing firm for eighteen months following graduation early in 1951. In "retirement," Mrs. McKee and her husband now own and manage a North Carolina golf course for which she does "all the operating and book work."

On November 11, 1950, Alpha Beta at Alabama initiated N. Dean Dickey, a senior ranking near the top of her class, and (apparently, if questionably, on a faculty basis) Mrs. Catherine E. McGinty, a graduate student en route to becoming the university's first Ph.D. recipient (a) of her gender and (b) within a business field. As Catherine Miles, the latter Alpha Beta alumna would build a major accounting department during long service as chairman at Georgia State, and make distinguished contributions to the literature of taxation, a field in which she enhanced her qualifications by earning a law degree. In 1981, Miles was honored by the American Accounting Association as the first female recipient of its Outstanding Educator Award.

During the week of November 14, 1950, at least three more chapters become coeducational. Caroline De Gagne, one of three women admitted by Zeta at North Dakota on November 14, would later in the year become a member of the honorary society Beta Gamma Sigma and win a competitive award from the state CPA society.

It was particularly fitting for Xi Chapter at Syracuse to be among tne pioneering groups in this area. Local secretary (and charter member) Solomon S. Buchman had in April 1930 wired his national counterpart Jacob B. Taylor to ask if women were eligible for the fraternity. Duly added to Xi's roster two decades later, on November 16, 1950, were junior Sonja Morrison, senior Marion Ward, and faculty member Cecilia Tierney. A chapter directory some years later listed the students as in turn a Long Island CPA and a "senior accountant" living not far from Niagara Falls. Tierney would go on

FIRST FEMALE MEMBER OF BETA ALPHA PSI

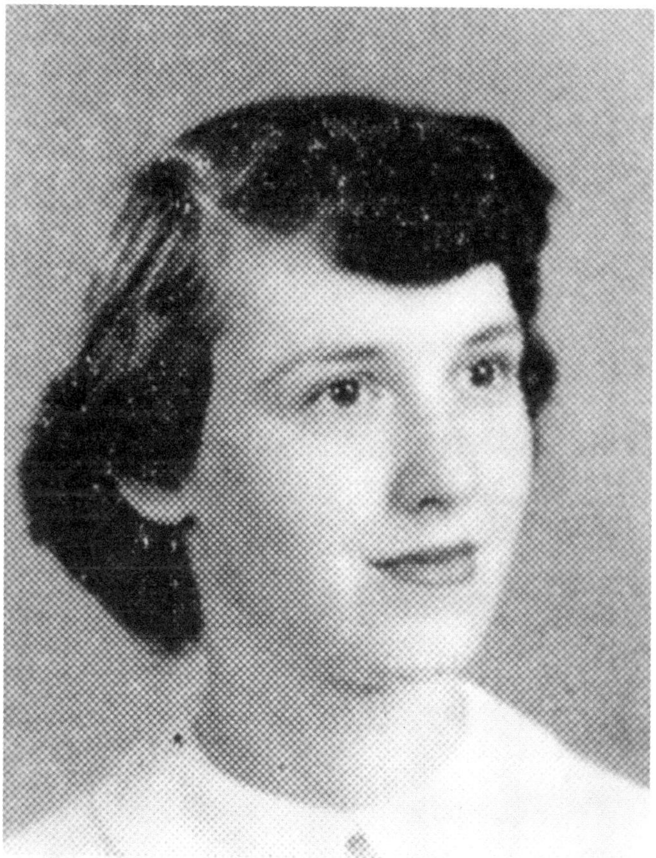

JEANNINE SKELTON, OMEGA '50

ONE OF THE EARLIEST FEMALE FACULTY MEMBERS
OF BETA ALPHA PSI

CECILIA TIERNEY, XI '50

to a varied career in teaching (Texas and Washington State), professional research (American Institute of CPAs), and industry (Phillips Petroleum).

Having earlier voted unanimously to admit women, in regular session at the College Women's Club, Lambda Chapter at Berkeley followed Syracuse into the fold by one day. Catherine De Motte Quire, Assistant Dean of Women, and Babette J. Barancik, a senior student, were initiated. Dr. Quire, a member of the Class of 1915 inducted on an honorary basis, had been a professor of economics at California, and earlier taught accounting or commerce at the University of Oregon, all-female Mills College, and Arizona State College. Miss Barancik, Class of 1951, would graduate from Berkeley's law school in 1954, and later likewise become a local faculty member. As Babette B. Barton, she is currently a full professor of law at her alma mater, specializing, appropriately enough, in taxation.

Finally, Omicron Chapter at Ohio State inducted six members of Lambda Alpha Sigma, an accounting sorority discussed later, prior to beginning regular biweekly meetings on November 30, 1950. One of them, Mrs. Barbara Scott, would serve in the spring as chapter _Newsletter_ correspondent.[6]

---

[6] _AAA Road Atlas: United States, Canada, [and] Mexico_, 1985 ed. (Falls Church, Va.: American Automobile Association, 1984), maps of New York state, pp. 74-77; Solomon S. Buchman, Xi Chapter, to J(acob) B. Taylor, transcript of telegram, April 15, 1930 (national files); Hasselback, _1984 Directory_, "Alphabetical by Individual," s.v. "Tierney, Cecilia V."; Local Chapter News," _Newsletter_ [3] (November 1950):20, (March 1951):16-29, passim, (May 1951):17-27, passim; Jeannine L. McKee to Author, September 10, 1985, quoted: "1981 Outstanding Educator Awards," _Accounting Education News_, October 1981, p. 7; "Roll of Honorary Members Initiated During the Past Year," _Newsletter_ [3] (May 1951):9; Smith, _Forty Acres_, pp. 43-44; University of California Alumni Association to Author, by telephone, November 12, 1984; _University of California, 1983-84: School of Law, Boalt Hall_ ([Berkeley: 1983]; San Diego: Career Guidance Found., College Catalog Collection on Microfiche, 1983-84 ed., CA-110), pp. 7, 18, 24-25; [S. M. Wedeberg], "Grand Council News," _Newsletter_ [3] (November 1951):12; [John Arch White], "Grand Chapter News," _Newsletter_ [3] (March 1951):6, (May 1951):6; and _Xi Chapter: 1966 Directory_, "Alphabetical Listing," s.v. "Clark, Sonja" (married name), "Tierney, Cecilia Veronia," "Ward, Marion L." (title quoted), chronological listing, s.v. "1929 - May," "1950 - November."

Even including the four units newly formed, nearly half the chapters would admit coeds during their first year of eligibility, signalling a very strong trend that would reach all but four groups over the next few years.

Rapid spread of coeducation

During the academic year 1950-51, 14 of the 30 chapters in existence by year's end had taken at least 46 women into active membership. In quoting a higher number, 49, the Newsletter editor clearly included "faculty" member Tierney among the four females attributed to Xi Chapter; probably counted "honorary" member Quire in recognizing three Lambda women; and, from chapter reports, should have cited just one coed for Alpha Epsilon, at Southern Methodist, rather than two. Other totals ranged from 9 at Alpha Gamma to 1 at both Gamma and Omega, also including the following numbers: Zeta, 3; Nu, 5; Omicron, 6; Pi, 6; Phi, 2; Chi, 2; Alpha Beta, 2; and Alpha Zeta, recently installed at Denver, 3. Although the four chapters installed in the spring of 1951 had initiated only men students as charter active members, each of them would soon bring women aboard. In addition, Alpha Lambda at Tennessee had included faculty member Julia Boyd in its first group.

Since 989 active members were initiated, in all, during 1950-51, these numbers are scarcely large. As discussed later, however, female accounting enrollments of the day were so low that the induction rate for women was notably high for a fraternity that was coeducational only in part. During the first year all eligible women from the senior class, such as Ward at Syracuse and Barancik at California, as well as those from the junior class were available for initiation. Also, female students may have frequently outperformed their male counterparts scholastically. The overall enrollment imbalance was typified by the initiation at coeducational Lambda Chapter in March 1951, wherein at least 23 of the 24 new members were male.

An interesting contemporary slant on enrollment patterns was provided by "Colonel" Sid Rucker, president of Alpha Epsilon Chapter at SMU. He reported early in 1952 that his group had thus far inducted only one female, because "any Texas woman with a smithereen of accounting marries some accountant before she has a chance to become eligible for our society."

Going coed in the fall of 1951 were Theta Chapter at Texas, Iota at Southern California, Tau at Maryland, and Alpha Lambda at Tennessee. At Texas, Edith Wood was promptly elected recording secretary, a local post that would by 1973 fall to women members another sixteen times. The only other office held by Theta women over those years (nine times in all) was that of corresponding secretary. With Texas and Maryland joining California and Ohio State in the coed ranks, only one sitting councilor was still associated locally with an all-male group. Past President Gould Harris of NYU, where Mu Chapter was destined to be one of the last few holdouts.

Half a dozen more chapters admitted their first woman active member in 1952, beginning in January with Alpha Iota at Arkansas and, as the first unit to include such members from the date of installation, Alpha Kappa at Ohio University. Following suit later in the year were Alpha and Beta Chapters, at Illinois and Oregon, and Upsilon and Psi, at Florida and Marquette. Alpha Iota, Beta, and Psi Chapters immediately or shortly put charter female members to work as local secretaries or secretary-treasurers, posts very often held by women in the early years even though the overwhelming majority of active members were male.

Alpha Chapter followed a developing pattern in voting unanimously in the fall of 1952 to extend membership to women. The issue had by implication been moot until then, because there had been no prospective female candidates at Illinois during the preceding two years. The subsequent initiation of three women, one a faculty member, received "considerable attention"

in the Champaign-Urbana press, and prompted the Newsletter correspondent to observe that "a touch of feminine beauty" would be a welcome addition.

Joining the ranks of coeducational groups in 1953 and 1954 were Rho Chapter at Minnesota, founded in 1932, and seven new or virtually new units. They included Alpha Eta at Michigan, Alpha Theta at Mississippi, Alpha Mu at Kentucky, Alpha Nu at Creighton, Alpha Xi at Detroit, Alpha Omicron at Michigan State, and Alpha Pi at Iowa. One or more women were charter officers of the last three chapters, formed in 1954. Professor Geraldine "Gere" Dominiak of Texas Christian University, an area councilor for the fraternity in the mid-1980s, was one of the original members of Alpha Xi.[7]

Charter or early women members of Beta Alpha Psi had been drawn in two cases from a preexisting accounting sorority.

Absorption of Lambda Alpha Sigma Sorority at Ohio State and Marquette

Both Ohio State and Marquette Universities had maintained chapters of Lambda Alpha Sigma, a professional accounting sorority having standards equivalent to those of Beta Alpha Psi. Immediately after the Grand Council approved the admission of women, Omicron Chapter at Ohio State voted unanimously to absorb the local organization through merger. Pending approval of a petition for formal merger submitted to the Council, Omicron inducted

---

[7]"Charter Members, Alpha to Gamma Xi," Newsletter 8 (50th anniversary ed., [1969]):19-20; "Local Chapter News," Newsletter [3] (May 1951 through May 1952), 4 (November 1952 through April 1955), both passim, [3] (March 1952):27, 4 (March 1953):45, both quoted; [Richard W. Metcalf], "Incoming Council Members," Beta Alpha Psi, The National Accounting Fraternity: Annual Report, 1983-1984, ed. [Metcalf], (Sarasota, Fla.: Dolphin Printing, [for National Council, 1984]), p. 19; Smith, Forty Acres, pp. 67, 74-78; [John Arch White], "Grand Chapter News," Newsletter [3] (November 1951):12; White, Secretary-Treasurer's Report, 1950-51, p. [4]; and Xi Chapter: 1966 Directory, chronological listing, 1950-51.

Beginning with the issue of April 1955, "Local" was omitted from the title of the chapter-report section of the Newsletter.

six Lambda Alpha Sigma sisters among the twenty-nine active members initiated during the fall quarter of 1950.

Meeting in Denver the folowing September, the governing body approved the Omicron request, providing explicitly for induction of the alumnae membership of the accounting sorority. For the first time, then, Beta Alpha Psi would confer upon graduates (or other former students) the same status as former active members, based on dissolution of the women's organization as a separate entity. Five of the ten former Ohio State coeds invited to join the fraternity were initiated at Columbus in December 1951.

The following year newly coeducational Psi Chapter at Marquette likewise sought permission to induct alumnae members of the local Lambda Alpha Sigma unit. By mail vote the Council granted unanimous consent, on the stipulations that each such candidate be certified as having met the fraternal grade requirements (already accomplished), be present for her initiation, and pay the regular fee of five dollars; and that the local sorority chaper, if not already defunct, be deactivated. The basic rationale for approval, applied at Ohio State as well, was that the seventeen women cited would be '"orphans"' without induction by Beta Alpha Psi.

Interestingly, only two of the sorority alumnae would be initiated at the next Psi Chapter ceremony. Apparently the fifteen others were either unavailable for the initiation, or not sufficiently interested to accept the chapter's invitation to membership.

No further information has been obtained concerning Lambda Alpha Sigma sorority. It is not otherwise mentioned in the Beta Alpha Psi files examined. More importantly, it was not cited in either the contemporary fifteenth edition (1949) of the authoritative fraternity reference work Baird's Manual, or the comprehensive Bicentennial edition (1976), listing a host of defunct

Greek-letter organizations. Nor was it listed in an earlier (1928) reference work on collegiate sororities. In light of these points, and the very low female enrollment of the day in accounting classes, the best conjecture is that Lambda Alpha Sigma was a relatively short-lived organization having few chapters.

In allowing Omicron and Psi Chapters to admit sorority alumnae, the Grand Council in effect distinguished sharply in status between the past active members of (a) partially honorary accounting societies coexisting with, and complementing, Beta Alpha Psi chapters; and (b) similar organizations preceding the formation of fraternal chapters, and ultimately replaced thereby. The former category could only have included women's organizations, since the installation of a Beta Alpha Psi chapter would have required, and signified, the termination of any local accounting group having comparable requirements. The second category represents local accounting organizations from which fraternal units emerged.

The Council would permit transfer of membership to Beta Alpha Psi only in the first case. An interpretation adopted in 1950, upon the motion of Councilor Charles Staehling, did recognize as eligible for charter membership all members of a successful "petition[er]" group, including any signers who might have left school during the interim prior to installation. This interpretation was made "retroactive for all chapters recently installed." It would be reaffirmed the following year, and another fourteen years later, in 1965 be incorporated within a new fraternal constitution.

Staehling's motion may have been prompted by circumstances at Alpha Gamma Chapter, established in the spring of 1949 at CCNY under the leadership of Professor E. I. Fjeld, Alpha '22, who more than twenty years earlier had founded Nu Chapter at Colorado. "Doc" Fjeld, identified above

as a participant in the Grand Chapter meeting of 1950, wanted to add to Alpha Gamma's charter membership not (merely) signers no longer registered as of the founding date, but students who had performed important "spade work" in earlier stages of the process leading to the successful petition. After conferring with Thomas and William Dickerson, President Gould Harris of NYU informed his friend at City College that pre-petitioner contributors to chapter formation who were no longer in school regrettably could not be initiated. He added, however, that current enrollment in "a single course" at CCNY would be sufficient to make the unspecified men eligible, noting also that they might eventually "be admitted by way of the honorary route."

Three years earlier, in the fall of 1947, the Council had dealt routinely with a more extreme request. A 1925 Syracuse University graduate who had belonged to Theta Phi Lambda, the predecessor of Xi Chapter, sought advice on joining Beta Alpha Psi. He had only recently learned that the local fraternity had given rise to a chapter of the national accounting body. After consulting his colleagues, Secretary-Treasurer W. E. Dickerson reported that it was the unanimous opinion of the Grand Council that "the granting of a Beta Alpha Psi chapter to local organizations does not entitle [prior] members of those organizations" to fraternal membership.

Of course membership could be conferred only by local chapters in any case, a point that was made in response to occasional other requests of the day for membership information. The more specific implication in the instance cited was that Xi Chapter would have no authority to grant alumni status to the Theta Phi Lambda member, identified as a public accountant and tax consultant practicing in Massena, New York.[8]

---

[8]Harold J. Baily, ed., Baird's Manual of American College Fraternities, 15th ed. (Menasha, Wis.: Collegiate Press, George Banta Publishing Co., 1949), pp. xv-xviii; Beta Alpha Psi National Constitution (rev. September 1, 1965), article 7, section 7; W. E. Dickerson to J. William Leary (Syracuse

Returning to the development of coeducation within Beta Alpha Psi, it is rather striking that as of the close of 1954 only four of the thirty-six existing chapters possessed (unlike their universities) an all-male identity, three of them from early fraternal sites. All four groups would continue to exclude women at least well into the 1960s, over a period of time during which new units consistently received such members promptly.

Four Long-term Holdouts--Delta, Mu, Sigma, and Alpha Delta--amidst Dominant Coeducation

As already documented, admission of coeds to Beta Alpha Psi chapters took hold early. After 1954, when all three additions to the fraternal roster had charter female officers, it was commonplace for entering local groups to initiate women members from the very start. A good example was Alpha Rho, installed at Baylor in 1955, prior, incidentally, to the printing of charter forms suitably reworded for a coeducational chapter. The four female charter members included Joy(ce) Smalley, who as Joyce Dean would serve in 1980-81 as the fraternity's second woman president. Initiated at the same time were future councilors Emerson Henke (faculty) and Joe Fritzemeyer.

An obvious exception was Beta Epsilon Chapter, formed in 1959 at Lehigh University, an all-male institution until 1971. Four other third-era units

---

'25) November 12, 1947; Grand Council Minutes Book, 1950, p. [3] (quoted), 1951, pp. 2-3; Gould L. Harris to E. I. Fjeld, November 22, 1950; J. William Leary to Beta Alpha Psi, October 30, 1947; "Local Chapter News," Newsletter [3] (November 1950):20, (March 1951):22, (March 1952):22, 4 (March 1953): 53; Ida Shaw Martin, The Sorority Hand Book, 10th ed. (Boston: Martin, 1928), pp. 78, 88, 95-96, 138 (Ohio State sororities), 171; John Robson, ed., Baird's Manual of American College Fraternities, 19th ed. (Menasha: Baird's Manual Found., 1977), pp. xiii, 878; Sheldahl, Alpha to Omega, p. 169; [S. M. Wedeberg], "Grand Council News," Newsletter [3] (November 1951):3; and Wedeberg to Mary Jane Hachmeister, Secretary of Psi Chapter, November 28, 1952.

The four letters cited above are contained in the Grand Council's "Policies" File, 1947-53, and each correspondent except Leary has been quoted.

CHARTER MEMBERS OF THE ALPHA RHO AT BAYLOR, INCLUDING THREE FUTURE COUNSILORS

Joyce Smalley (Dean), seated, fifth from left; Joe R. Fritzemeyer, standing, sixth from left; Emerson O. Henke, standing, fifth from right.

ALPHA RHO'S ENTRY FOR HOMECOMING QUEEN, 1955

JOYCE SMALLEY (DEAN)
Homecoming parade at Baylor, prior to the game with Texas Christian. Smalley's escort for the dance was Alpha Rho member Joe Fritzemeyer.

were likewise installed after 1954 without female representation. Women were inducted within a year, however, by Alpha Sigma at Cincinnati, Beta Delta at Texas Tech, Beta Zeta at Loyola of New Orleans, and Beta Theta at Penn State. In the two cases at least in which this occurred later during the term of installation itself, there was probably no constitutional exclusion to start with, but only an absence of eligible female students.

Four older chapters, however, would hold out against coeducation for some time. They were Delta at Washington and Mu at New York (until 1965), Sigma at Wisconsin (May 1967), and Alpha Delta at Pennsylvania (probably 1967-68, when two women appeared in the chapter's yearbook photo). All four chapters were represented on the Grand Council between 1950, marking the beginning of fraternal coeducation, and 1965. Gould Harris of NYU was elected president at the meeting at which the admission of women was approved. Later presidents included J. C. Gibson of Wisconsin in 1954-55, Williard E. Stone of Penn in 1958-59, and Julius A. Roller of Washington in 1964-65.

The late appearance of women within Alpha Delta may have only reflected local enrollment patterns. Characterizing the Wharton School as having been "largely a men's" unit until after his 1960 departure, Stone recalls no women "being proposed [for the chapter] and being denied" admission in his day.

Mu Chapter finally admitted women in May 1965. The four female initiates were included in a listing of the group's new "brothers," illustrating that old habits die hard. Present-day faculty advisor Ely Kushel, who joined the teaching staff in 1955, attributes the lag to low female enrollment and leadership by "Twentieth Century men with nineteenth century mentalities." In later years, in any event, it was in part a byproduct of unconstitutional alumni domination of the New York chapter, documented in chapter 4.

An interesting anecdote relating to Sigma at Wisconsin reveals that "local option" in this area extended to <u>classes</u> of membership. In

September 1952 local secretary Kimberly Peterson wrote Secretary-Treasurer S. M. Wedeberg concerning, among other things, whether the chapter was entitled to initiate a female faculty member. "Miss" Peterson was promptly advised that, "having apparently approved admitting women members," Sigma could routinely induct the professor on a "faculty" basis. Noting that he was "a Mister, not a Miss," Peterson thereupon restated his question: Could "Miss Lins" be admitted without "opening our chapter to active student female membership?," Wedeberg replied that "local option" would permit the local group to "vote to restrict . . . [female] membership to women faculty members" if it so wished. A few months later, on February 12, 1953, Professor Lins was duly initiated.

Firsthand authoritative information is available in the case of another laggard, Delta Chapter, from future Beta Alpha Psi president Fred J. Mueller (muller), a holder of three local offices, 1953-54, who returned to campus in 1956 as a faculty member. Professors Roller (1946-57) and Mueller (1957-63) were Delta's only postwar faculty advisors until Gerald Cleveland, under whose leadership coeds were finally admitted, assumed the post in the fall of 1963.

The University of Washington chapter, which had several years earlier held its annual spring banquet at the Women's University Club downtown, directly addressed the issue of gender discrimination at a regular Tuesday evening dinner meeting in 1955. The discussion leader was Genevieve Michel, CPA, a professional employee in the campus controller's office who had been one of the very few women accounting majors during her own student days at the school. Ms. Michel, who would herself have met Delta Chapter scholastic requirements, was an outspoken advocate of the inclusion of women students, as attested by a contemporary of hers as a student and later as a member of the state society of CPAs who took a different viewpoint.

Specifically, Fred Mueller recalls that as chapter advisor he would repeatedly be "lambasted" by Michel for the maintenance of an all-male organization, receiving letters in that vein "not less than every three months." In the same regard, very articulate women accounting majors of the day sometimes "almost violently assaulted" him, verbally.

Why, then, did Delta Chapter resist coeducation? Certainly it was not because the admission of women would have materially expanded chapter size, since female enrollment in accounting classes at Washington in the late 1950s was still extremely low. Looking back, Mueller estimates that usually "at best" only one woman would have been eligible for induction at each initiation ceremony. The main reason for maintaining a male-only unit in Seattle was much more interesting, in human terms.

It seems that many potential members, particularly among the numerous military veterans enrolled, were married, normally about 60% overall. Often the wives were home with infant children. Maintaining a long tradition of holding weekly dinner meetings, Delta was subjected to a national standard of 80% attendance at regular sessions, although it would soon receive a concession related in chapter 12. Eligible students would often express doubt about joining Beta Alpha Psi because their wives objected to the weekly commitment. Professor Mueller thus started to make a point of meeting with wives in advance to explain the importance of the fraternity to professional education in accounting, and urge them not to keep their men from reaping the benefits available. He found it extremely helpful in this regard to be able to point out that the chapter did not admit women members, and had no plans to do so, and feels that his task would have been far more difficult had even minimal participation by coeds existed.

In essence, it was felt that, with female enrollment in accounting so low, the exclusion of women from Delta Chapter on balance saved considerably

more members for the group than it left out. Whatever may be the merits of such a position, Mueller recalls with satisfaction that for years to come he would receive Christmas cards from former students who thanked him for persuading their wives to excuse them from dinner on Tuesday evenings.[9]

The University of Washington was of course scarcely exceptional in attracting few females to accounting classes in the 1950s. Throughout the nation the overwhelming proportion of majors were male, even while, by at least one significant indicator, women were becoming somewhat more involved in the accounting profession. Given such a context, the levels of female initiation within the fraternity were reasonably impressive. More importantly, perhaps, women members often had important chapter responsibilities, occasionally those of top leadership.

Low Initiation Rates amidst Lower Enrollment Levels, and Disproportionate Responsibility

Enrollment--Overwhelming male majorities throughout the decade

In 1951 (as defined within exhibit 1), as Beta Alpha Psi began admitting female members, more than fifty thousand men and fewer than six thousand

---

[9]"Alumni News," Newsletter 5 (November 1957, April - November, 1959, April 1961, Spring 1962), 6 (Spring 1964, Fall 1965), references to Delta Chapter; "Directory," [2] (November 1946 - May 1947):3; Hamilton Elliott, University of Pennsylvania Archives, to Author, August 22, 1985; "Grand Chapter: Chapter Representatives," Newsletter [2] (November 1947 - May 1949), [3] (November 1949 - May 1952), 4 (November 1952 - April 1957), 5 (November 1957, April 1959 - Spring 1962), 6 (Spring 1964), 2nd inside page, s.v. "Delta"; Grand Council Minutes Book, 1951, pp. 2-3, 1955, p. 3; Ely Kushel, Mu Chapter faculty vice-president (FVP), to Author, March 10 (quoted), July 8, 1986; "Local Chapter News," Newsletter 4 (May 1953):83, (March 1954):144, (April 1955 - April 1957), 5-6 (issues cited under "Grand Chapter"), passim, reports on Delta and Alpha Delta in particular, 6 (Fall 1965):268; Fred J. Mueller to Author, by telephone, November 12, 1984, quoted; "National Chapter Members," Newsletter 6 (Fall 1965):[248]; "National Council," Beta Alpha Psi, The National Accounting Fraternity: 1979-1980 Annual Report, ed. [James W. Pattillo, (Notre Dame, Indiana: For National Council, 1980)], p. 2; Sheldahl, Alpha to Omega, p. 42; Williard [E. Stone] to Author, [October 1985], quoted; Roy S. Tuttle, three-term Sigma FVP, to Author, August 9, 1985; and Nan E. Young, University of Washington Archives, to Author, August 9, 1985.

women received bachelor's degrees in business studies from American colleges and universities. Although separate figures are not available for specific fields, those available for later years of the decade leave little doubt that the gender imbalance in accounting would have been substantially greater still. Over the next several years the number of women graduates in business held fairly steady, while, as World War II veterans left the classroom and another military buildup occurred, there was a decline of approximately one-third in male graduates. During the last half of the decade, however, the male totals rose significantly, to 47,629 in 1960, while female business graduates declined markedly in number, to only 3,893 in that year. At graduate-degree levels the disproportion was usually much greater than in regard to four-year degrees.

Full details for six years from the decade are given in exhibit 1. Cited also, more importantly, are comparative statistics on accounting degrees conferred in 1956, 1958, and 1960. Cumulatively, they show that only some 1,300 undergraduate degrees were earned by women from a total of more than 30,000 awarded, a rate of 4.3% that was exceeded only in the earliest year included. It is hardly surprising, then, that in none of the three years did female students earn as many as one-twentieth of the master's degrees conferred in accounting.

Even so, women were making some degree of progress professionally within the contemporary accounting field. In particular, during the 1950s the number of female CPAs in the United States rose from 600 to 1,500, ten times that of 1940. Higher education was of course still only one source for entry-level preparation in a day in which but three states had as yet restricted certification to college graduates. Most women who became certified worked for small firms, conducted their own practices (about one-half in 1942), or worked in industry. Generally speaking, the larger

EXHIBIT 1

DEGREES CONFERRED IN BUSINESS AND ACCOUNTING, CLASSIFIED BY LEVEL AND GENDER, FOR SELECTED YEARS, 1951-60

Year[a]	All business fields		Accounting	
	Bachelor's	Master's	Bachelor's	Master's
1951				
Men	52,320	4,045	Data not available until 1956	
Women	5,917	310		
1953				
M	35,431	3,734		
W	5,275	301		
1955				
M	35,564	3,088		
W	6,091	248		
1956				
M	38,101	2,953	8,409	423
W	4,094	153	419	16
1958				
M	47,286	3,896	10,411	452
W	3,968	145	437	22
1960				
M	47,629	4,476	10,311	447
W	3,893	167	458	23

SOURCES: "Education," *Statistical Abstract of the United States* (Washington, D.C.: U.S. Government Printing Office, for Department of Commerce, Bureau of the Census): 73rd ed. (1952), p. 128; 75th (1954), p. 199; 77th (1956), p. 131; 79th (1958), p. 130; 81st (1960), p. 129; 83rd (1962), p. 137. The imbalances naturally extended to the doctoral level as well, as in 1958, when 104 men and 5 women received doctorates in business fields overall, and 16 of the 17 accounting degrees were earned by men (81st ed.).

[a]In accordance with the notation of the source documents, reference is intended to the *academic* years ending during the calendar years cited. The practice followed in reporting *summer* graduates has not been determined.

accounting firms, the "Big Fourteen" of the 1950s, were not yet interested in hiring female accountants.

Given the extreme enrollment imbalance of the time, female membership within Beta Alpha Psi would necessarily remain low during the third era. At that, it was somewhat higher than the nationwide enrollment disparities would have suggested.

Initiation data (incomplete) for three years

As already noted, it appears that only 46 of the 989 (or perhaps 990) students admitted to active status in the fraternity in 1950-51 were women, representing 4.65%. Including only the fourteen chapters that had so far exercised the local option, however, the rate was virtually doubled, at 9.2% (of 500). As the numbers of newly coeducational chapters and groups retaining all-male identities both declined, the two rates naturally moved toward convergence.

Exhibit 2 itemizes official initiation data, classified by sex, for the first year. Incomplete data, drawn mainly from Newsletter reports and representing well over half of the initiation totals in each case, are given also for the years 1954-55 and 1959-60. The following female induction rates were obtained:

	1954-55	1959-60
For all chapters	6.9%	5.7%
For coeducational chapters only	8.5%	7.1%.

Coincidentally or not, these figures are consistent with a slight decline overall in the female portion of contemporary accounting enrollments. Even so, the rates for the final year of the era are significantly higher than the female segment, 4.25%, of 1960 graduates.

EXHIBIT 2

SELECTED THIRD-ERA INITIATION DATA (ACTIVE MEMBERS), CLASSIFIED BY GENDER

Chapter	1950-51		1954-55		1959-60	
	M	W	M	W	M	W
Alpha	15				21	4
Beta	24		15		12	1
Gamma	29	1	12			
Delta	43		31		25	
Epsilon					7	1
Zeta	13	3			17	
Theta	43		24	1	24	3
Iota	26				15	1
Lambda	45	2	30	7	12	2
Mu	24		25		13	
Nu	18	5	12	2	25	3
Xi	29	3	20	2	19	3
Omicron	47	6	29	2	30	2
Pi	26	6	5	2	8	1
Rho	18		16	1	8	
Sigma	46		41		32	
Tau	19		13		14	1
Upsilon	26					
Phi	22	2	20		9	1
Chi	23	2			7	1
Psi	28		15	2	18	2
Omega	24	1	9		16	
Alpha Beta	27	2	24	3	28	2

EXHIBIT 2--Continued

Chapter	1950-51 M	1950-51 W	1954-55 M	1954-55 W	1959-60 M	1959-60 W
Alpha Gamma	60	9	29	2	69	1
Alpha Delta	56		33		18	
Alpha Epsilon	24	1	22	3	13	1
Alpha Zeta	67	3	27	2	14	1
Alpha Eta	55		17	2		
Alpha Theta	22		17	2	12	
Alpha Iota	18		18		8	
Alpha Kappa			5	1	4	1
Alpha Lambda	27				7	3
Alpha Mu			15	3	15	1
Alpha Nu			3		5	
Alpha Xi			11		9	
Alpha Omicron			13	1	26	2
Alpha Pi			25	1	20	
Alpha Rho			17	4	10	
Alpha Sigma			24	1	5	
Alpha Tau			21	3	4	
Alpha Upsilon					17	2
Alpha Phi						
Alpha Chi					3	1
Alpha Psi					5	1
Alpha Omega						
Beta Alpha					15	1
Beta Gamma					8	

EXHIBIT 2--Continued

Chapter	1950-51 M	1950-51 W	1954-55 M	1954-55 W	1959-60 M	1959-60 W
Beta Delta					11	1
Beta Epsilon					16	
Beta Zeta					10	
Beta Eta					22	1
Beta Theta					42	
TOTALS (OVERALL)	944	46	638	47	748	45
COED CHAPTERS ONLY	454	46	508	47	592	45.

SOURCES: Alpha Mu Chapter: 1969 Directory (as cited in note 10), pp. 2 (honorary, faculty members), 17-18 (initiation lists for last two years covered); "Charter Members, Alpha to Gamma Xi," (note 10), pp. 19-20; "Local Chapter News," Newsletter [3] (March 1952):37, 4 (May 1953):92, (November 1954 - November 1955), 5 (November 1959 - November 1960); [Herbert E. Miller], Secretary-Treasurer's Report, 1959-60, pp. 4-5; A. J. Penz, Secretary-Treasurer's Report, 1954-55, p. 4; [S. M. Wedeberg], "Grand Council News," Newsletter [3] (November 1951):12; [John Arch White], "Grand Chapter News," Newsletter [3] (March 1951):6, (May 1951):6; White, Secretary-Treasurer's Report, 1950-51, p. [4]; and Xi Chapter: 1966 Directory, lists of initiates for years covered and of "Honorary Members," last three years.

The figures given for the second and third years are incomplete. In addition, a handful of available names from those years have been disregarded because of gender ambiguity. The numbers given for 1950-51, yielding a total of 990 initiates, are taken from Secretary-Treasurer's White's report. He gave an overall total of 989 new active members, however, a number consistent with the audited financial report for the year. [Wedeberg], "Grand Council News," Newsletter [3] (November 1951):10.

Full records for the 1950s are available for Xi Chapter at Syracuse and Alpha Mu at Kentucky. Xi initiated 242 active members from November 1950, when it became coeducational, through April 1960. Of that group no more than 19, or 7.8%, were female. The rate was considerably higher at Kentucky, beginning with the spring of 1953, at 13.6% (23 of 169, omitting one name and classifying an ambiguous one as feminine). Exhibit 2 includes the pertinent records from both chapters.

Ironically, the charter memberships of the first three chapters formed in the next era, representing Loyola of Chicago, Mississippi State, and Los Angeles State, were entirely male. The latter two groups would soon admit coeds, however, and with occasional exceptions women would grace the initial memberships of the chapters formed thereafter in the 1960s. Even so, the comprehensive list of charter members presented in the Golden Anniversary Newsletter (1969) reveals a continuing pattern of low female representation.[10]

These and similar membership data from the third era do not, of course, depict the nature of feminine participation within Beta Alpha Psi. Considerable information is available concerning chapter officership, however,

---

[10]Alpha Mu Chapter of Beta Alpha Psi: Membership Directory, University of Kentucky (Lexington: Alpha Mu Chapter, 1969), pp. 2, 17-18 (listing of initiates, April 1953 through May 1960); "Alumni News," Newsletter 5 (Fall 1961):433, (Spring 1962):483, 6 (Spring 1964):97; "Chapter News," Newsletter 5 (Fall 1961):457-58, (Spring 1962):505, 6 (Spring 1964):119-20; "Charter Members, Alpha to Gamma Xi," Newsletter 8 (50th anniv. ed.):20-22; Gary John Previts, "American Accounting Education: Contributions from the Past, Data about the Present, Trends for the Future," 8th Texas CPA Education Conference, October 29, 1982, p. 6; E. L. Slocum, "The Lady Ages Well" (commemorative note on fiftieth anniversary of American Woman's Society of Certified Public Accountants), Accounting History Research Center, Particularis de Computis et Scripturis 2 (Winter 1984):4, source of information on public accounting; Professor Edward G. Sutula, Saint Joseph's University to Author, conversation (Philadelphia, Pa.), December 5, 1984, source of term "Big Fourteen"; and Xi Chapter: 1966 Directory, chronological listing of initiates near end, November 1950 through April 1960.

indicating that women members in general exercised chapter responsibilities well out of proportion to their numbers, although largely within offices associated with gender stereotypes.

Women chapter officers of the third era, including four presidents and one FVP

As already noted, many women served as chapter secretaries or secretary-treasurers. Chapters often elected separate secretaries and treasurers, and sometimes separate recording and correspondence secretaries as well. Since communication with the Grand Council was based largely on internal record-keeping, the latter division of duties involved closely related roles. By and large, women officers of the day served in one or more areas of secretary-treasurership, as defined in exhibit 3. Usually included within the correspondence function, although not mentioned in the national "statutes" from which the exhibit is drawn, was preparation of chapter reports for the *Newsletter*.

Looking back a generation or more later, the highly disproportionate number of women serving as chapter "secretaries," in particular, is apt to elicit either amusement or irritation, or a combination of both. No doubt gender bias was often involved, and many chapters having huge male majorities were more than willing to impose laborious record-keeping and correspondence duties upon women members. Exhibit 3 shows clearly, however, that typical responsibilities of female officers were extremely central to chapter operations, particularly inasmuch as a national chapter competition program had been implemented the very year that women became eligible for the fraternity.

Women occasionally, to be sure, served in other local offices. Although not required by the governing Council, chapters usually maintained

EXHIBIT 3

SECRETARY-TREASURER DUTIES IN THIRD-ERA CHAPTERS

CHAPTER VII

Duties of Chapter Officers

Section 73. The duties of the Secretary-Treasurer shall be as follows:

(a) To keep correct minutes of each meeting of the Chapter.

(b) To forward to the Secretary-Treasurer of the Grand Council the following:

(1) A correct and complete list of all initiates, their names, addresses, class of membership and other data on provided blanks within ten days after an initiation.

(2) A list of chapter officers and their addresses within one week after their installation.

(3) The national initiation fee of five dollars for each initiate (active membership) within ten days after the initiation. In case organization funds must be disbursed through university officers, extension of time can be granted by the Grand Secretary upon request from the faculty vice-president.

(4) Audited financial statements covering the chapter year not later than July 15.

(c) To fulfill, generally, such additional duties as may be required of him by the Grand Council or by the Chapter Constitution, the By-Laws, Resolutions, or vote of the chapter.

Reprinted from "National Statutes, National Constitution and Statutes (as amended September 1, 1953), by (and of) Beta Alpha Psi Fraternity.

a vice-presidency, presumably in most instances to provide for a readily available presidential stand-in (or replacement). The first female vice-president was apparently Edith Tanenbaum, elected by Alpha Gamma, at City College, in the fall of 1951. In the spring of 1955 Nu Chapter at Colorado, Xi at Syracuse, and Rho at Minnesota all had women veeps, and in succeeding years Alpha Gamma (in a repeat performance), Upsilon at Florida, and Beta Alpha at Indiana would follow suit.

Three of these chapters, further, would elect a female _president_ during the third era. In February 1954, Kay Blandford assumed the top post within Nu Chapter, joined by a vice-president who served also as Colorado's _Newsletter_ correspondent. The latter officer was Stephen A. Zeff, who in the years ahead would become a prominent accounting educator and scholar, a Beta Alpha Psi National Advisory Forum Member (1979-82), and an American Accounting Association editor and (in 1985-86) president. At the faculty level, the Boulder group included future AAA president Wilton T. Anderson, the chapter advisor, and Robert S. Wasley, Zeff's resident landlord of the day, each of whom would later serve as national president of Beta Alpha Psi.

Rosemarie Haberman was the president of Alpha Gamma Chapter at CCNY in the fall of 1956, being joined by two other female officers. Finally, Phyllis Wilson briefly headed Beta Alpha Chapter at Indiana during the spring of 1959, having moved up from vice-president. The faculty advisor to the chapter at Bloomington, which had been established slightly more than a year earlier under his leadership, was Leon E. Hay.

The reference to Professor Hay, finally, calls to mind another future national president of Beta Alpha Psi, whom he would eventually join on the

NU CHAPTER, 1954: A FEMALE PRESIDENT, AND THREE FUTURE LEADERS IN ACCOUNTING EDUCATION

Seated: President Kay Blandford, fourth from left; Vice-President Stephen A. Zeff, second from right; and Professor Robert S. Wasley, far right. Standing, directly behind Wasley (blemished photo) : Faculty Vice-President Wilton T. Anderson. Anderson would later head both Beta Alpha Psi and the American Accounting Association, and Wasley and Zeff would serve as presidents of the fraternity and the AAA, respectively.

University of Arkansas faculty. Doris M. Cook enjoys an enduring place within fraternal history as the first woman councilor, and first woman president (1976-77). It is more pertinent to note at this point, however, that she was also the first woman *faculty* vice-president. Having herself been initiated on a faculty basis four years earlier, Cook was elected to the leadership post at Alpha Iota Chapter in December 1956, and would continue in that capacity for more than eight years. Professor Cook was the fraternity's only woman faculty leader of the third era.[11]

Gender had not been the only nonscholastic basis for prewar exclusion from Beta Alpha Psi. With tacit constitutional sanction, local chapters had been permitted to discriminate on a racial or a religious basis as well, providing the setting for another significant facet of postwar expansion.

"Opening the Gates" to Racial and Religious Minorities

As illustrated in volume 1 in regard to Jewish students, the "local option" policy adopted for introduction of women into the fraternity had traditionally existed, much more invidiously, on matters of race and religion. Although no relevant change was made in basic fraternal law, changes in attitude at both national and local levels, in keeping with much broader cultural developments, would substantially eliminate such

---

[11] "American Accounting Association," *The Accounting Review* 55 (July 1980), 60 (October 1985):inside front cover; Doris M. Cook to Author, interview (San Antonio, Texas), March 21, 1980; "Grand Chapter," *Newsletter* [3] (November 1950 - May 1952), 4 (November 1952 - April 1957), 5 (November 1957, April 1959 - Spring 1960), 6 (Spring 1964):3rd page (including cover); Leon E. Hay to Author, interview (Cleveland, Ohio), May 2, 1980; "Local Chapter News," *Newsletter* [3] (November 1951):25, 4 (March 1953):60, (March 1954):147, (April 1955):247-49, (November 1956):364, 5 (November 1957):25, (April 1959):189, (November 1959):244, 6 (Fall 1965):278; [A. J. Penz], "Chapter News Review," *Newsletter* 4 (May 1954):174; and Robert S. Wasley to Author, interview (Denver, Colo.), March 23, 1980. Zeff's national Beta Alpha Psi service is documented in the *Annual Report* issued each year, 1979-82.

DORIS M. COOK, CPA, 1946

ALPHA ITOA CHAPTER, INCLUSIVE OF TWO FUTURE COUNCILORS, IN 1956

First row: Professor Doris Cook, second from left; FVP Nolan E. Williams, far right.

membership bias in the third era. In particular, Jewish students were welcomed into the fraternity in large numbers, and black students, although still a minute presence within relevant accounting classrooms, were admitted to Beta Alpha Psi chapters across the land.

Historical Background, in Review, and Evolution of an Affirmative Council Attitude

Article 3, section 2 of the first national constitution of the fraternity, adopted in 1921, asserted membership standards of "scholarship, practicability, and sociability," after having cited the same factors within the preamble. Throughout the third era, "practicality" and sociability continued to be listed with scholarship as entry criteria (article 6, section 4 or 5).

Consistent with such language, as reported in volume 1, it was decided at the landmark 1927 meeting presided over by Eric Kohler that matters of eligibility for minority racial or religious groups should be left to the chapters themselves. In a portion of the resolution that seems to have had negligible effect, the local groups were advised to confer with the Grand Council on specific issues of the kind.

At the same meeting, of course, the stage was set for the regrettable expulsion (in effect) of Eta Chapter at Boston University, based on its predominantly Jewish membership. Open discrimination against Jewish students by chapters at major schools on both coasts was also cited. Thomas Dickerson of Pi Chapter at Western Reserve stated in 1980 that black students were in practice excluded from the prewar fraternity. His judgment was impressionistic only, and if correct a notable exception is in any case cited later. It seems credible enough, even so, granting that enrollment patterns of the day would have rendered the issue moot in most cases.

There is compelling evidence that the Grand Council of Dickerson's

day did not wish to perpetuate earlier practices in these areas. Failure to delete from the constitution the highly questionable language cited was evidently a matter of inadvertance rather than of policy, just as other archaic language would be retained until the document was fundamentally revised in the mid-1960s. In 1967 Professor Dickerson recalled that he and his colleagues on the early postwar Council had:

> promoted and helped to bring about complete integration in B. A. P. chapters, resulting in the admission to membership of _any_ eligible accounting major, regardless of religion, race, color, creed, or sex.

Twelve years later the 1948-49 fraternal president identified "[m]eeting the requests of qualified women and minority groups for the privilege of membership in BAP" as having been among the "most pressing problems" facing the leadership of his day. He went on to state that during 1949 "the Grand Council recommended that all racial, religious, and color bars to membership be eliminated," although no independent documentation of official action has been found. Dickerson reiterated these points in a 1980 interview, mentioning that in response to this process one or two chapters had actually threatened to withdraw (citing one of the early groups), although no such action had actually been taken.[12]

Before turning to fraternal developments underlying these recollections, it is useful to place matters within the larger contemporary context of declining racial and religious bigotry within American society.

---

[12] Beta Alpha Psi Fraternity, "National Constitution," _National Constitution and Statutes_ (September 1953, August 1958), article 6, section 5; _Beta Alpha Psi National Constitution_ (September 1965), article 9; Tom (Thomas M.) Dickerson to A. J. Penz, February 1, 1967, indented citation (emphasis in original); Dickerson to Author, November 1, 1979 (quoted), April 19, 1980, interview; "National Constitution," _National Constitution . . . [and] National Statutes of Beta Alpha Psi Fraternity_ (September 1947), article 6, section 4, (September 1949), article 6, section 5; and Sheldahl, _Alpha to Omega_, pp. 115, 172-77, 821. The several constitutions cited were quoted, including the 1921 document presented in the last source, pp. 821-25.

The Broader Social Environment: Declining Bigotry within Contemporary American Culture

One of the most positive legacies of the Second World War was a substantial reduction, over time, in such prejudice:

> It was as though the confrontation with the ultimate racist society had shaken America to its underpinnings and made imperative the earliest possible realization of the constitutional promise of equality.

As the monstrous crimes of the Holocaust were revealed, strong feelings of guilt and dismay emerged concerning discrimination practiced against Jewish people, in particular. The 1947 Oscar-winning movie Gentleman's Agreement, featuring Gregory Peck as a newspaperman posing as a Jew in order to document American anti-Semitism, "caused a sensation at the time," according to a reliable film source. More significantly, the formation in 1948 of the State of Israel, and her immediate diplomatic recognition by the United States, generated particular ethnic pride among Jewish Americans and signalled the goodwill of their countrymen. The same year Brandeis University, named for a legendary Supreme Court justice, was founded in Massachusetts as the nation's first nonsecular Jewish university. The Anti-Defamation League of B'nai B'rith ("Sons of the Covenant") continued to combat religious and racial discrimination and promote intergroup understanding.

Within higher education, the untenability of excluding Jews from faculty positions had become manifest during the war, as departments spared from such bias had flourished through the addition of outstanding Jewish refugee scientists and scholars. Such developments naturally benefited homegrown Jewish scholars as well. For example, during the Depression years there had been scarcely a handful of Jewish professors of English literature at major universities, notably including Lionel Trilling at Columbia. A young man destined to become an extraordinary scholar of English Romantic poetry was able to find academic employment, beyond a proprietary business

college in Baltimore, only after his thesis advisor removed the last sentence from an otherwise glowing recommendation: '"Unfortunately, Mr. [Earl] Wasserman is a Jew"'. Yet within two decades "it seemed every English department in the country was brimming over with Jewish professors and students."

Closer to the accounting field, according to one source there were three Jewish economics professors nationwide in 1927. By 1980, sixty thousand of America's nearly six million Jews were teaching within higher education.

Discrimination against black Americans was of course particularly widespread and deep-seated. In keeping, however, with the significant wartime contributions made by blacks, both at home and overseas, it too was starting to recede in the early postwar years. President Truman established two commissions in 1946 to study race relations, and two years later ordered the desegregation of the armed forces and was returned to office after he and his party had endorsed "sweeping legislation looking toward racisl equality." Later, black and white troops fought well together on the front lines in Korea, and, in probably the most pivotal event of the century in America's struggle for racial justice, the Supreme Court (in 1954) declared school segregation unconstitutional.

Also, Jack Roosevelt "Jackie" Robinson, an Army veteran who had been a superb four-sport athlete at UCLA, had in 1946 become the first black player of the century within organized baseball, and a year later begun a brilliant Hall of Fame career with the Brooklyn Dodgers. Although other outstanding black players had promptly entered the major leagues, the color barrier would not be lifted on all teams until 1959.

With respect to Beta Alpha Psi, the most important difference between blacks and Jews was that the latter group were far more likely to attend college, particularly schools at which fraternal chapters existed, or would be formed, during the third era. Relatedly, as public accounting practice

evolved toward genuine professionalism, it would naturally have attracted an ethnic group strongly associated with both business and professional life. A. J. Penz indeed recalls first hearing references to accounting as "Jewish engineering" during a brief wartime teaching assignment at Rensselaer Polytechnic Institute, a major center of more conventional engineering studies.

Black enrollment in higher education had traditionally been very low, and of course was not even permitted at certain state-supported chapter sites in the third era. Many black students who did attend college were attracted to traditionally black institutions like Fisk, Howard, and Wilberforce Universities, Tuskegee Institute, and a number of public colleges in southern and border states. Inquiries concerning possible formation of Beta Alpha Psi chapters were received during the third era from four such schools. They were Atlanta University, representing a group of affiliated colleges, and three "land-grant" institutions: Southern University (in Louisiana), Tennessee (A. and I.) State, and Virginia State.[13]

---

[13]Red Barber, 1947--When All Hell Broke Loose in Baseball (Garden City, N.Y.: Doubleday & Co., 1982), pp. 52, 54-55; [Barron's] Profiles of American Colleges: Descriptions of the Colleges, 14th ed. (Woodbury, N.Y.: Barron's Educational Found., 1984), s.v. "Georgia, Morris Brown College" (Atlanta University affiliate), "Tennessee, Tennessee State University," "Louisiana, Southern University and A & M College," "Virginia, Virginia State University"; The College Handbook, 1984-85, 22nd ed. (New York: College Entrance Examination Board, 1984), s.v. "Massachusetts; Brandeis University"; Arnold Forster and Benjamin R. Epstein, The New Anti-Semitism (New York: McGraw-Hill, 1974), p. 2, quoted; Funk & Wagnalls New Encyclopedia [1981] ed. (c1979), s.v. "B'nai B'rith," quoting translation of the name; Leslie Halliwell, Halliwell's Film Guide, 4th ed. (New York: Charles Scribner's Sons, 1983), s.v. "Gentleman's Agreement," quoted; Edward Kierch, Where Have You Gone, Vince DiMaggio? (Toronto and New York: Bantam Books, 1983), p. 43; Clarence E. Lovejoy, Lovejoy's College Guide, 15th ed. (New York: Simon & Schuster, 1981), s.v. "Tennessee, Tennessee State University"; A. J. Penz, Secretary-Treasurer's Reports, 1953-54, p. 7, 1954-55, p. 8; Penz to Author, interview (Tuscaloosa, Ala.), August 15, 1984, quoted; Richard Reeves, American Journey (New York: Simon and Schuster, 1982), pp. 280-il; Eric Solomon, "Baseball, Johns Hopkins, Earl Wasserman, and Me," Johns Hopkins Magazine 35 (April 1984):16, quoted; S. M. Wedeberg, Secretary-Treasurer's Report, 1952-53, p. 6; [Nolan E. Williams], Secretary-Treasurer's Reports, 1957-58, p. 4, 1958-59, p. 5; and Joel Williamson, The Crucible of Race: Black-White Relations in the American South Since Emancipation (New

With full support from the Grand Council, Jewish students became prominently represented within Beta Alpha Psi in the early years of the third era.

Ending of Anti-Semitism within Beta Alpha Psi

Even without action at the national level, there was prompt movement away from prior local discrimination against Jewish students. For example, such students were clearly predominant within Mu Chapter at New York by the early 1950s, even though a member had been expelled in 1930 upon the realization that he was "not a Christian, with the result that he was not on cordial terms with the rest of the members." As other instances, Pi Chapter at Western Reserve admitted many Jewish members, in keeping with an official policy of nondiscrimination adopted in 1950, and Gamma at Northwestern, earlier a source of objection to the Boston chapter, did so as well.

The Grand Council strongly encouraged such developments by approving chapter formation at institutions having large Jewish enrollments. The best example was the installation of Alpha Gamma in May of 1949, as the second new chapter, at the City College of New York, a municipal tuition-free institution that had always been extremely popular among the large Jewish population of the city. Five years later the business school would

---

York and Oxford: Oxford University Press, 1984), pp. 483-84.

Even a quarter century after the end of the third fraternal era (1984-85), some 250,000 of the 1,100,000 blacks attending American colleges and universities were enrolled in the nearly 100 predominantly black institutions. Dave Evans, Harvard University admissions office, to Bryant Gumbal (NBC News), televised interview, Today, December 17, 1984, and Gumbal's prefatory remarks.

The reference to Gentleman's Agreement warrants noting that in 1949 one Gregory H. Peck was elected secretary of Iota Chapter at Southern California, appropriately enough, and served as the Newsletter correspondent. "Local Chapter News," Newsletter [3] (November 1950):15.

be renamed in honor of one of CCNY's most distinguished former students, the Jewish financier and statesman Bernard M. Baruch (1870-1965). In 1968 it would become a constituent part of Bernard M. Baruch College, a new institution within the City University of New York.

One night after the Alpha Gamma ceremony, Alpha Delta Chapter was chartered at the University of Pennsylvania, another school attracting many Jewish students. President Thomas Dickerson conducted both installations. Joining Penn in the Beta Alpha Psi fold, seven years later, was its sister Philadelphia institution Temple University. A quarter-century earlier, as reported in volume 1, a petition from the latter school had been turned down under circumstances suggestive of an anti-Semitic bias.[14]

The third era found black membership in, for example, several chapters reactivated after the war. Even though it has grown significantly from the very low levels of that day, black participation within Beta Alpha Psi has remained notably limited over the quarter century since 1960.

Racial Integration of the Fraternity

Illustrating the early postwar racial integration of the fraternity, at least a third of the chapters existing throughout the period initiated one or more black members during the third era. One unit, possibly not included among those chapters, had *earlier* inducted a black graduate student

---

[14]Thomas M. Dickerson, "Two New Chapters Installed," in "Grand Chapter News," ed. [John Arch White], *Newsletter* [3] (November 1949):10-11; *Funk & Wagnalls*, s.v. "Baruch, Bernard Mannes"; [W. B. Jencks], "Grand Council News," *Newsletter* [4] (November 1956):342-43; "Local Chapter News," *Newsletter* [3] (March 1951):27, 4 (November 1952):18, (March 1954):148, (November 1954): 223, (April 1956):310, member listings replete with "Jewish" names; Lovejoy, *Lovejoy's College Guide*, s.v. "New York: City University of New York, Bernard M. Baruch College . . ."; A. J. Penz to Author, interview, August 15, 1984, quoted; Sheldahl *Alpha to Omega*, pp. 173, 720; and Anthony Yocis, Mu Chapter president, to Jacob B. Taylor, July 1, 1930 (national files).

destined to become a prominent educator and governmental accountant. The slow entry of blacks into the fraternity was in keeping with severe limitations of professional opportunity pointed up by the cases of respective black midcentury graduates of Berkeley (a Lambda member) and Western Reserve. Even given a far more favorable external environment, and the absence of any indication of lingering racial bias within the fraternity, black participation in Beta Alpha Psi, and the accounting field in general, remains disproportionately low in the present day.

A distinguished prewar initiate:
Rho brother William L. Campfield

In the course of investigating the scope of recent participation by blacks, it came to light that an outstanding black governmental accountant and educator had entered Beta Alpha Psi prior to 1940. New York University alumnus William L. Campfield was initiated by Rho in May 1937, just before receiving his M.B.A. degree from Minnesota. A contemporary active member of the chapter, incidentally, was future Touche Ross chairman Robert M. Trueblood, who would be honored posthumously by election in 1974 to the Accounting Hall of Fame.

Bill Campfield was naturally cited in the nationwide Directory issued in 1939. He was then serving as an accountant and secretary at Johnson C. Smith University, a predominantly black school located in Charlotte, North Carolina, although his "[p]ermanent" home address was the Tuskegee Institute in Alabama. Twelve years later, in 1951, Campfield completed a doctorate in accounting at Illinois. His dissertation "An Inquiry into the Nature of Judgment Formation and its Implications to the Public Accounting Profession" was developed under the supervision of early Beta Alpha Psi president A. C. Littleton.

Over a long professional career still in progress in the mid-1980s, Dr. Campfield has taught at some twenty colleges and universities, mostly on visiting appointments. He has served, for example, at the predominantly black institutions Morgan State (Maryland) and Florida A. and M.; the more diversified minority-oriented school Florida International; the comprehensive public universities Illinois, Ohio State, and South Carolina; and the Jesuit university San Francisco. In the fall of 1985, Campfield began his fifth year on the faculty at Florida International, in Miami. He was lecturing at San Francisco, incidentally, at or around the time that the school submitted a third-era inquiry (1952-53) concerning the possible formation of a Beta Alpha Psi chapter.

It was in California in the fifties that Dr. Campfield began a distinguished career of public service with the U.S. Army Audit Agency. He held several managerial positions with the agency at national headquarters in Washington before moving to the General Accounting Office, where he was based for the last six years of a two-decade career of federal service.

From January 1952, as a lecturer at the University of San Francisco, through October 1970, as associate director of the General Accounting Office, the Rho Chapter alumnus contributed eleven articles to the world-renowned American quarterly The Accounting Review. Befitting his credentials as a certified public accountant, governmental auditor and staff training specialist, and collegiate educator, Campfield's principal topics were professional education, training, and practice within public accounting and (inclusive of government service) internal auditing. Validly or not, on an honorary basis he was inducted in 1969 by a second fraternal unit, Theta at Texas.[15]

---

[15] Barron's Profiles, s.v. "Florida: Florida Agricultural and Mechanical University; Florida International University," "Maryland, Morgan State University"; Thomas J. Burns and Edward N. Coffman, The Accounting Hall of Fame: Profiles of Thirty-six Members ([Columbus, Ohio]: College of

In the early postwar years, black students at several universities would join Bill Campfield within the Beta Alpha Psi ranks.

A survey of the 21 "old" chapters

Method of inquiry - archival research by correspondence

Black participation in the fraternity of the third era has been surveyed among the twenty-one chapters reactivated after the war, from Alpha to Omega. Information was already available only in the case of Theta at Texas, as profiled by C. Aubrey Smith in his historical study of the local accountancy program. In an attempt to develop solid, if incomplete, information on the other chapters, the archival staff at each of the other twenty universities was asked to inspect campus yearbooks from 1946-47 through 1959-60 for photographs of the local Beta Alpha Psi chapter. The basic request was to identify the earliest black member observed, although in several cases additonal information was provided.

Eighteen archivists were able to comply with the request, one through a substitute approach in the absence of fraternal yearbook photos. Past or present chapter sources supplied the information in the other two cases. A number of respondents noted inherent limitations of the approach--missing chapter photos and/or absence of certain members from groups photographed.

Administrative Science, Ohio State University, 1976), pp. 69, 80, 82; William L. Campfield, initial pages of the 11 Accounting Review articles listed by Previts and Committe in the source cited below; Campfield to Author, by telephone, October 1, 1985; James R. Hasselback, comp., Prentice-Hall Accounting Faculty Directory: 1980-81 (Englewood Cliffs: Prentice-Hall, 1981), and 1984 Directory, individual listings, s.v. "Campfield, William L."; Hermann C. Miller, ed., Beta Alpha Psi, The National Accounting Fraternity: Directory ([Columbus: Grand Council, 1939]), s.v. "Rho Chapter: Campfield, William L.; Trueblood, Robert M."; Gary John Previts and Bruce L. Committe, comps., An Index to the "Accounting Review," 1926-1978, and Proceedings of the AAUIA, 1917-1925 (Sarasota, Fla.: American Accounting Association, 1980), part 1, s.v. "Campfield, William L."; Smith, Forty Acres, p. 67; and V. K. Zimmerman, "The Long Shadow of a Scholar," The International Journal of Accounting: Education and Research 2 (Spring 1967):7.

On occasion, as observed by one archivist, the racial identity of a member might not be evident. Despite these limitations, black membership was verified for six of the twenty chapters besides Theta, and more or less conclusively ruled out for a numer of others.

The oldest Beta Alpha Psi unit was probably the first or second one to initiate a black member during the era, leading to an officership appointment.

Summary of findings

Late in 1947 both Alpha at Illinois and Omicron at Ohio State admitted a black member. Frederick C. Ford was then elected treasurer at Illinois for his final semester prior to graduation at the close of the academic year. Ford was president of the student senate during the same term in 1948, and for the full year was president of a black social fraternity on campus, Kappa Alpha Psi. He would successfully complete the CPA examination in 1952.

In December 1947, on the same occasion as future Illinois professor Norton M. Bedford (discussed in chapter 6 as a prominent critic of the fraternity's "activity" program), black student Farnham (John) E. Mosley was initiated at Ohio State. Carl J. Character was admitted by Omicron three years later, and there may have been a third black member in 1953-54.

The earliest black members identified from Lambda Chapter at the University of California were John Branch and Warren G. Parker, of the respective Classes of 1949 and 1950. Unable upon graduation to find an accounting firm that was "willing to hire a black person," Parker began a career with the Bureau of Internal Revenue, soon to be reorganized as the Internal Revenue Service. Based mainly in the San Francisco area, he would serve as a collection officer, field tax examiner, and (beginning in 1967)

employee plans specialist. Counting military service in the China-Burma-India theater, 1943-45, and brief stints as a civilian employee of the Naval Supply Center in Oakland, he retired in January 1986 with thirty-nine years of federal employment. Warren Parker married his "childhood sweetheart" while at Berkeley, and they have four children and three grandchildren.

Also in California, Iota Chapter at USC initiated several members of Asian ancestry during the third era, but the only known black participant was Edward Smith, who served as treasurer in the fall of 1955. Across the continent at Mu Chapter at New York, the lone black depicted in available sources was a member of the 1959-60 group not identified by name.

The first black member of Theta at the University of Texas was inducted in the spring of 1957. Luzine B. Bickham, a doctoral student in business administration who already held two degrees from Michigan, would later become business dean at Texas Southern University, a predominantly black institution in Houston. At the installation of Delta Xi Chapter at Texas Southern in 1975, the principal speaker was a distinguished alumnus who had been initiated by Beta Alpha fifteen years earlier while pursuing graduate work at Indiana. Dr. Joe J. Cramer, Jr. has since moved, by way of an interim professorship at Southern Cal, from Penn State to Howard University.

Concerned by a pattern of very low black involvement in accounting studies at Texas, the local department and Theta Chapter in 1970, or thereabouts, undertook a program aimed at recruitment of talented black students from the state's high schools and junior colleges. Chapter members have since then made many visitations to the schools to interview such students, although Aubrey Smith reported in 1980 that the results of such recruiting efforts had been disappointing.

One of the most explicit third-era initiatives on behalf of equal opportunity within Beta Alpha Psi was taken by Pi Chapter at Western Reserve

FIRST BLACK MEMBERS OF RHO (PRESUMABLY) AND THETA CHAPTERS

WILLIAM L. CAMPFIELD, RHO '37,
as NYU undergraduate in mid-thirties

LUZINE B. BICKHAM, THETA '57

A 1950 LAMBDA CHAPTER LUNCHEON MEETING:
AN EARLY BLACK MEMBER, A COUNCILOR, AND THREE FUTURE EDUCATIONAL LEADERS

Seated, front table: Warren G. Parker and three-term Sigma faculty advisor (through '86) Roy E. Tuttle.
Seated, back table, future American Accounting Association president Maurice Moonitz.
Standing, Councilor (and chapter FVP) Charles C. Staehling and future AAA president Lawrence L. Vance.

in February 1950. A new bylaw was adopted which stated that '"membership shall not be restricted because of race, creed, color, or religion"', a position strongly supported by Past President Tom Dickerson, head of the accounting department. Three months later, directly prior to his graduation, black student Marion Jones was admitted to Pi membership.

Granting that the evidence is highly inconclusive in a few instances, no black members have been identified within any of the remaining fourteen chapters surveyed. Photographs were evidently available throughout the third era for Beta at Oregon, Delta at Washington, Sigma at Wisconsin, Psi at Marquette, and Omega at Miami of Ohio, and throughout the 1950s for Gamma at Northwestern and Xi at Syracuse. The respondent from Washington, who found no black members in a search that extended through 1964, was careful to point out that some current members were always absent from the photos. In the same connection, it is noteworthy that the 1951 yearbook photograph of Omega included no reference to Jeannine Skelton, a midyear graduate who in the fall had become Beta Alpha Psi's first coed member.

Examination of Northwestern yearbooks beginning in 1949 revealed no black members of Gamma Chapter over the next twenty years, although a broader negative report was discounted due to 1951 listings of an hispanic and a Japanese name. Similarly, although Oklahoma State began admitting black students in 1949, no such individuals were identified within Chi Chapter through the 1960s. No blacks were enrolled prior to the sixties at Florida or (at the undergraduate level) LSU, the sites of Upsilon and Phi, and in the latter case no black members were noted before 1978-79. Zeta Chapter at North Dakota, a school drawing its students primarily from a sparseley populated area having few minority residents, had no black candidates during the third era because there were no black accounting majors on campus. Indeed, it is believed that as of 1985 there had been only

one such student at Grand Forks.

The report concerning Nu Chapter at Colorado identified three "orientals" and one "Filipino or Latin" within the third-era membership, but no blacks. The negative report obtained regarding Rho at Minnesota, William Campfield's chapter, was based on sources limited to 1946-52 and 1954-55. Maryland, finally, had no black accounting majors prior to third-era councilor S. M. Wedeberg's retirement in 1963. The university had been racially segregated before losing one of the pertinent Supreme Court cases of 1954.[16]

The case of a 1950 M.B.A. graduate of Western Reserve not affiliated with Beta Alpha Psi illustrates the compelling need of the day to open the

---

[16] Archivists (including assistants or other staff members) to Author, 1985: Jennifer Allen, Florida, August 29; Kathleen E. Bledsoe, Oklahoma State, September 24; Judy Bolton, Louisiana State, October 7; John A. Brenna, Colorado, August 6, enclosure, quoted; R. Scott Brown, Wisconsin, August 9; C. W. Butler, Miami (Ohio), August 2; Amy S. Doherty, Syracuse, August 1; Raimund E. Goerler, Ohio State, August 1; Lois G. Hendrickson, Minnesota, September 11; Bob Ickes, Southern California, August 5; Joshua Lazerson, Northwestern, July 30; Elizabeth Liu, New York (NYU), August 22; Gisella J. Lozada, Louisiana State, August 12; William J. Maher, Illinois, July 30; Tracy J. Muench, Marquette, July 31; K. Keith Richard, Oregon, August 7; Jeffrey Rollison, Case Western Reserve, September 4; Marie Condon Thornton, California, August 2, enclosure; and Nan E. Young, Washington, August 9.

Other sources: "Chapter News Items," Newsletter [2] (March 1947):8, (May 1947):10; Joe J. Cramer, Jr., "The Nature and Importance of Present Value in Financial Accounting," Part 1, The Arthur Andersen Chronicle 37 (September 1977):37, attached capsule biography; Funk & Wagnalls, s.v. "Internal Revenue Service"; John Gillett, Zeta Chapter faculty vice-president, to Author, September 5, 1985; James R. Hasselback, comp., Prentice-Hall Accounting Faculty Directory: 1979-80 (Englewood Cliffs; 1980), individual listing, s.v. "Cramer, Joe J."; Hasselback, 1984 Directory, individual listing, s.v. "Cramer Jr., Joe J."; "Local Chapter News," [2] (March 1948): 10, (November 1948):11, [3] (May 1950):19, quoted, (November 1950):20, (May 1951): [16], 4 (November 1952):14, (November 1955):281, (April 1956): 312, 5 (April 1961):394; [Robert S. Maust], "New Chapters of Beta Alpha Psi," Beta Alpha Psi, The National Accounting Fraternity: Annual Report / 1976, ed. [Maust, (National Council: 1976)], p. [8]; Warren Parker to Author, August 20, 1985, quoted; Smith, Forty Acres, pp. 68, 68n; C. Aubrey Smith to Author, two-reel recorded response to interview questionnaire, June 1980, part 1; Texas Southern University: 1983-85 General Catalog [and] Bulletin ([Houston: 1983]; 1983-84 Microfiche Catalogs, TX-60), pp. 1, 87-88, 329, 333 (listing Bickham as a professor of general business); University of California Alumni Records to Author, by telephone, August 8, 1985; and S. M. Wedeberg to Author, February 13, 1986.

the door of opportunity to blacks interested in accounting.

A third-era case study from Western Reserve

Elmer J. Whiting, Jr., Howard '44, entered night school at the university's Cleveland College soon after joining the General Accounting Office, in the spring of 1945, as an auditor of Navy Department construction and training outlays. Department head Tom Dickerson over a period of time "pulled strings" to obtain permission for him to take the CPA exam in a state, Ohio, in which no black person had as yet been certified. After promptly completing the exam, Whiting needed an opportunity to meet the experience requirements. Professor Dickerson suggested that he form a partnership with his brother, an accountant in Detroit. In the fall of 1946 the accounting firm "Whiting and Whiting" accordingly opened offices in the brothers' repective cities.

Fully three years later, the Ohio State Board of Accountancy invited Whiting for an interview in Columbus, at the time not an uncommon element of the qualifying process, and somewhat reluctantly he accepted. Having made a highly favorable impression on the board, he received the coveted CPA credential along with his master's degree in 1950, being counted nationally (he recalls) among the first twenty blacks to become certified.

Whiting at once joined the American Institute of Accountants and, under Tom Dickerson's sponsorship, the Ohio Society of CPAs, and was cordially received at the society's 1950 banquet. In a day in which only high school graduation was required of Ohio CPAs, new professional opportunities did not arise for the new M.B.A. product, however. Over a series of "lean" years he continued to build his own practice, while pursuing studies at the Cleveland-Marshall School of Law (since absorbed by Cleveland State). After receiving his J.D. degree in 1955, Whiting for sixteen years combined public accounting with a limited practice of corporate and tax law. The next five blacks

certified in Ohio met experience provisions at least in part within his firm.

Following a 1972 merger, Whiting served five years as an audit partner i the Cleveland office of Ernst & Ernst. He then moved to the national office, also in Cleveland, as as a specialist in state and local government. After retiring from Ernst & Whinney in 1982, Whiting became president of a family-owned consulting firm serving the not-for-profit realm.

Accounting opportunities for qualified blacks, such as 1984-85 Pi Chapter president Lonnie Sloan of Case Western Reserve (incorporating Case Institute of Technology), are of course incomparably better in the 1980s than those open to Elmer Whiting a third of a century earlier.[17] Yet Beta Alpha Psi itself provides disturbing reminders that black men and women are still only sparsely represented within accounting practice and education. In concluding the chapter, a useful comparison may be made with a much larger group traditionally showing low enrollment in the field, namely, women.

Limited present-day participation by blacks, inviting comparative reference to women

Beta Alpha Psi has in a variety of ways proved its commitment to the full inclusion of blacks and other minorities. Chapters have been formed at predominantly black Texas Southern and North Carolina A and T (Zeta Sigma); the second alumni councilor was black; the fraternity has assisted the American Institute in conducting a minority scholarship program; and AICPA minority recruitment manager Sharon L. Donahue served a 1977-80 term on the National Advisory Forum. Sometimes receiving initial financial support

---

[17] Thomas M. Dickerson to Author, interview, April 19, 1980, quoted; Victor A. Feldmiller, executive director, Ohio Society of CPAs, to Author, July 30, 1985; Lovejoy, Lovejoy's College Guide, s.v. "Ohio, Cleveland-Marshall School of Law"; Previts, "American Accounting Education," p. 6; Linda M. Stillabower, Pi Chapter faculty adviosr, to Author (by telephone), November 19, 27, 1984; and Elmer J. Whiting, Jr. to Author, October 15, 1985, quoted.

from the National Council, local chapters have also taken a variety of pertinent initiatives, including recruitment of minority students (as cited earlier regarding Theta at Texas), and provision to inner-city residents and/or business firms of free professional services. Black member Warren Moorehead of Beta Phi accepted a plaque at the 1970 National Chapter meeting at Maryland for a Newsletter essay on Sacramento State's new "Community Business Service Center," adjudged the year's outstanding contributed manuscript.

Yet as of August 1984 only two black persons had either served on the Council or the Advisory Forum, or received a national award for faculty advisors. The 1977-78 alumni councilor was Leroy Tanker of Alpha Beta at Alabama, and one of the Outstanding Faculty Vice-Presidents of 1979-80 was Larzette G. Hale of Delta Omega at Utah State, who as a doctoral student at Wisconsin in the 1950s would have been barred from all-male Sigma Chapter. Judging in particular from pictorial coverage in the nine "annual reports" issued through 1984, a similar pattern of no more than minimal participation had extended to other Beta Alpha Psi programs and activites, including student-centered areas.

By and large, however, comparably low involvement by women is documented in the reports. Only two women had served as national officers by 1984, Doris Cook and Joyce Dean, and only three others had served on the National Council as alumni or area representatives. None of the 27 "Accountants of the Year" had been female. Only 7 of the 72 faculty vice-presidents honored over the years and 4 of the 71 Forum members were women. A somewhat higher proportion of 1984 faculty advisors were female, 20 out of 155 (excluding two cases not classifiable by name).

At the student level, however, women had truly come to the fore in terms of Beta Alpha Psi involvement. Excluding a few names difficult to

classify, they comprised approximately 45% of the chapter presidents and 43% of the "National Scholars" (participants in any of five fraternal activities) listed in 1984, rates very much in line with a report issued a year later that 48% of all new accounting graduates were women. Consistent with earlier enrollment patterns, as recently as 1978-79 more than 70% of local chapter presidents had been male.[18]

Such data clearly foreshadow much higher levels of recognition for women throughout the fraternity than have been recorded to date. A similar prospect will emerge for minority groups as talented young men and women from such ranks become increasingly attracted to the study of accounting, and go on to develop outstanding professional careers in the field. The several "reminders" of low black participation to date were cited only to

---

[18]"Arthur Andersen & Co. Sponsors Richard S. Claire Awards," "Outstanding Faculty Vice Presidents . . .," or comparable title, Newsletter 9-14 (Spring 1971, Winter, Spring, 1972, Fall, 1972-75), pictorial coverage; Barron's Profiles, s.v. "North Carolina, North Carolina Agricultural and Mechanical State University"; "Beta Alpha Psi [or National] Advisory Forum Meets," Newsletter 14-15, 17 (Fall, 1975, 1976, 1978), pictorial coverage; Beta Alpha Psi Annual Report, 1975-76 through 1983-84, passim; "Former Accountants of the Year," Beta Alpha Psi, The National Accounting Fraternity: 1982 Annual Report, ed. [Henry R. Anderson, (National Council, 1982)], p. 18; Hasselback, 1984 Directory, individual listing, s.v. "Hale, Larzette G."; Robert S. Maust to Author, by telephone, September 18, 1985; [Metcalf], ed. 1983-84 Annual Report, pp. 4-8 ("National Scholars"), 31-38 ("Chapter Information"), 39 ("Prior [FVP Award] Recipients"), [40] (past alumni and area councilors); Warren Moorehead, Beta Phi Chapter, "Community Business Service Center Opened in Sacramento," Newsletter 8 (Spring 1970):3; [Fred J. Mueller], "Changes in National Council," Beta Alpha Psi . . .: Annual Report / 1977, ed. [Mueller, (National Council, 1977)], p. 3; "The National Chapter: 1978-79," Beta Alpha Psi . . .: Annual Report / 1979, ed. [Thomas J. Burns, (National Council, 1979)], pp. 1-2; [Patillo], ed., 1979-80 Annual Report, pp. 6 ("National Advisory Forum"), 12 ("Outstanding F.V.P. Awards"); Robert R. Randall, ed., "Data Sheet," Management Accounting (U.S.) 43 (July 1985):18; [Harold R. Royer], "Community Projects Encouranged by National" and "More than 100 Beta Alpha Psi delegates . . .," Newsletter 9 (Winter 1971):2; [Charles W. Taylor], "Drake Students and Accounting Aid Society Benefit Des Moines Community" and "Psi Chapter to Aid Direct Assistance Program in Milwaukee," Newsletter 8 (Spring 1970):2; and [Robert S. Wasley], Secretary-Treasurer's Report, 1969-70, p. 1.

draw attention to the continuing challenges presented to accounting educators in this regard, particularly those involved at any level within Beta Alpha Psi.

In Transition

To simplify coverage, only the 21 chapters reactivated after the Second World War were surveyed regarding the admission of black students to fraternal membership. The expansion of the Beta Alpha Psi roster during the third era to 31 new sites changed the profile of the organization as surely as did the enlargement of membership opportunity reviewed in this chapter.

CHAPTER 2

ROSTER EXPANSION IN THE THIRD ERA: STEADY GROWTH, DIVERSIFICATION, QUALITY CONTROL, AND LOCAL INITIATIVE

During the third era the chapter roster was more than doubled from the prewar total of twenty-one groups. Thirty new units were formed, ranging from Alpha Beta at Alabama in 1948 to Beta Theta at Penn State, a latter-day football rival of the Crimson Tide's, in 1960. In addition, Epsilon Chapter was reinstated at Oregon State in 1959. Beyond the numerical realm, this expansion significantly broadened the Beta Alpha Psi community, especially through marked elaboration of earlier precedents.

Starting more than two years before the first new chapter was installed, inquiries were generally received each year from a good number of interested campuses. Establishing a strong requirement of quality control (professional accreditation), and scrupulously avoiding any appearance of recruitment, the Grand Council would nonetheless miss few opportunities to cultivate new chapter possibilites. Such prospects commonly emerged on the initiative of local faculty members who were fraternal alumni. After 1951, initiation teams visiting from established chapters would ordinarily assist the presiding councilor at installations, whose costs were borne at least in part by the new local units through the academic year 1955-56. Many schools first expressing interest during the postwar expansionist era would in later years be added to the fraternal ranks.

The installation at Alabama was preceded by inquiries from numerous

other campuses, and an unsuccessful petition from an eventual chapter site of special historical interest. Resuming contact with the fraternity over this same period, 1946-48, were two former Beta Alpha Psi locations, one of which was denied permission to seek readmittance. The other school was cited above in regard to reinstatement near the close of the era.

Inquiries Prior to the First Postwar Installation

General Overview

In the spring of 1946, Secretary-Treasurer Elwell received letters concerning possible chapter formation from professors at Loyola of New Orleans, and the University of Missouri. He undoubtedly forwarded basic information on Beta Alpha Psi, but nothing more would be heard from either university at the time. Loyola was destined to be one of the last entrants of the third era, while Missouri would show no further interest until the 1960s.

From the fall of 1946 through the spring of 1948, thirty-six institutions expressed some level of interest in forming chapters. Secretary-Treasurers Kendrick and W. E. Dickerson faithfully answered each inquiry. The College of William and Mary, Clarkson College in upstate New York, and the University of Alabama each inquired in both academic years, with the latter school tendering a petition that would lead to the first installation of the era. The full list of colleges and universities indicating an interest in chapter formation during the years 1945-48 is presented as exhibit 4.

Besides Alabama, only City College of New York, Arkansas, Southern Methodist, and Missouri were at the time members of the American Association of Collegiate Schools of Business. As explained later, such an affiliation was adopted in 1947 as a constitutional requirement for eligibility. Each of the "accredited" schools except Missouri would form a Beta Alpha Psi chapter over the following three years. Later in the period,

EXHIBIT 4

SOURCES OF CHAPTER FORMATION INQUIRIES, 1945-48[a]

1945-46

1. Loyola of New Orleans
2. Missouri

1946-47

1. Alabama
2. Alpha, N.J. (proprietary business col.)
3. Arizona State
4. Arkansas State
5. Boston Col.
6. Chattanooga (Tennessee at Chattanooga)
7. City Col. of New York
8. Clarkson
9. Fenn (Cleveland State)
10. Louisville
11. Mississippi State
12. Northeast Jr. Col. of LSU (Northeast Louisiana)
13. Pennsylvania Military (defucnt)
14. San Jose State
15. Wichita (Wichita State)
16. William and Mary

1947-48

1. Akron
2. Alabama
3. Arkansas
4. Arkansas State
5. Baldwin-Wallace
6. Bowling Green State
7. Cincinnati
8. Clarkson
9. Golden Gate
10. Kansas State
11. Louisiana Polytechnic (Louisiana Tech)
12. Miami of Florida
13. Michigan State
14. Mississippi Southern (Southern Mississippi)
15. Oregon State
16. Rider
17. Southern Methodist
18. Stetson
19. Valparaiso
20. Washington State
21. Western Union (Westmar)
22. William and Mary
23. Wittenburg

SOURCES: Cleveland State University Bulletin: Undergraduate Studies, 1983-85 ([Cleveland]:1983; 1983-84 Microfiche Catalogs, OH-4), p. 1; W. E. Dickerson, Secretary-Treasurer's Report, 1947-48, p. 4; F. H. Elwell, Secretary-Treasurer's Report, 1942-46, p. 6; H. W. Kendrick, Secretary-Treasurer's Report, 1946-47, p. 5; Lovejoy, Lovejoy's College Guide, s.v. "Kansas, Wichita State University," "Louisiana: Louisiana Tech University; Northeast Louisiana University," "Tennessee: Tennessee, University of, at Chattanooga"; and Westmar College - Preparing You for Success in Life and Your Career, 1983-85 ([LeMars, Iowa: 1983]; 1983-84 Microfiche Catalogs, IA-13), p. 3.

[a]Changes in short-form institutional names since the year of inquiry are shown parenthetically. The demise of Pennsylvania Military College is documented in exhibit 7, note b.

however, chapters would be established also at Loyola, Michigan State, Cincinnati, Bowling Green, and Louisiana Polytechnic, after each school had become eligible. The association, always known in fact simply as the "AACSB," is cited subsequently as the "AAcSB" to distinguish it from the present-day American "Assembly" of Collegiate Schools of Business.

One institution formally petitioned for a chapter prior to Alabama, and another one sought consent to do so. An application from San Jose State College was rejected at the annual meeting in 1947 following "considerable discussion." San Jose had originally expressed interest just prior to Pearl Harbor, as reported in volume 1, apparently representing the first state college in California to contact the Grand Council. Along with San Diego State, site of the first pertinent chapter, the school was thus a pioneer in the development of the fraternity's principal family of chapter sites.

Having twice renewed contact with the Council during the interim, San Jose State would submit another petition nine years later. Since the business school remained unaccredited, that application could only have been a purely local initiative. The Grand Council routinely rejected the second petition, having found "nothing new in the picture." Thirteen years later, in 1969, Gamma Xi Chapter would be installed at San Jose.

Two Former Chapter Sites

William and Mary requested permission in 1947 to apply for a new charter, or for the reinstatement of Kappa Chapter, whose charter had been returned a year after formal deactivation of the group in December 1939. The request from Willimsburg was denied, ostensibly because the school lacked AAcCSB credentials. Apparently, however, the circumstances under which Kappa had originally been disbanded would have precluded any chance of favorable action.

As reported in volume 1, in the mid-1930s accounting studies at William and Mary had been absorbed by the economics department. More importantly, perhaps, the introductory course had been moved to the junior-year curriculum, thus preventing students from qualifying for Beta Alpha Psi, by the rules of the day, until at least the midpoint of the senior year. These developments were no doubt highly instrumental in the apparent cessation of all fraternal activity at the school after 1935.

In his 1947 request, Professor Wayne F. Gibbs no doubt advised Secretary-Treasurer Kendrick that a business department had been reestablished in 1942, and it is assumed that the curricular problem cited had been dispatched at the same time. The Council had not been persuaded in 1939, however, that local academic reorganization had justified four years of total chapter inactivity (a viewpoint drawing some support from a letter received from the chapter advisor himself). Instead, the group had "severely critici[z]ed" Kappa Chapter, as led by Gibbs, for having "refused or neglected to abide by the Statutes of the fraternity."

The oldest 1947 councilor in point of service, outgoing president James McConahey, had been elected during the 1939 meeting, and so had no first-hand knowledge of the earlier preceedings. He and his colleagues accordingly consulted earlier secretary-treasurer Hermann C. Miller and one or more of the other 1939 councilors prior to the meeting at which the new request from Willimsburg would be considered. In part because the earlier members were "very much opposed to reinstatement," there was no support for such action within McConahey's Council. With the adoption at the same 1947 meeting of a constitutional amendment restricting new chapters to AAcCSB-approved schools, reinstatement of Kappa would have been the only possible basis at the time for readmitting William and Mary.

The following year, in 1948, Professor Gibbs made another request

on behalf of such action. Since the matter was not mentioned in the minutes submitted by Secretary-Treasurer William Dickerson, it may not have even been considered at the Council meeting of that year. Finally, correspondence with Gibbs or others at the Virginia School led to an expectation in 1952 that a petition for reinstatement would be submitted, but no application was forthcoming.

In 1947-48 another early fraternal site requested information on the possibility of reestablishing a defunct chapter, namely, Oregon State (formerly Oregon Agricultural) College. Epsilon Chapter had been deactivated fifteen years earlier following state-imposed termination at Corvallis of all degree programs in nonclerical business fields. During the preceding four years, however, Oregon State had housed a degree-granting Division of Business & Industry, about to be succeeded by a School of Business and Technology offering a degree concentration in accounting.

In the summer of 1949 charter Epsilon brother Alton L. Peterson wrote Secretary-Treasurer William E. Dickerson concerning possible reactivation. He was advised that the essential conditions would be (a) AAcCSB membership and (b) existence of "a strong accounting department with [a] sufficient number of accounting majors." In numerical terms, at least, the department was probably in a strong position, since by 1950 the business school was the largest academic division on the Corvallis campus.

In 1952 incoming president Staehling presented a report to his fellow councilors concerning Oregon State, and was instructed to decide whether a petition should be invited. Although accreditation had not been attained, the only specific requirement cited was satisfaction that "the conditions which [had] caused the interruption of activities" had been corrected. Staehling's basic task, then, was to determine whether Oregon State had

resumed "a complete accounting curriculum," as the Grand Council had been advised. Former councilor McConahey was of the opinion that the institution continued to offer "only such accounting courses . . . as needed by an agricultural school."

President Staehling duly verified that a full-fledged accounting program had been restored at Corvallis, and the Grand Council voted at its annual meeting in 1953 to reactivate Epsilon. A year later, however, the Council reversed itself by ruling that Oregon State "would have to apply for a new chapter on the same basis as other schools," after Staehling had reported that there was "not enough interest manifest" at the campus to justify reactivation. Evidently no initiative would be taken at the local level until the fall of 1957, and a formal petition may have been delayed for yet another year. Epsilon Chapter was finally reinstalled in the spring of 1959, which notably was a year before Oregon State was readmitted by the accrediting body.[1]

The thirty-one institutions establishing fraternal chapters between the

---

[1]W. E. Dickerson to Alton L. Peterson (Epsilon '22), August 1, 1949, Policies File, quoted; Dickerson, Secretary-Treasurer's Report, 1947-48, p. [4]; Fayette H. Elwell, Secretary-Treasurer's Report, 1946-47, p. 6; Wayne F. Gibbs to Hermann C. Miller, March 14, 1983 (copy enclosed, McConahey to Wedeberg, February 6, 1952); Grand Council Minutes Book, 1947, pp. [2] (quoted), 3, 1952, pp. 3, 4 (quoted), 1953, p. 2, 1954, p. 2 (quoted), 1956, p. 3 (quoted); Jeanne Heywood, Office Mgr., Oregon State University Archives, to Author, January 29, 1985; H. W. Kendrick, Secretary-Treasurer's Report, 1946-47, p. 5; "[Local] Chapter News," Newsletter 5 (1959):224; Jas. M. McConahey to S. M. Wedeberg, February 6, 1952, January 28, 1953, both quoted; "Members of the Accreditation Council," AACSB Membership Directory, 1984-85 ([St. Louis: American Assembly of Collegiate Schools of Business, 1984]), pp. 16-24; A. J. Penz, Secretary-Treasurer's Report, 1954-55, p. 8; Alton L. Peterson to Dickerson, July 23, 1949, Policies File; Kristin M. Peterson, Oregon State University Archives, to Author, August 24, 1983, enclosed page on "School of Business and Technology: Chronology," 1880-1965; Charles F. Schlatter, Grand Council Minutes ("Meeting of the Grand Council," December 28-29,) 1932, p. 1 (copied from Alpha Chapter files soon to be disposed of, July 1980); Sheldahl, Alpha to Omega, pp. 168, 739-40; Wedeberg to McConahey, February 13, 1953; and [Nolan E. Williams], Secretary-Treasurer's Report, 1957-58, p. 4.

fall of 1948 and the spring of 1960 may usefully be classified in terms of three primary variables. One of them, in particular, invites subclassification reflecting expanded roster breadth.

A General Profile of Third-era Installation Sites

The three categories are the (1) geographical location, (2) source of controlling authority (public or private), and (3) level of urbanization of (as appropriate) the school or community. The first and third variables are approached in terms of workable division into four regions and three levels, respectively. Public institutions are subclassified by the controlling governmental unit, and state schools further by (in particular) the geographical range of the principal student market, while privately supported colleges and universities are divided primarily between church-sponsored campuses and other nonpublic schools.

Geographical Distribution

The geographical regions selected are western, central, southern and border, and eastern. The most striking pattern in this regard was the low representation of the Pacific and Rocky Mountain states. Aside from the return of Oregon State, only Denver (1950) and San Diego State (1960) entered the fraternity from the west, understood to exclude Texas. Twenty other schools from the region expressed interest at one time or another, ranging from a Wyoming junior college to an institution (Los Angeles State, as one campus of California State University was then known) that would be chartered at the outset of the next era. Unsuccessful petitioner San Jose State submitted inquiries in four separate years, as already noted, and Arizona State did so three times. By 1984 thirteen of the nineteen institutions had earned Beta Alpha Psi charters, excluding only one professionally accredited school,

although the unit at UCLA had been short-lived.

Counting Los Angeles State, accredited in 1960, six western schools submitting inquiries but not forming chapters in the third era were contemporary AAcCSB members. The others were Arizona, UCLA, Fresno State, Washington State, and the University of San Francisco. In the last three cases the inquiries either preceded accreditation or occurred in the year it was attained. The Universities of Utah, Santa Clara, and Wyoming also held the required membership, during all or part of the era, but evidently did not register interest in Beta Alpha Psi. Of all the western schools cited, only Santa Clara had not formed a fraternal chapter by 1984. During the third era, finally, the only western councilors were H. W. Kendrick of Colorado and Charles Staehling of Berkeley, the presidents of the fraternity in 1947-48 and 1952-53.

In classifying by region the twenty-eight other chapters formed in the third era, Ohio and Texas, each the site of three new units, are regarded in turn as central and southern states. Based on these conventions, the regional totals are ten chapters in both the central states and the southern or border region, and eight in the east. With the admission of Michigan, Michigan State, Iowa, and Indiana, only Purdue University from the "Big Ten" athletic conference lacked a Beta Alpha Psi chapter. From the south, broadly construed, four schools likewise entered from both the "Southwest" and "Southeastern" conferences, in addition to Louisiana Polytechnic Institute and Loyola of New Orleans.

There were interesting regional patterns among the new chapter sites in terms of source of governing control.

"Public" vs. "Private" Control, and Related Distinctions

Nineteen chapters were established during the period at publicly

supported institutions, two of them representing, as a new category for Beta Alpha Psi, municipal schools. The state colleges and universities differed notably in primary educational missions, including scope of the intrastate student market. Representing virtually a new species of sites, half of the twelve private schools were controlled by religious bodies.

Nineteen public institutions

Two municipal campuses

Seventeen of the public institutions were state colleges or universities, joining fifteen earlier chapter locations in that regard. The City College of New York, a 1949 installation site, and the University of Cincinnati, added six years later, were instead maintained by their respective municipalities. The New York campus, which continued (with its sister city schools) to offer strong academic programs to local residents on a tutition-free basis, was discussed earlier in regard to its high Jewish enrollment.

Cincinnati, which would in 1977 become a state school, was distinctive in another way, operating an essentially "cooperative" business college. During an academic year divided into six seven-week terms, students would alternate periods of study and intervals of practical work experience. For example, first-year Alpha Sigma initiate Thomas Williams, who would become a distinguished educator at Texas and Wisconsin, worked for two public accounting firms as an undergraduate student at Cincinnati, 1953-58.

Approximately half of the cooperative students would be taking classroom work at any given time. Since all members were enrolled on such a basis, this meant that Alpha Sigma chapter was divided into two separate sections. A report from 1960-61 indicated that a measure of integration of the two units had been achieved through featuring talks by currently employed student members at the beginning of each term's program.

Seventeen state institutions

The seventeen state-controlled schools added to the roster represented an interesting geographical distribution and, more importantly, a variety of overall educational missions. They comprised two of the three sites in the west, six of the ten in the central states, and seven of the ten in the south or border region, but only two of the eight locations in the east.

With an exception noted below, all state colleges and universities chartered by Beta Alpha Psi before the war had represented one or both of two species. They were (a) the primary general-purpose public institutions in their states, and/or (b) "land-grant" schools specifically committed to higher education in "agriculture and the mechanic arts."[2] A dozen new chapter sites of the third era were consistent with this tradition, but five

---

[2]The "land-grant" system was established following the passage in 1862 of the Morrill Act, providing for the transfer to each state of 30,000 acres of public land (or an equivalent "scrip" certificate) per United States senator and representative from the state. These grants were made specifically to fund higher education in "agriculture and the mechanic arts," although from the outset there was a commitment to curricular breadth rather than narrow vocational training. Later legislation, including a second Morrill Act (1890), extended the program significantly.

By 1929 colleges and universities in all 48 states and the territories of Alaska, Hawaii, and Puerto Rico had been designated, or established, as land-grand schools. There were 69 such institutions, generally one per jurisdiction unless racial segregation were practiced, in which case there were separate schools for white and black students.

While continuing to offer regular programs in agriculture and engineering, most of the 72 land-grant institutions of the present day are broadly based universities rather than "A. and M." colleges. In a recent year some 20% of the undergraduate degrees, 25% of the master's degrees, and 40% of the doctorates awarded in the United States were conferred by these schools, which now depend upon federal sources for less than one-tenth of their funding. Henry S. Brunner, Land-Grant Colleges and Universities, 1862-1962 (Washington, D.C.: U.S. Government Printing Office, 1962), pp. 2-4, 43-44, 75-78; and Funk & Wagnalls, s.v. "Land-Grant Colleges."

Six land-grant schools were chartered by Beta Alpha Psi in the prewar years. Besides Oregon State, where the chapter would of necessity be deactivated during the second era, they were Illinois, California, Ohio State, Minnesota, and Wisconsin.

others were not.

Michigan State and Penn State, established in 1855 as the nation's very first agricultural colleges, joined five other "land-grant" schools as homes of new Beta Alpha Psi chapters. The other institutions were Oregon State (readmitted), West Virginia, Arkansas, Tennessee, and Kentucky. Along with Penn State, the last four schools were also indisputably the principal public universities of their states.

Chapters were also formed during the third era at the leading general-purpose public institutions, not of the A. and M. character, of five states. They were Indiana University and the Universities of Alabama, Michigan, Mississippi, and Iowa.

Two new chapter sites represented a modification of historical patterns. Louisiana Polytechnic Institute and Texas Technological University were both akin to the land-grant tradition in their special commitment to applied scientific education, but not formally a part of it. Louisiana State and Texas A. and M., along with schools established for black students, had received land-grant designation within their states prior to the opening of Louisiana Tech and Texas Tech (using current nomenclature), respectively.

Finally, three chapters represented sequels to Omega, chartered at Miami in the spring of 1942 just prior to wartime deactivation of the fraternity. Located in southwest Ohio, Miami was an excellent "regional" state university, directing its major attention to serving a portion of the state. Joining the Beta Alpha Psi fold in the third era were three more such schools, two of them located in the same state as Miami. In 1952 Alpha Kappa Chapter was formed at Ohio University, located across the state in Athens, and three years later Bowling Green State, from northeast Ohio, became the site of Alpha Upsilon. In the spring of 1960, finally, Beta

Eta was established at San Diego State College, in California.

Three of these four regional schools would provide national presidents of Beta Alpha Psi during the fourth era. Future presidents C. Rollin Niswonger of Miami and Vern E. Odmark of San Diego State were the charter faculty advisors to their chapters. Odmark's immediate successor was Harvey E. Donley, an early faculty leader at Bowling Green who had known him originally as a fellow doctoral student at Missouri. The chartering of San Diego State foreshadowed a remarkable series of installations within the California state college (later "university") system. Over the next two decades chapters would appear on campuses in Los Angeles, Sacramento, San Francisco, San Jose, Fresno, Long Beach, Fullerton, Chico, Northridge, and Hayward.

Among the "private" colleges and universities chartered in the third era, one-half (six of twelve) were sponsored by religious groups, and two others held less formal church affiliations.

Twelve private schools, six under religious sponsorship

Psi Chapter at Marquette, installed just prior to the wartime deactivation, marked the first Beta Alpha Psi unit formed at a church-sponsored school. It is pertinent to note that, although a strong wave of anti-Catholicism swept through the southern United States (in particular) between the two world wars, there exists no record of a fraternal legacy of discrimination against Catholic students.

During the third era, four additional Jesuit institutions joined the Beta Alpha Psi ranks, namely, Creighton, Detroit, Fordham (for many years the only eastern Catholic school represented), and Loyola of New Orleans, along with DePaul University, controlled by the Vincentian Fathers. In that day and time the governing boards of Catholic colleges and universities

throughout the nation were confined to clergymen, a practice that would end over the following generation. Chapters would later be formed at Loyola of Chicago, Notre Dame (governed by the Congregation of Holy Cross), Seattle, San Francisco, San Diego (an "independent" Catholic school), Seton Hall, and Saint Louis (which had in 1965 initiated the appointment of lay, and women, trustees).

These installations reflect a serious commitment by Catholic schools to business and accounting education. Of particular note, through 1984 nine of the twenty-eight campuses affiliated with the remarkably learned Jesuit order were fraternal sites.

One other church school was added to the fraternal ranks during the third era, namely, Baptist-sponsored Baylor University. In later years local units would be established at institutions affiliated with four other religious denominations, namely, Texas Christian, Brigham Young, Pacific Lutheran, and Emory. Although, like Emory, they enjoy historical ties to the Methodist Church, third-era sites Southern Methodist and Denver are governed by independent boards. They must accordingly be classified as non-sectarian universities, along with the remaining four schools chartered during the period.

Representing Philadelphia and two famous steel cities, the latter sites were all from the same eastern state, but were notably diverse overall. Included were Pennsylvania, an Ivy-League campus; Temple, a working-class commuter school; Lehigh, an all-male engineering institution in Bethlehem; and Pittsburgh, a general-purpose university from Western Pennsylvania's leading city. Temple and Pitt (destined to lose its fraternal charter after terminating the undergraduate accounting program) would become "state-related" schools in the mid-1960s.

The references made thus far in the profile of new chapter sites point

up wide diversity in level of urbanization of the local environment, possibly a factor relevant to chapter activity levels. Generally speaking, the public colleges and universities were located within "college towns" or cities of comparatively modest size, while their private counterparts represented large cities, in some instances the nation's largest urban areas.

Chapter Locations: Large Cities, Smaller Urban Areas, and College Towns

Thirteen new Beta Alpha Psi groups of the third era were located in urban areas having 1950 populations, within the city proper, ranging from 251,117 (Omaha) to 7,891,957 (New York). The next largest cities, Knoxville, Tenn. and (as of the following census) Lubbock, Texas, were the homes of some 125,000 people, while regional marketing and manufacturing center Waco, Texas had nearly 100,000 inhabitants by 1960.

Four locations then smaller than the three just cited were also moderately urbanized. Lexington, Kentucky, a major regional commercial center, was the focal point of a noted livestock, horse breeding, and agricultural area; Ann Arbor (soon, like Lexington, to grow appreciably) and East Lansing, Michigan were located in turn relatively near metropolitan Detroit and adjacent to a state capital (Lansing) of reasonable size; and Bethlehem was an important steel-producing city. Unquestionably the remaining eleven chapter sites, however, would best be described as "college towns," owing their primary identification to the colleges and universities located therein.

Five of the new chapters were placed in the three largest American cities of the time, New York, Chicago, and Philadelphia, and another was established in fifth-ranked Detroit. At the other end of the scale were the groups founded in such towns as Tuscaloosa, Ala., Oxford, Miss., Iowa City, State College, Pa., Bowling Green, Ohio, and Bloomington, Ind.

The two municipal institutions naturally enough represented large

cities (New York and Cincinnati). Almost as a matter of course, however, the state colleges and universities were located in the smaller communities. The only one found in a large city was San Diego State College. Among the dozen private institutions, by contrast, only Baylor and Lehigh, of moderate-sized Waco and Bethlehem, were not located in large environments.

This classification of sites may be relevant to the prospective level of chapter activity. Major urban environments naturally afford more opportunity for off-campus activity than do smaller communities, and generally provide for more commuter students as well. One would thus conjecture that chapters located in the larger cities would tend to be less active than those found in college towns or smaller urban environments. This notion, brought out by fourth-era councilor Leon Hay in an interview, will be reviewed in chapter in discussing competitive results of the chapter/ratings activity program.[3]

---

[3]"AACSB Accreditation Council"; "The Association of Jesuit Colleges and Universities," Saint Joseph's University: Colleges of Arts and Sciences, College of Business and Administration Catalog, 1984-1985 (Philadelphia: Saint Joseph's University Press, 1984), p. 212; Barron's Profiles, s.v. "Colorado, University of Denver," "Georgia, Emory University," "Illinois, DePaul University," "Texas, Texas Christian University," and pp. [1 (front matter), liv]; The College Blue Book, 19th ed., 5 vols., vol. 1: Narrative Descriptions (New York: Macmillan Publishing Co., 1983), s.v. "Pennsylvania: Pittsburgh, University of; Temple University"; Thomas M. Dickerson to Author, interview, April 19, 1980; W. E. Dickerson, Secretary-Treasurer's Report, 1948-49, p. 5; Harvey E. Donley to Author, interview (Cleveland, Ohio), May 2, 1980; "Education - American Colleges and Universities," four-year schools, The World Almanac and Book of Facts, 1985 (New York: Newspaper Enterprise Association, 1984), pp. 215-31, s.v. "Brigham Young Univ.," "Emory Univ.," "Pacific Lutheran Univ.," "Southern Methodist Univ."; Funk & Wagnalls, s.v. "Ann Arbor," "Bethlehem, city of Pennsylvania," "Lansing," "Lexington, city in Kentucky," "Waco"; "Grand Chapter: Chapter Representatives," Newsletter 5 (November 1960):297; Hasselback, 1984 Directory, individual listing, s.v. "Williams, Thomas H."; Leon E. Hay to Author, interview (Cleveland), May 2, 1980; H. W. Kendrick, Secretary-Treasurer's Report, 1946-1947, p. 5; Kendrick, "Welcome," Newsletter [2] (May 1942):5; "[Local] Chapter News," Newsletter 4 (April 1956):321, 5 (November 1960):341, 347; Lovejoy, Lovejoy's College Guide, s.v. "California: San Diego, University of," "Indiana: Notre

The profile of the third-era expansion just developed is partially summarized in exhibit 5.

From virtually the beginning of the era, possible chapter sites were strictly limited by a constitutional requirement foreshadowed by an ambiguous prewar resolution. External events would require later clarification of the eligibility condition. After exceptions were allowed in granting three of the next nine charters (1954-56), the exacting eligibility requirement approved (unconditional "accreditation") would become firmly entrenched within Beta Alpha Psi. Even so, an interesting variation of opinion on the matter exists among former fraternal presidents.

Evolution and Application of the Requirement of AAcCSB Membership

Emergence of the Constitutional Requirement

Anticipatory resolution of 1940

At its annual meeting in Chicago in December 1940, the Grand Council had:

> go[ne] on record in favor of establishing as a standard for consideration of petitions for new chapters, membership of the institution, from which the petition is submitted, in the American Association of Collegiate Schools of Business.

This action had been taken after the Council had deferred action on a petition from Ohio University (having the ultimate effect of negating it), and rejected applications from Armstrong College (of California) and, for the second year running, Creighton University. Coincidentally, a petition

---

Dame, University of," "Ohio: Cincinnati, University of"; [Metcalf], ed., 1983-84 Annual Report, inside front cover ("Former . . . National Presidents"), pp. 31-38 ("Chapter Information"); Rev. Joseph A. Sellinger, S.J. (president of Loyola College) to Author, conversation (Baltimore, Maryland), January 14, 1985; Smith, Forty Acres, pp. 178-79; [Nolan E. Williams], Secretary-Treasurer's Report, 1958-59, p. 5; Williamson, Crucible of Race (chapter 1, note 13), p. 472; and World Alamanac, 1985, p. 252.

EXHIBIT 5

A PROFILE OF THIRD-ERA ROSTER EXPANSION

	Source of Controlling Authority						Community--Urbanization Level		
	Public				Private				
	City	--State--			Religious	Nonsectarian	Large city	Smaller urban area	College town
		Primary &/ or land-grant	Regional	Technological					
Western Schools									
Denver						X	X		
Oregon State		X							X
San Diego State			X				X		
Central Schools									
Michigan		X						X	
Ohio			X						X
Creighton					X		X		
Detroit					X		X		
Michigan State		X						X	
Iowa		X							X
Bowling Green			X						X
Indiana		X							X

EXHIBIT 5--Continued

	Source of Controlling Authority						Community--Urbanization Level		
	Public				Private				
	City	--State--			Religious	Nonsectarian	Large city	Smaller urban area	College town
		Primary &/ or land-grant	Regional	Technological					
Central Schools (continued)									
DePaul					X		X		
Cincinnati	X						X		
Southern or Border Schools									
Alabama		X							X
Southern Methodist						X	X		
Mississippi		X							X
Arkansas		X							X
Tennessee		X						X	
Kentucky		X						X	
Baylor					X			X	
Louisiana Polytechnic				X					X

EXHIBIT 5--Continued

	Source of Controlling Authority						Community--Urbanization Level		
	Public				Private				
	City	--State--			Religious	Nonsectarian	Large city	Smaller urban area	College town
		Primary &/ or land grant	Regional	Technological					
Southern or Border Schools (continued)									
Texas Tech				X				X	
Loyola of New Orleans					X		X		
Eastern Schools									
City College, NY	X						X		
Pennsylvania						X	X		
Pittsburgh						X	X		
Temple						X	X		
West Virginia		X							X
Fordham					X		X		
Lehigh						X		X	
Penn State		X							X

submitted by the latter institution after the war would raise a critical issue regarding a policy descended directly from the 1940 resolution.

That resolution was notably ambiguous, for it could be construed to mandate an eligibility condition for Beta Alpha Psi charters, or only to signal the Grand Council's support for such a condition, without actually establishing it. On the face of it, there would have been no particular point in an action of the latter kind, given that the Council had full authority to translate its will into operating policy. Yet there is compelling evidence that what was intended was merely, per literal interpretation of the minutes, a statement of support for an AAcCSB eligibility requirement. On this interpretation, the govening body did not wish actually to commit itself on the matter as yet, but was establishing a base for making a definite policy decision later on.

Strong circumstantial evidence is provided, first, by the secretary-treasurer's report, and subsequent Council minutes, of 1947. Contrary to the normal practice of his successors, Secretary-Treasurer H. W. Kendrick made no reference to affiliation with the American Association in listing the sixteen schools that had submitted inquiries in 1947. Nor did he do so in observing that a petition had been submitted by San Jose State, a preliminary application had been made by William and Mary, and a formal application (not to be forthcoming) was expected soon from Clarkson College. Yet of all the institutions listed, only Alabama and CCNY were professionally accredited. Similarly, according to Kendrick's minutes the San Jose petition, which presumably would not even have been made had the school been advised that it was ineligible for consideration, was rejected "after considerable discussion," rather than out of hand.

Further, it is very unlikely that a relevant policy adopted seven years

earlier would have been misunderstood, or overlooked, by the Council of 1947. Not only had newly appointed councilor Kendrick succeeded Hermann Miller as secretary-treasurer directly after the 1940 meeting, but 1947 (retiring) president McConahey had attended that session as a first-year councilor.

The matter became academic, in any case, through action taken by the Grand Council at the same New York session at which the first postwar petition was considered.

Constitutional amendment of 1947

On the motion of President McConahey, the governing body in 1947 approved an amendment of article 7, section 1 of the fraternal constitiution. The new provision stipulated that "[c]hapters of the Fraternity shall be established only at colleges and universities which are members of the American Association of Collegiate Schools of Business."

McConahey observed several years later that the Council had "received so many inquiries from Normal Schools [teachers colleges], Agricultural Colleges, and Business Colleges, that we felt some such rule was necessary." He felt that without the requirement the Council would receive frequent petitions from such institutions, "some of which might cause the members some embarrassment in refusing as well as trouble for existing chapters," and that in any event the fraternity was assured of continuing sufficient demand from "first grade schools."

Following adoption of the amendment, the secretary-treasurer would routinely distinguish in the annual report between AAcCSB members and other schools (usually the larger group) in reporting inquiries received concerning possible chapter formation. Occasionally included among the latter group were narrowly vocational institutions, although in the years to come

many schools of that kind would substantially broaden their programs.

Undoubtedly the councilors felt that the action taken in New York had been definitive. They could not foresee that just two years later the AAcCSB would introduce distinct classes of membership, or that during the early 1950s there would be essentially a "moratorium" on accreditation activity. One effect was the formation of chapters at two schools having only qualified AAcCSB credentials.

Advent of Membership "Classes," and Admission or Retention of Five Schools Lacking "Full" Status

Three membership categories, and three established sites having reduced or nonexistent status

In 1949 the association adopted a threefold classification of members, as "full," "associate," or "provisional associate." A year later, Zeta Chapter site North Dakota (admitted to membership in 1929) was reclassified as an associate member, and in 1951 it was reduced to provisional associate status. There is no indication that the Grand Council took immediate note of the new AAcCSB approach, or of North Dakota's diminished standing. However it was to be construed in light of membership gradation, the fraternity's new constitutional requirement was certainly not intended to be retroactive, in a day in which chapter sites Western Reserve and Oklahoma A. and M. enjoyed no recognition by the association.

"Full" and "associate" membership were distinguished in part according to the degree of <u>autonomy</u> exercised by the business school within the college or university. Required in either case, however, were sufficient budgetary, curricular, and personnel independence to permit maintenance of "an adequate program of instruction." Other factors considered included teaching load, faculty balance in terms of academic rank, salary structures, and curricular

breadth. The full statement of contemporary "Standards for Membership," as revised in 1953, is reprinted as exhibit 6.

Similar considerations presumably governed the distinction between associate and "provisional" associate status, which was dropped after only four years. Grand Council correspondence of the early 1950s implies, however, that associate membership tended to be regarded positively, as a step toward unqualified affiliation, and provisional membership negatively, as a precarious position indicating urgent need for corrective action.

The issue of proper interpretation for the eligibility condition was raised late in 1951, probably for the first time, in correspondence between President John Arch White and his successor Charles C. Staehling. They were agreed that "the differences [between associate and full levels] are minor and that associate membership is regarded as only a step to full membership."

A year later, two-time prewar petitioner Creighton University applied for a Beta Alpha Psi chapter. Creighton was an associate member of the AAcCSB, having been admitted originally, in 1949, with only provisional status. The Omaha school presented an accounting faculty whose six members included four men with doctorates (at least one of them in accounting) and four CPAs. The sticking point was the absence of unqualified accreditation.

Application by associate member Creighton following admission of (as it turned out) provisional associate member SMU

President Staehling had evidently changed his mind on the issue over the past year, for he wrote in regard to the Creighton position that "if we yield on this we weaken our entire basis for chapter membership qualification." In response, Secretary-Treasurer Wedeberg proposed that the fraternity evaluate associate members case by case, but "draw the line" against admitting schools having only provisional status. He accordingly requested

EXHIBIT 6

STANDARDS FOR AAcCSB MEMBERSHIP IN 1953

STANDARDS FOR MEMBERSHIP IN THE AMERICAN ASSOCIATION OF COLLEGIATE SCHOOLS OF BUSINESS

(1) For membership a school or college shall be a distinct and independent degree recommending unit responsible directly to the central administrative authority of an institution of higher learning. The unit shall have such active support as to indicate continuous commitments for the conduct of a professional program, adequate in itself and comparable to those offered by other professional schools.

(2) For associate membership an applicant should preferably possess the same degree of independence required for full membership. However, when full independence does not prevail, the Executive Committee may recommend associate membership provided it is convinced that the applicant possesses sufficient autonomy as to curricula, budget, and faculty personnel to insure the development of an adequate program of instruction.

(3) The curricula shall approximate, quantitatively and qualitatively, the standards in effect in recognized collegiate schools of business, due allowance being made for the meeting of regional or other special objectives. A portion of the four years of college work for the undergraduate degree may be taken in some other college, such as a liberal arts or engineering college of approved standards. At least forty per cent of the 120 semester hours or its equivalent required for the bachelor's degree must be taken in business and economics subjects; the major portion of the courses in this group shall be in business administration. At least forty per cent of the 120 semester hours or its equivalent required for the bachelor's degree must be taken in subjects other than business and economics provided that economic principles and economic history may be counted in either the business or non-business groups. With respect to the latter, breadth not specialization is the objective.

(4) As the foundation for training in administration, instruction shall be offered in the fields of economics, accounting, statistics, business law, finance, marketing, and production or industrial management. In general, candidates for the undergraduate degree shall receive basic instruction in each of these fields. Opportunities beyond the basic course shall be available in at least three of the above fields.

(5) The teaching and administrative staff shall possess the qualifications, experience, professional interests, and scholarly productivity essential for the successful conduct of a collegiate school of business. In judging the teaching staff, consideration is given to the percentage of student credit hours taught by those having the doctorate or other appropriate terminal degree, and to research or professional experience. There shall be at least five faculty members, exclusive of those in general economics, of professorial rank (assistant, associate or full professors) giving full time to instruction in business administration, the majority of members of the teaching staff shall give the greater part of their time to instruction and research. The number of teachers and their distribution among ranks and fields shall be adequate to provide effective instruction at all levels offered.

(6) Members of the instructional staff should not teach freshman-sophomore work in excess of fifteen credit hours a week, or junior-senior or graduate work in excess of twelve credit hours a week. A member of the instructional staff should not ordinarily teach more than two subject-matter fields in any one term. In judging the instructional load, consideration should be given to the total academic and professional responsibilities borne by each member of the teaching staff.

(7) The school shall have adequate laboratory, library, and other facilities for the pursuit of its objectives, and the suitable accommodation of its faculty and students. The interpretation of adequacy will be less rigorous in the case of an associate member.

(8) The school shall have been established and in operation for such a period of time as to make it possible to evaluate its character and policies.

(9) An institution at which a graduate degree in business is granted shall be eligible for full membership only.

(10) No institution subject to undue political influence may become or remain a member or associate member.

(11) Any member or associate member that does not maintain Association standards shall be placed on annual probation for a period not to exceed three years and, if not restored to membership or associate membership during this period, shall be suspended. Suspension may be imposed for cause without a prior period of probation.

(12) Each applicant for membership or associate membership shall be inspected by a committee of one to three persons. The Executive Committee may fix such inspection fee as it deems proper to be paid by the applying school.

(13) The Secretary shall each year assemble and distribute to the members and associate members such information as the Executive Committee may consider helpful to them. He shall also make such inquiries of members and associate members as will show whether Association standards are being maintained. When in the opinion of the Executive Committee a school is not maintaining these standards, an inspection committee shall be appointed to investigate and report.

(14) Membership in, or official information of, the Association may not be used for advertising or other promotional purposes. Membership in the Association may be indicated, however, by a bare statement that the institution is a member.

This statement of standards is subject to annual review.

Unless otherwise indicated these requirements apply to both members and associate members.

Effective April 23, 1949.

Amended April 18, 1953.

Reprinted, with the consent of the American Assembly of Collegiate Schools of Business, from _Standards for Admission to the American Association of Collegiate Schools of Business_ ([St. Louis: AACSB, 1953]), pp. [2-3].

detailed information, from the AAcCSB, concerning Creighton's specific situation.

A confidential reply explained that the Jesuit institution had orginally been granted only provisional status, due to (a) heavy teaching loads, (b) poor faculty balance, (c) low salary scale, (d) low budget, relative to income, and (e) lack of adequate core courses. Following documentation that progress had been made in all areas, and that the last deficiency had been removed entirely, the membership had been upgraded the following year, in 1950.

There had been no opportunity since then for further review of the case because of a special development within the AAcCSB that had already been of concern to the Grand Council. Specifically, since 1950 there had been a virtual "moratorium" on accreditation activity by the association, in keeping with a request made by the National Commission on Accreditation. Comprised of college and university presidents, that group had been formed in 1949 with the intent of consolidating all forms of academic accreditation within the regional accrediting agencies. Until resumption of normal operations, there was no prospect of a further visitation to the Omaha campus, an essential condition for the conferring of full membership.

The generally favorable report submitted by the accrediting agency was undoubtedly a pivotal factor in the Council's eventual approval of the application from Creighton. The methodical investigation conducted by the governing body would continue beyond that point, however. Specifically, President J. C. Gibson undertook his own "personal investigation" of the petitioner's college of commerce early in 1953, possibly in part through the unusual step (at the time) of a campus visit, and several past fraternal presidents were consulted on the matter.

The issue of fairness raised in Creighton's favor by the temporary suspension of accreditation activity was underscored by the status of four existing chapter sites, one of them in particular. Not only were Western Reserve, Oklahoma A. and M., and North Dakota either unaffiliated with the association or merely a provisional associate member, but Southern Methodist, admitted to the fraternity more than two years after adoption of the eligibility requirement, held only provisional standing.

SMU, a member since 1925, had apparently been downgraded to that tenuous level the very month, April 1950, that Alpha Epsilon Chapter had been founded there. It seems certain that no one on the Grand Council was aware of this development at the time, and indeed the best inference is that the matter remained unrecognized until Professor Wedeberg discovered the reclassification while evaluating Creighton's position in the fall of 1952. At least on the surface, SMU faculty sponsor Lionel E. Gilley had been seriously derelict in not advising the Grand Council of the development, and 1949-51 Secretary-Treasurer White had been remiss in not reviewing the current AAcCSB membership listing. The provisional status of North Dakota may also have been unknown until the fall of 1952.

Accreditation activity was resumed at normal levels in 1953, when Michigan State, San Francisco, and Santa Clara gained AAcCSB membership, after the aforementioned commission abandoned its consolidation program. Four of the schools just discussed acquired full membership over the next several years, but the oldest of the five chapter sites lost even its limited accreditation.

Full accreditation of four of the schools after 1953, but loss of AAcCSB standing by North Dakota

In 1953, also, the "provisional" category was dropped, and North

Dakota and Southern Methodist were duly raised to the associate level. SMU and Creighton became full members of the AAcCSB in 1955 and 1960 respectively, while Western Reserve and Oklahoma State (formerly A. and M.) both joined the fold in 1958.

North Dakota would, however, continue at the lower status (renamed "provisional membership" in 1958) until 1961. In that year the school was dropped from the AAcCSB roster. Coming at a time by which all other Beta Alpha Psi schools evidently were fully accredited, this extraordinary development naturally generated serious concern within the Grand or National Council of the 1960s.

For example, 1960-61 president Herbert E. Miller favored the revocation of the Zeta charter. That action would never be taken, however, even though the chapter site would remain unaccredited for a generation. Recalling the North Dakota issue as a "perennial question" during his own period of service, fourth-era councilor Leon Hay noted in a 1980 interview that the venerable chapter formed in Grand Forks in 1923 continued in the years following the loss of accreditation to be reasonably active, and function fairly well. North Dakota finally became reaccredited in the business field in 1984, being added to the roster of the Accreditation Council (at the undergraduate level) within the American Assembly of Collegiate Schools of Business (AACSB). Since 1963, accreditation has been defined in terms of undergraduate and graduate (master's-degree) levels, rather than grades of membership.

Returning to the third era, it scarcely seems coincidental that the Beta Alpha Psi constitution was amended in 1953, the year of resumption of normal accreditation activity, to clarify the eligibility requirement adopted six years earlier. Three early exceptions would be made, however, to the rigorous policy adopted.

Strict Reinterpretation of the Eligibility Requirement, but Less Strict Enforcement

Meeting at the University of North Carolina late in the summer of 1953, the Council voted to insert the word "full" in front of the word "membership" within constitutional article 7, section 1, thereby limiting charter candidates to full members of the association. It was emphasized, in the minutes, that such affiliation should not be considered "conclusive evidence of meeting the requirements of Beta Alpha Psi." For example, there was consensus agreement at the same meeting that at the "absolute minimum" a petitioner should have a hundred accounting majors in the junior and senior classes. The implication was left that the petition from the University of Detroit had foundered on this basis, at least in part, although the school would be chartered the following spring.

Undoubtedly President Staehling was not the only councilor who felt that failure to require full AAcCSB membership would significantly compromise the fraternity's standards. The governing body was presumably also unconfortable, however, about the prospect to having to evaluate the credentials of associate members case by case, as had been done regarding Creighton.

Ironically, just one year later the Grand Council would vote <u>unanimously</u> to waive the full membership requirement, to lay the way for approval of a petition submitted by associate member Baylor University (raised to full status in 1959). No explanation for this exception was provided in the minutes. The next year, 1954-55, inquiries were received from two new associate members, Bowling Green State and Louisiana Polytechnic. Although they would not achieve full AAcCSB membership until 1958 and 1959, respectively, chapters were installed at both schools during the academic year 1955-56, just before the Council "reaffirmed" official policy.

It may be pertinent that all other new inquiries of 1954-55 had arrived

from schools unaffiliated with the accrediting body. Since, as discussed below, the fraternity was not disposed to circularize material on chapter formation to nonchartered AAcCSB members, strict application of the eligibility provision would occasionally have threatened to interrupt roster expanison of the third era. Yet 1955-56 secretary-treasurer W. B. Jencks would observe in his annual report that "a tidal wave of students" were anticipated over the next fifteen years, and ask rhetorically whether it would not be appropriate to consider strengthening both the chartering and membership standards of the fraternity as a means of coping with "the advancing hordes."

Finally, as earlier noted, Epsilon Chapter at Oregon State was readmitted to the fraternity, in 1959, a year before the modern-day business school at Corvallis became accredited. Evidently the Grand Council remained willing to relax current eligiblity requirements to a degree in assessing a candidate for readmission that had withdrawn from the fraternity prior to the war. It seems more important to bear in mind, however, that Oregon State was clearly a highly credible candidate for AAcCSB membership in 1959.[4]

---

[4]Charles J. Dirksen and Lawrence C. Lockley, "Development of Collegiate Schools of Business and Activities of AA[c]CSB," The American Association cf Collegiate Schools of Business: 1916-1966, by Dirksen, Lockley, et al. (Homewood, Ill.: Richard D. Irwin, 1966), p. 12; "Grand Chapter," Newsletter [3] (November 1950):3; Grand Council Minutes Book, 1939, p. [5], 1940, pp. [1-2], 1947, p. 2, 1953, pp. 1, 3, 1954, p. 3, 1956, p. 4, quoting nonopening pages after 1939; Hasselback, 1984 Directory, individual listing, s.v. "Bausch, Norbert G."; Leon E. Hay to Author, interview, May 2, 1980; [W. B. Jencks], Secretary-Treasurer's Report, 1955-56, p. 3; H. W. Kendrick, Secretary-Treasurer's Report, 1946-47, p. 5; Lovejoy, Lovejoy's College Guide, s.v. "Oklahoma, Oklahoma State University"; Jas. M. McConahey to S. M. Wedeberg, January 28, 1953, quoted; "Members of the [AACSB] Accreditation Council"; Herbert E. Miller to Author, interview (Columbia, S.C.), April 18, 1980; "National Constitution," National Constitution and Statutes (1947, 1953), article 7, section 1; A. J. Penz, Secretary-Treasurer's Report, 1954-55, p. 8; Charles G. Staehling to S. M. Wedeberg, November 24, 1952, quoted; Staehling to John A[rch] White, December 13, 1951, quoted; Standards for Admission to the American Association of Collegiate Schools of Business ([St. Louis: AAcCSB, 1953)], four-page pamphlet, quoting p. [2]; James A. Viehland, Associate Director of AACSB, to Author, January 29 (preceding item

The accreditation requirement has over the years become one of Beta Alpha Psi's most firmly entrenced policies, and there is no reason to expect it to be relaxed in the foreseeable future. Yet interviewing conducted in 1980 among former fraternal presidents revealed, amidst prevailing strong support, a measure of significant objection to the policy.

Variation in Viewpoints Among Former Fraternal Leaders

More than a dozen leaders commented on the desirability of maintaining the requirement of AACSB accreditation for fraternal sites. Most of them favored the practice as a practical necessity for quality control. It was felt that the National Council had neither the time, expertise, nor financial resources that would be needed to conduct its own evaluations of business schools not recognized by the assembly; and that in any case the political dimensions of any such alternate "accreditation" program could only damage the reputation and credibility of the group.

Related points were raised by Vern Odmark and fifth-era councilor Thomas J. Burns. Odmark felt that the "honorary" aspect of election to Beta Alpha Psi presupposed an independent validation of "quality" business education, while Burns observed (as had James McConahey in the early 1950s) that

---

enclosed), February 6, 1985; Wedeberg to D. E. Gilliland, Jr., Executive Director of AAcCSB, December 15, 1952; Wedeberg to McConahey, February 13, May 2, 1953; and Wedeberg to Staehling, November 28, December 14, 1952, January 2, 1953.

All fraternal correspondence is from the Policies File except the three items involving James McConahey, which are from the McConahey File. Although he did not specifically identify the two members, W. E. Dickerson in 1947-48 was the first secretary-treasurer to mention AAcCSB affiliation in reporting the schools that had made inquiry concerning chapter formation (p. [4]). He disregarded the matter in his 1948-49 report (p. 5.), but all later secretary-treasurer reports of the third era specifically identified AAcCSB members in listing inquiries.

without the AACSB connection Beta Alpha Psi would be "flooded" with requests from highly problematic schools.

Charles W. Taylor, the first president of the fifth era (1970-71), basically endorsed the pragmatic case for maintaining the accreditation rule. He noted that it allowed the National Council to concentrate upon the accounting programs and organizations at potential chapter sites, and pointed out also that accounting education had indirectly benefited from the general upgrading of standards attributable to the AA(c)CSB. At the same time, he asserted that accreditation in itself had very little bearing upon the quality of accounting departments, and that it had always been recognized that many good programs were housed at schools not enjoying the credential.

Critics of the policy rejected the premise that without the AACSB connection the Council itself would have to get into the business of accreditation. Wilton T. Anderson, a fourth-era councilor, held that the "market" would always identify quality accounting programs, pointing to the acknowledged quality of departments at Pace (asserted, in 1980, to be the third largest source of Arthur Young recruits), Bentley, and Golden Gate. Williard Stone observed, similarly, that there were "some damned good accounting departments" within non-AACSB institutions, although in going on to state that nearly all undergraduate programs in accounting were reasonably good he seemed to invite Tom Burns' argument for the screening function served by the accreditation rule.

Third-era leader Nolan E. Williams objected to the policy from a somewhat different standpoint. In his view, the basic requirement for chartering should be simply that there exist at the school "a good strong accounting group" having been active over a period of time, traditionally recognized as a necessary condition, but not a sufficient one. Anderson's proposal

concerning evaluation of quality could of course readily be combined with Williams' emphasis upon organizational activity. At any rate, the Arkansas professor disagreed with his career-long colleague Doris Cook, who felt that to sever the AACSB linkage would leave the fraternity in the untenable role of an alternate or supplemental accreditor of some kind. Leon Hay, interviewed just prior to joining the Arkansas faculty, basically agreed with Cook. Support for the requirement was registered also by Hollis A. Dixon, Harvey Donley, Emerson Henke, A. J. Penz, and (in 1985) Harold L. Royer.

During the year 1968-69, Councilor Robert S. Wasley headed a committee concerned mainly with Beta Alpha Psi policy toward branch campuses. Contrary to Wasley's present-day viewpoint, it recommended that the AAcCSB linkage be severed, and that the National Council develop a questionnaire suited to the evaluation of accounting departments. The matter was taken up somewhat later by a study group that included a former councilor and two current or future ones. Herb Miller opposed the accreditation requirement, while (as in more recent interviewing) Robert S. Maust and Tom Burns supported it.[5] Broader review of the issue during the early 1970s, when Professor Henke was critical of traditional policy, is discussed in chpater 12.

Throughout the third era, the Grand Council maintained a passive

---

[5]Wilton T. Anderson (quoted), and Doris M. Cook, to Author (San Antonio, Texas), March 20, 1980; Thomas J. Burns to Author (Cleveland, Ohio), May 3, 1980, quoted; Hollis A. Dixon to Author (Tucson, Arizona), March 22-23, 1980; H(arvey) E. Donley, "Beta Alpha Psi: Minutes of National Council Meeting, August 23-23, 1969 . . ." (National Council Minutes, 1969), p. 4; Donley, and Leon E. Hay, to Author (Cleveland), May 2, 1980; Hasselback, 1984 Directory, school listing, s.v. "University of Arkansas"; Emerson O. Henke to Author (San Antonio), March 21, 1980; Robert S. Maust to Author (Morgantown, West Va.), July 14, 1980; Vern E. Odmark to Author, August 13, 1980, quoted; A. J. Penz, Williard E. Stone (quoted), and Charles W. Taylor, to Author (Columbia, S.C.), April 18, 1980; Harold L. Royer to Author, September 4, 1985; Robert S. Wasley to Author (Denver, Colo.), March 23, 1980; and Nolan E. Williams to Author (San Antonio), March 21, 1980, quoted. All sources cited in part by location were interviews, separate for each person cited, while the letters from Odmark and Royer served the same function by mail.

approach to the initiation of interest in forming chapters, which very often rested in large part upon the influence of local faculty members who were fraternal alumni. Campus accounting clubs or societies, possibly formed expressly for that role, served as forerunners to Beta Alpha Psi units. Installation officers from the Council were commonly assisted by initiation teams representing established chapters.

Chapter Formation, from Initial Inquiry to Installation

Generation of Interest: Full Reliance on Local Initiatives

With AAcCSB membership, temporarily (in practice) including associate status, recognized as a basic requirement for eligibility, one might think that the Grand Council of the "postwar expansionist era" would periodically have contacted the deans of nonchartered association members concerning possible chapter formation. There is no record, however, that such action ever occurred during these years, although Secretary-Treasurer Wedeberg sent copies of the *Newsletter* of November 1952 to the deans of all business schools represented in the association.

A *passive* approach to the initiation of local interest in chapter formation enjoyed traditional support within Beta Alpha Psi. In particular, the Grand Council had in December 1930 gone "on record":

> as not favoring the circularization of material to Universities and colleges not represented on the chapter roll purporting to solicit invitations from said Universities and Colleges for chapters of Beta Alpha Psi.

On the same occasion, as reported in volume 1, the Council had identified nine potential chapter sites at which personal contacts might permit inquiries to be made.

Fifty years later, 1953-55 Secretary-Treasurer A. J. Penz recalled that any kind of circularization regarding possible chapter formation would

likewise in his day have been regarded as "unethical" solicitation. This viewpoint could only have been strengthened within the Council by the ban on solicitation of clients enforced by the AI(CP)A from 1922 until the late 1970s. By way of practical justification of the policy, Penz noted that a school motivated to apply for a Beta Alpha Psi charter entirely on an independent basis "was almost always a good bet." From his point of view, at any rate, even personal initiatives of the kind sanctioned a generation earlier would have been suspect.

Clearly the main impetus for development of new chapters continued to be provided by local faculty members who were themselves alumni of the fraternity. Examples of such influence from the third era include the following professors:

1. Alabama--A. J. Penz, Phi Chapter
2. City College--E. I. Fjeld, Alpha (and Nu Chapter founder)
3. Michigan--Herbert Miller, Rho
4. Ohio--Tom Grant Wingfield, Gamma
5. Kentucky--Russell Grady, Upsilon (assisted by Wendell E. Beals, Gamma)
6. Arkansas--William R. Rives, Phi, and Nolan E. Williams, Chi and Theta
7. Detroit--Louis Matusiak, Alpha
8. Iowa--Daniel L. Sweeney, Alpha Eta
9. Cincinnati--Charles Griffin, Theta
10. Louisiana Polytechnic--William R. Rives, Phi
11. Indiana--Leon Hay, Alpha
12. Texas Tech--Fred W. Norwood, Theta
13. San Diego State--Vern Odmark, Rho.

Rives (pronounced "Reeves"), the charter faculty advisor at two schools, left Arkansas at the close of the installation year and was directly succeeded in his chapter post by Williams. Although unlike the others (or first men) listed he was not the charter faculty vice-president, department chairman Matusiak was apparently the only Beta Alpha Psi alumnus on the staff at Detroit. Among the eight faculty members at the school who were admitted by Alpha Xi Chapter directly after its formal installation was John W. McAuliffe, the group's first advisor.

Beta Alpha Psi alumni were not available at all chapter sites, of

course, to serve as faculty leaders. In such cases, the charter membership would of necessity include the faculty vice-president himself. In one such instance, William F. Schmeltz, the department chairman, was the first chapter advisor at Bowling Green State. After a year, he was succeeded in that role by Howard H. Kane, a colleague who had likewise been initiated on installation night.

Two of the founding faculty advisors died during the third era, one of them only a few months after the installation. Russell Grady guided Alpha Mu Chapter at Kentucky from its founding in the spring of 1952 until his death approximately six years later. His "photographic ability" had permitted Newsletter editor S. M. Wedeberg to publish three photographs of the chapter installation, representing (except for a small likeness of President C. Aubrey Smith in 1937) the first photos ever to appear in the publication.

Tom Wingfield organized Alpha Kappa Chapter at Ohio University in 1951-52 after having been elected to Gamma at Northwestern as an M.B.A. candidate the prior spring. Like Northwestern M.B.A. alumnus Tom Dickerson, he had received his undergraduate degree from Bowling Green College of Commerce in Kentucky. Only in his mid-twenties, Wingfield was found dead in his room during the summer of 1952. Although foul play was not suspected, no cause of death was determined.[6]

---

[6]Barry C. Broden and Stephen E. Loeb, "Professional Ethics of CPAs in Tax Practice: An Historical Perspective," The Accounting Historians Journa 10 (Fall 1983):83, 93; T. M. Dickerson, "Two New Chapters Installed," Newsletter [3] (November 1949):10; Grand Council Minutes Book, 1930, p. 2, quoted; [W. B. Jencks], "Grand Council News," Newsletter 4 (April 1956):301, 343-44; [Jencks], "[Local] Chapter News," Newsletter 4 (April 1957):406; [W. E. Karrenbrock], "Beta Alpha Psi's National President," Newsletter [2] (November 1937):[3] (containing only photo found in Newsletter until May 1952); "Letters from Local Chapters," Newsletter [2] (November 1941):13; "Local Chapter News," Newsletter [3] (November 1951):27, 4 (November 1955): 295-96 (titled "Chapter News" in second case); James M. McConahey, "History of Beta Alpha Psi," Newsletter [2] (May 1949):7; Fred W. Norwood, and Vern E. Odmark, to Author by telephone, January 22, 1985; [A. J. Penz], "Grand

Although only limited information is available, it is evident that new Beta Alpha Psi chapters were formed out of operating accounting clubs or societies, including local fraternities.

Fraternal Chapters as Outgrowths of Accounting Clubs or Societies

The best firsthand account available of the development of a fraternal chapter out of a preexisting student organization is presented in chapter 7 as part of the essay material contributed by Professor Penz, founder of Alpha Beta Chapter at Alabama. Penz had understood that such a group must have been in active operation for at least two years, but found that some flexibility existed. Advisory committees of 1954-56 developed a revised application questionnaire. As related in chapter 11, however, clearly defined evaluation standards may not in practice have emerged until later.

The Newsletter writeups of the second and third postwar installations, at City College and Pennsylvania in May 1949, refer specifically to the predecessor "accounting societies." The "organization committee" of Gamma Mu Beta at CCNY (named in honor of late department chairman G. M. Brett) assisted with the ceremonies in New York that replaced the fraternity with Alpha Gamma, while Penn's accounting group accepted the Alpha Delta charter.

Alpha Upsilon Chapter was formed at Bowling Green in 1955 as the successor to Phi Alpha Chi, a local honorary society whose alumni included the

---

Council News," Newsletter 4 (May 1954):166-67; [Penz], "New Chapter to be Installed," Newsletter 4 (November 1954):212; Penz to Author, interview, April 18, 1980, quoted; Warren Reininga (accounting professor, Ohio University) to Author, November 26, 1984; William R. Rives to Author, by telephone, January 26, 1985; William F. Schmeltz (retired dean at Bowling Green State) to Author, by telephone, January 30, 1985; Smith, Forty Acres, pp. 166-67; [S. M. Wedeberg], "Grand Council News," Newsletter [3] (May 1952):5 (quoted), 6; [Wedeberg], "In Memoriam [re Tom Wingfield]," Newsletter 4 (November 1952):12; [Wedeberg], "New Chapter at Ohio University," Newsletter [3] (March 1952):8; Who's Who in America 34 (1966-67), s.v. "Dickerson, Thomas Milton"; and [Nolan E. Williams], "Grand Council News," Newsletter 5 (April 1959):151.

charter Beta Alpha Psi advisor, Professor Schmeltz. With the installation at Fordham in the spring of 1957, Alpha Omega replaced an organization that had enjoyed "a long history as a local club."

As documented in chapter 6, however, the prior accounting club was maintained (or reorganized) at certain new chapter sites. They included Louisiana Tech, where a club had been formed two years before the chartering of Alpha Chi "with the intention of affiliating with Beta Alpha Psi" once the school had obtained professional accreditation; Indiana, where the nonfraternal group had predated Beta Alpha by some thirty years; and Michigan State and Lehigh, the respective homes of Alpha Omicron and Beta Epsilon.

The Grand Council sometimes discussed the matter of evaluating local accounting organizations, in the course of periodic consideration of policy actions that might be taken concerning "weak chapters." In particular, at the annual meeting held in Seattle in 1956 the group actually adopted a new rule requiring of all future candidates for charters "a two-year (counting the year of acceptance as a full year) pledge period" (emphasis added). This new condition would have supplemented any accounting club requirement.

President A. J. Penz had been stricken with pleurisy and pneumonia while en route to Seattle, and thus made it no further than a hospital in Missoula Montana. He thoroughly opposed the Council's action, as being calculated seriously to impede fraternal growth, and notified his fellow councilors of his position after returning to Tuscaloosa for the fall semester. Apparentl the dissent registered by Penz was persuasive, for the formal pledging requirement would be rescinded, by mail vote, even before Secretary-Treasure W. B. Jencks issued the annual minutes.

In summary, the Grand Council continued to rely very heavily upon local faculty contacts in evaluating petitioners. Professor Herb Miller, whose service was divided between the third and fourth eras, observed in a

1980 interview that in that day of a smaller "family of teachers" he personally knew one or two faculty members on each campus that might be a candidate for an installation. He did not recall any instances of rejection of a petition during his five years of service, 1958-63.

More generally, while it was noted on occasion that AAcCSB credentials did not guarantee acceptance into the fraternal roster, it appears that, but for a year's delay in the chartering of Detroit, at most one accredited school applied unsuccessfully for a charter during the third era. Following visits by Secretary-Treasurer Penz and Councilor Wayne E. Shroyer (well before the time of "site visitation"), Washington of St. Louis may have submitted at least a provisional petition in the spring of 1954. Penz had been especially interested in meeting Professor William S. Krebs, a member of the select group notified thirty-five years earlier by Hiram Scovill of the founding of Beta Alpha Psi. The two councilor's reports have not survived.

Krebs' colleague Dr. Norton M. Bedford, soon (as discussed in chapter 6) to become a leading critic of the fraternal activity program, had left at mid-year. The department also included a business law specialist, the university treasurer, and a Michigan doctoral candidate. Evening "associate" and "certificate" programs were offered in addition to regular degree work. In light of the rule of thumb that a school needed at least a hundred junior or senior accounting majors, perhaps Washington's program was considered too small to support an effective chapter. President S. M. Wedeberg, unable (like A. J. Penz) to recall any details, tends to doubt that a formal petition was filed.

It seems fair to conclude that the Grand Council was prepared to err on the side of leniency in granting charters, to extend the benefits of Beta Alpha Psi to as many deserving students as possible. The activity program and the practice of periodic visitation were considered adequate protection against chapter failure, in general, although charter revocation

would be available as a last resort.

Installation ceremonies always featured a current, or very recent, councilor assisted by a local or visiting "team."

Third-era Installation Ceremonies

President Tom Dickerson installed each of the three chapters formed in 1948-49, at Alabama, CCNY, and Penn. Through the spring of 1960, current councilors presided over all installations except those at Denver, Ohio, and Oregon State, at which for geographical reasons just-retired councilors H. W. Kendrick, W. E. Dickerson, and Wayne Shroyer did the honors. Herb Miller officiated at San Diego State during a visiting professorship at Stanford.

In another respect, however, the first two ceremonies would not be typical of the period, in that the charter initiations at Alabama and City College were not conducted by "visiting teams" from nearby chapters. At Tuscaloosa, five local professors who belonged to four established chapters assisted Dickerson, including A. J. Penz, Phi '47. A group composed of accounting chairman E. I. Fjeld, Alpha '22, two honorary members of Mu Chapter at neighboring NYU, and Councilor Harris from that campus served the same function in New York. The following night in Philadelphia, however, a team from Tau Chapter at Maryland, headed by future councilor S. M. Wedeberg, joined the fraternal president in installing Alpha Delta at Penn.

Three of the next four installations, at Denver, Michigan, and Mississippi, were conducted with the assistance of local teams, or perhaps (in the second case) by visiting councilors alone. At Michigan, none of the eleven faculty members who were fraternal alumni was cited as having assisted President Gould Harris and Past President W. E. Dickerson in a ceremony that inducted seven additional professors and twenty-four students. At Ole Miss, John Arch White (whose visit permitted a trip to his birthplace, twenty miles

away) was joined by three alumni of two chapters who lived in the region. A year earlier at Southern Methodist, however, he had been assisted by a group from his own Theta Chapter at Texas. Less information is available regarding the chapters formed at Arkansas and Tennessee in the spring of 1951, although apparently no outside team participated in the ceremony at Fayetteville.

After 1951, visiting initiation teams were ordinarily engaged. Of the twenty installations for which records have been found, groups from other chapters participated in seventeen cases. The exceptions occurred at Pittsburgh in 1955, where the four Omicron or Alpha Delta brothers involved were apparently alumni members living in the area; at Texas Tech in 1959, where a local group comprised of four Theta alumni and one Chi alumnus were on hand; and the following spring at Penn State, where local faculty members affiliated with other chapters again constituted the initiation team.

The general pattern was strongly favored by Professor Wedeberg, who observed during his tenure as secretary-treasuere that:

> I have seen installation by local teams and by visiting teams. An experienced team from another chapter is far superior, and the officers . . . can give a great deal of helpful advice to the incoming officers of the new chapter.

The official from the University of Maryland went on to note that, if the visiting team drove to the installation, "the additional cost should not be excessive." Concerned specifically with potential arrangements for a ceremony at Creighton, Wedeberg identified Councilor J. C. Gibson of Wisconsin as the "logical" installation officer, and suggested that he might wish to "reward" Sigma Chapter for being 'very much "on the ball" this year' by taking the local faculty advisor and student officers along with him to serve as the assisting team. "Gibby" and his chapter representatives would indeed conduct the ceremony at Omaha in the spring of 1953.

SIGMA CHAPTER TEAM ABOUT TO DEPART FOR IOWA TO INSTALL ALPHA PI, DECEMBER 1954

From left, Bob Page, Faculty Vice-President J.B. Bower, Grand Council president J.C. Gibson, Don Beffa, and Bob Brogan.

Although the group travelled a longer distance than usual, this case illustrates the common practice of employing an initiation team from the presiding officer's own chapter. Such an approach naturally reduced travel costs, which until the fall of 1952 were solely the responsibility of the new chapter itself.

In the interests of encouraging the use of outside teams, Secretary-Treasurer Wedeberg proposed in 1952 that the Grand Council pay installation costs in excess of $25.00. At the annual meeting, however, section 23 of chapter 2 of the national statutes was amended only to restrict the chapter's liability to $5.00 per each charter member, inclusive of the faculty and honorary categories. Even this limited concession probably contributed to the general practice thereafter of having visiting teams on hand.

An interesting example was the installation of Alpha Chi at Louisiana Tech in the spring of 1956. Fraternal president A. J. Penz and three officers of Alpha Beta drove to Ruston from Tuscaloosa (a distance of some 350 miles by present-day route I-20) for the evening ceremony and banquet, and then returned during the night in order not to miss the next day's classes. The group's level of classroom attentiveness that following day is not recorded.

Later in 1956, relevant statutes were amended again, this time in contrary directions that on balance reduced costs to new chapters. The installation fee (covered in statute section 21) was doubled, to $50.00. More than offsetting this change, however, was the assumption of _all_ travel costs, for installing officers and (officially cited for the first time) visitation teams, by the fraternity's national treasury.

The initiation ceremony conducted directly following the presentation of a charter was in keeping with fraternal ritual of the day. For example,

Faculty Vice-President William J. Schlatter (whose father Charles had been an early Beta Alpha Psi leader) and the three other officers of Alpha Eta Chapter at Michigan assisted Secretary-Treasurer Penz during the insallation of Alpha Xi at Detroit in 1954. Using "an abbreviated ritual," they initiated eight members of the accounting faculty. Then "[t]he full ritual" was conducted for purposes of admitting thirty-five active members:

> The blindfolded candidates were guidend into the room where they concentrated on the significance of the ritual. The candidates then presented themselves for the second part of the ceremony before the linen covered table whch had the large letters, B, A, and Ψ in front. A lighted insignia was the focal point flanked by red tapers on either side. Following the initiation, the new members were congratulated by the initiation team and faculty. Dr. Penz presented each new member with a Beta Alpha Psi membership certificate.

A generation later, Professor Penz recalled that the rationale for blindfolding was that, permitted only to listen to the ritual, candidates would be able to appreciate its full significance, without distraction. To the pleasant surprise of both men, incidentally, the first person whom Penz met after arrival at the University of Detroit was one of his former students at LSU. Preston Lebreton subsequently introduced him all over campus in ths same way: "I want you to meet my old prof."

Like chapter initiations generally, installations were capped by <u>banquets</u>. At Detroit the entire evening's activities were conducted at Buck's Redford Inn, and at Iowa all events totk place at Bill ["Goober"] Zuber's Dugout in the nearby Amana Colonies, operated by a former American League pitcher who had returned to his native Amish roots in eastern Iowa. At Michigan State, where nearly the same Alpha Eta team assisted two months after the Detroit ceremony, "[t]he festive occasion was brought to a close with a banquet at one of the many dining rooms in the [student] Union." It appears that all installation activities at West Virginia also occurred on campus. In a third approach, taken at Arkansas and, apparently, Louisiana

Tech, formal ceremonies conducted at the school were followed by a meal at an outside restaurant or club.[7]

Coverage of roster expansion may be concluded by reference to the overall record of inquiries received from interested schools during the third era. It is highly revealing in showing both how promptly the Grand Council was prepared to act in approving plausible candidates, and in foreshadowing chapter formation at many other campuses in later years.

Third-era Inquiries, Prompt Council Response, and Seeds for Later Chapter Formation

Inquiries for the three fraternal years ending in 1948 have already been

---

[7]AAA Road Atlas, maps of Alabama (pp. 6-7), Iowa (40-41), Louisiana (46-47), Mississippi (50-51); T. M. Dickerson, "Two New Chapters Installed," p. 10 (cited in note 6); [W. E. Dickerson], "Grand Chapter News," Newsletter [2] (March 1949):6; "Grand Chapter," Newsletter [3] (November 1950):3, (March 1952):3, 5 (April 1959):156, 6 (Spring 1964):[72]; Grand Council Minutes Book, 1953, 1955, 1956, and 1958, p. 3, 1952, p. 2, 1956, pp. 2, 4 (quoted), 7, 1963, p. 1; Hasselback, 1984 Directory, individual listing, s.v. "Schindler, James S.; Leon E. Hay to Author, interview, May 2, 1980; [W. B. Jencks], "Grand Council News," Newsletter 4 (November 1956):343, 344 (quoted), (April 1957): 381; [Jencks], Secretary-Treasurer's Report, 1956-57, p. 4, quoted; "Local Chapter News," Newsletter [3] (November 1949):25, (May 1951):27, (November 1951):26-27, 4 (November 1954):218, 224, (April 1955):248, 254, 259, 5 (April 1959):191, (November 1959):224, (November 1960):348; Beryl H. Manne, Washington University Archives, to Author (by telephone), April 4, 1985, quoted; Herbert E. Miller, "Biographical Data - April 1967" (Golden Anniversary Files), p. 1; Miller to Author, interview, April 18, 1980; Hermann C. Miller, ed., Beta Alpha Psi Directory, s.v. "Alpha Chapter: Schlatter, W. J., "Theta Chapter: Merriman, Edwin E.; Smith, L. Edwin"; "National Statutes," National Constitution and Statutes (1951, 1953, 1958), chapter 2, section 23; "News from the Chapters," Newsletter [1] (May 1932):5; [A. J. Penz], "Grand Council News," Newsletter 4 (May 1954):166-67, quoted (2nd indented citation), (November 1954):206, 207 (quoted); Penz to Author, interview, April 18, 1980 (quoted), and by telephone, January 7, 1985; Joseph Reichler, ed., The Baseball Encyclopedia, 4th ed. (New York: Macmillan Publishing Co., 1979), s. v. "Pitcher Register: Bill Zuber"; William F. Schmeltz to Author, by telephone, January 30, 1985; Sheldahl, Alpha to Omega, pp. 127, 129; [Charles C. Staehling] ("Charlie") to [Penz] ("Andy"), April 4, 1954 (McConahey File); [S. M. Wedeberg], "Grand Council News," Newsletter 4 (May 1953):76; [Wedeberg] "New Chapter at Ohio University," Newsletter [3] (March 1952):8; Wedeberg, Secretary-Treasurer's Report, 1951-52, p. 2; Wedeberg to Staehling, December 14, 1952 (Policies File), 1st indented citation; [John Arch White], "Grand Chapter News," Newsletter [3] (November 1950):9, (May 1951):5; Nolan E. Williams to Author, interview, March 21, 1980; and [Williams], "Grand Council News," Newsletter 5 (April 1959):151.

documented. Of the thirty-eight schools involved, a petition had been rejected from San Jose State, none had been permitted from William and Mary, one had just been received from Alabama, and one anticipated earlier would soon be received from City College. The latter two institutions would of course join the Beta Alpha Psi fold in 1948-49.

Over the full fifteen years of the third era, inquiries on chapter formation arrived from 161 sources, more than five times the number of schools chartered, as listed (with years) in exhibit 7. Among parties not establishing chapters at the time, the list included:

a. Three proprietary business colleges (nos. 5, 21, and, in transition to regular collegiate status, 12), and five other strongly business-oriented schools (nos. 54, 56, 83, 112, 122)

b. Four junior colleges (nos. 24, 46, 101, 118)

c. Three foreign institutions (nos. 33, 42, 88)

d. Two correspondents citing no affiliations (nos. 55, 93)

e. Fourteen Catholic colleges (nos. 16, 18, 34, 63, 68, 76, 80, 124-27, 130, 132, 133)

f. Nineteen other church-sponsored schools (nos. 1, 14, 25, 44-46, 67, 73, 87, 95, 105, 106, 111, 118, 138, 149, 150, 156, 161)

g. Six state colleges in California (nos. 27, 53, 70, 72, 123, 131)

h. A military college (no. 115)

i. A branch campus of 1957 installation site Indiana, covered by the university's AAcCSB membership (no. 60)

j. Two institutions (nos. 23 and 147) later chartered despite elimination or phasing out of the undergraduate accounting program.

Four schools inquiring in 1959-60 would form chapters the following year, namely, Loyola of Chicago, Mississippi State, Los Angeles State, and Georgia State, as would Tulane, an institution that had shown interest in three prior years. Otherwise, besides five western universities cited earlier (nos. 8, 23, 53, 130, and 154), the only professionally accredited

EXHIBIT 7

SOURCES OF THIRD-ERA INQUIRIES:
A COMPREHENSIVE LISTING[a]

---

1. Adrian, MI, '58
2. Akron, OH, '48
3. Alabama, AL, '47, '48
4. Alfred, NY, '51
5. Alpha, NJ (local bus. col.),[b] '47
6. American, DC, '56
7. American International, MA, '55
8. Arizona, AZ, '54, '60
9. Arizona State, AZ, '47, '49, '59
10. Arkansas, AR, '48, '50
11. Arkansas State, AR, '47, '48
12. Armstrong, CA, '49
13. Atlanta, GA, '55
14. Baldwin-Wallace, OH, '48
15. Baylor, TX, '54
16. Benedictine Heights,[b] OK, '59
17. Bloomfield, NJ, '52
18. Boston Col., MA, '47
19. Bowling Green State, OH, '48, '55
20. Bridgeport, CN, '49, '50
21. Bryant & Stratton, IL or NY,[c] '59
22. Butler, IN, '55
23. California, Los Angeles (UCLA), CA, '57
24. Casper Jr. Col.,[d] WY, '51
25. Centre, KY, '50
26. Chattanooga,[d] TN, '47
27. Chico State,[d] CA, '59
28. Cincinnati, OH, '48, '54
29. City Col. of New York,[d] NY, '47
30. Clarkson, NY, '47, '48, '51
31. Connecticut, CN, '54, '55
32. Creighton, NE, '53
33. Dalhousie, NS (CANADA), '53
34. Dayton, OH, '56
35. Delaware, DE, '52
36. Delta State Teachers,[d] MS '52, '59
37. Denver, CO, '50
38. DePaul, IL, '50, '51
39. Detroit, MI, '53
40. Drake, IA, '49, '52
41. Drexel, PA, '50
42. East, Univ. of, PHILLIPINES, '55
43. Eastern New Mexico, NM, '59
44. East Texas Baptist, TX, '55
45. Elmhurst, IL, '60

EXHIBIT 7--Continued

46. Emmanuel Missionary, GA,[e] '60

47. Fairleigh Dickinson, NJ, '58

48. Fenn,[d] OH, '47, '54

49. Florida Southern, FL, '55

50. Florida State, FL, '49, '50, '55

51. Fordham, NY, '53

52. Francis T. Nicholls State,[d] LA, '60

53. Fresno State,[d] CA, '59, '60

54. Georgia State,[f] GA, '50, '60

55. Gober, Mr. E. C., NY, '52

56. Golden Gate, CA, '48

57. Hawaii, HI, '54, '60

58. Hillyer,[d] CN, '52

59. Indiana, IN, '49, '56, '57

60. Indiana at Indianapolis,[d] IN, '52

61. Indiana State Teachers,[d] IN, '57

62. Iowa, IA, '54

63. John Carroll, OH, '57

64. Kansas State, KS, '48

65. Kent State, OH, '52

66. Kentucky, KY, '51

67. Lafayette, PA, '50

68. LaSalle, PA, '55

69. Lehigh, PA, '49, '58

70. Long Beach State, CA, '60

71. Long Island, NY, '51, '59

72. Los Angeles State,[d] CA, '58, '60

73. Louisiana Col., LA, '49

74. Louisiana Polytechnic,[d] LA, '48, '55

75. Lousiville, KY, '47, '59

76. Loyola of Chicago, IL, '55, '60

77. Loyola of New Orleans, LA, '46, '59

78. Luther, IA, '53, '59

79. Maine, ME, '50

80. Manhattan, NY, '52

81. Massachusetts, MA, '49, '55

82. Memphis State, TN, '56

83. Menlo, CA, '51

84. Miami, FL, '48, '50, '53 '58, '59

85. Michigan, MI, '49

86. Michigan State, MI, '48, '54

87. Millikin, IL, '55

88. Mindanao,[b] PHILLIPINES, '53

89. Mississippi, MS, '51

90. Mississippi Southern,[d] MS, '47, '48, '49

EXHIBIT 7--Continued

91. Mississippi State, MS, '60

92. Missouri, MO, '46

93. Monchs Corner (town), SC, '54

94. Montanta State, MT, '57

95. Muskingham, OH, '50

96. Nevada, NV, '60

97. New Mexico, NM, '50, '53

98. New Mexico State, NM, '55

99. North Carolina, NC, '53

100. Northeastern, MA, '55

101. Northeast Jr. Col. (of LSU),[d] LA, '47

102. North Texas State, TX, '51

103. Northwestern State, LA, '49

104. Norwich, VT, '57

105. Oakwood, AL, '59

106. Ohio Northern, OH, '50

107. Ohio, OH, '51

108. Oklahoma, OK, '54, '60

109. Oklahoma City, OK, '50

110. Oregon State, OR, '48, '53, '58

111. Ouachita Baptist, AR, '52, '55

112. Pace, NY, '53

113. Panhandle A and M,[d] OK, '58

114. Pennsylvania, PA, '49

115. Pennsylvania Military,[b] PA, '47

116. Pennsylvania State, PA, '55 '56, '58, '59

117. Pittsburgh, PA, '54

118. Presbyterian Jr. Col.,[b] NC, '49

119. Queens, NY, '55

120. Quinnipac, CN, '58

121. Rhode Island, RI, '55

122. Rider, NJ, '48, '51, '56, '59, '60

123. Sacramento State,[d] CA, '55

124. St. Bonaventure, NY, '51

125. Saint Joseph's, PA, '50

126. Saint Louis, MO, '53

127. Saint Norbert, WI, '54

128. Sam Houston Teachers,[d] TX, '59, '60

129. San Diego State, CA, '56, '59

130. San Francisco, CA, '53

131. San Jose State, CA, '47, '50, '55, '56

132. Seton Hall, NJ, '49, '55

133. Siena, NY, '51

134. Southern, LA, '58

135. Southern Methodist, TX, '48

136. Southwestern Louisiana, LA, '55, '58

EXHIBIT 7--Continued

137. Southwest Missouri State, MO, '55, '58

138. Stetson, FL, '48, '59

139. Suffolk, MA, '60

140. Temple, PA, '53

141. Tennessee, TN, '49

142. Tennessee Agri. and Indust. State,[d] TN, '54, '59

143. Texas, Agri. and Mechan. Col. of,[d] TX, '49, '56

144. Texas Technological,[d] TX, '49. '56

145. Texas Western,[d] TX, '58

146. Toledo, OH, '54, '55

147. Tulane, LA, '51, '54, '56

148. Tusculum, TN, '56

149. Upsala, NJ, '56

150. Valparaiso, IN, '48

151. Virginia State, VA, '53

152. Washburn, KS, '50

153. Washington of St. Louis, MO, '51, '54

154. Washington State, WA, '48

155. Wayne,[d] MI, '50

156. Western Union,[d] LA, '48

157. West Liberty State, WV, '59

158. West Virginia, WV, '56

159. Wichita,[d] KS, '47, '50

160. William and Mary, VA, '47, '48, '52

161. Wittenburg, OH, '48.

SOURCES: Barron's Profiles, pp. 1143-51; Lovejoy, Lovejoy's College Guide, pp. 371-80; Secretary-Treasurers' Reports, 1943-46 through 1959-60; and Charles Straughn and Barbarasue Lovejoy Straughn, eds., Lovejoy's College Guide, 16th ed. (New York: Monarch Press, Simon & Schuster, 1983), pp. 541-49. The reference is to the index of each collegiate manual (passim).

[a]The fraternal years of the inquiries, as defined by successive secretary-treasurer's reports, are designated by the later calendar year. For example, the period between July 31, 1957, and July 31, 1958 is shown as 1958. Reporting dates ranged from July 31 (1954-60) to August 31 (1948-51). The listing excludes the year of chapter installation at a school made previous contact with the Grand Council during the third era.

[b]Schools no. 5, 16, 114, and 118 apparently no longer exist. Neither Barron's Profiles (1984), Lovejoy's College Guide (1983 or 1981), the College Board's Handbook (1984-85), nor the College Catalog Collection

on Microfiche series (1983-84 or 1982-83) cites or includes (a) a proprietary business college in Alpha, N.J., (b) Benedictine Heights of Tulsa, Oka., (c) Pennsylvania Military of Chester, Pa., or (d) Presbyterian Jr. College of Moxton, N.C., or a successor institution (s.v. "New Jersey," etc.). Only the last two and three sources are relevant to cases a and d, respectively.

The locations of schools b-d were determined from a comprehensive 1966 source that did not list the junior college, and the 1948-49 secretary-treasurer's report. [College Catalog Collection on Microfiche:] Index by State and Name [and] Index by Name, May 1984 (microfiche), fully indexing 1983-84 and 1982-83 series; W. E. Dickerson, Secretary-Treasurer's Report, 1948-49, p. 5; and "Directory of Colleges and Universities," The Random House Dictionary of the English Language: The Unabridged Edition, [1st] ed. (1966), U.S. listings, pp. 1677-90, s.v. "Benedictine Heights C.," "Pennsylvania Military C."

Mindanao College of Davao City, The Phillippines, entry no. 88, was not cited in the Random House listing of "Major Foreign Universities" ("Directory," pp. 1691-96). None of the 26 Phillippine schools listed (perhaps a full national roster in 1966, although more recently in excess of 40 colleges and universities were attributed to the country) was located in Davao, the third largest city in the Phillippines. Located on the same large island, some 100 miles away in Marawi City, is Mindanao State, founded in 1961 (s.v. "Phillippines"). Funk & Wagnalls, s.v. "Phillippines, Republic of the."

[c]Secretary-Treasurer Nolan Williams gave no address for Bryant & Stratton Institute, exhibit entry 21, in his 1958-59 report (p. 5). The inquiry almost certainly came from either Chicago or Buffalo. The brothers H. B. and J. C. Bryant, who in partnership with their brother-in-law H. D. Stratton developed a "chain" of forty-eight proprietary business colleges prior to and during the Civil War, each retained ownership and management of one school after the system was dissolved in 1866. The Chicago school remained in family hands for approximately a century thereafter, while as of 1981 descendants (great-grandchildren) of Dr. J. C. Bryant's continued to operate the business college at Buffalo.

Since 1973, when a branch campus was opened in nearby Rochester, another link in the original chain, a modern-day Bryand & Stratton system has evolved, based in Buffalo. By 1981, campuses existed also in two other nineteenth-century sites, Syracuse and (metropolitan) Cleveland, and in Santa Barbara California. Bryant & Stratton: Buffalo, 1983-84 Bulletin ([Buffalo, N.Y.: 1983]; 1983-84 Microfiche Catalogs, NY-2), p. 26; "The International Business College Association," Harper's Weekly, October 13, 1866, pp. 653-54; and Linda Mamuscia, "Business Education in America--A Bit of Yesterday and Today," unpublished M.B.A. Comprehensive Paper prepared under Author's supervision [School of Management, Syracuse University, 1981], pp. 9-10.

EXHIBIT 7--*Continued*

[d]The short-form names of a number of the schools have changed since the third-era inquiries were made. New institutional names include:

- #24 Casper College (still a two-year school)
- 26 Tennessee at Chattanooga (merger
- 27 California (Cal) State at Chico
- 29 Baruch (splitoff)
- 36 Delta State
- 48 Cleveland State
- 52 Nicholls State
- 53 Cal State at Fresno
- 58 Hartford (merger)
- 60 Indiana-Purdue at Indianapolis
- 61 Indiana State
- 70 Cal State at Long Beach
- 72 Cal State at Los Angeles
- 74 Louisiana Tech
- 90 Southern Mississippi
- 101 Northeast Louisiana
- 113 Oklahoma Panhandle State
- 123 Cal State at Sacramento
- 128 Sam Houston State
- 142 Tennessee State (merger)
- 143 Texas A & M
- 144 Texas Tech
- 145 Texas at El Paso
- 155 Wayne State
- 156 Westmar
- 157 Wichita State.

The major source is *Lovejoy's College Guide* (1981), by Lovejoy, s.v. current (full) names, as cited within the respective state listings. All California State campuses are listed in the same section, s.v. "California: California State University and Colleges, The." Other sources are "Directory," *Random House Dictionary*, s.v. "United States, Chico State C."; exhibit 4; *University of Hartford Bulletin: Undergraduate, 1983-84* (West Hartford, Conn., 1983; 1983-84 Microfiche Catalogs, CN-8), p. 14; and *Wayne State University: Bulletin, 1984-86* [Detroit, 1984]; San Diego: Career Guidance Found., College Catalog Collection on Microfiche, 1984-85 ed., MI-13-14), p. 6.

[e]Although the Georgia school's catalog states that the current name was adopted in 1939, Emmanuel Missionary has tentatively been identified with Emmanuel College of Franklin Springs., Ga., a two-year school of the International Pentacostal Holiness Church that in recent years has offered a four-year program in Christian Ministries. Another Emmanuel College is a Catholic women's school in Boston. Emmanuel School of Religion in Johnson City, Tennessee, sponsored by Christian Churches and Churces of Christ, was not opened until 1965. *Barron's Profiles*, s.v. "Massachusetts, Emmanuel College"; "Directory," *Random House Dictionary*, s.v. "United States, Emmanuel C." (2 entries); *Emmanuel College, a Two-Year Co-Educational Liberal Arts College Founded in 1919: 1983-85 Bulletin* (Franklin Springs, Ga., [1983]; 1983-84 Microfiche Catalogs, GA-8), pp. 3-5; and *Emmanuel School of Religion: Announcements for 1984-86, Twentieth and Twenty-first Years* ([Johnson City, Tenn., 1984]; 1984-85 Microfiche Catalogs, TN-22), p. 4.

[f]Before Georgia State College (now University) joined the Beta Alpha Psi roster in 1961, the school had enjoyed four prior identities. The inquiries of 1950 and 1960 had arrived from the Atlanta branch of the University of Georgia, and the Georgia State College of Business Administration, respectively. Lovejoy, *Lovejoy's College Guide*, s.v. "Georgia, Georgia State University."

schools listed that did not form chapters in the third era were Oklahoma, North Carolina, Washington of St. Louis (as already mentioned), and Drake, an associate AAcCSB member.

Two particularly significant features of the era overall, both documented in exhibit 8, were (1) the promptness with which local fraternal units were generally formed, and (2) the foundation laid for subsequent expansion. Sixteen of 31 charters were issued within two years of the first contemporary inquiry. Ten chapters were formed within one year, with those at Denver, Mississippi, and Creighton being established in the very year of the first postwar inquiry. In other cases, notably that of Loyola of New Orleans, serious interest would evidently not surface until considerable time had elapsed following the initial correspondence.

The pattern of prompt chapter formation would be continued with the five installations of 1960-61, granting that Georgia State (as a branch of the university at Athens) and Tulane had both expressed interest a decade earlier. More importantly, a total of 42 schools that had contacted the Grand Council during the third era would form Beta Alpha Psi chapters over the two dozen years ending in 1984.

Finally, 49 colleges and universities submitted inquiries during more than one (nonchartering) year of the third era. Faculty members at non-AAcCSB campuses were apparently not always deterred by the constitutional ineligibility of their schools, assuming reasonable local "memory" concerning earlier contacts. In particular, Rider College filed inquiries in five separate years following the adoption in 1947 of the accreditation requirement, and (besides Oregon State, the site of a deactivated chapter) Florida State, San Jose State, and, prior to its professional accreditation, Miami of Florida each did so three different years. A dozen other schools lacking

EXHIBIT 8

SITES OF PROMPT THIRD-ERA CHARTERING, BY ONE MEASURE, AND SEEDS SOWN FOR FUTURE ROSTER GROWTH

Sites of Installation within Two Years of First Contemporary Inquiry

Same fraternal year	Following year	Second year after
Pennsylvania	Ohio	Alabama
Denver	Kentucky	Baruch
Mississippi	Detroit	Southern Methodist
Creighton	Iowa	Michigan
	Baylor	Tennessee
	Pittsburgh	
	West Virginia	

Later Chapter Locations Making Third-era Inquiries

Fourth era, 1961-70	Fifth era, 1971-80	Sixth era, to 1984
Loyola of Chicago	Rhode Island	Clarkson
Mississippi State	Cal State at Long Beach	Nevada
California (Cal) State at Los Angeles	Washington State	Southern Mississippi
Georgia State	Cal State at Chico	Saint Louis
Tulane	Hawaii	Seton Hall
Miami of Florida	Texas A & M	
Arizona	New Mexico State	
North Texas State	Massachusetts	
Florida State	Drexel	
Arizona State	Delaware	
Cal State at Sacramento	Cleveland State	
Kent State	North Carolina	
Toledo	Kansas State	
Akron	San Francisco	
Missouri	Connecticut	
Drake	Wichita State	
UCLA	Wayne State	
Northeastern		
San Jose State		
Cal State at Fresno		

SOURCES: "Chapter Information," 1983-84 Annual Report, ed. [Metcalf], pp. 31-38; and exhibit 7. Present-day institutional names have been used.

the required membership contacted the fraternity twice after 1947, although they included a candidate for readmittance (William and Mary), and an institution (Penn State) about to become accredited, in time to form the last new chapter of the era.[8]

In Transition

The ample growth of the chapter roster by itself assured much higher student initiation totals as the third era progressed than had been posted before the war. The highest induction level occurred at the very beginning of such expansion, however, and in relative terms the totals of the early postwar years would seldom be approached during the fifties.

---

[8] Barron's Profiles, s.v. "California: Golden Gate University; Menlo College," "New York, Manhattan College"; "Directory of Colleges and Universities," Random House Dictionary (as cited in exhibit 7, note b), pp. 1677-90; "Education - American Colleges and Universities," World Almanac, 1985, pp. 215-31; exhibit 7, notes c, e, f; Leon E. Hay to Author, interview, May 2, 1980; [Emerson O. Henke], "Congratulations," Newsletter 5 (Fall 1961): 414-15; "Members of the [AACSB] Accreditation Council"; Sheldahl, Alpha to Omega, pp. 447-48, 724, 735, 738; and S. M. Wedeberg, Secretary-Treasurer's Report, 1951-52, p. 6.

The World Almanac and Random House items are cited as convenient complementary sources for (a) identifying church-sponsored institutions in general, and (b) distinguishing explicitly within that group between Catholic colleges and universities and other schools. The latter source makes no distinction between sponsorship or control, and lesser forms of affiliation. The Almanac's classification of Manhattan College in Riverdale, New York as a nonsectarian institution is not supported by Barron's Profiles, or by related sources consulted.

CHAPTER 3

ACTIVE MEMBERSHIP IN THE THIRD ERA: EARLY BOOM, ENHANCED ENTRY STANDARDS, AND MODERATING GROWTH

Active membership grew immensely in the early postwar years, due largely to massive enrollments by veterans drawing educational benefits. The historical total had nearly doubled by 1950, and, despite striking growth in the chapter roster over the next decade, and the admission of women, the era's highest yearly induction total had already been recorded.

Another war, and veterans' program, would contribute to marked fluctuation in membership totals during the fifties. The numerical effects of coeducation may have been more than offset by the moderate elevation, in 1949, of national scholastic requirements for admission to Beta Alpha Psi.

Massive Growth Between Two Wars: America's "Best Years," 1945-50

A bicentennial-year work covering American life between V-J Day and the outbreak of hostilities in Korea was titled "The Best Years, 1945-1950," in recognition of the peace and prosperity that had followed more than fifteen years of economic depression or world war. The postwar boom was nowhere more evident than in college and university classrooms, whose male populations were carried well above earlier peacetime levels by the lure of the monumental "G. I. Bill."

Reactivation was strongly accelerated in 1946-47, when more than twice as many students were initiated as ever before. That level would be far surpassed a year later, and in 1948-49 a new record destined to endure

throughout the third era, despite more than a doubling of the chapter roster, was comfortably set. Excluding new chapters, however, growth had already levelled off in the latter year, and there would be a significant decline directly thereafter. Reports available from or concerning unusually authoritative Beta Alpha Psi sources at the sites of the two largest chapters illustrate both instructional and administrative problems that arose in coping with the multitude of students of a day in which summer fraternal programs were not uncommon.

Extraordinary Growth in Higher Education, Fueled by the "G.I. Bill of Rights"

Male enrollment during the war

Between the academic years 1939-40 and 1943-44, the number of men enrolled in American colleges and universities, and the number receiving bachelor's or first professional degrees, declined by slightly more than 35% and 46%, respectively. The former figure is deceptively low, however, being based on the inclusion of some 270,000 "full-time military and naval" men in the enrollment totals at civilian institutions. Excluding those students from the 1943-44 enrollment figures (only), the comparative data for three years were as follows:

	1939-40	1941-42	1943-44
Enrollment	893,250	818,559	308,914
Degrees (bachelor's and first professional)	109,546	103,889	58,876.

Female enrollment and graduation numbers declined slightly (by approximately 4% and 9%, in turn) over the four years, incidentally, possibly reflecting the increased demand for women in the labor force.

With the end of the war, the trend was promptly reversed. The number of male graduates in 1945-46 was up only slightly, to 58,664, because degrees

are based on several years of study. Male enrollment was dramatically higher, however, standing at 927,662 students, an increase of some 350,000 over the comprehensive total (inclusive of military personnel) of two years earlier. This marked the beginning of several years of remarkable expansion in American higher education, based in large measure upon landmark legislation adopted before the war's end.

Early postwar enrollment

The outbreak of peace in and of itself freed for college entrance the vast pool of young men of traditional collegiate age who would previously have been needed in large numbers for military service. Further, a significant number of returning veterans would no doubt in any case have pursued higher education. Such a process was immensely enhanced, however, by the passage of the Serviceman's Readjustment Act of 1944.

Known far more commonly as the "G.I. BIll of Rights," this act funded unemployment allowances and home, farm, and business loans for millions of World War II veterans. It is cited here, however, because it also extended allowances to 7.8 million returning servicemen to finance education at the secondary, collegiate, or university level, or within almost any form of "adult education" program.

The impact of the G.I. Bill upon higher education during the four academic years 1946-50 is reflected in fall-term enrollment totals of the day:

Year	Male students	Veterans
1946	1,418,000	1,080,396 men and women
1947	1,659,249	1,098,647 men
1948	1,709,367	999,787 men
1949	1,721,572	836,690 men.

Although separate figures for male and female veterans were not obtained

for 1946, during the following three years only between 1.9 and 2.1% of all veterans registered were women.[1]

These figures indicate far higher enrollment than in the prewar year 1939-40, for which the total of fewer than 900,000 cited earlier represented the academic year rather than the fall term only. They also show an increase each year (even if a very slight one in 1949), as the number of veterans declined in both relative and (after 1947) absolute terms. As reported below, however, a more drastic decline in enrollment by former military men, combined with the Korean callup, would serve to reduce male enrollment in the early 1950s.

Against this background, it is not surprising that active membership in Beta Alpha Psi strongly surpassed any previous levels during the first few postwar years.

Rapid Fraternal Growth, Peaking in 1948-49

General overview

Volume 1 reported that five Beta Alpha Psi chapters inducted a total of 33 active members in the fall of 1945. There is no reasonable doubt that Theta, Mu, and Omicron Chapters added a total of 25 students at that time. The 8 new members recorded from Iota and Pi, however, might well have been inducted during the preceding summer instead, since their initiation fees were recorded by Secretary-Treasurer Elwell on October 1. A similar

---

[1]"Education," Statistical Abstract, 68th-71st eds. (1947-50), 68th, p. 136 (quoted), 69th, pp. 135-36, 70th, p. 125, 71st, p. 124; Funk & Wagnalls, s.v. "Education, Adult," "Veterans Administration"; Joseph C. Goulden, The Best Years, 1945-1950 (New York: Atheneum Press, 1976); Historical Statistics of the United States, Colonial Times to 1970, 2 vols. ("parts"), bicentennial ed. (Washington, D.C.: U.S. Dept. of Commerce, Bureau of Census, 1975) 1:383; Carl Rowan, "Bread Cast upon Education Waters Floats Back Silver and Gold," Jackson Daily News (Miss.), February 4, 1985, p. 15A (number of World War II veterans receiving educational benefits); and Sheldahl, Alpha to Omega, p. 747.

uncertainty exists concerning the unidentified Sigma member whose initiation fee was recorded by Secretary-Treasurer Kendrick the following October.

Action picked up considerably in the spring and summer of 1946. Thirteen local units (ten of which had been inactive during the fall) took in 141 men, assuming that the student just mentioned belonged to the summer class as Wisconsin. As documented in chapter 1, considerable initiation activity of the first postwar year occurred after Elwell wrote the chapters in April 1946 to urge prompt reactivation, as appropriate.

Annual initiation totals by chapter for the five years 1945-50 are presented in exhibit 9, combining the summer months in each case with the preceding academic year. With reactivation basically completed, 1946-47 constituted by far the leading initiation period in Beta Alpha Psi annals to that point. The twenty-one chapters admitted 756 active members, more than double the 369 men inducted eight years earlier, the largest previous group by a substantial margin. Fifty or more members were inducted at Texas, Ohio State, Berkeley, Florida, Marquette, and Syracuse. The 96 new Theta brothers represented the largest number of members as yet added by any chapter in a single year. At the other end of the scale, Tau Chapter at Maryland, reactivated early in 1947, initiated only 7 students.

The high totals of 1946-47 were only a prelude to explosive growth over the rest of the decade. The following year 1,056 men were initiated, an increase of fully 300, and an average of 50 per chapter. Omicron at Ohio State became the first chapter to surpass the century mark in a single year by inducting 134 members. The Ohio State faculty included Secretary-Treasurer W. E. Dickerson, Faculty Vice-President W. B. Jencks, and former president Hermann C. Miller, while (as noted presently) former president Jacob B. Taylor held particularly critical administrative responsibilities at the school.

EXHIBIT 9

YEARLY STUDENT INITIATION TOTALS BY CHAPTER, 1945-50[a]

Chapter	1945-46	1946-47	1947-48	1948-49	1949-50	Total
ALPHA		25	50	50	32	157
BETA	11	19	21	39	27	117
GAMMA	5	22	40	34	22	123
DELTA	9	41	63	84	87	284
ZETA	3	19	33	46	22	123
THETA	29	96	62	69	80	336
IOTA	2[b]	35	42	56	43	178
LAMBDA	25	60	56	77	90	308
MU		17	15	22	45	99
NU	5	18	28	27	41	119
XI	20	50	63[d]	62[d]	31	226
OMICRON	19	71	134	133	65	442
PI		14	11	34	23	82
RHO	7	23	65[e]	44	24	163
SIGMA	13[c]	44[c]	53	70	79	259
TAU		7	25	42	29	103
UPSILON		55	52	34	21	162
PHI		27	92	34	35	188
CHI	7	30	50	52	30[f]	169
PSI	6[b]	52	66	27	32	183
OMEGA	13	31	35	30	28	137
Subtotals	174	756	1,056	1,066	886	3,938

EXHIBIT 9--*Continued*

Chapter	1945-46	1946-47	1947-48	1948-49	1949-50	Total
Prior Sub-totals	174	756	1,056	1,066	886	3,938
ALPHA BETA				101	39	140
ALPHA GAMMA				82	77	159
ALPHA DELTA				42	83	125
ALPHA EPSILON					41	41
ALPHA ZETA					51	51
Annual Totals	174	756	1,056	1,291	1,177	4,454

SOURCES: Grand Council Cashbook, 1931-49, pp. 52-70 (even-numbered only); "Local Chapter News" (or equivalent column), *Newsletter* [2] (November 1946 - May 1949), [3] (November 1949 - November 1950), passim; Secretary-Treasurers' Reports, 1943-46 through 1949-50, current initiation data; and *Xi Chapter: 1966 Directory*, chronological listing for years covered, and honorary membership. The second and fourth sources were used in particular to identify summer initiations.

[a]Summer initiates are combined with those of the prior academic year.

[b]The eight Iota and Psi brothers whose dues were recorded in the cashbook (p. 52) on October 1, 1945, have arbitrarily been assigned to 1945-46.

[c]The Sigma member whose dues were recorded on October 25, 1946, in the first cashbook entry made by Secretary-Treasurer Kendrick on his return to office (p. 56), has been assigned to the prior summer, when twelve other students were inducted. The next two entries recorded summer initiations by Xi and Gamma.

[d]The cashbook and secretary-treasurer's report imply that 21 students were initiated by Xi in the fall of 1947, while the *Directory* and *Newsletter* (May 1948, p. 14) list 22 and 19 December inititates, respectively. The second total was used in the tabulation. The following year, however, the initiation figure indicated by the local source was reduced by one due to inconsistency with the other sources, including the *Newsletter* report of November 1949 (pp. 18-19). The discrepancy turned on the status of a student listed in the *Directory* as an initiate of May 1949, and as a Syracuse graduate of four months earlier (alphabetical listing, s.v. "Hildebrandt, John William").

EXHIBIT 9--*Continued*

[e]The total of 66 Rho initiates reported in the cashbook and secretary-treasurer's report appears to have mistakenly included an honorary member, based on erroneous payment of initiation fees for that individual. "Local Chapter News," *Newsletter* [2] (May 1948):16.

[f]Sixteen of the 47 new members reported by the secretary-treasurer had been inducted in the summer of 1949, and thus have been included in the prior year's figures. *Newsletter* reports indicate that 30 active members and 3 honoraries, one more than reported by the secretary-treasurer, were admitted in 1949-50, suggesting that once again initiation fees had been paid for an honorary member, leading to incorrect classification in the national records. "Local Chapter News," *Newsletter* [3] (November 1949):24, (November 1950):23-24.

With Omicron again leading the way, adding 133 new members, the record of 1946-48 would immediately be eclipsed by more than 20%, as 1,291 students joined the fraternity the following year. The increase was based on roster expansion, however, rather than overall growth among established chapters. Virtually all of the 235-member increase was based on the initiation of 225 students at Alabama, City College of New York, and Pennsylvania.

Inducting 101 and (on the late-May installation date) 82 students, respectively, the chapters at the first two new sites were ranked among the top four local units for the year. It is noteworthy also that 41 of 57 men reportedly initiated as "faculty" members that year were brought aboard in successive nights at City College (16) and Penn (25). Part-time instructors were assumed to be eligible for membership, in terms of "holding a position in the accounting faculty." Five years later, in 1954, the constitututtion would be amended to restrict induction to "full-time" personnel.

Even though the chapter roster would more than double by 1960, from 24 to 52, the year 1948-49 would mark the high-water point of the third era in number of active members admitted. Total new membership fell by nearly one-tenth the following year, to 1,177, despite the addition of chapters at Southern Methodist and Denver accounting for 92 initiates. Omicron admitted fewer than half as many students as the year before, at 65, while the three new chapters of 1948-49, two of them formed at the very close of that year, initiated 26 fewer men. Finally, Alpha Zeta at Denver followed the example set by Alpha Gamma and Alpha Delta a year earlier by inducting a large contingent of faculty members (19).

As the historical membership of Beta Alpha Psi was virtually doubled, initiation totals over the full five years ranged from 82 at one Ohio school, Western Reserve, to 422 at another one, Ohio State. Although both schools

represented large urban areas (with Cleveland having the much larger city population of the day), Omicron Chapter was based on a predominantly resident student body while Pi was highly dependent upon part-time students employed in the city. Other urban chapters that may have relied heavily upon nonresident students included Mu at NYU, which initiated only 99 members (nearly half of them in one year), and Gamma at Northwestern, with 123 new brothers. Yet Alpha Gamma at the City College of New York, certainly a commuter school, inducted just as many students on installation night as did Pi in five years, and Alpha Delta at Pennsylvania (in Philadelphia) exceeded that total by one in its first full year.

The declining initiation levels of 1949-50, marking the beginning of a sharp downward trend, reflected moderation of the massive postwar growth that had taxed the resources of campuses across the nation, filling classrooms in the summer months as well as during the school year. At the two campuses admitting the largest number of Beta Alpha Psi members, one prewar Grand Council president was a pivotal administrator in his school's strategic response to remarkable growth, while another one remained in the classroom to form an indelible memory of the special challenges facing contemporary accounting educators.

Adjusting to the hordes, during regular term and summers alike

Plant expansion at Ohio State, led by former president Taylor

The record initiation levels reported by Omicron Chapter in the late 1940s were in keeping with a '"veterans bulge"' at Ohio State that had pushed overall enrollment beyond 25,000 students. Lacking the physical facilities to handle such an enrollment, the university turned over the major responsibility for plant expansion, early in 1946, to newly appointed

business manager Jacob Taylor, who had recently returned from the army.

Under Taylor's leadership, temporary facilities were constructed to meet immediate needs, and "vigorous steps were undertaken to provide for fulfilling the long-range building plans of the university." Twelve new buildings were completed between 1948 and 1954, and major additions were made to several others. As of the fall of 1954, by which time former fraternal president Taylor had added the titles of vice president and treasurer of Ohio State University, another fourteen major construction projects were underway or on the drawing boards.

Coping with overflow demand at Texas, as recalled by former president Smith

A 1947 observation by department chairman, and Chapter advisor, John Arch White concerning the intense demands placed on the accounting program at Texas during the early postwar years was quoted in chapter 1. More recently, C. Aubrey Smith described those years as having been "harrowing indeed" at Austin.

A severe shortage of classroom space, relative to enormously increased demand, required that classroom work be conducted on Saturdays, and also "from 7 a.m. to 10 p.m. five days a week--an unheard of situation in earlier years when students looked with disdain on any class scheduled after one p.m." Relatedly, the teaching load that devolved upon the small permanent faculty (in a day in which the maximum salary locally for a full professor was $6,000) "was almost a disaster." Even with enlistment of a number of part-time instructors and (less promptly) several junior faculty members, accounting professors at Texas during this time were required to teach 9-12 semester hours of courses ranging from 50-150 students per section. They would also commonly supervise the work of 10-20 M.B.A. students and

"a substantial number of Ph.D. candidates."

More than 200 undergraduate degrees in accounting were conferred at Texas for three consecutive years, reaching a high of 265 in 1948-49. That total would not be matched at the university until more than twenty years later. In addition, "service courses were conducted for the thousands who concentrated in other business subjects or elected not to become degree candidates."

Several fraternal chapters conducted summer programs during the first years after the war.

Summer fraternal programs of the late 1940s

Veterans Administration data indicate that, in their eagerness to make up (so far as possible) for lost time, many World War II veterans attended school year around. Some Beta Alpha Psi units accordingly conducted summer programs, at a regular or reduced level. Apparently the most active chapter in this regard was Chi at Oklahoma A. and M. After reactivating in July of 1946, Chi conducted regular programs over the next four summers, including businss and professional meetings, initiation banquets, and other social functions. Twice a slate of summer officers were elected, and at least one other year new officers were installed immediately before the summer term.

In numerical terms, at least, Xi Chapter maintained one of the most productive summer programs of the years 1946-48, inducting 47 students in three August ceremonies. Iota at Southern California, Sigma at Wisconsin, and Upsilon at Florida were each active in two of those three summers. The officers of Delta Chapter at Washington developed a program for the following school year during the summer of 1947, and two years later the Seattle

group held a few informal meetings and a social function, and distributed copies of the annual yearbook. In addition, Gamma at Northwestern was reactivated in August 1946, Beta at Oregon apparently admitted 15 of its 19 new members of 1946-47 the following summer, and Phi at Louisiana State capped a year of remarkable chapter growth with a large initiation in July 1948.[2]

After summer programs had generally been discontinued, but immediately following the largest initiation year of the entire era, the Grand Council in 1949 raised _scholastic_ requirements for admission to Beta Alpha Psi, and clarified a related point, in constitutional amendments that may have been designed in some part to moderate chapter growth.

Raising of Scholastic Requirements for Active Membership, 1949

Minimum scholastic requirements for active membership had been adopted shortly after Beta Alpha Psi was organized nationally, and been maintained nearly intact for more than a quarter century. Eventually, in 1949, modestly higher grade requirements (which chapters could raise for local operating

---

[2]Beta Alpha Psi Fraternity, "National Constitution," _National Constitution and Statutes_ (1953, 1958), article 6, section 2, quoted; W. E. Dickerson, Secretary-Treasurer's Report, 1948-49, p. [7]; "Grand Chapters," _Newsletter_ [2] (November 1947): 3; Grand Council Cashbook, 1931-49, pp. 52-58, even nos. only; Grand Council Minutes Book, 1954, p. 3; W. B. Jencks, "Grand Council of Beta Alpha Psi: Report on Chapter Visitation," Pi Chapter, February 21, 1958 (_date of visit_), item 2.2, and Jencks to Councilors (attached), March 3, 1958 (Visitation Files, 1950-60); Jencks, Visitation Report--Gamma, February 24, 1958, item 2.2, and to Councilors (attached), March 3, 1958; "Local Chapter News" (or equivalent report), _Newsletter_ [2] (November 1946):8, 11, (May 1947):10, 16, (November 1947):15-17, (May 1948):18, (November 1948):16-18, [3] (November 1949):13, 24, (November 1950):23-24; [A.J. Penz], "Jacob B. Taylor . . .: Fifth Grand President of Beta Alpha Psi, 1931," _Newsletter_ 4 (November 1954):197-98, quoted; Sheldahl, _Alpha to Omega_, pp. 181, 314-15, 747, 757-59; Smith, _Forty Acres_, pp. 30-31 (quoted), 31n, 38, 148-52; W. E. Stone, Visitation Report--Mu, April 23, 1960, letter format (Mu Chapter Files, National Office); John A(rch) White to S. M. Wedeberg, March 10, 1952 (Policies File); Nolan E. Williams, Visitation Report--Alpha Delta, November 5, 1959, item 2.2; _World Almanac, 1985_, p. 252; and _Xi Chapter Directory: 1966_, chronological listing, s.v. "August - 1946; 1947; 1948."

purposes) were approved, and limitation of eligibility to accounting majors was unequivocally declared. Subject to minor refinement, the revised standards would endure almost as long as the original ones. A series of changes that began in 1970 have led to the policies of the present day.

Traditional Policy

While recognizing "scholarship" as a basic membership criterion, the national constitution adopted in 1921 contained only a highly general provision concerning academic requirements:

> Any male person duly registered in advanced [nonintroductory] accounting in a college or university of recognized standing and contemplating a continuance in accounting work shall be eligible to active membership in this fraternity.

A year later, the following specific conditions were added:

1. Students must have at least a B average "or its equivalent" in accounting courses, and a C average "or its equivalent" in all courses taken
2. They must pass a written examination administered by the chapter.

The reference made to "equivalent" averages was perhaps intended only to cover chapter sites, if any, at which the conventional letter grades were not used. In any case, it would be retained without special interpretation for more than three decades, extending even beyond the 1949 revision of one of the grade requirements.

In 1924 eligibility conditions 1 and 2 were evidently moved to a new body of elements, supporting bylaws or "statutes." The original draft revision of that year simply dropped the somewhat ambiguous phrase "contemplating a continuance in accounting work," but a substitute formulation suggested (probably) by retiring president Hiram T. Scovill may have appeared in the finished product. At any rate, the fundamentally revised constitution drawn up in 1927, and formally adopted (following refinement) a year later, confined eligibility to students "contemplating public

or private practice or the teaching of accounting." In 1929, finally, this very subjective condition was permanently dropped.

Beginning in 1928, the national statutes characterized active members as "duly registered . . . undergraduate or graduate students <u>in the department of accounting</u>" (chapter 5, section 52, emphasis added). It seems plausible to interpret this passage as restricting membership to male students <u>majoring</u>, or concentrating, in accounting.

Between 1929 and 1949, the only substantive change in scholastic conditions of eligibility was the elimination, at the close of 1932, of the examination requirement. Local chapters have to this day retained the option of administering entry exams. Article 6 of the constitution proper was revised to refer expressly (like the statutes) to students at both academic levels, and in 1936 the word "advanced" was inserted in statute 52 prior to "undergraduate or graduate students," underscoring the requirement of more than introductory accounting study.

If "advanced" accounting meant primarily the second-year ("intermediate") financial course, then students would have been constitutionally eligible for election as early as the first term of their junior year, under the presumed usual placement of that course within the curriculum. As a matter of general practice, however, they were not admitted before completion of at least part of the second-year work. For example, examination of directory records of Xi Chapter initiates at Syracuse, 1946-49, reveals that undergraduates were inducted between the second semesters of the junior and senior years, inclusive. Similarly, observations by a long-term Lambda advisor that are cited below imply that the Berkeley chapter required completion of more than a year of accounting. Further, based perhaps in part on the structure of local academic programs, students at Northwestern and Michigan were for a time, in the 1950s, rarely admitted to Gamma or Alpha Eta Chapter

until their senior years, creating an obvious problem of operating continuity.[3]

In 1949, any question of whether Beta Alpha Psi was limited to accounting majors was firmly resolved, and a significant change was made in grade requirements, though a lesser one than had first been planned. In keeping with the exacting evaluation standards often found in accounting departments of the day, there was no change in required accounting grades. Over the following decade, certain chapters would adopt higher eligibility standards for local use.

---

[3]Grand Council Minutes Book, 1924, pp. 1-2, 1929, pp. 4-5, 1936, p. [2]; W. B. Jencks, Visitation Report--Gamma, February 24, 1958, item 3.4., and to Councilors (attached), March 3, 1958; Jencks, Visitation Report--Alpha Eta and Alpha Omicron, October 31, 1959, letter format; "National Constitution," National Constitution [and Statutes] of Beta Alpha Psi Fraternity ([1936 revision], 1938, 1947), article 6, section 1, "National Statutes," chapter 5, sections 51-52; "National Constitution of Beta Alpha Psi," or comparable title, [1921], preamble ("scholarship" reference), and article 3, section 1 (indented citation), [1922], article 3, sections 2 (quoted), 3, [1924 draft], article 5, section 1, including handwritten insertion, [1927 draft], article 6, section 1 (quoted), 1929, article 6, section 1; "National Statutes of Beta Alpha Psi," [1927 draft], chapter 5, sections 51-52; Sheldahl, Alpha to Omega, pp. 120-23, 821-25 (1921 constitution); and Xi Chapter: 1966 Directory, chronological listing, s.v. "April - 1946" through "May - 1949."

Only typewritten copies of the constitutions from the 1920s have been located. The 1929 version, without statutes, appears in an unpublished manuscript representing the ealiest history of the fraternity. James M. McConahey, "History of Beta Alpha Psi (The National Accounting Fraternity): From Organization to October 31, 1948, Inclusive" ([Seattle, Wash.: 1949-54], with annual updates extending coverage through 1953), pp. 8-12.

All earlier documents (copied for fraternal files) were found in the six folders relating to Beta Alpha Psi contained within box 5 of the Hiram T. Scovill Papers, University of Illinois at Urbana-Champaign Archives, University Library, Urbana Ill. The 1924 constitution (proper), in the provisional form modified during the national convention at Evanston, Illinois was identified as such by reference to the comprehensive list of "amendments" found in the Scovill Papers. The 1927 draft of the constitution and statutes was enclosed with a letter to which it is attached in the files--Eric L. Kohler to chapter presidents, November 1, 1927.

Tau Chapter at Maryland would admit otherwise eligible first-semester juniors who had earned a straight-A average in the introductory accounting course. [S. M. Wedeberg] to James M. McConahey, November 12, 1952.

Raising the Overall Grade Requirement, Only, and Explicitly Requiring an Accounting Major

A protracted amendment process

One of the two changes made in 1949 occasioned no controversy within the Grand Council. In amending constitutional article 6, section 1, to confine eligibility to undergraduate or graduate students "majoring" in accounting, the governing body was probably only restating prior policy. If so, such clarification was long overdue, particularly in light of precedents at Illinois and (very briefly) Oregon, from the earliest days of the fraternity, for requiring two years of accounting of all business students. The term "major" was certainly understood to cover programs in which the degree was conferred in business administration with a "concentration" in accounting, an approach often taken at the graduate level, and occasionally found in baccalaureate study as well. Oregon State University, for example, has technically never awarded a degree in accounting, even though it was the fifth chapter site of Beta Alpha Psi, and was readmitted to the fraternal roster during the third era.

Meeting at the University of Michigan in September 1949, the Council also raised the overall grade-average requirement from the traditional C, while leaving unchanged the required B average in accounting. The amendment of the statutes (chapter 5, section 51) was not completed at Ann Arbor, however, because the following month the councilors reconsidered matters and altered the original decision.

Specifically, the vote taken at the annual gathering would have raised the minimum overall grade average by a full grade point, from C to B. That decision would be changed, however, in time to report in the November *Newsletter* that the new requirement was a B minus grade average in all courses taken. The impetus for reducing the new requirement was provided by

President W. E. Dickerson of Ohio State and Faculty Vice-President Julius Roller of Washington. In assessing the impact of a B/average requirement upon their respective Delta and Omicron Chapters, both men foresaw severe curtailment of membership, and exclusion of "many desirable members," even though Delta already required a grade average (2.5) higher than C.

Roller (who some years later would earn a graduate degree from Michigan) had apparently not been among the faculty advisors who had joined the Grand Council in Ann Arbor for a "round table discussion" following the annual meeting. That informal gathering, only the second recorded meeting of local representatives since 1924, and the first one since 1938, would lead the way to the practice of holding annual "Grand Chapter" banquets. The Delta faculty leader may have first learned of the prospective new grade requirement from former president McConahey, who at his Seattle address had early in October received preliminary Council minutes for use in extending to 1949 the brief "History" of the fraternity that he had prepared to commemmorate its thirtieth anniversary.

Professor Roller expressed his concern in a letter to Secretary-Treasurer John Arch White that was shared with President Dickerson and his immediate predecessor, Thomas M. Dickerson. The latter gentlemen had already discussed the matter, and Bill ("Dick") Dickerson had "raised a question" concerning the wisdom of requiring an overall 3.0 grade-point-average (on a 4.0-scale). A list of potential new Omicron brothers had revealed that "a number of students" whom he would "recommend highly" for membership had averages falling between 2.7 and 3.0.

Although he represented one of the smallest chapters of the time, Tom Dickerson (described by President Nolan Williams in 1959 as an "old school" advocate of an honorary emphasis) was initially more supportive of the eligibility rule adopted in Ann Arbor. He ultimately agreed, however,

that it would "work a hardship upon most of the chapters in recruiting a sufficient number of members each year to keep the chapters operating satisfactorily." He reported that his own group, Pi at Western Reserve, was experiencing such a problem.

President W. E. Dickerson accordingly offered a revised amendment changing the minimum average required for all subjects to "B minus or its equivalent, where there are four passing grades--A, B, C, D." It was approved by way of the affirmative votes submitted to Secretary-Treasurer White by the Dickersons and Councilors Gould L. Harris of NYU and Charles C. Staehling of Berkeley (newly appointed). A four-fifths vote was required. Although White's position is not recorded, his own chapter, Theta, was comparable in size to the original sources of objection to the higher requirement, Delta and Omicron.

There was an interesting contrast among the three chapters just mentioned, incidentally, regarding new membership totals recorded directly after the overall grade average required was lifted to B-. The number of students initiated at Ohio State fell by more than one half in 1949-50, from 133 to 65, while the totals at both Washington and Texas rose moderately (from 80 to 87 and 69 to 84, respectively). As previously implied, Delta's entry conditions had not been affected. The Theta results may have contributed to the chapter's adoption a year later of the higher scholastic requirement originally approved at the national level.

The Grand Council of the day did not define a B- average in grade-point terms, probably less through oversight than because there was no ready consensus on the matter. Councilors Harris and Staehling, whose own interpretations (one of them clearly inappropriate) differed, advanced interesting observations on the broader issues involved based on their own faculty experience.

<u>Conflicting interpretations of "B minus," and other commentary</u>

It appears from the remark quoted above that Bill Dickerson tended to equate B minus with a 2.7 grade average, a reasonable definition assuming that room should also be made for the grade C plus within the range between 3.0 (B) and 2.0 (C). Both Tom Dickerson and Charles Staehling favored the amendment on the assumption that B- represented a <u>2.5</u> average (the equivalent of half Bs and half Cs), however, and the latter councilor recommended that this interpretation be stated within the statutes. Finally, Gould Harris wrote that, since B- was not used at NYU, he would take the grade to be equivalent to <u>C</u>, a position by which the statutory change would have been meaningless.

No information is available concerning requests for clarification of the new requirement, although one might conjecture that chapters tended to split the difference between B and C at 2.5 grade points (or 1.5 on a 3.0 scale). Five years later, during the 1954 annual meeting at the University of Illinois, the Grand Council issued just such an "interpretation," without altering statute 51, itself. The outgoing councilor on that occasion was Professor Staehling, who had been elected to the governing body at the 1949 meeting during which the requirement had been raised, so briefly, to a B average.

Staehling (soon to retire) had nearly followed the 1932 example of Henry Rand Hatfield, his predecessor as Lambda Chapter's faculty leader, by declining appointment to the Council, but had reconsidered in time to participate in the mail balloting. In registering his vote for the B- requirement, he noted that President Dickerson's memo had at first startled him in reporting that the Grand Council had earlier favored a "3.0" overall average, since that would be a straight-A record at Berkeley. Having

quickly realized, however, that a 4.0-scale was being assumed, the incoming councilor suggested that the B- grade be defined as a 2.5 average, the equivalent of Lambda's required overall GPA.

Staehling had served at least nine years as a faculty vice-president, and had probably held that role also over the period 1943-46 (during which the Berkeley group had initiated students each year), except for a brief leave of absence in France as the accounting chairman at an American military college. Based on his local experience, he felt that the Council policy should take note of grade trends. Making reference to accounting studies rather than course work in general, his illustration indicates that Lambda, if not actually requiring two full years of accounting, had scarcely been willing to admit students who had finished only the introductory course.

Professor Staehling observed, then, that two students each having a B average in accounting might have acieved it in opposite ways, one through earning As the first year and Cs the next, and the other through the reverse sequence. He submitted that the latter student would unquestionably be more deserving of admission to an organization like Beta Alpha Psi, and proposed accordingly that the accounting requirements (assumed to exceed one year's completed study) include the absence of any sub-B grades after the introductory course. The new councilor added that "border-line cases" relative to scholastic requirements might best be resolved by the local chapters, "in the light of the particular circumstances of each case." Finally, he recommended (without discernible effect) that the amended policy not be published until the Grand Council had carefully considered issues of the kind cited.

Across the continent at New York University, Councilor Gould Harris, after equating the grade B- with a C, stated rather paradoxically that he

favored "maintaining very high scholastic averages, with reference to membership." In support of reducing the overall grade requirement below 3.0, however, Harris noted that he had become increasingly skeptical of the value of grades as indicators of "future success or failure." He proceeded to relate two anecdotes from his tenure at NYU.

It seems that his department had a number of years earlier adopted a policy by which students would have to maintain a B average from one term to the next in order to continue as accounting majors. Enforcement had proved to be "impracticable," due to circumstances like those described below:

> One of our students was told by our former Dean [the late Beta Alpha Psi president John Madden] that he did not think that he had an accounting mind, in view of some low grades he was getting. Years later, he came in to tell us that he had passed his C.P.A. examination and was also an Assistant District Attorney.
>
> Just this last summer [1949] I had a student in one class who had been getting A's in accounging but missed several lectures; [the student] should not have taken the final, but did so and got the lowest grade in the course.

Even with the increase in one of the two components, the third-era scholastic requirements in accounting (B) and all courses taken (B-) may not seem particularly challenging to students and professors conditioned to grading standards prevalent in the 1980s. There is no doubt, however, that they were genuinely restrictive.

A challenging scholastic requirement

Making specific reference to the B average required in accounting courses, several councilors from different eras have provided pertinent recollections or anecdotes. C. Aubrey Smith commented several years ago that even though only a C average had been demanded, overall, until after the war, the accounting requirement itself would generally have excluded

at least seventy per cent of majors in the field. In support of this observation, it is noted that Texas awarded 695 bachelor's degrees in accounting during the academic years 1947-50, primarily to male students, while Theta Chapter inducted 211 active members, some of whom had graduate standing.

Certain professors, and full accounting departments, developed reputations for particularly severe grading. Self-described as having received "mostly Cs" as a collegian at Iowa in the 1930s, Herb Miller recently recalled his mentor Sidney Winter as having been "feared for his high standards." Following the installation of Alpha Pi Chapter, according to Miller, Iowa students faced a disadvantage in qualifying for Beta Alpha Psi, because some of their accounting professors almost never gave an A.

Vern H. Vincent, who earned his doctorate at Michigan while Miller was teaching there, reported a similar recollection of Alpha Pi in a 1980 interview. From firsthand experience, further, he referred in the same regard to West Virginia, home since 1957 of Alpha Psi. He stated that only eight students taking more than two accounting courses during his twelve faculty years in Morgantown (1957-69) had received all As in the field.

The harsh grading at West Virginia did not keep the local chapter from twice leading the nationwide chapter activity competition during its first dozen years, under the respective leadership of future councilors Vincent and Robert Maust. According to Vincent's fellow fourth-era councilor Leon Hay, it was often said that Alpha Iota Chapter would never lead the points competition so long as Walter Cole served on the faculty at Arkansas, because he supposedly did not give As. Coincidentally or not, this statement would be borne out, despite several high finishes by the chapter in the years leading up to Cole's retirement (following forty-three years on the faculty) in 1969.

The references to Alpha Psi and Alpha Iota point up a particularly

controversial feature of Beta Alpha Psi scholastic criteria that would emerge in the 1950s, namely, the inclusion of member grades as a factor in activity program ratings. As discussed in chapter 6, this practice probably contributed in some cases to the maintenance of chapter eligibility requirements exceeding those specified by the national statutes.

Finally, Andy Penz provided another perspective on grading standards in a 1980 interview. Retired from Alabama since 1971, but having served as a visiting professor at several colleges and universities in the intervening years, the founder of Alpha Beta Chapter felt that modern-day "grade inflation" had clearly not become "rampant" in accounting, and thus concluded that the continuing fraternal requirement of a B average in the major field remained a significant scholastic standard.

If the national eligibility requirements of the 1950s were truly restrictive, it is especially noteworthy that a few chapters, at least, imposed higher ones in conducting their own operations. Five examples may be cited.

Five chapters adopting higher requirements

In the spring of 1950, on the eve of its first anniversary, and but a few months after the new policy was announced, Alpha Gamma Chapter at the City College of New York felt "compelled to raise the requirement for eligibility substantially above the minimum standards of the national constitution" (emphasis added). The "extremely high scholarship" records presented by many local candidates had apparently produced an embarrassment of riches, in the form of stronger demand for membership than the chapter officers considered desirable.

Even more interestingly, however, as of the fall of 1950 Theta Chapter

at Texas would admit only students having at least a B average in all courses. This group was of course the home chapter of Secretary-Treasurer John Arch White, who had served as its faculty advisor for nine years (not including wartime deactivation) prior to joining the council. Permitting Theta to qualify as a local "honorary" organization, the higher entry requirement may also have benefited the group in regard to the annual chapter "ratings" competition begun in 1950-51.

In the late 1950s, both Gamma at Northwestern and Alpha Omega at Michigan State were encouraged by visitation officers to reduce their local scholastic conditions to the national level. Alpha Omicron had adopted the same policy followed by Theta, while Gamma was requiring a 3.2 average in two years of accounting work, and "almost" a B average overall. National files indicate only that each group agreed to consider the recommended change.

Finally, Mu Chapter at New York University was likewise encouraged, in the fall of 1959, to reduce admission standards to the national level. This case was exceptional, however, in that scholastic requirements that included a B+ (soon to be reduced to a B) average overall were identified as one factor contributing to a serious constitutional problem (alumni dominance of the chapter) discussed later.[4]

---

[4]T. M. Dickerson to C. C. Staehling, October 24, 1949, and John A. White, October 24, 1949, quoted; [W. E. Dickerson], "John T. Madden," Newsletter [2] (May 1949):9; W. E. Dickerson to White, October 22, 1949, and enclosed statement, quoted; W. E. Dickerson, prefatory note to "History of Beta Alpha Psi," by James M. McConahey, Newsletter [2] (May 1949):6; "Directory," Newsletter [2] (December 1938):2, (March 1939 - May 1947):3; "Directory of Activities," Newsletter [2] (April 1937:10, (November 1937):11; H. E. Donley, Secretary-Treasurer's Report, 1968-69, p. 8; exhibit 9; "Grand Chapter," Newsletter [2] (November 1947 - May 1949):3; Grand Council Minutes Book, 1949, p. [2]; Gould L. Harris to W. E. Dickerson, October 20, 1949, quoted (two indented citations); Harris to White, October 25, 1949; Hasselback, 1984 Directory, individual listing, s.v. "Roller, Julius L.," "Vincent, Vern H."; Leon E. Hay to Author, interview, May 2, 1980; Jeanne

The constitutional provisions on scholastic requirements approved in 1949 would remain unchanged for more than twenty years, although policy "interpretations" made along the way would lend a measure of flexibility to the application of both grade conditions. More significant change would be delayed until the 1970s.

Evolution of Scholastic Requirements after 1949

During the third era

Less than two years after the overall grade average requirement had been raised, Iota Chapter at Southern Cal petitioned the Grand Council to permit the initiation of students, already graduated, who had satisfied

---

Heywood, Oregon State University Archives, to Author, January 29, 1985; W. B. Jencks, Visitation Report--Alpha Eta and Alpha Omicron, October 31, 1959, letter format; Jencks, Visitation Report--Gamma, February 24, 1958, items 2.2, 3.4, and to Councilors, March 3, 1958; Norman W. Kaylor, "The Beta Alpha Psi Chapter Activity Program, 1950-69," Newsletter 8 (50th anniv. ed., [1969]): 2-3; "Local Chapter News," Newsletter [3] (November 1949):12, (May 1950): 24, quoted, (November 1950):17, 4 (November 1952):17; Jas. M. McConahey to White, October 14, 1949; V. R. McDougle, University of Oregon, to H. T. Scovill, January 19, 1921 (Scovill Papers, Illinois); Herbert E. Miller, "Biographical Data - April 1967" (Golden Anniversary Files), p. 1; Miller to Author, interview, April 18, 1980, quoted; Miller. "A Synopsis," Issues in Accounting Education: 1983, ed. Richard E. Murdoch, (American Accounting Association, 1983), pp. 5 (quoted), 6; [Hermann C. Miller], "Meeting of Grand Chapter," Newsletter [2] (March 1939):5; A. J. Penz to Author, interview, April 18, 1980, quoted; Julius L. Roller to Author, by telephone, March 26, 1985; Sheldahl, Alpha to Omega, pp. 103-104, 272, 677-78, 732, 747; Terry K. Sheldahl, 'A Professional Accountancy Program from the 1920s: The University of Oregon's "Five Year Course"', working paper (Millsaps College, rev. 1985), pp. 16-18, 28; Smith, Forty Acres, p. 38 (references to 1948, 1949, and 1950 are equated with academic years), 72-73; C. Aubrey Smith to Author, tape recording, June 1980, part 1; C. C. Staehling to W. E. Dickerson, October 27, 1949, quoted; Staehling to White, October 27, 1949; W. E. Stone to Councilors, October 30, 1959, Visitation Report--Mu, April 23, 1960, letter format (Mu Chapter Files, National Office); Vern H. Vincent to Author, interview (Edwardsville, Ill.), July 21, 1980; [White], "Grand Chapter News," Newsletter [3] (November 1949):7 (quoted), 8-9; and Nolan E. Williams, Visitation Report--Pi, November 3, 1959, item 2.4, quoted.

All correspondence from October 1949, except McConahey's letter, is from the Policies File.

the minimum scholastic requirements on the basis of their final semester's grades. Independently, Alpha Gamma faculty advisor E. I. Field, assistant dean at the City College of New York, recommended to Secretary-Treasurer White in the summer of 1951 that such an approach be permitted. At its September meeting, however, the Council voted unanimously to reject the request from Iota, following "thorough discussion."

Three years later in 1954, in addition to formally defining a B-average as a 2.5 GPA (or 1.5 on a 3.0-base), the councilors adopted two "interpretations" that among other effects might permit the induction _before_ graduation of students meeting the grade requirements only at the close of their studies. First, it was agreed that in '"borderline cases"', involving marginal deviation from either scholastic requirement, a student could be elected by unanimous vote of chapter officers, including the faculty vice-president. Second, after thirty-two years of constitutional or statutory reference thereto, the Council finally defined an "equivalent" to a B average in accounting. Specifically, rank within '"the upper 30 percent of the combined juniors and seniors majoring or having primary interest [that is, concentrating] in accounting"' was cited as an equivalent qualification. This alternative measurement basis could possibly itself be stretched a bit to allow for "borderline cases."

The second policy interpretation was no doubt intended in part to help promote eligibility within chapters associated with accounting programs noted for their difficult grading. The use of the 30% figure also lends much credibility to Aubrey Smith's characterization of the B average in the field. Oddly enough, the _Newsletter_ writeup of the 1954 Council meeting, but not the minutes themselves, reported that a rule was also adopted _limiting_ undergraduate fraternal admission to 30% of junior and

senior accounting majors. Although no further reference to such a policy has been found, the idea of restricting membership to the upper tier of accounting students (based on accounting grades) would commend itself as a protection against relatively permissive grading standards.

As already indicated, no changes were made in the constitution or supporting statutes themselves. Even with coverage in a faculty advisor's manual, developments of the early 1960s related below suggest that the class-rank alternative to the required B average was inadequately communicated within the chapter roster. At the close of the third era, however, visitation officer Williard Stone recommended that Alpha Lambda at Tennessee "temporarily" adopt the "optional membership requirements" in order to build up membership from a very low base. It seems that the number of accounting majors at Tennessee had declined in 1958 and 1959, but that enrollment was expected to increase relatively soon.

Later developments

At the first "Grand Chapter" banquent of the fourth fraternal era, held at the University of Texas in the summer of 1961, an unidentified individual (probably a faculty advisor)

> suggested that the Grand Council consider the merits of an alternative test for eligibility for membership by the use of a specified upper percentage of the accounting majors in addition to the grade average test.

Just such an "alternative test" had of course already been on the books for seven years. Yet minutes prepared by Secretary-Treasurer Miller (who favored class rank as the primary approach) gave no indication that this information was conveyed, even though all six councilors, the four Council

presidents of the years 1955-59, and twenty-seven current faculty vice-presidents were on hand.

The 30% rule was reported, however, within the "Faculty Vice-President's Handbook," a document completed and distributed in 1957-58 by Secretary-Treasurer Jencks, at a cost of $310. Accordingly, when it was reported at the 1962 Grand Council meeting that "some" chapters had requested an alternative to the traditional requirement of a B average in accounting, "[t]he provision in the . . . Handbook allowing a chapter to base its initiates upon a percentage of juniors and seniors was read." Secretary-Treasurer Emerson O. Henke was asked to refer the appropriate chapters to this provision.

At the next national meeting, there was a development that on first reading represented a major change in the accounting requirement. "Eligibility" for election to active membership was defined in 1963 in terms of several conditions that included the completion of twelve semester hours, or the equivalent, in accounting. As discussed in chapter 10, however, this definition governed only an important change made in the "Chapter Activity Program," and did not alter constitutional provisions.

In 1965 the fraternal constitution as a whole was substantially revised, partially through replacement of separate "statutes" by expanded coverage under fifteen constitutional articles. The respective requirements of B and B- averages, or the "equivalent," were maintained. The traditional language of "registration in advanced accounting" was abandoned in favor of

the clearer statement that students were eligible upon completion of "a two-semester (or equivalent) introductory accounting course," and declaration of an accounting major. In addition, the new constitution expressly authorized chapters to require higher grades, and/or the passing of an entry examination, if they wished.

Substantive changes in scholastic requirements were finally made in the 1970s, beginning with the amendment of article 9, section 1, as of the beginning of 1971 to recognize two alternatives to the overall GPA requirement of 2.5:

a. A 3.0 average "on the most recent 60 [semester] hours of course-work attempted"
b. A 3.25 average "on the most recent 30 [semester] hours . . . ."

Additional conditions that could be imposed by local chapters were cited.

The National Council had actually stipulated originally a <u>3.5</u> average under the second of the two options adopted for the benefit of "the sutdent who was late in finding himself." In a development reminiscent of the events of 1949, the requirement had been reduced before the amended constitution was printed. Only later, however, would the Council refer explicitly to "semester" hours, and to "equivalent" academic credit.

In 1972 the accounting requirement was increased from one year to three semesters or five quarters, and (reflecting concern over grade inflation) Beta Alpha Psi membership was capped by limiting admission to students ranking scholastically within the <u>top 35%</u> of all students at their schools. Later the minimum accounting requirement was changed to three semesters or four quarters that included one term of the intermediate financial course, and generally comparable but higher eligibility conditions were specified for <u>graduate</u> students, including a 3.5 average in accounting.

By 1983, finally, the original 1949 requirement of an <u>overall</u> B average

(3.0) had been adopted for undergraduate eligibility, allowing for the substitution of a 3.25 or 3.5 average, respectively, on the most recent 30 or 60 semester hours. Remarkably, however, the requirement of a B average in accounting courses that was adopted in 1922 has remained intact.

A number of the eighty-four chapters replying to a 1980 survey maintained grade-average requirements that surpassed existing national standards. Conditions for qualifying as a campus "honor society" were probably often instrumental in such cases; and in noting at the time of the inquiry that fraternal policy encouraged chapters to set eligibility rules considered suited to local grading practices, Professor Doris Cook called to mind the top-35% specified limit. Several chapters reported grade requirements below official minimum criteria, more commonly at the graduate level.[5]

The elevation of grade requirements was no doubt eclipsed by factors relating to war and peace in producing sharply reduced initiation totals during the early 1950s, even as women joined the Beta Alpha Psi fold. It would have played a significant if indeterminate role, however, in the restrained membership growth recorded by the fraternity throughout a decade marked after its first years by steadily increasing enrollment levels.

---

[5]Beta Alpha Psi, "National Bylaws," National Constitution and Bylaws (1977, 1983, 1985), article 4, sections 1-2, quoted; Beta Alpha Psi Fraternity, "National Statutes," National Constitution and Statutes (1958), chapter 5, sections 51-52; Beta Alpha Psi National Constitution (1965, 1967, [1969], 1971), article 9, section 1, quoted; Thomas J. Burns to Author, interview, May 3, 1980; Doris M. Cook to Author, interview, March 21,1980; Hollis A. Dixon to Author, interview (Tucson, Arizona), March 22-23, 1980; Harvey E. Donley to Author interview, May 2, 1980; E. I. Fjeld to John A. White, July 24, 1951 (Policies File); Grand Council Minutes Book, 1951, p. 3 (quoted), 1954, p. 2 (quoted), 1956, p. 4, 1961, p. 7 (quoted), 1962, p. 3, 1963, pp. 6-7 (quoted); [W. B. Jencks], Secretary-Treasurer's Report, 1956-57, pp. 1-2; National Council Minutes, 1970 (double-spaced typescript), pp. 9, 10 (quoted), 1972, p. 8; [A. J. Penz], "Grand Council News," Newsletter 4 (November 1954):199-200; W. E. Stone, Visitation Report--Alpha Lambda, April 1, 1960 (letter format), quoted; and Robert S. Wasley to Author, interview, March 23, 1980. Also, Janice Gonzales (national administrator) and James W. Pattillo to all local chapters, March 24, 1980, requesting scholastic requirements; and the 84 responses.

Moderate Expansion During the Fifties

Enrollment Trends Based, in Part, on Matters of War and Peace

As related earlier, new membership had declined by more than a hundred students in 1949-50 despite the addition of two new chapters. Significantly, there had been a decline of approximately one-sixth from the preceding year in the number of vetetans enrolled on American campuses.

As World War II receded further into history, the latter trend was of course certain to continue, at an accelerated pace. More importantly, a new war began in the summer of 1950 when United Nations troops supplied primarily by the United States came to the defense of South Korea after it was invaded by North Korean forces. During the three years of fighting, male enrollment at U.S. colleges and universities was understandably down measurably from the levels of the late 1940s. Fall-term totals were as follows:

1950	1,560,392 men	557,136 veterans (male)
1951	1,390,740	375,974
1952	1,380,357	224,884.

In 1952 Congress enacted a new G.I. Bill to cover Korean War veterans. Over the next thirteen years some 2,400,000 of them would utilize available educational benefits, more than half at the collegiate level. With the end of the war, the enrollment of veterans exceeded 280,000 in the fall of 1953, and rose to the range of 445-475,000 during the years 1955-57 before dipping slightly below the 1953 level by the end of the decade. These numbers include women, who had comprised from 2.2 to 3.0% of the veterans enrolled in the three years 1950-52.

Exhibit 1, in chapter 1, documented an upward trend in the number of accounting graduates between the middle and end of the decade. Total collegiate enrollment increased dramatically following the end of the Korean

War, from fewer than 2,150,000 students in the fall of 1953 to more than 3,375,000 (including 2,160,000 men) six years later. There was a substantial increase each year during this period.[6]

The Beta Alpha Psi chapter roster exactly doubled during the Fifties, from 26 to 52 local units. Within the setting just sketched, one might have expected the post-Korean years to yield record levels of fraternal initiation. Expansion of that magnitude would not occur, however, although annual totals after 1953-54 always exceeded 1,000 students, and several chapters posted consistently strong induction levels.

Aggregative Initiation Data

The yearly initiation totals for the Fifties were as follows (listing 1950-51 as 1951, etc.):

1951	1952	1953	1954	1955	1956	1957	1958	1959	1960
989	889	760	885	1017	1222	1249	1157	1163	1119.[7]

[6]"Education," Statistical Abstract, 72nd ed. (1951), p. 121, 73rd (1952), p. 125, 74th (1953), p. 128, 76th (1955), pp. 125, 127, 77th (1956), p. 127, 79th (1958), p. 126, 80th (1959), p. 126, 81st (1960), p. 125; Funk & Wagnalls, s.v. "Education in the United States: Federal Legislation in the 20th Century," "Korean War," "Veterans Administration"; and "Military Sevices and Veterans' Affairs," Statistical Abstract, 79th ed., p. 258, 80th, p. 257.

[7]Alpha Mu Chapter: 1969 Directory, pp. 2 (honorary and faculty members), 17-18 (initiates for years covered); "Local Chapter News," Newsletter 4 (May 1954):191; Secretary-Treasurers' Reports, 1950-51 through 1959-60, current initiation data, 1957-58, p. 2, 1959-60, p. 4; and Xi Chapter: 1966 Directory, chronological listing for years covered, and honorary membership.

The 1957-58 and 1959-60 annual reports correct the aggregate totals presented in the respective preceding years. Otherwise the totals given are those officially reported, with very minor exception. As noted in the first chapter, an inconsistency in the 1950-51 report leaves the initiation total indeterminate between 989 and 990 students. Based in turn on the Xi and Alpha Mu directories, one student has been added to the 1957-57 total and one has been reassigned from 1959-60 to the preceding year. Finally, the Newsletter report cited supports the secretary-treasurer's total for Alpha Mu initiates of 1953-54 rather than the higher number (by one) given in the local directory.

The overall total was 10,450 new members, more than doubling historical membership (from the estimated 9,025 recorded previously).

In essence, the decade consisted of (a) declining induction levels, 1951-53, (b) expansion, 1954-57, and (c) renewed decline, 1958-60. Based on chapter averages, the 1959-60 results were lower even than those recorded seven years earlier, when only 760 students were admitted to the fraternity.

Secretary-treasurers' reports often included brief comments on active-membership trends. In the decade's first report, John Arch White correctly forecast continuation of a two-year decline in initiation totals "at least through 1953," based on expected further decreases in enrollment. Two years later S. M. Wedeberg asserted the positive side of the same coin in predicting that "the trend will be reversed within the next year or two." Coming less than a month after an armistice had been declared in Korea, that statement would be borne out promptly with a gain in 1953-54 of 125 new members (71 of them from new chapters) over the number posted the previous year.

Following the largest such increment of the fifties (a gain of 205 in new membership), Secretary-Treasurer W. B. Jencks advised his colleagues in 1956 to begin to plan for "the tidal wave of students anticipated in the next fifteen years," and confidently forecast the immediate achievement of an "all time high" in annual initiation level. He was nearly proved right in the latter regard, since the 1,249 students admitted in 1956-57 would represent the second highest total to that time. Despite the additition of eight new or (in the case of Epsilon at Oregon State) reinstated chapters, however, there would be a significant decline over the last three years of the third era.

In 1958 Secretary-Treasurer Nolan Williams expressed some concern about

the "untoward trend" that he felt had set in during the year just completed, but looked for improvement soon based on "[t]he expected increase in University enrollemnt." He reiterated this viewpoint a year later, after two installations yielding 98 members had barely sufficed to maintain aggregate new membership. Finally, Herb Miller observed matter-of-factly in his 1960 report that "a downward trend" had "been established."

A chapter formed in 1949 would by a wide margin set the pace on induction levels for the 1950s, being joined among the leaders by two groups created still later, while (among preexisting units) an extremely old chapter would bring up the rear.

Chapter Initiation Data--Highs and Lows

The identity of the leading chapter, numerically, of the 1950s was foreshadowed when Alpha Gamma initiated 159 students during its first twelve months of existence, beginning in May 1949. Over the next ten years the CCNY chapter inducted 609 students, ranging from 37 in 1952-53 to 94, the decade's highest annual total, three years later. Five times Alpha Gamma posted the fraternity's highest yearly total.

Ranking next, though far behind Alpha Gamma, were two still younger chapters and three early ones, each admitting between 350 and 400 active members during the ten-year span. The new chapters were Alpha Zeta at Denver and Alpha Eta at Michigan, founded respectively on the eve of the year 1950-51 and the following spring, while the old ones were Omicron, Sigma, and Theta.

At the other end of the scale, Beta Chapter at Oregon inducted only 139 active members during the 1959s, admitting merely 6 students in 1953-54. Five other chapters existing throughout the decade, counting three formed in its first year, initiated fewer than 200 members (from 174 to 192).

They were Alpha Theta at Mississippi, Alpha Iota at Arkansas, Pi at Western Reserve, Iota at Southern Cal, and Alpha Lambda at Tennessee.

Numerically the weakest chapter, however, was Alpha Kappa at Ohio University, which after initiating 17 students on installation night in January 1952 added only 78 more over the next eight and one-half years. After 1951-52, yearly induction totals at Ohio ranged between 7 and 15 students, and four times the chapter registered the lowest national total.[8]

Contemporary visitation officers noted, but were not exceedingly concerned about, the low initiation levels at Beta and Alpha Kappa Chapters. After a visit to Oregon in May 1952, Charles Staehling observed that recent turnovers in faculty leadership had left Beta "unable to develop any momentum," but that new Faculty Vice-President John H. Soha seemed to be 'just the man to put it "on the map" again'. A year later President Staehling attended an elaborate orientation meeting held by Beta for A and B students from the introductory course who might wish to consider an accounting major, and was highly impressed by the interest shown by the sixty or more such students attracted. In the fall of 1958, Councilor Wayne Shroyer found in Eugene a "very selective" chapter whose nine members, enjoying excellent faculty leadership,[9] were "really . . . on the ball,"

---

[8]The alphabetical inconsistency of assigning the name Alpha Lambda prior to Alpha Kappa was rooted in early fraternal history. For reasons unrecorded, the chapters formed in succession at Berkeley, NYU, and William and Mary during the years 1925-27 were designated Lambda, Mu, and Kappa rather than Kappa, Lambda, and Mu. A quarter-century later the inconsistency was confined to the letters Lambda and Kappa, since Alpha Mu at Kentucky was founded after Alpha Kappa at Ohio. Sheldahl, <u>Alpha to Omega</u>, p. 167.

[9]Professor Shroyer, elected to the Grand Council in 1953 while serving as accounting chairman at Denver, strongly complimented new Beta faculty vice-president Dale Harwood, perhaps in spite of his educational credentials (D.B.A., University of Washington, 1957). Apparently fearing a trend toward excessively theoretical instruction, Shroyer (B.S., M.S., Denver) is remembered by Vern Vincent to have observed that "I don't want

conducting a "very meaningful" program.

W. B. Jencks of Ohio State made two visits to Alpha Kappa at Ohio University, whose founding advisor Tom Wingfield, as earlier related, had died soon after the installation. In the fall of 1955, Jencks found an "enthusiastic" officer group at Athens, led by a very able faculty vice-president, W. H. Reininga, but a definite shortage of student members, constituting the major problem discussed. At the beginning of the term there had been only three actives, but the registration of the largest freshman class in the school's history was expected to help matters. In the spring of 1954 Ohio had reported a student enrollment of 4,231, approximately 550 more than Oregon. All six local accounting instructors were regular participants in Beta Alpha Psi activities, compared with three of ten, on the average, at Oregon.

An upturn registered at Ohio the following year, 1956-57, with the initiation of 15 active members (an increase of 8), would not be sustained. Even so, Professor Jencks was able to commend Alpha Kappa after a return visit in the fall of 1958, having found there a group of "active and enthusiastic" student officers supported by a new advisor exhititing "keen interest" in the chapter.

By the close of the third era, in conclusion, two old chapters had surpassed the 1,000 mark in historical active membership, Omicron at Ohio State (1,117) and Theta at Texas (1,025). Two still older groups, Alpha at Illinois and Delta at Washington, had each brought in more than 950

---

one of them goddamned Ph.D.'s teaching accounting for me." It seems unlikely that he would have looked any more favorably upon the D.B.A. degree. Hasselback, 1984 Directory, individual listing, "Harwood Jr., Dale S."; Vern H. Vincent to Author, interview, July 21, 1980, quoted; and [S. M. Wedeberg], "Grand Council News," *Newsletter* 4 (November 1953):106.

members, fully twice as many as Beta at Oregon.[10]

In Transition

Throughout the third era, active or student membership was of course only one category of affiliation with Beta Alpha Psi. Two of the other three forms of membership invited, and received, particularly important policy attention during the period.

---

[10]"Accredited U.S. Colleges and Universities," Information Please Almanac, 1955 (New York: Macmillan Co., 1954), pp. 257-71, s.v. "Ohio University," "Oregon, University of"; exhibit 9; "Grand Chapter," Newsletter 4 (November 1955):263; W. B. Jencks, Visitation Reports--Alpha Kappa, October 25, 1955, items 2.1 (quoted), 2.2, 2.4, 3.1, 3.4, December 4, 1958, items 2.1 (quoted), 2.4 (quoted), 3.4; Secretary-Treasurers' Reports, 1950-51 through 1959-60, current initiation data, 1950-51, p. [3], 1952-53, p. 4, 1955-56, p. 3, 1957-58, p. 5, 1958-59, p. 6, 1959-60, p. 4, each quoted; Sheldahl, Alpha to Omega, pp. 181, 747, 758; Wayne E. Shroyer, Visitation Report--Beta, December 17, 1958 (letter format), quoted; C. C. Staehling, Visitation Report--Beta, May 27, 1952, items 1 (commentary, quoted), 2.4 (quoted), 3.1; and Staehling to S. M. Wedeberg (Visitation Reports--Beta, Delta), June 4, 1953, quoted.

Alpha Gamma was inadvertantly omitted from the secretary-treasurer's listing in 1955-56. Based on the aggregate total given, of 1,222 new members inclusive of Alpha Gamma, 94 initiates were imputed to the City College chapter. This number was checked against contemporary Newsletter reports, listing 98 initiates for the year. Both fall and spring listings were prospective in nature, however, and 10 students were cited twice, implying a delay in their actual induction. It seems altogether realistic, then, that another 4 students listed in the spring would not in fact have been admitted to the fraternity during the year, reducing the total new membership to 94. "[Local] Chapter News," Newsletter 4 (November 1955): 289, (April 1956):321.

CHAPTER 4

HONORARY AND ALUMNI MEMBERSHIP: MAJOR TRENDS, POLICIES, AND PRACTICES

Throughout the third era, three categories of nonactive membership were recognized--faculty, honorary, and alumni. Designed for professors who were not Beta Alpha Psi alumni, membership of the first kind facilitated broad faculty participation in chapter activities while guaranteeing that any department could supply a fraternal advisor (of necessity a member). Occasional brief references are added to prior mention of faculty status.

Honorary membership was awarded to some 650 distinguished accountants, representing considerable professional diversity. Four years after issuing important guidelines concerning such membership, the Grand Council in 1954 sought to form a national alumni organization. Although the effort was abortive, several chapters reported significant initiatives in this area, and there was extensive periodical coverage of fraternal alumni. Their influence within one chapter, however, raised a serious constitutional issue.

Honorary Membership

Basic policy governing honorary membership had evolved significantly during the prewar years, for example through the introduction of separate faculty membership. Recommendations concerning the selection and initiation of honorary members, published shortly before a national "roll" of such individuals appeared, represented the leading policy developments of the third era. The Newsletter provided substantial profile coverage of honorary members, documenting general observance of the selection criteria.

Honorary Membership

Evolution of Governing Policy

Historical background

Like the Alpha Chapter document on which it was based, the constitution adopted in forming a national fraternity in 1921 extended eligibility for honorary membership to "anyone holding a position on the accounting faculty, or any prominent practicing accountant." The contextual restriction to male professors or accountants would not have imposed a significant limitation in a day in which there were only thirty-three women CPAs in the United States.

Three years later, in 1924, the faculty and practitioner criteria were respectively (within the draft constitution available) broadened and narrowed. Faculty personnel from "any college or university of recognized standing" were made eligible, seemingly a reasonable provision at a time at which the entry of Theta at Texas increased the chapter roster to merely eight schools. Practicing accountants, however, could be elected only if they were "certified public or chartered accountant[s]." Such a restriction was timely in the sense that certification programs had by 1923 been established in all states and the District of Columbia, but the unique emphasis placed upon public accounting seems questionable given the formation a few years earlier of the National Association of Cost Accountants.

The constitution drafted in 1927 at (in effect) the first Grand Council meeting restored the original faculty provision, which was clarified through express exclusion of graduate students from honorary membership. This reversion to prior policy may have been intended to enhance the opportunity for a new chapter to induct distinguished local professors who were not fraternal alumni. That option would, for instance, be denied Sigma Chapter in regard to Fayette H. Elwell, due to his honorary election to the Zeta brotherhood in 1926. Through another revision, practicing accountants

who were members of the American Institute of Accountants could be considered for honorary membership even if they were not CPAs. Reference to "chartered" accountants was eliminated.

At the close of 1936, honorary membership was opened up much further by extending eligibility, beyond local faculty members and "prominent" practicing accountants who were CPAs or Institute members, to "any prominent accountant." Two years later, finally, the overall category was subdivided by recognizing a separate class of "faculty" membership. "Honorary" membership was thus defined (by article 6, section 3) as being available, through election by a local chapter, to

> any prominent practicing accountant who is either a Certified Public Accountant or a member of the American Institute of Accountants, or to any prominent accountant.

The dual reference to certification and the American Institute was already redundant, because AIA membership had been restricted to CPAs since 1936. Nonetheless, this redundancy would be maintained through the third era, during which the section would be altered only (in 1958) to reflect the organization's new identity as the American Institute of "Certified Public" Accountants. Also maintained was a "statute" adopted in 1938 (chapter 5, section 55) by which honorary membership would be based upon "outstanding personal and professional attainments in the field of accounting--public or private."

Addition of the phrase "any prominent accountant" clearly eliminated the strong prior bias in favor of public practice. The accompanying statute may have allowed for the induction of <u>professors</u>, lacking significant practitioner experience, from nonchartered schools who had been notably active within leading professional organizations. In addition, distinguished <u>publication</u> in the field could have been considered "outstanding . . .

attainment" in "public" or "private" accounting.

In any event, prominent professors who were initiated as honorary members shortly before wartime deactivation presented impressive records of nonacademic "professional" activity. For example, accounting and statistics chairman Thomas Leland of the Agricultural and Mechanical College of Texas (Texas A&M), honored by Theta Chapter in 1939, had served two terms as president of the state CPA society before becoming its secretary. Similarly, Professors Thomas H. Sanders of Harvard and Herbert F. Taggart of Michigan were inducted by Tau at Maryland, in 1942, while on temporary leave as accountants within war-related federal agencies.[1]

Criteria for selecting honorary members were clarified in a policy statement of 1950, and the Grand Council later the same year recommended mimization of the fraternal initiation *ritual* in their regard. Several additional policy interpretations or decisions were rendered during the third era.

Third-era policy development

Guidelines for selecting honorary members

The Grand Council encouraged chapters to admit honorary members,

---

[1]Beta Alpha Psi Fraternity, "National Constitution," *National Constitution and Statutes* (1953, 1958), article 6, section 3, quoted, "National Statutes," chapter 5, section 55, quoted; Grand Council Minutes Book, 1936, p. (2), 1938, p. [3], 1958, p. [3]; "Letters from Local Chapters," *Newsletter* [2] (March 1942):12; Hermann C. Miller, ed., *Beta Alpha Psi Directory*, s.v. "Sigma Chapter: Elwell, Fayette H."; [Miller], "Introducing: Mr. Thomas W. Leland," *Newsletter* [2] (May 1939):5; "National Constitution," *National Constitution and Statutes of Beta Alpha Psi Fraternity* [1936], article 6, section 2, quoted, (1938), article 6, sections 2, 3 (indented citation), "National Statutes," (1938), chapter 5, section 55, quoted; "National Constitution of Beta Alpha Psi" [1921], article 3, section 3, quoted, [1924], article 5, section 2, quoted, [1927], article 6, section 2; Sheldahl, *Alpha to Omega*, pp. 4, 8, 85, 89; and E. L. Slocum, "The Lady Ages Well," *Accounting History Research Center Scripturis* 2 (Winter 1984):4.

most directly by for more than four years concluding a regular Newsletter feature, "Attention Chapter Officers," with the following sentence:

> It is recommended that at each initiation some well-known accountant be admitted as an honorary member.

This recommendation first appeared in the issue of May 1949.

Obviously assuming that constitutional provisions were not sufficiently clear, the Grand Council had the prior summer "informally agreed" to develop for the benefit of faculty advisors a body of "standards" for selecting honorary members. This intent was reiterated a year later, and a statement of guidelines was printed in the Newsletter of March and November, 1950. It is reprinted as exhibit 10.

The last sentence revealed that the "Directive" was intended to be advisory only, and not to impinge on local discretion. There is no indication that the Grand Council took serious objection to existing chapter practices in this area. Betweeen the two printings of the guidelines, Secretary-Treasurer White was instructed to write all chapters "complimenting them on the fine quality of their honorary members," although he was supposed also to remind them of the new guidelines.

Of particular interest is the reference to officership or other service within professional organizations as a mark of prominence. Service within the American Institute of Accountants would have been national in nature, while state society activity could have been at a chapter level as well as statewide. Although not mentioned, membership on a state board of public accountancy would certainly have been recognized as a major contribution. The remaining organizations cited offered opportunities for service at both national and local chapter levels. The Controller's Institute of America (later renamed the Financial Executives Institute) used the term "control"

EXHIBIT 10

NATIONAL GUIDELINES FOR SELECTION OF HONORARY MEMBERS, 1950

DIRECTIVE RE SELECTION OF HONORARY MEMBERS FOR BETA ALPHA PSI

Beta Alpha Psi has always been proud of the high caliber of men selected for honorary membership in our fraternity and earnestly desires to maintain the high standards set for such membership. Accordingly, may we urge each chapter to observe the following standards in their consideration of potential and prospective honoraries. Each one should have the reputation of having attained conspicuous success in the public or private accounting field in his community, and preferably throughout the nation. Such standing may be indicated, in part, by his work as an officer, director, or committee member in one or more of the following organizations: American Institute of Accountants; one of the state societies of Certified Public Accountants; National Association of Cost Accountants (national or chapter level); Controllers' Institute of America (national or control level); and Institute of Internal Auditors (national or chapter level). Another test is his contribution or contributions to the literature of accounting such as books, articles, monographs, and brochures. Such writings should be generally recognized as authoritative.

A further evidence of prominence in the field of accounting is that he may have spoken on accounting subjects before accounting and business groups.

All prospective honoraries should receive the approval of the local Faculty Vice President before the formal voting by a given chapter.

It is not absolutely necessary that an individual who is being considered for honorary membership be presently engaged in accounting provided, however, that he has at some time been regarded as an outstanding accountant. No business executive, no matter how prominent, should be chosen as an honorary member if he has not had an outstanding accounting background. The Grand Council believes that each chapter will maintain the high standards of the past in its selection of its own honoraries; therefore, no interference on the part of the Grand Council is intended.

Reprinted from "Grand Chapter News," by [John Arch White], Newsletter [3] (March 1950):5, (November 1950):6-7.

in place of "chapter."

The restriction of eligibility to accountants, or persons who have "at some time been regarded as . . . outstanding accountant[s]," was presumably essential for an accounting fraternity. As noted below, however, at least one deviation from such a principle was recognized in the case of "faculty" membership.

No reference was made to the induction of accounting professors serving at schools not having Beta Alpha Psi chapters. Many instructors were of course active in the professional organizations cited (as well as the American Accounting Association), and a number of them conducted auxiliary practices or had extensive nonacademic accounting backgrounds. Further, numerous "contributions to the literature of accounting" that were considered "authoritative" had emanated from academic sources.

Initiation guidelines

In the course of modestly revising the initiation ritual, to increase the emphasis on "professional" dimensions, the Council developed procedural recommendations regarding the induction of hororary members. At the meeting in 1949 it was proposed that a special ritual be developed for honorary membership. The only action taken at the time was a decision to contact the various chapters to determine their practices in this regard.

The following year it was decided that no separate ritual was needed. It was recommended, however, that (contrary to the practice, favored by S. M. Wedeberg, of Tau at Maryland) honorary initiates not be blindfolded, and take only a limited part in the regular formalities. Soon thereafter, incidentally, Alpha Gamma faculty advisor E. I. Fjeld would criticize the blindfolding element as being "too much on the order of horse-play," an objection which would have seemed particularly pertinent to honorary stuatus.

The Grand Council recommended that any candidates for honorary membership be escorted into the room directly before an initiation; be advised by the presiding officer that the ritual was intended primarily for the students, and that they should participate in it as instructed; and then be permitted to serve largely as observers of the proceedings, from seats (usually in the front row) providing "the best possible view of the initiation procedure." They would be asked to stand, along with the students, only for the administration of the fraternal oath.

Third-era councilor A. J. Penz recalls that these recommendations were widely followed. As an alternative, the Newsletter writeup of November 1950 suggested that honorary members be inducted separately during an initiation ceremony, by use of a modified version of the basic ritual (properly explained to them). This approach was used in admitting faculty members to Alpha Xi at Detroit and, apparently, Alpha Omicron at Michigan State on their installation dates in 1954, when no honoraries were admitted. A simplified induction procedure, excluding blindfolds, was followed by the initiation of the charter active members.

In rejecting a request made by an unspecified chapter, the Council in 1951 reaffirmed the traditional policy that no distinctive form of membership certificate, or "shingle," should be designed for honorary members. It was felt that "the majority of the honoraries would rather not have a certificate that distinguished their membership from that of student and faculty members."

Although the Newsletter announcement implied that a slightly different format would be used for honorary members, a basically similar position had been taken two years earlier when (following the lead of Iota Chapter at Southern California) the governing body approved the preparation of

membership cards, to be presented to honorary members at their initiations and to active members at graduation. One might assume that faculty members received their cards when they were initiated, and that active members not remaining to graduate did so on their departure from school. In the present day, wallet-sized "alumnus" cards certifying the induction of student members are commonly presented on the initiation date.

A number of other significant policy interpretations or decisions were made in the third era concerning honorary membership, promoting strong consistency of practice despite occasional exceptions.

Other policy interpretations or decisions

Several significant develments, 1950-54

One development was only a corollary of a much broader policy change. Women became eligible for honorary or faculty fraternal status at the same time as student membership. Indeed, a chapter choosing to remain all-male at the student level could if it wished admit females to the other membership categories. Few women, however, would actually be inducted as honorary members during the 1950s.

The Grand Council favored "faculty" rather than "honorary" membership for business school deans at Beta Alpha Psi schools, who were "considered to be members of the accounting faculty, regardless of background, training or experience." The eligibility of deans served of course to promote goodwill for the chapters on their home campuses. In response to a particular inquiry, Secretary-Treasurer S. M. Wedeberg submitted that the "ethics of salesmanship" would warrant reference to honorary membership at the time of the local dean's induction, although his official status would be that of a faculty member instead. No doubt assuming that deans

from nonaccounting fields, in particular, would rarely become regular participants in chapter activities, he observed that the two kinds of affiliation would be virtually identical in such a case.

By and large, the governing body was otherwise unprepared to relax the constututional restriction of faculty membership to "accounting" personnel. At its meeting in 1952, the Council explicitly opposed extending eligibility to professors from related academic fields (although past specialization in accounting would perhaps have been accepted). Two years earlier, however, a Council composed of three of the same members had decided that "non-accounting members of the faculty where taken into the Fraternity should be listed as faculty [rather than honorary] members." A reference made by S. M. Wedeberg during the interim to a "gentleman's agreement" to permit such membership suggests that he understood the 1950 position to apply primarily to deans, despite the broader language used. A degree of flexibility would in any case have accommodated nonaccounting educators having had professional experience in accounting. A governing group whose recently published guidelines had unequivocally opposed the _honorary_ initiation of nonaccountants lacking accounting backgrounds would have insisted on comparable restrictions (deans aside) at the faculty level.

Two rulings of the third era not involving faculty membership served somewhat to limit honorary inductions. In response to a 1952 inquiry, Wedeberg wrote that Sigma at Wisconsin was not entitled to admit a distinguished accountant who was already an honorary member of another chapter, Psi at nearby Marquette. The individual, in whose memory an annual award for faculty vice-presidents would some years later be created was Richard E. Claire of Arthur Andersen & Co. Interestingly, the secretary-treasurer did authorize Sigma to present Claire with a chapter pin or key, without actually initiating him, although no such action would be reported.

As earlier noted, the Grand Council encouraged chapters to admit at least one honorary member at each induction ceremony. Probably reacting particularly to recent practices within one chapter, however, the group ruled unanimously in 1954 that as a general policy no more than _two_ accountants should be initiated on each occasion. New honorary membership would thus have been limited in most instances to four persons a year. Exceptions to the two-member restriction could be made only with the consent of the fraternal president.

At a 1954 ceremony, Mu Chapter at New York had initiated _13_ honoraries, including a major general who had flown from Omaha, and lieutenant colonel he had picked up in Ohio. Mu had honored 15 accountants for the year, and 24 over two years. The five individuals honored by Omicron in 1952-53 represented the largest contingent recorded by any other chapter during the two years, although A. J. Penz recalls the Ohio State chapter (which had averaged nearly seven honorary initiates over the years 1947-52) as a leading source of relevant concern. There was of course no risk that Mu would run short of highly deserving candidates from its New York City base, and no doubt locational factors could justify exceptions to the new quota. Indeed, retired councilor Gould Harris of NYU may have received such an assurance while attending the 1955 council meeting in an advisory role. In any case, the primary intent of the numerical restriction adopted the year before was presumably to protect the "honor" associated with honorary membership.

A final policy decision, made at the same 1954 meeting, would from one standpoint have compromised that objective, however. In raising initiation fees to $7.50, from the $5.00 level that had prevailed for more than three decades, the councilors assembled in 1954 extended such fees to honorary (though not faculty) members. These actions were taken because the Grand

Council had over the prior three years operated "at a loss," and operating costs were continuing to increase. The issue of principle raised, as stated by an accountant invited in 1933 to join Pi Chapter at Western Reserve subject to a fee requirement, was whether an honor should be '"contingent on the payment of monies"'.[2]

Inevitably, deviations from these policies occasionally occurred.

Illustrative policy deviations

From time to time an individual was accorded "honorary" membership who was better suited to "faculty" status. A possible example was Dr. Catherine De Motte Quire, inducted by Lambda at Berkeley in Nobember in 1950 as the first female honorary member of the fraternity. Her case points up the uncertain fraternal status of professors or administrators from outside the accounting department, at a Beta Alpha Psi school, who enjoyed

---

[2]The citation is from Dougles S. Meaden, president of the Cleveland Chapter of the Ohio Society of CPAs, as quoted in J. P. March, president of Pi Chapter, to Jacob B. Taylor, March 17, 1932 (national files). Although March had understood that the chapter requirements were based on national statutes, Taylor replied on March 25, 1932, that "the usual practice of the fraternity" was "not to collect initiation fees from honorary members" (who still included faculty personnel).

Even so, as drafted in 1927 the statutes had provided for "A fee of $5.00 for each initiate," and identical language would appear in the 1936 version. The qualifying phrase "taken into active membership" was added in 1938, when separate faculty status was first recognized, and retained through 1953. Comparison of Newsletter reports from the period 1936-38 with cashbook data identifies two chapters that had submitted fees, unrefunded, for honorary initiates (Delta and Pi), and four that had not (Zeta, Omicron, Tau, and Upsilon). Beta Alpha Psi Fraternity, "National Statutes," National Constitution and Statutes (1953, 1958), chapter 2, section 21b, quoting earlier version; Grand Council Cashbook, 1931-49, pp. 21, 26-27, 30, 33, 35; Grand Council Minutes Book, December 1938, p. [3], 1954, p. 3, quoted (regarding 1954 amendments); [W. E. Karrenbrock], "Tau Chapter Installed," Newsletter [2] (December 1936):6, (November 1937):8-10, (December 1938):7, 11, 14; "National Statutes," National Constitution and Statutes of Beta Alpha Psi Fraternity ([1936], 1938), chapter 2, section 21b, quoted; "National Statutes of Beta Alpha Psi" [1927], chapter 2, section 21c, quoted; and Sheldahl, Alpha to Omega, p. 193.

significant accounting credentials.

Although consistent with her doctoral specialization she had been an economics professor at California before her appointment as the assistant dean of women at the university, Dr. Quire seems clearly to have been qualified by professional background for election to Beta Alpha Psi. She had at least briefly taught accounting elsewhere, and was a charter member (1944) of the San Francisco Chapter of the American Society of Women Accountants, a professional organization of women engaged in accounting practice or education, or closely related work, founded in Chicago in 1938. Her academic career would have made Quire an excellent candidate for "faculty" membership, in keeping with the Grand Council's discussion just two months earlier concerning induction of professors from other fields. Councilor Charles Staehling of Berkeley had attended the annual meeting.

The honorary induction of another professor involved more fundamental issues. During the year 1960 Mu Chapter at NYU initiated a distinguished finance and insurance professor at the school. Unless he had a background specifically in accounting that was not reported in the writeup, he was seemingly not qualified for election to Beta Alpha Psi. On a favorable interpretation of eligiblity, however, "faculty" membership would have been more appropriate than honorary status, granting that the Council had in 1952 retracted any opening earlier made to professors from related disciplines.

No question of eligibility could be raised in regard to the business dean at Oklahoma State, who was initiated in 1960 by Chi. Contrary to established policy, however, he was reported by the chapter as an honorary initiate rather than as a faculty member. More appropriate was the honorary classification of visiting professor David Solomons, inducted by Lambda at

Berkeley in 1953-54. A chartered accountant since 1936, he had become a prominent accounting educator at the University of London, and served on a major professional committee.

During the third era, at least a few nationally recognized accountants who had become honorary members of Beta Alpha Psi before the war were inducted again, by the same chapters as before or different ones. Although only the latter irregularity was cited above (in regard to Richard Claire), repeat initiation would have been considered equally deviant. William B. Castenholz, the winner of the 1931 fraternal book award, was re-initiated by Alpha Chapter in 1947, having first been honored at Illinois sixteen years earlier. Similarly, Clem Collins, a distinguished professor, dean, and governmental accountant who was president of the American Institute for two terms, was elected by Nu Chapter at Colorado both in 1933 and some twenty years later. Moreover, Eric A. Camman, a Peat Marwick partner in New York who had been president of the National Association of Cost Accountants, was initiated by Omicron at Ohio State both in 1941 and 1948. Another example was Professor William A. Paton of Michigan, initiated at Illinois as an honorary Alpha brother in 1932, prior to speaking on the topic "Writing Down Capital Assets," and 1947.

Paton, a part-time practicing accountant who served a record eleven years on the AIA's Committee on Accounting Procedure, is also listed in a 1951 source (questionably) as an honorary member of Omicron Chapter at Ohio State. Before the war, James F. Hughes, a president of two state societies, was granted honorary membership by both Mu and Xi. American Accounting Association President Thomas Leland of Texas A&M, cited earlier as an honorary Theta brother, was one of six accountants admitted to honorary membership by Omicron at a 1948 ceremony. In 1953 Tau at Maryland initiated author and former Northwestern professor H. A. Finney, Gamma '30 (honorary).

T. Coleman Andrews, a member of the Accounting Hall of Fame who was serving as Commissioner of Internal Revenue, was likewise honored by Tau in 1954, nineteen years after he had become an honorary brother of Kappa at William and Mary. As an independent candidate campaigning as a severe critic of the income tax system, Andrews would finish third to Republican Dwight Eisenhower and Democrat Adlai Stevenson in the 1956 presidential election. Later he was one of the founders of the archconservative John Birch Society.

The dual inductions were only symptomatic of serious shortcomings in maintaining records of honorary membership. According to Professor Vern Vincent, that process had reached a "chaotic" state by the time that he became secretary-treasurer in the 1960s.[3] During the third era, in any

---

[3] Denise S. Akey, ed., Encyclopedia of Associations: 1985, 19th ed., 5 vols. (Detroit: Gale Research Co., 1984), vol. 1, National Organizations of the United States, part 1, section 1, s.v. "American Society of Women Accountants"; American Society of Women Accountants to Author, by telephone, April 16, 1985; "Attention Chapter Officers," Newsletter [2] (May 1949):14, [3] (November 1949 - May 1952), 4 (March 1953 - November 1953), quoted; Carrie Black, president, San Franciso Chapter of American Society of Women Accountants, to Mary Jane Sheldahl (by telephone), April 24, 1985; Burns and Coffman, Accounting Hall of Fame, p. 81; John L. Carey, The Rise of the Accounting Profession, 2 vols. (New York: American Institute of Certified Public Accountants, 1969-70), vol. 2, To Responsibility and Authority, 1937-1969, p. 505; W. E. Dickerson to Alton L. Peterson, August 1, 1949 (Policies File); exhibit 10, quoted; E. I. Fjeld to John A. White, July 24, 1951, quoted (Policies File); [Dale E. Flesher], "T. Coleman Andrews Dies," The Accounting Historians Notebook 6 (Fall 1983):5; Grand Council Minutes Book, 1948, p. [2] (quoted), 1949, pp. 1, [2-3], 1950, pp. 1, [2-3] (quoting p. 3), 1951, p. 3 (quoted), 1952, pp. 1, 5, 1954, p. 3, 1955, p. 4; Nancy Harke, National Administrator of Beta Alpha Psi, to Author, by telephone, April 18, 1985; "Honorary Initiates," Newsletter 4 (March 1954): 137, (May 1954):168-69, 171, 5 (April 1960):265, (November 1960):318; "Honorary Members Initiated During the Past Year," Newsletter [2] (May 1941):11; "Local Chapter News," Newsletter [2] (May 1948):10, (November 1948):18, 4 (March 1953):51-52, (May 1953):86-87, (November 1953):121, (March 1954):185-86; [Richard W. Metcalf], "Outstanding Faculty Vice President Award," 1983-84 Annual Report, ed. [Metcalf], p. 2; Hermann C. Miller, Beta Alpha Psi Directory, s.v. "Alpha Chapter: Castenholz, W. B.," "Gamma Chapter: Finney, Harry Anson," "Kappa Chapter: Andrews, T. Coleman," "Nu Chapter: Collins, Clem W."; "National Constitution," National Constitution and Statutes of Beta Alpha Psi Fraternity (1938, 1947, 1949,

case, John Arch White and others had made significant efforts to develop and maintain adequate historical records in this area. In the course of seeking an orderly accounting, the Grand Council of the day extended considerable recognition to honorary members, through preparation of an historical "roll," regular publication of profiles of new honoraries, and other initiatives.

Council Recognition of Honorary Members

The 1951 Honorary "Roll"

In 1948 the Grand Council approved a program by which, receiving partial funding from the national treasury, each chapter would in accordance with a prescribed format prepare an annual directory of "its active, alumni, and honorary membership." Perhaps by inadvertance, no reference was made to "faculty" members. Prohibitive cost would require abandonment of the original objective in favor of a three-year schedule for the issuance of updated chapter directories.

In the fall of 1949 Secretary-Treasurer White asked the chapters to submit complete listings of their honorary members, so far as possible, so

---

1951), article 6, section 2; "News from the Chapters," Newsletter [1] (March 1933, unbound):5, quoted; William A. Paton, "Recalling George Oliver May and Me," The Accounting Historians Journal 8 (Fall 1981):92-93; [A. J. Penz], "Grand Council News," Newsletter 4 (May 1954):166, (November 1954): 206; Penz, Secretary-Treasurer's Report, 1953-54, p. 4; Penz to Author, by telephone, April 16, 1985; "Roll of Honorary Members Initiated During the Past Year," Newsletter [3] (May 1951):9; Secretary-Treasurers' Reports, 1947-48 through 1951-52; Sheldahl, Alpha to Omega, pp. 492-94, 765; Vern H. Vincent to Author, interview, July 21, 1980, quoted; S. M. Wedeberg to Nicholas Longo, Mu Chapter secretary, May 11, 1953 (Policies); Wedeberg to James M. McConahey, November 24, 1951, quoted; Wedeberg, Secretary-Treasurer's Report, 1952-53, p. 4; Wedeberg, Visitatation Reports--Tau, May 1954, item 3.4, Mu, June 4, 1954, items 2.2, 4; [John Arch White], "Grand Chapter News," Newsletter [3] (November 1949):7, (November 1950):7, quoted; [White], ed., "Roll of Honorary Members," Newsletter [3] (March 1951):11, s.v. "Paton, William A."; and Stephen A. Zeff, The American Accounting Association: Its First 50 Years ([Evanston, Ill.: American Accounting Association, 1966]), p. [94].

that he could prepare "an accurate [national] "roll of these brothers. This request was renewed a year later. Based on responses obtained from a "majority of chapters," and on other files, White developed a "Roll of Honorary Members" that was published in the Newsletter of March 1951. It listed 239 men, normally along with chapter affiliations and at least partial current addresses. The following issue included a supplementary listing of 24 honorary members of Mu Chapter

White acknowledged that the roll was "far from complete" and contained "some discrepancies," asking (apparently with immediate response from NYU) that chapter officers submit corrections and additions. Of the six oldest chapters, Alpha through Zeta, only Delta at Washington and the defunct Epsilon at Oregon State were represented. Except for Eta Chapter at Boston University, deactivated in 1928, members were listed from all other local groups formed before 1950, including (although T. Coleman Andrews was omitted) Kappa at William and Mary. Initiation dates, not listed, extended as late as the fall of 1950.

Chapter affiliation was left out in six cases, although it could usually be gathered from the address given. Regarding fraternal history, an interesting inconsistency concerned early Beta Alpha Psi presidents who had been admitted as "honorary" members prior to establishment of the "faculty" designation. Both William E. Cox of Delta and George E. Bennett of Xi were cited, while John Madden of Mu, Hermann Miller of Omicron, Fayette Elwell of Zeta, and James McConahey of Delta were not. Nor (as Alpha Chapter initiates) were the first three honorary members, and charter national officers, of the fraternity, Professors Hiram Scovill, A. C. Littleton, and E. J. Filbey.

Records for two chapters are available for comparative purposes. All

but one of the fifteen men who had been honored by Theta Chapter at Texas were included within White's roster. It must of course be borne in mind that the secretary-treasurer, himself an early Theta member, had spent his entire career on the Austin campus, a significant part of it as the chapter advisor. A more meaningful comparison, then, may be made in regard to Xi at Syracuse. The 1951 roll listed thirteen honorary brothers from that group, four fewer, through 1950, than a chapter source.

Capsule biographies are available from a regular *Newsletter* feature for many third-era honorary members.

Featured "Newsletter" profiles

Recent honorary initiates had been profiled in several *Newsletter* issues published prior to wartime deactivation. Occasionally very detailed, the individual items had each appeared under the caption "Introducing." After resuming his editorship, H. W. Kendrick published three biographical notices in May 1947 under the heading "Introducing New Honoraries of Omicron Chapter." Ironically, only one of the men would actually be initiated.

One of the Ohio State absentees would erroneously be cited again in March 1948, when Bill Dickerson launched a new series "Honorary Members Initiated During the Past Year." Classified by chapter, it was published annually (in March or May) through the academic year 1951-52. The series appeared twice yearly thereafter, taking the title "Honorary Initiates" just before the *Newsletter* became a semiannual periodical in 1954-55. Coverage, whose overall scope was not enlarged by the change in publication schedule, was based upon the submission of biographical material by the chapters. After reference is made to other initiatives taken or discussed by the Council in regard to honorary members, the profiles appearing over three selected calendar years are briefly characterized.

Other relevant initiatives

Distribution of the Newsletter

Work on a national roster of honorary membership contributed significantly, of course, to an objective of maintaining contact with such elements, at chapter or national levels. At the Grand Council meeting of 1949, incoming secretary-treasurer White "was instructed to include all honorary members on the Newsletter mailing list." It is entirely possible that this directive gave rise to the honorary "roll" project that began in the fall. Apparently White sent copies of the three 1949-50 issues directly to all honorary members for whom he obtained addresses, rather than distributing them through the chapters.

In 1951 the Council discussed the topic of regularly mailing the Newsletter, free of charge, to "alumni, faculty and honorary members." After hearing the secretary-treasurer's estimate of cost, the group decided that such a practice would be too expensive, and that instead "alumni subscriptions" should be offered at one dollar per year. Accordingly, in the November issue new editor S. M. Wedeberg inserted a notice that fraternal alumni who wished to receive the periodical should mail the subscription fee to their local chapter secretaries (who would presumably distribute the three yearly issues). The basis for the assumption that alumni members would see the notice is unclear. No specific reference was made to honorary initiates.

Three years later, however, in 1954-55, the Grand Council surveyed 366 honorary members concerning their interest in the Newsletter. It had just become a biennial publication, two "expanded" issues having replaced the previous quota of three per year. In a day of the "penny post card," a self-addressed card was enclosed for reply. All but 60 of the 272

respondents were interested in receiving the periodical, most of them favoring a subscription ("self-sustaining") approach. Ten honorary members mailed a dollar or, in one case, five dollars with their replies, providing for nearly all the "subscriptions" revenue of $15.50 that would be reported by the Grand Council for the year. From a broader perspective the effort appears to have been for nought, however, as national subscription revenue for the following year, 1955-56, would reach a grand total of one dollar.

In the early 1950s, finally, a more ambitious project was discussed.

Discussion of an "organization"

At the 1951 annual meeting, the Grand Council discussed the possibility of formally organizing either alumni or honorary members, or both groups. President Harris proposed that a "national" honorary group be formed, and agreed to "sound out" some honoraries on the matter. The topic was broached again the following year, from a "feasibility" standpoint, but no details are available. Serious efforts made in 1954 to form a national alumni organization that would include honoraries are documented within broader discussion of alumni membership.[4]

---

[4] [W. E. Dickerson], "John T. Madden," Newsletter [2] (May 1949):9; Grand Council Minutes Book, 1948, p. 1, 1949, p. [3], 1950, p. 1, 1951, p. 3, 1952, p. 4, 1954, p. 3, 1955, p. 3 (all quoted), 1950, p. 2, 1955, p. 2; "Grand Council of Beta Alpha Psi: Operating Statement, Year Ended December 31, 1956," Newsletter 4 (November 1956):341; "The Grand Council of Beta Alpha Psi: Statement of Income and Expense, for Year Ended July 31, 1955," Newsletter 4 (November 1955):271; "Honorary Initiates," Newsletter 5 (March 1954 - April 1957), 6 (November 1957, April 1959 - November 1960): "Honorary Members Initiated During the Past Year," Newsletter [2] (March 1948):8-9, (March 1949), [3] (May, 1950-52), 4 (March-May, 1953); "Introducing New Honoraries of Omicron Chapter," Newsletter [2] (May 1947): 5-6; H. W. Kendrick, Secretary-Treasurer's Report, 1946-47, p. [10]; "Local Chapter News," Newsletter [2] (November 1947):14, (November 1948):18, [3] (March 1951):21, 26; Hermann C. Miller, ed., Beta Alpha Psi Directory, s.v. "Alpha Chapter," "Delta Chapter: Cox, William E.; McConahey, James M.," "Mu Chapter: Madden, John T.," "Xi Chapter: Bennett, George E.," "Sigma Chapter: Elwell, Fayette H."; Sheldahl, Alpha to Omega, pp. 93-94, 172-74, 764-66; Smith, Forty Acres, pp. 64, 66, 71, 178; [S. M. Wedeberg],

First, however, the coverage of honoraries should be extended beyond the policy level to actual practice. The extensive records available from the third ere reveal a considerable magnitude of honorary induction throughout the third era, embodying impressive professional breadth and generally in keeping with the expectation of significant achievement and service.

Selected Contemporary Initiation Records

Induction totals, and "Newsletter" coverage

Beginning with the fraternal year 1946-47, the annual secretary-treasurer's report specified the number of honorary members initiated by each chapter. Granting that minor discrepancies were inevitable, notably occasional timing deviations from summer inductions of the first years, the fourteen reports through 1959-60 recorded the induction of 656 honorary members. Aggregated for three subperiods of four or five years each, these data are summarized in the first entry within exhibit 11.

Remarkable consistency in overall induction levels is revealed, despite the steady increases in the chapter roster that began in 1948. Of particular note is the strong decline in the totals reported by Omicron and Mu Chapters, which together initiated nearly one-fifth of the honorary membership added in the third era, after the Grand Council in 1954 limited honorary initiation to two members per ceremony.

More than 40% of the new honorary membership were profiled in the aforementioned Newsletter series begun in 1948 that was based on submission

---

"Grand Council News," Newsletter [3] (November 1951):16; [John Arch White], "Grand Chapter News," Newsletter [3] (March 1950):6, (March 1951):9, quoted; [White], ed., "Roll of Honorary Members," Newsletter [3] (March 1951):10-12; [White], ed., "Supplement[al] Roll of Honorary Members of Mu Chapter," Newsletter [3] (May 1951):13; and Xi Chapter: 1966 Directory, chronological listing through "1950 - November," and honorary listing (disregarding four faculty members initiated, 1947-50).

EXHIBIT 11

SELECTED HONORARY MEMBERSHIP DATA FROM THE THIRD ERA

Initiation Levels, 1946-47 Through 1959-60

Time Span	Number of initiates	Highest annual total	Lowest annual total	Omicron Chapter	Mu Chapter
1947-50	182	57	26	24	22
1951-55	234	55	35	27	29
1956-60	240	62	41	13	10
TOTALS	656			64	61

Professional Classification of 101 Honorary Members Profiled in "Newsletter," 1950, 1954, 1960

Management accountants	CPA partners, national firms	Other CPA partners	University personnel	Governmental accountants	CPA managers	State society administrators	Other
29	22	23	9	8	4	2	4

Contributed Professional Service--Number, among the Same 101 Members, Holding Selected Posts

AI(CP)A posts	CPA societies (statewide)	State accountancy boards	NA(C)A, national	Other acct. groups (nationwide)	Presidents of local chapters	Holders of one or more posts
22 (2)[a]	27 (16)	11	8 (3)	7 (3)	12	58

SOURCES: "Honorary Initiates," Newsletter 4 (March 1954):135-37, (May 1954):168-71, (November 1954):208-212, 5 (April 1960):264-68, (November 1960):317-21; "Honorary Members," Newsletter [3] (May 1950):5-10; and Secretary-Treasurers' Reports, 1946-47 through 1959-60, yearly membership additions. Several sources cited in note 5 provided supporting information.

[a]The numbers in parentheses represent organizational presidents.

of copy by local chapters. Excluding the calendar year 1958, for which the two issues have not been located, 272 honoraries were represented through November 1960, all but four of them apparently inducted prior to the beginning of the fourth era in the fall of 1960. Because all issues except those for 1958 are available, and because there commonly was a semester's lag in the reporting, it is useful to record coverage by the calendar rather than academic year of publication.

For the twelve years of available reports, then, an average of more than 22 new honorary members were cited, representing approximately a dozen chapters. There was enormous variation in the extent of coverage, however, which ranged from 42 members in both 1954 and 1959 to an average of 6 honoraries over the intervening years 1955-57. In 1957 exactly 3 members, from as many chapters, were profiled. The vast swings in coverage, in no way based on actual initiation levels, presumably in part reflected differing degrees of emphasis among *Newsletter* editors in soliciting copy from the chapters.

One point stands out above all others concerning the 272 honorary members introduced in the periodical through 1960: all but two of them were male. The only exceptions, both cited (in May 1951) at the close of the first year of fraternal coeducation, were the aforementioned Catherine Quire, Lambda '50, and Martha L. O'Sullivan, Iota '51. At the time of her induction at Southern California, Mrs. O'Sullivan was a partner within a Los Angeles CPA firm that bore her name, along with two others.

A useful picture of honorary induction in the third era has been constructed from the *Newsletter* features of the years 1950, 1953, and 1960. Representing approximately 15% of the total honorary membership added, this sampling reveals an impressive breadth of professional practice and service.

A sampling of 101 honoraries

The three years selected were the heaviest reporting years for honorary members, each covering from 30 to 42 men. Excluding individuals inducted in the fall of 1960, and hence in the fourth era, 101 honorary members from 31 chapters were represented. Their professional practice and service are summarized, in aggregate terms, in the second and third parts of exhibit 11.

A classification of practice

Each of the honoraries covered was classified under one of eight occupational headings, including a miscellaneous classification. Occasionally this required selection from among two or more fields of distinguished practice or employment. Another oversimplification, perhaps, was the inclusion of two internal auditors and three treasurers (by primary job title) among management accountants.

Nearly three-fourths of the initiates were classified as management accountants (29), partners within national CPA firms (21), or other CPA partners (23). The nine "[u]niversity personnel" included professors, deans, and a university accountant. The somewhat irregular initiations of accounting professors Clem Collins (also a dean) and H. A. Finney by outside chapters, and of an NYU finance professor by the fraternal unit on his campus, were cited earlier, along with the local inductions of visiting professor David Solomons and the Oklahoma State dean. Initiated also were an accountant serving as the dean at Golden Gate, by Lambda at Berkeley; an accounting professor visiting from Australia, by Alpha Eta at Michigan; and a Harvard professor with an extensive practitioner background, Russell H. Hassler, by Omicron at Ohio State.

The eight governmental accountants honored included three federal

tax officials and three defense department accountants, two of them from the Strategic Air Command. Also initiated in the third era were a state comptroller and a General Accounting Office auditor.

Among the four CPAs who had not as yet reached partnership status, the most unusual case was perhaps the induction by Beta Gamma at DePaul in the spring of 1960 of a university alumnus who had graduated only three years earlier. Two state society executives were honored by chapters geographically at opposite extremes from one another, Delta at Washington and Upsilon at Florida.

Finally, the four honorary members not classified under specific professional headings included the executive vice-president of the New York Stock Exchange and a branch supervisor for a credit corporation described as "[a]n outstanding authority" on automobile financing and retail credit, both admitted by Mu Chapter; a department head in an oil and gas company, honored by Chi at Oklahoma State; and the "office supervisor" of a power company, initiated by Alpha Beta at Alabama. The first two men, incidentally, were among fifteen honorary members of the NYU chapter included in the sampling.

The 22 partners from "national" accounting practices represented each of the present-day "Big Eight" firms. For example, Mu inducted a Price Waterhouse partner originally from New Zealand who was licensed to practice in 13 states, and Alpha Beta initiated the managing partner of Haskins & Sells in Atlanta, a CPA in 8 states who had been a partner in three of the firm's other leading offices. Several of the most prominent practitioners honored represented local or regional firms, however.

For example, William D. Cranstoun, Mu '49, was a founding partner of the prominent New York firm Hurdman and Cranstoun, a predecessor of the

international firm KMG Main Hurdman. His credentials included the presidencies of the New York and New Jersey CPA societies, and a total of 19 committee assignments within those organizations, in addition to substantial national service. Maurice Peloubet, another Mu initiate, had been active in the American Insitute as chairman of the Board of Examiners, author of educational materials, and committee member.

Alpha Kappa at Ohio University inducted Robert E. Witschey, the head of a West Virginia accounting firm who would later serve as president of the AICPA when the celebrated "investment credit" controversy erupted around the newly formed Accounting Principles Board. The many professional distinctions of Lambda initiate Anson Herrick included pioneering contributions to social accounting, beginning with analysis of the relief effort that followed the San Francisco earthquake of 1906.

Possibly the most versatile career belonged to Joseph J. Klein, admitted by Alpha Gamma at CCNY. Besides being a partner in both a law practice and an accounting firm in New York City, Dr. Klein had significant teaching experience, and was a noted author and editor in the field of taxation. Long before his election to the fraternity, one of his many books had been nominated in 1929 for the Beta Alpha Psi book award.

A few references have already been made to contributed professional service, identified by the fraternal guidelines as a major factor in selecting honorary members. The Newsletter writeups identified a majority of the individuals covered as having held positions within major national accounting organizations and/or served in high-level capacities at state or local levels.

Contributed professional service

At least 58 of the 101 men had held posts within national bodies such

as the American Institute or the National Association of (Cost) Accountants; state CPA societies or boards; or, at the presidential level, local chapters (usually in major cities) of national or state accounting organizations. Many of them had served in several such capacities. Included were two presidents of the AIA, Clem Collins and T. Coleman Andrews; three presidents of the NA(C)A, one of whom had also headed the Controllers Institute; one president each of the Federal Government Accountants Association and the American Accounting Association (Russell Hassler); and sixteen presidents of state CPA societies. In addition, Professor David Solomons had held positions in the United Kingdom comparable to the AAA presidency and an AIA committee assignment.

Two of the most distinguished management accountants admitted to honorary membership were both initiated by Omicron at Ohio State during the year 1953-54. George W. Schwarz, vice-president and treasurer of Wyandotte Chemical Corp., was the current national president of both the NACA and (unless he had just stepped down) the Controllers Institute. I. Wayne Keller, controller of Armstrong Cork, was Schwarz's immediate successor in the National Association post, having been honored by the organization four consecutive years for distinguished contributions to the "industrial accounting" literature.[5]

---

[5]Carey, Rise of Profession, vol. 1, From Technician to Professional, 1896-1936, p. 240, vol. 2, pp. 77-78, 102-104, 287-88, 320n; exhibit 11; "Honorary Initiates" and "Honorary Members," Newsletter, as cited in note 4, especially sources for exhibit 11, quoting Newsletter 4 (November 1954): 209, 5 (November 1960):318; Nancy Hopper, marketing secretary for KMG Main Hurdman, San Francisco, to Author (by telephone), April 25, 1985; "Local Chapter News," Newsletter [3] (March 1950):16, 4 (November 1954):218-29, (November 1960):329-31, 346; Secretary-Treasurers' Reports, 1946-47 through 1959-60; Sheldahl, Alpha to Omega, p. 454; and John A(rch) White to S. M. Wedeberg, March 25, 1952, attached biographical material on William D. Cranstoun (Policies File).

A second category of nonactive membership enjoyed prominent attention during the third era. At the first postwar meeting, the Council agreed that an updated directory of _alumni_ memebers was needed, and as policy evolved on that matter over the next eight years alumni status was recognized among other ways through introduction of a regular _Newsletter_ feature. After at least two chapters had established pertinent local groups, the founder and an early member of Beta Alpha Psi were major figures in an unsuccessful 1954 effort to establish a national alumni organization. Later the alumni of Mu Chapter at NYU took control of local operations to produce a constitutional conflict that would not be resolved for some time.

Alumni Membership

Developments Prior to 1954

Evolution of a policy on "directories," 1946-54

The principal alumni-related initiative by the Grand Council prior to wartime deactivation was the project that led to publication of a Beta Alpha Psi _Directory_ in 1939, under the editorship of Hermann C. Miller. At the first postwar meeting, in 1946, the Council voted "to issue a complete revision" of the directory, provided that satisfactory printing costs could be obtained. Local chapters were apparently asked over the following year tondevelop updated directory information.

Cost estimates obtained during the year were considered prohibitively high, so at the 1947 meeting the Council agreed to defer a final decision pending further inquiries. A year later, however, by which time the lowest bid obtained for production of 7,000 copies (in keeping with the approximate historical membership to date) had been $4,000, the governing body abandoned the project. Instead, local chapters were to be asked to prepare annual directories, with financial assistance from the Council, for

distribution to all other chapters. As mentioned earlier, this plan was itself scaled back substantially due to cost implications. In 1950 the suggested interval between directories was extended to three years, with the proviso that chapters should develop supplemental data during the interim. The latter condition was finally dropped in 1954, just after the Council had belatedly attempted to implement an ambitious program suggested five years before by an early fraternal alumnus.

Alton Peterson's proposal for a national organization, 1949

The matter of formal organization of Beta Alpha Psi alumni apparently was first brought to the attention of a national officer in the summer of 1949. Alton L. Peterson, CPA, a charter Epsilon brother at Oregon State (using the modern name) who had been an Internal Revenue Agent since 1941, suggested to Secretary-Treasurer W. E. Dickerson that the fraternity had "reached the age of maturity whereby . . . [it] should consider the organization, on a national scale, of an active alumni organization." He added that he would be very pleased to help form such a body, should the Council be interested.

Dickerson responded that he saw no need for a national alumni group, since most fraternal alumni would already be involved in one or more professional accounting organizations. The secretary-treasurer stated that "a number of the local chapters" had formed their own alumni groups, located at points having "a concentration of members." His own Omicron Chapter at Ohio State was represented by alumni groups in both Cleveland and New York.

The skeptical position taken by Bill Dickerson was certainly a reasonable viewpoint, and would indeed be repeated by fraternal leaders A. J. Penz and Thomas Burns in interviewing conducted more than three decades

later. Dickerson's fellow Delta alumnus S. M. Wedeberg, a Council colleague of Penz's for several years, would enthusiastically support Peterson a few years after the initial inquiry, however, in seeking to create a national alumni body. Interim developments may be noted first.

Distribution of "alumni membership cards," 1950

The Newsletter of November 1950 reported that during the preceding spring "alumni membership cards were printed and samples sent to all chapters." Presumably these were similar to, or identical to, the "membership cards" discussed earlier. Two or three chapters had reported sending the card, duly signed, to each alumnus in the course of requesting directory information. Editor John Arch White described the card as "a device to keep in contact with our alumni," although with the distribution of membership cards to student members at the time of their graduation there clearly could not have been any basis for a continuing effort of this kind.

Alumni subscriptions, and first discussion of an organization, 1951

As aforementioned, in 1951 the Grand Council decided that it could not afford to send the Newsletter to alumni (or other nonstudent) members free of charge, but would offer "alumni subscriptions" of one dollar yearly. Two years after the Newsletter announced the subscription rate, new editor A. J. Penz inserted a notice recommending that chapters remind alumni of it in correspondence regarding directory data or other matters.

In the same issue, dated November 1953, the title page first stated that the periodical was published "for actice, faculty, and honorary members," having earlier referred only to "active" members. Beginning with the next issue, it also included the line "Alumni Subscription Rate $1.00

a Year." Both messages would be continued at least through 1963-64. As earlier noted, the subscription opportunity yielded an underwhelming response.

In 1951 also, at the close of Bill Dickerson's term of service, the Council evidently first discussed, however briefly, the topic of an alumni organization. Outgoing president Gould Harris and incoming secretary-treasurer S. M. Wedeberg agreed to "sound out Mr. [John L.] Carey at the next meeting of the American Institute of Accountants about a national organization of alumni." Since this was the only reference made to alumni within a paragraph, from the minutes, concerning the possible organization of "honorary" members, it appears that some kind of approach that would jointly serve both membership groups was already being considered. As executive director of the American Institute, Carey would of course have been an excellent source of opinion on whether a fraternal alumni group could serve a purpose in the professional development of young accountants. Although no record is available concerning the discussion (if there was one) with Carey, his organization would two academic years later provide a base of positive support by way of a most authoritative fraternal spokesman. In the interim, a Newsletter series on alumni members had originated.

"Alumni News," beginning in 1952

The May 1952 issue of the periodical introduced a feature entitled "Alumni News," providing updates on former student members as submitted by their chapters. Editor Wedeberg included material from Alpha Chapter at Illinois, Alpha Beta (cited as Alpha "Eta") at Alabama, Lambda at California, and Tau at Maryland, in the last two cases featuring CPA examination success rates. Reports of March and May 1953 included coverage from Tau, Delta at Washington, and Alpha Mu (twice) at Kentucky, regarding which he was respectively the charter faculty advisor, an alumnus, and the installing

officer, as well as another CPA-exam survey, from Gamma at Northwestern.

The following year, under Editor Penz, "Alumni News" was devoted largely to plans underway to develop a national organization. With the abandonment of those plans, the feature would revert to its original format in April 1955, and be continued on that basis beyond the remainder of the era.

Having introduced the Newsletter series in 1951-52, it seems only fitting that two years later, as president of the fraternity, S. M. Wedeberg, Delta '24, would join Alton Peterson, Epsilon '22, in seeking to create the kind of organization proposed by Peterson several years earlier. A certain honorary member of the fraternity inducted even earlier, however, would provide the direct impetus for the unsuccessful initiative.[6]

A Significant, though Abortive, Organizational Effort - 1954

Professor Scovill's motivating role

Beta Alpha Psi founder Hiram Scovill was a member during the 1953-54 term of the American Institute's subcommittee on Improvement in Education and Training. One objective of the subcommittee was "to do something for

---

6 "Alumni News," Newsletter [3] (May 1952):17-18, 4 (March 1953):44, (May 1953):81, (March 1954):138-39, (May 1954):175, (April 1955):238-39, 6 (Fall 1965):304-316; Thomas J. Burns to Author, interview, May 3, 1980; Carey, Rise of Profession 2:508; W. E. Dickerson to Alton L. Peterson, August 1, 1949 (Policies File), quoted; Grand Council Minutes Book, 1946, p. 2 (quoted), 1947, p. 1, 1948, p. 1, 1950, p. [2], 1951, pp. 3 (quoted), 6, 1954, p. 3; "Local Chapter News," Newsletter [2] (March 1949):24; Hermann C. Miller, ed., Beta Alpha Psi Directory, s.v. "Delta Chapter: Dickerson, William E.; Wedeberg, S. M."; [A. J. Penz], "Grand Council News," Newsletter 4 (November 1953):112; Penz to Author, interview, April 18, 1980; Alton L. Peterson to W. E. Dickerson, July 23, 1949 (Policies), first of two letters; Sheldahl, Alpha to Omega, pp. 766-74; Title Pages, Newsletter 4 (May 1953): 65, (November 1953):[97], (March 1954):[129], 6 (Spring 1964):[71], each quoted, (Fall 1965):[249]; [S. M. Wedeberg], "Grand Council News," Newsletter [3] (May 1952):5; and [John Arch White], "Grand Chapter News," Newsletter [3] (November 1950):9, quoted.

Strictly speaking, "Alumni News" originated as a notice of the 1950-51 winners of a senior scholarship award. Newsletter [3] (November 1951):16.

the younger accountants in the larger cities in addition to looking after their purely technical training." It was felt in particular that expanded opportunities for organizational involvement were needed by aspiring CPAs just out of school. Even newly certified accountants, eligible for American Institute and state society membership, might stand to benefit from leadership opportunities within a group oriented toward entry-level professionals.

Scovill apparently contacted President Wedeberg on the possibility that a national Beta Alpha Psi alumni association, with local chapters, might serve such a function. As the secretary-treasurer of the prior two years, Wedeberg would have known of the "Policies" correspondence containing Mr. Peterson's offer to help establish such an organization. Peterson (who incidentally also had Washington state connections, having practiced public accounting there in the 1930s and perhaps earlier) was promptly asked for assistance. The Newsletter of March 1954 announced that he had already "devoted considerable time to develop plans for an alumni association and to create interest in the project." Both Wedeberg and Peterson discussed the matter in that issue and, more briefly, the next one.

In an article addressed to active members, the fraternal president expressed his thinking on the potential value of an alumni association having "chapters in the larger cities":

> A national alumni association . . . would enable you to continue your good fellowship and professional activities after graduation, It would also tend to fill the gap between graduation and the time you become eligible to join your state society of certified public accountants and other professional accounting organizations [requiring certification]. Local meetings might be on a quarterly basis, with at least one of the meetings held conjunctly [sic] with chapter initiations [assuming the presence locally of a Beta Alpha Psi campus]. Such meetings could be so arranged as not to conflict with meetings of state societies of C.P.A.'s, N.A.C.A., Internal Auditors, or Controllers.

Alton Peterson had already identified several "tentative objectives."

Working objectives

Three specific programs were cited, along with a relatively undefined role:

1. Providing a "strictly professional, high calibre employment service" for professional accountants, at cost for undergraduates and, following routine credit checks, at commercial rates for alumni (or other professional accountants)

2. Fostering interest among high school and college students in professional accounting, through lectures and supervision of AIA occupational tests

3. Developing a "student fellowship fund" for graduate study in accounting

4. Assisting the Grand Council and undergraduate chapters as appropriate.

Wedeberg had suggested that annual dues of two dollars would support alumni subscriptions to the Newsletter and "whatever objectives might be established." Peterson, however, foresaw the employment program, serving "non-member C.P.A.'s and executive accountants" as well as members of the fraternity, as the essential source of funding for the other endeavors. He had received encouragement and assistance in planning the effort from professional organizations in engineering and other fields.

The second objective stated would have been very attractive in light of a proposal that had been received "enthusiastically" at the 1952 Grand Chapter meeting, particularly by the seven past fraternal presidents in attendance. The latter group had included both Scovill and Eric L. Kohler, the latter of whom had as president of the American Accounting Association six years earlier developed the plan submitted to the fraternal gathering by the faculty advisor to Iota Chapter at Southern Cal. The proposal was that, to counter the "dusty notion of the bookkeeper with his green eye shade sitting on his high stool."

> the accounting profession combine to produce a vocational guidance film of some 40 to 50 minutes duration which would, in dynamic fashion, exhibit the varied activities of the accounting profession to all who may be interested.

Kohler had recommended an emphasis upon "the people, places, and particularly the ideas [bold print in original] which constitute the coin of the profession," within a film that would be especially of interest to young people considering possible career fields. Although Beta Alpha Psi was not prepared at the time to take on such a project, the interest generated at the meeting would have commended alumni efforts of an educational nature.

The further idea of developing a "fellowship fund" for graduate study would be put into practice in 1957 by the American Accounting Association, rather than Beta Alpha Psi. The fraternity would in 1960, however, contribute $1,000 to the AAA fund. President Nolan Williams' Council included a member of the association's Committee on Accounting Fellowships, Professor C. Rollin Niswonger.

During the spring of 1954 an "Alumni Committee" was appointed to develop plans for a national alumni organization.

Appointment of a committee

The Grand Council unanimously appointed four regular committee members:

a. Hermann C. Miller, a former fraternal president, Chairman
b. Alton Peterson, Secretary
c. Elmer Beamer, managing partner of Haskins & Sells, Cleveland office
d. Russell H. Morrison, Arthur Andersen & Co. consulting partner, Chicago.

Miller was perhaps selected in virtue of his editorship of the 1939 national Directory, the fraternity's major alumni undertaking to date. As the first president of Alpha Chapter, Morrison represented an excellent linkage with founder Scovill as well as a base within the nation's second largest city and one of its largest accounting firms.

In view of Miller's long career at Ohio State, Elmer Beamer, Omicron '52 (honorary), may have added relatively limited coverage from a geographical (as distinct from a professional-firm) standpoint. Within the American

Institute of Accountants, however, he was already notably involved in the field of professional education, as a member of the Commission on Standards of Education and Experience for CPAs (and past chairman of a subcommittee on educational training). The commission's report, in 1956, would have "tremendous impact on the thinking of all persons concerned with standards for the CPA certificate." In the 1960s Beamer would head the Commission on the Common Body of Knowledge for CPAs, which supervised the preparation of the AICPA study Horizons for a Profession (1967), and later a committee (popularly known as the "Beamer committee") that developed specific proposals for implementing the educational philosophy of that landmark work. The ten recommendations made by the Beamer committee, including the adoption in all states by 1975 of a five-year educational requirement for certification, were adopted by the Council of the American Institute in 1969. Elmer Beamer himself had entered the public accounting field in 1931, incidentally, following acquisition of "varied bookkeeping experience."

Alton Peterson, finally, had apparently left his position with the Internal Revenue Service by 1954, for he was described by President Wedeberg as a CPA practicing in Colorado Springs. Wedeberg, Secretary-Treasurer A. J. Penz, and Councilor Wayne E. Shroyer were named ex-officio members of the alumni committee. Geographically, University of Denver professor Shroyer would have provided Peterson with a direct link to the Council.

In reporting the committee appointments, S. M. Wedeberg encouraged graduating seniors to join together in trying to form "at least the nucleus of a local chapter" in the cities where they planned to work. In proposing that alumni and honorary members listed in local chapter directories be contacted, with a view toward scheduling a meeting for early fall, he seemed to be speaking primarily to students planning to take jobs near

ELMER BEAMER PRESENTS HASKINS & SELLS AWARD TO OMICRON MEMBER 1956

From left, Elmer G. Beamer, Ohio State accounting chairman James R. McCoy, Dean Walter C. Weidler, and Norman Schwartz, the honored student.

their campuses. At any rate, the president stated clearly that honorary members, who would rarely be found among the "younger accountants" who were intended to represent the focal point of attention, would be included within an alumni association. Somewhat quaintly (and, in juxtaposing "active" and "passive," ironically), he wrote that "the alignment of honorary members with the alumni is a logical affiliation[,] whereas the association with the active chapter per force of circumstance is of a passive nature."

As pointed up by the reference made to local inquiries, the vital question remained of whether significant numbers of fraternal alumni (and honoraries) would be interested in participating in such an organization. As its first order of business, then, the alumni committee surveyed prospective participants, in part through the local chapters. The results were so disappointing that the committee was promptly dissolved, and the effort abandoned. The governing Council would not consider the matter of alumni chapters again for another generation.

"Survey of Proposed National Alumni Association," Leading to abandonment of the effort

The only information located concerning survey procedures appeared in Alton Peterson's article "Survey of Proposed National Alumni Association," published in the Newsletter of March 1954. Peterson appeared to endorse Hiram Scovill's recommendation that some 240 alumni, of the approximately 12,000 members to date, "be invited to express their candid opinions on this proposal." Given a favorable response, the entire fraternal alumni roster would then be surveyed.

It is likely that a small-scale survey was conducted, although no evidence exists from fraternal financial records. Even if the mailing

would have been paid from the national treasury (not indicated), 240 letters would have cost only $7.20 in postage (or double that amount if return postage were enclosed) at contemporary rates.

Peterson requested that local chapters hold "round-table disucssion[s]" regarding the proposed organization, and send him their "suggestions, comments, and criticisms." Citing several pertinent questions, he also asked them to survey their own alumni in the course of collecting periodic dicrectory information, and to report summaries of the response obtained.

Whatever information was developed by Alumni Secretary Peterson concerning potential interest in a national association operating through local chapters was reported on his behalf by Secretary-Treasurer Penz at the Council meeting of September 1954. A second report on the issue was presented by Alumni Chairman Hermann Miller. Obviously the messages were not encouraging, because "[t]he consensus of those present was that not enough interest was reflected by alumni members to warrant any further action at this time." Accordingly, on Miller's recommendation the Council unanimously voted to terminate the committee, and thus end the attempt to form a national alumni organization. There would be no sequel to that effort over the following three decades, although the development during the period 1978-82 of national standards governing any local alumni groups that might be formed is covered briefly in chapter 16.[7]

---

[7]Carey, Rise of Profession 2:265, 266 (quoted), 276-84, passim; Committee on Accounting Fellowships (AAA), "American Accounting Association: Accounting Fellowship Program," "Special Features," ed. [Herbert E. Miller], Newsletter 6 (November 1960):6-7; Grand Council Income Statement, 1953-54, Newsletter 4 (November 1954):211; Grand Council Minutes Book, 1954, p. 3, quoted; "Honorary Members Initiated During the Past Year," Newsletter 4 (March 1953):38; "Local Chapter News," Newsletter 4 (March 1953):49, quoted; Alton L. Peterson to W. E. Dickerson, July 23, 1949, first letter (Policies File); Peterson, "Employment Service Contemplated for National Alumni Alton L. Peterson, "Employment Service Contemplated for National Alumni Association," "Alumni News," Newsletter 4 (May 1954):175, quoted; Peterson, "Survey of Proposed National Alumni Association," "Alumni News," Newsletter 4 (March 1954):138, quoted; Sheldahl, Alpha to Omega, pp. 70-71; [S. M.

Newsletter and visitation reports from the third era reveal occasional cases of strong interest by chapter alumni in participation within Beta Alpha Psi. Actual alumni chapters were formed in relation to at least two local units.

Local Chapter References, Including Two Alumni Chapters

As reported in volume 1, Delta Chapter at Washington enjoyed a long tradition of active involvement of alumni members in the annual spring banquet. Such participation was maintained after the war. For example, in 1950 more than two hundred "actives, faculty and staff, alumni, and guests" were present at the banquet, and selected alumni from the chapter's early years were introduced.

Although it was not founded at Pittsburgh until 1955, Alpha Tau quickly developed an alumni tradition of its own by inviting alumni from any chapter who lived in the local area to attend its meetings. On some occasions such fraternal alumni gave presentations. Updated listings were maintained through annual surveys conducted by the chapter, with the assistance of Pittsburgh CPA firms. Twenty-eight of the 50 persons in attendance at Alpha Tau's fall initiation banquet in 1957 were Beta Alpha Psi alumni members. During a visitation shortly thereafter, chapter officers suggested to Councilor Williard Stone that extra copies of the Newsletter be sent for distribution to interested alumni, and that through the periodical the Grand Council from time to time encourage alumni to contact nearby chapters.

Wedeberg], "Grand Council News," Newsletter 4 (November 1952):6,7 (second indented citation, original in bold print); Wedeberg, "President's Page: Alumni Committee Appointed, Irreproachable Associates Stressed," Newsletter 4 (May 1954):164, quoted; and Wedeberg, "President's Page: Beta Alpha Psi Can Afford an Alumni Association," Newsletter 4 (March 1954):132-33, quoted (including first citation).

At a visit a year later to Alpha Xi at Detroit, Stone found more alumni members (12) in attendance than active ones (8). The chapter was planning thereafter to hold an earlier fall initiation to provide for a larger membership base in the first part of the year.

As indicated earlier, Alpha Gamma Chapter at the City College of New York, founded in May 1949, recorded very high initiation totals in its first years. It is not entirely surprising, then, that a need was seen very early for an Alpha Gamma alumni organization. Such a group was formed in the fall of 1950, under the leadership of a local professor, for purposes of "keeping active the principles and ideals of Beta Alpha Psi."

An alumni organization was formed during the same year in relation to a far older chapter, following the first local alumni reunion. Gathered at the Commodore Perry Hotel in Austin on October 21, 1950, were Theta Chapter alumni inducted at Texas during eight prewar years, as well as members initiated in each of the past five years. The highlight of the formal program was a speech by honorary member Gay Carroll, comptroller of Humble Oil and Refining Co., that would be published in full as a ten-page article in the Accounting Review. As another feature, an alumnus spoke on the topic "What I See in the Graduating Active," and a student member followed with a speech concerning "What I Hope For in the Practicing Alumnus." The reunion was combined with the induction of 24 new Theta brothers, bringing the total number of chapter members in attendance to some 125.

One of the objectives of the Austin gathering was "to bring into being a cohesive alumni association," and a local alumni group was indeed formed. Named alumni president was Fred Edward Pflughaupt, Theta '26, a San Antonio CPA cited in volume 1 in regard to a light-hearted chapter anecdote

Tau at Maryland appears to have enjoyed significant alumni participation. Three alumni members spoke on careers respectively in public,

governmental, and corporate accounting at a 1956 chapter meeting.[8]

In general, the Grand Council of the third era welcomed continuing participation by alumni members in Beta Alpha Psi activities. In the case of Mu Chapter at New York University, however, the involvement was pervasive, and clearly unconstitutional. The problem was not finally resolved until the mid-1960s, more than six years after it was discovered during a routine chapter visitation.

Alumni Dominance at Mu Chapter, 1958-65

President Williard Stone visited Mu on October 25, 1958. He was highly impressed by the level of activity found, the excellence of local record keeping, the innovative maintenance of an "alumni vice-president" position and an "executive committee," and the high level of alumni attendance. Although not noted in the visitation report, the office just cited (which had been listed in the program of a 1954 Mu initiation banquet attended by S. M. Wedeberg) was not sanctioned by the national constitution.

Much more importantly, Stone found that <u>all</u> of Mu's officers were alumni members, and that such a situation had existed, without Council awareness, "for some time." Active members served only in committee posts, although the incoming secretary was usually elected from the roster of graduating seniors. A system of regular succession from one office to another, from secretary to treasurer to vice-president to president, was followed, much as on the Grand Council itself. Some 20-25 alumni members attended each meeting. Reportedly the active members, many of whom had

---

[8]Gay Carroll, "Some Challenges to Accounting," <u>The Accounting Review</u> 26 (January 1951):9-18; "Local Chapter News," Newsletter (3) (November 1950): 15, 17, 25, quoting first two pages; Hermann C. Miller, ed., <u>Beta Alpha Psi Directory</u>, s.v. "Theta Chapter: Pflughaupt, Fred Edward"; Sheldahl, <u>Alpha to Omega</u>, pp. 373, 379, 381; W. E. Stone, Visitation Report--Alpha Tau, December 11, 1957, letter format; [Stone], Visitation Report--Alpha Xi, October 2, 1958, informal summary; and S. M. Wedeberg, Visitation Reports--Tau, May 1954, item 3.4, [November 14, 1956], et al., item 3.4.

part-time jobs, did not object to alumni dominance, and in some cases had declined officership opportunities. The alumni members were considered better able to secure top speakers for chapter meetings, and most of them lived nearby. Stone concluded that the fraternity faced a genuine dilemma--Mu was a "healthy" chapter, but was clearly operating unconstitutionally.

At the following year's Council meeting, incoming secretary-treasurer Herbert E. Miller was instructed to inform Mu that a program for transferring officership to student members should be submitted prior to the 1960 annual gathering. Miller duly wrote the chapter president in September 1959, requesting submission of the plan by July 1, and expressing the Council's wish that "loyal alumni support and interest" be maintained.

The NYU group had the preceding spring elected a vice-president from the student membership, but this information had somehow not reached the Council. Past President Stone finally learned of this development in October, at which time Faculty Vice-President Frederick Horn (elected in 1952) proposed that Mu gradually turn over control to the active membership by transferring one office each year to student ranks. Ironically, Stone opposed such an approach, not because of its gradualism, but because of the jeopardy posed to the retention of alumni interest. He recommended instead that separate "active" and "alumni" chapters be formed, and hold joint meetings featuring guest speakers. Horn agreed to take this proposal up with the chapter, and also to attempt to have local scholastic requirements reduced to the national level in order to increase the small supply of student candidates.

In April 1960 Stone made a second visitation to the New York campus in Greenwich village, having an opportunity before meeting with a "special

caucus" of Mu representatives to spend thirty minutes observing "the world's finest beatniks" provide "a good sample of their best." Later, the chapter president, three other alumni, faculty advisor Horn, and department chairman Arnold Johnson reported on recent reforms (election of a student officer, ending of the "officer succession" practice, and reduction of grade requirements), and explained that Mu combined very devoted alumni and generally uninterested students. Most of them were persuaded by Stone, however, that low student interest might be due largely to alumni dominance, and that the primary objective of the fraternity was to help undergraduates develop leadership abilities. Chapter representatives opposed formation of a separate alumni organization unless it could be formally chartered by the Grand Council. Past President Stone accordingly asked them to submit to the Council a specific proposal for constitutional revision.

Although such a petition was not forthcoming, six Mu members spoke to the Council at the 1960 annual meeting, held at Ohio State. They were advised that the chapter must be turned over to student control, but that a constitutional amendment authorizing a separate alumni chapter could be considered. Stone's position that separate organizations were needed at NYU was generally accepted by his colleagues.

Although specific developments are not known, the secretary-treasurer was instructed a year later to commend Mu Chapter for progress that had been made in 1960-61, expressing hope that all local offices would be held by students within the year. Incoming president Herb Miller planned, at Council request, to attend an initiation ceremony at NYU during the 1961-62 school year, but was unable to do so because of a schedule conflict in one instance and the absence of timely notice in another.

A letter from the chapter was presented at the 1962 Grand Council

meeting, reporting that all officers elected in the spring had been active members at the time. It is clear, however, that the new officer group included graduating seniors, who thus would be alumni during their actual terms of service. President C. Rollin Niswonger visited Mu during the year 1962-63, probably (as requested by his colleagues) at the time of an initiation. His report led to a major decision at the next Council meeting. Incoming president Emerson Henke was instructed to write Professor Horn that the chapter would be placed on probation unless all officers were "duly registered students working toward a degree" within one year. Such a warning was finally issued in October 1963, five years after the unconstitutional chapter operations had first come to light.

A month later, retired councilor Herb Miller visited the NYU group. The evening began with a dinner at the faculty club of which student members had not been informed. Most of the "non students" were "just there to break bread and visit with their old buddies during dinner," and left prior to a regular meeting that featured an excellent speaker from industry. It was probably during dinner that Fred Horn informed the visitation officer that at the last chapter meeting he had made a "strong appeal" for an all-student officership, only to be immediately rebuffed.

By this point there were two student officers, and plans had called for Miller to be seated with them during the meeting. Instead, he was joined by the immediate past president and another "non student," who proceeded to render a "strong defense" of the chapter structure. Afterwards, Miller insisted upon meeting only with student members and pledges who indicated that they had not been aware that Mu's operating practices were "distinctive." The student officers tried repeatedly to defend the status quo. Miller told the students that the Council was still willing

to consider the formation of an alumni chapter, which could interact in various ways with the regular unit.

Concerned only that his attitude throughout the evening might have been overly '"tough line"', Professor Miller concluded his report by endorsing the contingency plan to place Mu on probation. A constructive proposal was finally submitted by the chapter in the spring of 1964, but by incredible irony none of the three relevant letters sent to Council officials was received. Under this plan, there would be four student officers, having primary responsibility for operations, plus an alumni president and vice-president serving in an advisory capacity. All members in good standing would have equal voting rights. The information submitted included the names of the current year's initiates and the six officer-elects.

Unaware of these developments, the Grand Council went ahead with earlier plans. President Julius Roller wrote Fred Horn in September 1964 that, effective immediately, Mu Chapter was on probation for a period not to exceed one year. Probation would be lifted during that period if arrangements were made for exclusive student officership, but the chapter would be deactivated after a year in the absence of such action. Once Horn expressed "deep schock" on behalf of his chapter, the mailing irregularities were identified a month later. After contacting his fellow councilors, however, Roller reported that the new structure was still not acceptable. The constitution provided <u>only</u> for student officers, other than the faculty vice-president, except that (in a provision that would be repealed a year later) the secretary-treasurer could be a faculty person.

Professor Horn responded that the chapter would act on the matter immediately after the resumption of classes in January, 1965. Because of

illness, however, he would not actually report substantive developments until March 6. On that date he wrote that Mu had elected four new student officers to replace the four students graduating in January, and (more importantly) had abolished the two alumni posts. With the full support of the Council, President Roller was thus able to write Professor Arnold Johnson at the close of the month that the probation had been lifted, "effectively immediately," having a few days earlier signalled this outcome in an appreciative letter to the faculty vice-president.

The reference made to Johnson, the author of a well-known textbook series in financial accounting, prompts a personal note in closing. While teaching at Oklahoma a quarter-century earlier, one of his students in three summer terms had been a high school and, later, junior-college instructor named Wilton T. Anderson, who had earned his master's degree in 1941. A councilor of '65, Anderson credits the NYU department head of the day with having been "an exceptionally gifted teacher and author"; and with having contributed significantly to his own academic career, and to his appointment in 1957 as director of education for the American Institute of Certified Public Accountants. He had held that post, placing him in charge of the preparation and grading of the CPA exam, until his resignation in 1960 to become head of the accounting department at Oklahoma State. Through initiation on a faculty basis in 1948, Professor Johnson, who had also taught at Tulane, was a member of Xi Chapter at Syracuse.

---

[9] Wilton T. Anderson, "Highlights of My Life and Career," Issues in Accounting Education: 1983, ed. Murdock, pp. 2-3; Beta Alpha Psi Fraternity, "National Constitution," National Constitution and Statutes (1958), article 4, section 3; Beta Alpha Psi National Constitution (1965), article 7, section 3; "Biography: Wilton T. Anderson," resume, [1969] (Golden Anniversary Files); Grand Council Minutes, 1964 (typescript with the more ample margins), p. 2; Grand Council Minutes Book, 1952, pp. 1-2, 1959, p. 3, 1960, pp. 1, 6, 1961, p. 2, 1962, p. 1, 1963, pp. 2-3; Frederick G. Horn to Julius Roller, October 7, 1964 (quoted), December 7, 1964, March 6, 1965;

In Transition

Through a former high-level employee who was an early postwar leader of the fraternity, one of the more prominent organizations with which honorary (and alumni) members were affiliated played a central role in one of the foremost policy developments ever recorded within Beta Alpha Psi. Specifically, the National Association of Cost Accountants provided the model for the famous "rating," or "activity," program introduced at mid-century.

Horn and Andrew Maxon, student vice-president, Mu Chapter, to Emerson O. Henke, May 28, 1964 (duplicate of letter of March 5, 1964); "Local Chapter News," Newsletter [2] (November 1948):18; Herbert E. Miller to James J. Kennedy, president of Mu Chapter, September 23, 1959, quoted; Miller, Visitation Report--Mu (combined with reports for Rho and Alpha Gamma), [November 19, 1963], quoted; Previts and Committe, comps., "Accounting Review" Index, part 2, s.v. "Johnson, Arnold W."; Roller to Horn, September 10, October 30, 1964, March 26, 1965; Roller to Arnold Johnson, March 30, 1965, quoted; Roller to National Council (and Miller), March 16, 1965; Joseph A. Silvoso, review of Advanced Accounting, rev. ed., by Arnold W. Johnson, The Accounting Review 36 (January 1961):171; W. E. Stone to Grand Council, October 30, 1959, quoted; Stone, Visitation Reports--Mu, October 25, 1958, April 23, 1960 (letter formats), both quoted; and S. M. Wedeberg, Visitation Report--Mu, June 4, 1954, attached program for "Semi-Annual Initiation Dinner." Also, Anderson to Author, July 5, 1986, quoted.

All the letters and visitation reports cited from the period 1959-65 were copied from Mu Chapter files at the National Office of Beta Alpha Psi, Sarasota, Florida.

At the American Institute, Wilton Anderson worked secondarily in the areas of university relations, at a time in which prevailing academic attitudes "were not complimentary to the . . . AICPA," and continuing education. He had been hired away from the faculty of the University of Colorado for a salary of $25,000, a very handsome income, from a professor's standpoint, in 1957. Anderson, "Highlights," as cited above, p. 2, quoted; and Anderson to Author, March 15, 1976 (conversation, University of Alabama), July 5, 1986.

CHAPTER 5

BUILDING A SYSTEM FOR CHAPTER MOTIVATION AND CONTROL: ORIGINATION AND STRUCTURAL EVOLUTION OF THE "ACTIVITY PROGRAM," 1950-60

As reactivation neared completion, and before the first postwar chapter was installed, the Grand Council in 1947 already saw the need for a central control system that would promote strong local operations. Three years later a program for "rating" chapter performance, developed by a councilor uniquely suited by prior professional experience for such a role, was introduced. The "T. M. Dickerson Chapter Rating Plan," within a few years to be renamed the "Activity Program," represented the most ambitious and enduring policy initiative of the third era.

The new control system was administered for the fraternity by the secretary-treasurer. The nine evaluation components of the original plan incorporated constitutional reporting requirements, and were strongly oriented as a group toward routine chapter operations. Although at least nominally the same categories were retained throughout the 1950s, only one element remained wholly intact, and fundamental revisions foreshadowed much later developments. Perhaps influenced by a critique submitted by the fraternal historian of the day, the Council had by happenstance revised the program even before final competitive results for the first year had been determined. Two particularly controversial elements, shown in the next chapter to have decisively influenced annual results, concerned grade averages of members and (through revision) attendance at meetings.

Development and Implementation of the "T. M. Dickerson Chapter Rating Plan"

The Planning Period, 1947-50

As reported in volume 1, the highlight of limited prewar consideration of a chapter rating program was the submission by Secretary-Treasurer W. E. Karrenbrock in 1937 of a letter of inquiry to faculty advisors. A decade later, the Grand Council in September 1947 "approved the drafting by T. M. Dickerson and committee of a rating plan of chapters to be submitted" at the next meeting. With reactivation nearly complete, and resumption in roster growth expected soon, it was time to look for ways to stimulate meaningful activity throughout the fraternity while fostering excellent communication with the local level.

Thomas M. Dickerson was chosen to spearhead the effort because for three years (1931-34) he had administered the Stevenson Trophy chapter competition within the National Association of Cost Accountants. The Gamma Chapter alumnus would evidently carry out his assigned role over the next three years as a "committee" of one, receiving "valuable suggestions" from Council associates. As he would much later observe, chapter-based organizations like Beta Alpha Psi and the NACA "needed a system through the use of which they could measure the efficiency of widely scattered operating units" to permit effective control.

Tom Dickerson presented a tentative ratings plan at the 1948 Council meeting, at which he was elected president of the fraternity. It was decided that a revised draft should be developed through mail communication among the councilors, and implemented by the following September. The revision was not made until that month, however, at the 1949 annual meeting. Dickerson was asked to make further refinements in the plan "and submit it to the chapters [for implementation] at an early date." Surprisingly enough,

the ratings plan would not be mentioned in the <u>Newsletter</u> during the year 1949-50, despite the appearance of an otherwise informative account of the Grand Council meeting.

Following further delay, the "T. M. Dickerson Chapter Rating Plan" was formally approved in September 1950, in Cambridge, Mass., during its architect's final Council meeting.

The Original Program, 1950-51

A full transcript of the original program is reprinted from contemporary minutes as exhibit 12. The plan was sent to all local chapters prior to the issuance of November's <u>Newsletter</u>, according to which it was intended

> to stimulate friendly rivalry among the various chapters and to afford the chapter officers some basis for measuring their accomplishments and to see what other chapters are doing.

A similar statement of objectives, expanded to three specific points, appears at the beginning of exhibit 12.

Among the nine evaluation items listed, the requirements of submitting (1) a chapter program for the year and (2) a financial budget, classified by academic term, were waived for the first year due to inadequate notice. Although charter administrator John Arch White, the faculty advisor at Texas on the occasion of Karrenbrock's 1937 initiative, was authorized to omit any other factors for 1950-51 that he considered impracticable, the secretary-treasurer would choose to implement all remaining items.

The plan incorporated certain constitutional responsibilities of chapter secretary-treasurers. Subsection 73b in chapter 7 of the current statutes required them to submit timely audited statement of receipts and disbursements (item 3) and initiation reports (no. 5). Also, provision 73a, requiring that "correct minutes" of chapter meetings be kept, was only a weaker version of item 4, while the catchall requirement of subsection 73c

EXHIBIT 12

TRANSCRIPT OF THE T. M. DICKERSON CHAPTER RATING PLAN, SEPTEMBER 1950

Chapter Rating Plan

Beginning with the academic year 1950-51 the Grand Council of Beta Alpha Psi will rate the activity of its chapters in accordance with the following chapter rating plan. The purposes of this chapter rating are to:

1. Set fourth the major responsibilities of each chapter and its opportunities for service to its members, its school, its community, and the accounting profession.

2. Enable each chapter to compare its effectiveness with that of other chapters.

3. Develop more active and stronger chapters in Beta Alpha Psi.

A chapter can earn a total of 6,000 points each year, distributed as follows:

	Points
1. Organization of Annual Program	1,000
2. Financial Budget	300
3. Financial Report	500
4. Regular Meetings	800
5. Inititations	600
6. Scholarship Standards	600
7. News Letter	900
8. Chapter Directory	800
9. Special Activities	500
Total	6,000

The rating will be made annually and will cover the period from September 1 to June 30, both dates included. A form is provided upon which to report each activity and the dates by which each report is due will be indicated. It will be the sole responsibility of chapter officers to render reports to the Grand Secretary as required. Each report must be approved by the Faculty Vice-President and submitted on or before it is due, to receive any credit for the activity covered. The number of points awarded for the report will depend upon the nature and quality of the activity and the report. The Grand Secretary shall determine and record the number of points to be awarded for each report. In each issue of the News Letter there will be published the cumulative standings of the various chapters so that the officers and members of each chapter will be able to compare the operating effectiveness of their chapter with that of the other chapters.

It is realized that the rules and the activity point awards may have to be changed from time to time in order that no undue hardship may be suffered by any chapter. Therefore, the Grand Council reserves the right to change or modify any feature of the rating plan if experience indicates such

changes to be desirable. All chapters will be rated under the plan. No measurement of chapter effectiveness can accurately reflect the many real but intangible benefits resulting from active chapter operations, but it is hoped that this rating plan will help the individual chapters and the Fraternity as a whole in achieving our major aims and objectives.

1. Organization of Annual Program. (Not to be rated in 1950-51). The full program of regular meetings for the academic year should be submitted to the Grand Secretary on or before November 1, indicating meeting dates, subjects and speakers where possible. The program must include at least 16 scheduled regular meetings, but not more than two in any one month. The list of speakers may include not more than eight selected from outside the undergraduate membership. Maximum, 1,000 points.

2. Financial Budget. (Not to be rated in 1950-51). A complete financial budget should be prepared covering chapter operations for the year, showing estimated revenues and expenses, by quarters or semesters, properly itemized, and mailed to the Grand Secretary not later than December 1. Maximum, 300 points.

3. Financial Reports. An audited financial report should be prepared and mailed to the Grand Secretary not later than June 30, showing actual revenues and expenses for each quarter or semester compared with the budget. To receive the maximum number of points for this activity, the audit must be certified by a CPA who may be a faculty or alumni member, but not the faculty vice-president. Maximum, 500 points.

4. Regular Meetings. A report of each regular meeting should be sent to the Grand Secretary within one week after the meeting, indicating the date, place, subject and speaker, and the number present of active members and of others. Maximum for each meeting, 50 points; total maximum, 800 points.

5. Initiations. Reports concerning initiations must be submitted to the Grand Secretary in accordance with the National Statutes and Chapter By-Laws. For properly reporting all initiations per year, maximum, 400 points. For having unblindfolded portion of the ritual properly memorized, maximum, 200 points; total maximum, 600 points.

6. Scholarship. A report should be submitted to the Grand Secretary during each quarter or semester, indicating the scholastic average of each active member for the preceding quarter or semester. Where a school or college does not make grades of its students available to the chapter secretary for this purpose, the grades as reported by the active members to the chapter secretary will be accepted. In order that a chapter may earn the maximum point award for this item, the grade average for each individual active member for each quarter or semester must be at least "B" (or its equivalend). Maximum, each quarter 200 points, each semester 300 points; total maximum, 900 points.

7. News Letter. Local chapter news items for publication in the News Letter should be submitted to the Grand Secretary on or before the dates announced by the Grand Secretary. The news items may combine much of the materials submitted in other reports but should be submitted in a form suitable for publication with a minimum of editing by the Grand Secretary. Maximum, each issue, 300 points; total maximum, 900 points.

8. Chapter Directory. A directory of chapter members, or an annual supplement, should be prepared and distributed to the chapter members and to the members of the Grand Council not later than June 1, in accordance with instructions issued by the Grand Secretary. Maximum, 800 points.

9. Special Activities. This item is intended to include special meetings held jointly with business and professional groups; job placement of members, activie participation in Red Cross or other fund drives; industrial tours; radio programs; accounting research; other activities of unusual or timely merit.

   Because of the wide variety and irregular occurence of such activities, the final award of points for this item will be made at the end of the academic year. However, a complete report covering each of such activities should be submitted to the Grand Secretary within one month of its occurrence or completion but not later than June 30. Maximum, 500 points.

Suggestions and Instructions for Submitting Reports. Friendly rivalry among local chapters had contributed greatly to the growth, development and usefulness of several of the large national and international professional, civic and service organizations. But of far greater value has been the training afforded the individual members who participated actively in the work of their chapters. The planning, organizing and conducting of chapter activities provides real training in executive and administrative leadership. Benefit derived by a member from any organization is in proportion to his active contribution to its successful operation. It is hoped that each member of Beta Alpha Psi will benefit greatly through the operation of this chapter rating plan, while increasing the prestige and usefulness of the Fraternity.

Organization. At the first meeting of the chapter after the details of the plan are available, the plan should be explained to the members and the necessary organization perfected for carrying out its provisions. The provisions governing each activity covered in the plan should be studied to determine what must be done and when it must be reported, in order to earn the maximum number of points for the chapter. Then committees may be appointed to work with the chapter officers in putting the plan into operation. A calendar indicating the schedule of reporting dates will be very helpful. During the first few weeks the most urgent matters will be the preparation of the program of meetings for the academic year, the preparation of a financil budget and the reporting of items for the News Letter.

Of course, of equal importance will be the regular chapter meetings and an early initiation of new members. The faculty vice-president can be particularly helpful while getting the plan started.

Reporting. Each activity itme must be reported separately on Form A, which will be supplied by the office of the Grand Secretary. Special forms will be provided next year for submitting the Financial Budget and Financial Report. This year each chapter is asked to prepare the Financial Report in whatever form seems best. The best of these two reports submitted will be given honorable mention in the News Letter each year.

In those cases where the space on Form A is not sufficient for reporting an itme in full, separate sheets may be used and attached to a copy of Form A. This is particularly true with respect to items 1, 2 and 3.

In all cases where there is the least doubt as to the rules or method of procedure, write to the Grand Secretary for further information.

SOURCE: [Thomas M. Dickerson], "Chapter Rating Plan," Grand Council Minutes Book, 1950, pp. [3-7], verbatim transcript.

that chapter secretary-treasurers fulfill any other duties imposed by the Grand Council probably encompassed element 8, "Chapter Directory." Omitting the 200 points from item 5 based on memorization of the ritual, those four areas represented 2,500 of the 6,000 points within the original program. Moreover, another 900 points were available through regular submission of *Newsletter* material (no. 7), a routine practice since 1931, discounting wartime deactivation.

In the latter regard, as reported in the periodical's spring issues of 1951, there was a daily penalty of 50 points for "late" copy received before the printing date. The 50 points assigned by item 4 to reports of individual meetings were divided evenly among timing (dispatch within one week) and each of the four specified points of descriptive content.

The limitation by element 1 of "outside" speakers (broadly defined) to no more than half of a schedule of at least sixteen regular meetings (normally two per month) reflected concern that chapters had become too dependent on guest presentations. For example, Delta Chapter's long tradition of reliance upon papers and panel discussions by active members had given way, according to James McConahey, to "total" dependence upon invited speakers. Based on the prevailing belief that such gatherings were "a waste of time," *alumni* attendance at Washington had declined to "a scattering few, with none at many meetings."

Perhaps the most critical, and controversial, element of the program was factor 6, concerning periodic reporting of active members' *grades*. It seemed clearly to invite the adoption of scholastic requirements exceeding the B- standard imposed by the national constitution, and also to discriminate against chapters located within the more rigorous grading environments. The relevant grading periods were the final term of the preceding academic year and the first semester, or first two quarters, of the

given ratings year.

On a semester basis, 100 points were available each term for simply _reporting_ member grades. Two hundred additional points would be awarded if each active member had earned at least a B average the preceding semester, while otherwise 100 points would be conferred if the chapterwide average had reached that level. Partial credit was available for lower aggregate averages, ranging on a 4.0-scale from 20 points for 2.50 to 70 for 2.70 to 95 for 2.95. Under the honor system allowed by the Grand Council, chapter grade reports could be based on information supplied by the members themselves.

In general, the ratings plan was oriented strongly toward routine operations. Even the elements not evaluated the first year, items 1, "Organization of Annual Program," and 2, "Financial Budget," involved regular planning and control functions. Only 500 of the 6,000 total points were allotted to factor 9, concerning "special activities" such as interprofessional meetings, job placement, charitable work, field trips, and manuscript preparation. One of the principal features of early program development was detailed interpretation of this area, and significant expansion of the weight assigned to it.

Initially, special activities, as well as financial reports (item 3) and chapter directory supplements (no. 8), were evaluated only at the close of the year. As a result, the two interim reports of chapter standings during the year 1950-51 were based entirely on factors 4-7. More interestingly, two significantly different reports of "final" standings would be issued in 1951.

Overview of the First Year

The _Newsletter_ of March 1951 reported results of the rating program

based on reports filed on "Form A" through January 31. Sigma and Tau Chapters at Wisconsin and Maryland were ranked highest, followed, in a third-place tie, by Theta and Omicron at Texas and Ohio State. All units except Mu at New York and Alpha Epsilon at Southern Methodist had been credited with points. The initiation of thirteen active members at SMU during the fall semester had evidently not been properly reported. Every other group had received at least partial credit in two or more of the four categories measured except Gamma at Northwestern and Phi at LSU, each of which had received the full 300 points available for submitting material for the fall Newsletter.

By April 15, 1951, Tau, Theta, and Alpha Beta at Alabama were the three top-ranked chapters, with the latter two units having identical point totals. Alpha Epsilon had earned full credit for a Newsletter report while Mu remained without points. Only nine chapters to date had submitted scholastic reports.

John Arch White announced "final" standings for 1950-51 in his secretary-treasurer's report, listing Theta, Alpha Zeta at Denver (formed the preceding summer), and Alpha Beta as the top three chapters, and Mu, Phi, and Alpha Epsilon as the three lowest-ranked groups among the 26 chapters that had existed throughout the year. Because the program represented a learning experience for all concerned, White had consciously exercised "leniency" in awarding points. Twelve chapters had received credit, ranging from 200 to 535 points, in the "Scholarship" category, while every group except Mu had earned Newsletter credits, although Alpha Epsilon (ranked last) had otherwise been shut out.

White's leniency was destined to be expanded, however, by way of an action taken by the Grand Council at its 1951 annual meeting. His successor

as secretary-treasurer, S. M. Wedeberg, was authorized to award partial credit for financial reports submitted by September 30, fully three months after the date specified in the program's third element. Wedeberg would ultimately give credit for financial reports received by October 26, presumably the cutoff date for the fall Newsletter.

This expression of generosity by the Council did not dislodge Theta from its first-place standing, based on the accumulation of 4,250 points out of a possible total of 4,700. It did, however, move Omicron and Tau into second and third positions, ahead of Alpha Zeta and Alpha Beta. Unlike the pattern of later years, no single factor stood out as pivotal, as the Texas chapter received maximum scores in four categories while losing 200 points each regarding scholarship and special activities and 50 points concerning regular meeting reports.

The last three positions were changed only slightly, as Phi moved into a tie with Mu for next-to-last place. Both chapters were surpassed, however, by Alpha Eta at Michigan, which had not even been installed until late in the school year, on March 19.

The outgoing president at the time the council had decided to develop a ratings plan offered Secretary-Treasurer White a thoughtful critique of the original program shortly after its adoption. Reference to his analysis provides a useful transition to coverage of modifications in program design made during the 1950s.

Critique of the Plan by Former President McConahey

For health reasons, the 1947 gathering at which Tom Dickerson was instructed to prepare a ratings plan would be James McConahey's last Grand Council meeting. Because of his appointment a year later as the Beta Alpha Psi historian, however, he would remain in close touch with the fraternity

until about a year before his death in 1955.[1] As a matter of course, John Arch White sent him a copy of the current minutes, including the "Plan of Rating of Chapters," on October 17, 1950.

Six weeks later, McConahey sent White a mixed review of the new program. He found nothing objectionable in items 5-8, provided that the "Scholarship" provision did "not put too much of a load on the officers." That reservation may have contributed to the adoption of a permissive policy on collection of grade data, which in any case would have fully allayed the expressed concern. The early Delta honorary member ('21) particularly welcomed the provision of credit, in item 5, "[f]or having the unblindfolded portion of the ritual properly memorized."

Professor McConahey was somewhat critical, however, of the remaining five evaluation elements. In regard to item 9, he made the procedural recommendation that reports of special activities be accepted in conjunction with regular Newsletter submissions. He commented as follows on factors 1-4:

1. Organization and Annual Report--Budgeting could be only tentative. Also, the formulation would limit chapter meetings to two per month, surely not the Council's intent

2. Financial Budgeting--A chapter operating on a quarter system but initiating students only semiannually might find it difficult to develop meaningful academic-term budgets

3. Financial Reports--The requirement that actual revenue and expense be

[1] In a most uncharacteristic slip of the (written) tongue, Editor A. J. Penz made an unfortunate choice of words in referring in a Newsletter item of May 1954 to the establishment at Washington of a "Memorial" library honoring Professor McConahey. The special collection had originated through the donation by "Jim" McConahey (known in his earlier years as "Mac") of his personal library, and was being enlarged through the efforts of Delta Chapter. [Penz], "Chapter News Review," Newsletter 4 (May 1954):175; and S. M. Wedeberg to Penz, February 8, 1954 (McConahey File).

compared with budgeted amounts each term would make the chapter audit too expensive: "Why not have the [chapter] secretary" make such a comparison?

4. Regular Meetings--To require reports within a week of the meetings "puts quite a load on some officer."

Secretary-Treasurer White responded immediately, and most appreciatively, to the former councilor's letter. He felt that preparation of even highly "tentative" annual schedules would be "most helpful" to the chapters, acknowledging that the stated limit on number of meetings would serve only "to set a standard for the purpose of grading." Foreshadowing a provision later adopted concerning the evaluation of "special activities," the Texas professor suggested that a means ought to be found for rewarding a chapter (like Delta) that met far more often than the average, without compromising primary emphasis upon program quality.

White by and large accepted point 2, noting that financial budgeting would have to be graded on "effort" rather than "relative accuracy." He implied that the Council was not rigidly committed to interim budgeting, but was mindful that an annual horizon might instead be "superior."

The secretary-treasurer did not address the third point, but observed in regard to the fourth one that the structure of "Form A" should facilitate the timely reporting of meetings. A designated member could complete it during or directly after a meeting, and it could be mailed without a covering letter. Finally, White agreed that it would be "quite satisfactory" to submit activity reports with regular Newsletter copy, given the understanding that evaluation would be deferred until meaningful comparisons could be made, at year's end.

McConahey's primary concern, overall, was that "adding too much detail" to the work of officers and other active members of a chapter could "interfere with their studies and result in all their work being skimped too

much." White accordingly concluded by proposing that chapters designate different members to handle each of the nine evaluation elements (conceivably not always possible, in very small chapters), and asking the retired Washington professor to "watch" the operation of the plan at Delta to see if "too much detail work" were required.

At the conclusion of White's presidency, nearly two years later, the Council would recommend that chapters elect or appoint an "assistant" or "corresponding" secretary, "responsible for the submission of Form A's on all chapter activities, including such items as the budget, program, and audited financial statements." Interestingly, the position corresponding secretary had existed at his own chapter, Theta, since 1949.[2]

The criticisms registered by McConahey provided part of the backdrop against which the Grand Council began as early as 1951 to modify the ratings program. The major directions of change are signified by the adoption a few years later of the modern name "activity" program.

---

[2]Thomas M. Dickerson to Author, November 1, 1979 (quoted), April 19, 1980, interview; W. E. Dickerson, "The President's Page," Newsletter [3] (November 1949, March 1950, May 1950):4, cited for nonreference to rating program, author imputed for 1950 columns; exhibit 12; Grand Council Minutes Book, 1947, p. 1 (quoted), 1948, pp. 1, [3], 1949, p. 1 (quoted), 1950, pp. 1, [3], [7], 1951, p. 5, 1952, p. 3 (quoted); Jas. A. McConahey to W. E. Dickerson, October 17, 1948; McConahey to A. J. Penz, March 22, 1954, last of his letters filed; McConahey to S. M. Wedeberg, September 25, 1951, August 20, 1952; McConahey to John (Arch) White, August 29, November 28 (quoted), 1950; Hermann C. Miller, ed., Beta Alpha Psi Directory, s.v. "Delta Chapter: McConahey, James M."; "National Statutes," National Constitution and Statutes of Beta Alpha Psi Fraternity (1949), chapter 7, section 73, quoting subsection a; "News from the Chapters," Newsletter [1, unbound issue] (May 1931):4-9, first such item to appear; [Penz], "In Memorium," Newsletter 4 (April 1955):239, reporting the death of McConahey on March 26, 1955; Sheldahl, Alpha to Omega, pp. 384-88; Smith, Forty Acres, pp. 73-74; [Wedeberg], "Grand Council News," Newsletter [3] (November 1951):14-15; [White], "Grand Chapter News," Newsletter [3] (November 1949):7-11, quoting p. 8, (March 1950):5-6, (May 1950):5, (November 1950):7 (quoted), (March 1951):8-9, (May 1951):6-8, quoting p. 8; White to Mcconahey, December 1, 1950, quoted; and White, Secretary-Treasurer's Report, 1950-51, quoted.

Evolution from the "Rating" Plan of 1951 to the "Activity" Program of 1960

John Arch White told his fellow councilors in 1951 that the new ratings program had "exceeded expectations" in its first year, while acknowledging that chapter acceptance had varied, and that accurate evaluation of activities, as reported, had not been feasible. He anticipated still better results the second year, when all nine factors would be measured. The Grand Council in 1951 altered the weights of the annual program and special activities categories, and the reporting requirements concerning financial condition.

Over the following nine years, further changes would be made in these three areas; the reporting of regular meetings would be transformed largely into an attendance requirement; and other elements would be altered in one way or another, if only by way of environmental change. Only item 5 of the original plan, "Initiations," would survive completely intact.

Annual Program

Submission by November 1 of an annual schedule of regular meetings, which had originally been allotted one/sixth of the 6,000 total points, was reduced to 800 points prior to the year 1951-52, when it was first evaluated. The credit deducted was transferred to the special activities category.

As indicated earlier, the basic specification was that a program include at least sixteen meetings, no more than half involving outside speakers, and that a minimum schedule provide for no more than two meetings in one month. The stated limit on nonstudent presentation (in contrast with "member participation in the form of papers, round table discussions, etc.") was characterized in the 1953 minutes as a "recommend[ation]," rather

than as a rule enforced in assigning points. This interpretation is consistent with the allocation, among the items sought, of 200 points for dates, 300 for names of speakers or discussion leaders, and 300 for topics or programs. Chapters, which were given partial credit for late submissions, were understandably not penalized in this category for deviations made from their original schedules.

In the spring of 1952 the officers of Alpha Delta at Pennsylvania politely suggested to visitation officer S. M. Wedeberg that the program element was one of several '"relatively unimportant"' categories whose weights should be reduced. This appraisal of the first ratings item was apparently not isolated, for two years later the Grand Council transferred another 300 points from the annual program to special activities. The respective point totals thus became 500 and 1,000, exactly reversing the original ones. Each informational component of category 1 was reduced by 100 points.

Emblematic of this limited shift in emphasis, the interchapter competititon was in 1954 renamed the Chapter "Activity" Program. During the first decade no other changes would be made in the weights of the nine program elements.

An early alteration made in financial budgeting provisions seems to reflect the influence of the fraternal historian of the day.

Financial Budgeting

As noted earlier, James McConahey had questioned the requirement that budgets be formulated for academic terms rather than full years. Although the matter was not mentioned in the 1951 minutes, during the following year the Newsletter specified that budgets "must cover a full year's operations," making no reference in that context to semesters or quarters.

Full-year budgeting would be stipulated and illustrated within an authoritative 1952 committee report dealing in particular with a program area in which significant changes both of substance and timing were made. These changes in financial reporting requirements resulted in part from constitutional amendment.

Financial Reports

Following a discussion of "the wide variety and the quality of financial reports submitted," the Grand Council in 1951 revised subsection 73b-4 from chapter 7 of the statutes. Whereas previously "[a]n audited statement of . . . receipts and disbursements" had been required, henceforth "[a]udited financial statements" (emphasis added) were mandated.

An authoritative interpretation for this requirement was already being developed. A year earlier, the Council had adopted the proposal of incoming president Gould Harris that a "uniform system" of chapter reporting be prepared. For this purpose, Harris had appointed a committee chaired by Haskins & Sells managing partner Arthur B. Foye, elected in 1958 to the Accounting Hall of Fame. Other members were Jack Seidman, like Foye a future president of the American Institute of (Certified Public) Accountants, Harris himself, two representatives from industry, and a governmental accountant.

With Seidman assuming the primary responsibility for the project, the Foye committee produced a chapter-level accounting system for presentation at the 1952 annual meeting. It provided, most pertinently, for a statement of "assets and liabilities," as well as a statement of "income" that differed from a report of "receipts and disbursements" only through the inclusion of receivable from members (unpaid dues) witin an otherwise cash-based system. The model formats are presented as exhibit 13, showing within the context of the income statement the format recommended

EXHIBIT 13

FORMATS RECOMMENDED IN 1952 FOR FINANCIAL REPORTING BY CHAPTERS

Income Statement[a]

_________________ Chapter

BETA ALPHA PSI

Statement of Income

_________________ to _________________

	Actual	Budgeted
Income:		
Initiation fees (__ members at $____)...............	$	$
Dues (__ members at $____).........................		
Badges and keys....................................		
Directory rebate from Grand Council................		
Proceeds from social activities....................		
Miscellaneous: [ruled lines added for consistency]		
________________________..................		
________________________..................	______	______
Total income.......................................	$______	$______
Expenses:		
Initiation fees to Grand Council...................	$	$
Badges and keys....................................		
Social activities..................................		
School publications................................		
Chapter publications...............................		
Stationery and postage.............................		
National [should be "Chapter"] directory...........		
Miscellaneous:		
________________________..................		
________________________..................	______	______
Total income.......................................	$______	$______
Net income...	$______	$______

EXHIBIT 13--Continued

Balance Sheet

__________ Chapter

BETA ALPHA PSI

Statement of Assets and Liabilities

____
(Date)

Assets

Cash:		
In bank (or on deposit with school organization)...	$	
Petty cash..	______	$
Receivable from members.............................		______
Total assets..		$______

Liabilities

Unpaid bills..		$

Surplus

Balance (last report date)..........................	$	
Add net income (or subtract net loss) from		
__________ to __________.......	______	
Balance (this report date)..........................		______
		$______

SOURCE: [Arthur B. Foye and Committee], "Beta Alpha Psi: Uniform System of Accounting to be Maintained by Each Chapter" [1952], pp. 6-7. Attachment, S. M. Wedeberg to Faculty Vice-Presidents, November 6, 1952.

[a]The dual income-statement items relating in turn to initiation and directories are covered, under Grand Council finances, in chapter 8.

for the annual budget. In compliance with his instructions, Secretary-Treasurer Wedeberg in November 1952 submitted the full committee report to the chapters, "with an addendum . . . setting forth other possible procedures, so as to provide for variations in size of chapters." Although not compulsory, at least "[f]or the time being," compliance with the uniform system was naturally "considered sufficient . . . to meet the requirements of audited financial statements."[3]

In terms of timing, the Grand Council in 1951 moved the financial reporting deadline for ratings purposes from June 30 to July 31 while retaining the statutory requirement that reports be filed within four weeks of the close of the chapter year. It was clearly intended that chapters select a fiscal year consistent with both provisions. Since a genuine possibililty of inconsistency remained, however, the statutes were amended in 1952 to require a closing date of April 30, "or at least one month before the end of the school year" (chapter 6, section 61), and a reporting date not later than July 31. A year later, in keeping with an advance in the Council's year-end from August 15 to July 31, the chapter reporting deadline for both statutory and ratings purposes was moved forward to July 15.

The most fundamental revision made within the entire program concerned the fourth evaluation factor, "Regular Meetings." It followed injection of limited flexibility into the scheduling area.

---

[3]Although "[f]ormal books" were not required, the system involved nine books or other records, inclusive of the two-part financial report. Procedures were outlined for cash receipts and disbursements, petty cash, and members' accounts, and a chart of accounts reflected within exhibit 13 was presented. Besides a short covering letter, the secretary-treasurer appended two pages to the seven-page statement submitted by the Foye committee, illustrating acceptable simplifications or other modifications. Any changes made at the local level were to be approved by the faculty vice-president and chapter auditor in keeping with considerations of "internal check and auditability." [Foye committee], "Beta Alpha Psi Uniform System of Accountint" (cited in exhibit 13), quoting pp. 1, 8. Wedeberg submitted the report proper and his "addendum" (pp. 8-9) in triplicate (covering letter).

Regular Meetings

Distribution of meetings

Whereas over the first two years no more than two meetings in a given month had earned credit, beginning in 1952 the secretary-treasurer enjoyed the discretion to accept a third report to offset arrearages for months in which it might not be feasible to conduct two regular meetings. This concession was made in response to familiar calendar conditions, such as short school months and final-exam months.

The requirement of sixteen meetings was retained. Near the end of the decade, however, the faculty advisors to Nu at Colorado, Alpha Sigma at Cincinnati, and Beta Alpha at Indiana recommended a reduction. In the last case, future fraternal president Leon Hay suggested that the standard be lowered by two meetings, noting that his chapter could not convene in January and experienced weak attendance (by then a serious ratings detriment) in May. Precisely such a change would be made in 1960.

The issue of number and distribution of meetings could be particularly acute at a school with a senior internship program in accounting. Tau at Maryland was inactive one month each winter on that basis. "A large percentage" of Alpha Zeta members at Denver and five Delta brothers at Washington were on leave over the 1952 winter quarter; and "[m]any members of Rho at Minnesota applied for winter assignments in public accounting six years later. It was reported in '56 that the "[f]ield work problem" at Michigan State left Alpha Omicron "dormant" during the winter term. At the annual meeting held later in the year, it was agreed that chapters "hampered" by internship programs could "make up meetings missed in the month preceding or month subsequent to" student absences. Although it assumed a minimal internship period, this limited concession no doubt helped Alpha Omicron improve significantly in category 4 from its very low 1955-56 base.

Without, apparently, disrupting local chapter schedules, field-work appointments substantially reduced active membership rosters for several weeks at Ohio State and Miami of Ohio. For example, 9 Omicron members were absent for the winter quarter of 1955-56, and 11 Omega actives were away for five weeks a year later. The respective annual initiation totals were 32 and 28 students.

The internship problem would in fact become more acute, potentially, in 1957, as standards governing a fundamental redefinition of the category adopted three years earlier were made much more rigorous.

<u>Redefinition as mainly an "attendance" requirement</u>

Responding to a suggestion made by Professor James B. Bower of Sigma Chapter at Wisconsin, the Grand Council in 1954 reassigned 40 of the 50 points under Regular Meetings to <u>attendance</u>, leaving only 10 for the timely reporting of date, place, and topic. Originally, full credit was given for 50% or higher attendance by active members, deducting one point for each per cent below that level. As noted later, within the special activities category provision was also made for <u>faculty</u> attendance credit.

Three years later, in 1957, the reguired rate of student attendance was raised to <u>80</u>%, for full credit, subject to the deduction of one point for each 2% shortfall. An express purpose of this marked tightening of the standard was to produce an element besides <u>scholarship</u> (item 6) that might be a "deciding" factor in the ratings program. In effect set forth a year earlier by Secretary-Treasurer Jencks, this objective would be promptly achieved.

Naturally an internship program would have substantially reduced attendance during a certain stretch of the year, assuming no interruption of chapter operations. Point totals earned by Omicron in category 4

after 1957, including the sixth highest score in 1957-58 (when Ohio State won the overall competition), imply that "active" membership was construed, equitably, to allow for the absence of interning students. In the extreme case of the "cooperative" system by which students at Cincinnati alternated seven-week terms of study and employment, Alpha Sigma attendance was naturally evaluated based on active members in residence at a given time.

The real area of controversy for the attendance requirement lay elsewhere, however. It was decidedly favorable toward chapters located on predominantly residential campuses in "college towns," and equally unfavorable toward those found at commuter-oriented schools in large urban areas.[4] In the former connection, for example, Councilor S. M. Wedeberg reported in 1952 after visiting Alpha Theta at Mississippi that the location was "ideal," because there was "not much to do in that area except to participate in university affairs." A somewhat similar viewpoint was perhaps implied by a reference made to attendance at Zeta, at North Dakota, in a report filed by W. B. Jencks several years later.

Visitation reports concerning chapters of the second kind repeatedly stressed problems of attendance. Examples included Gamma at Northwestern, Mu at NYU, Pi at Western Reserve, Alpha Gamma at CCNY, Alpha Delta at Penn, Alpha Tau at Pittsburgh, Alpha Phi at Temple, and Beta Gamma at Depaul. Indeed, the lack of student interest contributed heavily to alumni control at New York, a situation that was apparently not adequately revealed by the chapter reporting process.

In some cases many active members were evening students, as were 18 of the 30 Pi Chapter actives early in 1958. Oftentimes, also, many day

---

[4]In 1967, a future councilor would publish an article on characteristic problems of urban chapters, based in part on personal experience. James W. Pattillo, FVP of Iota Chapter at USC, "Metropolitan Area Chapters: Oh, the Disadvantages," Newsletter 7 (May 1967):3-5.

students had jobs. It was probably more in the latter regard that the advisor to Xi Chapter at Syracuse expressed "dismay" late in 1957 about prospects for securing adequate attendance to attract quality speakers. At DePaul in Chicago, where no classes were scheduled after 12:30, nearly all members held afternoon jobs. In the years to come, according to fourth-era councilor Leon Hay, strong "ethnic" bonds existing on campus would more than offset any environmental obstacles faced by Beta Gamma Chapter.

A major facet of coping with typical problems of an urban setting was of course selection of an appropriate <u>meeting time</u>. At the City College of New York, meetings began around 5:30 to permit day students to meet after class and night students before class. Selection of the day of the week was particularly critical, since "practically all students" were "daydodgers," meaning that they could not be expected to make a special trip to campus in order to attend a meeting. At NYU, by contrast, meetings were started at 8:00 or 8:30 P.M., so that evening students would be free to attend only their latter stages.

At Pittsburgh, where there existed no dormitories, members lived as much as twenty miles from campus, and the last bus departed at 6:30, meetings initially were held at midday (12:30). Such a practice was recommended in 1958 by Councilor Williard Stone to Alpha Omega at Fordham, whose only problem appeared to be that of securing adequate attendance at business meetings by the sixty active members. In the late 1950s, Alpha Tau at Pitt moved all nomination meetings to 8:00 <u>A.M.</u>

Regardless of environment, the 80% standard gave chapters special incentive to promote high attendance by active members. Theta at Texas reported some problems in meeting the new requirement, during the first

year, but as of April (1958) had failed only once to achieve maximum points. To stimulate attendance, Theta had started a practice of filing a "probation letter," with the accounting department and the placement office, for members having more than minimal unexcused absences. Councilor Jencks commented that such an approach would probably work only if the letter were placed in the student's "permanent file."

Even prior to adoption of the 80% rule, the officers of Omega expressed support for a policy of placing on inactive status any member having two successive "unexcused absences," although it is not recorded that such a practice was actually followed at Miami. Formed just prior to the 1957 revision of category 4, Alpha Psi at West Virginia immediately adopted a "compulsory" attendance policy by which students could be removed from good standing for nonattendance. Similarly, Williard Stone reported in December 1957 that Alpha Phi at Temple would soon seek Council approval for increasing its own penalty for absentees. Stone himself, however, was somewhat skeptical of punitive approaches to the attendance problem, feeling that "the only real solution" lay "in having better meetings of genuine interest and value to the members."

Somewhat ironically, just before it was strengthened the officers at Texas had recommended that the attendance requirement be increased to <u>100%</u>, for full credit, and also be increased in relative weight within the activity program. Within context, these suggestions were made in support of smaller chapters, which presumably tended to operate at a comparative disadvantage in the special activities field.

Although Theta itself was by no means a "small" chapter, the reference was revealing because of the raising, some years earlier, of local scholastic requirements. The same membership limitation device that had strengthened

the chapter's performance in the "scholarship" category would later assist in in earning full credit for attendance. According, indeed, to Theta alumnus (by transfer from Chi at Oklahoma A. and M.) Nolan Williams, the chapter would sometimes delay the initiation of eligible students until the senior year to assure high grade averages, a practice attracting council concern in the latter 1950s.

The scholarship provision itself was left virtually unchanged from the first year, while the revisions in two other categories were dictated by external environmental changes.

Areas of Minimal, or Environmentally Dictated, Revision

Scholarship

The only change relative to "Scholarship" was the raising in the fall of 1951 of the cutoff for credit under the third component, concerning the chapterwide grade average of active members. Whereas during the first year credit had been granted for as low as a 2.50 average (20 points),the new minimum was 1.65 (for 60). This revision was evidently made at the discretion of Secretary-Treasurer Wedeberg.

"Newsletter" and Directory

When the annual *Newsletter* publication schedule was changed from three issues to two, in 1954, category 7 was duly revised to allocate 450 points for each local news report, rather than 300. The penalty for late submissions was maintained at 50 points per day, rather than also being increased proportionately.

The 1954 change in the policy concerning chapter *directories* had a far greater impact on the activity program. Previously, each chapter had been expected to produce a full directory once every three years, and to issue

supplements in the two intervening periods. With the elimination of the latter requirement, category 8 became applicable only every third year. As a result, over the last six years of the third era the maximum point total available was 5,200 except for 1956-57 and 1959-60, when the preparation of new directories was required.

A lesser change regarding the category may have been made earlier. The directory requirement included distribution by June 1 to the full membership of the chapter for whom addresses were available. In 1952-53 Omicron Chapter at Ohio State had failed to satisfy this provision, evidently under somewhat special circumstances, and at the suggestion of Secretary-Treasurer Wedeberg had appealed the unspecified penalty assessed. At the 1953 annual meeting, the Grand Council had voted to reduce the penalty to 50 points, perhaps as a specific ruling rather than as a change of policy.

Even disregarding the doubling of the point total from 500 to 1,000, the special activities area underwent more alteration in the 1950s than any other category aside from regular meetings.

Special Activities

The first four years, 1950-54

Details regarding the evaluation of special activities are not available for the first four years of the program. Initially, however, it appears that an itemized ratings schedule was used under which a chapter could accumulate *more* points in category 9 than the listed maximum. According to two authoritative sources, Delta Chapter at Washington was in 1950-51 awarded 600 points for special activities, 100 more than the number officially available. Over the following two years, five chapters earned the new official maximum total of 700 points, all of them in 1952-53, but no excess credit was awarded.

Implying that more points had been available, the Grand Council ruled in 1953 that henceforth "the raw scores for activity No. 9" would "be so adjusted that the highest score w[ould] be 700 (or not more than 700)." If greater than 700, the highest itemized total would be divided into that number to obtain a "proration" index. Then the highest raw score would be translated as 700 points, and all lower ones would be prorated by using the caluclated rate.

In 1953-54, accordingly, Iota at Southern Cal received 700 special activities points by virtue of leading the pack with an aggregate raw score of (at least approximately) 1,700. All other itemized scores were prorated using an index of .41. This approach would be abandoned, however, after only one year.

Fundamental revision in 1954, and later refinements

Besides increasing the credit total to 1,000 points, the Grand Council in 1954 responded to two areas of concern by substantially changing the evaluation process for category 9. At a general level, the deferral of point assignments until year's end was thought to have impaired chapter "incentive," while the "proration" approach in particular was felt to have had a "discouraging effect." The councilors no doubt recognized in the latter connection that variations in size or environment would favor some chapters over others in regard to activities of certain kinds.

Based particularly on the counsel of Tom Dickerson, the Council identified thirteen activity areas, including a miscellaneous subcategory, providing for a total of 1,600 points. No more than 1,000 points would be awarded a chapter, however, and there would be no proration. Hence chapters would accumulate points through the year up to the lower of the cited totals,

after which additional activities would not be counted. The itemized schedule adopted is reprinted as exhibit 14.

To limit maximum credit to chapters conducting a varied program of special activities, no single subcategory was allocated more than 200 points. A group could not achieve 1,000 points without participating in a minimum of six areas. The listing reflects no clear bias with respect to chapter size or environment. For example, while an urban setting would lend a comparative advantage in arranging joint professional gatherings (item c), location in a college town might be more conductive to holding extra chapter meetings (g). Certainly there was no intent to offset any bias associable with the attendance requirements also introduced in 1954, granting that they were not initially very rigorous.

Three items listed in exhibit 14 warrant special reference. The provision of as many as 100 points for extra meetings (g) recalls to mind John Arch White's concession a few years earlier to James McConahey that chapters maintaining unusually large schedules ought somehow to be rewarded in the ratings program for doing so. Former president White himself had proposed at the Grand Chapter meeting held between Council sessions of 1954 that faculty attendance be factored into the program, as was done through item l. Finally, component h gave credit for publication of an alumni newsletter or submission of alumni news to the national editor, although in another major act at the meeting the Council abandoned the idea of forming a special organization for such members.

In fundamentally revising the special activities factor, the governing body took a first step toward an overall approach to the activity program that would emerge a generation later. Based on the diversification embodied in exhibit 14, it was considered "quite possible that there w[would] be a

EXHIBIT 14

REVISED POLICY ON "SPECIAL ACTIVITIES," 1954

With the help of Professor T. M. Dickerson, past president and originator of the Activity Program, the Council made the following changes in point allocation:

1. Program points were reduced to 500.
2. Special Activity points were increased to a maximum of 1,000.

The maximum of 1,000 points in special activities can be earned out of a choice of 1,600 points as follows:

(a)	Orientation meeting of all commerce students where Beta Alpha Psi participates and promotes the field of accountancy	2	@	100	200
(b)	Tutoring sessions	10	@	20	200
(c)	Joint professional meetings such as A.I.A., N.A.C.A., A.K.Psi, etc.	2	@	100	200
(d)	Field trips	2	@	100	200
(e)	Community Activity (Accounting help)				50
(f)	Subscriptions to A.I.A. and A.A.A. journals. Senior Accounting majors as denominator and all subscriptions in numerator; each 5% 25 points				100
(g)	Extra chapter meetings	4	@	25	100
(h)	Alumni News Letter or Alumni News reported to National for News Letter	2	@	50	100
(i)	Write-ups in newspaper mentioning local chapter	5	@	10	50
(j)	Chapter employment activity				100
(k)	Social and athletic activities	4	@	25	100
(l)	Faculty attendance at meetings 10 points each faculty other than F.V.P.				100
(m)	Miscellaneous activities				100
					1,600

Reprinted from "Grand Council News," by [A. J. Penz], Newsletter 4 (November 1954):201.

number of ties in the upper bracket." Relative to one category, the Council had accepted the suggestion of the faculty advisor to Chi Chapter at Oklahoma A. and M. "that an achievable standard be set for the Activity Program which would enable most chapters to achieve standard." In expressing this viewpoint at the Grand Chapter meeting, Professor George McCowen foreshadowed the appearance in the 1970s of a highly flexible program lending itself to the achievement by many chapters of maximum points in a given year.

In 1959 a new 100-point subcategory was added to the special activities listing, "Cooperation with other accounting organizations in programs or campaigns to promote interest in accounting careers." No changes were made in the weighting of other items. Examples cited of such activity were distribution of a contemporary pamphlet titled "Young Eyes on Accounting," and visitation with state society members to high-school career days. Three years earlier Alpha Tau at Pittsburgh had complained to visitation officer S. M. Wedeberg that an accounting symposium for student recruitment conducted with the state society (to which chapter members had devoted 200 hours in preparation) deserved four times the 25 points available under subcategory g, "Extra chapter meetings." Wedeberg encouraged Alpha Tau to request 100 points, leaving the matter to the discretion of Secretary-Treasurer Jencks.[5]

---

[5]Carey, Rise of Profession 2:511-12; exhibit 14; [Foye committee], "Beta Alpha Psi Uniform System of Accounting," p. 8, quoting "Addendum"; Grand Council Minutes Book, 1950, p. [3], 1951, pp. 4-5, 1952, p. 1, 1953, pp. 4-5, 1954, pp. 3, 6, 1957, p. 4, 1959, p. 3 (each quoted), 1951, p. 1, 1952, pp. 2-3, 5, 7, 1953, p. 1, 1954, pp. 4-5, 1960, p. 2; Leon E. Hay to Author, interview, May 2, 1980, quoted; [W. B. Jencks], "Grand Council News," Newsletter 4 (November 1956):339, quoted; [Jencks], Secretary-Treasurer's Report, 1955-56, pp. 4, [7], 1956-57, pp. 5, 9; Jencks, Visitation Reports--Zeta, March 28, 1958, item 2.2, Theta, April 14, 1958, nos. 2.2, 2.3 (quoted), 4 (quoted), Pi, February 21, 1958, no. 2.2, Omega, March 28, 1956, no. 2.3 (quoted), Alpha Omicron, May 11, 1956, no. 2.2 (quoted), Alpha Psi, November 18, 1957, no. 4; "[Local] Chapter News," Newsletter [3], full title, (March 1952):18, 28 (quoted), 4 (April 1956):315, (April 1957):396, 5 (November 1957):29; "National Statutes," National Constitution and Statutes of Beta Alpha Psi Fraternity (1949, 1951), chapter 7, subsection 73b-4, both quoted; C. Rollin Niswonger, Visitation Report--Nu, November 20, 1959,

In Transition

Since the points competition was intended, in part, to stimulate high-quality local operations, some form of recognition for leading chapters was clearly needed. A two-part "symbolic" reward system emerged early in a decade during which several chapters consistently finished high in the ratings, particularly on the basis of excellent performance in scholarship and, after 1957, attendance.

---

supplemental page; [A. J. Penz], "Chapter Activity Plan," 1953-54, Newsletter 4 (November 1954):213; [Penz], "Chapter Activity Program," Newsletter 4 (April 1955):241; [Penz], "Chapter Rating Plan Scores," 1952-53, Newsletter 4 (November 1953):107; Williard E. Stone, Visitation Reports--Xi, October 25, 1957, no. 4 (quoted), Alpha Tau, December 11, 1957, Alpha Phi, December 12, 1957, Alpha Omega, December 6, 1958, Beta Alpha, May 5, 1959, Beta Gamma (and Gamma), February 5, 1960 (letter formats in last five cases); [S. M. Wedeberg], "Beta Alpha Psi Chapter Rating Plan Results," 1950-51, Newsletter [3] (November 1951):14, 1951-52, 4 (November 1952):13; [Wedeberg], "Chapter Rating Plan," Newsletter [3] (March 1952):14; Wedeberg, Secretary-Treasurer's Report, 1952-53, p. 5; Wedeberg. Visitation Reports--Mu, June 4, 1954, no. 2.2, Tau, December 14, 1956 (et al.), no. 3.2, Alpha Gamma, June 3, 1954, no. 2.2 (quoted), Alpha Delta, May 8, 1952, nos. 2.3, 4 (quoted), Alpha Theta, November 13-15, 1952, no. 4 (quoted), Alpha Tau, November 27, 1956, nos. 2.2, 3.2; John A(rch) White, Secretary-Treasurer's Report, 1950-51, p. [5]; [Nolan E. Williams], Secretary-Treasurer's Report, 1957-58, p. [10]; Williams to Author, interview, March 21, 1980; and Willims, Visitation Reports--Theta, May 10, 1957, no. 2.3, Alpha Delta, November 5, 1959, no. 2.2, and Alpha Sigma, November 2, 1959, no. 2.3. Also, Burns and Coffman, Accounting Hall of Fame, pp. 23, 82.

CHAPTER 6

THE INTERCHAPTER COMPETITION IN ITS FIRST DECADE, A SERIOUS LOCAL CHALLENGE TO THE PROGRAM, AND AN EXPANDING COMMITMENT TO CHAPTER VISITATION

Counting retroactive coverage of the first and (in part) second years, the interchapter competition led from the start to special recognition for highly ranked groups. Examination of yearly results reveals the most critical factors within the evaluation process, identifies chapters consistently placed high or low in the standings, and permits limited generalization concerning campus environments favorable or unfavorable to strong performance.

A prolonged challenge to the activity program, from principle, was conducted by the _original_ fraternal unit. Alpha at Illinois represented an isolated failure for chapter _visitation_, a complementary program to which, as the chapter roster grew, the Grand Council became increasingly committed.

A Symbolic Reward System, and Competitive Results, 1950-60

Awards to Top Chapters: Certificates and a Rotating Plaque

At the 1951 Grand Chapter banquet, Professor T. M. Dickerson expressed gratification concerning the operation of his plan in its first year. He also recommended that some kind of award be presented each year to "winners of the competition." Three relevant proposals were made by banquet guests, including at least two former fraternal presidents:

a. Founder Hiram Scovill favored honoring the top three chapters each year with _certificates_ that "might be framed and hung in appropriate places"

b. Hermann Miller proposed the creation of an <u>illuminated scroll</u> that would be passed from one year's first-place chapter to the next, and on which would be recorded the name of each winning chapter and the year

c. It was also suggested that (following a tradition in the National Association of Cost Accountants) <u>banners</u> be awarded to the top finishers.

The Grand Council reconvened the day after the banquet, and on the motion of incoming president White "the Secretary was asked to proceed to order suitable banners for first, second, and third places in the chapter competition" of the year just ended. They were supposed to include the Beta Alpha Psi seal, chapter name, year, and competitive standing. In addition, new secretary-treasurer Wedeberg was instructed "to secure the price of drawings and specifications of a <u>permanent rotating award</u>" to honor first-place chapters (emphasis added).

For reasons not recorded, no banners would be produced. Nor were any bids or suggestions received in 1951-52 from the several firms contacted by Wedeberg regarding a rotating award. The secretary-treasurer had cited as a model a permanent emblem of selection to a '"Roll of Honor"' at Ohio State. Given that Professor Thomas Burns, a member of the staff since 1963, is unacquainted with any program by that name, the reference most likely was to the <u>Accounting Hall of Fame</u> created at Ohio State in 1950. Names of persons elected to that elite group are inscribed on a permanent <u>scroll</u> maintainted in the corridors of the university's business school. It is only fitting, then, that Professor Miller of Ohio State had recommended the preparation of a permanent scroll.

By default, Scovill's recommendation was adopted in 1952, and emblematic <u>certificates</u> were conferred upon the top three chapters from each of the first two years of competition. Those for 1951-52 were presented at the annual Grand Chapter meeting to Nu at Colorado, Omicron at Ohio State, and Alpha Beta at Alabama. The format is illustrated in the first part of

exhibit 15. As implied in the example, a certificate bore the name of the incoming president rather than the outgoing one, who would have served during the award year.

Secretary-Treasurer Wedeberg enlisted the aid of former fraternal presidents from Ohio State, on the advice of the Council, as he carried forth the objective of developing a rotating first-place award. Working from ideas suggested by Professors Hermann Miller and W. E. Dickerson, the L. G. Balfour Company during the year 1952-53 produced an appropriate plaque, at a cost of $84.65. It was presented to the year's leading chapter, Gamma at Northwestern, at the 1953 Grand Chapter meeting. The names of prior first-place groups Nu and Theta Chapters had also been engraved on the "trophy," along with the appropriate years. Six spaces remained for entering the names of future winning chapters.

The 1952 and 1953 gatherings commenced a tradition of presenting the first-place plaque and the three (or five) certificates, ordinarily to current faculty vice-presidents, at the yearly Grand Chapter meeting. During the latter year, however, six chapters were honored, based (as related below) on the recognition of ties for second and third places. The faculty vice-presidents of five of them were in attendance, while Councilor J. C. Gibson was present on behalf of Sigma at Wisconsin. Because the 1952-53 standings had not been finalized until a Council session of three days earlier, however, not all of the certificates were as yet available for presentation.

After Theta had in 1956-57 finished in first place for the third time, it was decided that the original plaque should be retired by the Texas chapter, and be replaced by a new one. The "quite big and heavy" plaque shown in exhibit 15 (second part) was duly shipped to Austin, where in 1985

EXHIBIT 15

EMBLEMATIC AWARDS FOR TOP CHAPTERS
Original First - place Plaque

EXHIBIT 15 Continued

Sample Certificate for Top Three of Five Chapters

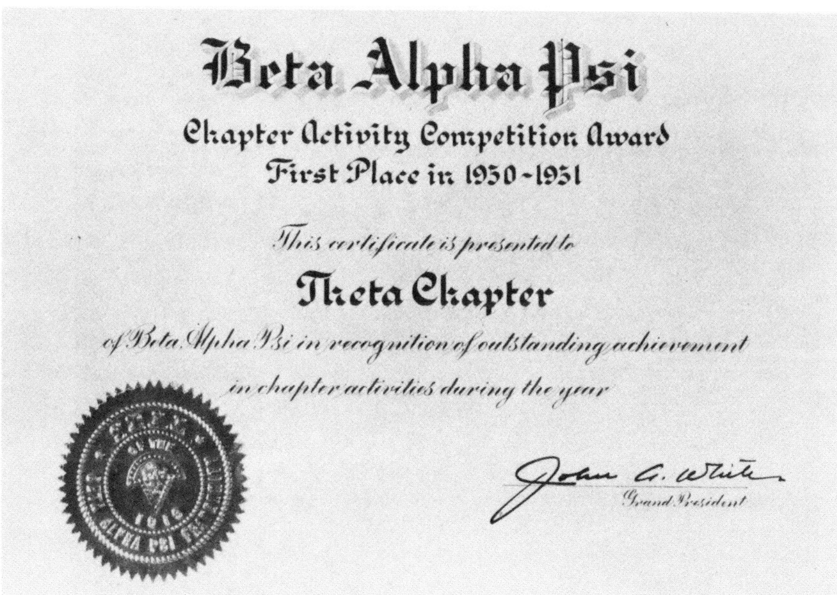

Photographs supplied by Professor Bobbe M. Barnes, faculty vice-president of Theta Chapter at Texas.

it would adorn the office of a recent recipient of the Outstanding Faculty Vice-President Award, Professor Bobbe M. Barnes. A plaque "identical" to the original one was supplied by Balfour, for $53.26, in time for presentation to Omicron in 1958.

Recognizing that the fraternal roster had grown substantially during the fifties, the Council in 1958 increased the yearly certificate awards from the top three chapters to the top five. Acting on the advice of an advisory committee made up of past presidents, the governing body rejected respective plans by which certificates and medallions would have been issued each year to the ten groups. Consideration of the latter options may have been an outgrowth of a decision made three years earlier to limit Newsletter reports of the annual standings to the first ten chapters.

Only one of the first three first-place chapters would enjoy continuing prominence in the ratings/activity program of the 1950s, leading a group of consistently competitive units. In general, they were distinguished by strong performance in the rather isolated nonprocedural categories.

A Synopsis of High-ranking Chapters

An overall concentration of leadership

Over the first decade, eight different chapters finished first in the annual competition. Only Theta led the field more than once, winning the competition in 1950-51, 1955-56, and 1956-57, under three different faculty vice-presidents. The other winners were:

1. Nu at Colorado, 1951-52
2. Gamma at Northwestern, 1952-53
3. Alpha Beta at Alabama, 1953-54
4. Alpha Delta at Pennsylvania, 1954-55
5. Omicron at Ohio State, 1957-58
6. Alpha Theta at Mississippi, 1958-59
7. Alpha Psi at West Virginia, 1959-60.

These results obscure, however, a prevailing pattern of high concentration of a select group of chapters among the leaders. As earlier mentioned, through 1958 certificates were awarded to the top three chapters, while in the next two years five chapters were honored. Exceptions to the original practice occurred in 1953, when six chapters were honored, and in 1955, when a fourth chapter was cited. In each case the chapters awarded certificates were tightly bunched in the point standings, standing well ahead of any others, and in the first instance ties (two- and three-way) were declared for second and third places.

In accordance with the practices (and exceptions) indicated, a total of 38 certificates were conferred during the 1950s, to a contingent of 16 chapters. Seven units received only one certificate, including first-place finishers Nu and Gamma. Four others earned two awards--Alpha Delta, Alpha Psi (which existed only in the final three years), Sigma at Wisconsin, and Alpha Zeta at Denver. The remaining 23 certificates were distributed among five chapters:

a. Theta, 3 firsts and 4 seconds
b. Omicron, 1 first, 3 seconds and 1 third
c. Alpha Beta, 1 first and 4 thirds
d. Alpha Theta, 1 first and 2 seconds
e. Alpha Iota at Arkansas, 2 thirds and 1 fifth.

The latter two chapters were formed during the first two years of the ratings program, while Alpha Beta had been installed less than two years before.

These five chapters, four from the southern United States, represented the leading general-purpose public universities of their states. Each school was located in either a moderate-sized state capital (Austin or Columbus) or a college town. Perhaps most significantly, all were predominantly residential universities, granting that (as illustrated by later reference

to low-ranking chapters) such environments provided no guarantee of even adequate performance.

Probably a more significant (if not altogether independent) factor is that all five chapters enjoyed extremely strong support from the local accounting faculties. Such support was virtually assured at Ohio State by the presence on campus of former councilors Hermann Miller (who died in 1955), Bill Dickerson, and Jacob Taylor, and of 1957-58 president Bill Jencks. Visitation reports of the day reveal a similar pattern in each of the other cases. Regular chapter involvement by all accounting professors was reported in some instances, including a 1960 visitation to Alabama, which had a 10-member staff. The lowest level of regular faculty participation was 8 out of 11 at Texas in 1957-58, representing "excellent" support according to visitor Jencks.

It is noteworthy that each chapter except Alpha Theta was represented on the Grand Council in the 1950s, and that the faculty advisor to that group in its first-place year (Charles Taylor) would eventually serve at that level. Broad faculty support was especially vital at Mississippi because, except for the chapter's first (full) year, 1951-52, Alpha Theta had replaced its faculty vice-president annually, a practice rather unlikely to enhance operating continuity. Within an accounting department reported as having five members in 1952 and four in 1960, six different men had already served as faculty advisor at "Ole Miss."

Before turning to the other end of the spectrum, the upper-tier standings may be analyzed briefly to identify the critical factors within the program so far as chapter placement was concerned.

Critical, or "differentiating," factors

For those factors calling simply for procedural compliance of one

PRESIDENT WILLIARD E. STONE PRESENTS FIRST-PLACE PLAQUE TO ALPHA THETA FVP CHARLES W. TAYLOR, 1959

kind or another, receipt of maximum credit would be essentially a matter of chapter discretion. Accordingly, one would expect the critical, or "differentiating," elements to be those at least partly nonprocedural, or non-"programmed," in nature. The results over the first ten years of the activity program fully support this expectation.

Throughout the decade, seven categories were basically procedural or programmed, considering that the annual plan and periodic budget (items 1 and 2) need not be correct forecasts of actual events, and two were not. The fundamental revisions made in 1954 reversed the roles of two elements, however. Item 6, the scholarship provision, was certainly not a programmed category, although chapters might increase the likelihood of attaining high credit by setting admission standards higher than national requirements. In the early years, also, the special activities element (no. 9) was essentially nonprocedural, particularly when a proration approach was used.

The special activities case was changed, however, by the 1954 revision that enabled chapters routinely to plan their point totals. Item 4 was largely deprogrammed at the same time, by making 80% of the credit dependent upon attendance. To be sure, the original requirement of only 50% attendance, for full credit, was not a difficult standard for many chapters. The later 80% requirement was far more demanding, although some control could be achieved through establishing local policies governing attendance.

During the first two years of the program, 1950-52, no clear differentiating factors were apparent. The chapters were learning the ratings process, with the result that achievement of maximum points in the procedural areas was less routine than it would soon become. Closest to perfection in those areas was Theta Chapter in year 1, when the Texas group earned all but 50 points in the five procedural areas that were evaluated. In the two

other categories, Theta obtained 400 of the 600 points available for scholarship, and 300 of 500 for a special activities.

By 1952-53, however, a predictable pattern had begun to emerge. The top six chapters (all honored with certificates) stood where they did largely through their performance in the special activities and, secondarily, scholarship fields. Four of them achieved the full 700 points available in the former area, and the two others received at least 590, while only one other chapter even topped 400 points in the category. Further, two of the top three chapters, Gamma and Theta, achieved maximum points in all seven procedural areas of the day, so that the 50-point difference between them was attributable entirely to the two categories just cited.

The following year, the pattern was more pronounced as four of top five chapters, representing an appreciable range of 380 points, each received maximum points in the seven procedural areas. After 1954, it would become increasingly broader and more entrenched as category 4, regular meetings, replaced number 9, special activities, as a nonprogrammed item. With an isolated exception of the fifth-ranking chapter in 1956-57, over each of the next six years from the top five to the top ten chapters had maximum scores for special activities, and also for every other category aside from (4) and (6).

During the decade no chapter achieved maximum points in scholarship. For the first three years of the attendance requirement, when it was set at 50% of active members, the lowest score attained in category 4 among the top five chapters was 784 out of 800, and maximum points were earned in 11 of the 15 cases. With the raising of the requirement to 80% in 1957, however, 800 points would be earned in the regular meetings category only once during the first two years, by Alpha Iota at Arkansas in 1957-58.

Competition was extremely keen in several years. The closest bunching

occurred in 1957-58, when only 23 points separated first-place Omicron Chapter and sixth-place Alpha Iota. The highest scores were earned by Alpha Psi in 1959-60 and Theta three years earlier, which finished respectively 37 and 38 points short of the maximum of 6.000, although the 5,181 points earned by Alpha Theta in the non-directory year 1954-55 represented the strongest performance recorded in the 1950s.

Ironically, in a visitation report issued virtually at the close of Theta's biggest year in terms of points, 1956-57, Nolan Williams stated that there was a "dangerous trend" of member inactivity at Texas, suggestive of an "honor[ary]" concept of Beta Alpha Psi. New faculty advisor Robert E. Seiler, who had served Omega Chapter at Miami in the same role after completing doctoral work at Alabama, had earlier been described by Councilor A. J. Penz as "on the inactive side," fraternally. At any rate, with the adoption the following summer of the 80% requirement, any such "trend" at Texas was promptly checked at least in terms of attendance.[1]

---

[1]Bobbe M. Barnes, Theta Chapter faculty vice-president, to Author, June 5, 1985, with enclosures; Thomas J. Burns to Author, by telephone, June 25, 1985; Burns and Coffman, Accounting Hall of Fame, p. 81; "Grand Chapter," Newsletter [3] (November 1951 - May 1952), 4 (November 1952 - April 1957), 5 (November 1957, April 1959 - May 1960):3rd p. (listing faculty advisors); "Grand Chapter Meeting," Grand Council Minutes Book, 1954-60, including reference to replacement plaque, 1958, p. [8]; Grand Council Minutes Book, 1951, pp. 5 (quoted), 6, 1955, pp. 2-4, 1957, pp. [3-4], 1958, pp. 1-[2]; Hasselback, 1984 Directory, individual listing, s.v. "Burns, Thomas J."; [W. B. Jencks], "Grand Council News," Newsletter 4 (November 1955):269, quoted; [Jencks], "In Memoriam," Newsletter 4 (November 1955):266; Jencks, Visitation Report--Theta, April 14, 1958, items 2.2, 3.1; [Richard W. Metcalf], "Outstanding Faculty Vice President Award," 1983-84 Annual Report, ed.[Metcalf], p. 2; National Association of Accountants: NAA Trophy and Banner Winning Chapters - 1925 to Present" ([New York: NAA, 1965]), 8 pp. supplied by Sophie Richards, NAA National Office, June 28, 1985; [A. J. Penz], "First Place Gamma Chapter, Northwestern University," Newsletter 4 (November 1953):110; [Penz], "Grand Council News," Newsletter 4 (November 1953):104-105; Penz ("Andy") to Jencks ("Bill"), note attached to Vititation Report--Omega, by Jencks, March 28, 1956, quoted; [Penz], "Rating Plan Scores," Newsletter 4 (November 1953):107; Secretary-Treasurers' Reports, 1953-54 through 1959-60, listings of chapter standings; Smith Forty Acres, pp. 74-75, 172; [S. M. Wedeberg], "Grand Council News,"

Just as there was a concentration of chapters at the top, so there were were other local units that commonly finished very low in the activity standings. Sometimes, at least, the chapter did not accept the emphasis of Beta Alpha Psi upon professional activity, as in the most conspicuous instance of consistently weak performance.

"Leading" Noncompetitive Chapters, Representative Factors, and a Prominent Case Study

General Overview

As just discussed, the top three chapters (generally) were honored each year until 1958, and the top five were recognized thereafter. Low-ranking groups may be cited on a parallel basis, omitting units (one of which, Alpha Mu at Kentucky, surpassed 12 established chapters after formation on March 29) created during a given year. Over the decade, 17 chapters were listed among the last three or (1958-60) five in the points competition. Only 6 groups were included more than once, and 4 more than twice.

Three chapters placed only once among the "leading" noncompetitive units were last in those years: Xi at Syracuse, 1952-53; Alpha Xi at Detroit, 1954-55; and Alpha Delta at Penn, 1959-60. Early in 1954, visitation officer A. J. Penz found Xi to be in a "disorganized state," based in part on conflict between the faculty advisor and the departmental and college administration, and absence of any other faculty participation. These

---

Newsletter 4 (November 1952):5-6; [Wedeberg], "Rating Plan Results," Newsletter [3] (November 1951):14, 4 (November 1952):13; Wedeberg, Secretary-Treasurer's Report, 1951-52, p. 7 (quoted), 1952-53, pp. 2, 5-6; Wedeberg, Visitation Report--Alpha Theta, November 13-15, 1952, no. 3.1; John A(rch) White, Visitation Report--Alpha Iota, May 21, 1952, no. 3.1; [Nolan E. Williams], Secretary-Treasurer's Report, 1957-58, p. 3, quoted; and Williams, Visitation Reports--Theta, May 10, 1957, nos. 2.2 (quoted), 3.1, Alpha Beta, February 22, 1960, no. 3.1, and Alpha Theta, February 22, 1960, no. 3.1. According to the filed reports, President Williams had also visited both Alpha Delta at Pennsylvania and Beta Epsilon at Lehigh on the same date, November 5, 1959.

problems had been resolved by the time of the next visit, more than three years later, but the fact that a very high proportion of active members held jobs had complicated chapter operations.

Alpha Xi and Alpha Delta represented schools with many nonresident students, located in two of the nation's largest cities. The Detroit chapter finished last in its first full year, having been formed only following a year's delay due to the marginal size of the local accounting program. A visitation in the fall of 1955, however, revealed that half of the eight members of the department regularly participated in fraternal activity. At Pennsylvania, problems posed by the prevalence of employed students and night classes were combined with a remarkable concentration of prelaw students among the active membership (all but two members in the fall of 1960). In keeping with the latter factor, "tax talks by lawyers" had come to dominate the chapter program.

Ironically, Alpha Delta had in 1954-55, under the leadership of Williard Stone, _led_ the annual competition. A similar contrast occurred at Gamma Chapter at Northwestern, which stood last in 1958-59, six years after leading the pack, and a year after finishing ahead of just two other units. Several of Gamma's problems have been noted in earlier coverage, including a mainly nonresidential membership within an urban environment twenty-five miles in length, a general policy limiting initiation to seniors, and high eligibility requirements. In addition, meetings (usually featuring a Chicago speaker) frequently conflicted with a CPA coaching course enrolling a number of local accounting majors. Still another complication was the time-consuming political career of Professor Ambrose M. Reiter, the faculty vice-president at Northwestern since 1955, and it was compounded by unusually low overall faculty interest in the chapter. Following Reiter's reelection in 1959 as a reform mayor of neighboring Skokie, Illinois, the Gamma membership selected

prior faculty vice-president F. Virgil Boyd as their '"honorary advisor"', to the embarrassment of both men. From a department of a dozen members (1958), eleven of whom belonged to Beta Alpha Psi, Boyd was the only other accounting professor to participate regularly in chapter activity.

Gamma was joined as a chapter twice ranked near the bottom by a still more conspicuously commuter-oriented urban group. Before the onset of alumni dominance, Mu at New York stood next-to-last in the first two years of the program.

Finally, four chapters often finished low in the points standings:

a. Alpha at Illinois - three firsts and one third (reverse-order ranks)
b. Beta at Oregon - one first, two seconds, and three thirds
c. Alpha Epsilon at SMU - one first, two seconds, and one third
d. Phi at LSU - one first, three seconds, and one fifth.

Like the frequent *highly*-ranked units, ironically, each of these chapters except Alpha Epsilon represented a predominantly residential public university in a college town or (in the last case) moderate-sized state capital.

Alpha's strong dedication to an "honor-society" concept, deemphasizing professional activity, is documented presently. The relevance of such an attitude to weak performance at Beta is much less clear. In 1948, Secretary-Treasurer W. E. Dickerson described the chapter as being in a "slump," holding few meetings other than initiation. Four years later, when Beta once again was not conducting regular sessions, visiting councilor C. C. Staehling cited a "lack of direction" on the part of a faculty vice-president whose midyear resignation, to devote full time to public accounting, had temporarily left the group without an advisor. As noted in chapter 3 relative to the low initiation levels found at Oregon, two later visitation reports were genuinely favorable, especially concerning faculty leadership. No doubt low membership (associated in 1958 with "very selective" standards) contributed somewhat to Beta's low standing in the activity

program, but with still lower induction rates Alpha Kappa at Ohio consistently posted a stronger performance.

Alpha Epsilon was afflicted by common problems of a major urban environment (Dallas), including student employment and evening classes, although regular participation by <u>all</u> six or seven members of the accounting department was twice reported. Just after the close of the third era, Emerson Henke reported that there was a lack of "cohesiveness" at Southern Methodist, and that the members tended to place social activities and work ahead of Beta Alpha Psi participation. Possibly the most serious problem, however, was the discontinuity that resulted from the chaper's general practice of delaying initiation until the senior year.

In the early years, of the ratings program, especially, Phi suffered from weak faculty support. During an early 1953 visit to Baton Rouge, Councilor Penz (a faculty alumnus of the chaper's) found that the faculty vice-president was none too knowledgeable about fraternal objectives, and that no one else in the department seemed interested in chapter activities. In addition, the new faculty advisor bore the responsibilities of departmental chairman. The program at Louisiana State was basically limited to periodic initiations, and Penz was unable to "get any rise . . . whatsoever" from chapter officers when he requested policy or operating recommendations from them.

Phi's condition had improved somewhat by the end of the 1950s, according to a visitation report by Nolan Williams. At least three of the six accounting professors at LSU had become involved in chapter activities, but Williams felt that faculty interest needed to be developed further. He had found the chapter officers, who were involved in numerous other campus activities, to have a very limited understanding of Beta Alpha Psi.

There was considerable variation during the 1950s in the point totals of low-ranking chapters, irrespective of the variation in total points available brought about by the 1954 policy revision on directories. Only Beta, in 1951-52, was credited with no points at all. The next lowest total was 450, posted twice by Alpha. By contrast, Gamma achieved nearly 2.000 points as the lowest ranked chapter of 1958-59, two years after Phi had earned more than 1,600 while placing last. The totals recorded by chapters ranked third lowest in the standings ranged from 735 points by Rho at Minnesota in 1951-52 to 2,332 by Nu at Colorado seven years later, when 800 fewer points were available.[2]

A prolonged challenge was waged against the activity program, as understood by the national leadership, by the oldest Beta Alpha Psi unit.

Alpha Chapter's Persistent Dedication to an "Honor Society" Concept

From the beginning, Alpha at Illinois strongly resisted participation

---

[2] AAA Road Atlas, p. 36; W. E. Dickerson to James M. McConahey, May 29, 1948, quoted; "Grand Chapter," Newsletter 4 (April 1955):231, (November 1955):263; Emerson Henke, Visitation Report--Alpha Epsilon, December 19, 1960 (letter format), quoted; W. B. Jencks, Visitation Report--Gamma, February 24, 1958, items 2.2, 2.4, and to Councilors, March 3, 1958; Jencks, Visitation Report--Alpha Epsilon, April 16, 1958 (letter), no. 3.1; [A. J. Penz], "Rating Plan Scores," Newsletter 4 (November 1953):107; Penz, Visitation Report--Xi, March 21-22, 1954, nos. 2.4, 3.1, and to faculty advisor Lauren Brush, March 29, 1954 (quoted); Penz, Visitation Report--Phi, February 23, 1953, nos. 2.3 (quoted), 2.4, 3.4, 4; Secretary-Treasurers' Reports, 1953-54 through 1959-60, listings of chapter standings; Wayne E. Shroyer, Visitation Report--Beta, December 17, 1958 (letter), quoted; C. C. Staehling, Visitation Report--Beta, May 27, 1952, nos. 1 (supplemental comment), 2.3 (quoted); W. E. Stone, Visitation Reports--Gamma, May 2, 1959, February 5, 1960 (letters), Xi, October 25, 1957, nos. 3, 4 (quoted), Alpha Xi, November 28, 1955, 3.1; R. M. Van Voorhis, Visitation Report--Alpha Delta, December 14, 1960 (letter), quoted; [S. M. Wedeberg], "Rating Plan Results," Newsletter [3] (November 1951):14, 4 (November 1952):13; and Nolan E. Williams, Visitation Reports--Phi, February 24, 1960, nos. 2.1, 3.1, and Alpha Epsilon, December 10-11, 1957, nos. 2.2, 3.1.

in the program, based on the premise that by tradition the chapter was an "honor society" that left professional activity mainly to a local "accountancy club." The first few years were capped by a notably unproductive visitation to the campus in 1955. Chapter performance improved somewhat near the close of the decade without any discernible change in underlying viewpoints, despite the harmonious coexistence elsewhere (and earlier at Illinois itself) of active chapters with accounting clubs or societies. Resistance to the activity program would indeed prevail at Illinois for another era, and beyond, until sanctions were finally imposed against Alpha in 1975.

The early years, 1950-55

Developments through 1953-54

The charter fraternal unit was a "problem chapter" from the outset of the rating program. During the first three years, Alpha earned points only for initiation reports and Newsletter submissions, except for 100 attained one year (of the 800 available) in the regular meetings category.

At the annual meeting following the third year of competition, the Grand Council in 1953 added to the constitution (article 7, section 5) a provision governing chapter noncompliance with constitutional or statutory responsibilities:

> The Grand Council shall notify any chapter in case of a delinquency. If such delinquency is not removed within three academic months from date of notification, such chapter shall be placed on probation for a period of six academic months. If at the end of probation said delinquency still exists, the Grand Council shall have the power to suspend or take any action it deems necessary for the good of the Fraternity.

This policy naturally included in its coverage any statutory requirements incorporated within the ratings program.

As implied above, Alpha Chapter had in particular not been complying

with basic financial reporting requirements. Nor did it advise the Grand Council in 1953 of a change in officership, contrary to chapter 7, subsection 73b, of the statutes. Secretary-Treasurer A. J. Penz had learned that the treasurership had changed hands only by happenstance, rather than through a report duly submitted by the chapter within one week.

In light of these delinquencies, and a much broader pattern of non-communication from Urbana-Champaign, Penz wrote the Alpha president and treasurer in December 1953 to report the Grand Council's serious concern. In his letter to chapter president James A. Hanley, he observed that Alpha was "not participating" in the ratings program, leaving the Council "in the dark," and called his attention to President S. M. Wedeberg's article "Friendly Chapter Competition" from the November _Newsletter_. Writing the local treasurer ten days later, the national secretary-treasurer enclosed a copy of the newly revised constitution, making express reference to the addition of the passage cited above.

Penz forwarded a copy of the first letter to Faculty Vice-President H. E. Breen, serving his _tenth_ year in the post (omitting 1943-46), and wrote him independently one or more times later in the academic year. There was no response from Breen, however, or (apparently) from the student officers. The 1953-54 ratings results themselves were scarcely encouraging. For the first time Alpha had finished _last_ in the standings, garnering, from initiations and periodical copy, just 700 points.

The stage was set for a more explicit challenge to the activity program by Alpha Chapter, operating under new faculty leadership.

Alpha challenges the program, fall 1954

The Grand Council coincidentally met on the Illinois campus late in the summer of 1954, as the fraternity continued its long practice of meeting

in conjunction with the American Accounting Association. Dean Paul M. Green of the College of Commerce and Business Administration, and Alpha president Harold E. Arnett, since 1962 an accounting professor at Michigan, welcomed the group assembled for the annual Grand Chapter banquet. One of the guests in attendance was Professor Norton M. Bedford, Omicron '47, the newly appointed faculty vice-president of the local chapter. He had moved to Illinois from Washington of St. Louis the preceding January.

The Council's concern about Alpha Chapter was evidently expressed to the new advisor during the course of the meetings, or very shortly thereafter. On September 30, 1954, Bedford wrote all five councilors to defend the practices of his chapter, and seek for it an exemption from participation in the activity program. He asserted that Alpha had functioned in essence as an '"honorary organization"' from the start, leading to the formation of a local '"accountancy club"' as a base for '"professional"' activity. The local membership objected to the fraternity's '"low"' scholastic requirements, and viewed involvement in the competitive program as a clear threat to chapter values. The faculty vice-president accordingly proposed that chapters be permitted <u>to withdraw</u> from the annual competition if they had genuine reasons for doing so.

As implied in volume 1, the fraternity had in fact originated at Illinois substantially as a professional organization, although a significant honorary element had emerged promptly. As indicated below more importantly, Alpha Chapter had maintained its professional commitment while cooperating with the accountancy club in that group's early years. Further, the reference made to Alpha's high scholastic requirements was not fully to the point, since the constitution defined only minimum standards, and those chapters that exceeded them stood to benefit in the critical scholarship element of the program. Nonspecific references of the day, and

reported 1966-67 requirements of a 4.5 average in accounting and a 4.3 average overall, on a 5.0-scale, support the belief that contemporary entry conditions at Illinois were unusually high.

Any historical inaccuracies on Bedford's part were fully understandable, since he had been appointed at Illinois only after the retirement of early fraternal presidents Hiram Scovill, A. C. Littleton, and Charles Schlatter, as well as charter secretary-treasurer E. J. Filbey. From the same generation of accounting professors, Lloyd Morey, far less identified with Beta Alpha Psi, was closing out his career by serving as president of the university.

The reaction of the Grand Council to Bedford's letter was uniformly negative, but restrained. Secretary-Treasurer Penz wrote his colleagues immediately after receiving it that he waas "astonished" by the viewpoint expressed, and considered the problem to be "quite serious." Observing that "Alpha wants all the rights and privileges without <u>any</u> responsibility" (his empahsis), he felt that the case was pivotal to fraternal policy. Penz suggested that President J. C. Gibson, from Wisconsin, name a councilor to handle the matter, seeking a solution based on "facts and figures, reactions and opinions [obtained] from all Councilors." Three weeks later, he volunteered to take the lead himself, while also suggesting that Wayne Shroyer, who was "quite experienced in handling difficult chapters" (an unclear reference), would be a logical choice for the assignment.

In the interim, the secretary-treasurer had received letters similar to Bedford's from chapter president Arnett and department head C. A. Moyer, Hiram Scovill's successor. He had written Arnett that the matter was being referred to a committee, presumably meaning a newly formed advisory group made up of past presidents Wedeberg (chair), Staehling, and White. Shortly thereafter, President Gibson asked "Wede" to contact "Charlie and

John Arch" in this connection. He felt that Alpha's request for exemption from the program should be granted only if "refusal . . . would be disastrous," but had more questions than answers concerning proper strategy. In particular, the president wondered whether either Scovill or Hermann Miller could be of assistance, asking whether the fraternal founder might instead "be on the other side."

No record exists of Charles Staehling's comments or suggestions on the issue. As fraternal president two years earlier, however, he had contributed a strong endorsement of the activity program to the Newsletter ('We have no category of "passive" membership'), and solicited from the aforementioned Professor Miller a brief article emphasizing the professional side of Beta Alpha Psi.

S. M. Wedeberg and John Arch White were in agreement that a reasonable level of activity should be expected from Alpha Chapter, but that it should not strictly be forced to participate in the activity competition. The latter concession was presumably not intended to relax statutory reporting requirements in any way, or undermine the new rule supporting them with disciplinary sanctions, but it did mark the first known Council anticipation of a "voluntary" interpretation of the activity program. Wedeberg added that the Grand Council should try to "appeal to their good sportsmanship" to secure acceptance of chapter competition at Illinois.

Both past presidents considered Bedford to be mistaken on basic points, beginning with the apparent assumption that Alpha had from its earliest days emphasized honorary elemets, to the exclusion of professional activity. Relatedly, the premise that in conducting a broad program the chapter would only be competing with the local accountancy club was challenged. Professor Wedeberg pointed out that Maryland's accounting club complemented Tau by

serving sophomores planning to major in the field, and juniors and seniors ineligible for initiation to the fraternity.

New councilor W. B. Jencks had a similar policy perspective, although, apparently after making inquiries at Ohio State, he rather surprisingly accepted the faculty vice-president's historical interpretation of the Illinois chapter. Perhaps his colleagues Jacob Taylor and Hermann Miller had developed a largely honorary image of Alpha from their prewar association on the Grand Council with Littleton, Schlatter, and W. E. Karrenbrock (who had moved from Illinois to UCLA during his own tenure).

At any rate, Jencks felt that it would be most unfortunate either to make the activity program merely optional, or to "push" the chapter to the point of withdrawing from the fraternity. He noted that at the Ohio State business school, where no accounting club had been formed, Omicron "compete[d] to a greater or lesser degree" with certain other Greek-letter organizations, yet coexisted in mutual harmony with each of them. The new councilor felt that the key to the issue lay in whether regular meetings were being conducted at Illinois; if they were, the chapter should be able to earn around 4,200 points, "a fair score."

Delta was cited at this juncture as a chapter that conducted more than an adequate program, inclusive of full constitutional compliance, without showing appreciable concern about accumulating points. Ironically, <u>Alpha itself</u> was reportedly rather active, in 1954-55, in efforts to "promot[e] closer relations between faculty and students" and, through joint meetings with other campus groups, "enlighten . . . members as to the problems faced by other factions of management." These citations from President Arnett's November <u>Newsletter</u> dispatch imply that a major part of the chapter's deficiency at the time lay strictly, as perhaps suspected by

Councilor Jencks, in the reporting area.

Jencks concluded by recommending that the Grand Council pursue with Norton Bedford a cooperative approach rather than one of confrontation. Unfortunately, if not surprisingly in view of the delicate balance the leadership wished to strike between making the activity program optional and strictly enforcing compliance, such cooperation proved to be very elusive, despite a significant effort made by Councilor Penz early in 1955.

An unproductive visitation by
A. J. Penz, February 1955

At some point in 1954, the secretary-treasurer wrote his good friend Dean Paul Green, Alpha '29, to share with him the governing body's serious concern about the local chapter. Since Penz would in 1980 relate it to the nonresponse by Faculty Vice-President H. E. Breen to his letters of 1953-54, this contact may have preceded Norton Bedford's letter, and even have contributed to the appointment of a new chapter advisor. According at an any rate to the third-era councilor, the dean "called the FVP [Breen] on the carpet," prompting a meeting among accountancy faculty to defend their colleague and protest Council "interfer[ence]" with chapter operations.

Against this background of policy disagreement and delicate personal sentiment, Penz visited the University of Illinois on February 19, 1955. He was greeted warmly at the train station (or airport) by Professor Bedford. Meeting with him on campus later on, Bedford and student members of Alpha Chapter "were most cordial and listened to what . . . [he] had to say."

The reception was otherwise very hostile, however. Penz stated in 1980 that he had been "practically crucified" by department head "Tee" Moyer and "ranking professor" Robert K. Mautz, Zeta '36. As a student, ironically, Mautz had epitomized the dual professional and scholastic commitment of Beta

Alpha Psi as the 1936-37 winner of the student manuscript contest. In 1984, Professor Penz tentatively recalled that even the retired Hiram Scovill had tended during the visitation to defend the honor-society policy concept.

This 1955 effort by Andy Penz would represent the second and last visitation at Illinois during the third era. President H. W. Kendrick (M.S. '29, Illinois) had in 1947 met with Professor Breen and the Alpha treasurer during a brief stopover at Urbana-Champaign en route home to the University of Colorado from a Grand Council meeting in New York. Later, W. E. Dickerson had planned to visit both Alpha, and Gamma at Northwestern; during his first year of retirement from the Grand Council, 1951-52, but had not carried through with those plans. Finally, the ambitious visitation schedules of 1957-59 drawn up by Presidents Jencks and Stone (note 8) assigned Alpha to J. C. Gibson and Nolan Williams, but neither man visited Illinois.

It is not as if, contrary to most signals received on the campus, Penz's trip had yielded constructive results. During the year 1954-55 itself, it is probable that Alpha earned points only for initiation reports and submission, twice, of Newsletter copy, although by inadvertance the chapter was omitted from an otherwise complete tabulation of annual results. As noted below, local performance would only be worse the following year. The absence of further visitation, representing (as noted later) a singular exception to practices of the latter 1950s, was probably based on a perception that the climate simply did not exist for a productive trip to Illinois.

More significantly, Alpha was permitted to continue to violate constitutional requirements without being placed on probation. Nor by 1960 had Beta, Alpha Epsilon, Phi, or any other "weak" chapter been disciplined for reporting deficiencies under the official policy on probation adopted seven years earlier.

Two observations made a generation apart by A. J. Penz shed considerable

light on this state of affairs. First, his expectation of October 1954 that "future policies w[ould] depend on" the handling of the Alpha Chapter problem seems to have been borne out. It may only be realistic to acknowledge that dealing decisively with the original fraternal chapter remained, thirty-five years after its founding, a delicate matter behaviorally and politically. Second, Penz recalled in 1980 that the Grand Council of his day had consciously taken a very lenient stance in this area, feeling that a chapter that had been unresponsive to the activity program was yet "not ready" to accept it.

Alpha clearly remained in the resistant category through the close of the decade, although significant improvement had at least temporarily been recorded.

The last years of the era, 1955-60

In 1955-56, the Illinois chapter reached rock bottom, earning points only in the Newsletter category, and even there only one-half credit (450). The following year there was significant improvement, though still a low ranking. Yet in 1957-58 the results reverted to the same level as two years earlier, representing less than one third as many points as any of the other forty-four chapters.

During the presidency of Bill Jencks, another effort was made in 1957-58 to effect a change of attitude at Illinois. On the eve of his fourth and last year as faculty vice-president, Professor Bedford had become acquainted with Secretary-Treasurer Nolan Williams during the 1957 Beta Alpha Psi and American Accounting Association meetings. Just before Christmas, the secretary-treasurer wrote the faculty advisor (who had incidentally more than a year earlier succeeded Charles Schlatter as the fraternity's

"registered agent" for legal purposes) to reiterate the Grand Council's opposition to local chapter practices.

Bedford's response was highly gracious in tone and equally resolute in substance, presenting essentially the same position as his controversial letter of 1954. The Illinois professor repeated that it was the express policy of Alpha to operate as an honorary group, and that the group would be reluctant to tread on the professional domain established by the accountancy club. Significantly, however, he added that Alpha did in fact "perform most of the activities suggested by" the competitive program, implying, as (within context) had earlier Newsletter reports from Alpha, that the major issue was the authority of Grand Council reporting requirements or expectations.

Perhaps the real crux of the Illinois position, as interpreted by Bedford, was that "assuring activities in an organization by means of competition for points is not especially desirable." Alpha Chapter wished largely to chart its own course, giving more weight than most units to the honorary side, and did not feel bound by a reporting program that seemed designed to limit chapter diversity. From the Council standpoint, the reference made to the motivational role of the activity program indirectly challenged its vital control function. Hence the faculty leader's assurance that Alpha would not wish to impose its own approach on chapters whose own traditions and values might invite a commitment to the activity program seemed only to follow, logically, from the independence he had asserted. Based on this minimal (at best) concession, Professor Bedford concluded that the Council could be assured of his chapter's cooperative intent, in recognition of the "definite addition to the accounting educational program of any university" represented by Beta Alpha Psi.

Alpha's performance improved substantially at the close of the decade, coincidentally or not, under the faculty leadership of Professor Donald Scadden, like his predecessor a future president of the American Accounting Association. In 1958-59 the Illinois unit finished squarely in the middle of the pack nationally, ranking 24th out of the 47 chapters in existence throughout the year. Total points earned had increased tenfold, from 450 to 4,318. The following year Alpha dropped to 42nd place, but still operated at a stronger level than before.[3]

---

[3] Norton M. Bedford to Author, by telephone, June 27, 1985; Bedford to Nolan E. Williams, January 6, 1958, quoted; Burns and Coffman, Accounting Hall of Fame, p. 43; "Directory," Newsletter [2] (December 1938):2, (May 1941 - March 1943):3; J. C. Gibson to A. J. Penz, November 5, 1954; "Grand Chapter," Newsletter [2,3] (November 1946 - May 1952):3, 4 (November 1952 - May 1954):3rd; Grand Council Minutes Book, 1947, p. 1, 1951, p. 4, 1953, p. 3, 1954, p. 2, 1956, p. 3 (quoted), 1954-60, nonreference to taking of disciplinary action against chapters; Melvin H. Greene, Alpha treasurer, to Penz, December 14, 1953; Hasselback, 1984 Directory, individual listing, s.v. "Arnett, Harold E."; Leon E. Hay, Visitation Report--Alpha, October 27, 1966, letter format; W. B. Jencks to Gibson, November 22, 1954; H. W. Kendrick, "Chapter Visitations," in "Grand Chapter News," ed. [W. E. Dickerson], Newsletter [2] (May 1948):6; "Local Chapter News," Newsletter [2] (March 1948):15, 4 (November 1954):214 (quoted), (April 1955):243; Beryl H. Manne, Washington University archives, to Author (by telephone), April 4, 1985; Hermann C. Miller, ed., Beta Alpha Psi Directory, s.v. "Alpha Chapter: Green, P. M.," "Zeta Chapter: Mautz, Robert K.," "Nu Chapter: Kendrick, H. W."; Miller, "President's Page," Newsletter 4 (March 1953):37; "National Constitution," National Constitution and Statutes of Beta Alpha Psi Fraternity (1953), article 7, section 5 (indented citation), "National Statutes," chapter 7, subsection 73b; "News from the Chapters," Newsletter [1] (March 1933, unbound):5; "Past Presidents" of the American Accounting Association, AAA Accounting Education News, November 1984, p. 6; Penz, "Beta Alpha Psi Activity Program," March 29, 1980 (prepared for Author), p. 2, quoted; Penz to Gibson ("Gibby"), October 25, 1954; [Penz], "Grand Council News," Newsletter 4 (November 1954):199, 202-203; Penz to (Grand) Councilors, October 4, 1954; Penz to Greene, December 18, 1953; Penz to James A. Hanley, Alpha president, December 8, 1953; [Penz], "Rating Plan Scores," 1953 (as cited in note 2); Penz, Secretary-Treasurer's Report, 1954-55, pp. 2, 5; Penz to Author, interviews, April 18, 1980, August 15, 1984, both quoted; Secretary-Treasurers' Reports, 1953-54 through 1959-60, listings of chapter standings, reference to reporting deficiencies, nonreference to disciplinary action; Sheldahl, Alpha to Omega pp. 65-66, 72-73, 76, 83, 85, 102, 581; C. C. Staehling, "President's Page," Newsletter 4 (November 1954):4, quoted; S. M. Wedeberg ("Wede") to A. J. Penz ("Andy"), February 8, 1954 (McConahey File); Wedeberg, "President's Page: Friendly Chapter Competition," Newsletter 4 (November 1953):100-102; [Wedeberg], "Rating Plan

In light of the relationship found at Illinois between the local fraternal chapter and accounting club, it is noteworthy that the two groups had not always been so sharply contrasted with one another, and that on several other campuses, in a development destined only to spread, active chapters coexisted very harmoniously with other accounting organizations.

Coexistent accounting clubs--other cases and viewpoints, even at Illinois

A contrasting local precedent

Except for a short-lived group predating Beta Alpha Psi, the first reference found to a nonfraternal club at Illinois is from the second Alpha Chapter report to the Newsletter, dated May 1932. The local brotherhood had attended an address by the president of the American Institute of Accountants, sponsored by the "Accountancy Club." The only outside speakers known to have addressed the chapter itself during the year were former Northwestern colleagues Eric Kohler and H. A. Finney, who had been guests at initiation banquets. Alpha's original correspondent, however, had anticipated that the spring program would feature "prominent men in the profession as speakers at dinner meetings."

The following year, at any rate, the chapter adoped a new policy in support of a major element of the Accountancy Club program. Alpha would

---

Results," 1951, 1952 (note 2); Wedeberg, Secretary-Treasurer's Report, 1951-52, p. 1; Wedeberg to Staehling ("Charlie") and John Arch White ("John"), with appended note to J. C. Gibson ("Gibby"), November 18, 1954; and Zeff, American Accounting Association, p. 67.

Except for Wedeberg's earlier letter, and Hay's visitation report, all correspondence cited was copied in 1979 from Alpha Chapter records maintained at the National Office. Each such item was quoted, including Wedeberg to Staehling and White, the source of the citations from Bedford's unavailable letter to the councilors of September 30, 1954. The absence of further third-era visitation at Illinois is documented in the final section of the chapter.

leave to the club the sponsorship of "speaker" meetings, featuring professors, accountants, or other appropriate guests, from on or off campus. This deferential gesture was not really sacrificial in nature, since all Alpha members also belonged to the club, and the excellent series of addresses scheduled were open to other "Commerce" students as well. It was reported in the spring of 1933 that the Accountancy Club had grown by some 100 members from the total of 197 listed in the fall. The fraternal chapter accounted for 56 of the members, 23 of whom were from the faculty.

This policy, followed again in 1933-34,[4] most certainly did not lead to an abandonment by Alpha of professional activity in its own name. To the contrary, it placed the focus squarely upon active student involvement. During this time the chapter was conducting biweekly dinner meetings featuring student discussion of current topics, in particular the presentation of senior theses one of which, in 1933, would earn for Alpha a fourth straight national manuscript award. The chapter itinerary for 1934-35, during which the only known off-campus speaker addressed an initiation banquet, included:

> making up a report on recommendations for improving the accountancy curriculum, [hosting] talks on some of the legal questions involved in

---

[4]The ten speakers listed in 1932-33, two of them for both semesters, included Professors Finney, William A. Paton, Lloyd Morey, and Paul Pettingill (a coauthor with Kohler), Beta Alpha Psi book award winner W. B. Castenholz, and local accounting instructor (and future dean) P. M. Green. After being inducted as an honorary member, Paton also spoke an Alpha initiation banquet. Sechduled speakers the next year included Green, Hiram Scovill, noted business law authority E. R. Dillavou, and James O. McKinsey, the originator of the accounting principles textbook series later associated with fraternal leader C. Rollin Niswonger, Alpha '31. "News from the Chapters," Newsletter [1] (March 1933, unbound):5, (October 1933):2; William J. Robert and Robert N. Corley, Dillavou and Howard's Principles of Business Law, 8th ed. (Englewood Cliffs, N.J.: Prentice-Hall, 1967), pp. vi-vii; and Sheldahl, Alpha to Omega, pp. 430, 492, 705, 707.

> accounting by instructors in accounting who are now taking law [courses], and . . . [conducting] a C.P.A. review . . . for the spring examination.

In summary, it is clear that activities of the Illinois accountancy club, in the early days, had not left the fraternal chapter (in A. C. Littleton's memorable words) "a mere key-wearing brigade whose members quit pushing after their initiation."

Visitation reports from the years 1956-60 identify six chapter sites besides Illinois at which there were accounting clubs or societies.

Other contemporary sites, and later developments

Such organizations were cited in connection with Alpha Omicron at Michigan State, Tau at Maryland, Psi at Marquette, Beta Alpha at Indiana, Alpha Chi at Louisiana Tech, and Alpha Lambda at Tennessee. Except for the first case, none of the clubs was perceived locally, or by the visitor, as either the primary base for "professional" activity, a rival to the Beta Alpha Psi chapter, or a redundancy. Visiting Michigan State in 1956, at the close of the chapter's second year, Secretary-Treasurer Jencks found that "an accounting club - the old bugaboo" was operating within a departmental environment that at the top, in the person of Dr. Edward Gee, favored a "mostly . . . honorary" approach to Beta Alpha Psi. Two and a half years later, however, President Williard Stone found in East Lansing an active chapter enjoying excellent faculty support under new department head James Don Edwards, destined in the 1970s to be recognized as the fraternity's first "Accountant of the Year."

Joint meetings were conducted more or less regularly by the local chapter and club in each of the other instances. The visitation officer attended such a session at both Louisiana Tech and Tennessee, at least. In all probability one or more combined gatherings were included among the

five 1956-57 (nonbusiness) meetings at Maryland that were observed by chapter founder S. M. Wedeberg. Tau officers favored maintaining this relationship with the accounting club, and there was some comembership. Much more controversially, chapter members "frequently" served as _officers_ of the nonfraternal organization.

At Indiana, an active accounting club had existed since the 1920s. Over the years it had become in substance very much like a model Beta Alpha Psi chapter, combining honorary and professional elements. Acoriding to Leon Hay, however, accounting firms that made recruiting visits to Bloomington were commonly unaware of the extent of such similarity. When Hay joined the Indiana faculty in the fall of 1954, after receiving his doctorate from Illinois, he found that the department chairman decidedly opposed seeking a Beta Alpha Psi chapter. This position was apparently rooted in personal distaste that the chairman had harbored toward Professor Scovill since his days as a student at Illinois during World War I.

During his third year on the faculty, Hay was able to secure consensus faculty support for creation of a fraternal chapter. It was understood that the accounting club would be retained as a vehicle for _all_ departmental majors. Following the installation of Beta Alpha late in 1957, the accounting club consponsored half of the sixteen regular chapter meetings each year. Professor Hay recalled many years later that the new Beta Alpha Psi chapter consciously adopted rather "exclusive" entry standards, not in order to function primarily as an honor society, but to protect the interests of the local club. After visiting Indiana in May 1959, President Stone reported that the two organizations were working very well together.

Newsletter reports reveal that similar cooperative relationships were found also at Minnesota and Lehigh, the homes of Rho and Beta Epsilon.

Two prominent chapter sites that did not maintain a separate accounting organization during the third era, or did so only briefly, would some years later find it desirable to establish such a body. In the former instance, an "association" would ultimately be formed at Ohio State to complement the work of Omicron Chapter. As a visiting professor there in 1980, Leon Hay found the Accounting Association to be doing well at a school featuring an "almost nauseatingly active" Beta Alpha Psi group.

At Alabama, the club giving rise to Alpha Beta was apparently reorganized, after the 1948 installation, as an auxiliary of the state CPA society. Seeming at the time to be "redundant," it was terminated within a few years. By the fall of 1973, however, the Alabama Accounting Society had been formed to serve in particular both as a "feeder" for the local chapter, lending an exposure to responsibility prior to initiation, and as a base for professional involvement by students not qualifying for fraternal membership. In 1980, A. J. Penz remarked that the society was "thriving" on a campus noted for a strong Beta Alpha Psi unit.

One of the most interesting accounting clubs of the present day functions both "separately and cooperatively" in relation to the next-to-last chapter formed in the third era, Beta Eta at San Diego State. It represents the nation's first student chapter of the National Association of Accountants. Far more controversially, the accounting club and fraternal chapter at the California State campus at Long Beach operated as <u>a single organization</u> during the Beta Alpha Psi presidency of Hollis Dixon (1973-75), an arrangement that appears to have contributed to a strong competitive performance by Gamma Omega. Dixon's efforts to generate a formal National Council policy on accounting clubs seem to have yielded only a preliminary review by his predecessor Harold Royer, whose own school (Miami of Florida) had earlier maintained a "good" club alongside Beta Xi. Although

another councilor was asked in 1975 to build upon Royer's contribution, no further action would be reported.

Former Beta Alpha Psi presidents known to regard an accounting club as potentially an excellent complement to an active chapter include Dixon, charter Beta Eta advisor Vern Odmark, A. J. Penz, Leon Hay, Thomas Burns, Harvey Donley, and James Pattillo. According to Pattillo, the "majority view" that has evolved within the fraternity is that such an organization can be highly beneficial in taking care of students not eligible (at least yet) for Beta Alpha Psi, providing a feeder for the chapter, and cosponsoring events. Dixon has suggested that at least one slate of proposed fraternal officers should perhaps belong to the accounting club, although (to spread leadership opportunities around) Beta Alpha Psi students should not serve as officers of the other group.

A dissenting (or "minority") opinion was expressed in 1980 by Thomas Dickerson, who considered an accounting club redundant for a Beta Alpha Psi school. In effect he agreed with Norton Bedford, and other Alpha representatives, that it was inappropriate for an accounting program too sponsor two "professional" organizations, while rejecting their call for a primarily "honorary" chapter.

In the latter regard, "the father (or mother)" of the activity program countered rather ironic suspicious voiced by Nolan Williams after visiting Pi Chapter in 1959. In Dickerson's mind, an accounting club was either merely a predecessor of a fraternal chapter, or a continuing organization at a school not chartered. After "retirement" to Tampa, as a faculty member and, later, the chief systems analyst at South Florida, the former Western Reserve professor contributed to the eventual installation of Delta Gamma a local chapter. Unlike, for example, Andy Penz, Leon Hay, and Tom Burns, Tom Dickerson did not have an opportunity to observe the

operations on a campus of coexistent accounting groups.

Despite the improved performance results recorded at the close of the third era, deep-seated objection to the activity program would endure at Illinois far beyond that point, leading finally to disciplinary action long deferred.

Continuing resistance at Illinois, culminating, in 1975, in probation

Late in 1966, Secretary-Treasurer Leon Hay, Alpha '47, had lunch on the Urbana-Champaign campus with Faculty Vice-President James Deskins, local student officers, and Norton Bedford, who was standing in for department head E. J. De Maris. In his visitation report, he stated that the two professors had taken "the offensive against the chapter activity program," and the chapter president had been "primed to present the case that Alpha chapter was proud of its long existence as an honorary."

Hay felt that "by dessert" he had convinced the students that they should be meeting more often, and be preparing and conducting their own programs. He doubted that more than limited progress was possible, because "the faculty d[id]n't want to bother," but predicted that by continuing "to apply pressure" on senior faculty members such as Bedford, Mautz, and De Maris "some degree of success" could eventually be achieved.

Even this very restrained level of optimism would be tested for some years to come. Robert Wasley, for example, recalls that he and three other "education zealots" who headed Beta Alpha Psi during the years 1968-72 (Professors Odmark, Donley, and Charles Taylor) became increasingly disturbed by the highly "independent" attitude expressed by Alpha toward the activity program.[5]

---

[5]By coincidence, Bob Wasley and Rollie Niswonger had joined Norton Bedford in 1950 as the first doctoral graduates in accounting from Ohio

Ironically enough, however, the National Council itself had come to approach participation in the activity program as fundamentally "voluntary" in nature, to be encouraged but not required. For a time, chapters were permitted to exempt themselves from the competition, just as Faculty Vice-President Bedford had requested for his group in 1954. This change in policy was no doubt welcomed at Illinois at a time by which, as bluntly stated by Professor Hay, Alpha was rarely interested "in doing anything, or reporting it if they did," an interpretation supported locally by Professor Frederick L. Neumann's recollection that by around 1970 the chapter was operating as a purely honorary organization. In fairness, Hay did cite Professor Robert L. Schlosser, later Coopers & Lybrand's national partner for continuing professional education, as a faculty advisor at Illinois from the (early) 1960s who had encouraged a fair level of activity.

Within a few years, the tide turned again, and the National Council began truly to enforce reasonable compliance with the activity program, through the threat of chapter probation. During "a long talk" in the fall of 1974, Alpha's new faculty advisor Kenneth W. Perry, a departmental member since 1950, explained to Secretary-Treasurer Fred Mueller the historical background of his chapter's weak condition. Although due to a leave of absence he would serve only a year as faculty vice-president, Mueller would

---

State. Three years earlier, Andy Penz had completed a broader Ph.D. program at the school by successfully defending a dissertation specifically in the management field. Another interesting coincidence is that Bedford's eight colleagues on the American Accounting Association committee that developed the noted monograph A Statement of Basic Accounting Theory (1966) included the charter Beta Alpha Psi president at Illinois, Russell H. Morrison. [Thomas J. Burns], The Ohio State University: The Ph.D. Program in Accounting, 1984 ([Columbus: Academic Faculty of Accounting, Ohio State University, 1983]), pp. 5-6; Hasselback, 1984 Directory, individual listing, s.v. "Penz, Anton J.": A. J. Penz to Author, by telephone, January 16, 1985; and Sheldahl, Alpha to Omega, pp. 66, 70-71, 70n.

later express the conviction that Perry had "done something to rekindle the spark of life" within the chapter.

Nonetheless, Alpha performed below minimum national standards in 1974-75, and in November 1975 was placed on probation, along with eleven other chapters. In notifying department chairman Bedford, most fittingly, of the action, Mueller acknowledged a special reluctance to move against the original fraternal group, but submitted that "it would be worse to waste a resource" capable of "benefit[ing] students, the university, and the profession." The secretary-treasurer expressed hope that the department head would support efforts to reverse a trend whose continuation would yield an "almost unthinkable" result, namely, the revocation of Alpha's charter.

Fortunately, the chapter performed acceptably in 1975-76, under faculty advisors Richard E. Ziegler (an interim replacement) and W. Morley Lemon, and was duly removed from probation. In her letter to Lemon, however, Secretary-Treasurer Joyce C. Dean cautioned that to maintain good standing Alpha must continue to satisfy constitutional requirements, and achieve specified point totals.

Two local developments, in particular, would assist the chapter in meeting these modest conditions. First, the Illinois accountancy club had been disbanded by 1973, reflecting a lack of student interest in relevant activity, but also leaving Alpha Chapter as the only available campus source for an extracurricular program in the field.

Second, and more importantly, faculty attitudes toward Beta Alpha Psi became substantially more positive, based in large part on major changes in fraternal policies and operations themselves. These developments included a highly flexible activity program; annual competitive programs, for active members, particularly suited to superior academic environments; expanding

fraternal visibility within the professional and business communities, notably through the National Advisory Forum and the "Accountant of the Year" awards; and an active policy of roster expansion, rendering charter revocation for deviant chapters less "unthinkable" than otherwise. Fraternal Accountants of the Year have included Norton Bedford and a "not insignificant" Illinois alumnus, General Motors chairman Thomas A. Murphy.

Within such a context, maintaining good standing in the fraternity naturally became more important to the accountancy department at Illinois. Senior faculty members like Bedford and Charles E. Smith, who in 1983 resumed the faculty vice-presidency he had held in 1978-79, recognized the importance of Beta Alpha Psi to their department, and the commitment to a reasonable level of activity that went with a charter. At a philosophical level, however, Professor Bedford observed in 1985 that he would <u>still</u> prefer having on campus separate honorary (or "academic") and professional organizations in accounting, while commending the fraternity for doing a "darned good job" in the professional area.

By the fall of 1982, finally, although Alpha had accepted substantially more than an honorary role, there once again were two accounting groups at Illinois. A new accountancy club was formed to enable students not in Beta Alpha Psi to hold regular meetings, participate in field trips, and in other ways complement their classroom studies in the field, in a day in which prospective employers increasingly looked for such experience. After three years, the present-day club was described by department head Neumann as "flourishing," with a membership that included a number of students from Alpha Chapter. Since the early 1930s, then, the accountancy club and fraternal unit at Illinois had come full circle, or remarkably

approached so doing.[6]

Probably more than by coincidence, the advent of the rating/activity program was followed soon by significant increase in the frequency of another prime vehicle for fraternal communication and control, chapter visitation.

---

[6][Henry R. Anderson], ed., 'Three "Giants" Named Accountants of the Year', Newsletter 17 (Fall 1978):1; Norton M. Bedford to Author, by telephone, June 27, 1985, quoted; Thomas J. Burns to Author, May 3, 1980; Burns and Coffman, Accounting Hall of Fame, pp. 21, 31; "Chapter Information," 1983-84 Annual Report, ed. [Metcalf], p. 31; [Doris M. Cook], "James Don Edwards, Outstanding Accountant of the Year," Newsletter 13 (Fall 1974):1; [Cook], "Norton M. Bedford, Accountant of the Year," Newsletter 15 (Fall 1976):1; Joyce C. Dean to W. Morley Lemon, October 13, 1976; Thomas M. Dickerson to Author, November 1, 1979, April 19, 1980; Dickerson to C. Aubrey Smith, January 18, 1969 (Golden Anniversary Files), quoted; Hollis A. Dixon to Author, March 22-23, 1980; Harvey E. Donley to Author, May 2, 1980; "Grand Chapter," Newsletter 5 (April 1961):351, 6 (Spring 1964):73; Grand Council Minutes Book, 1955, p. 6; Hasselback, 1979-80 Directory, individual listing, s.v. "Hay, Leon E."; Hasselback, 1984 Directory, individual listing, s.v. "Neumann, Frederick L.," "Perry, Kenneth W."; Leon E. Hay to Author, May 2, 1980; Hay, Visitation Report--Alpha, October 27, 1966, quoted; W. B. Jencks to J.C. Gibson, November 22, 1954; Jencks, Visitation Report--Alpha Omicron, May 11, 1956, nos. 2.2-2.3, quoted; A. C. Littleton to Robert J. McQuade, Mu Chapter president, April 13, 1927, Alpha to Omega, by Sheldahl, p. 330, quoted; "[Local] Chapter News," Newsletter 5 (November 1957):29, (April 1960):292; Fred J. Mueller to Norton M. Bedford, November 5, 1975, quoted; Mueller, Secretary-Treasurer's Report, 1975-76, pp. 1-2, 10, 13; "The National Chapter: 1978-79," 1978-79 Annual Report, ed. [Burns], p. 1; National Council Minutes, 1969, pp. 4-5, February 1974, p. 5 (nos. 10, quoted, 10.1), May 1974, p. 6 (no. 19), February 1975, p. 7 (no. 24), August 1975, p. 5 (no. 19), April 1976, p. 1 (no. 5); Frederick L. Neumann to Author, by telephone, June 24, 1985, quoted; "News from the Chapters," Newsletter [1] (March 1932):6, (May 1932):5, (March 1933):5 (each quoted), October 1933):2, (December 1934):1, 2 (indented citation), (March 1935):5; Vern E. Odmark to Author, August 13, 1980; James W. Pattillo to Author, August 8, 1980; A. J. Penz to Author, April 18, 1980; Gary John Previts, ed., Programs in Accounting: The University of Alabama, 5th ed. ([University, Ala.: Programs in Accounting and Information Systems, 1974]), p. 35; Sheldahl, Alpha to Omega, pp. 53, 65-66, 555-56, 693-94; W. E. Stone, Visitation Reports--Alpha Lambda, April 1, 1960, Alpha Omicron, October 3, 1958, Beta Alpha, May 5, 1959, letter formats; Robert S. Wasley to Author, March 23, 1980; S. M. Wedeberg, Visitation Report--Tau, December 14, 1956, et al., nos. 2.2, 2.3 (quoted), 3.3; and Nolan E. Williams, Visitation Reports--Pi, November 3, 1959, no. 3.1 (quoted), and Alpha Chi, February 23, 1960, no. 3.4.

All 1980 references are to interviews or, in regard to Odmark, a correspondence equivalent, and all subjects except Dickerson and Donley were quoted.

Chapter Visitation in the Third Era

In visitation terms, the third era divides readily into the subperiods 1946-51, 1951-57, and 1957-60. During the five years directly following the 1946 reactivation of the Grand Council, the practice was highly sporadic, and was only loosely structured by a checklist drawn up before the war. After the first year of the rating program, there emerged a moderate level of visitation, unified by a modernized reporting format. Conspicuously under presidential leadership, finally, there was in the late fifties a surge in such activity, consistent with the growth of the chapter roster in general, and a commitment to the enhancement of local programs in particular.

Low to Moderate Levels, 1946-57

The first five years

The principle of regular visitation that had survived even depression years, 1930-36, during which it could not be honored in practice was reaffirmed at the 1946 Council meeting. The three men gathered in Chicago made tentative plans to visit a chapter located in the immediate area, directly after adjournment (at no fraternal cost), and three other local groups, two of them in conjunction with business travel.

It seems clear, however, that no visits would be made in 1946-47, even to Gamma at Northwestern, whose first stages of reactivation became known to the designated visitor, Secretary-Treasurer Hazen Kendrick, only through a note received from the chapter in early fall. Neither Kendrick's official report for the year nor the 1947 Council minutes contain any evidence of visitation.

The report submitted by the secretary-treasurer in September 1947 observed that reactivation had been "difficult for many chapters," and that

> considerable . . . work remain[ed] to be done in acquainting the chapters with the routines to be accomplished and their responsibilites

in this and other areas.

The Council accordingly laid out an exceedingly ambitious plan by which all but one of the twenty-one chapters of the day would be inspected by one of the four continuing councilors before the next annual meeting. Phi at Louisiana State was apparently considered too remote geographically for a trip from Colorado by incoming president Kendrick, from Washington by his predecessor James McConahey (newly retired), or from Ohio by either of the councilors Dickerson.

Each of these men was assigned his "home" chapter, while four prospective sites were identified as more tentative than the others. Tom Dickerson was supposed to visit both Mu at New York and Xi at Syracuse, the local chapters of incoming councilor Gould Harris and outgoing member George E. Bennet. It was agreed that the fraternal treasury would cover travel costs up to an overall total of $1,000, representing barely more than one/third the $2,917 excess of "income" over "expense" (including no visitation costs) that would be reported for the following fiscal year.

To permit visitation, at a useful time in the chapter year, in the course of travel to a reasonably central convention site, there was a provisional decison to delay the next annual meeting until around the first of November. In 1948 the Grand Council did indeed assemble in Chicago at the end of October, rather than in Memphis fifty days earlier, marking (through 1985) the last annual, or summer, meeting not coordinated with the yearly national gathering of the American Accounting Association. Directly after the war, the AAA had moved its meeting time from the week between Christmas and New Year's Day to early September (to be changed to late August in 1956), routinely preceding the contemporary school year.

Ironically, however, no chapter visits would result from this one-time delay. In fact, beyond (unrecorded) "home" visits, only President

"Ken" Kendrick, the foremost advocate at the time of an active policy in the area, would conduct visitations under the 1947 plan. Ill health prevented Professor McConahey from travelling south in the spring of 1948 to inspect Beta at Oregon, and later from making the much longer trip to Chicago. Before reluctantly cancelling his train reservations, he had made plans to visit four chapters from the midwest, two of which (Gamma, and Rho at Minnesota) had been particularly slow to reactivate.

Kendrick's brief stop at Illinois in September 1947, noted earlier, represented the first of five visitations by the Colorado professor. Clearly on faculty leave, he added the others during a prolonged trip late in the year. In an interesting Newsletter article, Kendrick related highlights of a long journey that had led him in time to a neighboring state:

> I travelled some 4000 miles from Boulder, by way of Berkeley [Lambda Chapter, November 14], Los Angeles [Iota, December 3], and Texas [Theta, December 18], to reach the Oklahoma A and M campus [Chi, December 28].

Despite the date, some twenty Chi brothers, inclusive of faculty, had turned out for a dinner meeting.

In each case, the Beta Alpha Psi president had utilized a 12-point checklist, dating from 1939, that represented the only contemporary frame of reference for conducting visitations. Earlier, as editor, he had twice reprinted the list.

Nearly a year after his trip, Kendrick was reimbursed by the fraternity in the amount of $250, a total that would exceed total visitation expense over the next three years. Despite another exhibit of good intentions at the annual meeting, no visits would be recorded in 1948-49. The following year, Gould Harris and Bill Dickerson traveled respectively to Maryland and Syracuse, to inspect Tau and Xi Chapters, at a combined cost of $123. Especially since Tau had alreay reimbursed Harris for the $30 paid the

teachers who had filled in for him at NYU, President Dickerson felt bound to honor that item in his expense report (through payment to the chapter) along with the more standard ones.

The same two men conducted the three visitations of 1950-51. Presideent Harris paid a local call to Alpha Gamma at CCNY, and, at least in the capacity of banquet speaker, also visited Omicron at Ohio State, his alma mater. Dickerson traveled from Columbus to Oxford to inspect Omega Chapter at Miami of Ohio. The visitation expense of $112 yielded a grand total since 1946 of less than $500 for ten visits to as many schools.

With the ink not yet dry on tabulation of initial results under the new rating plan, the Council decided in 1951 to commence "a more extensive" visitation program featuring two new elements, only one of which was immediately implemented.

Increased activity, and structure, 1951-57

At the 1951 annual meeting, Gould Harris recommended that former councilors be invited to make chapter visits, a practice enjoying limited fraternal precedent that represented a logical approach to extending coverage. Not long after the formation, in 1954, of a "[president's] advisory committee," made up of the outgoing president (as chairman) and his two direct predecessors, past leaders would begin to make occasional visitations after leaving the Grand Council. The first such services were provided, in 1956-57 (three years before the committee formally addressed the topic), by S. M. Wedeberg.

More importantly, President Harris suggested that visitors "be provided with an outline of the points to be undertaken," as a basis for reporting results to the secretary-treasurer. Coincidentally or not, despite initial plans for ten visits during the year 1951-52, none had as yet taken place

by the beginning of March, when President John Arch White produced '"a rather hastily drawn check sheet for recording and reporting"' visitations. Secretary-Treasurer Wedeberg added a section covering "Methods, procedures or suggestions of value to other chapters." The result was the reporting form shown as exhibit 16. It would be used for the duration of the third era, although Williard Stone, particularly, would often file letters instead, and A. J. Penz liked to supplement reports with letters to local officers.

Just before summer vacation in 1952, finally, Councilors Harris, Wedeberg, White, and Charles Staehling visited five chapters, at an average fraternal cost (highest of the era) of nearly $79. For the 1951-57 subperiod as a whole, 28 different chapters were inspected, six of them twice and another one three times.

The three visits to Nu at Colorado were made by Wayne Shroyer of nearby Denver. Professors Shroyer and Wedeberg, of Maryland, each filed two reports on their respective home chapters, Alpha Zeta and Tau, while Wedeberg and A. J. Penz each visited two New York City chapters, Mu at NYU and Alpha Gamma at City College, on a single trip. The latter two men likewise each traveled, four years apart, to Mississippi to look over Alpha Theta Chapter. The only repetition that seems to have been prompted by chapter inactivity led, as already noted, to a favorable 1953 report by President Staehling on Beta at Oregon.

Among the ten chapters visited earlier, only Lambda at California, Omicron at Ohio State, and Chi at Oklahoma A. and M. were absent from the 1951-57 group. Through the spring of 1957, of the 39 fraternal units in operation for at least two full years, 30 had received at least one postwar visitor, while the newer chapter Alpha Chi at Louisiana Tech had already also been inspected. Schools not yet covered were Western Reserve,

EXHIBIT 16

VISITATION REPORT FROM ADOPTED IN 1952[a]

GRAND COUNCIL OF BETA ALPHA PSI
Report on Chapter Visitation

Visiting Councilman[b] ; Date visited
Name of Chapter

1. Records

1.1 Minutes inspected . Remarks

1.2 Books inspected . Remarks

1.3 Are financial affairs reasonably well supervised?
Recommendations

1.4 Chapter Roll inspected? . Remarks

2. Chapter Officers and Faculty:

2.1 Did you meet all chapter officers? . Remarks

2.2. Major questiond discussed (list below):

2.3 Suggestions from Chapter Officers (list below):

2.4 Faculty Vice-President. General impressions as to interest, ability, etc.:

3. General

3.1 How many faculty members on the accounting staff?
How many are Beta Alpha Psi members?
How many are actually active?
Comments

3.2 Does the chapter meet regularly?
3.3 Did you meet with the chapter?
3.4 Brief report on chapter meeting attended:

4. Methods, preocedures or suggestions of value to other chapters; (If their method of filing roll cards is especially good, describe method. If their bookkeeping method seems efficient, describe. If committee organization seems very effective, describe, etc.)

---

[a]To permit compressing the two-page form into a single page, without overcrowding, the ruled line(s) following each item have been omitted.

[b]"Councilman" seems to have been used as widely as "councilor" during the third era in referring to a member of the Grand Council.

Wisconsin, Alabama, Northwestern, North Dakota, Creighton, Iowa, Baylor, and Cincinnati, the last three of which had been on the roster for less than three years.

The local presence of third-era councilors Tom Dickerson, J. C. Gibson, and Andy Penz seemed sufficient regarding the first three cases--Pi, Sigma, and Alpha Beta Chapters. In addition, before Gibson's election in 1951 the Wisconsin group had on hand Dean Fay(ette) Elwell, the former president who on an interim appointment had submitted the first postwar secretary-treasurer's report, "to keep it in line."

During the middle six-year span, visitation expense ranged from $107 in 1954-55 to $412 two years later. Interestingly, the highest number of visits, seven, was recorded in 1953-54 at the second lowest total cost, $129. During that year, the University of Alabama provided transportation for the inspection of Upsilon at Florida by Penz, and the secretary-treasurer's stopover at Syracuse to observe Xi Chapter, as an extension of a trip to Detroit to install Alpha Xi, was probably included under another expense category.

The reference to Alpha Xi brings up a unique development of the same year not accounted for as visitation. Wayne Shroyer visited the University of Detroit prior to the vote on the school's second petition for a Beta Alpha Psi charter, and both he and Secretary-Treasurer Penz traveled to Washington of St. Louis during the year to evaluate a prospective petitioner. Shroyer's "site" visitation (using modern terminology) led to a favorable vote, whereas the two trips to St. Louis evidently had a negative effect on the other school's prospects, whether or not a formal application was ever filed. Shroyer's midyear journey to Washington University would have occurred, incidentally, at just about the time Norton Bedford left to join

the Illinois faculty. Newly retired from the Grand Council, the Denver professor would late in 1958 travel to Oregon State, just before or after visiting Beta at Oregon, as part of the process by which Epsilon Chapter was reinstated soon thereafter.

Under President Shroyer, the year 1956-57 was a transitional one for chapter visitation. At the annual meeting just prior to the fall term, the governing body had "[gone] on record as favoring a vigorous visitation program." Considering previous levels of activity, the eleven visits, at a cost of $412, upheld this promise. The year is classified within the middle subperiod, rather than the last one, in part because the president himself conducted only one visit. Over the balance of the third era, each of his three successors would individually visit more than eleven chapters during his year in office, as Beta Alpha Psi dramatically expanded the program.

Marked Expansion of the Program, and Presidential Leadership, 1957-60

The Grand Council in 1957 "renewed" its commitment of the preceding year by agreeing that the problem of "weak" chapters "could best be overcome by frequent visitations." Incoming president W. B. Jencks, an affirmed supporter of increased activity, reported that he could visit "a number" of local groups while on leave from Ohio State the following spring.

Largely on a geographical basis, and with very limited overlap, Jencks early in the year divided <u>all 43</u> existing chapters as potential visitation sites among himself his four fellow councilors, and advisory committee members Penz and Gibson. Each party was assigned his home-campus unit. Despite the earlier reference to "weak" chapters, the lists were basically organized by reversing the order of recency of visitation, including installation.

Jencks virtually achieved his personal target of 15 outside chapters as he made 14 visits during the year, 10 of them in as many weeks in the spring. Five additional trips were made by other councilors, including a visitation by Nolan Williams to a campus also covered by the president, Southern Methodist (Alpha Epsilon). Jencks' travel included the first visits in modern times to Northwestern, Western Reserve, and North Dakota, and the first inspections made at Creighton, Baylor, Cincinnati, Bowling Green, and newly chartered West Virginia. Total program cost nearly tripled, to $1,169.

These records would be short-lived. In the fall of 1958, President Williard Stone made potential "assignments" covering the 46 existing chapters among the five current and two most recent councilors. Based on evaluations made at the recent Grand Council meeting, he specifically identified 17 chapters as the prime subjects for visitation. Interestingly, a dozen of them had been visited, or installed, within the past year or two. More generally, Stone listed 34 of the 39 groups not represented by prospective visitors as having been inspected, or installed, since 1954.

During the year 1958-59, President Stone himself visited 15 chapters, having apparently not been reluctant to surpass his predecessor's total. Early in April, the Wharton professor advised his Council colleagues that he had an "opportunity" to visit Northwestern, DePaul, Indiana, and Ohio State four weeks later, which would enable him to "finish up . . . [his] chapter visits with a bang (and push Bill's record of 14 Chapters visited)" the preceding year. Bill Jencks would naturally have not have objected to an outside visitation for Omicron Chapter. Secretary-Treasurer Herb Miller graciously waived his prior claim to both Gamma and Beta Alpha, but cited a firm commitment to address the initiation banquet at Beta Gamma a week later. Stone visited DePaul during the spring of 1959, even so, as well as

the other three campuses listed.

Overall, 23 visitations were conducted during the year, at a recorded cost of $1,265. Besides Beta Gamma, Alpha Mu at Kentucky and Alpha Psi at West Virginia had two visitors. Twelve of the original 17 target chapters were covered, notably not including Alpha at Illinois, From a personal standpoint, Williard Stone's visit to Upsilon Chapter at Florida, following "quite a rough trip" by air, is noteworthy, since slightly more than a year later he would move to the southeastern school from the University of Pennsylvania.

The following year, 1959-60, President Nolan Williams of Arkansas headed an effort that led to 29 visitations at 27 schools, at a cost of $1,472. His own 13 visits included stops at 11 schools during respective five-day swings through Ohio, Pennsylvania, and Maryland in November and Alabama, Mississippi, and Louisiana in February. Williams' travel included the first formal visitation to Alpha Beta at Alabama, and a meeting with his predecessor's home chapter, Alpha Delta at Penn, that was carefully distinguished from an "inspection" in the usual sense. As past president, Stone contributed 7 visits, including follow-ups, at no cost to the fraternity, to trips by Williams to two Ohio schools, Miami (Omega) and Cincinnati (Alpha Sigma).

The dominance of the final three years is pointed up vividly in a tabulation of third-era visitation sites, officers, and costs presented as exhibit 17. Over that brief span, all fifty chapters installed before April 1960 were visited at least once except for Alpha at Illinois, Epsilon at Oregon State, Sigma at Wisconsin, and Alpha Iota at Arkansas. The first group has been discussed in detail, and the second one had been reactivated in 1959 after advance inspection by Wayne Shroyer. The other exceptions

EXHIBIT 17

THIRD-ERA VISITATION SITES, OFFICERS, AND COSTS

Number of Visits to Each Chapter, Classified by Subperiod[a]

		1947-51	1951-57	1957-60	Total			1947-51	1951-57	1957-60	Total
1.	ALPHA	1	1	0	2	23.	ALPHA BETA	0	0	1	1
2.	BETA	0	2	1	3	24.	ALPHA GAMMA	1	2	1	4
3.	GAMMA	0	0	3	3	25.	ALPHA DELTA	0	1	1	2
4.	DELTA	0	1	1	2	26.	ALPHA EPSILON		1	3	4
5.	EPSILON				0	27.	ALPHA ZETA		2	1	3
6.	ZETA	0	0	1	1	28.	ALPHA ETA		1	1	2
7.	THETA	1	1	1	3	29.	ALPHA THETA		2	1	3
8.	IOTA	1	1	1	3	30.	ALPHA IOTA		1	0	1
9.	LAMBDA	1	0	2	3	31.	ALPHA KAPPA		1	1	2
10.	MU	0	2	2	4	32.	ALPHA LAMBDA		1	2	3
11.	NU	0	3	1	4	33.	ALPHA MU		1	2	3
12.	XI	1	1	2	4	34.	ALPHA NU		0	1	1
13.	OMICRON	1	0	1	2	35.	ALPHA XI		1	1	2
14.	PI	0	0	2	2	36.	ALPHA OMICRON		1	2	3
15.	RHO	0	1	1	2	37.	ALPHA PI		0	1	1
16.	SIGMA	0	0	0	0	38.	ALPHA RHO		0	2	2
17.	TAU	1	2	2	5	39.	ALPHA SIGMA		0	3	3
18.	UPSILON	0	1	1	2	40.	ALPHA TAU		1	3	4
19.	PHI	0	1	1	2	41.	ALPHA UPSILON			1	1
20.	CHI	1	0	2	3	42.	ALPHA PHI			2	2
21.	PSI	0	1	1	2	43.	ALPHA CHI		1	2	3
22.	OMEGA	1	1	2	4	44.	ALPHA PSI			3	3

EXHIBIT 17--Continued

		1957-60			1957-60			1957-60
45.	ALPHA OMEGA	1	47.	BETA GAMMA	3	49.	BETA EPSILON	1
46.	BETA ALPHA	1	48.	BETA DELTA	1	50.	BETA ZETA	1

Number of Visits by Each Councilor, Classified by Subperiod

		Tenure, 1947-60	--Visitations-- 1947-51	1951-57	1957-60	Total	After tenure
1.	H. M. Kendrick, Colorado	1947-49	5			5	
2.	W. E. Dickerson, Ohio State	1947-51	2			2	
3.	Gould L. Harris, New York	1947-52	3	2		5	
4.	John Arch White, Texas	1948-53		1		1	
5.	C. C. Staehling, Berkeley	1949-54		3		3	
6.	S. M. Wedeberg, Maryland	1950-55		7		7	2
7.	A. J. Penz, Alabama	1952-57		9	2	11	2
8.	Wayne E. Shroyer, Denver	1953-58		5	4	9	4
9.	W. B. Jencks, Ohio State	1954-59		6	17	23	2
10.	W. E. Stone, Pennsylvania	1955-60		2	25	27	
11.	Nolan E. Williams, Arkansas	1956-60		1	16	17	
12.	R. H. Van Voorhis, LSU	1957-60			1	1	
13.	Herbert E. Miller, Michigan	1958-60			4	4	
14.	C. Rollin Niswonger, Miami of Ohio	1959-60			2	2	
	Totals		10	36	71	117	10

Reported Dollar Costs of Visitation

		1947-51	1951-57	1957-60	1947-60
1.	Yearly range	0-250	107-412	1169-1472	0-1472
2.	Total amount	485	1484	3906	5875
3.	Yearly average	121	247	1302	452
4.	Range of yearly averages per visit	37-62	18-79	51-62	18-79
5.	Overall unit average	48	41	55	50

SOURCES: Grand Council Minutes Book, 1947-60, p. 1 (Council membership), 1958, pp. [2-3], 1959, p. 2; Gould L. Harris to John (Arch) White, December 7, 1949 (Policies File); H. W. Kendrick, "Chapter Visitation," *Newsletter* [2] (May 1948):5-8; Secretary-Treasurers' Reports, 1946-47 through 1959-60, visitation; W. E. Stone, Visitation Report--Mu, April 23, 1960 (Mu Chapter files, National Office); and Visitation Files, 1950-60, 101 visits.

[a]Zeros appear only if chapters existed for two full years of the span.

were vestiges of the earlier economical practice of excluding from outside visitation the home chapters of current or recent councilors. Sigma stands out because it had not been visited earlier in the third era, either, although the Council had met in 1957 on the Wisconsin campus. Coincidentally, local professor J. C. Gibson was, along with Thomas Dickerson, one of only two councilors of the years 1947-60 not to conduct a recorded visitation.

Having moved to a normal three-year visitation interval, the Grand Council met with 19 of the 50 groups more than once during the years 1957-60. For example, Williard Stone's second trip to Mu at New York was prompted by the alumni problem documented in chapter 4, and five of his stops as president or past president embodied opportunities to visit schools covered by other officers the same year.

Visited three times were Gamma at Northwestern and Alpha Epsilon at SMU, identified through the activity program as notably "weak" chapters; and Alpha Tau at Pittsburgh, Alpha Psi at West Virginia, and Beta Gamma at DePaul. Stone twice visited both DePaul and Northwestern during trips to Chicago, one of them on American Accounting Association business. Each based in a neighboring state, Presidents Jencks and Stone called on Alpha Psi during their terms, respectively soon after installation and shortly before the completion (as a warmup for leading the nation in 1959-60) of a fourth-place competitive performance. The latter stop followed an unusual

[7] Reverse discrepancies between Grand Council minutes and secretary-treasurer reports for the two years 1957-59 have been resolved in favor of the former sources. In specifying reports given at the annual meetings, the minutes do not show a visit to Xi at Syracuse by President Jencks in 1957-58 (corroborating other evidence that he had made "only" fourteen visitations), but do cite for the following year a trip by Councilor Miller to inspect Alpha Psi at West Virginia. Grand Council Minutes Book, 1958, pp. [2-3], 1959, p. 2; and [Nolan E. Williams], Secretary-Treasurer's Reports, 1957-58, p. 4, 1958-59, p. 4.

visit to Alpha Tau, eighty miles to the north, that is recounted in chapter 8. By the summer of 1959 the Grand Council had learned that undergraduate business studies might be terminated at Pitt, raising the prospect that the local chapter would "have to be disenfranchised," and foreshadowing a problem that would in years to come (as covered in chapter 12) beset other chapters as well, including Gamma.

After a 1958 visit, President Jencks expressed concern based on the mayoralty responsibilities and other commitments of Gamma advisor Ambrose Reiter. A year later President Stone judged instead that the chapter was "fortunate in its F.V.P.," but encouraged Secretary-Treasurer Miller to "reinstate" plans for a broader visitation to Northwestern. Later, Miller agreed to travel to the campus during the year 1959-60 to determine whether action should be taken "to replace" the advisor in light of his outside duties. Instead, however, Stone would make a second trip, confirm the absence of faculty supervision, and recommend that in due course the Grand Council "suggest" a leadership change based on an informal policy limiting terms (within "weak" chapters) to five years. Ironically, Reiter was already in his fifth year in the faculty post, but it would not revert to Professor Virgil Boyd until the fall of 1961.

Just 11 of the 117 visitations recorded from the third era were conducted at the officer's home chapter or within the same locality, only two of them (counting Stanford visiting professor Herb Miller's visit to Lambda at Berkeley in 1960) after 1956-57. The strong financial commitment made to the program in the last three years was only increased by the raising of the milage rate for automobile trips, in 1957, from six to ten cents. Possibly reflecting the absence, from illness, of notably frugal president A. J. Penz, the Grand Council had a year earlier upgraded the coverage of travel by air or rail from "cost of transportation (including Pullman)" to

"[c]ost of first class transportation (including Pullman)."

Finally, the activity program was constantly a prime theme of coverage at visitations of the 1950s. As already noted, problems of compliance with attendance provisions were often discussed, especially on urban campuses. Local officers occasionally encouraged the Grand Council to seek additonal ways to publicize within the fraternal roster the activities and practices of successful groups, although contemporary annual minutes reveal no pertinent initiatives. Lambda at California proposed in 1958 that "programs for 10 or 15 of the better chapters" be incorporated within a formally printed revision of the manual of chapter operations contributed seven years earlier by retiring councilor W. E. Dickerson. The recommendation was timely in that Past President Jencks was then in the process of revising the manual, but visitation officer Nolan Williams would unavoidably miss the next annual meeting. After an earlier visitation, Williard Stone had made a comparable suggestion regarding the newly prepared faculty vice-president's handbook.[8]

---

[8] AAA Road Atlas, pp. 14, 95; [W. E. Dickerson], "Councilor Gould L. Harris," Newsletter [2] (November 1947):9; Dickerson, Secretary-Treasurer's Report, 1947-48, p. [2], quoted; Dickerson, Visitation Report--Xi, April 18, 1950 (Visitation Files. 1950-60, only entry before 1952); Dickerson to John A. White, January 7, 1950 (Policies File); exhibit 16; "Grand Chapter," Newsletter 5 (April 1961):351, (Fall 1961):403; Grand Council Minutes Book, 1951, p. 4, 1954, pp. 2-3, 1955, p. 3, 1956, pp. 3-4, 1957, p. 2, 1959, p. 3 (each quoted), 1946, p. 2, 1947, pp. 1-[2], 1948, pp. 1, 3, 1951, p. 6, 1956, p. 1, 1959, pp. 1-2, 7-8; Gould L. Harris to White, December 7, 1949 (Policies); Hasselback, 1984 Directory, individual listing, s.v. "Stone, Williard E."; [W. B. Jencks], "Grand Council Visitation Assignments, 1957-58" (Visitation Files); [Jencks], Secretary-Treasurer's Report, 1956-57, p. 2; Jencks, Visitation Report--Gamma, February 24, 1958, item 2.2, and to Councilors, March 3, 1958; Jencks, Visitation Report--Alpha Psi, November 20, 1957, letter format; H. W. Kendrick, "Chapter Visitation," Newsletter [2] (May 1948):5-8, quoting p. 7; [Kendrick], ed., "Chapter Visitations," Newsletter [2] (November 1946):351, (March 1947):403; Kendrick, Secretary-Treasurer's Report, 1946-47, pp. 3 (indented citation), 8 ("Expenses"); Jas. M. McCohahey to Dickerson, June 6 (reference to "Ken" Kendrick), August 3, September 5 (quoted), October 17, 1948; [Herbert E. Miller], "Dean Emeritus Fayette H. Elwell," Newsletter 5 (April 1961):355; Miller to President (W. E.) Stone and Councilors, April 7, 1959 (Visitation Files); Miller, Visitation Report--Lambda, May 9, 1959, letter; Secretary-Treasurers' Reports, 1948-49 through

In Transition

Councilor A. J. Penz has been identified as a leading figure of the third era both in activity program administration, and controversy, and in chapter visitation, although his most memorable contribution of the day has yet to be cited--the introduction of chapter *banners*. The service provided by Dr. Penz to Beta Alpha Psi would hardly end with the close of his membership on the Grand Council or the advisory committee. One of his leading contributions would indeed occur over a span of time roughly a quarter-century later, as the author of a remarkable collection of essays forming the base for a very special chapter.

1959-60, coverage of visitation; Sheldahl, *Alpha to Omega*, pp. 305-314, 318, 320 (visitation checklist); Wayne E. Shroyer, Visitation Reports--Beta, December 17, 1958, letter, Nu, January [1954], no. 4; Charles C. Staehling ("Charlie") to A. J. Penz ("Andy"), April 4, 1954 (McConahey File); W. E. Stone to (Grand) Councilors, April 3, 1959 (Visitation Files), quoted; [Stone], "Grand Council Visitation Assignments, 1958-59" (same source); Stone, Visitation Reports--Gamma, May 2, 1959, February 5, 1960 (with Beta Gamma), Upsilon (and Alpha Mu), March 16, 1959 (quoted), Omega, November 23, 1959, Alpha Sigma, November 28, 1959, Alpha Psi, April 24, 1959 (letters), Xi, October 25, 1957, no. 4; Visitation Files, 1950-60; [Nolan E. Williams], Secretary-Treasurer's Report, 1958-59, pp. 4, 10; Williams to Author, interview, March 21, 1980; Williams, Visitation Report--Lambda, December 16, 1958, no. 2.3, and to Councilors, December 24, 1959 (quoted); Williams, Visitation Reports--Alpha Beta, February 22, 1960, Alpha Delta, November 5, 1959, no. 1 (quoted); and Zeff, *American Accounting Association*, pp. 66-67.

CHAPTER 7

ESSAYS CONTRIBUTED BY COUNCILOR A. J. PENZ: A TREASURY OF REMINISCENCE AND COMMENTARY

This chapter is the product of an opportunity to provide a firsthand account, embodying breadth and depth alike well beyond the interview level, of experiences, recollections, and observations of a distinguished Beta Alpha Psi personality. Dr. A. J. Penz, emeritus professor of accounting at the University of Alabama, is widely recognized as a major contributor to the postwar development of the fraternity and one of its major exponents.

Nearly ten years after his retirement from the governing body, the National Council turned to Andy Penz for the development of an historical profile of the organization in commemoration of its forthcoming golden anniversary. The excellent booklet that resulted is covered within proper chronological sequence in chapter 11. Twenty-five years after the close of his presidential term, Penz was one of three past leaders invited by the Council in 1981 to meet for a videotaped exchange of fraternal reminiscence and commentary. He was unable to join Herb Miller and Fred Mueller on that occasion, in creating an inherently prized Beta Alpha Psi document, as Mrs. Penz was hospitalized for major surgery. In an earlier interview, Emerson Henke, who had known him personally at least since the installation of Alpha Rho Chapter at Baylor in 1955, had described Andy as "Mr. Beta Alpha Psi."[1]

---

[1] Henry R. "Hank" Anderson, "From the President," 1981-82 Annual Report, ed. [Anderson], p. 1; Emerson O. Henke to Author, interview, March 21, 1980, quoted; National Council Minutes, June 1981, p. 12 (no. 24); and A. J. Penz to Author, July 29, 1981.

At that very time in 1980, Penz was preparing a series of five essays to assist the author in developing a fraternal history then expected to require a single volume. This material covering postwar developments was retained for later use once it was decided to close initial coverage at 1945.

Following a biographical sketch, the present chapter is based on four of the 1980 essays, as (where pertinent) revised and extended over the years since they were composed. Not included, because of substantial overlap with earlier coverage, is "Beta Alpha Psi Activity Program," dated March 29, 1980. It was used as a source, however, regarding Secretary-Treasurer Penz's frustrating visitation to Illinois twenty-five years earlier. Covered in turn are the formation of Alpha Beta at Alabama, and a memorable practice within that chapter; the impact of the fraternity on professional education and practice, making special reference to the same local unit; and the creation and production of Beta Alpha Psi banners, representing a remarkable family tradition.[2]

Andy Penz's special commitment to Beta Alpha Psi is rooted in an educational outlook that itself began to take shape while he was still in high school.

---

[2]Three essays prepared later, in the spring of 1985, are of much biographical interest, but have been omitted for lack of Beta Alpha Psi themes. "International Accounting," submitted to the author on April 29, 1985, covers an assignment undertaken in Peru, from September 1965 to January '66, under the sponsorship of the State Department's Agency for International Development (AID). Dr. Penz prepared for translation into Spanish a basic cost accounting manual designed primarily for small businesses, and conducted extremely popular short-term lecture courses in several cities. "Guayana, S. A. (The Former British Guiana)," dated May 7, documents a month-long AID-sponsored teaching mission in Georgetown of early 1969. Finally, "A Glimpse of the Life of a Retired Professor," dated May 20, covers Andy Penz's active retirement, since 1971. Highlights of coverage are his courtship of Nashville widow Edith Bruder Orr in 1972, and their marriage that December; and teaching assignments at Nevada, Colorado, Virginia Commonwealth, Maryland, and predominantly black Stillman College, at his home base in Tuscaloosa.

Biographical Sketch

The Making of a Pragmatic Educator, Through 1947

A(nton) J(acob) Penz was born in Cleveland in 1906. His father was a custom tailor who worked for a firm that manufactured ladies' garments. As a high-school student, Andy worked afternoons and evenings at the May Company Department Store, staying on for a full year after his graduation in 1927 to earn money for college. Later at Fenn College, now Cleveland State University, he pursued a "cooperative" work-study program that included jobs with the May Company and other firms, including a Chandler Motors assembly plant and an electric products company. On campus he served as student council president and editor of the annual.

Such experiences helped establish A. J. Penz as a strong advocate, as well as a worthy exhibit, of the pragmatic educational philosophy of "learning by doing." He firmly accepts the related position, attributed to pragmatist John Dewey, that '"[t]he very process of association is educative"' (emphasis added), drawing the inference that "the informal association of faculty, students and practitioners is an integral part of higher education." It is naturally within this light that he interprets the role of Beta Alpha Psi as a professional fraternity.

Penz received a B.S. degree in electrical engineering in 1933, having also (being already "more interested in human engineering") completed all accounting courses that were offered. There was of course no local chapter of Beta Alpha Psi, although Dean Paul Anders had during Andy's time at Fenn College contacted the Grand Council on the possibility (not realistic) of forming a fraternal unit within the evening division.

The accounting study quickly paid dividends as the Depression-year graduate secured a job in Cleveland as a cost accountant with the firm Gulf

Refining of Delaware. In 1934 he became office manager for Starr Products, and began a master's program in education at Western Reserve that was completed within two years. Reflecting in 1980 on his first contact with graduate study, Penz recalled courses in educational and abnormal psychology and in the philosophy of education that had been "interesting" and "most useful" to his academic career. The master's candidate in education also studied accounting under newly arrived associate professor Thomas M. Dickerson. Even had he been specializing in the field, he would not have been exposed to Beta Alpha Psi because, for reasons related in volume 1, Pi Chapter was inactive at the time.

After a year as a cost analyst with the Cleveland Tractor Company, Andy Penz began his teaching career in 1937 as professor and chairman in the business department at Davis and Elkins College, a Presbyterian school in West Virginia located south of Morgantown a few miles west of the Alleghenies. During the next two summers he studied business administration at Northwestern. In June 1940 Penz left West Virginia to become manager of a proprietary business college at Greenwood, South Carolina. A year later he took a teaching job at a similar school in Jacksonville, Florida, but left after the fall semester upon being urged by acquaintances to raise his sights toward a career at "a reputable college or university."

As an important step in that direction, Andy resumed his studies at Northwestern midway through the 1941-42 academic year, and by the end of the following summer had completed an M.B.A. degree with a concentration in accounting. The business school had by this point introduced the "case" method of graduate instruction, coupled with a deemphasis upon Penz'a major field, ostensibly a purely technical subject. Classroom demonstrations were conducted in the use of "single-purpose" and "multipurpose" accounting

machines of the day, based on the processing of punched cards.

For the first time A. J. Penz was an accounting major, and indeed the M.B.A. would be his only degree specifically in the field in which he would pursue his academic career. Again, however, he did not become involved in Beta Alpha Psi, largely due to the brevity of his stay on campus. In addition, Gamma Chapter was by choice only moderately active, at best, during the year 1941-42. Observing a "policy of working on each meeting as it c[ame]," the group prepared "no definite schedule" of meetings. The first session of the year had occurred on November 30, a week before Pearl Harbor, amidst an expectation that there would be monthly meetings thereafter. The only further information available is that fifteen new members were initiated during the year.

With his M.B.A. in hand, Penz headed for Ohio State in the fall of 1942 to work toward a doctorate in business administration. For two years he was a full-time student, a teaching assistant, and a part-time auditor for W. E. Langdon and Sons, CPAs. The unusually broad program embraced comprehensive exams in <u>four</u> fields: accounting, economics, finance, and management, the area in which he completed his dissertation in 1947. After the fall of 1942, Omicron Chapter had been largely dormant during Penz's time at Ohio State, with Hermann Miller and Jacob Taylor both in service, so once again he had not been introduced to Beta Alpha Psi.

During the summer of 1944, the doctoral candidate in business who held a degree in electical engineering taught at Renssalaer Poyltechnic Institute, a prominent engineering school in upstate New York. In the fall, he moved on to Louisiana State as an assistant professor of accounting. One of his students the first year, as reported in chapter 1, was the future wife of fourth-era Beta Alpha Psi president Leon Hay.

More pertinently, Penz himself was married at Christmas 1945, to Arline Ruth Hassmer, a pediatric social worker who held two degrees from Western Reserve. They had met some fifteen years earlier through Arline's brother Wilford, a member of Andy's social fraternity, and since then she had worked for the Red Cross in Cleveland and the University of Pennsylvania Hospital in Philadelphia. Upon their arrival in Baton Rouge, the first caller on the Penzes was the dean of social work at LSU, who offered the bride an assistant professorship, beginning immediately. She accordingly joined her husband on the faculty over the next year and a half. Later in Tuscaloosa, she worked ten years, part time, at the Veterans' Administration Mental Hospital, developing proficiency in the psychiatric side of social work.

Although Phi Chapter was reactivated late in 1946, Andy Penz does not recall attending many chapter meetings, and he was not included among the initiates of the academic year 1946-47. Finally, however, he "came into the fold of Beta Alpha Psi the easy way" through election as a faculty member during the summer of 1947. Holding a newly minted Ph.D. degree, Penz left the campus at the close of the summer to become an associate professor at the University of Alabama.[3]

---

[3] AAA Road Atlas, pp. 110-111; Barron's Profiles, s.v. "West Virginia: Davis and Elkins College"; "Letters from Local Chapters," Newsletter [2] (November 1941):9, quoted; A. J. Penz, "How Alpha Beta Chapter of Beta Alpha Psi Was Established," [March 1980], p. 1 (opening paragraph, deleted from slightly edited version presented as essay no. 1); Penz, Resume, pp. 1, 3; Penz to Author, March 19, 1980 (quoted), June 15, 1982, January 16, 1985 (both by telephone, latter quoted), August 1, 12, 1985; [Prentice-Hall] Encyclopedic Dictionary of Business (New York: Prentice-Hall, 1952), s.v. "Business machines: [Nos.] 5-7," emphasis in original; Sheldahl, Alpha to Omega, pp. 752, 758, 817; Jerry E. Trapnell, 1981-84 Phi Chapter faculty vice-president, to Author (by telephone), July 25, 1985; [S. M. Wedeberg], "New Councilor A. J. Penz," Newsletter 4 (November 1952):11, quoted; and Who's Who in America 43 (1984-85), s.v. "Penz, Anton Jacob."

Phi Chapter alumni files consulted by Trapnell, reflecting dates supplied by the National Office, list Penz as an initiate of July 16, 1947. The summer initiation was recorded six days earlier in the contemporary cashbook, however. The erroneous reference made to 1946 as the year of

The most pertinent contributions made by A. J. Penz during his twenty-four years at Alabama were of course his work in establishing Alpha Beta Chapter, his service as faculty vice-president, and then his membership on the Grand Council. Two other particular highlights were likewise focused squarely on accounting education, namely, doctoral study locally, and effective introductory teaching nationally.

University of Alabama, 1947-71

Leadership role in doctoral program

A doctoral program with a major in accounting was introduced at Alabama in 1950. It thus joined Louisiana State, Penz's former school, as (east of Texas) the only southern or border-state universities to offer terminal degrees in the field during the 1950s. Ten doctorates were conferred through 1960, the first one in 1953, ten years after LSU had awarded its first such degree. Andy Penz served as a dissertation advisor in at least four cases, each involving an educational, pragmatic, and/or engineering theme. Two of his students wrote on higher education in accounting within selected southern states; one reinterpreted certain accounting concepts in light of "the requirements of a dynamic economic environment"; and the final one sized up potential implications for accounting practice of the new technical field operations research.

Dr. S. Paul Garner, Beta Alpha Psi's second Accountant of the Year, was

initiation, on the dedication page of the first volume, was based on a somewhat tentative recollection by Dr. Penz that was accepted without further inquiry. The correct year, ironically, was available from the resume cited above (p. 2). Grand Cashbook, 1931-49, p. 58; Penz to Author, by telephone, June 15, 1982; and Sheldahl, Alpha to Omega, p. [iii].

Penz has been listed in Who's Who since the 36th edition, dated 1970-71. The amended resume provides fuller and more exacting information, however.

the original driving force behind the Ph.D. studies at Alabama. Dr. Penz emphasized this contribution in a 1976 "Accountancy Day" campus tribute to his long-time dean in which he recalled, with due institutional pride, that in his day the Alabama doctoral program had helped populate numerous accounting departments across the south. He himself, however, merits considerable personal credit for the gratifying results cited. Succeeding Garner as department head in 1954, a year after being promoted to the full professor rank, Penz would serve in that role for sixteen years. During that period, forty-five men and women earned Ph.D.'s in accounting from Alabama, a total exceeded by 1970 by only seven American universities. A number of doctoral students were attracted to the department in 1960s by the availability of generous fellowship assistance under the National Defense Education Act of 1958, producing for a time "quite a heavy load" in dissertation advising.[4]

As a writer and editor, Dr. Penz's major nonfraternal contributions would also directly concern accounting education, although he earned a Lybrand certificate of merit from the National Association of Cost Accountants in 1951 for an article on standard costing in the steel industry.[5] In particular, he served as coeditor and lead author for two major studies

---

[4]Dorothy E. Brown, University of Alabama business librarian, to Author, August 13, 1985, quoted; [Doris W. Cook], "S. Paul Garner, Accountant of the Year," Newsletter 14 (Fall 1975):1; Funk & Wagnalls, s.v. "Education, Office of"; Hasselback, 1984 Directory, p. [viii], numbering consecutively from title page; "Local Chapter News," Newsletter [3] (March 1951):26; A. J. Penz, remarks delivered to Accounting Recognition Banquet (Accountancy Day), University of Alabama, February 25, 1976; Penz, Resume, p. 3; Penz to Author, August 1, 1985, quoted; Previts, ed., Alabama Accounting Program, pp. 14-15; and The University of Alabama Graduate Catalog, 1983-84 (University, Ala.: 1983; 1983-84 Microfiche Catalogs, AL:10), p. 30.

[5]A. J. Penz, "Standard Costs in a Small Steel Company," N.A.C.A Bulletin 32 (July 1951):442-44; and [S. M. Wedeberg], "New Councilor A. J. Penz," as cited in note 3.

issued by Southwestern Publishing Company for the American Accounting Association. They were focused on the opposite end of the spectrum from doctoral work, namely, the teaching of accounting principles.

Coeditor and contributor regarding two major AAA educational studies

One of Paul Garner's very first acts as president of the AAA in 1951 was to appoint a committee to prepare an "accounting teachers' guide," for purposes of (a) stressing the importance of elementary instruction in the field, and (b) enhancing standards and methods of teaching at that level. Appointed to the committee were Professors Leo Schloss (chairman) of Long Island University, Harry D. Kerrigan of Northwestern,[6] and A. J. Penz of Alabama. Early in 1953, just before the assignment was completed, future AAA research director Ralph L. Boyd of Oregon State replaced Kerrigan.

Schloss and his colleagues began, in 1951, by drafting an outline for a teachers' guide, and then revising it based on a small questionnaire survey conducted within the association. The following year pertinent manuscripts were obtained from 70 members, from among some 200 contacted, to provide a strong base of content. Eight chapter editors were appointed to organize this material for publication in book form.

Andy Penz was the only committee member to assume such responsibility, as the editor of chapter 1, although his two colleagues had likewise provide

---

[6] Kerrigan had served at least eleven years as faculty advisor to Gamma Chapter (1934-48, omitting three years of inactivity). The position appears to have been vacant for a time during 1933, following the departure for a leave of absence in New York of prior holder W. Mason Smith. "Directory," Newsletter [2] (December 1938):2, (March 1939 - March 1943):3, 3 (November 1946- May 1947):3; "Directory of Activities," Newsletter [1] (March 1933, unbound):9, (October 1933):9, (December 1934):7, (March 1935):16, (February 1936):[12], [2], (October 1936):10, (April 1937):10, (November 1937):11, (April 1938):2; "Grand Chapter," Newsletter [2] (November 1947 - November 1948):3; "News from the Chapters," Newsletter [1] (October 1933):3; and Sheldahl, Alpha to Omega, p. 747.

manuscript material. Other contributing authors included H. W. Kendrick (editor of chapter 3), John Arch White, Emerson Henke, H. J. Ostlund, a pre-war Beta Alpha Psi president, and William J. Schlatter, the son of another such leader. In a day of relatively limited copying capabilities, honorary Sigma member Richard Claire of Arthur Andersen, in whose memory annual faculty vice-president awards would later be named, "was responsible for reproducing the entire manuscript in its final stages." Claire, Tom Dickerson, and one other member served as vice-presidents of the AAA in 1952.

The result of the 27-month project was the publication in the summer of 1953 of the 258-page book Accounting Teachers' Guide, edited by Schloss, Boyd, and Penz. Although material from all 70 contributors appears to have been incorporated into the text, Paul Garner specified in his forward, in interrogative form, that content had been selected and edited on a fundamentally pragmatic basis:

> Is it useful?
> Will it make college and university accounting instruction more effective and thorough?
> Is it material which will be permanently helpful to the younger, more inexperienced instructors who enter the teaching ranks each year?
> And finally, has it been tested through the years for validity?.

The eight chapters bore the following titles:

1. "Professional Developments"
2. "Course Content and Conduct"
3. "A Well-informed and Better-guided Student"
4. "A More Effective Teacher"
5. "Teaching Aids"
6. "Testing"
7. "The Teacher's Self-Audit"
8. "The Student Evaluates the Teacher."

The last two components respectively provided an operational checklist for the accounting instructor in evaluating his or her own strengths and weaknesses as a teacher, and demonstrated that "student evaluations" were already in some measure an element of college and university teaching in the early fifties. To be sure, one of the twelve section headings within chapter 8 might prompt more objection in the mid-1980s than when it was

adopted: "Students Do Not Know What Elements Constitute Good Teaching."

The first chapter, comprised of 31 pages, presented under eleven headings the material submitted by editor Penz and seven other contributing authors. A number of the sections covered extremely broad topics, including the origins and evolution of (a) accounting, (b) teaching, and (c) the teaching of accounting; the nature of a profession, and ethical standards for the teaching profession; and the full range of occupational and career opportunities found within accounting.

One of the most interesting sections of the "Professional Developments" chapter was titled "The Future of the Accounting Teacher." It bore the undoubted mark of the editor, beginning with the second sentence: "Every act in association with others is educational." The author foresaw the eventual formation, possibly still "in the distant future," of schools of accountancy comparable to law and medical schools, offering professional instruction to students holding a bachelor's degree as an entry requirement. Preprofessional instruction in accounting would continue to be provided at the undergraduate level, however. Indeed, the day was foreseen that, because of the relevance "to the general understanding of our industrial economy" of a discipline incorporating elements from "law, finance, mathematics, statistics, economics, and business organization," accounting would ultimately become established as "a requisite in every college curriculum."

Read more than three decades later, these projections seem conceptually well-founded, but still visionary from a practical standpoint.[7] A prediction

[7] It was also forecast that "in the foreseeable future a doctor's degree together with adequate business experience, w[ould come to] be considered essential for all college teachers of accounting" (p. 16). The first component would be realized in 1969, when the AACSB upgraded faculty educational standards in the field to the doctoral level, four years after the AAA had endorsed such a position. Standards adopted later for the accreditation of accounting programs, moreover, would include significant "certification"

made regarding accounting practice, also sounding very much like a contribution originating with chapter editor A. J. Penz, was destined to be realized much sooner. Penz (by assumption) foresaw the rise of "[t]he science of accounting engineering," or "professional controllership":

> Within it will be all the services in office systematizing, financial interpreting, budgeting, cost control, and assistance in management decisions. . . . [I]t will be a service to hundreds of thousands of businesses which do not have available a full-time controller.[8]

Although its application is scarcely confined to, or concentrated upon, the small business realm, it is clear that such a field has emerged as a major component of public accounting practice, under the name "management advisory services." A bit ironically, Andy Penz's last Ph.D. student would advocate in a 1968 thesis a limitation in the scope of CPA work in this area.

Finally, the opening chapter of Accounting Teachers' Guide made specific reference to Beta Alpha Psi. Within a discussion of accounting opportunities

---

and "experience" requirements for departments (or other administrative units) as a whole. "Accreditation Standards and Interpretations for Accounting Programs," American Assembly of Collegiate Schools of Business: Accreditation Council Policies, Procedures, and Standards (St. Louis: AACSB, [1984]), pp. 40-42, quoted; Milton R. Blood, Director of Accreditation, AACSB, to Author, August 21, 1985; and Gary John Previts and Barbara Dubis Merino, A History of Accounting in America: An Historical Interpretation of the Cultural Significance of Accounting (New York: John Wiley & Sons, Ronald Press div., 1979), p. 283.

[8]Leo Schloss, Ralph L. Boyd, and A. J. Penz, eds. (editorial committee), Accounting Teachers' Guide (Cincinnati: South-Western Publishing Co., for American Accounting Association, 1953), p. 20 (immediate indented citation). This concept of accounting engineering was credited in a footnote (p. 20n) to Maurice H. Stans. Although his distinguished professional career would lead to his election in 1960 to the Accounting Hall of Fame, Stans' public reputation was destined to be tarnished by his association with fundraising improprieties within the Republican presidential campaign of 1972. Thomas J. Burns, capsule review of The Terrors of Justice: The Untold Side of Watergate, by Maurice H. Stans, The Accounting Review 55 (January 1980): 235; and Burns and Coffman, Accounting Hall of Fame, pp. 63, 79-80, 82.

The American Institute of Accountants established a committee on management services in 1953. Carey, Rise of Profession 2:482.

for women, the subject of one section, it was pointed out that fraternal membership was, by then, "open on an equal basis to men and women."

During the presidency of Herbert Miller, 1965-66, a committee was formed within the AAA to determine whether the instructors' guide should be revised, replaced, or allowed simply to go out of print. The decision was to develop a major revision, retaining the basic format of the original study. As a result, a successor committee was appointed in 1966 to prepare the revision. The seven members included Dr. Penz and future Beta Alpha Psi president James Pattillo, faculty vice-president of Iota at Southern California. Members Penz, Clarence G. Avery of Northern Illinois, and Doyle Z. Williams of Texas Tech were then selected to form an editorial subcommittee, and thus function in essence as editors of the new study. Williams, who in the course of the project would join the staff of the American Institute of CPAs, served as chairman of both the full group and the subcommittee.

The work of Williams' committee led to the publication in 1968 of _A Guide to Accounting Instruction: Concepts & Practices_. Opting for substance over form, the group designated the book as a second edition. In keeping with the development or expansion since 1953 of several important teaching devices, material was included "on the instructional dimensions of business games, the case method, instructional television, computers, and programmed instruction." In addition, the remarkable spread, and increasing formality, of "student evaluation" required the complete revision of chapter 8, supported by inclusion, in the appendix, of "widely used evaluation forms." The author of that final chapter (reference to "editors" had been dropped) was James Pattillo, who during the project had moved from USC to Louisiana State. He likewise had prepared the preceding chapter, retitled

"The Instructor Evaluates the Student and Himself" due to material added on assessment of students well beyond the grading function.

Six of the seven members of the full committee served as chapter authors, including the three subcommittee members. Dr. Penz's chapter, "Introducing the Profession" (pp. 1-24), was mainly a modest revision of his 1953 essay. Unlike the original chapter, however, it made more than passing reference to Beta Alpha Psi. A full page was devoted to the formation of the fraternity and its development as a significant contributor to collegiate education in accounting.

During the interim between the two AAA studies, Penz had served as a vice-president of the association in 1961-62, and as a member of the editorial committee of the Institute of Internal Auditors, 1960-63, publisher of the periodical The Internal Auditor. In the latter capacity, he had borne specific responsibility for the "Education and Practice" section of the journal, and contributed a number of editorials to that section.[9]

During Andy Penz's first year at Alabama, he had spearheaded an effort that, starting from scratch, had produced the year's only application for a Beta Alpha Psi charter. With the approval of the petition early in his second year, the stage was set for a career of exceptional service to the fraternity that would always include dedicated involvement in the work of

---

[9]American Accounting Association, Committee to Prepare a Revised Accounting Teachers' Guide, [ed.], A Guide to Accounting Instruction: Concepts & Practices, 2nd ed. (Cincinnati: South Western, for AAA, 1968), pp. [iv-ix], numbering consecutively from first inside page (blank), quoting pp. [v-vi, ix]; Dorothy E. Brown (note 4) to Author, August 13, 1985; James W. Pattillo, "Metropolitan Area Chapter: Oh, the Disadvantages," Newsletter 7 (May 1967):3-5; A. J. Penz, "Introducing the Profession," Guide to Instruction, ed. AAA committee, pp. 1-24, especially pp. 18-19; Penz, ed., "Professional Developments," Teachers' Guide, ed. Schloss, Boyd, and Penz, pp. 1-31, passim, quoting pp. 15, 26, 28; Penz, Resume, p. 2; Schloss, Boyd, and Penz, edsl, Teachers' Guide, pp. iii-xiii, quoting pp. iv-v, vii-x (chapter titles); Doyle Z. Williams to Author, August 12, 1985 (postmark); and Zeff, American Accounting Association, p. [95].

the first postwar, and double-letter, chapter.

Essays Concerning Alpha Beta Chapter: Its Founding, a Memorable Tradition, and a Continuing Commitment to Professional Service

The founding of Alpha Beta is covered in the first of three essays focused on the local unit. Others deal with a heartwarming twelve-year annual tradition at the Penz home and an illustration of the distinctive role played by a Beta Alpha Psi chapter in the educative process. With the full consent (and indeed encouragement) of Dr. Penz, occasional limited editorial changes have been made in this and later essays for purposes of stylistic continuity (to a degree), effective transition, updating, and avoidance of redundancy or minor factual discrepancy. Rather than risking distraction through use of quotation marks throughout the text, an appropriate notation is used to identify each page that begins with essay material.

Essay No. 1, March 1980: "How Alpha Beta Chapter of Beta Alpha Psi Was Established"

"After Phi Chapter was reactivated during my last year at LSU, I was immediately impressed with the viability of the organization in the educative process and the profession of accountancy. Upon my arrival at the University of Alabama in 1947 as associate professor of accounting, I was surprised to discover that there was no B.A.Psi chapter or any accounting student organization.

When I brought up the question at a faculty meeting, it was revealed that Professor William Whitney and a group of students had looked into the matter the previous year, but found that there was not enough student response or enthusiasm for an organization. Thus the subject was dropped. My overt interest, however, prompted the chairman of the department, Dr.

S. Paul Garner, to appoint me as a committee of one to pursue the matter further.

This committee charge I found somewhat perplexing. Confronted with the report of the previous year's failure, being new on the faculty and unknown to most of the upper-level students, would I be able to engender enough student support, interest, and enthusiasm for a student organization? My chances for success were at best doubtful.

Eager to establish my mark on the teaching staff, I promptly contacted the Grand Council (now the National Council), and soon received the procedures and other requirements for chartering a new chapter. The major requirement posed a hurdle. An existing and functioning accounting student organization or club was required. The previous year's apathy or lack of interest notwithstanding, I issued a bulletin, distributed to upper classes for announcement, calling for a meeting of interested students in Room 308, Commerce Bldg. I expected about 8 to 10 students to show up, which I thought would make a good nucleus with which to start organizing. When I entered the 50-seat room at the appointed time, I was overwhelmed. About 80 students had showed up.

This was the first of many pleasant surprises and pleasures I had in working with upper-level and high-ranking accounting students. I briefly presented the advantages and benefits of an accounting organization. The applause that followed assured me of interest and support. In order to have a B.A.Psi chapter we had to have an accounting club. I appointed a committee of students to draw up an organization plan for an accounting club. At a meeting the following week, a constitution and bylaws were approved and officers were elected, and a functioning club was underway.

--Essay no. 1 (continued)--

The first order of business was to make formal application for a Beta Alpha Psi charter. A discouraging prerequisite was revealed in the fine print. The accounting club had to have a history of two years' successful operation. Since the students were primarily juniors and seniors, they would all be graduated before a B.A.Psi chapter could be installed. Undaunted, we discovered that the application form did not call for a date of origin for the accounting club, and since we did have a viable and strong club, it was decided to send in an application. If everything went right, at least the junior members of the club could become charter members, locally, of B.A.Psi.

In the light of the fact that the accounting program at the University of Alabama had a national reputation, and possibly because the Grand Council of B.A.Psi was eager to expand and become active following the lull of the W.W.II years, the question of the accounting club's length of existence was not raised. Negotiations continued, the Grand Council approved the application, and Alpha Beta Chapter was installed during the fall semester of 1948. Prof. Thomas Dickerson of Western Reserve U. (now Case Western) was the installing officer.

As might have been expected, I was nominated by the chapter for the faculty vice-presidency and subsequently approved by the Grand Council. I served in this position until 1952, when I was elected to the Council. Since one could not be a member of the Grand Chapter, made up of F.V.P.'s, and also serve on the Grand Council, Alpha Beta Chapter had to have a new advisor. Successful operations continued under Dr. Robert H. Van Voorhis, as Alpha Beta in 1954 became the first double-letter chapter to come in first in the relatively new activity program. Over the years it would

consistently rank among the top ten chapters in the country."

A year after his election to the Grand Council, Dr. Penz and his family commenced a particularly meaningful Alpha Beta tradition at their home that would reinforce the fraternal themes of responsibility and association. It originated, however, in response to a paternalistic social policy of the day that extended beyond the campus to the broader community.

Essay No. 2, March 1980: "Alpha Beta Chapter Banquets in a Ratskeller, 1953-64"

'In 1953 Tuscaloosa County was dry, being located in the Baptist belt. The previous year we had held the initiation banquet at the Cotton Patch in Green County, which was wet, but afterwards we had been told in no uncertain terms that we were in violation of a university rule that no university-related function could be held in a place that served beer.

When plans came up for the 1953 initiation banquet, an impasse developed. B.A.Psi members, many of them GIs, felt that they were mature enough to gather where they wished, yet all of the desirable spots were ruled off limits, with the result that final arrangements were delayed so much that when other places were considered, there were none available for the scheduled date.

One evening at dinner I casually mentioned the predicament. After a moment's reflection, Mrs. Penz suggested that we have the banquet at our house. "At our house!" I exlaimed. "At best we could seat twenty-four in the dining room, but that would not nearly be enough," I remarked. "No, no," she replied, "we could have it in the basement with a 'Ratskeller' motive." "But the basement is not finished," I continued. We had built the house

that year and moved in during August. Since I was my own contractor, many details remained to be completed. Mrs. Penz insisted that <u>we</u> could have the basement ready in the two weeks that remained before the scheduled banquet. From past experience I was apprehensive about the editorial "we". The "we" usually meant that I had to do it.

At the next B.A.Psi meeting, I extended the invitation with considerable misgiving, but to my amazement students agreed that it was a great idea and they were delighted to accept. With this acceptance, feverish preparations began with committee appointments for food to be catered, decorations, entertainment, refreshments, etc., until there were no more members left who were not on a committee of one kind or another. As anticipated, I was a committee of one to paint the concrete walls in the basement, an area of over 2,100 square feet divided into three rooms.

The enthusiasm that students displayed became infectious. Normally it would have taken years to finish the basement, but with the time limit it was finished in good order. In two evenings and with the help of a few six-packs, the decorating committee did an excellent job, with multicolored streamers and balloons covering the unfinished ceiling. Popping the balloons added to the merriment.

The faculty all helped out with card tables and chairs, and Mrs. Penz in no time had dozens of checkered table cloths of various colors ready to create a Ratskeller, cabaret, atmosphere. Only one insurmountable shortage was encountered. There were not enough wine bottles available to serve as candle holders for each table. When we mentioned this fact, we promptly had numerous volunteers to serve on the committee to empty wine bottles to make candle holders.

--Essay no. 2 (continued)--

As an emergency measure, the banquet was a huge success. In the privacy of our home, the students and their dates, wives, or guests were throughly relaxed and had an enjoyable evening. The Penz family enjoyed it no less. Alton and David, 6 and 5 years old respectively, basked in the attention they received while helping to clear tables. The overall consensus was that the party be repeated next year. Even the Duke, a semi-Dalmatian, and Tiger, an alley cat, were much in favor of repetition, as they feasted on table scraps for the next two weeks.

Mrs. Penz and I were much pleased with the effectiveness of the affair. The sociality was enhanced by the plan that no two faculty and no two actives sit at the same table. The interaction among faculty and students, actives and initiates was tremendous, achieving one of the objectives of B.A.Psi.

Arranging an affair of this magnitude on short notice, some short-comings were bound to develop. For instance, plastic knives and forks were inadequate for one-half of a barbecued chicken. However, that did not keep some of the men from going back for a second half.

Parking facilities were woefully lacking. Off-street parking was necessary, as the drive in front of the house was wide enough for only two cars, and a ditch a yard deep running the entire length of the 250-feet frontage necessitated parking cars like sardines in the back of the house and in the driveway.

In anticipation of a repeat performance the next year, corrective action was taken. The City of Tuscaloosa was called on to fill in the ditch, which the boys helped to level and to sod. The wooded lot was surveyed with the Penz boys pointing out to Dad that if you take this tree out there would be room to park a car between two other trees. Thus a number of pine trees

--Essay no. 2 (continued)--

became victims of the saw and ax to make room for parking.

To make the next event more convenient, we acquired stainless flatware; and to reduce the borrowing of tables and chairs, we ordered four Monroe folding tables and enough chairs to seat 40 people. As the chapter membership increased, however, additional equipment had to be ordered until we could seat from 82 to 87 people in 1964, as I recall, 25-30 more than had attended the first banquet.

When the 1954 banquet came around, Alton and David, now 7 and 6, with flashlight in hand, assumed the responsibility for orderly parking. This activity went smoothly with the exception that Alton, who was stationed at the lower level, stopped every car coming up Beech Hills and waved it into our yard. One chap finally pleaded with Alton, "Look bud, I'm tired and all I want to do is go home. Won't you let me pass?" On the other hand, David, who was stationed at the upper drive, came to me with tears flowing down his cheeks, "Daddy, Alton is parking all the cars and I don't have any. I assured David that the lower level would be filled in no time and then all the remaining cars would be his to park. Consoled, he went back to his station.

The second banquet in 1954 established a tradition. It surpassed the success of the one in '53. The singing of folk songs and spirituals until the late hours of the night left Sigmund Romburg's "Student Prince" in the shade. Certainly singing, "For they cut down the old pine tree, " was most appropriate, except that the pine tree ended in the fireplace. The singing may have lacked the harmony of an a cappella choir, but with song sheets in hand and everyone participating, the volume was tremendous. The only mishap occurred when the candles on the table in front of the roaring

--Essay no. 2 (continued)--

fireplace melted and drooped.

This tradition continued for twelve years. As the boys grew older they not only helped in many ways, but also supplied the entertainment. One year Alton constructed an electronic question and answer device. When one pointed to the correct answer a bell would ring. To the delight of Alton, everyone wanted to try it. The following year, David, not to be outdone, constructed a six-foot robot with head turning and heart beat indicated by a flashing red light. The robot answered questions of yes and no in morse code. In subsequent years the boys delighted the group by forming a combo with members of the high school band.

But all good things have to come to an end. Mrs Penz died in the spring of '63, but the boys, having been imbued with the spirit of Beta Alpha Psi, insisted that the banquet must go on. On it went in the fall of '63 and '64. In the fall of '65, however, Alton went to Ohio State and David to Michigan State, while I headed for Peru, S.A. under a State Department program, lecturing on financial and accounting control for small business entrepreneurs. With all of us away from home, the chain was broken.

The end of this tradition was inevitable. Alpha Beta Chapter was growing while the facilities of our home were limited. In recent years the fall banquet, with about 250 people in attendance, three times the largest number ever seated at our home, has been held at the sumptuous North River Yacht Club. One might say to Alpha Beta Chapter, "You have come a long way, baby."

According to John Dewey's philosophy, education is not a preparation for life, it is a part of life. In retrospect we can see that the congenial atmosphere created admirable camaraderie among students, while the informal

FRONT AND REAR VIEWS OF THE PENZ HOME, SITE OF A DOZEN
ALPHA BETA BANQUETS, 1953 - 64

ANDY AND EDITH PENZ AT HOME IN TUSCALOOSA, JUNE 1985

setting fostered interaction among students, faculty, and practitioners (honorary initiates). Being responsible for various activities of the function taught students to shoulder responsibilities. All these pleasant experiences are subjects for reminiscence for years to come.

At various professional meetings, I am often asked what the boys are now doing.[10] Alton finished in math and physics at Cornell, where he transferred after his freshman year at Ohio State, and earned a doctorate in urban and public affairs from Carnegie-Mellon, in Pittsburgh. Before recently taking a position in Washington, D.C. with the Building Owners and Management Association, International, he taught at Carnegie-Mellon and commuted to Washington to conduct research in energy conservation. David completed his degree in mechanical engineering at Michigan State, and for some years has been a consulting engineer in Atlanta. He is a vice-president, and a cofounder, of the Emprise Corporation, Consulting Engineers.

In conclusion, the contribution these extracurricular activities made to higher education in accounting and the accounting profession cannot be overestimated'.

In a brief 1980 essay supported by a sample of program material relating to Alpha Beta Chapter, Dr. Penz further illustrated the theme

---

[10]This paragraph has been updated to July 1985. A. J. Penz to Author, July 23, 1985.

Early in 1984, Dr. Penz retitled the 1980 essay, and made minor refinements in the text. A contemporary published source indicated banquet attendance in 1953. "Local Chapter News," Newsletter 4 (March 1954):103; Penz, "Alpha Beta Chapter" (original title), copy of essay with isolated handwritten changes of (based on date of submission to author, withoug covering letter) January 1984; and Penz to Author, February 15, 1984 (making further changes), August 12, 1985 (addressing a minor discrepancy).

just stated. Because his commentary assumed familiarity with the supporting items, the presentation in this case is interspersed with appropriate background content.

Essay No. 3 (Supplemented), March 5, 1980: "The Impact of Beta Alpha Psi on University Education and the Accounting Profession"

'When Alpha Kappa Psi and Delta Sigma Pi were formed at New York University in 1904 and 1907, respectively, one of their major objectives was to inform the public or bring it to public attention that business administration (B.A.) in higher education had substance. Classical educators were prone to look down their noses on B.A. in a sense that there were no merits that warranted higher education prestige. This attitude is further emphasized by the fact that Phi Beta Kappa had no room for B.A., and as a consequence Beta Gamma Sigma came into being.

When the Harvard Business School was established in 1908, it was felt that it would reflect unfavorably on Harvard Yard. Hence it was shunted off across the Charles River with its own campus.

The struggle to become established still prevailed when Beta Alpha Psi was formed in 1919. Hence one of the objects was "to promote the accountancy profession." How was this carried out? It was a slow beginning, but representative current material concerning Alpha Beta illustrates the internal operation of one chapter in the "promoting" process'.

Dr. Penz had enclosed four main items from the 1979-80 academic year at Alabama, including the schedules of (a) chapter activities for the spring semester and (b) annual "Accountancy Day" events, and the programs for (c) the annual "Accounting Research Convocation" and (d) the "Accounting Recognition Banquet" conducted as the final Accountancy Day event. A

month later he would submit an announcement of an April address to Alpha Beta by past National Advisory Forum member William R. Gifford of Price Waterhouse, and the program for the spring banquet of the Alabama Accounting Society, the professional club on campus. The chapter schedule, prepared before Gifford's appearance had been scheduled, listed a variety of professional, organizational, business, and social gatherings, three of which featured guest or sponsoring accounting firms. On successive days in February, Alpha Beta had conducted an orientation for the 'Volunteer Income Tax Assistance Program" ("VITA"); been a leading participant, as discussed below, in Accountancy Day activities; and held a VITA clinic.

The research convocation had the preceding fall brought to campus 11 prominent accounting scholars and professional accountants, and 65 representatives of doctoral faculties or (in nine cases) national accounting organizations, for a two-day seminar on the topic "Seeking Full Disclosure." National Advisory Forum member A(rthur) Clarence Sampson, Jr., chief accountant for the Securities and Exchange Commission, had served on the convocation faculty, and new Beta Alpha Psi councilor Richard W. Metcalf had been the delegate from the University of Nebraska. Sampson, Tau '51, and 1952-53 president of the Maryland Chapter, had earlier in 1979 been designated the fraternity's "Accountant of the Year" within government. The convocation staff had acknowledged the assistance of one organization besides the sponsors: Alpha Beta Chapter. That support had probably included such routine but vital functions as providing local or Birmingham airport connections for guests and transporting them to the opening banquet at the North River Yacht Club.

For Accountancy Day, which had occurred just a week prior to the date of Penz's essay, the Beta Alpha Psi chapter had served in particular as the

coordinator of the evening banquet, and members had received many of the nineteen awards or honors conferred on that occasion. Banquet sponsors had included each of the "Big Eight" accounting firms and a host of corporations and smaller CPA firms. Among the some 500 people in attendance were 10 practicing accountants who had earlier met with regular classes as "Professors for a Day." A likeness of the Beta Alpha Psi seal appeared on the cover page of the day's program.

The stated purposes of Accountancy Day were to provide recognition to students for academic excellence or imminent graduation, and "to provide an opportunity for interaction between representatives of the business community and accounting students and faculty at The University."[11] Andy Penz, who had been on campus a week earlier for Accountancy Day, not surprisingly picked up on the latter point in concluding essay no. 3:

"In the program for the day, students from the Alabama Accounting Society operated the hospitality room, where 'interesting people were met over a cup of coffee'--Maxwell House. At the reception and subsequent banquet every effort was made to visit and talk with students. At dinner faculty and the businessmen did not sit together as they generally do, but

---

[11] "[Accountancy Day] Program" ([University of Alabama, February 27, 1980]), one-page typescript; "Alpha Beta Chapter, Beta Alpha Psi: Schedule of Activities, Spring 1980," one-page typescript, quoted ("VITA"); "Beta Alpha Psi Meeting [, Alpha Beta Chapter]," April 3, [1980], announcement; [Burns], ed., 1978-79 Annual Report, pp. 6 ("Accountant of the Year Awards"), 18 ("Regional Meetings), 23 ("National Advisory Forum"); "Local Chapter News," Newsletter [3] (March 1952):24, 4 (November 1952): 23, (March 1953):52; [Fred J. Mueller], "National Advisory Forum," 1976-77 Annual Report, ed. [Mueller], p. 4; 1979 Accounting Research Convocation: Seeking Full Disclosure (School of Accountancy, University of Alabama), November 16-18, 1979, folder; A. J. Penz to Author, March 5, (source of essay no. 3), April 5 (memo), 1980, enclosing the Alabama items; School of Accountancy, Beta Alpha Psi, and Alabama Accounting Society, Accountancy Day ([University of Alabama]), February 27, 1980, folder; and The University of Alabama Accounting Society, 8th Annual Spring Banquet, April 4, 1980, folder.

they were interspersed among students in order to establish rapport. Students, of course, learned by doing--assuming responsibility for organizing and coordinating the activities for the day. Yes, the faculty and staff helped, but working together constituted a laboratory on human relations that is unsurpassed by any lab in the natural sciences.

Accountancy Day is just one of the activities listed on the spring schedule of Alpha Beta Chapter. Multiply all of these activities by 136 chapters [from early 1980], some better and some worse, and you come up with an educational extra-curricular activity that is bound to have its favorable effect or impact on the educative process, on the profession of accountancy, and the business community."

From a national standpoint, A. J. Penz is of course much more noted for his service as a member of the Grand Council, and later as the fraternal historian, than for the founding and nurturing of Alpha Beta Chapter that led to his appointment in 1952. Probably the foremost contribution was a project that took shape during his last year on the Council and would become a remarkably enduring enterprise of the Penz _family_.

Beta Alpha Psi Banners: A Fraternal "and Family" Tradition

General Background

In 1980, Andy Penz cited as his major national service to the fraternity the creation of the chapter _banner_ that since the late 1950s has identified every local unit. Primarily in order to enhance the initiation ceremony, as discussed below, but also to provide a symbol that might help soothe any ill feeling generated by the activity program, he first proposed the making of banners at the 1955 Grand Council meeting. During the next

year, he produced a Council banner in provisional form, using it as a backdrop in presenting the Alpha Chi charter to the dean at Louisiana Polytechnic Institute in May 1956.

President Penz missed the 1956 annual meeting in Seattle after being stricken en route, during a family stopover at Yellowstone National Park, by pleurisy and double pneumonia. In his absence, the Council authorized the president's advisory committee to proceed with work on "the idea of a banner." As a practical matter, the project was placed in the hands of incoming committee chairman Penz.

For a number of years, incidentally, "attending the August [or September] annual BAPsi and AAA meetings constituted the Penz family vacation." Shortly after being hospitalized in 1956 in Missoula, Montana, Andy told his doctor that he must leave for an important meeting just three days away. The response was that he could indeed leave for Seattle, but would never get there. Penz and his family averted a prolonged stay in the west, however, as he flew back to Tuscaloosa accompanied by his colleague R. H. Van Voorhis (about to move to LSU, and soon to be appointed to the Council) and Arline and the children drove back together with Dean and Mrs. Paul Garner. In the company of the Garners a year earlier at the University of Pennsylvania, Andy had suffered a kidney stone attack while on the dance floor, and been rushed by his wife to a nearby hospital admission office to which, as "her old stomping ground, she knew the shortest distance." Between two nights at the university hospital, he had been able as "a fugitive from" the facility to participate the next day in a full round of Grand Council work.

Over the months that followed the return of the Penzes from Montana

in 1956, the visual design for the banner was improved measurably from the original one by showing the fraternal and chapter names in highly visible gold lettering (rather than black), and adding a gold border. The Council banner was redesigned similarly. Fourteen chapter banners were produced during the year, two of them being used (possibly in a questionable manner, as discussed below) at installations. Within another year, thirty-one more banners had been made and delivered, leaving out only newly installed Beta Gamma at DePaul. That omission was promptly rectified during the academic year 1958-59, when only three other new productions were needed and banners were routinely prepared thereafter in time for advance delivery to new chapters.[12]

The Penz contribution had only begun with the design of the banner, as indicated within the following essay.

Essay No. 4, April 4, 1980:
"Beta Alpha Psi Banners"

'After Alpha Beta Chapter was installed in the fall of 1948, we started with plans for the spring initiation. The ritual called for the pointing out of the rising sun and cross keys, but we had nothing to point to. One of the members created a metal insignia in the form of a lamp. When light the rising sun and cross keys would show in a golden glow with white pearls reflected around the edges. This excellent creation worked beautifully

---

[12]Grand Council Minutes Book, 1956, pp. 5 (quoted), 7, 1957, pp. [3-4] 1958, p. [2], 1959, p. 3; S. Paul Garner and A. J. Penz to Author, conversation (Tuscaloosa, Ala.), July 28, 1983 (one day after author's initial kidney stone attack); [W. B. Jencks], "Chapter Installed at Louisiana Polytechnic Institute." Newsletter 4 (November 1956):353, accompanying photo; A. J. Penz to Author, April 18, 1980 (interview), August 1, 12 (quoted), 1985; Author to Penz, August 5, 1985; and [Nolan E. Williams], Secretary-Treasurer's Report, 1958-59, p. 3.

when the initiation was held in one of the classrooms.

As the initiates became more numerous and the ritual was performed at a local hotel, a number of drawbacks developed. The lighted symbol had to be placed on a desk or table, and the second and third rows of initiates still had difficulty viewing it.

I mentioned this problem at a Grand Council meeting, and suggested that we ought to have a chapter banner that could be hung on the wall high enough so that everyone in the audience could see it. It would also be used to indicate official meetings. The Council agreed with me, and, true to form, appointed me a committee of one to look into the matter.

First, of course, a design was needed. To incorporate the fraternity colors of black and crimson posed a problem. Too much black would reflect mourning. We finally arrived with an accent of black in the form of the insignia on a crimson background. The gold letter and border were chosen for legibility and good photographic reproduction.

With the design approved by the Council, I sent out requests for bids to two or three manufacturers. Quotations varied from $50 to $75 per item depending on the number ordered at one time, and changes from one banner to another, such as in length of chapter name.

Mrs. Penz had made some good suggestions on the design of the banner, so when the bids came in I mentioned the price. On her own initiative she called some yardgoods stores to get the price of felt, and before I knew it she came up with a cost that was less than half of the lowest bid price. Since she loved to sew and the project evidently appealed to her, she volunteered to make the banners at $20 each (raised to $25 in 1959). The Council recognized a good deal when they saw one, and gave Mrs. Penz the

go-ahead sign; and thus began a labor of love.

Since each of the active chapters was scheduled to receive a banner, a system of production had to be devised. Out of hard cardboard I cut out the alphabet in two sizes, one in large letters for Beta Alpha Psi and one in smaller letters for the chapter name. Next came the pattern for the insignia and the curvature for the letter arrangement for the main title. Basting of the applique was too slow a process. Instead, rubber cement was used to mount the letters on the background before the final sewing.

Mrs. Penz was thoroughly familiar with fabrics. She chose a good quality wool felt and production got under way. Shipments of the banners began in the fall of 1956. A photograph made of the Alpha banner by Alpha Beta active member Howard Nunley, prior to its shipment from Alabama to Illinois, appeared in the Newsletter of April 1957, [and was reproduced for this chapter].

While the activity program had created a degree of divisiveness, the banner project turned out to be a milestone of cohesiveness of the organization.[13] The following selected responses pleased Arline and me no end, but are also indicative of the good reception the banners had:

Norman Slagle, Alpha Lambda

> The banner is quite beautiful and all of Alpha Lambda would like to express their appreciation for it. You and Mrs. Penz are to be commended for the excellent job which you have done

Stuart B. Mead, Alpha Omicron

> I want to extend my sincere thanks for the beautiful banner presented to us by the Grand Council. The members are very proud of it and will see that it is appropriately displayed

---

[13] Endorsing Penz's interpretation of it, Williard Stone stated in 1980 that the banner program had brought new "vitality" to the chapters. Stone to Author, interview, April 18, 1980, quoted.

PRESIDENT A. J. PENZ IN HIS OFFICE, 1955

THE FIRST BETA ALPHA PSI BANNER: ALPHA CHAPTER, 1956
(White border partially visible at top.)

--Essay no. 4 (continued)--

Julius Roller, Delta

- I received the banner recently and must say that it is a beautiful thing, and I know the members of the Chapter will appreciate it very much

Russell S. Grady, Alpha Mu

I received the beautiful B.A.Psi banner for our Chapter in today's mail, and I think the Penz family has done a wonderful job

Nolan E. Williams, Alpha Iota

All the members have expressed their admiration and appreciation for this gift from the Grand Council, and it certainly is a beautiful banner. As best as I can tell, the workmanship is perfect

Wayne E. Shroyer, Alpha Zeta

Received the banner and awarded it to the Chapter, and believe me, they were very much impressed, as was I. Tell your wife she did an outstanding job, and I wish to take this opportunity in behalf of the fraternity to express our appreciation to her and you for all the effort and thought you put into it for us

S. M. Wedeberg, Tau

The very attractive banner arrived some time ago. Borgie [Mrs. Wedeberg] and I are the only ones who have seen it so far, and we think it is an excellent artistic job. I am certain that Tau Chapter members will be pleased to receive the banner

R. K. Jaedicke, Rho

The banner is certainly a well-done piece of work. Please be assured that we will make frequent use of it. I understand that Mrs. Penz had a major part in this project, so please convey the appreciation of the Minnesota Accounting staff and the actives of Rho Chapter to her

Bob Seiler, Theta

The banner is a beautiful piece of work, and I think you and Mrs. Penz certainly deserve a note of thanks for your work in promoting the idea and preparing the banners. We have used it at every one of our meetings since it arrived, and it adds considerably to the decor and atmosphere

Jacqueline Van Dam (secretary), Alpha Xi

We have received the banner and have displayed it at our meetings and our initiation banquet last night. Congratulations on a job well done! It is very striking, and we have received many compliments on it.

These letters among many others were really heartwarming for us, and reassuring to the Grand Council that the banner program was a tremendous success. On top of these accolades, however, the Penzes had yet another surprise.

My being chairman of the Department of Accounting at the University of

Alabama, the staff frequently gathered at our house for one purpose or another. Some of the ladies showed unusual interest in our belongings. Questions were raised such as "Who are your silversmiths? What is your silver pattern?" The ladies closely scrutinized the sterling flatware. We felt that the behavior was unusual, but gave it no further thought.

At the next national meeting the mystery came to light. The Grand Council presented Arline (Mrs. Penz) a pair of sterling candelabra in the Chantilly pattern of our flatware. Arline was overwhlemed with surprise, and with humbleness and tears of joy accepted this beautiful token of appreciation.[14]

These candelabra are still the most prized possesion in the Penz family. They are not only beautiful, but can be used in three different settings. With the arms and center insert removed, a pair of low candle holders result. Inserting the stem pieces makes a pair of high-level candle holders. When the arms are attached, the candelabra shine in their full glory.

Arline continued making the banners until her death in the spring of 1963. Since I was the helper and had observed the operation, I made a feeble attempt to produce the next banner. I was quite proud of my accomplishment and showed it to David, my son, when he came home from high school. After viewing it critically he remarked, "Daddy, that won't do. It is not as

---

[14]While president's advisory committee member Penz was temporarily out of the room, the Grand Council at its 1958 meeting had approved the purchase of an appropriate gift for Mrs. Penz, at a cost not to exceed $100.

The 1958-59 secretary-treasurer's report implies that the candelabra had been "sent" to Mrs. Penz <u>before</u> the 1959 meeting in Boulder, Colorado, in which case she would have been "overwhelmed with surprise" upon their arrival a bit earlier. Even in that event, there might have been a "token" presentation, or other observance of the gift, during the Grand Chapter banquet. Grand Council Minutes Book, 1958, p. [2], 1959, pp. 5-6; A. J. Penz to Author, August 12, 1985, quoted; and [Nolan E. Williams], Secretary-Treasurer's Report, 1958-59, p. 3 quoted.

perfect as mother made them. I can make a better one." At age 15 David not only took on the responsibility of turning out perfect banners, but also improved the procedure and added grommets.

With proper anticipation of needs and good use of vacations and holidays, David managed to keep the Beta Alpha Psi banner project going through his four years at Michigan State. I feared that it would be in a precarious state of flux upon his graduation in 1969, but as he began a professional engineering career he continued to make all fraternal banners. As a joint venture with his wife Lisa, David continues to this day to make the banners. Because they have maintained this uninterrupted family tradition, arrangements have already been made for David and Lisa Penz in due time to receive the candelabra.

After thirty-odd years, the labor of love continues on behalf of a well-founded nationwide organization that has as its motto idealism, sociability, and practicality. I am confident that much of this motto has rubbed off on the entire Penz family'.[15]

From the beginning three main <u>uses</u> for the chapter banner were specified, although at least by appearance another one (inherently nonrecurring) would sometimes be found. Careful instructions would be sent concerning the preservation of banners in good condition.

Uses, and Careful Maintenance, of Banners

The commencement of the "banner" tradition was announced in the

---

[15]The last two paragraphs have been updated, and concern expressed to another former councilor in 1969 about the continuity of the family project has been added to the text. A. J. Penz to Author, August 12, 1985; and Penz to C. Aubrey Smith, February 4, 1969 (Golden Anniversary Files).

Newsletter of April 1957, carrying the photograph of the Alpha Chapter banner. After citing Past President Penz as the "driving force" behind the two-year project, and briefly describing the resultant product, Editor W. B. Jencks cited three uses for the new chapter symbol, and explained how it should be cared for. These specifications were included in a one-page statement, left virtually unchanged over time, that was sent for many years with each new banner.

Three mutually consistent contexts for _displaying_ a banner were specified:

a. On a _permanent_ basis, within an appropriate setting like the faculty advisor's office, a chapter bulletin board, or a glass-enclosed showcase

b. At _chapter meetings_, either as a backdrop for the speaker's table or a drape across the front of the podium

c. At _initiations_, during which (in keeping with Dr. Penz's basic idea) the constituent symbols could "be pointed out to the initiates at the proper time."

The announcement said nothing about using the banner as a background for chapter _installation_, granting that such a reference would have had no practical application to a readership representing schools already chartered. Such display was inappropriate in that the chapter would not truly exist prior to the formal presentation of the charter. As Penz wrote in 1984,

> [T]he National Council has a banner which should be used whenever the Council meets. At the installation ceremony of a new chapter, the Council banner should be used. After the chapter has been installed and at the subsequent banquet, the new chapter banner can be raised.

On the surface, however, this logically questionable use was illustrated in the _Newsletter_ just three pages after display settings a-c were cited. Editor Jencks himself was shown presenting the Alpha Psi charter to the business dean at West Virginia against the background of the _Alpha Psi_ banner. A similar photo would appear in the following issue relative to the installation (the same month) of Alpha Omega at Fordham, under the

caption "[Councilor] Stone Presents Charter to Dean McGinley." Still more interestingly, retired Councilor A. J. Penz was depicted a few years later handing a charter to the dean at Mississippi State with the Beta Kappa banner in full view.

There may well be less in these photographs than meets the eye, however, even discounting the rather apparent "posing" found in the last case. Richard W. Metcalf, the 1983-84 president, reports that installation pictures of the present day are commonly taken <u>after</u> the ceremony, "usually at the banquet," by which time the chapter banner would properly have been raised. Similarly, the three photos just cited may have represented reenactments rather than actual charter presentations.

The initial announcement provided instructions for taking quality care of the banners, "made of high grade wool felt." A moth-proof container was furnished for storage purposes, and dry cleaning at least every other year was advised in the event of permanent display. Any creases were to be removed through "[s]team" (later changed to "[l]ight") pressing.

Eventually, however, wool felt would no longer be available in the United States, and David and Lisa Penz would have to settle for synthetic fibers instead. In the fall of 1976, they adopted a new approach to <u>packing</u> banners as a means of minimizing the effects of lower-quality fabric. The acrylic fibers now used do not drape as well as wool felt, and are more difficult to work with. At the same time, they do not require mothproofing, for storage. Andy Penz is assured by his younger son that in "the long run the acrylic fibers will be quite satisfactory."

After reading a draft version of this chapter while visiting his father during the Thanksgiving holiday of 1985, David Penz elaborated somewhat on these points:

> Today's felt is 100% acrylic. It is better to work with than the wool/synthetic blends which were all we could find for many years, though the acrylic does not compare to the 100% wool available 30 [?] years ago. The acrylic holds its shape better than wool, is strong, durable, and mothproof. It does crease more easily than wool, and is more dificult to press.
>
> Therefore, we started and continue the practice of rolling the banner around a cardboard core tube for shipping and storage. The banner then is inserted into a plastic bag and then into a cardboard shipping carton. We buy the cardboard boxes, but in the beginning could not find the right sort of bags and so made these out of plastic sheets. Last year we bought a large "reel" of plastic in tube form, and [we] now have enough packaging material for the <u>next 30 years</u>! [emphasis in original].

Each of the nine fraternal <u>regions</u> of the present day also has its own banner, to be transferred among member chapters from year to year, as noted in discussing regional meetings in chapter 14. According to David Penz, regional banners "have a tendency to become lost and quite frequently require replacement."

Finally, while A. J. Penz was a member the president's committee considered a proposal that small banners or medallions be presented each year to the top ten chapters in the activity program, for attachment to the regular banner. After much discussion, the committee submitted a negative recommendation in 1958, and the matter was dropped from further consideration.[16] There presumably was concern that such attachments would in the

---

[16] [Grand Council], The Beta Alpha Psi Banner" [(1956-57)], one-page transmittal notice presumably used through 1963-64; Grand Council Minutes Book, 1956, p. 5, 1957, p. 1, 1958, p. 1; [W. B. Jencks], "Beta Alpha Psi Banner," <u>Newsletter</u> 4 (April 1957):378-79, quoted; [Jencks], "Dean Coleman Accepts Charter from Secretary Jencks," <u>Newsletter</u> 4 (April 1957):381, photograph; [Robert S. Maust], "New Chapters of Beta Alpha Psi," <u>1975-76 Annual Report</u>, ed. [Maust], p. [8]; [Richard W. Metcalf], "Regional Meetings," <u>1983-84 Annual Report</u>, ed. [Metcalf], p. 21; Metcalf to Author, August 1, 1985; [Herbert E. Miller], "Congratulations," <u>Newsletter</u> 5 (April 1961):357, photo; [National Council], "The Beta Alpha Psi Banner" [(1964-65)], transmittal notice used at least through 1975-76; A. J. Penz to Author, January 1, 1984 (1st indented citation), August 1, 1984 (quoted), February 1, 14, 1986; David Penz ("dp"), handwritten note sent by his father under separate cover from last letter, presented (with minor punctuation

case of consistently high-ranking units provide a serious distraction from the banner itself.

In Transition

Interesting anecdotal material from the third era has been supplied by several councilors besides Dr. Penz. Part 1 may thus be concluded on a light note after a vital remaining facet of Beta Alpha Psi evolution is documented in conjunction with a variety of programs and practices funded, namely, the financial development of the accounting fraternity during the postwar period up to 1960.

---

change) as 2nd citation; David and Lisa Penz to Fred J. Mueller, October 27, 1976; and [Nolan E. Williams], "Chapter Installed at Fordham University," Newsletter 5 (November 1957):9, photo. The virtually identical Grand and National Council "Banner" statements, and the substantially overlapping item attributed to Jencks, were quoted.

CHAPTER 8

GRAND COUNCIL FINANCES IN THE THIRD ERA, A SELECTION OF PROGRAMS AND PRACTICES FUNDED, AND AN INVENTORY OF ANECDOTES

Most of the six "perennial dimensions" discussed in selected chapters of the earlier volume have already been covered more or less extensively in regard to the third era. Two chapters were devoted to membership growth; important symbolic initiatives and interprofessional connections were respectively identified relative to the activity program and both honorary and alumni membership, in particular; and the preceding chapter included significant interprofessional and anecdotal material in developing an extensive "personal" profile of A. J. Penz.

Financial aspects of third-era operations have been discussed only incidentally, however, as within the section on chapter visitation. Furthermore, preparations for observing the fiftieth anniversary of Beta Alpha Psi yielded a large supply of excellent anecdotal material from the third era that has yet to be tapped. Accordingly, in this concluding chapter of part 1 the evolving financial condition of the Grand Council, 1946-60, is documented in reasonable detail; a variety of programs and practices that were funded during the period are covered both in their own right and from a financial standpoint; and substantial fraternal lore is related, some of it associated with more serious fraternal "dimensions."

Evolution of the Council's Financial Condition, 1946-60

The rapid rise in membership years fueled notable prosperity for the fraternity in the early postwar years. Based on membership trends and other factors, a cyclical financial pattern was thus begun that is revealed both in fund balances of the third era and in selected operating statements. Overall, there was excellent growth in the financial holdings of the Grand Council as emphasis was placed upon investment that would keep current cash balances relatively low while maintaining a strong liquidity position.

Changes in Fund Balances, 1946-60

The Grand Council of the third era followed proper accrual practices, in general, in reporting annual income or loss.[1] At no time, however, did it hold material receivables or nonmonetary assets, or bear significant debt. By and large, then, the financial development of the fraternity was reflected in periodic changes in (a) current cash holdings and (b) financial investment balances, representing for all practical purposes the "funds" held by the organization.

As discussed a bit later, investment over the years was comprised of three classes of government bonds and of savings and loan balances.

---

[1]The "honorarium" paid in arrears to the secretary-treasurer was not accrued, since the amount was not specified until the Grand Council meeting at which his report was submitted. Chapter reporting discrepancies or brief timing lags produced slight deviations, occasionally, in the reporting of membership revenues, notably in the recognition of 1959-60 of fees for fourteen students inducted the prior spring. [Herbert E. Miller], Secretary-Treasurer's Report, 1959-60, pp. 1, 4-5; and [Nolan E. Williams], Secretary-Treasurer's report, 1958-59, pp. 5-6, 15.

Two other departures from a strict accrual basis are noted, or implied, later. A substantial "advance" paid relative to the 1947 Grand Council meeting was reported as an expense of the preceding fiscal year, and the earnings on savings accounts and two bond investments were recognized on an appropriate legalistic or contractual basis.

Although the latter assets were extremely liquid, the term "cash" was reserved for checking accounts and any funds on hand. Respective balances for even-year reporting dates (subject, in the summations, to slight rounding distortion) were as follows:

	1946	1948	1950	1952	1954	1956	1958	1960
Cash	$2,570	$ 7,100	$ 6,863	$ 7,236	$ 3,804	$ 4,330	$ 2,995	$ 1,321
Investments	5,137	5,681	9,830	9,883	12,023	18,860	21,424	19,897
Total	$7,708	$12,781	$16,693	$17,118	$15,827	$23,190	$24,419	$21,218.

The final financial statements of the second era were dated November 30, 1942. The cash and investment balances had been, respectively, $955 and $4,753. The increase in the investment total, by 1946, was based on updated cash surrender values of the bonds held. In regard to cash, the fraternity had in the interim taken in $2,734 and expended only $711. Since Fayette Elwell had become secretary-treasurer, in April 1943, upon Hazen Kendrick's entry into military service, receipts (of $1,680) had surpassed expenditures by more than six-to-one, based largely on initiations during the late spring of 1943 and the year 1945-46, and the absence of Council meetings and *Newsletter* publication.

The tabulation above reflects striking trends in the two asset categories: a cash balance moving significantly downward after 1952, and an investment amount steadily growing through 1958. Following roughly equivalent dollar declines between the last two dates cited, cash represented just one-sixteenth of total funds at the close of the era. In a time of rising costs and declining revenues, limited withdrawals from savings accounts had been made in the late 1950s to keep the fraternity solvent. Indeed, although a cash balance of $3,875 had been reported at July 31, 1959, there was a brief delay in completing reimbursement of the participants in the

Grand Council meeting of the following month because it had reached a precariously low level.[2]

The fund totals overall reflect a cyclical pattern in fraternal finances that was broadly consistent with initiation trends as covered in chapter 3. The dramatic rise between 1954 and 1956 was based on a major boost in entry fees,and their extension beyond student entrants, as well as on growing membership. The cyclical pattern discerned is borne out by four operating statements from the third era.

Cyclical Operating Results, as Revealed by Four Statements

In 1946-47, the Grand Council reported income of $2,075, based on a ratio of revenue to expense of two-to-one, even though the listed Council meeting expense of $602 covered not only the 1946 gathering but also $250 in advance payments relating to the following one. From this base, reported income increased in 1947-48 by 40%, to $2,915, a total destined to be surpassed only once by 1960.

Even given the highest initiation level of the era, income fell by 20% in 1948-49 as expense rose substantially more than revenue. Over the next four years, the two elements of income generally moved in reverse directions until a net loss of $1,075 was recorded in 1952-53. A record income level of nearly $3,700 two years later was attributable in considerable part to an increase in the initiation fee from $5.00 to $7.50, its extension to

---

[2]F. H. Elwell, 1942-46 Secretary-Treasurer's Report, pp. 1-3; "Financial Statements," Newsletter [2] (November 1948):7, [3] (November 1950):10; "Grand Council of Beta Alpha Psi: Audit Report . . .," 1951-52 (issued by LeRoy L. Lee, CPA), exhibit A, 1953-54 (Joseph E. Lane, CPA), exhibit A; Grand Council Cashbook, 1931-49, pp. 50, 52, 54; Herbert E. Miller to A.J. Penz, September 25, 1959; and Secretary-Treasurers' Reports, 1955-56, 1957-58 through 1959-60, balance sheets.

honorary members, and a continuing spurt in new membership following the Korean War. During the latter fifties, operating performance declined once more, however, as new initiations again trended downward, and costs of visitation, Newsletter publication, and (by and large) Grand Council meetings rose sharply. This decline culminated in 1959-60 in a loss of more than $3,000, nearly three times the previous "high."

To point up this cyclical operating pattern in some detail, the income or operating statements for the two years of highest income (1947-48 and 1954-55) and highest loss (1952-53 and 1959-60) are shown as exhibit 18. They reveal that the principal items of revenue after initiation fees were royalties, on fraternal badges, and investment earnings. The leading source of expense already covered was visitation, a major element only on the last statement shown.[3]

Discussed below are three consistently large expense items--the annual meeting, the secretary-treasurer position, and the Newsletter. Another major item to be covered is the partial funding, at three-year intervals after 1954, of chapter directories.

Investment opportunities taken by the Grand Council of the third era were generally consistent with earlier practices, but expanded in scale, as the fraternity moved toward minimizing its idle funds without incurring significant risk.

Investments

During the first half of the third era, Grand Council assets consisted primarily of checking account balances and investments in government bonds.

---

[3] W. E. Dickerson, Secretary-Treasurer's Report, 1946-47, p. [8]; exhibit 19; and Grand Council Minutes Book, 1954, p. 3. All other operating statements of the era have also been consulted in preparing this subsection.

EXHIBIT 18

FOUR GRAND COUNCIL OPERATING STATEMENTS FROM THE THIRD ERA

1947-48

GRAND COUNCIL BETA ALPHA PSI
Statement of Income and Expense
August 11, 1947, to August 31, 1948

INCOME

Initiation Fees Earned		$5480.00
Royalties on Badges		651.11
Duplicate Shingle Reimbursement		7.00
Increase in Redemption Value — U. S. Savings Bonds		223.76
Total Income		$6361.87

EXPENSES

Express and Shipping	$ 27.08	
Chapter Supplies	232.04	
Printing, Postage and Stationery	160.10	
Clerical Expense	497.75	
Certificates	820.70	
Newsletter Printing	739.33	
Secretary's Honorarium — 1947	500.00	
Supplies and Miscellaneous	14.37	
Council Meeting Expense	434.32	
Corporation Filing Fee	1.00	
Refunding Initiation Fees of Prior Year	20.00	
Total Expenses		3446.69
Excess of Income over Expenses		$2915.18

1952-53

THE GRAND COUNCIL OF BETA ALPHA PSI
STATEMENT OF INCOME AND EXPENSE
For the Year Ended August 15, 1953

Income			
Initiation Fees		$3,815.00	
Royalties on Jewelry		358.97	
Interest on U. S. Government Bonds		256.36	
Charter Fees		25.00	
Duplicate Certificate Reimbursements		13.00	
Subscriptions to the "News Letter"		2.00	
Total Income			$4,470.33
Expenses			
Grand Chapter Expenses:			
Council Visitation Expense	$ 284.25		
Council Meeting Expense	1,229.29		
Secretary's Honorarium	100.00		
Fidelity Bond Expense	25.00		
Corporation Filing Fees	1.00		
Chapter Installation Expense	63.00		
Total Grand Chapter Expenses		$1,702.54	

EXHIBIT 18 --Continued

1952-53 (cont'd)

Chapter Expenses:			
News Letter Expense	$1,428.65		
Membership Certificates	613.20		
Chapter Supplies	36.77		
Directory Expense	316.40		
Scholarship Expense	8.40		
Total Chapter Expenses		2,403.42	
General Expenses:			
Clerical Expense	$ 319.48		
Postage, Printing, and Stationery	217.39		
Telephone and Telegraph	8,85		
Miscellaneous and Supplies	232.54		
Miscellaneous Reimbursed Expenses	660.18		
Total General Expenses		1,438.44	
Total Expenses			5,544.40
Net Loss			$1,074.07

1954-55

THE GRAND COUNCIL OF BETA ALPHA PSI

Statement of Income and Expense

For Year Ended July 31, 1955

INCOME		
Initiation Fees	$7,890.00	
Royalties on Jewelry	274.32	
Interest on Investments	346.36	
Charter Fees	100.00	
Duplicate Certificate Fees	15.00	
Subscriptions to "News Letter"	15.50	
Total Income		$8,641.18
EXPENSES		
Grand Chapter Expenses:		
Council Visitation Expense	$ 107.69	
Council Meeting Expense	1,165.20	
Secretary's Honorarium	100.00	
Fidelity Bond Expense	25.00	
Corporation Filing Fee	1.00	
Chapter Installation Expense	37.95	
Total Grand Chapter Expenses	$1,436.84	
Chapter Expenses:		
News Letter Expense	$ 882.60	
Membership Certificates	773.50	
Chapter Supplies	86.86	
Scholarship Expense	14.00	
Total Chapter Expenses	$1,756.96	
General Expenses:		
Clerical Expense	$ 248.71	
Postage, Printing, and Stationery	192.07	
Telephone and Telegraph	22.44	
Miscellaneous Supplies	184.42	
Reimbursed Expenses	1,100.00	
Initiation Fee Refund, Prior year	4.00	
Total General Expenses	$1,751.64	
Total Expenses		$4,945.44
Net Income		$3,695.74

EXHIBIT 18 --Continued

1959-60

GRAND COUNCIL OF BETA ALPHA PSI
OPERATING STATEMENT
Year Ended July 31, 1960

Income:			
Initiation fees			$ 8,880.00
Installation fees			150.00
Royalties on jewelry			428.33
Miscellaneous			7.50
Subscriptions to News Letters			3.00
Duplicate certificates reimbursement			35.00
Interest on investments			665.36
Total income			$10,169.19
Expenses:			
Grand Chapter Expenses:			
Visitation expenses	$1,472.03		
Council meeting	2,825.64		
Secretary's honorarium	1,600.00		
Fidelity bond expense	25.00		
Corporation filing fee	2.00		
Faculty vice-presidents' awards	250.00	$6,174.67	
Chapter Expenses:			
Installation expense	$ 217.39		
Charters printed	57.50		
Chapter banners	105.00		
Membership certificates	1,007.20		
Chapter supplies	228.22		
Directory expense	1,674.80		
News Letter expense	2,280.60		
Scholarship certificates	19.60	5,590.31	
General Expenses:			
Clerical expense	$ 727.86		
Postage, printing, stationery	526.84		
Telephone and telegraph	29.96		
Miscellaneous	145.34	1,430.00	13,194.98
Net Loss			$3,025.79

Reprinted from Newsletter [2] (November 1948):7, 4 (November 1953):109, (November 1955):271, 5 (November 1960):305.

After 1953, savings accounts were added, soon surpassing bonds as the largest of the three components. Bonds acquired in 1949 provided a modest source of cash through the fifties, while highly liquid time deposits helped the fraternity pay the high costs incurred in the decade's closing years.

U.S. government bonds

As related in volume 1, the fraternity had early in 1939 acquired five $1,000 series D bonds, maturing in ten years, at $750; and in the spring of 1942 had purchased $950 in series F defense bonds, maturing in twelve years, for $703. These holdings were reported at July 31, 1946, at current redemption values of $4,400 ($880 each) and $737, respectively.

Beginning with the first anniversary of acquisition, six years earlier, the surrender value of the D bonds had through February 1, 1946, increased by $50 semiannually. The regular increment would be $100 thereafter. Hence, as noted by Secretary-Treasurer Fay Elwell, the cash value reported in 1946 would rise to $4,500 the very day following the reporting date.

The cash-value accumulation of the $9,500 in series F bonds, issued at 74% and bearing an effective interest rate of 2.53%, was more complex. During the nearly four years between the last wartime report (dated November 30, 1942) and the first postwar statement, the valuation had increased, above cost, by only $34. After an addition of $20 was reported for the year 1946-47, yielding a total amount of $757, the balance would grow at a constant or progressive rate to $914 at August 15, 1953, six and one-half months prior to maturity. Interest earnings were recognized in accordance with the cash-value schedule. Besides helping to finance the war, defense bonds had served to "combat inflation" during the war years by diverting funds from the extremely competitive market for consumer goods.

Reflecting its prosperity immediately after reactivation, the fraternity's cash balance had risen by the end of fiscal year 1947-48 to $7,100, substantially exceeding even the combined maturity values of the two sets of investments. With the maturity early in 1949 of the $5,000 series, it was clearly time to make one or more large new investments. On February 12, 1949, Secretary-Treasurer Dickerson accordingly purchased at face value $9,000 in twelve-year series G bonds, earning 2.5%. Interest in the amount of $112.50 was *distributed* semiannually. Since changes in the (lower) cash surrender value could hardly be accounted for as interest revenue, this investment was always reported at cost. Although the regular dates for interest distribution were February 1 and August 1, three sets of financial statements issued following the adoption in 1953-54 of a closing date of July 31 indicated that the second calendar-year payment had been received by that date.[4]

The next Grand Council investment was made upon the maturity of the defense bonds, early in 1954. In light of financial problems of the day, however, higher liquidity was needed than was provided by government bonds. Secretary-Treasurer A. J. Penz thus turned to an investment outlet that had been utilized in earlier times, under a prior name, and for good measure provided a slightly higher earnings rate.

---

[4]F. H. Elwell, Secretary-Treasurer's Report, 1942-46, p. 4; "Financial Statements," *Newsletter* [2] (November 1948):6-7, [3] (November 1949):5-6, (November 1950):10-11, (November 1951):9-11; "Grand Council Audit Report," 1951-52, 1952-53 (LeRoy L. Lee), 1953-54, 1954-55 (Joseph E. Lane, Jr., by supposition); Grand Council Cashbook, 1931-49, p. 69; Grand Council Minutes Book, 1939, p. 1; [H. W. Kendrick], "Annual Meeting of the Grand Council," *Newsletter* [2] (March 1942):14-15; [Kendrick], "Grand Council Notes," *Newsletter* [2] (March 1943):6-7; *Prentice-Hall Dictionary*, s.v. "Savings bonds," quoted; Secretary-Treasurers' Reports, 1942-46, 1946-47, 1955-56 through 1959-60, financial statements; and Sheldahl, *Alpha to Omega*, pp. 789-90.

Savings deposits, 1954-60

The series F bonds had been purchased in 1942 based on proceeds from the liquidation at par of $700 in "building and loan" securities. It seems fitting, then, that their maturity twelve years later helped finance a sizable deposit establishing a "savings and loan" account. By 1954, many "building" and loan associations were known instead as "savings" and loan firms (although the former name remained the primary entry within Prentice-Hall's business dictionary of the day). More importantly, such organizations had generally shifted their principal sources of capital from "share" deposits of various kinds to regular "savings" accounts and systematic savings plans known as "bonus" accounts.

Because of operating losses, the Beta Alpha Psi cash balance had declined by nearly 20% over the two years directly preceding Andy Penz's election as secretary-treasurer in September 1953. Nonetheless, the checking account remained slightly in excess of $6,000. With the maturity of the series F bonds in February 1954 at $950, the fraternity was in a good position to make a major investment. Accordingly, Penz opened a regular savings account in the amount of $3,000 at a savings and loan association in Birmingham, Alabama. Earnings of 3% were credited quarterly and compounded semiannually, and were accounted for in the year credited rather than on a strictly accrual basis. Funds could be withdrawn "without notice."

In his 1953-54 audit report, Professor Joseph E. Lane, Jr. of Alabama, who was at the time working toward his law degree at the university, questioned the formal authority of his colleague Secretary-Treasurer Penz to make the savings and loan deposit. Presumably in light of the statute by which a secretary-treasurer could "disburse money only under the authority of the Grand Council, or the President," Lane recommended that the Council

explicitly authorize that officer "to properly invest unneeded cash." No reference to the matter appears in the 1954 minutes, however.

As noted earlier, the financial condition of the fraternity improved dramatically in 1954-55, producing a net income of approximately $3,700. Accordingly, in two equal installments Secretary-Treasurer Penz deposited an additional $4,000 in the S & L account. The following year, his successor W. B. Jencks made a further investment in the account of $2,500 bringing the balance by July 31, 1956, to $9,860, inclusive of $360 in total interest earnings. Since the maximum insured deposit of the day was $10,000, Jencks proposed in his annual report that "we cease making deposits" to the Birmingham account.

In actual fact, Jencks in 1956-57 made an additional deposit of $140 to bring the balance to the insurance maximum, and subsequently had the interest distributed to the fraternity as earned rather than added to the account. In addition he opened a $2,000 account, earning 3.5%, with a savings association in his own city, Columbus, Ohio. When Nolan Williams became secretary-treasurer in the fall of 1957, then, Beta Alpha Psi held $12,000 in savings.

During his first year, Williams left the two accounts untouched. At a common interest rate of 3.5% compounded semiannually, the result was a total interest accrual of approximately $425. By this point, the cash balance (checking) had reached one of its lowest postwar levels, at $2,995. Accordingly, early in the fiscal year 1958-59 the secretary-treasurer withdrew slightly more than $1,350 from the Alabama account to reduce the balance, prior to the accrual of any new earnings, to $9,000, comfortably under the maximum insured level. This infusion of cash permitted a vital increase of

$880 in the cash balance as the fraternity began the "directory" year 1959-60.

Finally, as secretary-treasurer in the final year of the third era Herbert Miller found the availability of highly liquid investment assets even more welcome than had his predecessor. With declining initiation revenue and costs far higher than in any prior period, the cash balance fell to its lowest postwar total, at $1,321. The bulk of that amount, $1,000, was based on a withdrawal from one of the savings accounts. Although the balance was still precariously low, it seemed adequate in light of the imminent maturity, on February 1, 1961, of the $9,000 series G bonds.

The net result of the deductions and interest accruals of the years 1958-60 was to leave a total of $10,896 in the two savings accounts, representing slightly more than one half of total fraternal assets.[5]

The financial reports naturally document a variety of interesting programs or practices funded by the Grand Council of the third era. They include chapter directories; academic achievement awards; Grand Council fraternal badges; faculty vice-president awards; and secretary-treasurers' "honoraria." Reference is made first, however, to the funding of Grand Council (and Grand Chapter) meetings and of Newsletter publication, which was resumed directly after the first postwar gathering.

---

[5]Beta Alpha Psi Fraternity, "National Statutes," National Constitution and Statutes (1953), chapter 1, section 13, quoted; "Grand Council Audit Report," 1951-52 and 1952-53, exhibit C, 1953-54 (quoting auditor's opinion), 1954-55, 1958-59 (Douglas Walker & Co., CPAs), exhibit "D," schedule "1"; Hasselback, 1984 Directory, individual listing, s.v., "Lane, Joseph E., Jr."; [W.B. Jencks], Secretary-Treasurer's Report, 1955-56, pp. 1 (quoted), 10, 1956-57, pp. 1, 12, 14; [Herbert E. Miller], Secretary-Treasurer's Report, 1959-60, pp. [11], [13]; A. J. Penz, Secretary-Treasurer's Report, 1953-54, p. 1, quoted; Prentice-Hall Dictionary, s.v. "Building and loan associations," quoted; Sheldahl, Alpha to Omega, p. 790, quoted; and [Nolan E. Williams], Secretary-Treasurer's Report, 1957-58, pp. 1, 13, 15-16.

Selected Programs or Practices Funded During the Third Era

Meetings of the Grand Council, and Grand Chapter

Based on travel reimbursements made to participants, the first four post-war Grand Council meetings ranged in cost from $353 to $684. The gatherings in Chicago in 1946 and 1948 each cost less than $400, while the meetings of 1947 and 1949 in New York and Ann Arbor each reduced the fraternal treasury by well over $600. The differences were based less on geographical factors, however, than on attendance by only three of the five councilors in 1946; and the absence in 1948 of Past President James McConahey of Seattle, who had accounted for more than $200 of the amount paid out for the earlier Chicago meeting.

After 1949, the <u>lowest</u> cost incurred for the annual meeting was nearly $1,100, and well over twice that amount was incurred three times. There were five principal variables: (a) geographical location relative to participant residences; (b) number of participants; (c) terms of travel reimbursement; (d) length of meeting; and (e) coverage, if any, beyond travel or other costs of participation. The first factor was controlled by the fraternity only when, in 1948, the meeting was not coordinated with the convention of the American Accounting Association.

There were five positions on the Grand Council throughout the third era. After 1946, the full group were present nine times through 1959, and only one member was absent the other four times. With the establishment in the fall of 1954 of the president's advisory committee, however, the two most recently retired councilors were invited to attend the annual meeting on the same reimbursement terms as current members. One or two past councilors were present each year thereafter. At the 1959 gathering, the advisory

group recommended that the two retired councilors be assigned two or three visitations per year to "earn . . . their keep," and justify their (nonvoting) participation in the meetings.

As indicated at the close of chapter 6, the terms of travel reimbursement were upgraded over the years. In 1953, they were reported as six cents per mile driven plus $10 per diem (based on 300 miles, later raised to 350), or the cost of public transportation "(including Pullman)." Three years later the nondriving alternative was changed to the cost of "first class" transportation, and in 1957 the mileage rate was raised to ten cents.

The first two meetings lasted only a day each, although the second one was conducted before the AAA convened. In 1948 there was a two-day meeting, and the shortest duration thereafter was three days. The fraternity was ordinarily in session during at least part of each day of the association's two- or (after 1954) three-day convention, and frequently met also before and/or after that event. The lengthened Grand Council functions gave rise at least by 1953 to an additional element of reimbursement, namely, $10 per diem for the meetings themselves, raised to $15 at the five-day meeting two years later.

Finally, in 1949 a significant new cost was added with the commencement of annual Grand Chapter banquets. The dinner held in Ann Arbor that year contributed to an increase of some $250 in costs over the preceding year even though two councilors, Tom and Bill Dickerson, hailed from the neighboring state of Ohio. In 1950 the expense rose from $640 to $1,092 for a meeting and dinner in Cambridge, Massachusetts, a remote location for members Charles Staehling of California and John Arch White of Texas.

Between 1950 and 1954, inclusive, the cost ranged from $1,092 to $1,340, incurred for the 1951 gathering in Denver. After the president's advisory committee was formed, the lowest total was slightly more than $1,500, for a 1955 meeting in Philadelphia which only five of the seven eligible participants attended. More than $2,750 was spent on the 1956 meeting in Seattle, for which full travel costs (perhaps computed on the basis of the destination point) were paid for hospitalized president A. J. Penz. Still more costly, at $2,826, was the meeting at Boulder, Colorado in 1959 that Secretary-Treasurer Nolan Williams missed because of a death in the family.

Except for the second meeting, for which the $250 advance paid to President McConahey was charged to the preceding year, the costs of Grand Council meetings were always fully accounted for in the fiscal years in which they took place. For example, the 1959 cost was reported in the income statement for 1959-60.[6]

The second highest expense item reported that year concerned a program that had been reinstated immediately after the first postwar meeting, namely, publication of the fraternal Newsletter.

The Fraternal Newsletter

The Newsletter did not change materially during the third era. It continued to be devoted primarily to news reports from local chapters preceded

---

[6]W. E. Dickerson, Secretary-Treasurer's Report, 1946-47, p. [8]; "Financial Statements," Newsletter [2] (November 1948):7, [3] (November 1949):6, (November 1950):11; Grand Council Cashbook, 1931-49, pp. 57, 59; Grand Council Minutes Book, 1946 through 1959, p. 1; 1947, p. [3], 1949, p.[3], 1953, p. 5 (quoted), 1954, p. 3, 1955, p.3, 1956, p. 4 (quoted), 1957, p. [3], 1959, pp. 7, 8 (quoted); [Herbert E. Miller], Secretary-Treasurer's report, 1959-60, p. 1; A. J. Penz, Secretary-Treasurer's Report, 1954-55, p. 2; and Zeff, American Accounting Association, pp. 66-67.

by a selection of "Grand Council News." Continuing a practice begun before the war, annual balance sheets and operating statements were published (normally in November). Periodic reports on "honorary" and "alumni" members became established features, as observed in chapter 4. As also previously indicated, regular coverage of the activity program began in 1950-51.

The principal change was the replacement of the March and May issues, in 1954-55, with a single spring issue published in April. Five years earlier a handsome full-color cover page had been added.

Almost immediately, Newsletter costs were far higher than before the war. Hazen Kendrick reported an expense of only $253 for the three issues brought out in 1946-47, only moderately higher than prewar amounts. Under the editorship of Bill Dickerson the following year, the costs (printing and distribution) nearly tripled, to $739, and the addition of a record number of new members and increases in total pages from 56 to 76 pushed the cost to nearly $1,100 in 1948-49. John Arch White obtained a favorable printing bid in the last year of the forties to reduce the cost by more than $200, despite the expenditure of $54 for the new cover page.

From a higher base, a similar pattern prevailed over the five years 1950-55, with costs rising to more than $1,400 in 1952-53 only to fall to less than $900 two years later. Under Editor S.M. Wedeberg, the printing process was changed from photo-offset to regular press printing on coated paper, and total pagination was raised to a new high of 96. Naturally as the chapter roster grew, more space tended to be needed for chapter news. In 1954-55, however, with the announced shift to two "expanded" issues the page total fell to 68. Editor A. J. Penz had reduced costs the preceding year, when 20,000 issues were produced, by obtaining lower printing costs and using the "book rate for parcel post" in mail distribution.

During the last five years of the third era, however, there was a steady increase in publication cost, to a level slightly in excess of the 1952-53 level six years later, and finally to a much higher total, $2,281, in 1959-60. Herb Miller explained the large increase of his first year as editor, an amount nearly as high as total Newsletter costs of the mid-1950s, in terms of printing costs in the Ann Arbor area as contrasted with his predecessor Nolan Williams' community in Arkansas. Over these final years of the third era, in keeping with steady growth in the number of chapters, page totals gradually moved to a new high of 100 printed pages in the last year.[7]

A second significant publication program authorized in 1946 was intended as an updating of an earlier national initiative. Due to cost considerations, however, the directory project would soon be decentralized as an activity of local chapters every third year.

Partial Funding of Chapter Directories

The evolution of directory policy has already been covered in broad outline. Directly after the war, the Council decided to develop a new national directory to replace Hermann Miller's volume of 1939, and simultaneously sought updated information from the chapters and solicited bids from printing companies. Because of high printing costs, the project was abandoned late in 1948 in favor of partially funding the production of yearly

---

[7]"Financial Statements," as cited in note 6; Grand Council Minutes Book, 1954, quoted; Newsletter, [2]-5 (November 1946 - April 1960, omitting 1958); Secretary-Treasurers' Reports, as cited in note 6, and 1948-49, p. 2, 1949-50, p. 1., 1952-53, p. 2, 1953-54, p. 1 (quoted), 1959-60, p. 2; and Sheldahl, Alpha to Omega, p. 661.

directories by the chapters. Two years later the requirement was changed to production of a full directory every three years, and annual supplements in between, while in 1954 the latter requirement was dropped.

During the year 1946-47, "[t]he majority of chapters responded" to the request for new directory information. For reasons of economy, and of ready identification of all changes, the data received were recorded along with standard new-member information in the "current roll card file." During the year, printing bids were obtained ranging from $2,625 to $3,750, but an increase of between five and ten per cent seemed imminent based on rising costs of scarce materials. Since these quotations were considered very high, and not all chapters had yet been heard from, the Grand Council voted provisionally in 1947 to defer until the next meeting a decision on the directory project. A mail vote would be taken during the interim, instead, should prices "materially lower than those at hand" emerge.

Printing prices were in fact moving rapidly in the other direction, so that _the lowest_ bid obtained between the 1947 and 1948 meeting was $4,000, for offset production of 7,000 copies, approximately matching the historical membership of the day. Since that quotation exceeded by more than $550 _total_ expense reported for the year 1947-48, the cost seemed clearly prohibitive. A further consideration was that in making such an expenditure the governing body would not be contributing a cent toward helping chapters defray the costs of developing the required data.

Accordingly, after rejecting all printing bids receiving, the Grand Council in the fall of 1948 voted to reimburse the chapters, in part, for the preparation of annual directories according to prescribed specifications. Probably under the leadership of Secretary-Treasurer W. E. Dickerson, the following requirements were soon laid out:

1. Issuance every spring
2. "[I]nclusion of name, address, business connection and such other data as may be appropriate for each member of the chapter, active, alumni, faculty and honorary"
3. Separate classification of members by their residential localities
4. Listing of alumni (former student) members by initiation year
5. Submission of two copies to the Council, and single copies to each member with an available address and each of the other chapters.

More specific matters of format were left to the discretion of the local officers.

Chapters would be reimbursed in the amount of ten cents for each current address provided. For the first year of the reconstituted directory program, 1948-49, only 5 of the 21 chapters existing throughout the period submitted directories, "all of which appear[ed] to be very satisfactory." A total of $174 (rounded) was accordingly disbursed to Iota at USC, Omicron at Ohio State, Sigma at Wisconsin, Tau at Maryland, and Phi at LSU, estimated to represent less than half of total cost to the chapters. Delta at Washington and Theta at Texas were reported to have directories in progress.

The following year, all of these chapters except Iota prepared directories, along with Zeta at North Dakota, Lambda at California, and Alpha Delta at Pennsylvania. A total of $411 was quoted as directory expense, some $40 higher than would have been accounted for by the 3,3713 names listed. Since apparently four of the nine directories deviated significantly from published requirements, it is evident that no penalty had been exacted for such deficiency. Secretary-Treasurer White's report summarized inconsistencies between the directory listings and the national roll card files.

At the same time that the requirement was initially scaled down to production of one full volume every three years, in the fall of 1950, the directory program was incorporated, as item 8, within the new chapter rating plan. Through 1954, chapters were eligible for the full 800 points each

year so long as they complied with the maximum three-year interval between directories and issued proper supplements in the interim.

The reduction in directory requirements naturally reduced chapter costs, and hence reimbursement cost to the Grand Council, at a time of prospective major roster expansion and, through the chapter competition, newly created incentive. At this time also, or (in light of the leniency exercised in evaluating chapters in 1950-51) within a year, the Council imposed strict standards requiring proper verification of current addresses. In 1953 the question was raised of whether "negative" confirmation would suffice, particularly the nonreturn of letters of inquiry marked "return postage guaranteed." After lengthy discussion, it was concluded that only "positive" verification was admissible.

Over the four years, 1950-54, yearly directory expense ranged from $221 to $491. The latter figure was recorded after the Council had voted in 1953 to fund all directories on the same basis, even if a chapter were to produce a full volume each year, on the premise that preparation more frequently than required was a "desirable practice." With the elimination a year later of the requirement of interim supplements, the fraternity reversed course. Thereafter, no provision was made at the national level for submitting interim data, and funding was provided only in the two "directory years," 1956-57 and 1959-60.

At the Grand Chapter meeting immediately preceding the first of those years, Faculty Vice-President Julius Roller of Delta Chapter questioned whether chapter directories were worth the high cost of production. During "active discussion" of the matter, a consensus emerged that directories were worthwhile, but that the Grand Council "should consider increasing its subsidy." There was also "an almost unanimous feeling" that the distribution

of directories to other chapters served no useful purpose. Upon reconvening, accordingly, the Council in 1956 doubled the "subsidy," to twenty cents per verified address, and dropped the requirement of distribution to other chapters.

Over the year that followed, $1,376 was expended from the national treasury in support of chapter directory production. Of the 44 chapters that had been formed through the spring of 1957, 32 submitted directories, and 22 of those units received maximum activity credit of 800 points. Formed April 30, 1957, Alpha Omega at Fordham earned full credit simply by accounting for its charter membership.

Finally, 38 of the 52 chapters existing by year's end submitted directories in 1959-60, all but one of them receiving the full 800 points. Rho at Minnesota earned one-half credit. Total directory cost for the Council was $1,675.[8]

Two important initiatives were undertaken late in 1948 to recognize outstanding scholarship, although only the "symbolic" one would last beyond the first year.

Two Awards for Academic Achievement

Awarding of a scholarship in 1949

As related in volume 1, the Grand Council had in December 1940 approved an annual $250 '"graduate scholarship in accounting"' at the same time as

---

[8] [W. E. Dickerson], "Grand Chapter News, " Newsletter [2] (November 1948):5 (quoted), 6, (March 1949):5; Dickerson, Secretary-Treasurer's Report, 1948-49, pp. 1, 3 (quoted), 6; "Financial Statements," Newsletter [2] (November 1948):7; Grand Council Minutes Book, 1947, p. 1 (quoted), 1948, p. 1, 1953, pp. 3-4 (quoted), 1956, pp. 4, 7 (quoted); H. W. Kendrick, Secretary-Treasurer's Report, 1946-47, pp. 5 (quoted), 6; [W. B. Jencks], Secretary-Treasurer's Report, 1956-57, pp. 1, 6, 9; "National Statutes," National Constitution and Statutes of Beta Alpha Psi Fraternity (1947), chapter 5, section 54; A. J. Penz, Secretary-Treasurer's Report, 1953-54, p. 2; and [Nolan E. Williams], Secretary-Treasurer's Report, 1959-60, pp. 1, 8.

officially terminating the eleven-year manuscript contest, but would not make an award prior to deactivation. Members holding accounting degrees from Beta Alpha Psi schools who were commencing graduate work in the field at such institutions were eligible. At the first postwar meeting, in 1946, a motion was approved not to offer the scholarship during the coming year, and the matter was not mentioned in the 1947 minutes.

The Council finally renewed the scholarship plan at its meeting late in 1948. There were short _Newsletter_ notices in November 1948, within a summary of the gathering, and March 1949, under the heading "Are You Eligible for the $250 Scholarship Award [?]." Applications were supposed to be received by Secretary-Treasurer Bill (or "Dick") Dickerson by April 10, including (a) a summary of the student's academic record, statements of (b) practical experience and (c) objectives and fields of special interest, and (d) the names of two academic references. Prewar specifications, incidentally, had required _five_ letters of reference. The $250 award would "be granted to the member whose past record and future plans g[a]ve the greatest promise of outstanding graduate work."

The award was made to John C. Dieckman, Nu '48, a 1949 graduate of Colorado who was remaining on campus to pursue an M.S. degree. He had learned of the opportunity from Past President Hazen Kendrick, one of his professors, who had recommended that he apply for the scholarship. One-half of the amount was before the close of the fiscal year ending August 31, 1949, and the remainder was expended after the student had submitted "a progress report of his scholastic activities." Completing his graduate studies in December 1950, a semester before the degree was formally conferred, John Dieckman immediately joined a CPA firm on San Francisco from which he would retire in 1984, following twenty-nine years as a partner.

The firm is known in the present day as Muncy, McPherson, McCune, & Dieckman.[9]

No further references has been found to the scholarship program, suggesting that it simply faded from Council consciousness with the introduction of chapter competition, the admission of women members, and the beginning of a significant visitation effort. As noted in chapter 4, one of the items on the agenda of the proposed national alumni association in 1954 was a graduate scholarship program, and six years later (at a time of very high fraternity expense) Beta Alpha Psi contributed a thousand dollars to the fellowship fund of the American Accounting Association.

A far more enduring (and less expensive) award for outstanding academic performance was also introduced in 1948-49.

Chapter scholarship certificates

At least as soon as it was reactivated under the war, under the faculty leadership of future Councilor J. C. Gibson, Sigma Chapter at Wisconsin had introduced an emblematic certificate award for the senior member having the highest scholastic average. For the year 1946-47, the winner was Leroy Bruechert, a Phi Beta Kappa student who had accepted a position with Arthur Andersen & Co. in New York.

---

[9] [W. E. Dickerson], "Are You Eligible for the $250 Scholarship Award[?]," Newsletter [2] (March 1949):5, (quoted); [Dickerson], "[Grand] Chapter News," Newsletter [2] (November 1954):5; [Dickerson] Secretary-Treasurer's Report, 1948-49, pp. 1, 6 (quoted); John C. Dieckman to Author, September 5, 1985; "Financial Statements," Newsletter [3] (November 1950):11; Grand Council Minutes Book, 1946, p.2, 1947, pp. 1-[4], 1948, p. 1; [Hazen W. Kendrick], "Announcement of Beta Alpha Psi Scholarship Award," Newsletter [2] (March 1941):5; Sheldahl, Alpha to Omega, pp. 567, 585 (quoted); and UCB (University of Colorado at Boulder) Alumni Association to Author, August 26, 1985.

Sigma recommended that the Grand Council introduce such a "scroll" award on a national basis by which each chapter could annually honor its top senior student. At the 1947 meeting, this proposal was approved, pending agreement with the chapter on the design of the new certificate, and arrangement with the Chas. A. Belz Co. for production at a cost not exceeding one dollar per unit.

During the year that followed a draft design was submitted to Belz, producing an estimated cost of $110 for an engraving plate and $45 for the preparation of 100 certificates. Based on this estimate of "fixed" and "variable" costs, the Council voted in 1948 to proceed with development of the certificates, to be awarded by each chapter

> to the Beta Alpha Psi member of each graduating class who is a candidate for an undergraduate degree and who has attained the highest cumulative scholastic average to the end of the term immediately preceding his graduation.

The use of the masculine possessive pronoun was of course not of a generic nature in a day in which the fraternity was still an all-male organization.

With the approval of his colleagues, Secretary-Treasurer Dickerson submitted the slightly revised final design to Belz early in 1949, and a hundred certificates were produced at a cost to the fraternity, as estimated, of $155. The form is reproduced as exhibit

For the academic year 1948-49, only Sigma, Xi at Syracuse, Tau at Maryland, Psi at Marquette, and newly formed Alpha Beta at Alabama awarded the emblematic scroll, although other chapters expressed interest. Recipients Robert Kaiser of Xi and Edgar M. Gober, III of Alpha Beta would respectively become a financial executive on Long Island, and accept a position with the Tennessee Valley Authority upon graduation.

The following year Tau and Psi from the original group were joined by 11 additional participants in the program, and in 1950-51 16 local units

EXHIBIT 19

BETA ALPHA PSI SCHOLARSHIP CERTIFICATE

B E T A A L P H A P S I

SCHOLARSHIP AWARD

This certificate is presented to

by____________________________chapter of Beta Alpha Psi in

recognition of outstanding scholarship in the field of accounting.

Date this_______________day of________________________

at the____

President of Grand Council	Seal	Chapter President
Chapter Vice-President		Chapter Secretary

SOURCES: W. E. Dickerson to John A(rch) White, January 25, 1949, and enclosure (reproduced above); and White to Dickerson, January 31, 1949, conferring approval of the design. Policies File.

awarded the scroll. The full listing available for the latter year reveals not only the designation of the first female award recipient (in the first year of coeducation), Ruth Merves of Pi Chapter, but also the awarding of two or more scrolls by Xi, Theta at Texas, and Alpha Gamma at CCNY. Rather than equivalent grade averages for top students, the latter cases involved awards for multiple graduating classes of the year, from respectively the fall, spring, and (at Texas) summer terms.

Although local interest would steadily decline in the later years, the scholarship certificate continued to be awarded at least until present-day academic awards began to emerge in the early seventies. A. J. Penz inserted an attractive notice on the program in the Newsletter of November 1953, and beginning in 1956 it was for several years promoted in the April issue. Regular or frequent chapter participants of the third era included Iota at Southern California and Alpha Beta at Alabama. USC conferred the award semiannually, for the fall and spring classes, at the "Honoree Banquet" held for students having received As or Bs in accounting the preceding term. After the first year, costs of the certificate program ranged from \$3.50 to \$21.00 except for \$54.80 in 1951-52 and \$103.20 five years later, totals that imply major replenishment of the supply.[10]

---

[10] AAA Road Atlas, p. 77; "Alumni News," Newsletter [3] (November 1951):16, (May 1952):19; Beta Alpha Psi, Xi Chapter: 1972-1974 Directory (Syracuse, N.Y.: [1972]), alphabetical listing, s.v. "Kaiser, Robert H."; "Chapter News Items," Newsletter [2] (May 1947):15, W. E. Dickerson to John A[rch] White, January 25, 1949 (Policies File); "Directory, Newsletter [2] (May 1947):3; "Grand Council Audit Report," 1954-55, exhibit B; Grand Council Minutes Book, 1948-7, p. 3 (quoted), 1948, p. 1 (quoted), 1949, pp. 1, 3; "Grand Council News," Newsletter (April, 1956-57, 1959-61), 4 (1956):305, (1957):382, 5 (1959):149, (1960):253, (1961):354; "Local Chapter News" or "Chapter News," Newsletter [3] (November 1949):19, 26, 4 (November 1952):27, (November 1954):216, (April 1955):246 (quoted), 253, (November 1955):281-82, (April 1956):312-13, (November 1956):363-64, 5

Another important addition was made to Beta Alpha Psi "symbolism" through action taken at the 1953 annual meeting.

Grand Council Badges

As related in volume 1, diamond pins had been made for early presidents of the fraternity. In 1953, the Grand council voted to

> provide each Councilman with a crown set pearl badge [emphasis added], with a grand officer's bar attached, for use at chapter installations, chapter visitations, and . . . official meetings and local chapter meetings only. The engraving on the grand officer bars are to be suitable for proper identification.

The plans were to purchase a new badge each year for the immediate past president, permitting the retiring councilor to retain his badge for any subsequent official business. Otherwise, badges would be transferred "to successors in office at the end of each year." Five badges were accordingly produced by the Balfour Company during the year 1953-54 at a cost, to the fraternity, of $115.20. Because a full set of badges were always to be held by the Council, this amount was presented on the 1954 and 1955 balance sheets as an asset cost. Beginning in 1956, at the close of Bill Jencks' first year as secretary-treasurer, the badges were reported at the nominal amount of one dollar. The cost of replacement badges is identified in none of the income or cash statements of the day. In all likelihood it was accounted for as a "miscellaneous" item rather than as a deduction from royalties paid by Balfour on fraternal jewelry.

In 1957, Past President Andy Penz gave his badge to 1950-51 president Gould Harris on the occasion of the latter's retirement from NYU, no doubt

---

(November 1957):38; A. J. Penz, Secretary-Treasurer's report, 1953-54, p. 2; Penz, "Scholarship Certificates," Newsletter [4] (November 1953):109; Robert S. Wasley, Secretary-Treasurer's Report, 1970-71, pp. 1, 10; White to Dickerson, January 31, 1949 (Policies), and White, Secretary-Treasurer's Report, 1949-50, p. [4].

during a visitation to Mu Chapter. In recognition of this gesture, the Grand Council later in the year approved the production of a replacement badge for retiring member Penz. Also in 1957, incoming secretary-treasurer Nolan Williams was asked to check with Balfour on the creation of a jeweled fraternal key with attached gavel for presentation to former presidents (if they wished) in place of the badge. Such a key was made for retiring councilor Wayne Shroyer in 1958,at a cost of $24.30.[11]

Throughout the third era, in continuation of a prewar practice, payments were made to secretary-treasurers in recognition of their unique services to the fraternity, although indications are that in substance they largely represented reimbursements. During the last six years of the period, small monetary awards were made annually to ten faculty advisors in a program tied jointly to the chapter activity competition and the yearly Grand Chapter meeting.

Disbursements to the Secretary-Treasurer and to Faculty Vice-Presidents

Secretary-treasurer "honoraria"

The secretary-treasurer was responsible for all day-to-day operations of the fraternity, including the recording and collection of fees for new

---

[11] "Grand Council Audit Report," 1953-54, exhibits A, C, 1954-55; Grand Council Minutes Book, 1953, p. 4 (quoted), 1957, p. [2]; Secretary-Treasurer's Reports, 1955-56 through 1959-60, financial statements; Sheldahl, Alpha to Omega, pp. 211-15; and [Nolan E. Williams}, Secretary-Treasurer's Report, 1957-58, p. [3].

Prior to the National Council meeting in 1971, the widow of third-era councilor W. E. Dickerson carried out her husband's wishes by presenting his fraternal pin to his former graduate student at Ohio State, Secretary-Treasurer Robert Wasley. Incoming president Wasley accordingly advised his colleagues that it would be unnecessary to acquire for him the pearl pin or

membership, the issuance of member certificates, the collection of annual reports from the chapters, all treasurership functions, annual reporting by the Grand Council, communication with prospective chapter sites, maintenance and distribution of annual minutes, and, after 1950, stewardship of the chapter activity program. In addition, virtually all other fraternal correspondence, at the national level, was conducted through the secretary-treasurer's office. It is not surprising, then, that the Grand Council had from its early days provided modest annual payments as "honoraria" for holders of that position.

The highest amount paid to a secretary-treasurer prior to the war was the $400 approved for Hermann Miller at the close of 1940. The payments made to H. W. Kendrick after each of the next two years had reverted to the prior $300 level. At the first postwar meeting, which he was unable to attend, it was agreed to pay Fayette Elwell $500 for his services since April 1943, most of which had of course been rendered since reactivation had commenced during the preceding year.

In each of these cases, and throughout the third era, payments to the secretary-treasurer were made <u>subsequent to</u> the year of service, based on approval at the annual meeting. Because the amount was not set in advance, they were necessarily accounted for on a cash basis rather than through accrual. Although in practice there was generally an upward progression in the scale, the approach taken offered the Grand Council an opportunity to adjust the amount paid to both the actual financial condition of the fraternity and the level of unreimbursed cost having been absorbed by the officer.

---

key customarily given retiring presidents. Dickerson had evidently received such a pin at the Golden Anniversary observance in 1969. Hollis A. Dixon, Secretary-Treasurer's Report, 1971-72, p. 1; and National Council Minutes, 1968, p. 9, 1969, p. 11.

As a potential incidental benefit, the Council was not placed in the position of increasing the provision at the close of a secretary-treasurer's term for the benefit of his successor.

For his services in 1946-47, Secretary-Treasurer Kendrick was paid $500. During the next four years, W. E. Dickerson and John Arch White, in turn, were compensated (in arrears) at an annual rate of $750. Each payment was reported as an "honorarium."

From the minutes prepared by Secretary-Treasurer S. M. Wedeberg in 1952, however, it seems apparent that a major part of this expense item was actually belated <u>reimbursement</u> for costs of fraternal business that had been borne by the officer. At a time of declining revenue at rising expense, the Council that year approved Wedeberg's motion that the honorarium be reduced to $100. At the same time, however, it authorized an additional payment to him of $660 to cover "local transportation and other types of expenses for which auditable vouchers or receipts c[ould] not be secured conveniently," and also the cost of the annual audit, which constitutionally was absorbed by the secretary-treasurer. A bookkeeping change had thus been made to account more accurately for essentially the same level of expenditure approved the previous four years.

During the next four years, 1953-56, the Grand Council took a similar approach, authorizing payment of $100 as an honorarium and from $900 to $1,200 as reimbursement for relevant costs of "auditing, traveling, depreciation, etc." In his 1956-57 financial reports, however, Bill Jencks reported the full amount paid him for the preceding year as an honorarium. Finally, from 1957 through 1960 the Council reverted to earlier practice by approving simply the payment of an honorarium to the secretary-treasurer, in the amount of $1,600, and beginning in 1958-59 the payments were reported accordingly.

Although not financially pertinent, it is interesting to note that the fraternity had an acting secretary-treasurer at the close of the third era. When offered appointment to the Grand Council, in 1958, Herbert E. Miller was a busy as ever in his career in his collaboration with H. A. Finney on their celebrated textbook series. Since the new councilor would become secretary-treasurer within a year, he told President Jencks that he could accept only if his wife Lenore, an accounting major, would be permitted to conduct the activity program, in full, and assume other major responsibilities of the position. These terms were accepted, and thus during the two years 1959-61 Lenore Miller completely ran the activity program, maintained all financial records at the national level, and wrote all checks on behalf of the Council.[12]

With an improved financial condition in the mid-1950s, the fraternity introduced a monetary award for faculty vice-presidents, and on a one-time basis financially rewarded top-ranked chapters.

Payments to FVPs attending Grand Chapter meeting

At some point between the 1954 and 1955 annual meetings, the Grand Council voted to pay $25 each to the ten faculty vice-presidents attending the next Grand Chapter meeting whose chapters were highest ranked in the year's activity competition. This award, intended "in part as an incentive and in part to defray expense of attending the meeting," was approved at the

---

[12]"Financial Statements," "Grand Council Audit Reports," Secretary-Treasurers' Reports as cited in note 4, income statements only; Grand Council Minutes Book, 1946 through 1960, quoting minutes of 1952, p. 5, 1953, p. 5; Herbert E. Miller to Author, interview, April 18, 1980; and Sheldahl, Alpha to Omega, pp. 790-92.

forthcoming Council meeting, and promptly became established as a regular practice.

The following year, in 1956, the governing body took an isolated action intended to yield limited student participation in the Grand Chapter meeting. It voted to invite the top three chapters in the coming year's activity program to send a delegate of their choosing to the 1958 meeting, recognizing that the standings might not be established in time to permit orderly planning for the 1957 gathering. The student delegates were to be reimbursed for the cost of first-class transportation, and be paid $10 per travel day and $25 toward costs incurred at the meeting.

During the year that followed, however, it was decided to leave to the discretion of the chapters the use of funding provided. Later, by mail vote, Secretary-Treasurer Nolan Williams was directed to send respectively $250, $150,and $110 to Theta at Texas, Alpha Theta at Mississippi, and Sigma at Wisconsin for their first-, second-, and third-place rankings. The latter two chapters placed their monies in scholarship funds, while Theta reserved $100 for financing the next chapter directory and placed the balance in an "accounting education" (presumably scholarship) fund.[13]

There exists ample material, finally, for covering the lighter side of life on the early postwar Grand Council.

Supplementary Anecdotes from the Third Era

Substantial anecdotal material provided by A. J. Penz from his own experience was included in chapter 7. Coverage of the third era is

---

[13] Grand Council Minutes Book, 1955, p. 4 (quoted), 1956, p. 3, 1958, p. [4]; Secretary-Treasurers' Reports, 1955-56 through 1959-60, income statements; and [Nolan E. Williams], Secretary-Treasurer's Report, 1957-58, p. 7 (quoted).

concluded on a similar note relative to several other Beta Alpha Psi leaders, based on files developed separately by Penz and an earlier president in connection with the fraternity's golden anniversary. Ten anecdotes are drawn from these sources, after they are identified in general terms, and a composite story told by Thomas Dickerson is substituted for a bit of third-era lore involving him that was used in volume 1.

Source Files Developed by Andy Penz and Aubrey Smith

During the first week of 1967, Andy Penz was appointed fraternal historian in preparation for observing the half-century milestone less than three years away. Later in January (or, in an instance of delayed acquisition of a current address, in mid-February) he wrote the eighteen other living presidents retired from Council service, from Eric Kohler to Emerson Henke. The objective was to identify unrecorded "significant events, humorous incidents, (or interesting) remarks about associates" that could be used "to inject . . . personalities and humor into the history." Excellent copy was obtained, in particular, from Tom Dickerson, S. M. Wedeberg, and Williard Stone, as well as earlier councilor C. Aubrey Smith. In the end, however, Penz was unable to include such material in his booklet due to certain limitations imposed upon the project.

In the fall of 1968, Aubrey Smith of Texas was invited to deliver an informal address the following August at the fiftieth-anniversary banquet. With considerable time to prepare his speech, he followed in Penz's footsteps by contacting his fellow past presidents in the "expectation" that they "would supply an anecdote, situation, point of interest, quotation and/or reference, humorous or serious, concerning some aspect of Beta Alpha Psi" that he could "weave into" the address.

Smith, whose letter opened (on the same line as the salutation) with the plea "Help! Help! I need your Help!," hoped that each of them could "recall at least one whiz bang of a story or incident that w[ould] be of genuine interest to those in attendance."

In essence, Smith had been asked to supply at the banquet anecdotal coverage of the kind having been excluded from Penz's commemorative history. Andy Penz not only briefly summarized the family "banner" project and his untimely hospitalization, in Montana, of 1956, but also sent on summaries of anecdotes sent him by Councilors Wedeberg and Stone, and offered to share with Aubrey Smith the entire file that he had collected. As it was, material provided by Penz, Wedeberg, Stone, Gould Harris, Nolan Williams, and councilors serving in other eras was more than ample as a base for an outstanding commemorative speech. Unfortunately, and indeed ironically, Professor Smith was forced to cancel his trip to the Beta Alpha Psi festivities in 1969 after both he and his wife became ill while visiting Ireland, and her recovery was delayed somewhat.

The bulk of the material collected by the Alabama and Texas councilors is belatedly presented in the remainder of this chapter. Other stories from the two files appeared in the first volume, or are used in covering the 1960s.[14] The eleven items of fraternal lore that follow (one of them

---

[14]Wilton T. Anderson to A. J. Penz, January 5, 1967 (Penz History Files, 1966-69); Penz to Emerson Henke, Eric L. Kohler, and seventeen other former councilors, January 19, 26, 30, or February 13, 1967, identical letters (Penz Files), quoted; "Past Presidents of Beta Alpha Psi," *Newsletter* 6 (Fall 1965):320; Penz to C. Aubrey Smith, February 4, 1969, with enclosure (Golden Anniversary Files, source likewise of Smith's letters to to Penz and to or from Taylor); Sheldahl, *Alpha to Omega*, pp. 274-77, 314-18, 817; Smith to Penz, January 7, 1969, quoted, same letter apparently sent to all other living ex-councilors; Smith to Charles W. Taylor, August 14, 1969; and Taylor to Smith, December 16, 1968.

Among Penz's 1967 letters to former fraternal leaders, one (to Henke)

collected independently) are classified respectively in terms of weather, two different chapters, and other accounting organizations.

Weather-induced Obstacles to Fraternal Travel, by Highway, Air, and Rail

Snowstorms delayed the official formation of Alpha Mu at the University of Kentucky in 1952 and forced an early termination of a visitation swing through Michigan in the fall of 1955. Cold weather was the prime factor in a "miserable" trip to Pittsburgh in the winter of 1958-59 for what turned out to be a most unusual visitation. Councilors Wedeberg and, in the latter two cases, Stone travelled respectively by car, plane, and train.

A snow-delayed installation at Kentucky

On the morning of March 28, 1952, "a sunshiny day," Secretary-Treasurer S. M. Wedeberg and Tau Chapter advisor John A. "Jack" Daiker left the Maryland campus bound for Lexington, Kentucky to install Alpha Mu the next evening. In that pre-interstate day and time they had chosen to drive northwest on "old route 40" to its conclusion just short of Washington, Pennsylvania, south of Pittsburgh, and then to cut over to "old route 50" for a trip across Ohio, finally turning due south at Cincinnati. Hitting a most unexpected snowstorm shortly before reaching Washington, they decided to stop there for lunch and wait for conditions to clear. The storm "got worse and worse," however, so the travelers stayed overnight in the small Pennsylvania city that was the hometown of Wedeberg's undergraduate

---

was misdated January 19, 1966, while another one was addressed to William E. Cox, who along with J. C. Gibson had died the preceding year. [Vern E. Odmark], "Past Presidents Cox, Gibson Die," Newsletter 7 (February 1967):5.

professor and Delta brother James McConahey, an alumnus (B.S. '96, M.S. '99) of the local college, Washington and Jefferson.

The next morning driving "was a little slow," as Wedeberg and Daiker encountered many one-way bridges on the roads between the two main highways. Perhaps they were also "too leisurely in driving and eating on the way." At any rate, by the time they arrived in Lexington the newspaper photographer and university officials outside the school had given up waiting, and a picture of the presentation of a charter had been "improvised" in the absence of the Council representative and the Alpha Mu document he was carrying from Maryland. Sill on hand, fortunately, were an initiation team from Miami of Ohio headed by Professor Glenn G. Yankee, all twenty-three initiates, four other Beta Alpha Psi members, including designated FVP Russell S. Grady, and the business dean.

After arrival, Jack Daiker was introduced as "the biggest man in accounting." He then "broke the ice" (no pun intended) by explaining that his singular professional status was the reason that he and Secretary-Treasurer Wedeberg had been late--"the car was overloaded and couldn't make the hills in high gear." Everything went well from that point on, and thanks to the charter faculty advisor three pictures were produced for the Newsletter, marking the beginning of photographic coverage within the periodical. By the time they arrived back, uneventfully, in College Park, the visitors from Tau Chapter had logged 1,185 miles.[15]

---

[15] AAA Road Atlas, p. 45,50-51, 88-89, 95; James M. McConahey to S. M. Wedeberg, April 22, 1952; [A. J. Penz], "James M. McConahey . . .: Grand President of Beta Alpha Psi, December 1941 to September, 1947," Newsletter 4 (March 1954):134; [Wedeberg], "Grand Council News," Newsletter [3] (May 1952):15-16; Wedeberg to McConahey, April 16, 1952; Wedeberg to Penz, December 10, 1967, quoted; and Wedeberg to C. Aubrey Smith, February 8, 1969, with enclosure, quoted.

KEY PARTICIPANTS IN INSTALLATION OF ALPHA MU AT KENTUCKY, 1952

Installation officer JACK DAIKER (left), and FVP RUSSELL S. GRADY

Installation officer S. M. WEDEBERG

Another snowstorm shortened the first visitation trip of the most active Grand Council visitor of the third era.

Eleven hours at a Michigan airport in lieu of a visitation

Directly after Thanksgiving vacation in 1955, new councilor Williard Stone flew from Philadelphia to Detroit to conduct, at the University of Detroit (Alpha Xi), the first of three visitations planned in Michigan. The following night he attended a meeting of Alpha Eta at the nearby University of Michigan. The final stop was supposed to be at Michigan State, home of Alpha Omicron.

The faculty vice-president at Michigan took Stone to "the old Willow Run Airport" in Detroit around 1:00 P.M. on the third day of the trip, to board a plane for East Lansing. Just prior to boarding, however, the traveler was informed that a timely departure from that destination would be "very doubtful in view of a rather serious blizzard which was on its way." Needing to conduct classes the next day at the Wharton School, he decided to cancel the Michigan State visit and return, on a standby basis, to Philadelphia.

Councilor Stone would later describe the remainder of a long day as follows:

> As each flight left, and they were leaving late because the blizzard was now really raging outside, I stood and watched every person arrive and take their seat. . . [I]t was twelve o'clock that night before I got on my own flight[,] which left about two hours late. . . . [At] the old Willow Run Airport, . . . the seats were plain unshaped boards. After eleven hours, a certain part of my anatomy was shaped exactly to fit the board seat.[16]

---

[16]A. J. Penz to C. Aubrey Smith, February 4, 1969, enclosure; Williard E. Stone to Penz, February 6, 1967, quoted (indented citation); Stone to

A still less comfortable travel experience would lead to an unusual reception somewhat more than three years later for President Stone.

A bumpy, cold, and long train ride, from Philadelphia, to a subdued reception in Pittsburgh

Early in December 1957, Williard Stone paid "a very pleasant visit" to Alpha Tau Chapter at Pittsburgh, and as president the following year he wished to make a return trip, also calling upon Alpha Psi at West Virginia and, possibly, visiting Washington, D.C. before returning to Philadelphia. Traveling by train, Stone would make it to the nation's capital earlier, and under different circumstances, than he could have planned.

Writing to Andy Penz and Aubrey Smith eight and ten years after the fact, Stone recalled having left for Pittsburgh on a Friday afternoon, or evening, "in the very coldest part of the [w]inter" of 1959. Contemporary records, which include reports of all fifteen of his presidential visitations _except_ the one to Pitt, imply that the trip actually began on _April 15_, no doubt an unseasonably very cold day. Boarding the B & O sleeper in late afternoon or early evening, the fraternal leader shortly retired to an upper berth. As the temperature continued to fall, he "almost froze to death" despite having a generous supply of blankets. It seems that the car had square wheels, so that the traveler "bounced and jogged enough that there was a continuous bellows effect between the mattress and the covers which forced out the warm air and sucked in the cold." Finally, "[a]fter what seemed [like] an interminable night," the train pulled into the station. The only problem was that the route was an indirect one, and Stone

---

Smith, January 16, 1969, quoted; and Stone, Visitation Reports--Alpha Xi, November 28, Alpha Eta, November 29, 1955.

had arrived in Washington rather than Pittsburgh. After another "several . . . miserable hours," he finally reached his destination.

Upon arrival, the visitation officer telephoned Alpha Tau advisor Stanley F. Jablonski, who had been "a gracious host" the year before. As the first tipoff that something was amiss, the Pitt professor was at first completely silent. Later, just 4 to 6 students showed up for a meeting of an admittedly small chapter that would initiate only 14 active members during the year, and the local secretary did not recognize the guest speaker from Philadelphia. Furthermore, the faculty vice-president "bawled the daylights" out of the members who had assembled, as if they were responsible for the embarrassingly low attendance.

This "fiasco" seems all the more bizarre in that a forthcoming visit by President Stone, scheduled for April 16, was reported by Alpha Tau's correspondent in the April Newsletter. The reasons were never revealed, although it appears that the faculty advisor had somehow forgotten that the fraternal leader was coming to the campus.[17]

As faulty vice-president of Alpha Delta, and later as immediate past president at the national level, Williard Stone was a visitation host and an installation officer on memorable occasions that directly or indirectly involved the University of Pennsylvania chapter.

---

[17]"Grand Chapter," Newsletter 5 (April 1959):147; Grand Council Minutes Book, 1959, p. 2; "[Local] Chapter News," Newsletter 5 (April 1959):187; Williard E. Stone to A. J. Penz, February 6, 1967, quoted; Stone to Author, interview, April 18, 1980; Stone to C. Aubrey Smith, January 16, 1969, quoted; Stone, Visitation Reports--Alpha Tau, December 11, 1957 (letter format), quoted, Beta Psi, April 24, 1959.

Two Instances of (at Least in Part) Alpha Delta Lore

FVP Stone's analogical defense of the activity program

In covering early response to the rating/activity program in chapter 6, it was noted that during a 1952 visit by Secretary-Treasurer S. M. Wedeberg the Alpha Delta brotherhood objected to the credit assigned several reporting provisions which they considered relatively insignificant. At the same time, they insisted that more points should be assigned for plant and office visits.

After Wedeberg had tried without success to persuade his audience that each element of the program was worthwhile, charter faculty advisor Stone (silent to that point) directed remarks in turn toward several different members. Specifically, he raised rhetorical questions pertinent, apparently, to their particular recreational interests, as illustrated by the following indirect statements:

> 'When you play tennis, you play according to the rules, don't you, even if you do not like those rules?'[18]

> 'When you play golf, you play according to the rules, don't you?'

After raising a series of such "questions," the future councilor, by analogy, drew the following conclusion:

> 'If we are going to play the game of chapter competition, we should play the game according to the rules'.

As the final installation officer of the third era, in the spring of 1960, Past President Stone encountered no travel problems, unlike Professors Wedeberg and Daiker in their journey to Kentucky eight years earlier. He

---

[18] S. M. Wedeberg to A. J. Penz, December 10, 1967, quoted.

had to resort, however, to a temporary substitute for the most basic installation document.

Presentation of a "rival" charter at Penn State

In preparing for the installation of Beta Theta at Penn State, "there was a slip-up in securing the necessary supplies and the charter." Through "[a] bit of scurrying around," installing officer Stone was able to obtain adequate materials aside from the official symbol that would uniquely define the new chapter. Accordingly, he borrowed the charter of his own chapter, Alpha Delta at Pennsylvania, and handed it to Dean Ossian MacKenzie in the picture-taking ceremony at Pennsylvania State. Since "there exists a bit of rivalry" between the two schools, as respectively the leading private and public universities in the state, and since Professor Stone of Penn was a 1933 graduate of Penn State, there was a degree of irony to the incident. Serving at Penn State under Mackenzie, a prominent leader of the American Association of Collegiate Schools of Business, was associate dean David H. McKinley.[19]

Williard Stone was part of a captive audience in the first of three anecdotes involving Mu Chapter at NYU in general, and Council Gould Harris (at least as a source) in particular.

---

[19]Dirksen, Lockley, et al., AAcCSB:1916-1966, pp. v-vii, ix, identifying Ossian MacKenzie as a prime contributor to the official AAcCSB history; [W. B. Jencks], "Williard E. Stone Elected to Grand Council," Newsletter 4 (November 1955):277; Eugene J. Kelley, business dean at Pennsylvania State University, to Author, August 29, 1985; and Williard E. Stone to A. J. Penz, February 6, 1967, quoted.

Three Incidents Relating to Mu Chapter

"Concluding" remarks by Professor Harris

President Stone's visitation to New York in October 1958 is notable primarily for having revealed alumni dominance within the local chapter. A light-hearted anecdote also came out of the trip, however.

Stone had taken the train from Philadelphia, and intended to return that night on a train leaving at 9:00. With that end in view, he presented "a very reasonably lengthened talk," after which former Beta Alpha Psi president Harris got up to thank him for his "apt and concise" remarks. As luck would have it, the brief talk had reminded the retired NYU professor of a recent trip to Spain, on which he chose to reminisce in much detail. As a result, the fraternal president departed for Philadelphia at 12:05 A.M.

Whatever may have been the merits of his extemporaneous speech to Mu Chapter in October 1958, Gould Harris was evidently a prominent speaker in the field of cost accounting. During his last year on the Grand Council, 1951-52, he had made no fewer than eleven addresses to NACA chapters in New York, Pennsylvania, and Ohio, four of them to his home New York City group, on topics including profit planning and overhead costing. He had also spoken at two conferences held that year on his own campus.[20]

Harris' own favored anecdotes likewise involved Mu Chapter, by way of either a local meeting or a prominent honorary member and chapter speaker.

Not fit for a "mixed audience": A coed's logical solution

As Harris was about to address a Mu Chapter initiation, one of the young men present sought to direct his attention to a particular kind of content:

---

[10]Williard E. Stone to A. J. Penz, February 6, 1967, quoted; and [S. M. Wedeberg], "Grand Council News," Newsletter (3) (May 1952):7.

'"Professor, you haven't told us any stories recently"'. There were women in attendance, although perhaps only in the capacity of dates or wives, given that Mu would not become coeducational until several years after the professor's retirement. The Beta Alpha Psi leader responded accordingly: '"I haven't heard any [stories] recently that I thought I could tell to a mixed audience"'. At that point, one of the women offered the obvious solution: '"Send the boys out"'.

Jack Seidman and the scarcity of "great men"

In the spring of 1951, President Harris was honored by Mu Chapter at its twenty-fifth anniversary banquet, held on Park Avenue. Honorary initiates on that occasion included senior partner Arthur Foye of Haskins & Sells, a member of the Class of 1914, and tax authority J. S. "Jack" Seidman from Seidman & Seidman, another local alumnus. As related in chapter 5, both men were appointed during the year to a committee to prepare a uniform accounting system for Beta Alpha Psi chapters, and respectively as chairman and chief draftsman they would be the major figures in producing the eventual report.

Seidman was the principal speaker at the 1951 Mu banquet, and his speech on ways of committing fraud that are difficult to detect, based on case histories, received a glowing writeup in the Newsletter. Eighteen years later the speaker would be recalled by Gould Harris as "probably my best student in all the years I taught at NYU." In the same letter to Aubrey Smith, however, he passed on a story that Mr. Seidman had told on himself, presumably concerning a different speaking engagement, but one for which the praise (in advance) was as lavish as in the case of the periodical report just mentioned.

It seems that Mrs. Seidman was in the audience one evening when her husband was introduced with '"a great buildup"' that simply '"enthralled"' him. Throughout his ensuing speech, '"the chairman's rapturous comments kept ringing"' in his mind to the point that, later, he could not even remember what he had said. Heading home in a cab, Seidman was at first '"still lost in the reveries of that introduction"', but in time turned to his wife and said, '"You know, there are very few really great men in this world"'. Her response finally undid the effects of the effusive introduction: '"Not only are there very few great men in this world, but there's even one less than you think"'.[21]

The final three anecdotes relate in one way or another to two of the nation's leading accounting organizations, the American Accounting Association and the National Association of (Cost) Accountants.

Stories Having an AAA or NACA Dimension

Conscientious immediate work on initiation ritual

At his first Grand Council meeting, Professor Charles Staehling was asked in 1950 to draft a revision of the initiation ritual, with a view toward

> making the initiation work more smoothly, securing greater emphasis on the professional nature of the fraternity, and making minor changes in line with current practices of the various chapters.

Having evidently exchanged correspondence on the matter with other members, Councilor Staehling presented a tentative revision at the 1951 meeting, the first one attended by S. M. Wedeberg. It was felt that further work was

---

[21] Gould L. Harris to C. Aubrey Smith, [1969], quoted; and "Honorary Members Initiated During the Past Year," Newsletter [3] (March 1952):9-10.

needed on the project, and Wedeberg was asked to assist Staehling in that regard.

The two councilors were so conscientious about their assignment that they began working intensively on it at once, in Denver, "while the old timers [other councilors] attended AAA meetings and otherwise seemed to enjoy life." The Council as a whole were not satisfied with the initial results of their collaboration, however, so further refinements were developed through correspondence over the next year, leading to the approval of a modified ritual in 1952. As recalled by Wedeberg,

> the amusing part was that Staehling and I took the job seriously and waded right into it, instead of attending the AAA meetings in between our meetings and then doing the revision later at our leisure.

Somewhat ironically, Professor Wedeberg had severe misgivings about the project, fearing that "any revision would tend to ruin a very effective ritual." The traditional ritual had made an indelible impression on him during his own induction, by Delta at Washington, nearly thirty years earlier. There was strong pressure for at least modest change, however, based for example on the suggestion from some quarters that the Beta Alpha Psi ritual contained "a stronger oath than the oath of office for the supreme court or president of the U.S." Although details are not available, it is noteworthy that the Grand Council did not at this time eliminate the "blindfolding" element of the initiation ceremony.[22]

---

[22]Grand Council Minutes Book, 1950, p. 1, first indented citation, 1951, p. 1, 1952, p. 1; [Grand Council], "Procedures for Pledging, Initiation, and Election and Installation of Officers of Beta Alpha Psi," revised 1961, 6-page typescript, pp. 1-2; and S. M. Wedeberg to A. J. Penz, December 10, 1967, quoted.

At the 1952 meeting during which the Council adopted the proposed revisions, concern was expressed that "some chapters did not adhere strictly to the initiation ritual." A different viewpoint was taken by Williard Stone several years later when he commended a modification made by Xi

As its last act of the third era, the Grand Council made a monetary contribution to the American Accounting Association that signified a change in operating attitudes having, in the recollection of its leading official proponent, a humorous dimension.

"New dealers" award money to AAA fellowship fund

At the 1960 meeting, President Nolan Williams moved that $1,000 be given to the AAA's graduate fellowship fund established during the presidency (1958-59) of Councilor C. Rollin Niswanger. The motion was seconded by Past President Stone, and then passed unanimously. The check apparently was drafted and presented before the end of the association's annual meeting.

This action seems remarkable in light of the cash balance of $1,321 reported at July 31, 1960, and the loss of $3,026 reported for the year ending on that date, even given the imminent maturity of $9,000 in government bonds. A year earlier, indeed, the fraternity had temporarily been insolvent following the national meeting after a cash balance of $3,875 had been reported at July 31, 1959. It does not seem surprising, then, that 'some of the past presidents . . . were quite alarmed that control of the organization had fallen into the hands of '"new dealers"'. Irreverently, Williams would describe the supposed heresy as the belief in, "of all things, spending the organization's funds."

Retiring member Williard Stone was the only past president on the Grand Council in 1960. Wayne Shroyer was present at the meeting in a nonvoting capacity as a member of the president's advisory council, but for

---

Chapter at Syracuse as having "added much to the simplicity and dignity of the ceremony." Grand Council Minutes Book, 1952, p. [3], quoted; and Stone, Visitation Report--Xi, November 12, 1959 (letter format), quoted.

unexplained reasons Bill Jencks was absent from the gathering at his own Ohio State campus. Nolan Williams remembers Jencks, Shroyer, and Andy Penz as a group of "[c]onservative accountant-type people," emphasizing "public trust," who were very reluctant to expend funds. Yet it was under Jencks' leadership that the visitation program had been immensely enlarged, and Williams credits Shroyer with strong support for the program dispensing $250 annually to faculty vice-presidents. These points would tend to push the alarm about fraternal "new dealers" back at least as far as Professor Penz, recalled by Williams as the most frugal Councilor figure of his day, 1956-61.

The 1960 meetings at Ohio State, incidentally, had brought back to the campus an alumnus who had attended the 1916 meeting in Columbus at which the AAA, under its original name, had been organized. At a Grand Chapter gathering attended by five chapter advisors later to head Beta Alpha Psi, Gould Harris spoke to the faculty vice-presidents and other chapter representatives with whom he was seated (who perhaps did not include FVP Doris Cook of Alpha Iota) as "you young fellers."[23]

Anecdotal coverage may be concluded by reference to the councilor of the third era other than Harris, the first research director (1920-25), having a major connection with the National Association of (until 1957) "Cost" Accountants, namely, Thomas Dickerson.

---

[23] Grand Council Minutes Book, 1960, pp. 5, 7-8; Leon E. Hay to Author, interview, May 2, 1980; Herbert E. Miller to A. J. Penz, September 25, 1959; [Miller], ed., "Special Features," Newsletter 5 (November 1960):314-15 (material provided by three-member AAA committee that included Professor Niswonger), with accompanying photograph; Sheldahl, Alpha to Omega, p. 706; Nolan E. Williams to Aubrey Smith, February 12, 1969, quoted; and Zeff American Accounting Association, p. 7.

Recollections by Tom Dickerson of the NACA's "Doc" McLeod

Since a 1948 story from Dickerson was used in the first volume, it seems only fair to draw upon his pre-Council days at this point. Tom Dickerson's model for the chapter rating program had of course been the NACA competition that he had administered for three years in the 1930s. His boss had been "Doc" McLeod, a colorful figure briefly described in volume 1 who is memorialized within the modern-day NAA through the exclusive Stuart Cameron McLeod Society.

According to Dickerson, McLeod could be a rather difficult personality at times. Three incidents, in particular, seem far more amusing when they were recalled in a 1980 interview than they had as factual episodes nearly half a century earlier. When hired by McLeod in 1931 at the then handsome salary of $4,000, the future fraternal leader was promised a yearly raise of $500. Instead, the only change in his pay was a reduction of five per cent. One fall he stood in for Doc McLeod at the annual clambake held by the Boston NACA chapter. A year later, after another clambake had taken place, Dickerson was asked by Boston acquaintances why he had not attended. A bit of inquiry revealed that the invitation extended him had stopped in the boss's office. Finally, through an employment-related competition (most likely) the administrator of the Stevenson Trophy program won an expense-paid trip to Bermuda, only to be denied permission to go by Stuart Cameron McLeod.[24]

---

[24]Thomas M. Dickerson to Author, interview, April 19, 1980; [W. E. Dickerson], "Councilor Gould L. Harris," Newsletter [2] (November 1948):9; and Sheldahl, Alpha to Omega, p. 12.

In Transition

As Beta Alpha Psi entered the 1960s, several major policy issues were emerging, or were about to surface, to set an agenda for a fraternal decade of undramatic but pivotal reform. The fourth era, 1961-70, embodied continuity with the fifties through reasonable roster expansion, conclusion of the coeducation process, and reform (finally basic) of the activity program. All the while, the organization was undertaking significant modernization on fronts ranging from governing law to fraternal symbolism. It was within such an environment that, partially through a new contribution by a leading third-era councilor, a fraternity founded in 1919 observed a notable milestone.

PART 2. THE MODERATE REFORMIST (or FOURTH) ERA, 1961-70

CHAPTER 9

MODERNIZING THE FRATERNITY WITHIN CONVENTIONAL BOUNDS: CONSTITUTION AND COUNCIL STRUCTURE, INCLUSIVE OF A SEPARATE EDITORSHIP

The "Moderate Reformist Era" of the sixties was a period of modernizing reform throughout Beta Alpha Psi, beginning with constitutional revision providing one source for an altered operating structure of the renamed "National" Council. One important structural change was the appointment of a separate editor to bring out a much improved *Newsletter*. As covered in the following two chapters, equally significant change occurred in the activity program, the fraternity's foremost behavioral vehicle; the initiation ritual, its leading symbolic element; and policy on chapter formation, the readiest expansion base. In addition, important programs were begun to assist or reward faculty vice-presidential service. Several reforms reflected the leadership of particular councilors.

The reference made to moderation is not meant to imply the absence of fundamental change in important areas. It is intended rather to signify that Beta Alpha Psi operations were updated, and upgraded, in several major realms without enlarging the overall program, materially, or changing the basic nature of the organization. No innovations of the 1960s had the magnitude of the interchapter competition started in the preceding decade, or of several initiatives taken during the following one to democratize the fraternity. Fourth-era councilor Vern Vincent would later observe that during his tenure "Big things didn't happen--at least we didn't think they

did." Even so, the modernizing reform of the sixties enabled Beta Alpha Psi, as it approached and passed (in 1969) the half-century mark, to adapt to dynamic educational and professional environments.

The most antiquated area within the fraternity at the outset of the fourth era, aside at least from the initiation ritual, was basic governing law as expressed in the constitution and statutes. The reform task posed was identified and embraced at the 1963 annual meeting.

Reworking of the National Constitution, 1963-65

Thirty-five years after the completion of the last such endeavor, the Grand Council voted in 1963 to revise the constitution and supporting statutes *fundamentally* over the following year. Under the leadership of the outgoing president, the project would in fact take two years, although significant progress had been made prior to the 1964 meeting. The fully unified constitution finally adopted embodied pervasive formal change, of multiple kinds, and very significant substantive revision as well. Changes in nomenclature extended to the Council itself.

A Project to Rewrite Fundamental Fraternal Law

Background: No fundamental change since the twenties

When the Grand Council met at Stanford in 1963, the fraternity was governed by a constitution and body of statutes that had not been reworked, overall, since Eric Kohler and A. C. Littleton had over the year that followed carried through the massive revision mandated at the pivotal convention held in Chicago in 1927. The structure of the dual document had remained intact, as shown in exhibit 20, part 1.

The constitution proper consisted of a preamble and nine articles that bore the same titles in 1958 (the year of the most recent edition) as thirty

EXHIBIT 20

COMPARATIVE STRUCTURES OF BASIC FRATERNAL LAW, 1928-58 AND 1965

Part 1 - Constitution and Statutes, 1928 and 1958

Articles	Chapters
1. The Supreme Law	1. Duties of Officers of Grand Council
2. Purpose	2. National Revenue of the Fraternity
3. Government of the Fraternity	3. General Provisions
	4. Investigations and Charters (1928) New Chapter Investigations and Charter (1958)
4. The Grand Council	
5. The Grand Chapter	5. Membership Qualifications
6. Membership	6. Chapter Organization and Procedure
7. Chapters	7. Duties of Chapter Officers
8. Insignia	8. Amendments (1928) Amendments to the Statutes (1958)
9. Amendments (1928) Constitutional Amendments (1958)	

Part 2 - Constitutional Articles of 1965

1. Name
2. Purposes
3. Insignia
4. Organization
5. National Council
6. National Chapter
7. Creation of Local Chapters
8. Classes of Membership
9. Eligibility for Membership
10. Duties of Members of the National Council
11. Revenues and Expenses of the National Council
12. Expulsion of Members
13. Government of Local Chapters
14. Duties of Chapter Officers
15. Amendments

SOURCES: Beta Alpha Psi Fraternity, "National Constitution and Statutes" [1927 draft]; Beta Alpha Psi Fraternity, National Constitution and Statutes (1958); and Beta Alpha Psi National Constitution (1965). The 1928 and 1958 constitutions, but not the 1965 document, included a preamble.

years earlier, with the slight exception that an adjective had been added to the last one, "Constitutional Amendments." The statutes (or bylaws) still consisted of eight chapters, comprised of sections 11-89, with the titles of numbers 4 and 8 having been made somewhat more explicit. Although there had of course been a number of changes through the years in specific content, the overall continuity was extraordinary.

The constitution retained terminology or usage that by 1963 was archaic, as in the reference by article 2 to an objective of promoting "cordial intercourse" among members, and the designation of the governing body or the roster of faculty advisors as the "Grand" Council or Chapter. In addition, the preamble's reference to "Sociability" as a basic fraternal principle only conjured up earlier practices within some chapters of religious, ethnic, or racial bias. Furthermore, very narrow and piecemeal revision of the constitution had yielded complicated formulations of simple rules, as in the doubly redundant restriction of honorary membership (article 6, section 3) to

> any prominent practicing accountant who [wa]s either a Certified Public Accountant or a member of the American Institute of Certified Public Accountants, or . . . any prominent accountant.

Against this background, President Niswonger proposed in 1963 that the Council rewrite its basic governing documents.

<u>Approval of Niswonger's recommendation, and progress during the year 1963-64</u>

Beyond recommending revision that would cover format, style, and substance alike, Niswonger set forth a list of possible changes (not recorded) that were "favorably received" by his four colleagues. On the motion of Herbert Miller, the Grand Council voted "to completely revise the constitution and the statutes" in time for approval at the next meeting. It was

suggested that the president's advisory committee take the lead, most appropriately in that the members for 1963-64 were Professors Niswonger and Miller. Due to the death from lung cancer a year earlier of the 1960-61 president R. H. Van Voorhis, one slot on the past presidents' group was vacant.

Noted textbook author Rollie Niswonger took primary responsibility for a redrafting process that would require two years. He is remembered by fellow councilors Vern Vincent and Wilton Anderson as "the master English stylist," able to find the "best" way to express an idea; and a "tower of strength," a "beautiful writer" with a "flair for words" and a knack for concise expression. Herb Miller, according to Vincent, assisted his immediate successor as fraternal president as an excellent "idea man" for the project.

Both members of the advisory committee attended the 1964 annual meeting at Indiana, and Niswonger led a discussion of constitutional revision that was focused on "substantive changes." Several alterations were approved, taking immediate effect, all of them in the statute category except the final one:

1. Incorporation of an already recognized alternative to the national eligibility standard of a B average in accounting and a B- average overall, namely, standing among the top 30% of junior and senior students
2. Reduction of required number of chapter meetings (business, program, or banquet) from 14 to 8, "reasonably distributed throughout the academic year"
3. Incorporation of chapter fiscal-year options previously announced
4. Restriction of voting privileges to active members
5. Provision for FVP attestation to chapter compliance with constitutional requirements (simplifying audit reports)
6. Increase of the Council term to six years, and elimination of the president's advisory committee.

It was also agreed to clarify the "faculty" category of membership, in keeping with the existence of somewhat different institutional criteria for identifying the faculty. In actual fact, items 1 and 4 would be discarded or altered before a new document was ever printed.

The 1964 Grand Council felt a special sense of urgency in completing the basic revision underway because a "large" supply of constitutions and statutes available a year earlier, for distribution to new members, had dwindled to 700 copies. February 1, 1965, was thus set as a target publication date, raising the possibility that the governing body would need to meet in special session. The most recent printing, from the year 1961-62, had evidently been a reproduction of the 1958 combined edition, the sixth one issued since 1947. Sepcifically, the minutes reveal no amendments over the period 1959-61; available files contain no editions dated between 1958 and 1965; and the earlier edition appears within two distinct covers, differing somewhat in the script employed.

In actual fact, the revision process would move more slowly than planned. An interim reprinting of the existing constitution and statutes would thus have been essential to accommodate the nearly 2,000 members inducted during 1964-65. Although no further evidence is available, contemporary secretary-treasurer Vern Vincent tentatively recalls having undertaken "significant editing" for a reprinting inclusive of minor revision. A printed insertion found in a copy of the 1958 constitution and statutes that lists amendments reflected in that edition points up one approach to updating that could have been used.[1]

---

[1]Wilton T. Anderson to Author, interview, March 20, 1980, quoted; Beta Alpha Psi Fraternity, "National Constitution," article 2, article 6, section 3 (both quoted), "National Statutes," _National Constituion and Statutes_ (1958); Beta Alpha Psi Fraternity, _National Constitution and Statutes_ (1953, 1956); Beta Alpha Psi Fraternity, "National Statutes" [1927 draft]; exhibit 20; Grand Council Minutes, 1964, agenda and (referring to 8-page copy employing more ample margins) pp. 1, 3 (quoted), 4; Grand Council Minutes Book, 1959-61, 1962, p. 1, 1963, pp. 1, 5 (quoted), 10; [Emerson O. Henke], Treasurer's Report, 1961-62, p. 2, 1962-63, p 2 (quoted); _National Constitution and Statutes of Beta Alpha Psi Fraternity_ (1947, 1949, 1951); A. J. Penz to Author, interview, April 18, 1980; Sheldahl, _Alpha to Omega_, pp. 114-23, 706-707; [Vern H. Vincent], Secretary's Report, 1964-65, pp. 11-12; and Vincent to Author, July 21, 1980 (interview), January 25, 1986, both quoted.

Completion of the Project by Fall 1965

As a result of the expansion of the Grand Council to six members, Rollie Niswonger's term had been extended through 1964-65. On July 29, 1965, he issued a summary of the new constitution that he would submit a month later, listing twenty-three "important" changes. The list incorporated three of the policy changes approved a year earlier, and probably only by inadvertance omitted the reduction made in required number of local meetings. Reference to the alternate percentile standard for academic eligibility had been deleted, and (although not mentioned in the summary) the new constitution would extend chapter voting privileges to faculty members. Previously, the statutes had permitted chapters to extend the vote to alumnus or honorary members, if they wished, while stipulating that _all_ members were eligible to vote on prospective members.

Niswonger's summary, which presumably had been sent to the other five councilors on the date cited above, generally provided "[t]he basis for the exact wording" that was adopted during the annual session. It was inserted, along with three related points, in the annual minutes. Revisions not already noted may be classified under five headings, beginning with changes in format, terminology, and style.

Format, terminology, and style

For the first time since the adoption of a dual structure in 1924, the basic laws and rules of the fraternity were consolidated within a single document, based on the lack of any practical need to distinguish between constitional and statutory provisions. In place of 9 articles and 8 chapters, the new constitution containted 15 articles, as listed in part 2 of exhibit 20. Ironically, as fraternal operations continued to grow in scope and complexity the National Council decided in 1974 to revert to a dual structure,

C. ROLLIN NISWONGER,
Principal Draftsman of New Constitution of 1965

leading to the publication three years later of an expanded document comprised of a very brief constitution and a highly detailed body of "bylaws."

Many of the new articles of 1965 were comparable to prior elements. Sequence was significantly revised, however, to secure "a more orderly progression" from general to specific levels, and from national to local topics. For example, because of its national character the coverage of fraternal insignia constituted the third article rather than the eighth. The relatively detailed kind of coverage of national and local levels alike that had previously appeared in the statutes was placed primarily within the latter part of the new document.

The most important terminological change was the replacement of the word "Grand" with the word "National" in designating the Council itself and the collective Chapter. Niswonger objected to the former term because of its customary association, especially, with fraternal lodges. Relatedly, the new document referred to the fraternal president and secretary-treasurer as "national" officers rather than as officers of the "Council." Also, "active" members were redisignated as "student" members, probably on the expectation that faculty, "alumnus" (formerly "alumni"), and even honorary members would often or sometimes participate actively within a chapter.

Significant stylistic changes were also made, particularly through verbal simplification and reduced capitalization. For example, the terms "national council" and "national chapter" were no longer capitalized (although the traditional form, used in this study, would reappear in 1977), and material identified as "extraneous verbiage" had been dropped. The preamble, attesting to principles of "SCHOLARSHIP, PRACTICALITY AND SOCIALIABILITY," had been eliminated, and the statement of "Purpose[s]" in article 2 materially simplified (dispensing, for example, with references to

"cordial intercourse").

Constitutional changes imposed at the Council level have been cited only in part.

National Council

As indicated, the membership was increased to six persons, each serving a single term of six years, and the president's advisory group was abolished. The immediate past president was no longer considered an "officer," but was recognized as vice-president in the sense of designated presidential stand-in. Duties of the councilors were carefully defined, and the functions of the secretary-treasurer, in particular, were "more accurately delineated" than before.

Coverage of fraternal finances was both enhanced and imporved. The revenue section was clarified, and National Council expenses were covered for the first time, partially through clarifying the secretary-treasurer's relevant authority.

One of several significant changes made concerning the National Chapter enlarged that advisory body.

National Chapter, and chapter roster

The "Grand" Chapter had consisted of incumbent councilors and faculty vice-presidents. The new constitution added all living past councilors to the group, thus providing a formal base for their continued participation in the fraternity. Having always been most welcome at the annual banquet, former councilors would now be invited to the annual business meeting held with faculty advisors.

The functions of the National Chapter were "enlarged and clarified." Express reference was made to National Council referral of matters to the

advisory body; and to presentation by faculty leaders "for [Council] consideration such proposals as they m[ight] consider conducive to the welfare of the fraternity."

Significant revisions or additions were made concerning the creation of new chapters. Petitioners were officially restricted to "[o]rganized" accounting groups made up of students academically "eligible" for Beta Alpha Psi, and the required number of students was increased from 10 to 15. A revised enumeration of application contents omitted any reference to a prior "extra-legal and unnecessary" requirement (not cited in the prior statutes) for data on the distribution of teaching responsibilities among academic ranks. Express provision was made for the election to membership of otherwise eligible petitioners who were no longer in school, but initiation in abenstia (for anyone) was disallowed.

Several changes were made in the coverage of student (or other forms of) membership, including symbolic dimensions.

Membership and insignia

Membership categories and pertinent eligibility criteria were clarified, through simpler or more descriptive formulation. For students, the archaic reference to registration in "advanced" accounting was restated in terms of completion of a full-year's introductory course. The broadening of faculty membership that had occurred over the years was finally recognized formally through reference to the "instructional, research or administrative staff" of Beta Alpha Psi institutions. Honorary members were defined simply as members who, at the time of initiation, were neither students nor (in the expanded sense) faculty of the school, having been selected based on "prominence in the field of accounting and . . . possess[ion of] those qualities" fostered by the fraternity. Finally,

alumnus membership was redefined to include onetime faculty, as well as student, members no longer associated with the initiating school.

"Eligibility" for faculty membership was covered only in part, through reference to "[f]ull-time members of the accounting faculty." The minutes announced that the general restriction of honorary induction to two persons at each initiation would be dropped, but it had in fact not previously been recorded at the constitutional or statutory level. Four years earlier, in 1961, Secretary-Treasurer Emerson Henke had been asked to review that restriction, and make any appropriate clafification on allowable "excep-tion[s]." In any event, over the five years 1965-70 only three chapters would exceed four honorary initiates in a single year. Alpha Upsilon at Bowling Green and Mu at NYU inducted six such members in 1965-66 and 1966-67, respectively, one more than were brought in by Xi at Syracuse during the latter year.

The coverage of membership insignia was expanded, through description of the fraternal badge adopted in 1922 and the pin (previously not mentioned) that had become associated with pledges. A relic from the days (pre-1950) of an all-male fraternity was finally dropped, the rule restricting the wearing of badges to members, "their mothers, wives, sisters, and fiances."

New articles 13 and 14, finally, governed local chapters and their operations, introducting several changes beyond the reduction in number of required meetings and the provision for a broader range of fiscal years.

Local chapter operations

The traditional provision for the approval of new faculty vice-presidents by the Council was eliminated, as a "meaningless formality." To guard against the perpetuation of weak faculty leadership, however, it was held that a person should "ordinarily" not hold the post for more than

three successive years, two fewer years than under prior policy.

The special responsibilities of the chapter secretary regarding compliance with reporting requirements of the constitution and the activity program led the National Council to separate the secretary and treasurer positions. In the interests of more democratic operations, the prior authority of chapter executive committees, or officer groups, to amend local constitutions or codes of regualtions was withdrawn.

Finally, the new constitution more explicitly stated the scope of Council disciplinary authority over the chapters. Going beyond the assertion of authority "to withdraw from any chapter the power to exercise all or any part of its functions," and to "suspend" a local unit, it referred directly to "revocation" of the charter. For chapters formally notified that they were "not functioning properly" or were "delinquent in [their] financial obligations," the Council as before (in reference to "delinquency") provided for a grace period of three months, after which a six-months' "probation" would take effect. Suspension or charter revocation could be approved beyond that point.[2]

The reorganization of the National Council, and restatement of the responsibilities of its members, were vital elements of the constitutional

---

[2] Beta Alpha Psi, National Constitution and Bylaws (1977); Beta Alpha Psi Fraternity, "National Constitution," National Constitution and Statutes (1958), preamble, article 6, section 1, article 7, sections 4-5 (all quoted), article 6, section 3, "National Statutes," chapter 4, section 43, chapter 5, sections 54 (quoted), 55; Beta Alpha Psi National Constitution (1965), quoting articles 5-9, 13; Grand Council Minutes, 1964, p. 5; Grand Council Minutes Book, 1961, pp. 2 (quoted), 4; [Leon E. Hay], "National Council News," Newsletter 6 (Fall 1965):255; Hay to Author, interview, May 2, 1980; Emerson O. Henke to C. Aubrey Smith, February 6, 1969 (Golden Anniversary Files); National Council Minutes, 1965, pp. 1, 5-6 (quoted), 7, February 1974, p. 3 (no. 5); Secretary-Treasurers' Reports, 1965-66 through 1969-70, chapter initiation totals, especially 1965-66, p. 15; and Sheldahl, Alpha to Omega, p. 105.

changes of the mid-sixties. A further major change was imminent, the creation of a separate national editorship, while the formation at the close of the decade of a new advisory committee would set the stage for expanding the Council's traditional meeting schedule.

Reorganization of the Council

Expansion of the Council and Clarification of Responsibilities, 1964 and 1965

Essence of Reconstitution

The essence of National Council reconstitution has already been indicated, namely, expansion to six members, serving six-year terms, and abolition of the president's advisory group. By adding a second past president to each year's Council, the former action provided the rationale for the latter one. Observations made by Herbert Miller suggest that the advisory body may have functioned in part to prolong, to seven years, the active service of councilors reluctant to depart from their principal role on the national accounting scene. Both Miller and C. Rollin Niswonger "strongly supported" these changes approved in 1964, having the effect of immediately ending Miller's formal affiliation with the Council after six years, five of them as a member.

Emphasis was placed, in the new constitution, on clear statement or restatement of councilor *duties*. Article 10, "Duties of Members of the National Council," is accordingly reprinted as exhibit 21. The references made to the president and secretary-treasurer called attention to potential areas of reform or reorganization that by and large were only discussed during the fourth era.

EXHIBIT 21

COUNCILOR DUTIES AS SET FORTH IN THE 1965 CONSTITUTION

ARTICLE X—DUTIES OF MEMBERS OF THE NATIONAL COUNCIL

Section 1. The national president shall preside at meetings of the national council and the national chapter, appoint special committees, submit proposals for courses of action to the national council, provide for the installation of new chapters, prepare recommendations for chapter visitation, suggest nominees for membership on the national council, and seek to promote the successful operations of the local chapters and the welfare of the fraternity in general.

Section 2. The immediate past national president shall advise and assist the national president in the performance of his duties and assume the duties of the national president in the event of his absence or incapacity.

Section 3. The national secretary-treasurer shall be the principal executive officer of the fraternity and as such shall be responsible for the maintenance and safekeeping of all records, correspondence, and properties not otherwise assigned. He shall record the minutes of the meetings of the national council and the national chapter, administer the chapter activity program, determine the recipients of prize awards authorized by the national council, assume responsibility for fraternity publications, promptly inform the local chapters of amendments to the constitution, and in all other respects carry out the duties associated with the office of secretary. He shall also collect the revenues owed the fraternity, disburse money for authorized purposes, maintain appropriate records, arrange for an annual audit by a CPA approved by the national council, supply a fidelity bond for such amount as the national council shall direct, and in all other respects carry out the duties associated with the office of treasurer.

Section 4. All members of the national council shall be expected to attend meetings, respond to requests for mail ballot and answer other correspondence promptly, participate in the program of chapter visitation, perform special duties assigned by or under the authority of the national council, and seek to further the interests of the fraternity.

Reprinted from Beta Alpha Psi National Constitution (1965).

Presidential leadership in selection of councilors

An interesting addition to the stated responsibilities of the president was that of "suggest[ing] nominees for membership on the national council." By long-standing practice, the outgoing president would take especial responsibility in regard to the selection of the incoming councilor. As observed by Vern Odmark, the president "spearheaded" this very important annual initiative, but a candidate would be invited to join the Council only following "a thorough discussion and agreement" among the members.

Geared to compatibility and continuity, this approach promoted a kind of "good-old-boys'-club" atmosphere that on balance, as recalled by Herb Miller, worked very well. The selection of new councilors in Miller's day involved "very nebulous intangibles" that included (a) moderation in general outlook and (b) commitment to the objectives of Beta Alpha Psi. No "radical" or basically "indifferent" person would be invited to serve.

According to Williard Stone, whose five-year term ended on the eve of the fourth-era, an absolute condition for election to the Grand Council of his day was clear support for the activity program. A particularly strong recommendation was a track record of service as faculty vice-president of a highly ranked chapter. The Council also looked for professors who were highly visible within the accounting community, nationwide, <u>so long as</u> they were clearly associated with Beta Alpha Psi activity.

The latter point may be illustrated by reference to the cases of three nationally prominent accounting professors who were candidates for election to the Grand Council in the late 1950s. Two of them became councilors, following a negotiation process that assured that their textbook writing and other professional commitments would not be jeopardized. Both had been identified with the origin of well-established, though not leading, chapters.

The third professor, however, was ultimately not invited to join the Council, because he (beyond alumni membership) and his school were not associated with the fraternity.

As observed in the preceding chapter, Herb Miller accepted his post in 1958 on the basis that the secretary-treasurer duties of 1959-61 would be delegated to his wife Lenore. His commitment to Beta Alpha Psi was evident from his leadership role in the founding of Alpha Eta at Michigan, and his service as the charter faculty advisor, 1951-53.

A second noted textbook writer was appointed in 1959. Rollie Niswonger, who joined the Council as the immediate past president of the American Accounting Association, had been the initial FVP of Omega at Miami of Ohio, serving two years separated by wartime deactivation. Furthermore, he brought to the Grand Council a potentially unique perspective as the first councilor representing a regional state university, just as his chapter had been the first one to be formed at such a site. Niswonger's election to the "off-year" position, not slated for the secretary-treasurership, was presumably a simpler matter than Miller's appointment a year earlier.

Another person considered for the 1959 opening, months in advance of the annual meeting (indicating the participative approach taken that year),[3]

---

[3]At the 1962 meeting, three men were discussed as possible candidates for the Council vacancy that would arise a year later. From that group, Wilton Anderson would be elected in 1963, and Charles Taylor four years later. Grand Council Minutes Book, 1962, p. 8.

The reference made to the writing careers of Miller and Niswonger warrants memtion of a professional sacrifice made by Vern Vincent on behalf of Beta Alpha Psi. At the time of his appointment to the Grand Council in 1962, Vincent was nearing the completion of an accounting theory text for publisher Richard D. Irwin (Homewood, Ill.). That project would become a casualty of his service, particularly, as 1963-65 secretary-treasurer, but he has had "no regrets" about having accepted the fraternal appointment

was Professor Walter F. Frese (frā-zē) of Harvard, later a member of the standards-setting Accounting Principles Board. Frese, Alpha '29, had taught at Illinois for six years during the 1930s, but not served as a faculty advisor to the very independent chapter located there. He had joined the Harvard faculty in 1956 following a distinquished career featuring twenty years with the U.S. Treasury Department, and eight years as charter director of the Accounting Systems Division within the General Accounting Office (GAO).

Frese's governmental service had ranged from establishing accounting systems for the disbursement of New Deal relief funds, to representing U.S. interests relative to the Stablization Board of China, to playing a major role in reorganizing federal accounts at the GAO. His commitment to accounting as a '"civilizing [social] force"' had been strengthened by his experiences as a Japanese concentration camp inmate following the capture of Hong Kong on Christmas Day, 1941. The prisoners' misery "had been mitigated by the perceptions of fairness engendered by the community's meticulous system of accounting for every transaction."

Walter Frese had perhaps been recommended to the Grand Council by Eric Kohler, whom he would later credit with a major contribution to the "[t]urn-around" in GAO operations. It is noteworthy that Kohler had been one of only four former councilors present at the 1958 Beta Alpha Psi banquet. In any case, the only documentation that exists in regard to Frese's possible appointment to the Council is a letter of March 1959 addressed by Councilor Miller to President Stone. Miller began by stating that he was supporting

---

(Vincent to Author, interview, July 21, 1980). In 1965 Irwin brought out the first edition of Eldon S. Hendricksen's noted text Accounting Theory.

the position already expressed by Andy Penz, the senior advisory committee member.

The first-year councilor wrote glowingly of the values and achievements of his "good friend" of long standing, fellow Iowa native and University of Iowa graduate "Walt" Frese. The issue, as he saw it, was whether the Grand Coucil should appoint a member "from a school that ha[d] never had a chapter of Beta Alpha Psi and no doubt never w[ould]" have one. Miller's answer was unequivocal:

> I think such a move could be offensive to the faculties who for many years have cooperated with Beta Alpha Psi and given time and effort to local chapter affairs.

Conceivably Herb Miller would have taken a more favorable viewpoint had Frese recently been identified with a "cooperative and enthusiastic" fraternal chapter, granting that a question of <u>institutional</u> support for Beta Alpha Psi service (identified as an important factor by Vern Vincent) would still have arisen. At any rate, his position that national prominence in accounting higher education (largely based in the particular case, at the time, on an outstanding professional career) did not by itself qualify a person for Council membership would prevail in 1959, and apparently not be questioned thereafter. Frese would become recognized as one of Harvard's foremost accounting educators, concentrating in the financial area. He held the first literally "accounting"-designated professorial chair at his school, although Robert N. Anthony had earlier been appointed to such a post in "Management Control" within the '"control" area' in which both men taught.

However much internal participation there may have been in selecting new councilors, no formal provision was made for external involvement, although such an initiative was considered. In 1962 the Grand Council agreed to discuss a year later the desirability of appointing an "outside" committee to nominate candidates for the annual opening. At the next

meeting, incoming president Emerson Henke was instructed "to solicit suggestions from all faculty vice-presidents" on this matter through a letter that would also request "nominations for the council member to be elected" in 1964. Response from the local level is not recorded, however, in the minutes from the latter year.

In 1965, before the Council turned to the reworking of the constitution, incoming president Vern Vincent asked whether all his colleagues were "favorable" to the "prevailing practice" that vested in the presidency "the major responsibility" for new councilor selection. That approach was agreed to be "more effective" than any alternative. President Julius Roller observed later during the meeting, however, that he had requested suggestions on potential appointees from past presidents. It was subsequently decided that Vincent should instead write the faculty vice-presidents in that regard, redlecting clear informal movement toward a more democratic procedure.

Finally, in 1968 the annual meeting opened (following routine approval of the prior year's minutes) with "general discussion of the criteria for selection" of councilors. A "consensus" was registered that there shold be no change of approach. Several factors were identified as pertinent to the selection, including:

> demonstrated interest in the Fraternity; successful FVP service; availability of time to do the job; geographic location; faculty rank . . .; and general enthusiasm for the job and the organization.

In addition, 1968 presiding officer Leon Hay would later note that reasonable extra-geographic diversity was sought in the nature of schools represented on the National Council.

The faculty rank preferred was full professor, on the premise that national service to Beta Alpha Psi might interfere with activity more

pertinent to academic promotion. Regarding geography, the Council would in 1969 adopt a policy of communication by the members with chapter advisors in their respective regions, as defined by the national president. Although it had been carried out only partially in the interim, this control concept was reiterated a year later on the urging of retiring councilor Hay, only to be abandoned by 1970-71 president Charles Taylor due to concern that it would "fragment" the fraternity. As an alternative approach to regionalism, endorsed at the 1971 annual gathering, Taylor preferred that councilors host breakfast meetings for faculty advisors attending regional meetings of the American Accounting Association.

The traditional approach to councilor selection inevitably led to a degree of Council inbreeding, as illustrated by an anecdote related by Harvey Donley. In 1960 or thereabouts, Donley, his friend (from graduate school) Vern Odmark, Emerson Henke, and Wilton Anderson were included among the delegates to a Ford Foundation seminar sponsored, in Williamstown, Mass., by the University of Chicago. It was on that occasion that Donley become acquainted with both Henke and Anderson. Coincidentally or not, it is a matter of record that these four men would each serve as the president of Beta Alpha Psi over the seven-year period 1963-70.

The constitutional restatement of national secretary-treasurer duties pointed up effectively their increasing scale, a matter that had begun to raise concern by the close of the third era.

Restatement of secretary-treasurer duties, and measures suggested or adopted for reducing their burden

The coverage of secretary-treasurer responsibilities was a good example of the simplification sought by Rollie Niswonger. The opening reference made to their bearer as "the principal executive officer of the fraternity"

set the stage for a concise statement of duties freed from technical formalities such as affixation of the fraternal seal, and points of detail such as the title of the national periodical and the dollar amount of required bonding.

The official responsibilities of the position had become increasingly burdensome with the further growth of the chapter roster, primarily in regard to administration of the activity program. The secretary-treasurer was expected, relatedly, to keep the president apprised of those chapters that "needed" visitation, encouragement, or other attention. According to Leon Hay, Council presidents based their visitation decisions largely on secretary-treasurer input. Advancement toward regional communication with chapters promised to lessen the load on the secretary-treasurer in keeping the pulse of the fraternity, nationwide.

The increasing demands of the position had attracted the attention in 1959 of the president's advisory committee. Chairman W. B. Jencks, Wayne Shroyer, and A. J. Penz had forecast a truly onerous workload within another decade, leading them to propose that the Grand Council "consider seriously" in 1960 the immediate appointment of an "executive secretary" having at least a five-year term. Such an individual, presumably serving on a salaried basis would be a nonvoting administrative official.

Probably in part for financial reasons, the recommendation made by the Jencks committee was apparently ignored at the time. Nor was action taken when the idea was broached at the 1964 meeting, although the secretary-treasurer "was authorized to secure whatever clerical help m[ight] be needed in the conduct of Grand Council business." Leon Hay recalls, however, that former secretary-treasurer Andy Penz expressed interest in the mid-'60s in serving as a "permanent administrator" for the Chapter Activity Program. The viewpoint taken by the National Council was that it was not

"a good idea to have a permanent grader of Form A's," since any individual would have particular "strengths and weaknesses" for the job.

In the mid-1960s, during the AAA secretary-treasurership of future councilor Joel Fritzemeyer, the American Accounting Association (a) established "permanent" headquarters in Evanston, Illinois, ending the traditional practice of moving from the campus of one secretary-treasurer to that of another; and (b) appointed Paul L. Gerhardt as a full-time executive secretary. These developments prompted the National Council to explore the possibility of obtaining certain administrative services from the new association office.

Specifically, at the 1966 annual meeting Secreatry-Treasurer Leon Hay, on the motion of incoming president Wilton Anderson, was instructed to contact incoming AAA president Lawrence L. Vance on

> the possibility of Beta Alpha Psi['s] utilizing the AAA office in Evanston as a central point for the procurement, storage, and distribution of publications and for maintenance of permanent membership files.

Focusing on the printing and distribution of fraternal materials, Hay duly contacted Vance, and subsequently met with the executive committee of the other organization. Gerhardt himself, having only recently assumed office, did not take a definite position on the matter. Ultimately, the AAA "gently" rejected Hay's proposal, based on the uncertainty of whether the new central office could "assimilate" services to Beta Alpha Psi. Professor Hay later observed that a "radical" change that had occurred in executive committee orientation, featuring much increased emphasis by the association upon scholarly research, had hindered the fraternal cause.

During the year 1966-67, however, a major transfer of responsibility that is discussed presently was underway within the Council, serving to remove the printing area from the secretary-treasurership. Three years

later, in 1969-70, Secretary-Treasurer Robert Wasley was authorized to employ a paid assistant to handle correspondence. The Council paid $2.50 per hour for services, normally twelve hours weekly, that "made the administrative side of the fraternity a smooth and easy operation." A student assistant assigned to Wasley by the University of Colorado also helped out with the Beta Alpha Psi work. The burden of the office was further reduced that year as an incidental consequence of a newly extended local option discussed in chapter 10, namely, nonparticipation in the activity program.

It is worth notice, in passing, that section 4 of article 10 marked a constitutional advance simply by stating the basic responsibilities of nonofficer councilors.[4] Those ranks were destined soon to be reduced,

---

[4]Robert N. ("Bob") Anthony to Author, August 11, 15, 1986, both quoted; Beta Alpha Psi Fraternity, "National Statutes," National Constitution and Statutes (1958), chapter 5, section 13; William W. Cooper and Walter F. Frese, "Turnaround at the GAO," pp. 127-56, Eric Louis Kohler: Accounting's Man of Principles, ed. Cooper and Ijiri, (Reston, Va.: Reston Publishing Co., 1979); "Directory," Newsletter [2] (November 1942 - March 1947, 4 issues): 3; "Directory of Activities," Newsletter [1] (October 1933, December 1934, March 1935), [2] (November 1937, April 1938); "Directory of Officers," Newsletter [1] (March 1931 - March 1933); Harvey E. Donley to Author, interview, May 2, 1980; exhibit 21, quoted; "Former Beta Alpha Psi National Presidents," 1983-84 Annual Report, ed. [Metcalf], inside front cover; "Grand Chapter," Newsletter [2-3] (May 1951 - November 1953):3rd; Grand Council Minutes, 1964, pp. 4, 6; Grand Council Minutes Book, 1959, p. 7, 1960 (nonreference to advisory committee proposal), 1963, p. 4 (quoted); Leon E. Hay to Harvey E. Donley, March 30, 1967 (filed with fourth-era visotation reports, as cited in chapter 10, note 3), quoted; Hay to Author, May 2, 1980 (interview), January 14, 1986, both quoted; [David Irons], "Walter F. Frese, Arthur Lowes Dickinson Professor of Accounting, Emeritus: Distinguished Service Award," pp. [14]-15, 17 (each quoted), 16, Course Development & Research Profile, 1983 (Boston: Harvard Business School, 1983), citing Frese as a recipient of "the highest recognition given by the Harvard Business School" (p. [9]); Kaylor, "Chapter Activity Program, 1950-69," p. 2; Herbert E. Miller, "Biographical Sketch - April 1967" (Golden Anniversary Files), p. 1; Miller to Author, interview, April 18, 1980 quoted; Miller to Williard E. Stone, March 5, 1959 (provided by A. J. Penz), quoted; Hermann C. Miller, ed., Beta Alpha Psi Directory, s.v. "Alpha Chapter: Frese, W. F."; National Council Minutes, 1965, pp. 2 (quoted), 4, 1966, p. 5 (quoted), 1968, p. 1 (quoted), 1969, p. 1, 1970, p. 1, 1971, pp. 4 (quoted), 5; Vern E. Odmark to Author, response to interview questionnaire, August 13, 1980; Sheldahl, Alpha to Omega, pp. 264-65, 708, 747; Stone to Author, interview, April 18, 1980, quoting pp. 14-15; [Robert S. Wasley], Secretary-Treasurer's

however, as just a year after approving the new body of fraternal law the National Council would signal an important change in its internal structure through action taken in the publication area.

Establishment of a Separate Editorship, 1967

A decision to reform the "Newsletter"

From its inception in 1931, the Newsletter had not changed materially in format. Through the advent of a printed periodical in 1936, and the later addition of photographs and further upgrading of physical appearance, the publication had remained a vehicle primarily for chapter reports (commonly on very routine topics) and related material, and secondarily for Council news, information, and commentary.

Dated Fall 1965, the last available Newsletter of this kind was a 6 x 9 magazine bearing (as at least a recent innovation) a glossy cover featuring the fraternal seal. It contained 73 pages, consisting mainly of local reports (35 pages), honorary and alumni coverage (18), and "National" news (9). Other material included lists of National Council and Chapter memberships, a roster of past presidents, a summary audit report, jewelry information, President Vincent's "Letter," and a classic letter sent to Mu Chapter by A. C. Littleton in 1927.

With the continued growth of the chapter roster, larger and larger issues were required, at steadily increasing cost. By 1964-65, publication costs for, at least primarily, the Newsletter were nearly two thousand dollars, more than one-sixth of total expense. Not surprisingly, then, discussion in 1965 of the secretary-treasurer's report promoted a question

---

Report , 1969-70, pp. 1, [11] ("Financial Analysis," p. 1, quoted); Nolan E. Williams to Author, interview, March 21, 1980; Who's Who in America 35 (1968-69), s.v. "Frese, Walter Frederick"; and Zeff, American Accounting Association, pp. 82, [95].

> as to whether the original purpose of this publication could not better be achieved by a different approach, as by emphasizing articles more or less scholarly in nature to be written by student members.

It was agreed to raise the issue for discussion at the National Chapter meeting, and to have President Julius Roller attempt to secure for inspection by the Council several copies of the _Balance Sheet_, a periodical issued by Alpha Omega at Fordham that had been commended to him. The latter reference brings to mind the observation made in 1930 by A. C. Littleton that a national periodical would be hard-pressed to match _Mu's News_, issued at NYU.

The minutes of the 1965 faculty vice-presidents' meeting indicate only that the Council's concern about the _Newsletter_ was mentioned, and that participants were encouraged to submit "ideas for change" to incoming secretary-treasurer and editor Leon Hay. The fall issue did not mention any prospect of a new format. Hay's National Council agenda for 1966 stated possible options of (a) changing the periodical to "a brief, frequent, newsletter, edited by [the] Secretary-Treasurer," or (b) "appoint[ing] an editor not now on [the] Council" to produce a true "magazine." In view of cost considerations, it was probably assumed in the latter case that the editor would be a past or newly appointed councilor, or somewone otherwise associated with the fraternity, rather than a commercial consultant.

Instead of committing itself to either of these options, or some other alternative, the National Council elected in 1966 to take an experimental approach to _Newsletter_ modernization that was destined to yield fundamental change. Leon Hay agreed to prepare "as soon as possible," in "tabloid rather than magazine format," an issue mainly covering the annual meeting. Looking ahead, second-year councilor Vern Odmark was

> charged with responsibility for editing subsequent 1966-67 issues; format, content, and frequency to be chosen by him to attain the

objective of improving communications between the national office and student members and chapter officers.

Odmark's assignment in effect signalled the restoration of a national editorship separate from the secretary-treasurership. Such a post had previously been held only by H. D. McGirr, whose Keys of Beta Alpha Psi magazine had been abandoned in 1931 after two issues, due to prohibitive costs. Cost reduction, ironically, was also a prime objective in the sixties, together with developemnt of a publication more interesting and meaningful that the traditional Newsletter. If not inherently necessary for achieving such purposes, a separate editorship was very logical given the expanding noneditorial burdens of the secretary-treasurer (the administrator of the chapter activity program), and the absence otherwise of well-defined prepresidential responsibilities for the "off-year" Council appointee.

During the transitional year 1966-67, a strong base was laid for what President Wilton Anderson would later describe as a "true newsletter."

The transitional year, 1966-67

Secretary-Treasurer Hay brought out his last Newsletter in October 1966, one far different in size, content, and appearance from the magazine of the past. It consisted of three connected 8 1/2 x 11 sheets, printed on both sides with the third sheet folded inside the others. Coverage was divided equally between general news of the fraternity at the national level (the August meetings, the top fifteen chapters of the preceding year, and new installations) and detailed instructions on the current activity program. Although the abandonment of the traditional format was not explicitly noted, a three-paragraph notice headlined "National Needs News Letter News" related that chapters should henceforth submit:

> stories of wide interest and appeal to student members . . . [, covering, for example,] exceptionally interesting programs; or . . . services rendered . . . to the university, community, or to the accounting profession.

Members were admonished not to "waste time, effort, and postage on dry, dull lists of names or recitations of events"--the very kind of material that had been a staple of the periodical from the start.[5]

Councilor Odmark, identified as the "Editor," brought out two additional six-page tabloids during the year, dated February and May, 1967. They included five major articles on issues relating to the fraternity, accounting education more generally, and/or professional accountancy. The authors were three faculty advisors, including future president James Pattillo from USC and a colleague of the editor's at San Diego State; an Arthur Young partner in San Diego; and Leo Herbert of the General Accounting Office. President Anderson contributed a "Letter" to each issue, dealing respectively with the recruitment by chapter members of able accounting

---

[5]An effort to secure more interesting Newsletter copy had been initiated at the 1960 annual meeting, through the approval of a new column "report[ing] on special features, projects, or traditions peculiar to any given local chapter." The idea had been to draw material initially from contemporary councilors themselves, and to continue the column, if it proved popular, with the assistance of the local chapters. A 1962 change in activity program coverage of submissions to the periodical, identified in chapter 10, may have been related in part to this initiative.

Two of the first four issues published during the fourth era contained such a column, titled "Special Features" in November 1960 and "Activity Program Notes" in Spring 1962. Although devoted largely to the American Accounting Association fellowship fund, the former item included an excellent writeup, presumably contributed by Councilor Nolan Williams, on a "pledge week" tradition observed within Alpha Iota at Arkansas. The 1962 article included very brief notices from Beta at Oregon and Epsilon at Oregon State (reporting a joint activity), Delta at Washington, Iota at Southern California, Upsilon at Florida, and Alpha Sigma at Cincinnati. The two issues available for the four academic years 1962-66 (dated Spring '64 and Fall'65) do not include a special features column. Grand Council Minutes Book, 1960, p. 5, quoted; [Emerson O. Henke], "Activity Program Notes," Newsletter 5 (Spring 1962):467; and [Herbert E. Miller], ed., "Special Features," Newsletter 5 (November 1960):314-16, quoting p. 316.

majors from the high schools, and the value of graduate study in the training of accountants.

A full page of "chapter reports" in the new mold, covering 24 chapters, appeared in February. One notice reported that future councilor Joe R. Fritzemeyer had been (re)appointed FVP of Alpha Pi at Iowa, succeeding future councilor Richard Metcalf. On other pages, there were more detailed writeups of special academic or community services offered by Alpha Theta at Mississippi, Delta at Washington, and Alpha Kappa at Ohio, and a feature article on two awards created by Omicron at Ohio State. Other material in Odmark's first issues included interim activity program standings (in both issues), a chapter directory (in May), an announcement that A. J. Penz would be preparing a fifty-year history of the fraternity, obituary notices, and one of the last *Newsletter* price lists on fraternal jewelry.

The following year, the goal of featuring *student* articles was achieved.

Fall, Winter, and Spring issues, 1967-70

The issuance of three *Newsletters* a year promptly became standard. In line with the practice of the years 1961-66, when the periodical had appeared semiannually, issues were dated by season, namely, Fall, Winter, and Spring. The latter two issues were dated the same calendar year. A summer edition was published in 1969 to commemorate the fraternity's golden anniversary.

Vern Odmark continued as editor for the year 1967-68, being succeeded for the last two years of the fourth era by Charles Taylor. A system was thus established by which, after holding no office during the first year, each councilor would serve during his second or third year either as editor

or secretary-treasurer. Previously the councilor elected in the first year of a secretary-treasurer's term would not be an officer during the three years prior to his presidency. At the 1969 annual meeting the National Council began a practice of awarding on honorarium to the editor by approving a payment of $500 to Professor Taylor for his services during the preceding year. On Taylor's motion, a similar payment to Vern Odmark was authorized in 1970 in belated recognition for his editorship of 1967-68.

Beginning with the issue of Winter 1968, the Newsletter ordinarily consisted of 8 pages, through the placement of one two-sheet folder within another, although there were successive 12- and 4- page issues in 1970. Beginning in Fall 1967, each issue had a distinct color, representing (except for the golden anniversary issue) some shade or another of green, brown, or blue.

Like its counterpart of the previous year, the first Newsletter of 1967-68 was divided equally between national news and detailed activity-program instructions. The winter issue, however, featured three articles prepared by student members, or based on information supplied by them. Covered were the winning strategy employed by Beta Omicron at Arizona in the latest points competition; suggestions for effective job interviewing; and the approach taken by Tau at Maryland to overcoming the hazards, discussed by James Pattillo a year earlier, of an urban environment. The aforementioned Littleton letter of 1927 was reprinted again, there were short notices on the activities of several chapters, and interim point standings were listed. President Hay contributed a message concerning fraternal structure and programs at the national level, and their relationship to local operations. Also included was part 1 of a discussion of student responsibilities by Southern Cal Professor A. N. Mosich that would be completed in

the spring Newsletter, the final one edited by Odmark.

That issue otherwise featured five articles by student members, and writeups (by the respective directors, one of them in collaboration with an associate) on the research programs of both the American Institute of CPAs and the National Association of Accountants. A page of chapter news, "Chapters' Dotted Shorts," also appeared, along the interim chapter standings.

With a pattern now established, over the two years 1968-70 the fall issue concentrated on national news and the activity program, while student articles, local chapter news, and interim standings were featured in the winter and spring. During the period there were two messages from the national president.

The issues of Fall 1968 and Winter 1970 contained amusing (at least from a distance) errors. In the former case, two of the several photographs published showed President Hay presenting awards for second and third places, respectively, in the 1967-68 activity program to the faculty advisors of Alpha Upsilon at Bowling Green and Beta Pi at North Texas State. Both FVPs were incorrectly identified, as acknowledged by Editor Charles Taylor in the following Newsletter.

An article appearing in the winter of 1970 reported that Gamma Mu at Drake, where Richard Metcalf was the faculty officer, had established an "Accounting Aid Society," a pioneering

> pilot program . . . offer[ing] consumer accounting services to lower income persons, small businesses, and non-profit organizations who normally c[ould not] afford to pay a CPA firm for such purposes.

The headline over the article read "Drake Students Create Possible Future National Problem" (emphasis added). A follow-up report on the "program" appeared in the following issue, along with otherlocal chapter articles

illustrating the "Social Force" of accounting.[6]

The refashioning of the periodical required some change in the activity program, due to provision of credit for chapter submissions. Before turning to fourth-era development of that program, an initiative of 1960-70 is noted that related only indirectly to Council structure, but would lead to significant change in operating procedure.

Establishment of Long-Range Planning Committee

Five years after the president's advisory committee was disbanded, the National Council reached a "consensus" in 1969 that incoming president Harvey Donley "should appoint a long-range planning committee for the fraternity." It was suggested that Donley, senior past president Leon Hay, and former councilor Emerson Henke, perhaps along with other individuals, might serve as charter members. Donley related his plans to form such a group at the National Chapter business session.

A committee was formed over the following year, but evidently had not met as of the 1970 annual gathering. On that occasion incoming president Charles Taylor agreed to chair the group, and was authorized to call a meeting at his discretion. The new Texas doctoral graduate saw the formation of the advisory body as a base for implementing a suggestion made to him by

---

[6]Grand Council Minutes, 1964, p. 4; Grand Council Minutes Book, 1963, p. 2; [Leon E. Hay], "News Letter Needs News," Newsletter 7 (October 1966): 2, 3rd indented citation; [Hay], Secretary-Treasurer's Report, 1966-67, p. 6 (Iota and Beta Eta FVPs); National Council Minutes, 1965, p. 2, 1966, p. 6 (1st and 2nd citations, respectively), 1965, p. 11, 1966, agenda (both quoted), 1969, p. 7, 1970 (double-spaced version), pp. 12, 14; John Neubauer, Gamma Mu, "Drake's Students Create Possible Future National Problem" [sic], Newsletter 8 (Winter 1970):8, 4th citation; Newsletter 7-8 (October 1966 - Spring 1970); Sheldahl, Alpha to Omega, pp. 695, 596-97, 622-26, 644-47, 656; Charles W. Taylor ("C. W. T."), "Accounting--A Social Force" (thematic contents of issue), Newsletter 8 (Spring 1970):1; [Vern H. Vincent], Secretary's Report, 1964-65, p. 1; and [Robert S. Wasley], Secretary-Treasurer's Report, 1969-70, p. [7], Gamma Mu FVP.

Professor C. Aubrey Smith--that the National Council should assemble more than once per year because of the increasing scope of its responsibilities. Accordingly, in May 1971 Hay and Henke (cited as "Hinkle" in Robert Wasley's minutes) were joined by five of the six sitting councilors for a two-day session in Las Vegas, the concurrent site of an American Accounting Association business meeting. Harold Royer had been unable to attend. The full group formed the "committee."

Hollis Dixon had joined Arizona State visiting professor Leon Hay in Phoenix for a flight to Nevada. Dixon had forgotten about his original plans to take a small aircraft to Las Vegas, and thus not told his family that he had made new travel arrangements. Upon arrival, he learned that the other plane had crashed, with no survivors. At, perhaps, another meeting during his early years on the Council, Tucson rancher Dixon was informed that his cattle had become sick.

During each of the following two academic years there was a similar meeting except that Emerson Henke was the only noncouncilor present in 1971-72, and only the Council were on hand the following year. In effect the "Long-Range Planning Committee" had quickly become the identity of the National Council assembling at midterm to discuss important policy issues. Finally, in 1973-74 the "committee" terminology was dropped, and the Council began its present-day practice of meeting <u>twice</u> each year prior to the traditional "annual" conference.[7]

---

[7]Hollis A. Dixon, Long-Range Planning Committee Minutes, December 1972, p. 1; Harvey E. Donley and Leon E. Hay to Author, interviews, May 2, 1980; Ron Fritch, "Visiting Ernst & Whinney Professor: Leon E. Hay," <u>The Sun</u>, Omicron Chapter newsletter, Winter 1980, p. 7; Robert S. Maust, Long-Range Planning Committee Minutes, December 1971, p. 1; National Council Minutes, 1969, pp. 7 (quoted), 10, 1970, p. 14, February 1974, p. 1, May 1974, p. 1; Smith, <u>Forty Acres</u>, p. 194; Charles W. Taylor to Author, interview, April 18, 1980; and Robert S. Wasley, Long-Range Planning Committee Minutes, May 1971, pp. 1-2, quoted.

In Transition

Unlike either basic fraternal law or Grand Council structure, the foremost initiative undertaken by Beta Alpha Psi over the third era had been revised significantly by the close of the period. Revision of the activity program would be continued until a more fundamental reform was instituted in the late 1960s. By then a logical step had been taken to enhance the value for faculty vice-presidents of the annual National Chapter gathering, and a second major program designed to benefit them would be initiated in 1970. Finally, the formalities of member initiation, like the constitution (inclusive of statutes), were significantly modernized during the sixties after having resisted major change since the fraternity's early days.

CHAPTER 10

MODERNIZING THE FRATERNITY WITHIN CONVENTIONAL BOUNDS: ACTIVITY PROGRAM, FACULTY VICE-PRESIDENCY, AND INITIATION RITUAL

Gradual revision in the Chapter Activity Program had led to significant reform by 1969. At that point it was restructured as an *optional* area of participation, on the notion that it could not adequately accommodate all legitimate styles of chapter operation, although reporting requirements essential for control purposes were maintained. The activity program was a major theme of early annual "workshops" conducted for faculty vice-presidents beginning in 1967, a focal point in selecting "outstanding" FVPs for an awards program commenced three years later under the sponsorship of a leading accounting firm. Like the highly "substantive" activity program, the "symbolic" initiation ritual was revised moderately and later fundamentally during the sixties, leading (as in the cases of constitutional and periodical reform) to the abandoment of an increasingly outmoded format.

Up to 1969, the activity program was refined and improved in several areas, and in response to criticism received from the local level the Council showed a willingness to consider further change on an experimental basis At the golden anniversary meeting, however, much more basic change was approved.

Chapter Activity Program

Moderate Reform Through 1968-69

The major developments up to 1969 concerned chapter meetings,

"scholarship" provisions, initiations, and Newsletter contributions. Coverage of the latter two areas was revised, in part, based on external events, including reassessment of the scholarship area.

Required meetings

As related in chapter 5, the Grand Council had in 1960 reduced the number of meetings required for full credit under item 4, "Regular Meetings," from 16 to 14, as had been recommended in particular by Leon Hay of Beta Alpha at Indiana. A chapter could earn credit for both a business meeting and (under item 5) an "initiation" on the same date, but no additional multiple credit.

The total points under category 4 had been lowered, accordingly, to 700. When the number of required meetings was decreased four years later to 12, however, the credit assigned per meeting was doubled, to 100, yielding an overall increase of 500 points for the category. The same year item 9, "Special Activities," was raised by another 300 points, based in part on an increase in recognized "Extra chapter meetings" under subcategory 9g, and a doubling of credit for each extra session from 25 to 50 points. As required regular meetings had declined from 16 to 14 to 12, the number of "extra" meetings credited had advanced from 4 to 6 to 8.

The revisions of 1964 were made by Councilors Hay, Emerson Henke, and Vern Vincent after the annual meeting. Three years later, finally, a significant change was made in the structures of items 4 and 9g, without changing their respective point totals (1,200 and 400). Category 4 was renamed "Meetings with Programs" to signify that business meetings were no longer included. For full credit, eight program gatherings were required. Business meetings would henceforth be covered only in subcategory 9g, in

conjunction with additional program sessions.

One controversial feature of item 1 was not changed during this period. The pivotal requirement of 80% attendance by student members was retained, although clarifications that were developed afforded chapters a small measure of flexibility in defining student membership for that purpose.[1]

"Scholarship" (item 6), identified in chapter 6 as the other critical factor in the early activity program, remained a bone of contention through much of the fourth era.

"Scholarship" requirements

Two principal lines of objection were raised against item 6: first, that the rule was unfair to chapters that admitted students based on national eligibility standards, rather than higher ones; and second, that it was also unfair to chapters operating within severe grading environments. The first concern was addressed in the early sixties, to the detriment of the home chapter of a leader about to join the Council, and apparently to the confusion of certain local units. The second one elicited an experimental initiative, at the prompting of another future national president, that proved unproductive.

Highly restrictive admission

Background to Council action. At the Grand Chapter meeting in 1962,

---

[1]"Chapter Activity Program," Newsletter 5 (November 1960):312; Grand Council Minutes Book, 1960, pp. 2-3; [Leon E. Hay], "Chapter Activity Program Instructions for 1966-67," Newsletter 7 (October 1966):4-5, 6 (quoted); National Council Minutes, 1964, p. 5, 1966, p. 7, 1967, p. 8 (quoting new title of category 4); [Vern H. Vincent], "Chapter Activity Program: Basis for Rating Activity Reports, 1963-64," Newsletter 6 (Spring 1964):79; [Vincent], Secretary's Report, 1964-65, pp. 9-10; and [Robert S. Wasley], "1969-70 Instructions for Activity Program," Newsletter 8 (Fall 1969):6.

it was observed that, in light of the typical advantage enjoyed by "graduate"-oriented chapters regarding grade averages, there had been a tendency within some chapters "to admit only a limited number of initiates each term" from among those who were eligible by national standards. An obvious approach was the local imposition of high grade requirements, yielding a membership academically more elite. Alternatively or additionally, a chapter might require a high number of academic credits in accounting, or otherwise (on a judgmental basis) defer the election of undergraduate students. Especially demanding entry requirements would potentially benefit chapters not only relative to scholarship provisions, but also in the critical area of attendance (as addressed by activity item 4), granting that higher dependence on graduate students might just as well have a negative effect in that regard.

The top-ranked chapters of the first three years of the fourth era were Theta at Texas, 1960-61, and Beta Alpha at Indiana, 1961-63. Both units employed restrictive entry requirements leading to preponderant graduate-level influence. Incoming president Niswonger reported the Indiana situation at the 1962 meeting. Theta alumnus (by transfer) Nolan Williams noted in an interview that Texas would often delay the election of undergraduates to permit further tracking of academic performance. By 1967-68, however, the period of graduate-student dominance at Theta had passed. because of activity program changes reported below, particularly restrictive membership policies could be costly. In addition, the chapter's interest in the annual competition had decidedly waned.

High grade requirements were as apt to be associated with an "honor-society" orientation as with a points strategy, as illustrated by

Alpha at Illinois and Alpha Omicron at Michigan State after incentives for lower ones had been introduced. Alpha, whose distaste for the activity program was documented earlier, as of 1966-67 required a 4.5 grade average in accounting and a 4.3 average overall, on a 5.0-scale. A year later, when the chapter president had informed visiting councilor Wilton Anderson "that he was not interested in serving as an officer in a professional [or non-honorary] organization," Alpha Omicron had maintained respective requirements of 3.2 and 3.0 averages, on a 4.0-base. A similar case was Rho at Minnesota, noted for an oral qualifying exam. In 1963 alumnus Herb Miller, who had two years earlier moved from Michigan to Michigan State, had referred within a visitation report to Rho's "high" grade requirements.

Data have not been obtained from the early 1960s on accounting credit-hour criteria recognized at the local level. The constitutional minimum requirement of enrollment in "advanced" (meaning "intermediate") accounting implied that completion of a one-year's course, ordinarily embodying 6-8 semester hours or 9-12 quarter credits, was sufficient. Information from a few years later indicates that at least 12 semester hours or the equivalent, which by then had become a maximum national standard, were often required.

Alpha Omicron apparently combined its relatively high grade restrictions with the quarterly equivalent of 12 required semester hours in accounting. The latter condition effectively delayed entry until late in the junior year. In the fall quarter of 1967, only two students were invited to join the Michigan State chapter from among some 300 junior and senior accounting majors. Ironically, Beta Psi at Kent State reportedly was a "large" unit (in 1968), "particularly in proportion to the number of accounting majors"

on campus, despite maintaining a still higher requirement--the equivalent of 10 semester hours in the field _beyond_ the introductory course. The latter chapter followed the national B/B- scholastic standard.

Credit requirements equal to those of Alpha Omicron were in effect at two traditionally weak chapters, Gamma at Northwestern and Pi at (Case) Western Reserve; and also within Beta Iota at Loyola of Chicago, and newly formed Gamma Kappa at the University of Nebraska--Omaha. Georgia's strong Beta Omicron group required 20 quarter hours plus grade averages comparable to those recognized at Michigan State. Pi Chapter observed an alternate rule by which majors who had completed 9 semester credits in the field with an A average were eligible for membership from an accounting standpoint.

At Georgia and the Nebraska campus, at least, admission in the latter 1960s required the completion of intermediate accounting. Under either of two settings, however, such a condition would not have delayed participation in Beta Alpha Psi. First, accounting instruction was still on occasion begun in the freshman year, as had until 1961 been the case at Pennsylvania, site of Alpha Delta. At DePaul, where the prerequisite was only four quarters of accounting, students could be elected to Beta Gamma as early as the second term of the _sophomore_ year.

Second, Sigma at Wisconsin followed the practice of including "pledges" in chapter activities during the first semester of the junior year. The idea of "having pledge classes among the first or second year students in accounting" was positively received when broached by a faculty advisor during the 1970 National Chapter meeting. Perhaps at a later date, Chi at Oklahoma State began a practice of designating top-ranked sophomores as affiliated "associates," eligible to begin attending chapter meetings. Under a concept endorsed by the Council in 1974, prospective initiates

could even enjoy "the rights and privileges of membership" (except for holding an office) in advance of their formal induction.

In stating instructions for "pledging," the Grand Council itself had in 1961 endorsed membership limitation unrelated to academic work:

> Only those who express a sincere willingness to take an active part in the activities of the Fraternity and to serve their university and the accounting profession should be invited to pledge.

Such a commitment could be sought during "personal interviews" conducted with students academically eligible for election to membership. President Bill Jencks had written in 1958 that "some Chapters question[ed] candidates for membership at length" on their "ability and expectation to attend meetings," a policy evidently under consideration ten years later by recently formed Gamma Eta at Akron, which wished otherwise to admit anyone who was "eligible." As an interesting variation on the same theme, Beta Mu at Georgia State was reported in 1967 to be sometimes excluding students who were "very near graduation," based on lack of time to serve the chapter. Having no clear relationship to activity points, this approach stood in marked contrast to a policy of deferring the election of undergraduates.

Certain highly-ranked chapters of the early 1960s may well have required more than 12 accounting hours, or otherwise commonly delayed admission until the senior year. This supposition is based upon action taken by the Grand Council in 1963 to deal with the activity program bias, within the scholarship area at least, toward highly restrictive eligibility.

Action by the Grand Council, 1963. The discussion at the close of the 1962 meeting of this bias, and the consequent incentive to restrict admission significantly, produced a suggestion that the chapter activity programs be revised to provide credit based on the proportion of students "eligible"

by national standards who were invited to join a chapter. This proposal was favorably received, and Secretary-Treasurer Emerson Henke was instructed to survey the chapters over the coming year to determine their eligibility criteria and admission practices. The Council resolved to pursue the matter at the 1963 meeting.

Although no information is available regarding a canvass of chapters, significant action was taken in 1963. Leon Hay, who would join the governing body a year after the meeting, recalls having been told, "privately," that the changes had been made to keep his Beta Alpha chapter from winning the first-place trophy a third successive time. As a matter of record, the Indiana group would fall to third place in 1963-64. Broader factors appear to have been considered, in any case.

The approach taken was to amend category 5, "Initiations," to provide for earning from 5 to 30 points twice yearly by inviting from 70 to 90% of nationally "eligible" students, as defined, to become members. "Eligibility" for this purpose was defined compatibly with the national constitution, requiring an average of B in accounting and B- overall, with one conspicuous exception. Whereas constitutionally students who had completed as few as 6 semester hours in accounting could be initiated, the activity program amendment identified eligibility with the completion of 12 such credits, or the equivalent. In addition, a prior term in residence and, to limit pressure for induction of part-time students, current enrollment for at least 10 (semester) credit hours were required.[2]

---

[2]As clarified in activity program instructions, the new rule was applied in modified form. Specifically, in determining percentages all students invited to join the chapter were counted, whether or not they were "eligible" in the special sense defined. For example, students asked to become members based on fewer than 12 semester credits completed in accounting would be included in the tabulation. The practical effect was to liberalize the rule,

It is important to stress that the amendment of item 5 neither altered constitutional criteria for eligibility, nor contradicted them. Chapters were entirely free to induct accounting majors who had completed a full-year's introductory course with a B average and achieved a B- average overall. They would be penalized in the points competition, however, if they extended invitations to fewer than 90% of students who had completed 12 hours in accounting, and satisfied the other requirements. In effect, the Council had identified 12 semester credits as the maximum acceptable requirement for invitation to membership, given suitable grade averages. The fact that this level exceeded the constitutional minimum by one to two courses suggests that chapters were sometimes deferring induction decisions even beyond that point.

At the 1965 National Chapter banquet (following the Council meeting at which the term "National" had been adopted), President Julius Roller "urged" the assembled faculty leaders "to keep in mind" that the 12-hour

---

through making equal additions to the numerator (eligible students invited to join) and the denominator (total eligible students).

The instructions also originally cited "junior standing" (along, by implication, with completion of sufficient accounting work to be constitutionally eligible) as an "alternative" to the 12-hour requirement. Although he had not mentioned it in the minutes, Secretary-Treasurer Vincent apparently believed that such a provision had been approved at the 1963 Grand Council meeting. No doubt finding it difficult to discern a rationale for the "alternative," or to imagine conditions under which it would be preferred, the Council in 1964 registered a "unanimity of opinion" in favor of the 12-credit element in unqualified form. Grand Council Minutes, 1964, p. 1, quoted; and [Vern H. Vincent], "Chapter Activity Program: Basis for Rating Activity Reports, 1963-64," _Newsletter_ 6 (Spring 1964):80, quoted.

It is conjectured that the 1963 Council may have approved, instead, a contingency provision by which an academically qualified student completing 12 accounting hours before the close of the _sophomore_ year need not be considered "eligible" for program purposes. In view of schedule patterns already noted, such a condition would not have been unusual at DePaul, the home of Beta Gamma.

standard pertained only to the evaluation of activity category 5, and did not supersede the traditional requirement of the constitution. There is evidence of misunderstanding in this area, however.

Specifically, on a visit to Gamma Epsilon at Toledo in 1967 Harvey Donley found that the chapter had identified "eligibility" as defined in the '"90% rule"' with constitutional provisions, and on that basis required 12 hours of accounting work for admission. Such an error would only undermine the intent of the program revision, by leading some chapters to make admission more, rather than less, restrictive. In the specific case of Gamma Epsilon, the misinterpretation had generally delayed election until the senior year, leaving the chapter largely dependent on graduate-student leadership. Donley commented that he would "wager" that "many" chapters were unclear on the vital distinction involved.[3]

---

[3]Wilton T. Anderson to Author, interview, March 20, 1980, quoted; [Anderson] (name penciled in), Visitation Report--Alpha Omicron, November 2, 1967, quoted; Barron's Profiles, s.v. "Illinois, Northwestern University"; Beta Alpha Psi Fraternity, "National Constitution," National Constitution and Statutes (1958), article 6, section 1, quoted; Thomas J. Burns, "Student Involvement Key to Effective Chapter," Newsletter 8 (Fall 1969):5; H. E. Donley, Visitation Reports--Gamma, May 17, 1968, Pi, April 15, 1968, Beta Eta, April 27, 1967 (quoted), Beta Iota, May 17, 1968, Beta Mu, April 27, 1967 (quoted), Gamma Epsilon, April 6, 1967 (quoted); [Grand Council], "Procedures for Pledging, Initiation, and Election and Installation of Officers of Beta Alpha Psi," rev. 1961, p.1, quoted; Grand Council Minutes Book, 1962, pp. 3, 8 (quoted), 1963, pp. 6-7 (quoted); Leon E. Hay to National Council, December 11, 1967, memorandum supplementing visitation reports on Gama Kappa and two other chapters; [Hay], Secretary-Treasurer's Report, 1966-67, p. 2; Hay to Author, interview, May 2, 1980, quoted; Hay, Visitation Reports--Alpha, October 27, 1966, Beta Psi, May 17, 1968 (quoted); W. B. Jencks to Robert Jaedicke, FVP, May 7, 1958, attached to his Visitation Report--Rho, May 1, 1958; Kaylor, "Chapter Activity Program, 1950-69," p. 2; "[Local] Chapter News," Newsletter 5 (November 1959):223; Herbert E. Miller, "Biographical Sketch - April 1967" (Golden Anniversary Files), p. 1; Miller, Visitation Report--Rho, Fall 1963, quoted; National Council Minutes, 1965, p. 11, 1970, p. 17, May 1974, p. 3 (no. 6.4), each quoted; Vern E. Odmark, Visitation Report--Theta, March 11, 1968; [Charles W. Taylor], "Past Presidents of Beta Alpha Psi," Newsletter 8 (50th anniv. ed., [1969]):11; Taylor, Visitation Report--Beta Upsilon, December 11, 1967; R. H. Van Voorhis, Visitation Report--Alpha Delta, December 14, 1960; and Vern H. Vincent,

The 1963 revision only partially alleviated concern over the Scholarship category, in any case, as best illustrated by objection registered from the University of Iowa.

Severe grading standards

Background, with special reference to Alpha Pi. As observed particularly in chapter 3, regarding the modest elevation made during the third era in national eligibility requirements, certain Beta Alpha Psi schools were known for unusually difficult grading. It was primarily for this reason that an alternative percentile option had been introduced by which rank in accounting courses among the top 30% of junior and senior majors was counted as equivalent to a B average.

This concession was very limited, not extending to the requirement for a B- average in all courses completed. Further, there was no alternative interpretation for the overall B average for preceding terms specified, at chapterwide and individual levels alike, in the Scholarship section of the activity program. Reference within activity category 6 to the "equivalent" of a B average related to an alternative grade notation, ordinarily numerical, rather than a percentile criterion. Use of the alternate standard for

---

Visitation Reports--Upsilon, [March 22, 1967] (quoted), Beta Epsilon, February 22, 1968 (reference to Sigma's "Pledges"), Beta Rho, [March 23, 1968], Gamma Eta, March 12, 1968 (quoted).

The visitation reports cited, from the 1960s, are drawn from a file of 38 reports (sometimes combined in groups of two or three) and 6 related letters, memoranda, or notes available from the two years 1966-68 and from the falls of 1960 and 1963. This tabulation counts Miller's joint 1963 reports on Mu (cited in chapter 4 relative to alumni domination at NYU), Rho, and Alpha Gamma. Only part of Vincent's combined coverage of visits to Upsilon and Beta Rho is available. At the 1960 annual meeting the Grand Council had abandoned the use of a visitation form, leading frequently to very brief memoranda in the years to come. Grand Council Minutes Book, 1960, p. 3.

admissions purposes might well only jeopardize a chapter's prospects in a category that had proved so critical to activity-program results. As documented in chapter 6, a relatively few points had often separated the top several chapters of the fifties.

One of the most severe chapter sites from a grading standpoint was Iowa, where Alpha Pi adhered to the national grading standard, probably in its basic version. Following a 1958 visit to his graduate alma mater, President W. B. Jencks (M.A. '35) had not commented on scholastic conditions as he commended the local faculty for giving "almost solid backing and cooperation" to the chapter. A few years later, the Iowa business school graduated a class whose top 10%, academically, owned a cumulative average of less than B.

Dick Metcalf, who taught at Iowa from 1963 to 1966, recalls that accounting chairman Gilbert Maynard did not give As, and that he and his three other colleagues (who included Joe Fritzemeyer) were required to submit their own grades through Maynard. Even though Alpha Pi members would have had the required B average in accounting when initiated, the departmental grading standards left top students with little or no cushion for maintaining such marks overall, within a very strenuous environment, even if they maintained their grades in the major field.

Feeling "adversely penalized" by this situation, the Iowa chapter requested in 1962 that a _percentile_ option be approved for assigning points in the Scholarship category. Based on later developments, it was probably recommended that rank among the top 20% of junior and senior business majors, or relative to the most recent graduating class, be accepted as "equivalent" to a B average. The Grand Council rejected the request at the annual meeting, and no further comment was recorded in the minutes.

Less than two years later, in April 1964, Councilor Wilton "Andy" Anderson made a visitation to Alpha Pi. It is clear that the problems posed for the chapter by the difficult grading at Iowa were seriously discussed, for at the next Council meeting Anderson was asked to solicit a written proposal from new FVP Metcalf on possible means for alleviating them. In due course, a limited experiment with an alternative interpretation was approved in 1965, only to be aborted through limitation in fact to the source chapter.

Approval of an experiment in 1965, undermined by minimum implementation. The heart of the proposal that emanated from Iowa was that '"a rank as high as that attained by the upper 20% of the prior year's graduating class"' in business be accepted as an alternative to a B average, under item 6, for both individual and collective averages. The frame of reference was the second semester of the senior year. The proposed "Metcalf amendment" also provided that to be eligible for the alternative interpretation, a chapter would have under item 5, "Initiations," to define eligibility for membership comparably. In the latter regard, the reference groups specified were the top 20% of the preceding year's accounting graduates, for grade averages in the major field, and the top 25% of all business graduates, for averages overall. In effect a new substitute for the traditional B/B- standard had been recommended.

The Council decided in 1965 to experiment with the Iowa proposal minus, on the ground that they could not practicably be imposed for test purposes, the alternate eligibility criteria. The plan was to invite a few selected chapters to report item 6 during the coming year, 1965-66, on a dual basis, using in turn the conventional rule and the percentile alternative. Besides

Alpha Pi, Secretary-Treasurer and incoming president Vern Vincent identified as good candidates for dual reporting his own Alpha Psi chapter at West Virginia (also noted for difficult grading), Beta Epsilon at Lehigh, and Beta Xi at Miami of Florida. During the National Chapter meeting that followed, both Metcalf and Beta Epsilon advisor Robert Mills "strongly urged" the need for alternative scholarship and eligibility provisions.

Vincent would probably have included Upsilon among desired test chapters had he been familiar at the time with grading practices at Florida, where Williard Stone had served as department chairman since 1960. On visitations of March 1967, he would learn that (by best estimates) fewer than 15% of Florida's accounting graduates in an average year belonged to Beta Alpha Psi, compared to around 30% of the class at Florida State, the home of Beta Rho. '"Tough grading"' was the reason given for Upsilon's low admission rates.

Somewhat ironically, Beta Xi had led the chapter competition just completed, receiving 586 of a possible 600 points on scholarship. Alpha Psi, ranked third, had been first a few years earlier. None of the four chapters cited had received fewer than 540 points in category 6.

Lehigh, an engineering-oriented school of strong academic reputation, had a very small chapter even though it followed the traditional B/B- eligibility rule, occasionally "stretching a little below 2.5 overall where a student's more recent record was up around 3-point overall."

The experiment was apparently very limited. Only Alpha Pi at Iowa appears to have reported Scholarship on a dual basis in 1965-66, perhaps because of difficulties in assembling pertinent grade information. Even in that case the alternate reporting system was revised somewhat for reasons of practicality. Because the grade averages for business graduates of the

prior year were not readily available to Alpha Pi, in a day of growing concern for student privacy, the chapter referred instead each semester to the college-wide grade average of the prior term. The top 20% range remained the standard of comparison.

As recalled by faculty advisor Dick Metcalf, the alternate method did yield a higher point total for Alpha Pi than the official one. The difference would have been inconseqnential, however, in a year in which the chapter fell thirty-five notches in the national rankings, to 55th place, an event attributed by Secretary-Treasurer Leon Hay to the FVP's preoccupation with relocating from Iowa. Because the experiment with dual reporting had been so isolated, the National Council had virtually no data to refer to when it met in 1966, and there is no evidence that the matter was even discussed. Metcalf, a graduate student of Hay's at Indiana, left for Drake in the fall of 1966, and would have a hand in the establishment there of Gamma Mu the following year.

Andy Anderson visited Alpha Pi a second time in the fall of 1967. His brief report did not mention grading, except in a puzzling statement that the year's president-elect had "flunked out." The main concern expressed was that the Iowa chapter might be drifting into an "honor society" concept under the faculty vice-presidency of John H. Smith, an alumnus of Alpha at Illinois.

Although nothing would come of the discussion of the Metcalf amendment, a change occurring in 1970 would substantially disarm criticism concerning scholarship, attendance, or any other sensitive element of the activity program. That year the National Council awarded commemorative plaques to <u>the top eight</u> chapters in the activity program rather than only the first-place group, making fine disciminations less consequential than before from a

symbolic standpoint. Four years later, in 1974, the scholarship component was finally replaced by a disclosure provision concerning fraternal pledges.[4]

As mentioned above, one important concern about Scholarship was handled by adding yearly credit of up to 60 points under item 5, "Initiations," based on the proportion of nationally "eligible" students who were invited to join the chapter. Later the weight assigned to that category was further increased, and the distribution of initiation points was substantially changed due to an important symbolic development.

Initiations

In 1965-66, the maximum credit assigned to category 5 was increased by 140 points, to a total of 800, by adding 70 points for each of two properly reported (and fee-remitted) initiations. For each initiation, 100 points were still assigned for proper memorization of the non-"blindfolded" part of the initiation ritual.

Three years later, in 1968, the blindfolding was eliminated as part of an overall simplification of the ritual, as discussed below. Accordingly, the points previously granted for memorization were reassigned to proper reporting and fee remission, to a total of 370 per initiation.

The remaining major change up to 1969 was required by the alteration

---

[4] [Wilton T. Anderson], Visitation Report--Alpha Pi, October 31, 1967, quoted; Grand Council Minutes, 1964, pp. 4-5; Grand Council Minutes Book, 1954, p. 2, 1962, p. 8; Hasselback, 1984 Directory, individual listing, s.v. "Barnes, B. L." (an Iowa professor), "Metcalf, Richard W."; W. B. Jencks, Visitation Report--Alpha Pi, March 25, and to Councilors, April 2, 1958 (quoted); National Council Minutes, 1965, pp. 3-4, 11 (quoted), 1970, p. 3; [A. J. Penz], "William B. Jencks Elected to Grand Council," Newsletter 4 (November 1954):203; [Vern H. Vincent], "Chapter Activity Program," Newsletter of (Spring 1964):80 (quoted); [Vincent], Secretary's Report, 1963-64, p. 1, 1964-65, pp. 9-10; and Vincent, Visitation report--Beta Epsilon, February 22, 1968, quoted.

of the _Newsletter_.

"Newsletter"

In 1962, four years before the traditional periodical format was abandoned, a noteworthy change was made in assigning points under category 7, _Newsletter_. Whereas previously 450 points were available twice yearly for timely submission of a chapter report for publication, 50 points per report were reassigned that year to "qualitative evaluation" of the material. They would be awarded only for "organization and content . . . judged to be of the quality reasonably to be expected of a student member of Beta Alpha Psi."

With the decision of 1966 to experiment with new approaches to the _Newsletter_, it was necessary to change item 7, for the year 1966-67, even though the exact shape of recasting was uncertain. Accordingly, the category was reduced in weight from 900 points to 600, and it was required that copy "be of general interest to student members of the Fraternity," rather than "mere lists of meetings and . . . of names of initiates." As before, two submissions were required.

With the periodical established in the new format, Councilors Vern Odmark, Harvey Donley, and Charles Taylor developed a new approach to its coverage within the activity program during the National Council meeting of 1968. Item 7 was eliminated as a separate category in the program, but the 600 points reappeared as subcategory f in item 9, "Special Activities." _Four_ timely submissions on topics of "general interest to student members" were required for full credit. The maximum length was set at three typewritten pages, double spaced.

Some chapters registered strong objection to the modernized _Newsletter_,

according to 1967-69 secretary-treasurer Donley, probably based on the activity program consequences. One of them was probably Alpha Iota at Arkansas, cited as having generally been "rather unpleasant" regarding point allocations. Between the developments of 1966 and 1968, Past President Wilton Anderson had reported on a visitation to Fayetteville, in part, as follows:

> Much time was spent in complaining because they received only 250 points on the copy for the Newsletter. (They did not receive the 50 bonus points because they did not report on anything unusual).[5]

In combination with one another, the various revisions just discussed, and a variety of lesser ones, produced a distinctly different program of interchapter competition in 1969 than had existed nine years earlier. Yet at the golden anniversary meeting that year, based on committee recommendations, the program was altered more basically than throughout the fourth era to that point, perhaps than even since its inception in 1950. The most striking reforms were the substantial separation of the activity competition from areas of constitutional compliance, and the concurrent restatement of competitive participation as a chapter <u>option</u>.

Fundamental Revision of 1969: Restructuring the Activity Program, and Making it Optional

<u>Committee work of 1968-69, and consequent reports</u>

At the 1968 National Chapter meeting, President Hay reported that he would be heading a "study group" over the coming year to review the chapter activity program that he had administered during the two years 1967-67.

---

[5] [Harvey E. Donley], "1968-69 Instructions for Activity Program," <u>Newsletter</u> 8 (Fall 1968):8; Donley to Author, interview, May 2, 1980; "Chapter Activity Program," <u>Newsletter</u> 5 (Spring 1962):468; Grand Council Minutes Book, 1962, p. 3, quoted; [Leon E. Hay], "Chapter Activity Program Instructions for 1966-1967," <u>Newsletter</u> 7 (October 1966):5, 6 (quoted; and National Council Minutes, 1965, p. 8, 1966, p. 7, 1968, p. 6.

Secretary-Treasurer Donley commented on the same occasion on the "apparent enigma" by which a trend toward elimination of "sharp discrimination" in awarding points coexisted with "consensus" support, still, for a "competitive flavor." The latter point had been established when at a National Chapter meeting the preceding year a proposal to replace numerical ranking with division of chapters into several performance categories had been "overwhelmingly" rejected.

The Newsletter of Winter 1969 announced the appointment of Hay's committee, and encouraged the chapters to spend meeting time during the year in

> discussion of the role the Fraternity should play in helping the members develop the knowledge, abilities, and attitudes that w[ould] promote their personal progress and the contribution of the accounting profession to society.

Chapters were asked to send their suggestions to the National Council.

As listed, the committee was composed of former presidents Leon Hay (as chairman) and Vern Vincent; former faculty vice-presidents James Pattillo of Iota at USC and Lyle C. Steinmeier of Zeta at North Dakota; and current FVPs Earl F. Davis of Beta Upsilon at Georgia and Vernon E. Pontius of Beta Lambda at California State, Los Angeles. Future councilor Pattillo had moved to LSU, and Steinmeier was on leave in Michigan working for Haskins & Sells.

The committee functioned primarily through correspondence and telephone communication, but met in South Bend, Indiana in conjunction with the Council meeting of 1969. Apparently based on the absence of the other three persons appointed, only Hay, Pattillo, and Steinmeier were listed as committee members in the annual minutes.[6] The latter two men had represented

---

[6]Vern Vincent had in June 1969 moved from West Virginia in time to teach summer school at Southern Illinois at Edwardsville. The term ended the same day as the National Council meeting, on August 25, and Vincent was

chapters that environmentally were polar opposites. Just as Los Angeles was one of the foremost metropolitan chapter sites, Grand Forks was one of the most isolated and remote. Pontius, also representing a Los Angeles unit, and Davis, reporting in 1986 no recollection of a committee appointment, were from chapters formed during the decade that had shown strength in the activity program.

Another 1968-69 committee, headed by ex-councilor Julius Roller, studied an issue pertinent to reform of the activity program, namely, problems faced by chapters located within predominantly (or wholly) graduate-school environments. Such units tended to favor an honorary slant toward the fraternity, and correspondingly to look with some disdain upon interchapter competition. Roller's committee, made up of the chairman and two faculty vice-presidents, conducted one or more meetings during the year in addition to communicating at long distance.

At the national meeting in 1969, Past President Hay recommended a detailed "substantial revision" of the activity program. A report was read from the Roller committee that made four recommendations very relevant to the activity program, in particular that the "competitive aspect" be eliminated. Based on the reports of the two committees, and evidence that certain chapters were in one way or another ill-suited to existing requirements, the National Council decided "to introduce more flexibility into the program and attempt to provide, in part at least, for the preferences and differing interests and needs of the various chapters." The result was fundamental change that would restructure the Chapter Activity Program beginning,

---

on hand the next evening for the golden anniversary banquet. National Council Minutes, 1969, pp. 1, 11; Vern H. Vincent to [C.] Aubrey Smith, June 27, 1969 (Golden Anniversary Files); and Vincent to Charles W. Taylor, June 8, 1969 (Golden Anniversary).

immediately, with the year 1969-70.

A fundamentally new program

There were two very basic changes. First, "constitutional" requirements for remaining in good standing within the fraternity were expressly identified, as proposed by the Roller committee, and largely eliminated from the points competition. Those annual requirements were the holding of at least one initiation; the conduct of at least seven other meetings; and the timely submission of an audit report.

Second, chapter participation in the competitive program was made optional. A predominantly graduate-student chapter, a group otherwise favoring an honorary emphasis, or a more active unit that found reporting provisions of the activity program burdensome could avoid such involvement without any jeopardy to its standing in the fraternal roster.

Structure of the new program

As restructured, the activity program consisted of seven elements:

1. Plan of Activities - 500 points
2. Financial Plan - 300
3. Student Participation in Activities - 1,600
4. Initiations - 400 (two initiations properly reported)
5. Scholarship - 600
6. Chapter Involvement in Campus or Community Activities - 1,000
7. Chapter Involvement in Professional and Fraternity Activities - 1,000.

Item 4 clearly overlapped with constitutional requirements. It was intended to encourage participating groups to hold multiple initiations by awarding 200 points each for two ceremonies properly reported and accounted for. The initiation category had been reduced to a weight of 400 points out of 5,400, from 800 points out of 6,000 (exclusive of "directory" years), in part through eliminating the credit previously given for liberal eligibility policies. With the Scholarship category remaining intact at 600 points,

within a smaller overall point total, it was only enhanced as a critical factor in the chapter rankings. The Council may have assumed that chapters having particularly restrictive academic requirements would tend not to participate in the annual competition.

The 1,600 points in item 3 were allocated based on the allotment of 100 points for each of 12 chapter activities securing the participation of at least 80% of student members, and 4 program meetings prepared and presented by such members. The place in the activity program of member attendance, the second critical discriminating factor identified in chapter 6, was thus enhanced, granting that the imminent large expansion in the number of chapters recognized with plaques would reduce the visibility of small point differences.

Finally, items 6 and 7 significantly expanded upon the former "Special Activities" element. Each of the two sets of instructions specified a variety of activities assigned a total of 1,600 points. Under item 7, four submissions to the Newsletter could yield 400 points, in total.[7]

More than half of the chapters elected to compete in the first "optional" annual activity program, marking the start of an experiment destined in some fashion to last for five years.

"Optional" participation

The first year, 1969-70. Forty-eight of the eighty active chapters

---

[7] Earl F. Davis, to Author, January 24, 1986; [Harvey E. Donley], Secretary-Treasurer's Report, 1968-69, pp. 15-16; Donley, Visitation Report--Zeta, April 27, 1967; [Leon E. Hay], Secretary-Treasurer's Report, 1966-67, p. 6; Hay to Author, January 7, 1986; National Council Minutes, 1967, p. 8, 1968, pp. 10-11, 1969, pp. 4-5 (all quoted), 9; Lyle C. Steinmeier to Author, January 8, 1986; [Charles W. Taylor], "Committees Appointed: Professors Hay, Wasley Named Chairmen," Newsletter 8 (Winter 1969):2, quoted; "Top 15 Chapters Listed in '67-68 Activity Program," Newsletter 8 (Fall 1968):3; and [Robert S. Wasley], "1969-70 instructions for Activity Program," Newsletter 8 (Fall 1969):3.

participated in the points competition of 1969-70. In keeping with the recommendation made by the Roller committee that the option not be available during the first two years of local operations, they included Gamma Omicron, established at Fresno State in December 1969. Although such a rule had been adopted, Gamma at San Jose State, founded the prior spring, was listed (without comment) among nonparticipating chapters. As a related point, chapters having been placed on probation would be required to take part in the activity program.

Nonparticipating chapters during the first year included Theta, which had one top honors a record four times over the first eleven years of the activity competition, but not been in serious contention since 1961-62; Alpha and Beta, associated with an honor-society emphasis, particularly in the first case; Delta and Omicron, traditionally active units that had not placed particular emphasis on points accumulation; Gamma, Pi, and Rho, relatively weak urban-centered groups; and Alpha Pi and Beta Epsilon, already identified as centers of special concern about the scholarship category.

After 9 top-three finishes in the first 12 years of the program, Theta at Texas had after 1962 moved in the direction of Delta at Washington and Omicron at Ohio State, as characterized above. During the years 1967-69, under the faculty leadership of Kermit D. Larson, there was somewhat of an honorary emphasis within the chapter. In discussing Theta's decision not to participate in the activity program, C. Aubrey Smith wrote in 1973, or thereabouts, that the officers wished to pursue certain "local activities . . . not recognized for points." Although Smith may have been unaware of the breadth of coverage that had developed within the interchapter competition, his recitation of chapter activity at Texas as of the early seventies was impressive:

> The usual programs at which outstanding practitioners, business and governmental executives speak . . .[;] production of a chapter directory; sponsorship of an awards-day banquet; holding joint meetings with other professional accounting organizations; securing funds for an awarding scholarships; . . . sponsoring, promoting and directing at least one out-of-town field trip annually . . .[; and taking a leadership role in] supplying income tax advice and service to certain segments of the community in need thereof.

In administering constitutional compliance in 1969-70, Secretary-Treasurer Robert Wasley permitted chapters to substitute a second initiation for a program or business meeting. Accordingly, four chapters that did not participate in the activity program, including Delta at Washington (under FVP Julius Roller), were judged to be in compliance with only six non-initation meetings. Five of the nonparticipating chapters still failed to report enough meetings, with Gamma at Northwestern (featuring its final undergraduate class) and Beta Zeta at Loyola of New Orleans reporting none at all, at least on an acceptable basis. Only those chapters and Mu at New York violated the initiation requirement, in one case by not remitting fees.

Nine of the 32 chapters that did not engage in the points competition reported <u>10 or more</u> meetings, other than initiations. Leading the way were Beta Xi at Miami of Florida with 16, Alpha at Illinois with 14, and Gamma Xi at San Jose State with 13. Alpha's performance was not entirely out of character, in that the chapter had seemed in the past to be more resistant to the reporting requirements of the activity program than to conducting at least a modest annual program.

The National Council voted unanimously in 1970 to continue the new activity-program structure. Reporting requirements were soon increased for nonparticipants, however, and by the last year of a voluntary arrangement there was only a formal difference between the two classes of chapters.

Evolution, and conclusion, of the voluntary structure, 1970-74. Except for initiations and officer elections, the minimal reporting required of nonparticipating chapters was at first year-end in nature. As discussed in chapter 12, Omicron and Delta had agreed to provide fuller information under an experimental reporting plan. In 1970 the council decided that other noncompeting units should "be urged to submit annual summaries of their activities," exceeding minimum requirements, although there is no record of positive response. The following year the policy was changed to require nonparticipating chapters to report *semi*-annually, and in 1973, on the motion of former Delta student and faculty officer Fred Mueller, monthly reporting was reinstated for *all* units.

The only "option" that existed during the year 1973-74 was whether or not to be ranked, competitively, given that "only chapters electing to have their points published w[ould] be eligible for monetary and other awards made on the basis of chapter activity." On that diminished basis, the fraternal experiment with a voluntary activity program was concluded as of that period. In 1974, by which time "attendance" provisions had been reduced significantly, and at which point traditional "scholarship" coverage was eliminated, full participation in program was restored as a requirement for all chapters. To remove any reluctance to comply, however, the National Council agreed that point totals should be disclosed only within a chapter-alphabetical format, and only at an itemized, noncumulative level. In that form, midyear results would be shown in the *Newsletter*, and final ones would be made available at the National Chapter meeting.[8]

---

[8] *Beta Alpha Psi National Constitution* (1971), article 14, section 4; Thomas J. Burns to Author, interview, May 3, 1980; [Harvey E. Donley], Secretary-Treasurer's Report, 1968-69, p. 8; Kaylor, "Chapter Activity Program, 1950-69," p. 4; [Robert S. Maust or Fred J. Mueller], "Changes in Reporting Chapter Activities," *Newsletter* 12 (Fall 1973):5; Mueller to Author

The activity program of the fourth era is covered further in chapter 11, in reference to leading local chapters of the sixties and pertinent recognition and awards. At this point, attention may be turned to two major programs that were established near the close of the period for chapter advisors.

Two New Programs for Faculty Vice-Presidents

In 1967, annual "workshops" were begun for faculty vice-presidents in connection with the meeting of the National Chapter. Two years later, planning was underway for an FVP awards program that would begin in 1970 in memory of its principal initiator, Richard S. Claire.

Annual FVP Workshops, 1967-70

Initiation of the program

On the recommendation of incoming president Andy Anderson, the Council voted in 1966 to sponsor a "Faculty Vice-Presidents Workshop" a year later during the first day of the American Accounting Association meetings at Penn State. The plan was to start with a luncheon, and conclude prior to the association's evening meal. Anderson was appointed to supervise the planning, and to select "faculty" for the first workshop from among the advisors at leading chapters. All incoming or continuing FVPs, as of August 1967, would be invited to the workshop.

Two potential topics were suggested in 1966 for coverage a year later at the first workshop:

the effect on the Fraternity of increasing numbers of universities

---

interview, November 27, 1979; National Council Minutes, 1969, p. 4, 1970, p. 6 (quoted), 1971, pp. 2-3, 1972, pp. 5-7 (nos. 6.2-3, 6.11), 1973, p. 12 (nos. 32.1-2), May 1974, p. 6 (no. 19), August 1974, p. 6 (no. 1-e); Vern E. Odmark, Visitation Report--Theta, March 11, 1968; Smith, Forty Acres, pp. 69, 70 (indented citation); and [Robert S. Wasley], Secretary-Treasurer's Report, 1969-70, pp. 6-8. A passage from the 1973 minutes suggests that semi-annual reporting had not taken hold among nonparticipating chapters (National Council Minutes, 1973, p. 12, no. 31.0).

> abandoning undergraduate programs and accounting and business administration in favor of graduate programs . . ., and the effect . . . of metropolitan colleges with predominantly evening programs.

President Anderson agreed to seek operating advice from FVPs serving at "successful" chapters found within programs catering to graduate or evening instruction, and share his findings through the Newsletter or the 1967 workshop.

The graduate-school setting, discussed in detail in chapter 12, was addressed by the aforementioned Roller committee of 1968-69. Broadened coverage of chapters from "metropolitan" chapters drawing, in particular, many commuter students was provided in 1967 by an article appearing in the May Newsletter and by one of two workshop panels engaged. James Pattillo, representing Iota at Southern Cal (although relocating to LSU), contributed the article and chaired a panel session that also featured William Kimball of Psi at Marquette and Gerald Cleveland of Delta at Washington. A concurrent session led by Charles Taylor of Alpha Theta at Mississippi (chairman), Samuel Frumer of Beta Alpha at Indiana, and Hollis Dixon of Beta Omicron at Arizona addressed issues of special interest to faculty vice-presidents from primarily residential campuses, in particular (despite the inclusion of a panelist from Tucson) nonurban ones.

A telling contrast existed between the two groups of sources for the charter workshop "faculty." The three chapters from residential schools had ranked first in four of the preceding nine activity-program competitions. Dixon's unit had led the pack in the year just completed, 1966-67, and would do so again two years later. Taylor had incidentally been the faculty leader of not only of the frontrunning Ole Miss chapter in 1958-59, but also, as a doctoral student having faculty rank, first-place Theta at Texas two years later. The three metropolitan-chapter panelists, however, did not represent

first-place units, or ones that were consistently highly ranked. This difference was in keeping with the notion expressed at their session that the activity program was somewhat biased against urban commuter-oriented sites, particularly relative to attendance provisions.

Pattillo's workshop was focused on the activity program, problems of motivating student activity, membership eligibility requirements, program meetings, and alumni activities. Most of the suggestions made were of a conventional nature, such as asigning a job to every member (subject to strong supervision), encouraging faculty attendance, holding occasional breakfast meetings, capitalizing on relevant advantages of metropolitan settings, and presenting programs on interesting, stimulating, and (sometimes) controversial topics. A more novel idea expressed was that of charging newly initiated members for the cost of future chapter activities, granting that assessment of chapter dues was perhaps not unusual.

Approximately 40 FVPs had preregistered for the workshop session concerning primarily residential campuses, and another 15 for the other program. Actual total attendance was lower, however, at 41 persons, apparently including the panelists. Each participant received $15 from the National Council, marking a replacement for the traditional award of $25 to the faculty advisors of the top ten or (beginning in 1963) fifteen chapters represented at the National Chapter meeting.

Adjudged a clear success, the workshop program was continued.

General-purpose workshops, 1968-70

The six 1967 panelists had included three future councilors, Professors Taylor (just elected), Dixon, and Pattillo. During the three years 1968-70, five future councilors served as workshop faculty, namely, (1) Harold Royer (twice) of Beta Xi at Miami of Florida, (2) Joyce Dean of Alpha Rho at

Baylor, (3) Thomas Burns of Omicron at Ohio State, (d) Robert Maust of Alpha Psi at West Virginia, and (e) Richard Metcalf of Gamma Mu at Drake, relocating to Nebraska. Other discussion leaders were Ronald Olson of Tau at Maryland, who had led that metropolitan chapter to first place in 1965-66; and William Keane of Delta Sigma at Notre Dame, the host institution in 1969; and Donald Jones of Beta Pi at North Texas State. Five of the chapters cited finished in first place in the activity program during the 1960s.

Starting in 1968, the sessions were plenary in nature, designed to address in two or three hours all manner of topics relevant to effective chapter operation. Indicative of discussion coverage was a Newsletter article published by Tom Burns directly after his 1969 leadership role. That contribution, "Student Involvement Key to Effective Chapter," is reprinted as exhibit 22.

Beginning in 1968, honoraria of $100 were paid to the workshop leaders in lieu of the regular $15 per participant. Attendance over the three years, besides panelists and councilors, ranged from 20 to 30 faculty advisors. At the 1970 National Chapter meeting "many" faculty vice-presidents questioned the need for the $15 payments, and the following year they were discontinued.[9]

Tom Burns and Bob Maust were charter (honored) participants in another

---

[9] [Harvey E. Donley], Secretary-Treasurer's Report, 1967-68, treasurer's section, p. 1; Grand Council Minutes Book, 1963, p. 5; Kaylor, "Chapter Activity Program, 1950-1969," pp. 2-3; National Council Minutes, 1966, pp. 6 (quoted), 7, 1967, pp. 4-5, 1968, pp. 11-12, 1969, pp. 6, 10-11, 1970, pp. 17 18 (quoted), 1971, p. 4; [Vern E. Odmark], "Problems of Urban, Rural Chapters Discussed in Workshops at Confab," Newsletter 7 (Fall 1967):2; James W. Pattillo, "Metropolitan Area Chapters: Oh, the Disadvantages," Newsletter 7 (May 1967):3-5; Secretaries', or Secretary-Treasurers' Reports, 1960-61 through 1966-67 (omitting unavailable 1962-63 report), listing of annual chapter standings; Smith, Forty Acres, pp. 43-45, 151, 194; and Robert S. Wasley, Secretary-Treasurer's Report, 1970-71, p. 10.

FVP WORKSHOP LEADERS OF 1968,
INCLUDING TWO FUTURE COUNCILORS

JOYCE C. DEAN and HAROLD L. ROYER
with RONALD OLSON of Tau Chapter (on right).

EXHIBIT 22

OMICRON FVP THOMAS BURNS' 1969 ARTICLE
ON CHAPTER ACTIVITIES, NATIONWIDE

Student Involvement Key to Effective Chapter

By Thomas J. Burns
Faculty Vice President
Omicron Chapter
The Ohio State University

In a recent questionnaire survey of chapter activities to which 39 responded, practically every chapter reported that the extent to which chapter activities were effective was directly dependent upon the degree of student participation in these activities. The stress on student involvement, while in marked contrast to the programs of earlier decades when many of the present faculty advisors were actives, is in keeping with the trend towards greater student participation in the affairs of their college, university and community. This relationship was found in all types of activities undertaken by chapters and often strongest in many of the chapters consistently ranked as outstanding by the national council.

For example, the Beta Omicron Chapter at the University of Arizona, the top ranked chapter in the national competition last year, reported their most effective activities to have been:

(1) The actives, in cooperation with Tucson High School Counselors, speaking to various high school classes on accounting careers; and

(2) The actives serving as financial advisors to Junior Achievement groups in the community.

Another outstanding chapter of the past year, Beta Xi, University of Miami, reported their most effective activity to be a public speaking contest for actives on a current accounting topic. Cash prizes and accounting magazine subscriptions were awarded to the winners by the Miami Chapter of the NAA. Other most effective activities by Beta Xi were their actives conducting the audit of the university newspaper and a study of the AICPA's "Common Body of Knowledge" report together with an evaluation of Miami's accounting courses, again by the actives. The West Virginia University Chapter, Alpha Psi, another outstanding chapter of last year, reports that its most effective activity was one similar to Miami's[,] namely a student-faculty debate on the relevance of the curriculum to these objectives and the effectiveness of various instructional approaches. The Ohio State University Chapter, Omicron, reports that its actives reviewed proposed accounting curriculum changes and prepared a written critique of the proposed changes.

The most effective activities for the Alpha Iota Chapter at the University of Arkansas last year were the actives' conducting a ticket sales program for a Boy Scout Expositon and the actives' appearing on a program

for the Arkansas Teachers of Accounting. Several chapters reported tutoring among their most effective activities. These include: Alpha Upsilon (Bowling Green State University); Alpha Psi (Temple University); Beta Alpha (Indiana University); Beta Chi (San Francisco State University); Beta Chi (San Francisco State University); Gamma Zeta (Southern Illinois University); and Beta Sigma (University of Notre Dame). Two chapters, Beta Alpha at Indiana University and Phi at Louisiana State University[,] report their most effective programs to be those on CPA exams. The former conducted a program on preparing for the CPA exams and the latter held review sessions for its actives for six Sunday afternoons prior to the CPA exams.

Gamma Eta, Akron University, reports tours by its actives as its most effective activity. One field trip was made to Firestone's new EDP center and another to Price Waterhouse's offices in Cleveland. Similar tours to offices of CPA firms were reported by the Beta Xi Chapter (at the University of Miami), the Alpha Mu Chapter (at the University of Kentucky) and the Sigma Chapter (at the University of Wisconsin). The Omicron Chapter (at Ohio State University) reports tours to an airplane manufacturer and to a steel mill; both were personally conducted by the vice presidents of finance, Omicron alumni. A tour of the local plant of a national brewery was also enjoyed by the actives at Ohio State. Successful tours, by Beta Omicron at the University of Arizona, include one to an airplane manufacturer, too, as well as one to the IRS and Bell Telephone.

Alpha Mu (at the University of Kentucky) reports its most effective activity to be the information booth for the university. Beta Sigma at the University of Notre Dame conducted tax return help sessions for the underprivileged. The same chapter conducts an audit of student government. Similar audits by actives of the Community Chest, Heart Fund Drives and League of Women Voters were reported by other chapters.

The Beta Sigma Chapter (Notre Dame) actives also work with the South Bend Model Cities office to provide financial advisory services to families in underprivileged areas. The actives at Ohio State University contacted[,] through their counselors, senior high school students in 40 inner-city high schools in the eight largest cities in Ohio; these students were brought to the campus, tested (AICPA and Strong) by the actives and oriented in an all-day program. Students recruited under this program, are offered scholarships by public accounting firms[;] and once enrolled, are counseled by actives.

This chapter reports that a panel session of student actives who have taken both public accounting and industrial firm internships always provides an effective program and that panel sessions of young alumni, whether on the merits of a graduate degree or on what a young CPA does, are also particularly effective. The most effective activity for the Ohio State Chapter last year was their all day seminar based on the recommendation for booking executory contracts from the AAA's statement of 1966. Eighteen chapters of Beta Alpha Psi sent undergraduate student delegates; each student was required to present a position paper on either leases or pensions and all participants and moderators were fellow students. The national council officers

were observers and Professor Neil Churchill of Harvard, a member of the AAA committee who wrote the statement, was the speaker at the end of the day. (Copies of the seminar papers and proceedings will be available upon request from the Omicron Chapter in the late fall).

A tradition of the University of Minnesota chapter was reported on most favorably. This chapter gives an oral exam to each pledge on a pre-announced question; and the examining panel consists of actives and faculty. The San Francisco State College Chapter, Beta Chi, also reports favorably on examining candidates informally in a joint discussion meeting. In electing officers, several chapters report asking the candidates to make campaign speeches or prepare in writing their qualifications and the ideas they would try to implement if elected. Some chapters indicated that the more competition there was in the election of officers the more effective the elections[,] particularly where the qualifications of those running for office was communicated adequately. One chapter mentioned that the "Best officers are almost always the best students." Notre Dame has its retiring officers write brief reports of their duties, accomplishments and problems for the benefit of the incoming officers. Ohio State uses a council to train junior class students for officerships. The Iota Chapter at the University of Southern California gives a "Most [ ]nspirational Active" award upon the basis of the vote of its actives. The Gamma Zeta Chapter at Southern Illinois University awards a fraternity key to the member who has contributed the most to chapter activities. Another chapter each year makes an award to its "outstanding alumnus;" only the actives of the chapter may nominate or vote for the alumnus.

Reprinted from Newsletter 8 (Fall 1969):2-5. The next-to-last paragraph supplements the information presented a bit later in the chapter on Omicron's first student seminar.

FVP program initiated during the fourth era, in this case at its very end. Several of their successors would likewise become national leaders of the fraternity.

Richard S. Claire Award

Development of program, 1968-70

At the 1968 annual meeting, Wilton Anderson cited recent correspondence with Richard S. Claire of the Arthur Andersen Foundation concerning an institutional "interest" in providing "some tangible support of Beta Alpha Psi." A long-time Arthur Andersen partner, Claire was mentioned earlier as an honorary member of Psi at Marquette whom Sigma at Wisconsin had wished (contrary to fraternity policy) to initiate similarly in 1952. He had attracted the attention of accounting educators a quarter-century prior to the Council meeting through a 1944 article proposing the creation of '"a professional school or schools"' of public accounting, an idea that had promptly been challenged by former councilor C. Aubrey Smith.

On Anderson's motion, the National Council in 1968 directed incoming president Vern Odmark to contact Claire in an effort to obtain funding for (1) plaques to be presented each year to the top three chapters in the points competition, and (2) a cash grant to be awarded to the first-place unit, preferably to be used for local scholarships. Over the year 1968-69, however, the discussion was redirected to the idea of funding an awards program for faculty vice-presidents. Independently of his discussions with Odmark, Richard Claire arranged for his firm's graphics department to assist Editor Charles Taylor in bringing out the golden anniversary Newsletter.

Before meeting with Claire during the 1969 gathering in South Bend, the council reached preliminary agreement that recipients of any FVP award

should be selected by a committee of present and past councilors assembled to review written nominations. "[T]he amount and nature of documentation" that should be required regarding nominations were also discussed at the outset.

Later on, at President Odmark's invitation, the Arthur Andersen representative met with the governing body. Claire explained that his organization was willing to assist Beta Alpha Psi financially "in its program emphasizing scholarship and chapter excellence," with a view toward indirectly promoting '"good classroom teaching"'.

Afterwards, the National Council appointed incoming president Harvey Donley to draft a proposal for funding that would be circulated by mail among his colleagues, for refinement purposes, and then submitted in final form to Mr. Claire. The general understanding was that he would propose the funding of an average of three $500 awards annually for outstanding FVPs, with the Council deciding each year the exact number of awards, from zero to five. It was also suggested that the program should include the award of at least three plaques or medallions to faculty vice-presidents, "and perhaps ten plaques to outstanding chapters." Commemorative plaques had been mentioned during the discussion with Claire, possibly without reference to a specific number of chapters.

Richard Claire died prior to the next annual meeting. During the fraternal year 1969-70, however, an agreement was reached with the Arthur Anderson Foundation for an annual grant of $2,000. At the 1970 meeting policies were developed for an awards program limited to FVPs, and the first recipients were chosen, inclusive of two future councilors.

Initiation of the award in 1970

The agreement with the foundation specified only that the annual grant

would be distributed at Council discretion to faculty vice-presidents who had provided outstanding service to Beta Alpha Psi and excellently promoted the accounting profession among students. At the 1970 meeting it was decided that the award should be conferred upon present (either retiring or continuing) faculty advisors based on (a) length of service, (b) performance of chapters served for two or more years, and, secondarily, (c) community service. Although a concern was expressed that some means should be found to honor former FVPs who had made outstanding contributions, a consensus developed that the fraternity's objectives could best be served by limiting the award to current advisors.

After agreeing on basic policy, the Council selected the first year's winners of the $500 "Richard S. Claire Award," perhaps only ratifying a decision already reached informally. On President Donley's nomination, the professors honored were Thomas Burns of Omicron, Robert Maust of Alpha Psi at West Virginia, Lowell Dodds of Beta Eta at San Diego State, and William Grasty, of Gamma Lambda at Virginia Tech (who was moving to another school). No reference was made to an independent nominating committee, and indeed it was agreed that "all decisions as to who should receive the awards would be kept in the hands of the National Council."

At the closing business session in 1970, the Council reviewed the policy that had been adopted on the FVP award with Arthur Andersen representatives Claude Rodgers and Ray Terrell, both of whom endorsed it. They requested that Secretary-Treasurer Bob Wasley contact the home chapters of the four designated recipients to arrange for presentation of the cash awards at a Beta Alpha Psi meeting on campus. Since Professor Grasty was relocating to Murray State in Kentucky, future National Advisory Forum member Rodgers indicated that the foundation would defray the expense for him to return

to Virginia to receive the award.

Bob Maust recalls that individualized commemorative plaques were presented to him and the other winners (or, in one case, a stand-in) during the 1970 National Chapter banquet, implying that for practical purposes the recipients had been identified prior to the August meeting. Lowell Dodds was represented in absentia by his San Diego State colleague Wallace Harned. The $500 checks, along with an additional plaque, were presented on the respective campuses by local-area Arthur Andersen partners.

Maust's two FVP plaques are shown as exhibit 23. Five National Council plaques were conferred at the annual banquet of 1971, although two more had to be placed on order after it was decided to honor seven professors that year. As a variation, at the symbolic level, Arthur Andersen representatives awarded medallions embedded in lucite at the chapter ceremonies of 1971-72.

The four men honored in the first year of the award presented chapter records ranging, from a competitive viewpoint, from good to excellent. One of them had in addition already made significant contributions to Beta Alpha Psi from regional and national standpoints.

Prior fraternal records and achievements of charter recipients, especially Tom Burns

As of 1970, Burns had been a faculty advisor for four years, Grasty and Maust since 1967, and Dodds for two years. Until it had elected not to compete in 1969-70, Tom Burns' Omicron Chapter had ranked from 11th to 13th in the annual competition, over a period in which at least 13 chapters were given special recognition (receiving $50 cash prizes). Under alumnus Bob Maust's leadership, Alpha Psi had finished number 1 the first year, and

EXHIBIT 23

NATIONAL COUNCIL AND ARTHUR ANDERSON PLAQUES PRESENTED TO CHARTER OUTSTANDING FVP ROBERT MAUST

Photographs supplied by Professor Robert S. Maust of Alpha Psi at West Virginia.

among the top ten chapters thereafter. William Grasty's Gamma Lambda unit, founded in the spring of 1967, had in its first three years placed 23th, 8th, and 3rd, respectively. Finally, Lowell Dodd had helped Beta Eta finish in 8th place, nationally, in 1969-70.

In summary, the initial selections for the Claire award suggested that the National Council was not looking simply at chapter standings, but that a highly respectable record in that area would normally be expected. Not addressed in 1970 was the bearing on the award process of the new option, exercised at Ohio State, of nonparticipation in the activity program.

The most visible record of contribution to the fraternity and to accounting education belonged to Thomas Burns. His leadership role at the 1969 workshop, and related survey of chapter activities, have already been noted. Over the last two years of the fourth era, the Omicron advisor had also initiated the Beta Alpha Psi "student seminar," and prepared an excellent pamphlet on doctoral education in accounting. The latter project was completed in 1970 under partial funding by the Council, which arranged for distribution of the publication to all chapters. In 1981 the fraternity would publish a revised version of the pamphlet, Academic Careers in Accounting, reprinted (in slightly updated form) three years later.

On May 10, 1969, Burns' Ohio State chapter had hosted a "student seminar" concerning lease and pension contract proposals made in the 1966 American Accounting Association monograph, A Statement of Basic Accounting Theory. The original plan was to invite student delegates from the eight other chapters located in Ohio, and from the other "Big Ten" universities (probably excluding Purdue, which did not as yet have a fraternal chapter). Perhaps because the chapters at Northwestern, Indiana, Kent State, and Akron appointed no representatives, students attended also from several

other chapters in the region--those at Lehigh, Loyola of Chicago, Southern Illinois (two delegates), Detroit, and DePaul. Of the twenty student members present, including three from Ohio State, only Elaine Theus from Pi at Case Western Reserve was female. The 1969 gathering commenced a tradition that, largely through continuing leadership by Omicron Chapter, would become a nationwide function.

The Richard S. Claire award was likewise destined to become a fixture within the fraternity. The Arthur Andersen initiative marked the beginning of a wave of professional institutional support that would make possible many of the programs undertaken by the National Council during the 1970s. It is of equal interest as an indicator of future Beta Alpha Psi leaders beyond the chapter level.

The Claire award through 1984--
An index of leadership talent

Through 1984, 72 faculty vice-presidents had been honored, in numbers ranging from two in 1972-73 to seven in both 1970-71 and 1983-84. Eighteen of the 50 chapters represented had provided more than one winner of the award, including Gamma Lambda at Virginia Tech with four recipients, and Alpha Psi at West Virginia and Delta Beta at California State, Fullerton, with three each.

Six of the eight professors appointed to the National Council, at (in current terms) the "board-of-directors" level, from 1976 through 1984 had earlier received the Claire award. They were Joyce C. Dean, Jack E. Kiger (honored under unusual circumstances, as related in a later chapter), Henry R. Anderson, David E. Tinius, Richard J. Murdock, and Jan R. Williams. Six of the nine "area" councilors through 1984, besides Murdock, had likewise been so honored. Julius A. Roller of Delta at Washington is a unique case

RICHARD S. CLAIRE
(along with strands of his wife's hair)

DELEGATES TO FIRST OMICRON STUDENT SEMINAR, 1969*
*One additional student attended the seminar.

in having been selected as an outstanding faculty vice-president, in 1971, after his retirement from the Council.

As of 1984 the Richard S. Claire Award included $1,000 in cash, presented by the sponsoring Arthur Andersen Foundation, and separate plaques from the sponsor and the fraternity. Faculty vice-presidents who had led their chapters to (a) "position[s] of excellence" in the activity program and (b) active participation in several of the fraternity's regional and national activites, and had otherwise (c) emphasized the importance of Beta Alpha Psi at campus, community, and professional levels, were eligible for consideration. Nominations from the five area councilors had been solicited in the course of making the 1984 selections.[10]

The final area of fourth-era reform discussed in this chapter represents the "symbolic" realm. The most important policy development in that area was the approval in 1968 of a substantial simiplification, and demystification of the fraternal initiation ritual. A relatively minor revision made

---

[10] [Henry R. Anderson], "Omicron Chapter Hosts Seventh National Student Seminar," Newsletter 17 (Winter 1979):1; [Thomas J. Burns], Ohio State Ph.D. Program (as cited in chapter 6, note 5), p. 10; Burns to Author, interview, May 3, 1980; Burns, for National Council of Beta Alpha Psi, Twenty Questions and Some Answers about Academic Careers in Accounting ([National Council, 1984]); Hollis A. Dixon, Secretary-Treasurer's Report, 1976-72, p. 1; Robert S. Maust to Author, by telephone, February 10, 1986; [Richard W. Metcalf], "Outstanding Faculty Vice President Award," 1983-84 Annual Report, ed. [Metcalf], p. 2; [Fred W. Mueller], "National Advisory Forum," 1976-77 Annual Report, ed. [Mueller], p. 4; National Council Minutes, 1968, pp. 2-3, 1969, pp. 6-7, 8 (quoted), 1970, pp. 2-4, 7, 13-15; "Prior Recipients of Outstanding Faculty Vice Presidents' Awards," 1983-84 Annual Report, ed. [Metcalf], p. 39; [Harold E. Royer], "Arthur Andersen & Co. Foundation Sponsors Richard S. Claire Awards," Newsletter 9 (Spring 1971):6; [Royer], same title expanded, Newsletter 10 (Fall 1971):1; [Royer], "Arthur Andersen Foundation Awards to Outstanding Faculty Vice Presidents," Newsletter 9 (Winter 1971):1 (with separately captioned photo); Smith, Forty Acres, pp. 133-34 (quoted), 134n; "Student Delegates to Beta Alpha Psi Seminar at Ohio State University . . ." (photograph), Newsletter 8 (Fall 1969):7; [Charles W. Taylor], "Chapter News," Newsletter 8 (Winter 1969):6; and Taylor to Richard S. Claire, June 3, 1969 (Golden Anniversary Files).

at the beginning of the fourth era had been insufficient to prevent increasing criticism that much of the ritual was archaic.

Basic Revision of the Initiation Ritual, 1968

The Prior Ritual

A modest revision, credited to Williard Stone, 1961

As noted in chapter 8, Councilors C. C. Staehling and S. M. Wedeberg had revised the ritual somewhat in the early fifties. At the 1960 meeting, retiring councilor Williard Stone agreed to review the initiation ceremony over the following year, for purposes of recommending new changes. His report in 1961, which may have embodied contributions by other advisory committee members Bill Jencks and Nolan Williams as well, led to the approval of several changes that year, incorporating certain suggestions generated during the Council meeting itself.

The 1961 formulation of the ritual is the earliest one available, and there is no direct record of the changes that it reflected. Three visitation reports from the late 1950s shed light on the matter, however. Two of them recorded Stone's approval of local modifications of the ritual that he had observed on visits to Tau at Maryland and Xi at Syracuse.

It is apparent that until 1961 the ceremony required the candidates to be led out of the room, midway, to remove their blindfolds. President Jencks had criticized Rho Chapter at Minnesota for having omitted this feature at a 1958 initiation in favor of having the initiates "just remove the blindfolds" where they were standing. Jencks felt that "quite a bit was lost," perhaps the major point of the blindfolding, by this simplification.

Past President Stone had a very different reaction, however, to a similar modification observed at Syracuse late in 1959. The Xi candidates had remained standing throughout the blindfold component of the ceremony, and

then been seated. Stone felt that "[t]he absence of the somewhat awkward shuffling and shuffling noises which accompany being blindly led out of the room [had] added much to the simplicity and dignity of the ceremony." He commented that he would favor altering the ritual accordingly. Having the opportunity less than two years later to develop a revision of the ceremony, it is clear that he recommended just such a change, and that it was approved.

In the spring of 1959, President Stone had attended a visitation at Maryland. In his report, he noted most approvingly that Tau's president had closed the ceremony by greeting each new member by name, awarding his or her Beta Alpha Psi key, and shaking the new member's hand. He commended this innovation for making the initiation "much more impressive and personal" to the initiates, adding that personal awarding of keys (and certificates, if available) "should be a part of every initiation." Once again, Williard Stone would later seize the opportunity to amend the ritual based on an approved local practice.

Another point merits passing reference. Specifications sent to Leon Hay prior to the installation of Beta Alpha at Indiana in 1957 stated that student candidates should be advised in advance of six '"Key Words"' on which they might be asked to comment "at the initiation." These words, actually phrases, were the titles of the basic principles of conduct identified in the fraternal code of ethics presented to the new members directly after the formal ceremony. It was presumably within that context that any recitation might occur. The revised instructions of 1961 mentioned possible oral or written examination on ethical standards following the "pledging" of students, although it appears that the six fundamental principles remained subject to brief coverage at the subsequent initiation.

These changes, and any others that may have been made, still left a

ceremony that could at the time have been considered either quaint or archaic, as the following summary indicates.

The ritual of 1967-68

In preparation for the regular initiation ceremony still followed in 1967-68, the pledges were lined up alphabetically by name, to facilitate the distribution of fraternal insignia, and blindfolded. They were then marshalled into a room illuminated by candlelight (and, perhaps initially, electric lights as well) in which chapter officers and members had already assembled, and congregated in a semicircle around the officers. As explained by A. J. Penz, the blindfolding was intended to shield the students from all distractions, so that they might concentrate fully on the spoken ritual.

The chapter president began the initiation by making a statement to the candidates concerning fraternal standards and objectives, after which the treasurer secured their formal assent to those principles. The president then introduced the vice-president to explain in detail the personal attributes required of accountants. More than a single-spaced page was recited of analogy with balance sheet accounts. For example, "Capacity" and the temporary foibles of "Youth" were current assets and liabilities, respectively; "Character" constituted fixed assets; and there were no fixed liabilities. After summary reference was made to the "candidates' personal balance sheets," the president followed with a brief homily on the further development of Character and Capacity and "extinguish[ment]" of any personal liabilities.

At that point, electric lights (if used) were shut off, and the students removed their blindfolds. The president presented several paragraphs recommending that they cultivate "scholarship, morality, and congeniality," and

then asked the treasurer to administer the oath. After the candidates had in unison repeated their commitments, in a series of segments, the president extended congratulations, and promised to be the first person to grip the hand of each new member after the secretary had explained the symbolism of the fraternal badge and motto. The secretary duly referred to the "rising sun" and "crossed keys," and the derivation of the fraternal name from Greek terms broadly translated as "Scholarship, Sociability, and Practicality" (emphasis deleted).

Finally, the president called each new member forward, presented the key or pin and (if available) certificate,[11] and offered "the hearty handclasp of brotherhood." Each initiate was then greeted by the other chapter

---

[11] During at least the tenure of 1967-69 secretary-treasurer Harvey Donley, the National Council did not send membership certificates to chapters prior to initiation ceremonies. This practice was based on a broader policy (continued by Bob Wasley) of not crediting chapters with new members until all reporting and payment requirements had been satisfied; and, historically, in an official policy governing student initiates that had been published in 1936. In the latter regard, Secretary-Treasurer S. M. Wedeberg had observed in 1953 that the fraternity was pleased to honor advance orders, nonetheless, except for chapters that were habitually delinquent in accounting for initiations. A Newsletter notice of Fall 1970 indicates that by then certificates were once again routinely supplied in advance, based on three weeks' notice.

Donley made an exception to his certificate policy for the 1968-69 honorary induction, by Beta Theta at Penn State, of Comptroller General Elmer B. Staats, the head of the General Accounting Office. Ironically, the initiation of the U.S. official was not reported or paid for at the time, and hence was not recorded until the following year. Staats' address to the chapter was published in the national periodical. "Attention Chapter Officers," Newsletter [3] (May 1952):16-17; [Harvey E. Donley], Secretary-Treasurer's Report, 1968-69, p. 6; [W. B. Karrenbrock], "Instructions for New Officers," Newsletter [2] (October 1936):3; [Harold L. Royer], "Membership Certificates for Initiations," Newsletter 9 (Fall 1970):6; [Elmer B. Staats], "Comptroller-General of the United States Elmer B. Staats -- On Management Accounting," Newsletter 8 (Winter 1970):1, 4-6, 10-12; [Robert S. Wasley], Secretary-Treasurer's Report, 1969-70, p. 5; and S. M. Wedeberg to W. B. Jencks, January 3, 1953 (Policies File).

officers and all active members present.[12]

Although only scattered evidence is available, local criticism of the traditional ritual aparently mounted as the fourth era progressed, despite the refinements of 1961. The National Council appointed its incoming member of 1967 to form a committee to develop a fundamental revision, and a new ritual, destined largely to withstand prominent criticism in the seventies, was duly approved a year later.

Criticism of the Ceremony, Leading to Simplification and Demystification by the Taylor Committee

Evidence of dissatisfaction

Chapter visitation would have been the leading indicator of local sentiment concerning the initiation ceremony. Unfortunately, fourth-era visitation reports are available only from the falls of 1960 and (restricted to Herbert Miller) 1963, and for the period 1966-68. During the five years following the revision attributed mainly to Williard Stone, no reference to criticism of the ritual appeared in the annual minutes. They do record that in 1964 President Emerson Henke had presented a Theta chapter proposal, not adopted, that activity-program credit be eliminated for officer memorization of the unblindfolded part of the text.

---

[12] Beta Alpha Psi, The National Accounting Fraternity, The Principles of Professional and Personal Conduct, rev. 1954, pp. [3-4]; [Grand or National Council of Beta Alpha Psi], "Beta Alpha Psi: Instructions to the Candidate," [c1961-67], one-page typescript on "Keywords"; [Grand Council], "Procedures for Pledging, Initiation, and Election and Installation of Officers," rev. 1961, pp. 1-6 (officer section absent from copy), quoted except for p. 2; Grand Council Minutes Book, 1960, p. 3, 1961, p. 2; [National Council], "Procedures for Pledging and Initiation: Beta Alpha Psi," "rev." 1967 (no change noted from 1961 version); A. J. Penz to Author, interview, April 18, 1980; W. E. Stone, Visitation Reports--Xi, November 12, 1959, Tau, April 30, 1959 (letter formats), both quoted; Nolan E. Williams to Leon E. Hay, November 27, 1957; and [Williams], "Procedure for Installation of Beta Alpha Chapter of Beta Alpha Psi at Indiana University, December 5, 1957," [1957], pp. 2, 3 (quoted).

More to the point, Harvey Donley was asked during a visit to Gamma Beta at South Carolina in the spring of 1967 why blindfolding was still used. Although his response is not recorded, the visitation officer observed in his report that the chapter had raised, "perhaps[,] . . . a good question." As an indication that there existed more than isolated criticism of the ritual, Donley noted a year later after a visit to DePaul that Beta Gamma had been "one of the few chapters" in his experience to express general support for the current version, including the analogical section on assets and liabilities.

By the spring of 1968, however, revision was already well underway, a development that had "delighted" Pi Chapter at Case Western Reserve and pleased Beta Psi officers at Loyola of Chicago, although neither group had made specific recommendations.

The thrust of most of the criticism received had no doubt been captured in the 1967 minutes, reporting that President Wilton Anderson had appointed incoming councilor Charles Taylor

> to chair a committee to prepare a draft of an initiation ritual designed to meet the objections of those who consider the present ritual as _archaic_ and somewhat _juvenile_, yet preserve and emphasize the dignity and traditions of the ceremony [emphasis added].

Taylor had been authorized to appoint from two to four faculty vice-presidents to assist him in the project, and to conduct one or more meetings, as needed, at fraternal expense. A secondary assignment of the committee would yield the condensation made in 1968, as discussed in volume 1, of _The Principles of Professional and Personal Conduct_, the fraternal code of ethics.

Three FVPs served on Taylor's committee: James A. Gunn, Jr. of Chi at Oklahoma State, James W. Deskins of Theta at Texas, and Hollis Dixon of Beta Omicron at Arizona. Gunn and Dixon had recently earned doctorates from

Arkansas, and Deskins was a 1965 product of the doctoral program at Texas, where Taylor remained in candidacy. Presumably meeting only once, in late February, at a cost of $528, the committee produced a proposed revision for distribution to the five other councilors by July 1, 1968. At the August meeting, final action was taken to produce a briefer, simpler, and perhaps more dignified initiation ritual, stripped of much of the ornateness and mystery of the past.

A fundamentally revised ritual

The general approach taken was to simplify the ceremony by eliminating verbose, outdated, and/or pretentious elements. Blindfolding was eliminated, subject to the provision that lighting should be "subdued" throughout. After the president listed the purposes of the fraternity and urged the pledges to participate in activities, and accept a responsible place in Beta Alpha Psi and thence the accounting profession, the treasurer elicited an affirmation of the purposes and responsibilities.

The vice-president then gave a one-paragraph statement of the personal and professional qualities required of accountants, absent the "balance sheet" format, and the president followed with a brief commendation of (a) intellectual curiosity, (b) high professional responsibility, and (c) tolerance of others. At this point, the treasurer administered the oath. Finally, the secretary explained the emblem, much as before; the president welcomed the new members to the fraternity, as a group; and the officers and other members present greeted their new associates. No reference was made in the printed ritual to the presentation of jewelry or certificates, or to a fraternal handshake.

The Taylor committee had very ably discharged its assigned responsibility, as quoted above. Yet even the modernized ritual would draw

criticism from significant sources.

Survival of prominent criticism in the '70s

In 1970 Herb Miller left Michigan State to become a partner with Arthur Andersen & Co., at the international headquarters in Chicago. In an interview provided ten years later, he referred to attending a Gamma Chapter initiation shortly thereafter. The Northwestern unit assumed inactive status in the fall of 1970, however, after having apparently met only once the preceding year, to hold an initiation that would not be properly accounted for. The ceremony mentioned by Miller was probably conducted, then, in May 1973, when Gamma was reactivated. By then undergraduate business studies had been terminated at Evanston, so that the revived fraternal chapter was strictly a graduate-level organization.

Miller found that many of the Northwestern students considered the initiation ritual to be "kindergarten" or "adolescent" in character, despite the basic revision made in 1968. He promptly telephoned a councilor to suggest that further change in the ceremony would be necessary if the fraternity Psi were to retain chapters, within major universities, catering to advanced students.

In the fall of 1973, the Arthur Andersen partner participated in a special Beta Alpha Psi committee meeting held in Chicago, along with Bob Maust (chairman), Tom Burns, and two other individuals. Miller was once again critical of the ritual, and the committee overall felt that it should be made "more meaningful." The group even objected to the use of the word "fraternity," which was considered "demeaning to students." It should be borne in mind that the "social" organizations especially identified with the term were none too popular on many campuses in the late '60s and early '70s.

The word "fraternity" was of course retained. By the year 1977-78, at least, the ritual would embody a slightly different structure, but reflect no basic change. The explanation of the emblem and the formal assent to fraternal purposes and responsibilities had been repositioned to precede, directly, the administration of the oath. Terminologically, "professionalism" had been substituted for "practicality." Taking part in the installation of Zeta Alpha at Purdue in the spring, Tom Burns found that the printed ritual in use during the year 1979-80 had omitted a line of text.[13]

In Transition

The final realm of fourth-era reform to be covered concerns a major theme of the preceding period--expansion of the Beta Alpha Psi roster. Although less dramatic than developments of the late sixties within the activity and initiation fields, significant changes in policy emerged, gradually, in this area as new chapter formation kept pace with the prior decade, leading up to a well-planned golden anniversary celebration in 1969.

---

[13] Beta Alpha Psi, The National Accounting Fraternity, Initiation Ritual for Student, Faculty, and Honorary Members, rev. 1968, quoting p. 1 (of 2); Beta Alpha Psi, "New Member Initiation," New Member Initiation [and] Officers' Election and Installation, rev. [1977-78], pp. 1-[5]; Hollis A. Dixon, Secretary-Treasurer's Report, 1972-73, p. 9; H. E. Donley, Visitation Reports--Pi, April 15, 1968 (quoted), Beta Gamma, May 17, 1968 (quoted), Beta Iota, May 17, 1968, Gamma Beta, April 27, 1967 (quoted); Grand Council Minutes Book, 1962-63; National Council Minutes, 1964-66 (especially 1964, p. 5), 1967, p. 3 (quoted), 1968, p. 7, 1973, pp. 3-4, (no. 5.0), February 1974, p. 2, (no. 3.8, quoted), February 1977, p. 3 (quoted); Hasselback, 1984 Directory, individual listing, s.v. "Dixon, Hollis A.," "Gunn Jr., James A.," "Deskins, James W.," "Taylor, Charles Wallace"; Herbert E. Miller to Author, interview, April 18, 1980, quoted; Michael W. Sedlak and Harold E. Williamson, The Evolution of Management Education: A History of the Northwestern University J. L. Kellogg Graduate School of Management, 1908-1983 (Urbana: University of Illinois Press, 1983), p. 119, Sheldahl, Alpha to Omega, pp. 398-99; Charles W. Taylor to A. J. Penz, January 26, 1968; [Vern H. Vincent], Secretary's Report, 1963-64, p. 1; Robert S. Wasley (name omitted from first report), Secretary-Treasurer's Report, 1969-70, pp. 5-6, 1970-71, pp. 1, 7; and Who's Who in America 43 (1984-85), s.v. "Miller, Herbert Elmer." Also, Thomas J. Burns to Author, May 3, 1980.

CHAPTER 11

A MORE ACTIVE POLICY OF ROSTER DEVELOPMENT IN A DECADE OF THIRTY INSTALLATIONS, CAPPED BY THE GOLDEN ANNIVERSARY OBSERVANCE OF 1969

The Postwar Expansionist Era was so named, in part, because the chapter roster had been significantly expanded, from several standpoints, during the period. Yet the Grand Council had played a rather "passive" role in the development of new chapters. Through the activity program and, in particular, extensive visitation, the Council had started by the close of the era to take more responsibility for the nurturing of new units.

That trend would continue during the fourth era, while the Grand or National Council assumed a more "active" part in the process leading up to Chapter formation itself. Revealing several interesting patterns, an overview of the thirty chapters created during the sixties provides a useful backdrop for interpreting policy developments at three stages. Just before the final installation, the fraternity paused in 1969, following three years of preparation, to observe its fiftieth birthday.

Expansion, from Beta Iota to Gamma Omicron

Not counting the reinstatement of Epsilon at Oregon State in 1959, the same number of chapters were admitted to the fraternity during the ten academic years 1960-70 as over the fifteen years 1945-60, namely, thirty. Since, however, no installations had been made before December 1948, the proper comparison is between 12 years and 10. In addition, earlier expansion had been impeded somewhat by the AAcCSB accreditation "moratorium" of 1950-53.

The thirty chapters formed from the fall of 1960 through the spring of 1970 are shown, by academic year, in exhibit 24. Without classifying sites in the detail provided in chapter 2, several summary observations are useful. First, there was a strong preponderance of "public" institutions over "private" ones. The latter category included only four denominational institutions and four nonsectarian universities. Loyola of Chicago, Notre Dame, Texas Christian, and Brigham Young represented the Roman Catholic, Disciples of Christ, and Mormon religious traditions. Tulane, Miami of Florida, Drake (historically linked to the Disciples), and Northeastern were also added to the Beta Alpha Psi fold. Like third-era expansion site Cincinnati, Northeastern was noted for a "cooperative" education program by which students interspersed classroom work with gainful employment.[1]

Second, new entrants included the Universities of South Carolina, California at Los Angeles (UCLA), Georgia, Missouri, and Arizona; and three land-grant schools besides the last three locations, namely, Mississippi State, Florida State, and Virginia Polytechnic Institute (Virginia Tech).

Third, following San Diego State from the spring of 1960, five members of the large system (tuition-free for state residents) eventually known as California State University were chartered. They were identified at the time

---

[1]A 1968 visit to Cincinnati made Secretary-Treasurer Leon Hay aware of an officership dilemma faced by Alpha Sigma at Cincinnati. The two distinct groups of "coop" students (not inclusive of all accounting majors) would each alternate classroom study and employment over four ten-week terms, so that each class would be away while the other one was on campus. Alpha Sigma elected a single set of officers annually, raising the possibility that "key officers" might be gone "ten weeks out of the middle of the chapter year."

Neither Hay nor the faculty advisor at Cincinnati was enthusiastic, however, about the plan proposed at Northeastern to elect two separate slates of officers. The secretary-treasurer suggested that in light also of incresing adoption of quarter and trimester systems, it was time to "re-examine the concept of a nine-month school year" that was "implicit" in activity program instructions. Leon E. Hay, Visitation Report--Alpha Sigma, April 19, 1968, quoted.

EXHIBIT 24

CHAPTERS INSTALLED DURING FOURTH ERA

1960-61

1. Beta Iota, Loyola (Chicago)
2. Beta Kappa, Mississippi State
3. Beta Lambda, Los Angeles State[a]
4. Beta Mu, Georgia State
5. Beta Nu, Tulane

1961-62

6. Beta Xi, University of Miami
7. Beta Omicron, Arizona
8. Beta Pi, North Texas State

1962-63

9. Beta Rho, Florida State
10. Beta Sigma, Notre Dame
11. Beta Tau, Arizona State

1963-64

12. Beta Upsilon, Georgia
13. Beta Phi, Sacramento State[a]
14. Beta Chi, San Francisco State

1964-65

15. Beta Psi, Kent State
16. Beta Omega, Texas Christian
17. Gamma Alpha, Brigham Young
18. Gamma Beta, South Carolina

1965-66

19. Gamma Delta, Houston
20. Gamma Epsilon, Toledo

1966-67

21. Gamma Zeta, Southern Illinois (Carbondale)
22. Gamma Eta, Akron
23. Gamma Theta, Missouri
24. Gamma Iota, UCLA
25. Gamma Kappa, Municipal University of Omaha[a]
26. Gamma Lambda, Virqinia Polytechnic Institute

1967-68

27. Gamma Mu, Drake
28. Gamma Nu, Northeastern

1968-69

29. Gamma Xi, San Jose State

1969-70

30. Gamma Omicron, Fresno State.[a]

SOURCES: Secretaries' or Secretary-Treasurers' Reports, 1960-61 through 1969-70.

[a]Present-day institutional names are indicated in the text.

as Los Angeles, Sacramento, San Francisco, San Jose, and Fresno State Colleges. Along with San Diego State, these schools obtained "university" status in the following decade. Three years after the 1961 installation, the first campus was renamed California State, Los Angeles, and the Sacramento and Fresno sites would later be similarly redesignated.

Fourth, Toledo, Akron, and Nebraska at Omaha formed chapters while they were city-supported institutions, known in the last case as the Municipal University of Omaha. Each school was reconstituted as a regional state university within less than two years. Nebraska at Omaha thereby became the first "branch" university to appear within the Beta Alpha Psi roster, ironically preceding the main campus at Lincoln by several years.

Fifth, several other "regional" or "emerging" state universities were chartered, representing sharply different levels of development. They included Georgia State, Arizona State, North Texas State, Southern Illinois, Kent State, and Houston, a private institution until 1963. The respective sites of Beta Mu and Beta Tau provide an interesting contrast. At the time of the installation in 1961, Georgia State enrolled only 3,126 students as it was about to shed its narrow identity as Georgia State College of Business Administration, its fourth distinctly different identification in less than fifty years of existence. Former teachers' college Arizona State, however, had grown from fewer than 4,000 students in 1954 to 13,300 by the time it became a chapter site nine years later.

Sixth, a number of major metropolitan areas were represented, including Chicago, Los Angeles, Houston, San Francisco, New Orleans, and (by way of the Tempe suburb) Phoenix. Miami (through Coral Gables), Omaha, and Akron, having city populations in 1960 of approximately 290 or 300 thousand, were also included. The most remarkable growth locations were in Arizona, where

during the fifties Phoenix and Tucson had respectively quadrupled in size, to some 439,000 and 212,000 people.

Seventh, an interesting geographical pattern emerged. Only two schools from the northeast or (inclusive of Virginia) middle Atlantic area were chartered--Northeastern and Virginia Tech. Based on the conventions adopted in chapter 2, the other three regions were divided very evenly: western, 9; southern or border, 10; and central, 9. Different classifications of the three chapters each from Texas (south) and Ohio (central) would have shifted the proportions materially.

The cumulative result of fourth-era additions (aside from Fresno State) was shown in the fiftieth-anniversary map that appeared in the commemorative *Newsletter* of 1969. Prepared at the suggestion of Past President Leon Hay, and apparently designed by the Arthur Andersen Foundation graphics department, the map is reprinted as exhibit 25. A line drawn across the United States, longitudinally, at the Minnesota-Iowa boundary reveals very few chapters--east, central, or west--to the north. New England was represented only by the recently installed Gamma Nu at Northwestern, and aside from New York City the state of New York had only Xi Chapter at Syracuse. The most densely populated area, fraternally, included Illinois, Indiana, Ohio (with nine chapters), and neighboring areas in Wisconsin, Michigan, Pennsylvania, and West Virginia. Fifteen states, in addition to Alaska and Hawaii, had no Beta Alpha Psi chapters. Except for Texas and California, with seven units each, only ten chapters were located west of Omaha.

Eighth, the expansion of the fourth era (assisted after 1964 by the admission of women members, finally, at Washington, New York, Wisconsin, and Pennsylvania) enabled the fraternity to post large membership increases. The downward trend of the late fifties was only superficially reversed in

EXHIBIT

GOLDEN ANNIVERSARY MAF

Beta

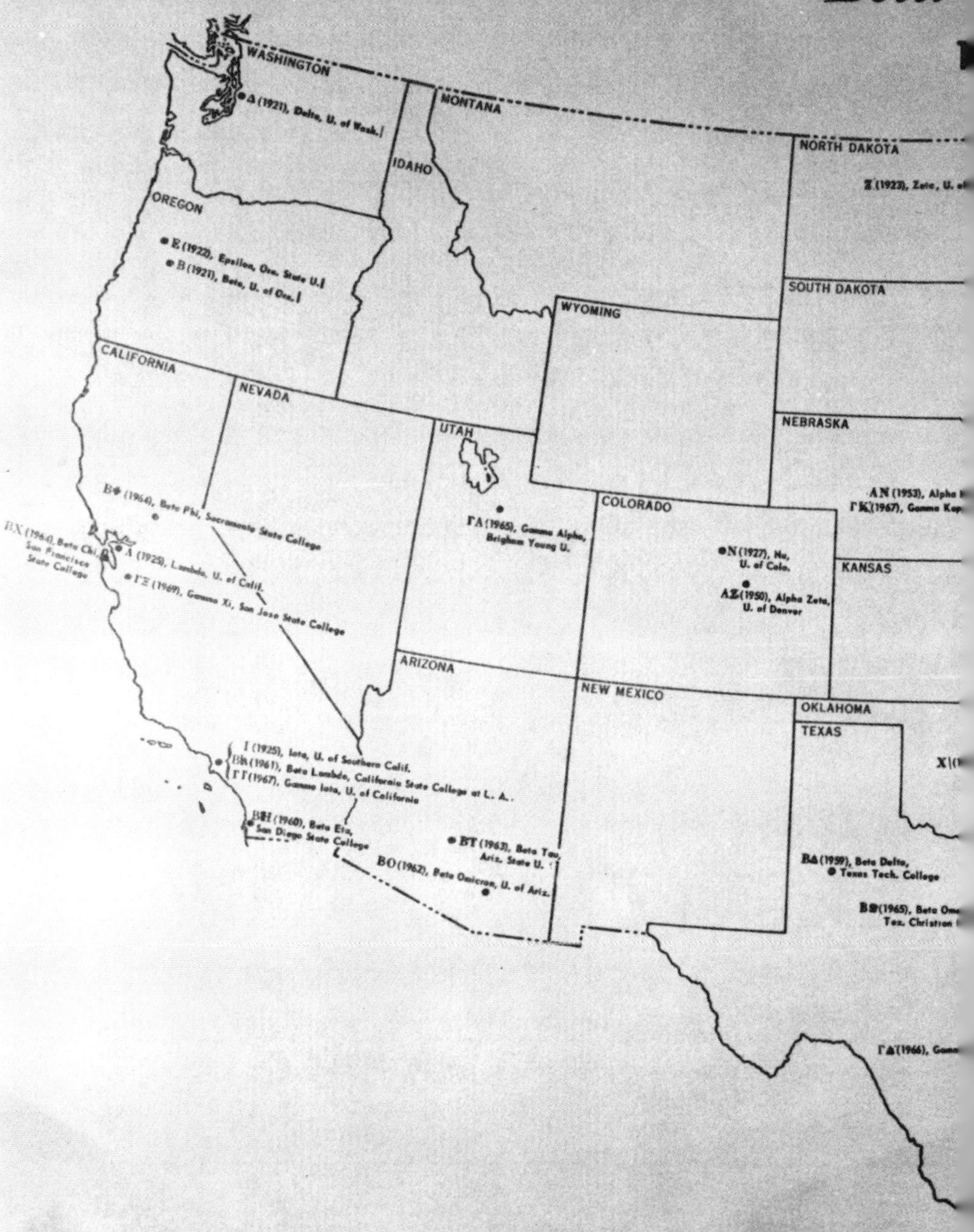

OF THE CHAPTER ROSTER

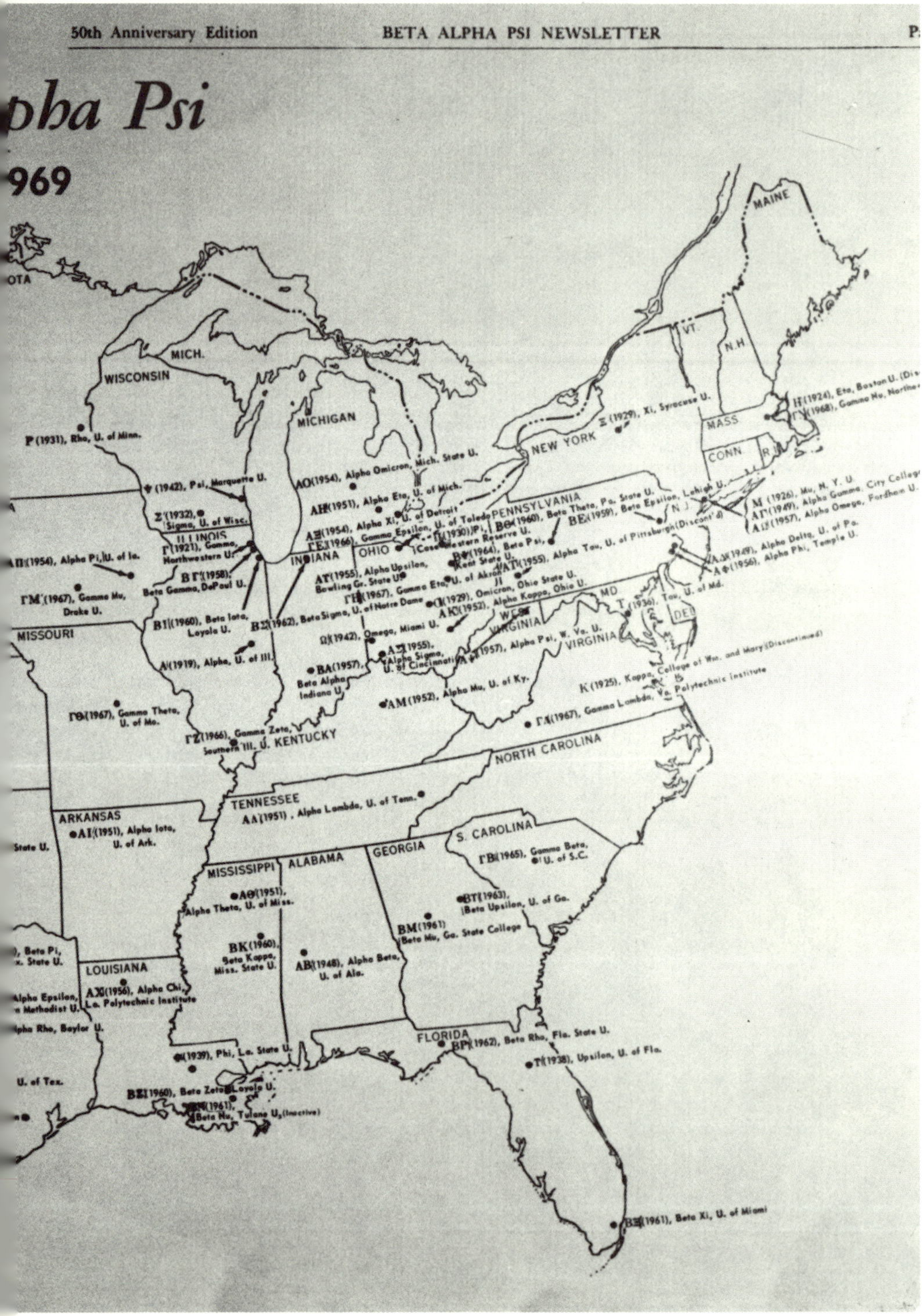

the year 1960-61, when the number of students initiated rose by 77, to 1,196, only because the five new chapters inducted 122 active members. Two years later, however, 1,631 students entered Beta Alpha Psi; the total ranged from 1,794 to 1,873 during the three years 1963-66; and from 2,153 to 2,384 students were admitted annually over the period 1966-70, disregarding the immaterial effect of deferring recognition in the case of initiations not properly accounted for.

The only significant decrease was recorded in 1969-70, when there was a decline in new membership of 180 despite the induction of 54 students by newly installed Gamma Omicron at Fresno State. The first "draft lottery" of the Vietnam War period was conducted on December 1, 1969, marking the end of undergraduate student deferments. Throughout the fourth era, the initiation fee remained at $7.50, but a rise to $10.00 was approved in 1970, effective the following January.

Finally, there was a marked slowdown in roster expansion during the last three years of the decade. Following seven years in which, with one exception, from three to six chapters had been formed annually, only four new units were organized during the period 1967-70. It is probably only coincidental that the charter fee was doubled, to $100, in 1967. As the era ended, however, the national Council tentatively accepted petitions arriving from Rhode Island and Northern Illinois, pending favorable visitations under a newly approved program cited below.[2]

---

[2]"Accredited Colleges and Universities," Information Please Almanac, 1955, p. 257; Barron's Profiles, s.v. "California: California State University" (general description); Brunner, Land-Grant Colleges, pp. 75-78; "Cities Growth and Decline," World Almanac, 1985, p. 252; "Education: American Colleges and Universities," The World Almanac and Book of Facts, 1962, 1964, 77th, 79th eds. (New York: World-Telegram and The Sun, 1962, 1964), 77th ed., p. 517, 79th ed., pp. 513, 525; exhibits 25, 26; Funk & Wagnalls 21, s.v. "Selective Service System," quoted; [Leon E. Hay], Secretary-Treasurer'

The temporarily slow growth reflected, in part, a more critical and deliberative approach to charter approval that represented the middle link within a more active Council policy toward chapter development. The other components were the assumption of some initiative in the genesis of interest in charter acquisition, and (dating from the late fifties) prompt visitation of new units in a day in which a modernized conception of that practice had emerged. Through the involvement of another academic organization, the first stage of the process was related to a broader interprofessional effort of the day that yielded little return at the time.

Initial Generation of Interest: Contacting Accredited Business Schools (a Basis for an Interprofessional Digression)

Traditional "Passive" Approach

As related in chapter 2, throughout the third era the Grand Council had studiously left the full initiative, in the process leading to chapter establishment, with local groups of accounting professors and students. Methodical effort of any kind to generate interest in forming a Beta Alpha Psi chapter would have seemed professionally unethical to councilors of the time, smacking of solicitation. Just after sending a 1952 Newsletter to the deans at schools recognized by the American Association of Collegiate Schools

---

Report, 1966-67, p. 2; Lovejoy, Lovejoy's College Guide, s.v. "California--California State Universities and Colleges, The: California State University, Fresno; . . ., Los Angeles; . . ., Sacramento; San Diego State University; San Francisco State University," "Florida: Miami, University of," "Georgia: Georgia State University," "Iowa: Drake University," "Louisiana: Tulane University," "Massachusetts: Northeastern University," "Nebraska: Nebraska, University of, at Omaha," "Ohio: Akron, University of; Toledo, University of," "Texas: Texas Christian University"; National Council Minutes, 1967, pp. 6-7, 1970, pp. 9-10; Secretaries' or Secretary-Treasurers' Reports, 1960-61 through 1969-70, new active or student membership totals ("Analysis of Membership Changes"); and L. L. Vance, ed., "News Notes," The Accounting Review 38 (October 1963):875, 39 (July 1964):811, indicating renaming of Los Angeles State College.

of Business, ironically, S. M. Wedeberg had noticed a 1930 Council resolution opposing the "circularization of material" to promote chapter formation.

As a supporting point, also noted earlier, it was felt that chapters formed without any outside promotion would ordinarily be the work of highly motivated students and faculty members providing a strong base for successful operations.

Beta Alpha Psi had from early times relied mainly on advocacy by professors who were alumni and/or faculty members, and other promotion through "word of mouth," to spread its message to prospective new campus sites. Relatedly, the organization had gained visibility through annual meetings coordinated with those of the American Accounting Association, and (especially) councilors who were active in that body. Leon Hay, who as councilor-elect had sat in on most of the 1964 annual meeting attended by Miller as an advisory committee member, recalls that Herb Miller and Andy Anderson would "shuffle back and forth" between Beta Alpha Psi and AAA committee sessions. The two future presidents of the association were members in 1964 of respective research and education committees.

A passive approach of this kind had produced impressive expansion during the first fifteen postwar years. Yet it was apparent that many AAcCSB schools did not have a Beta Alpha Psi chapter, and had shown little or no interest in forming one. By the 1960s, also, the "small family of teachers" that had in Miller's nostalgic phrase made up the academic accounting field had begun to grow beyond the point that a figure of his prominence would have personal contacts on virtually any campus holding professional accreditation. During the fifties the AAA itself had grown in membership from 3,849 (more than double the 1946 level) to 10,151, granting that the nonacademic segment included therein rose from 60% to 70% during the period 1948-65.

It appears that ethical reservations about making a modest effort to initiate interest in the fraternity had by the early '60s disappeared from the Grand Council. Promotional activity was centered on the basic standard of charter eligibility.

Contacting New AAcCSB Schools, and Related Actions

The Council began early in the fourth era to inform newly accredited schools that they were eligible for consideration for a Beta Alpha Psi chapter. Emerson Henke, appointed in 1960, recalls that such an approach was a routine practice in his day. It remained so throughout the period, as in effect pointed out by Vern Odmark in noting that "[i]t was the policy of the National Council to write to new members of [the] AA[c]CSB and to invite inquiries from them regarding the formation of a chapter." As a matter of course, these notices would have cited potential benefits of chartering for a school and its students.

In 1966 a further step was taken. Secretary-Treasurer Hay was asked to prepare and circulate to all councilors a list of all professionally accredited schools that were not associated with the fraternity. Each Council member would then indicate institutions that he would be prepared to contact on behalf of Beta Alpha Psi. Through this approach, and no doubt a substantial contribution by Anderson himself, 1966-67 president Wilton Anderson recalled some years later that all the (approximately fifty) AAcCSB schools not as yet chartered had been approached during his term. Although expansion was minimal over the final three years of the decade, the former councilor felt that the efforts made that year had eventually been very productive.

Attending as a representative of the fraternity, finally, Anderson's

successor Leon Hay "informally discussed" Beta Alpha Psi with various deans present at the 1968 annual meeting of the AAcCSB. Included were administrators from institutions that were still only "prospective" members of the association, and not as yet professionally accredited.[3]

President Hay had attended the meeting based on a policy adopted by the National Council that was intended to promote interaction between Beta Alpha Psi and other professional organizations. Although directly relevant to chapter formation only in the case of the accrediting agency, that initiative warrants brief attention.

A Brief Digression Concerning a Broader Interprofessional Initiative of the Day

The accrediting agency, and nonacademic accounting organizations

It was decided at the 1967 annual meeting that beginning that year the fraternal president, or a councilor designated thereby, should attend the yearly gatherings of the AAcCSB and the major national organizations, besides the AAA, related to accounting. Specifically cited were the American Institute of CPAs, the National Association of Accountants, and the Financial Executive Institute (FEI). The fraternity would finance such travel in anticipation that the other professional bodies would duly recognize its representative during their meetings. Beta Alpha Psi would reciprocate by inviting the other organizations to send delegates to the annual fraternal

---

[3]"AACSB Accreditation Council"; "American Accounting Association Committees--1964," The Accounting Review 39 (April 1964):513-15; Wilton T. Anderson to Author, interview, March 20, 1980; Grand Council Minutes Book, 1930, p. 2, quoted; Leon E. Hay to Author, interview, May 2, 1980, quoted; Emerson O. Henke to Author, interview, March 21, 1980; Herbert E. Miller to Author, interview, April 18, 1980, quoted; National Council Minutes, 1966, p. 2, 1968, p. 2 (quoted); Vern E. Odmark to Author, August 13, 1980, quoted; A. J. Penz to Author, interview, April 18, 1980; S. M. Wedeberg to C. C. Staehling, December 14, 1952 (Policies File); and Zeff, American Accounting Association, pp. 83, 85-[86].

banquet.

A potential defect in this plan was that the fraternity did not conduct a meeting comparable to the annual conventions sponsored by the AICPA, NAA, FEI, etc. At any rate, although he attended other national gatherings during his term, President Hay evidently appeared as a representative of Beta Alpha Psi only at the AAcCSB conference, at a cost to the National Council of $258. Prior inquiry had generated "little interest in recognition" of his organization at the accounting functions.

The American Institute convention of 1967 occurred during the first month of Leon Hay's presidency. Despite initial indications that education director Guy W. Trump (a former dean at Emory) would arrange for formal recognition of the fraternity, Hay learned before leaving for the Portland gathering that the honorary member of Theta at Texas had neglected to do so. Two years later, however, Trump would see to it that copies of the institute's "Beamer Report" on education and experience requirements for CPAs, discussed in chapter 4, were mailed to all local Beta Alpha Psi units.

From discussions with Mississippi State (and future Georgia) business dean William C. Flewellen, Jr., Alpha Beta '49, the president was hopeful that a working relationship could be established with the Financial Executives Institute, on whose education committee the former Alabama accounting professor served.[4] Nothing would come of that prospect, however, as Hay

---

[4]Two years earlier, Flewellen had served as national president of the Accounting Careers Council, an outgrowth of an American Accounting Association initiative of the fifties to develop a careers booklet targeted toward high school students. The program had soon attracted support from the AICPA, NAA, FEI (while still known as the Controllers Institute of America), and the Institute of Internal Auditors. By the time of Flewellen's presidency (1965-66), "substantially more than one million copies" had been distributed of the leaflet Young Eyes on Accounting (revised in 1962 by Rollie Niswonger and two other professors), and a second booklet had also been favorably received. The Careers Council, later absorbed by the American

encountered "a hell of a time" trying to persuade other FEI leaders that a traditional accounting education was an appropriate base for a career as a financial executive. Finally, the 1967-68 president felt that another councilor might wish to represent Beta Alpha Psi at the National Association of Accountants convention, since he was not an NAA member, but no delegate was sent.

The accrediting agency differed fundamentally, of course, from the other organizations. Because fraternal charters were restricted to member universities, its annual meeting offered a unique opportunity to promote Beta Alpha Psi to potential chapter sites. President Hay accordingly recommended in 1968 that the national president plan each year to attend the AAcCSB convention, or to send another councilor as an official delegate.

Vern Odmark, the next fraternal president, felt that his principal role in that capacity was

> the nurturing and growth of Beta Alpha Psi [so] as to promote the fraternity through inter-relations among the National Council, the faculty vice-presidents, chapter student members, AA[c]CSB, AAA, AICPA, FEI, and other organizations.

Nonetheless, he apparently followed Hay's example in limiting his official travel to the AAcCSB meeting. Visiting at Ohio State, Odmark attended the Detroit function at approximately the same cost submitted by Leon Hay the

---

Institute, was by then an independent body supported by the five organizations, conducting a highly decentralized "nationwide program of promoting accounting as a career among college and pre-college students." Its top officials, however, had been appointed by AAA president Herb Miller.

Niswonger had played a significant role in the development of the original AAA endeavor. It seems fitting, then, that one of the activity program changes adopted during the 1959 meeting at which he was elected to the Grand Council provided for points credit under category 9, Special Activities, "for things such as distribution of Young Eyes on Accounting." Akey, ed., Encyclopedia of Associations, vol. 1, part 1, section 1, s.v. "American Institute of Certified Public Accountants"; Grand Council Minutes Book, 1959, p. 3; and Zeff American Accounting Association, pp. 70-73, 71n, quoting pp. 71n, 72.

year before. Secretary-Treasurer Harvey Donley from nearby Bowling Green was also present. Donley probably continued the pattern as president in 1969-70, while the relevant travel cost incurred by President Charles Taylor the following year ($739) suggests that he represented the fraternity at one or two additional meetings.

Later, in 1974, it was decided that the immediate past president should also represent Beta Alpha Psi at the annual AACSB ("Assembly") gathering. Past President Harold Royer had observed that as a delegate the preceding year "most of his time" had been "spent getting acquainted and finding out how things were done," rather than promoting fraternal objectives.

At the 1969 annual meeting, two councilors agreed to "represent" Beta Alpha Psi based on committee assignments held with two major organizations. Editor Taylor served on the AICPA committee on academic relations, and incoming secretary-treasurer Robert Wasley was a member of the FEI education group. Incoming American Institute president Louis M. Kessler addressed the fiftieth-anniversary banquet that followed, and other guests included NAA past president James Meredith.

The efforts made by the fraternal leadership of the latter part of the fourth era to establish institutional ties with other accounting organizations were a prelude to major achievements of the 1970s. They included the creation of the National Advisory Forum, the development of a truly "national" yearly meeting, and the mergence of external funding for a broad array of fraternal activities.

Reference should be made also to the remaining organization mentioned by Vern Odmark.

American Accounting Association

Beta Alpha Psi had from its origins enjoyed a warm relationship with

the American Accounting Association. Herb Miller recalls that during his Council tenure there was no sign of institutional conflict. Beginning in 1958, the two organizations had met on the same dates. The Grand Council would convene on a Monday morning, and adjourn following a brief Wednesday morning session. The Tuesday evening Grand Chapter banquet marked the fraternity's "night" during the coordinated gatherings, although a popular reception held early in the evening by textbook publisher Richard D. "Dick" Irwin provided "free booze" that sometimes led faculty vice-presidents to forget to attend the subsequent banquet.

To reduce the heavy schedule overlap between the Grand Council meeting itself and the technical program conducted by the AAA, the Council in 1964 advanced its starting time to Sunday morning. By the close of the fourth era, however, there were scattered signs that the fraternity and the educators' association were drifting apart. Beta Alpha Psi continued to broaden its chapter roster and national leadership base as the American Accounting Association moved toward a strong research orientation that seemed increasingly removed, in particular, from undergraduate professional instruction.

The latter development may be traced largely to two independent developments: expansion in 1965 of the authority enjoyed by the AAA research director; and emergence by 1970 of The Accounting Review as a full-fledged '"refereed"' scholarly journal. In terms of leadership, it is noteworthy that 10 of the 19 Beta Alpha Psi presidents of 1948-67 were included (usually later) among the association's 54 vice-presidents, 1952-66, while through 1985-86 no subsequent councilor had held that post. In twenty years, only four fraternal officials had served on the American Accounting Association executive committee: Wilton Anderson, as president and past president; Herbert Miller, in the latter capacity; and Leon Hay and Thomas Burns, as

directors of education.

Possibly the earliest indication that the two organizations were diverging somewhat from one another was the fraternity's inability in 1966-67 to arrange for clerical assistance from the association's new national office. In recalling that 1968-71 presidents Vern Odmark, Harvey Donley, and Charles Taylor, and he himself (the 1971-72 leader), were primarily "accounting education" men, interested above all in the teaching of the discipline, Robert Wasley felt that a degree of estrangement existed by his time on the Council. Taylor observed at the time that "the AAA ha[d] not considered accounting education to be its primary concern."

Probably relative to his service on the long-range planning committee of the early seventies, Emerson Henke sensed that the association regarded the fraternity more as a "necessary appendage" than as a vital partner within the educational field. Initial discussion at the time of the program to become known as the Accountant of the Year award contemplated a yearly AAA luncheon presentation; and although the association (which had begun to consider a similar award of its own) formally endorsed the proposal, the response was unenthusiastic. Even so, there is no evidence at all that any serious friction had developed, and indeed Odmark (who at the time still looked to the other organization for primarily educational leadership) has described relations between the two groups as having been "excellent" in his day.[5]

---

[5] AAA Road Atlas, pp. 53, 86; "American Accounting Association," The Accounting Review 58 (January 1983):inside front cover; "American Accounting Association Committees--1966-67" through "1985-86" (excepting "1982-83"), The Accounting Review 41-57, 59-61 (January, 1966-82, 1984-86):initial page of annual item; [Harvey E. Donley], Secretary-Treasurer's Report, 1967-68, p. 1; Grand Council Minutes, 1964, p. 1; Grand Council Minutes Book, 1949-63, p. 1 (meeting dates), 1958-63 (times of opening, closing, and banquet sessions), 1963, p. 4; Leon E. Hay to Councilors, October 2, 1967; Hay to Author,

In returning to the topic of chapter formation, it is noted that Wilton Anderson, who had broadened the effort to contact accredited schools outside the Beta Alpha Psi fold, is remembered by Vern Vincent as a "numbers man" who strongly promoted fraternal expansion. Another side of the coin, however, pointed up a second major difference from earlier practice that emerged during the 1960s--more intensive scrutiny of petitioning groups prior to approval of charters, accompanied by a more deliberative formal procedure at that stage.

More Scrutiny of Petitioning Groups within a More Deliberative Process of Charter Approval

Development of an Active Policy

The third-era Grand Council had been largely passive not only at the beginning of the process leading to chapter formation, but also at the stages of (a) petitioning and (b) charter approval themselves. It would be an over-statement to say that an AAcCSB-accredited school that could provide a nucleus of ten petitioning students and a supervising professor could receive a Beta Alpha Psi charter for the asking. Based on the recollection of A. J. Penz concerning the formation of Alpha Beta at Alabama, there was some level of

---

interview, May 2, 1980, quoted; Emerson O. Henke to Author, interview, March 21, 1980, quoted; Robert S. Maust, Long-Range Planning Committee Minutes, December 1971, pp. 2 (quoted), 6; Herbert E. Miller to Author, interview, April 18, 1980, quoted; National Council Minutes, 1965, p. 1, 1967, p. 4, 1968, p. 2 (quoted), 1969, pp. 2, 11-12, 1971, p. 5, 1972, p. 11 (no. 30.0); Vern E. Odmark to Author, August 13, 1980, indented citation and quoted AAA reference; Smith, Forty Acres, p. 67; [Charles W. Taylor], "AICPA to Distribute Committee Report to BAPsi Chapters," Newsletter 8 (Fall 1969):4; [Taylor], "Past Presidents, 1919-69," p. 15; Taylor to Author, interview, April 18, 1980; Wasley, Long-Range Planning Committee Minutes, May 1971, pp. 1-[2]; Wasley, Secretary-Treasurer's Report, 1970-71, p. 10; Wasley to Author, interview, March 23, 1980, quoted; Who's Who in America 35 (1968-69), s.v. "Trump, Guy Winston," 43 (1984-85), s.v. "Flewellen, William Crawford, Jr."; Zeff, American Accounting Association, pp. 67, 87-88, 90, [94-95]; and Stephen A. Zeff, "On Communicating the Results of Research," The Accounting Review 53 (April 1978):472, quoted.

expectation even before the beginning of the rating/activity program that a petitioner would already have a functioning accounting club or society. Further, as observed in chapter 2 action was deferred for a year on the application submitted by Detroit in 1953, due to concern about the relatively small size of the accounting program, and a similar issue may have arisen when Washington of St. Louis expressed interest in chapter formation.

With the possible exception of the latter school, however, no instance has been identified from the third era of either rejection (viewing Detroit as a case of deferred approval) of a petition by the Grand Council, or of discouragement of an interested group from filing one. It is not surprising, then, that by the time that Leon Hay was appointed in 1964 there was a general feeling that earlier councilors had (in his words) been "a bit too automatic" in approving chapters. The perception had developed, externally, that a Beta Alpha Psi chapter, if wanted, "went with" professional accreditation in business.

Hay, Andy Anderson, and others established a firm requirement that interested schools would have to submit evidence of capacity to operate reasonably effective chapters. The constitution, as revised in 1965, for the first time made explicit reference to a need for prior "[o]rganized accounting groups." In practice, those groups would have to establish a record of activity and student participation consistent with the expectations for a Beta Alpha Psi unit. Initially at least a year of prior operation was required. By 1970, it was generally understood that an accounting club could give rise to a chapter only after at least two years in existence, during which it held a minimum of eight meetings a year, four of them presented by student members.

At the 1970 meeting, the last provision was reinterpreted as a

"recommend[ation]," since the overriding issue was whether '"the chapter [would] be capable of mounting a successful program"'. To facilitate a judgment on that point, the National Council approved a practice of "site" visitation, by which petitioning campuses would be visited prior to deciding on their qualifications. The objective was to determine in advance the attitudes of faculty members, the department chairman, the business dean, and others regarding the fraternity and its purposes.

Before turning to some illustrations of the elevation of standards in the fourth era for the approval of a charter, two further constitutional provisions of 1965 should be noted. First, as pointed out in chapter 9 the minimum number of student petitioners, newly identified as needing to be "eligible" for student membership, was raised from 10 to 15. The evident intention was to guard against the admission of chapters that might be too small to function effectively, or that might be too dependent upon a small nucleus of members.

Second, a critical change was made in the process of voting on a petition. According to the 1958 statutes, the current Grand Council president would after conducting any appropriate investigation "submit his recommendation" to each councilor, who would then send back his own vote. Sometimes, of course, applications would be considered during the annual meetings, providing an opportunity for general discussion and careful deliberation. There was no requirement, however, of true consultation. Furthermore, the president was accorded special influence within the process.

Such an approach was logical so long as the vote was little more than a formality, with approval almost assured. It was not suited, however, to the more discriminating posture that had emerged by the mid-sixties. Accordingly, the new constitution provided that each councilor would "transmit

his comments and vote to all other members," having received the application from the secretary-treasurer. In the event that any negative votes were cast, or "serious reservations" expressed, the president was authorized to conduct further inquiry, and (if deemed appropriate) to defer definite action to the next session of the National Council, where a majority vote would decide the issue. The new approach clearly promised broader participation and consultation.

Some documentation exists of the higher chartering standards of the fourth era, leaving approval far from "automatic."

Examples of Enhanced Standards

At the 1964 annual meeting during which Leon Hay was elected, the Grand Council set aside an application received from Toledo, "recommending that the accounting faculty and students give strong support to an organization there such as an accounting club for at least a year before applying again." By August 1965, the Council was still not fully satisfied that Toledo was ready to conduct a successful Beta Alpha Psi program. Approval was thus made conditional upon "a definite showing" by the end of the fall semester "that the student group . . . ha[d] planned and carried out a strong program," including "a considerable amount of student activity." Presidents Julius Roller (1964-65) and Vern Vincent (1965-66), and Secreatry-Treasurer Hay, were asked to evaluate the group at midyear. Clearly they were satisfied, for Gamma Epsilon was installed at Toledo in May 1966.

Although records are incomplete, some documentation exists for Professor Hay's statement that the Council "sat on" (or rejected) certain petitions. Hofstra University, on Long Island, first applied in the summer of 1968, and submitted another application the following year. On Hay's

motion, the 1969 petition was rejected unanimously, although the door was left open for reconsideration once certain problems had been addressed. Specifically, the councilors were concerned with (a) low student participation in accounting club programs, (b) limitation in regular daytime faculty, (c) possible shortage of eligible students, and (d) "changing standards of [the] AA[c]CSB, particularly with regard to faculty," probably referring to upgraded formal requirements. Hofstra apparently did not reapply during the year 1969-70. Delta Pi was finally installed there in 1976.

St. John's (of New York) and Delaware likewise petitioned in 1968. Both applications were returned, presumably with an explanation of relevant deficiencies. St. John's reapplied the following year, but the National Council deferred any action pending further correspondence. Through 1984, the school had not formed a chapter. Delaware did not pursue the matter further over the final two years of the era, but Delta Phi would be formed there in 1977.

By the late 1960s, as earlier noted, the formation of new chapters had slowed to a trickle. Harvey Donley, the last national president of the decade, was particlarly insistent on strict compliance with all requirements.

Despite the general impression of high standards for approval of a charter, two reservations should be noted. First, the process led to the chartering of UCLA, based on the full satisfaction of established criteria, as it was moving toward a wholly graduate program. Gamma Iota was destined to be one of the few failed chapters in Beta Alpha Psi annals. Second, Vern Vincent believes that the Grand or National Council even of his day was apt to be too readily swayed by a "big spiel" that might be made by any one of the members on behalf of a particular school.[6]

---

[6]<u>Barron's Profiles</u>, s.v. "New York, Hofstra University"; Beta Alpha Psi Fraternity, "National Statutes," <u>National Constitution</u>

Although advance "site" visitation was not established within the petitioner evaluation process until 1970, the fourth-era Council placed strong emphasis on making an early visit to a newly established chapter. Several relevant reports are available illustrating a modernized interpretation of visitation purposes.

Timely Visitation to New Chapters, Illustrating a Revised Interpretation of Chapter Visits

General Overview

The remarkable upswing in visitation recorded during the three years 1957-60 had as one element provided for the first or second visitation to every chapter formed during that period (before April 1960) and the three preceding years. For obvious reasons there were no post-installation visits during the fourth era to the chapters formed at its very close, Beta Eta at San Diego State and Beta Theta at Penn State, established in April and May, 1960.

President R. H. Van Voorhis visited Penn State, however, late in the calendar year 1960 as part of a four-campus trip that also included stops at three other Pennsylvania chapter sites--the University of Pennsylvania, Temple, and Lehigh. The only other visitation of the year was conducted by Emerson Henke of Baylor at nearby Southern Methodist, home of Alpha Epsilon. The severe reduction in the program was probably based on the large operating

---

and Statutes (1958), chapter 4, sections 41-43, 44 (quoted); Beta Alpha Psi National Constitution (1965), article 7, sections 1-5, quoting nos. 1, 4; "Chapter Information, 1983-84," 1983-84 Annual Report, ed. Metcalf, pp. 31-38, especially s.v. "Delta Pi," "Delta Phi"; [Harvey E. Donley], Secretary-Treasurer's Report, 1968-69, p. 4; Donley to Author, interview, May 2, 1980; Grand Council Minutes, 1964, p. 4, quoted; [Leon E. Hay], Secretary-Treasurer's Report, 1965-66, p. 2; Hay to Author, interview, May 2, 1980, quoted; National Council Minutes, 1965, p. 8 (quoted), 1969, pp. 2, 3 (quoted), 1970, pp. 8-9 (quoted); Vern H. Vincent to Author, interview, July 21, 1980, quoted; and [Robert S. Wasley], Secretary-Treasurer's Report, 1969-70, p. 3.

deficit, $3,026, absorbed the preceding year.

After the Grand Council finances had barely exceeded the breakeven level in 1960-61, there was a second year of very lean visitation, as indicated by an expenditure of only $293 for such activity, marking a $27 increase. President Herbert Miller, newly arrived at Michigan State, traveled to Loyola of Chicago in October for the fall initiation banquet at Beta Iota, founded a year earlier. Three months later, after beginning a visiting professorship at Stanford, he spent three days at Los Angeles State, where Beta Lamda was in its first full year of operation. During the visit Miller addressed both a group of "pledge candidates" assembled at a local professor's home, on the history of Beta Alpha Psi, and a gathering open to all accounting majors (and other interested parties) at the school. Although no documentation exists, there is every reason to believe that the fraternal president would also have visited Beta Eta at San Diego State, which he had installed two years earlier, during the winter or spring of 1962.

During the year 1961-62, the fraternity reported a net gain of $2,669. The Council was thus prepared at the 1962 annual meeting to declare that "an extensive visitation program" would be conducted during the following year. More pertinently, the councilors agreed that "newly established chapters should be visited soon after installation," affirming a practice that was already well established. Moreover, it was observed in 1962 that the "philosophy" underlying the program had changed from an "audit" emphasis to one of "visitation and counsel," a development considered "desirable."

The elimination two years earlier of the visitation report form had signified a change in outlook. Although never completely "sold" on the need for visitation as a general practice, President Miller, who always

supported "individual choice" by chapters regarding level of activity (subject to a reasonable minimum standard), favored the positive emphasis upon chapter "assistance" that was asserted in 1962. At the Grand Chapter meeting two years later, President Emerson Henke stated, pointedly, that visitations were by that time "in no sense inspection trips."

The difference should not be exaggerated. Visitation officers had always hoped to assist chapters with their programs, in significant measure through detailed inspection of the kind reflected in exhibit 15 (chapter 6), and had rarely if ever described their objectives primarily in negative, disciplinary terms. Indeed, the Grand Council of the 1950s was unusually tolerant of chapter inactivity, having so far as is known never even threatened, seriously, to take disciplinary action, whereas a decidedly firmer policy emerged following (in particular) the clear identification made of constitutionally enforced requirements in 1965. Even so, within a day and time in which financial auditing would often have been perceived as a negative, fault-finding process, a difference only in degree between "audit" and "counsel" understandings of visitation would have been important.

The policies declared in 1962 of "extensive" visitation in general, and early travel to new chapters in particular, were certainly carried out in the years to come. At a cost of $1,570, twenty-seven chapters were visited during the year 1962-63, including for apparently the very first time Sigma at Wisconsin, founded thirty years earlier. For the balance of the decade, total yearly visitations ranged in number from 16 to 29, costing an average of $1,073 during the years 1963-66, and from $1,592 to $1,756 (one of three figures over $1,700) thereafter.

The 1962-63 sites included the six campuses, aside from Loyola of Chicago and Los Angeles State, that had been chartered over the preceding two years. They were Mississippi State, Georgia State, and Tulane from

1960-61, and Miami of Florida, Arizona, and North Texas State from the following year.

Of the 22 chapters installed during the eight years 1962-70, 18 were visited during their first full year of operation. Gamma Beta at South Carolina and Gamma Xi at San Jose State received Council visits two years after their formation. Gamma Zeta at Southern Illinois and Gamma Omicron at Fresno State, founded in 1966 and (as the last new chapter of the era) 1969, were the exceptions. Their first visitations were delayed until the fifth and (at the earliest) fourth complete years, respectively.

Past President Wilton Anderson of Oklahoma State began a trip to Southern Illinois at Carbondale late in the fall of 1967, visiting Alpha Iota at Arkansas the first evening. Upon arrival the next day in Springfield, Missouri, he checked on road conditions with the state's highway patrol. Advised to turn back due to icy bridges and underpasses and a 40% prospect of snow, Anderson telephoned the Gamma Zeta FVP to report that he would have to cancel the visit. The call revealed that the chapter's major problem was weak attendance by graduate students.

Fresno State may have originally been on the agenda for a first-year visit, given that Secretary-Treasurer Robert Wasley called during 1970-71 at three other California State campuses and Berkeley as well. As it was, there is limited circumstantial evidence that Gamma Xi was finally visited three years later (the first period since 1961-62 for which full visitation records are not available) by Fred Mueller of Washington.[7]

---

[7]Wilton T. Anderson to Harvey Donley, December 5, 1967 (Visitation Files); "Chapter News," Newsletter 5 (Fall 1961):457, (Spring 1962):506 (quoted); exhibits 15, 24; "Grand Chapter," Newsletter 5 (Aptil 1961):350, (Fall 1961):402; Grand Council Minutes, 1964, p. 8, quoted; Grand Council Minutes Book, 1962, pp. 1-2 (quoted), 1963, pp. 2-3; [Leon E. Hay], Secretary-Treasurer's Report, 1966-67, p. [17]; [Emerson O. Henke],

Seven first-visitation reports of the sixties are on file, including two from the fall of 1960 concerning late installation sites of the fourth era.

Seven First-visitation Reports

Lehigh and Penn State, from an intensive visitation swing of fall 1960

President R. H. Van Voorhis of Louisiana State visited Beta Epsilon at Lehigh and Beta Theta at Penn State, along with two other Pennsylvania chapters, over a very busy two days in December 1960. Originally he was scheduled to spend an evening with Alpha Delta at Pennsylvania, call on Alpha Phi at Temple and Beta Epsilon the next day and evening, and complete his assignment at Penn State the third night. The scheduled early afternoon flight from New Orleans was cancelled, however, and Van Voorhis did not arrive in Philadelphia until 10:00 P.M.

The next day he met separately with the chapter officers at Penn and Temple in the morning; had lunch with Alpha Phi Chapter as a whole; flew to nearby Bethlehem, and met with the Lehigh officers; and then participated in a Beta Epsilon dinner meeting. The Grand Council president was joined the next morning by his parents, who had driven from their home in New Jersey to transport him to State College, 180 miles from Bethlehem. The Penn State visitation consisted of dinner with the Beta Theta officers, and an evening chapter meeting. At each of the three regular meetings,

---

Treasurer's Report, 1961-62, p. 1; Herbert E. Miller to A. J. ("Andy") Penz, January 16, 1962 (supplied by Penz); [Miller], Secretary-Treasurer's Report, 1960-61, pp. 1, 3; Miller to Author, interview, April 18, 1980, quoted; National Council Minutes, February 1974, p. 1 (no. 1), May 1974, p. 2 (no. 3); Secretaries' (first two years) or Secretary-Treasurers' Reports, 1963-64 through 1972-73, visitation listings (1968-69, p. 3, 1972-73, p. 4, otherwise pp. 1 and/or 2); and [Robert S. Wasley], Secretary-Treasurer's Report, 1969-70, p. [12] ("Financial Analysis," p. 2).

Van Voorhis spoke briefly on "the operation of Beta Alpha Psi as a professional fraternity." After spending the night at the Nittany Lion Inn (bringing his three-day hotel bill to $24.38), he accompanied his parents on their return home, and subsequently flew back to New Orleans from New York.

The reports covering the two non-Philadelphia chapters were very short, embodying around fifteen typewritten lines. At Lehigh, where the chapter had been formed in May 1959, the faculty vice-presidency had just been assumed by former dean Carl E. Allen, Alpha '25, who was cited in volume 1 as the author of an important early study (1927) of collegiate instruction in accounting. Allen, who had returned to the faculty after retiring as dean, had been at Lehigh since the '30s. President Van Voorhis was hosted in Bethelehem, however, by charter FVP Wendell P. Trumbull, a future editor of The Accounting Review.

The Beta Epsilon dinner meeting attracted nearly all "active" members. The visitor found the chapter to be operating "nicely," having only the inherent problems of a new unit in "getting going, building up tradition, [and] passing on know-how from old officers to new." Despite somewhat high grade requirements and "strict grading" within the department, the chapter seemed large enough to operate satisfactorily.

At Penn State, Beta Theta conducted a professional meeting on the topic "integrated data processing," held (in accordance with a practice being established by the new chapter) at a social fraternity house. The fraternal president was favorably impressed by the chapter officers, and remarked that a relatively selective admissions policy at the university had apparently given rise to "an alert group of accounting majors."

The remaining reports available for first visitations are from the two

ROBERT H. VAN VOORHIS, 1960-61
FRATERNAL PRESIDENT, IN CLASSROOM

years 1966-68. An anecdote for this period concerning installation travel also deserves mention.

Five visits from 1966-68, and an installation anecdote

President Wilton Anderson was critical of the faculty vice-president to Gamma Delta at Houston following a visit during the fall of 1966, indicating that he might need to contact the department chairman in the spring concerning a replacement if chapter faculty leadership did not improve. Since no change would occur at that level, the problem apparently, to Anderson's satisfaction, took care of itself. Of the 72 chapters existing from the start of the year, Gamma Delta ranked 56th in the 1966-67 activity program.

On a trip to nearby Toledo in the spring of 1967, Harvey Donley of Bowling Green State found that Gamma Epsilon was conducting about half its meetings jointly with a local accounting club. The major problems found were typical of an urban campus--"too many night classes, [and] students living off campus." Donley commented also on "the remarkable lethargy of this faculty," other than the chapter advisor, by which they "me[t] classes and disappear[ed]." The departmental chairman conducted a law and/or CPA practice, and there was no secretarial staff. As noted in the preceding chapter, Gamma Epsilon had wrongly identified the '"90% Rule"' governing membership for activity program purposes with constitutional eligibility requirements, leading to overdependence upon graduate-student members.

Also in April 1967, Donley found that Gamma Beta at South Carolina was likewise very reliant on graduate students. A meeting with twelve members and three professors was hampered by noise from the heating and cooling equipment. Criticism raised that the activity program placed undue emphasis upon routine matters such as meeting and financial reports, and not enough

upon service projects, was generally consistent with the reforms developed by the Hay committee two years later. As mentioned in chapter 10, the continued use of blindfolding within the initiation ritual was also questioned by Gamma Beta. Donley concluded that the South Carolina chapter had considerable potential, but that weak faculty leadership and "quite keen" competition for the members' time from the professional fraternity Delta Sigma Pi, and other campus groups, had hindered its progress to date.

Late in 1967 Vern Odmark visited Gamma Iota at UCLA, which he had installed the prior spring, attending an initiation banquet that had attracted two faculty colleagues of "capable and energetic" chapter advisor Corine Thompson Norgaard. Odmark reported that local president Wayne Label, later to join Vern Vincent on the staff at Southern Illinois at Edwardsville, was "an enthusiastic young man" who "ha[d] the chapter off to a fairly good start." He noted that the problem of attendance had been addressed by the metropolitan chapter, so far successfully, through "holding monthly Saturday morning meetings." Such a pratice had been instituted by Beta Eta at San Diego State, under charter faculty vice-president Odmark, several years earlier. The meetings here had started early, at 7:30, to accommodate students who had Saturday jobs.

The only criticism raised by the visitation officer was that, "[a]s might [have] be[en] expected from UCLA," the unblindfolded part of the ritual had not been memorized. As observed in the next chapter, however, the National Council would quickly find much more serious shortcomings at Gamma Iota, which would end the decade in a very precarious position.

The fifth report was submitted by Vern Vincent in March 1968 following a visit to Gamma Eta at Akron. He characterized the student-presented program as "weak" in content, and was "discouraged" that it had generated no

questions or discussion. The principal obstacle facing the chapter seemed to be the outside employment, for twenty or more hours weekly, of the students with "the best leadership" qualities, raising problems of proper formal compliance with activity program requirements. Positively, Gamma Eta stood to benefit from "a strong feeling of rivalry" felt at Akron toward neighboring Kent State, the home of Beta Psi chapter.

A closely related anecdote is available, finally, in lieu of the first-visitation report that would have been filed by Anderson in the fall of 1967 had weather conditions not aborted his planned trip to Southern Illinois. On an installation assignment the previous spring, President Anderson had enjoyed an excellent reception at Missouri, the new site of Gamma Theta, following a "difficult trip" from Oklahoma.

Anderson had intended to fly to Columbia from Tulsa, via Ozark Airlines, which he would later recall as having been "known quite widely as the type" of carrier that "cancel[led] flights at the slightest hint of bad weather." After some delay, his flight was cancelled, and he boarded a plane for Kansas City with the intention of making connections there for completing the trip to the University of Missouri. In Kansas City there was a further delay before the regularly scheduled flight to Columbia (approximately 125 miles away) was also called off.

With time running out for purposes of conducting the installation, the Beta Alpha Psi leader "finally made arrangements to charter a flight from Kansas City to Columbia." Two years later, he recalled the experience as follows:

> The small plane could make the flight even with a fairly low ceiling. We had a tremendous head wind to buck going to Columbia. The clouds settled lower and lower. Rain started falling. The pilot searched the map for alternate airports in case we had to land in a hurry. Our ground speed average was something like 65 or 70 miles an hour.

In the lobby of the destination airport, Anderson by coincidence met the immediate past president of the American Accounting Association, Herb Miller, who later recalled that the traveler had "looked pretty harried" at the time. After an excellent installation, the return trip was apparently uneventful.[8]

Except for the installation already planned at Fresno State, fourth-era expansion was complete when the National Chapter gathered in 1969 to observe the golden anniversary of Beta Alpha Psi. Relevant preparation had been underway since the appointment three years earlier of 1968-69 president Vern Odmark to supervise such activity. The milestone was recognized through three initiatives involving prominent participation by former councilors: the preparation of a fifty-year fraternal history and a related commemorative Newsletter; and the hosting by the National Council of a particularly meaningful banquet.

Observing Beta Alpha Psi's Golden Anniversary, in 1969, Following Three Years of Preparation

Development of a Commemorative History: Andy Penz's *Fifty Years* Project, 1966-69

First-year developments, 1966-67

Appointment of the historian

Meeting in the fall of 1948, the Grand Council had voted to observe the thirtieth anniversary of Beta Alpha Psi by inviting absentee (and retiring)

---

[8]"American Accounting Association Committees--1966-67," *The Accounting Review* 41 (January 1967):197; Wilton [T. Anderson] to C. Aubrey Smith, March 28, 1969 (Golden Anniversary Files), indented citation; Anderson, Visitation Report--Gamma Delta, October 17, 1966; *Barron's Profiles*, s.v. "Missouri, University of Missouri/Columbia"; "Chapter News," *Newsletter* 5 (November 1959):246-47, quoting Alpha Phi, Beta Epsilon, Beta Theta reports; Harvey E. Donley, Visitation Reports--Gamma Beta, April 27, 1965, Gamma Epsilon, April 6, 1967; Hasselback, *1979-80 Directory*, school listing, s.v. "S[outhern] Illinois, Edwardsville"; [Leon E. Hay], Secretary-Treasurer's Report, 1966-67, p. 4; Herbert E. Miller to Smith, February 25,

member James McConahey to prepare a fraternal history. The result, by and large, was a summary of available national minutes, 1922-48, that would be extended yearly by the former Washington professor through 1953. Eventually a 57-page typescript, the history had been published only by way of two Newsletter articles representing (a) a synopsis of the original material and (b) the 1949 installment.

In 1966, incoming president Wilton Anderson was asked to invite an appropriate person to prepare a half-century history, after receiving nominations and suggestions from other councilors. During the fall a consensus selection for the appointment emerged. Early in December, Vern Odmark wrote A. J. Penz that the National Council would "very much like" for him to prepare the booklet. The newly appointed editor tentatively envisioned a 5 x 8 or 6 x 9 pamphlet covering fraternal "highlights" in only 10-12 pages, foreshadowing constraints under which the project would be conducted.

Having immediately accepted the assignment, Penz was officially appointed by President Anderson in January 1967. His initial response to Odmark had included the following observation:

> I always associated historians with old, senile people, with long beards, milling over dusty archives in the hope of recapturing their ill spent youth. It is incredible that it should happen to me[,] but I always have been able to cope with the inevitable.

The Alabama department head lost no time himself in securing access to appropriate archives, as one of two principal initiatives undertaken early in 1967.

1969 (Golden Anniversary); Hermann C. Miller, ed., Beta Alpha Psi Directory, s.v. "Alpha Chapter: Allen, C. E."; Vern E. Odmark, Visitation Report--Gamma Iota, December 4, 1967, quoted; Sheldahl, Alpha to Omega, pp. 16n, 25-27; R. H. Van Voorhis to Herbert E. Miller, December 14, 1960, concerning visitation reports of same date; Van Voorhis, Visitation Reports--Alpha Delta, Alpha Phi, Beta Epsilon, Beta Theta, December 14, 1960, quoting last three items; and Zeff American Accounting Association, p. [95].

Two prompt initiatives

Penz promptly contacted Secretary-Treasurer Leon Hay concerning inspection of historical files held by the secretary-treasurer. They included the McConahey compliation; bound and unbound Newsletters, perhaps not including the incomplete 1931-36 volume; the bound minutes through 1963; "a couple of boxes of materials" recently delivered from early councilor Jacob Taylor's papers at Ohio State; and "miscellaneous material" that probably included financial statements and the early postwar McConahey and Policies files.

The new historian traveled to Indiana at the first opportunity, perhaps during the 1966-67 semester break, and spent two days in Hay's office "mulling over" the available material. He took some of it back to Alabama with him, and soon was sent additional items by Professor Hay.

In addition, as related in chapter 8, Penz during January 1967 (except for a brief delay in one case) wrote all living retired councilors to solicit content that "normally would not be in the minutes":

> [W]ould you jot down for me any significant events, humorous incidents, remarks about associates that occurred during your tenure. I am trying to inject some personalities into the history rather than just recite dates and facts.

The nineteen letters sent out included one addressed to William Cox of Washington, who had died the preceding spring. Penz had also written future councilor Robert Wasley to seek a current address for an ex-colleague at Colorado, only to learn that Hazen Kendrick also was deceased. The very recent death of the historian's Grand Council contemporary J. C. Gibson of Wisconsin had come to his attention prior to the drafting of a letter.

At least two thirds of the eighteen living former Council members responded, but only C. Aubrey Smith, Tom Dickerson, S. M. Wedeberg, and Williard Stone supplied information. Their anecdotes were related in volume

1 or in chapter 8. W. E. Karrenbrock, who had become a real-estate investment consultant after retiring from UCLA, acknowledged that one "interesting" incident had come to mind, but added that "to report it would be a criticism of one of our retired deans." No record exists of a response from either Fred Woodbridge or Gould Harris, both of who would submit excellent anecdotal material to Smith two years later. Another apparent nonrespondent was Charles Staehling, who had been addressed by his onetime fellow councilor Penz as Professor "Stealing," and would be cited in the published product as C. C. "Straehling."

Following Andy Anderson's request for a "a brief progress report" on his project, Dr. Penz submitted a "Tentative Outline" about a month before the 1967 annual meeting. The response was less supportive than he had hoped.

Penz's "Tentative Outline,"
and the Council's response

Ten topics were identified, in sequence. The first three of them were of a background nature:

1. "History and Background of Professional Fraternities" - European, American, and business-related
2. "The Professional Fraternity Role in the Educative Process" - European vs. American, and evolution in the United States
3. "Accounting Education Differentiation Process" (not further explained).

Regarding Beta Alpha Psi specifically, Penz identified seven areas: (a) origin and growth, in concert with professional accounting; (b) organization and operation; (c) selective membership; (d) financial administration; (e) chapter operation and motivation; (f) chapter diversity; and (g) future role, in several respects. He was assuredly outling a project that would well exceed the limits proposed seven months earlier by Vern Odmark.

In his covering letter to Anderson, Andy Penz implied that he wished to meet with the national Council the following month, "to get . . . comments,

suggestions, and ideas." In August 1967, he accordingly presented his own "progress report." The outgoing president followed, not by asking for questions or discussion, but by stating, in one or two minutes, that the history should focus on topics a and b; not exceed twenty double-spaced typewritten pages; and be drafted in preliminary form by the following July 1.

Although he said nothing at the time, the appointed historian was troubled by this response, and in part for that reason let the project slide over the next several months. Amidst his misgivings, he developed a draft in the early summer of 1968 that was reasonably consistent with National Council expectations.

Development of a draft, in the summer of 1968, amidst misgivings

The historian's "uneasiness"

After eight months without communication, President Leon Hay sent a polite "reminder" to Professor Penz in mid-April of 1968 concerning the specifications given by his predecessor. Having finally finished working on the revision of the AAA Accounting Instructors Guide, discussed in chapter 7 the Alabama department head indicated that he would have "ample time available" to complete a short manuscript by July 1.

Several weeks later, Penz wrote Hay that although he had for two weeks been "working diligently and exclusively" on the project, he had not as yet overcome a certain "uneasiness" about the "directives" laid down earlier. He asked for clarification of Council intentions in sponsoring the project, the restrictions of size and scope, and the absence of any effort to secure a foundation sponsor for the history. In his opinion, Beta Alpha Psi should develop a document that might be useful for many years to come, providing "as complete a history as possible."

Hay replied that a majority of councilors favored the production of a capsule history for distribution at the anniversary banquet, and that there was some thought that a more scholarly study would be very expensive and have limited readership appeal. He added that if anyone wished to prepare such a book as "a labor of love," it would be gratefully received for the fraternal archives.

During this period, in the early summer of 1968, Andy Penz was in touch with Secretary-Treasurer Harvey Donley, on isolated details, and the University of Illinois commerce librarian, concerning potential Beta Alpha Psi files. Advised that six folders of fraternal material were included within the Hiram T. Scovill Papers, he would have a brief opportunity to review them (in August 1970) only well after his booklet was in print. Penz considered writing charter Alpha president Russeell H. Morrison, and possibly other original members, but apparently did not do so.

The first draft was completed in time for submission of six copies to President Hay, for distribution to the other councilors, during the third week of July, 1968.

Submission of the first draft, and councilor reaction

The original manuscript probably included substantial coverage of the varieties of fraternal organizations in (at least) the United States, and incorporated anecdotal material supplied by Professors Smith, Wedeberg, and Stone. Although it was surely longer than the twenty pages requested, response seems to have been fairly favorable, overall. Wilton Anderson, who was "a bit reluctant" to propose major changes, recommended three minor stylistic revisions; reduced discussion of the academic fraternity system; and consideration of reference to activity program evolution. He thought

that the booklet should list all chapters with the installation years, charter presidents, and initial faculty advisors; and the historical sequence of national presidents.

Vern Odmark, who described the paper as "an excellent job," endorsed the inclusion of such tabular material, and made several specific stylistic recommendations. Without apparent effect, he proposed that the booklet be dedicated to, and display a picture of, founder Hiram Scovill.

Harvey Donley was more critical. He listed nineteen "Petty Details" of style or content, and asserted that undue emphasis had been placed on "setting the stage, " and not enough on "actual history," including names, dates, listings, and rosters. The secretary-treasurer also felt that author Penz had tended to "editorialize" at times, in a manner generally consistent with present-day Council viewpoints, but still in departure from historical objectivity. Overall, Donley suggested that "Andy" be "very diplomatically steer[ed] . . . in a slightly different direction."

At the 1968 meeting, the National Council discussed the project "at length,' asking Leon Hay to advise the author of the changes desired. In addition, Councilors Anderson, Odmark, and Bob Wasley were appointed a committee to review revised material, and arrange for publication.

Revision and publication, 1968-69

Two-stage completion of manuscript

During the subsequent fall term, Hay duly "suggested" to A. J. Penz "a number of changes to the manuscript," and in mid-January President Odmark requested a progress report. Penz promised to submit an appropriate revision shortly, and declared that the committee should "feel free to make further" alterations, although "[o]bviously" he did "not agree with all the changes indicated." Odmark attributed such differences to a committee system that

involved "a group of people, each one with different ideas." In response to a reference made to the availability at Alabama of "quite reasonable" multilith facilities, he also reported that Secretary-Treasurer Donley of Bowling Green was planning to arrange for printing at his campus.

Submitting four copies of a revised manuscript on February 18, 1969, shortly before leaving for a five-weeks' teaching assignment in Guyana, South America (chapter 7, note 2), Andy Penz noted that among other changes "some . . . extraneous material" had been deleted. It had included the writeup of anecdotes that he had sent two weeks earlier to assist Aubrey Smith in his own assigned role concerning the anniversary observance. By this time a decision had been made to list existing chapters and their 1968-69 faculty vice-presidents (given that no listing of charter leaders was on file), and the historical sequence of national Beta Alpha Psi presidents.

Penz remained unclear on the use planned for the history. He had tried to produce a summary that would be "informative" for students, embodying "a narrative of related events subject to interpretation and philosophy," and hoped that in some form it could be provided to student <u>pledges</u>, possibly as an element of the initiation process.[9] Beyond the idea of distribution at the golden anniversary banquet, however, the only suggestion emanating from the National Council came from Harvey Donley:

The chapters will be interested in obtaining a few copies each year for

---

[9]Penz added a pointed criticism of the newly simplified initiation ritual: "At the rate it [the ritual] is being abbreviated, its entire significance will be lost in short order." His only recorded advice to committee chairman Charles Taylor a year earlier had been to "[k]eep in mind that the ritual is geared to the undergraduates and basically involves symbolism." As a new councilor in 1952, he had welcomed the condensation, and placement '"in . . . proper sequence"', of the fraternal oath emerging from the efforts of S. M. Wedeberg and C. C. Staehling. A. J. Penz to Vern E. Odmark, February 18, 1969; Penz to Charles W. Taylor, January 19, 1968; and Wedeberg to Staehling, November 28, 1952 (Policies File), all sources quoted.

> several years at least[,] and perhaps all the active members should be given a copy at least next year.

In addition, Vern Odmark wrote the author at the conclusion of the review process, in May 1969, that he had already found several occasions to refer to the manuscript for source material, and was sure that the booklet would continue to be useful to fraternal leaders.

Councilors Odmark, Anderson, Wasley, and (serving largely in a coordinative capacity) Donley had made "[r]elatively few changes" in the revised manuscript, primarily corrections of minor errors of detail. Having thus succeeded in satisfying the National Council, the historian admitted to remaining frustration about the project: "The lack of time and the other constraints I had with the History prevent [plural form supplied] me from having any sense of accomplishment in writing it."

Ironically, the booklet would not be printed quite on time for the distribution that had been planned from the beginning.

Printing, completed _after_ anniversary banquet

On Secretary-Treasurer Donley's suggestion, it was decided to have Editor Charles Taylor arrange for the _Newsletter_ publisher in Mississippi to print the Penz history as well. President Odmark, through Donley, asked Taylor to secure cost quotations for one, five, and ten thousand copies. Ultimately, 5,000 copies were produced at a total cost of $716.10.

The main contents of _50 Years: Beta Alpha Psi, 1919-1969_ are shown as exhibit 26. The 4 1/2 x 6 (vest-pocket-sized) booklet contained 31 pages of text, and 6 pages of listed material on presidents and chapters, as described above. The cover was black rather than (as proposed by Donley) scarlet, with white and red lettering for the title and a white representation

EXHIBIT 26

CONTENTS OF A. J. PENZ'S COMMEMORATIVE 50 Years

CONTENT

iv

Reprinted from 50 Years: Beta Alpha Psi, 1919-1969, by A. J. Penz, ([University, Miss.: Rebel Press & Office Supply Co., for] National Council, 1969. On the title page, unlike the cover, the dates appear prior to the fraternal name.

embossed, of the fraternal seal. The author was identified, along with the six 1968-69 councilors, directly after the title page.

The booklet was unfortunately not ready until two weeks after the August banquet, although the manuscript had been sent to the printers more than six weeks in advance. Author Penz had been honored in that capacity during the commemorative ceremonies. Besides distribution to councilors, past and present, and faculty vice-presidents, copies were probably made available for the 2,277 new members (in all categories) initiated during the year 1969-70. In that case, the remaining supply would have been inadequate for the following year's group of 3,046 new student, faculty, and honorary members. In any event, the booklet was reprinted near the end, apparently, of the reporting year ending June 30, 1972. The only changes were a minor revision in the cover, an updating of the presidential and chapter lists, and the deletion of FVP names. By early 1980, when pertinent files were sent for the new history project underway, only a few dozen copies of 50 Years remained on hand, divided between the two versions.[10]

---

[10] Wilton T. Anderson to National Council, August 6, 1968, quoted; Anderson to A. J. Penz, January 5, July 11, 1967; Esther M. Clausen, Commerce Librarian at Illinois, to Penz, June 25, 1968; Thomas M. Dickerson to Penz, February 1, 1967, Hollis A. Dixon, Secretary-Treasurer's Report, 1971-72, p. 4, 1972-73, p. [1]2; Harvey E. Donley, "Comments on the Penz Manuscript," [August 1968]; Donley to Vern E. Odmark, May 1, 1969; Donley to Penz, July 22, 1968, February 14, 1969; Donley to Charles W. Taylor, May 26 (quoted), 30, 1969; Grand Council Minutes Book, 1948, p. [2]; Gould L. Harris to C. Aubrey Smith, [1969] (Golden Anniversary Files); Leon E. Hay to Penz, January 13, 1967 (quoted), April 17, 1968, June 18, 1968 (quoted); W. E. Karrenbrock to Penz, February 19, 1967, quoted; Karrenbrock to Taylor, June 28, 1969 (Golden Anniversary); James M. McConahey, "History of Beta Alpha Psi," [1949-53], manuscript; McConahey, "History of Beta Alpha Psi," ed, W. E. Dickerson (assumed), Newsletter [2] (May 1949):6-9; McConahey, "History of Beta Alpha Psi (1949)," Newsletter [3] (March 1950):6-8; National Council Minutes, 1966, pp. 5-6, 1967, pp. 5 (quoted), 6, 1968, p. 8 (quoted), 1969, p. 11, 1971, p. 6; Vern E. Odmark to Donley, April 8, May 12 (?), 1969; Odmark to National Council, August 9, 1968, quoted; [Odmark], "Past Presidents Cox, Gibson Die," Newsletter 7 (February 1967):5; Odmark to Penz, December 6, 1966, January 13, 21, May 22, 1969, all quoted; Penz to Anderson,

Independently of the Penz study, Charles Taylor developed a significant body of historical data for a commemorative Newsletter prepared in the summer of 1969. As part of the project, however, he obtained another significant contribution from the official historian.

Editor Taylor's Commemorative Newsletter

Vern Odmark had presented "tentative plans" for the golden anniversary celebration a year in advance. The first item listed was the issuance of "A special edition of the Newsletter, with articles by early presidents, to be distributed at the dinner." A month later, in September 1968, President Odmark had suggested that Editor Taylor:

1. Promptly write the living former presidents, at addresses enclosed, "to give them time to get their thoughts together and something on paper"
2. Request pictures "of these illustrious men"
3. Ask Andy Penz to contribute "a short article" on faternal history.

Along partially different lines, a special issue having permanent value to Beta Alpha Psi would be developed over the succeeding year. Former

---

July 26, 1967, with enclosed outline, both quoted; Penz to Business Library at Illinois, June 19, 1968; Penz to Donley, June 10, 12, 19, 1968, February 6, 1969; Penz, 50 Years (as cited in exhibit 26), especially pp. i-ii, 22 (implying that the author had not seen the earliest bound Newsletter volume), 32-[37] (appendices, revised in 1972), quoting p. 32; [Penz], handwritten list of ex-councilors' addresses, [January 1967], notes on Scovill Papers, August 26, 1970; Penz to Hay, January 10, 1967 (relative to his appointment), April 22, June 10 (quoted), 26, July 18, 1968; Penz to Emerson O. Henke, January 19, 196[7], W. E. Karrenbrock, February 13, C. C. St[aeh]ling, January 30, and 16 other former councilors, January 19, 26, or 30, 1967, 2nd indented citation; Penz to Vern E. Odmark, December 13, 1966 (1st citation), January 15, February 18, May 29, 1969, all quoted; Penz to C. Aubrey Smith, February 4, 1969, with enclosure (Golden Anniversary); Penz to Robert S. Wasley, January 17, 1967; Rebel Press & Office Supply Co., Oxford, Miss., to Beta Alpha Psi, invoice no. 16693 ($76.10), September 9, 1969; Sheldahl, Alpha to Omega, pp. 276-77, 315-18, 815, 817; Smith to Penz, July 10, 1967; Taylor to Penz, July 10, 1969; Wasley to Penz (addressed as "Al"), February 8, 1967; S. M. Wedeberg to Penz, December 10, 1967; and Frederick W. Woodbridge ("Fred") to Smith ("Aubrey"), March 3, 1969 (Golden Anniversary). Except for his own letter to Smith, items attributed to the general anniversary files do not refer to Penz's history project. Seven additional replies to his letter to ex-councilors are available.

president Penz did provide an historical article, supplementing rather than summarizing 50 Years, and Odmark himself added a future-oriented statement. The fraternal map shown as exhibit 25 was prepared. Otherwise, three major contributions were developed: (a) a listing of charter members of each chapter, 1919-69; (b) brief profiles, with photographs, of all national presidents of the first half century; and (c) summary annual and cumulative information on results in the interchapter competition begun in 1950.

Contributed articles on fraternal history and prospects

Penz on "Origin and Growth"

Early in May of 1969, a few weeks after returning from South America, A. J. Penz asked Charles Taylor for basic specifications on an article he had agreed to write for the anniversary Newsletter. He assumed that it "should not be too long," in order to be clearly distinct from the historical booklet, but should be complete enough to be "self-contained." Taylor deferred to the author's own best judgment on length, within a range of two to five printed pages, requesting submission by July 1.

A week late, Penz mailed the editor an article titled "The Origin and Growth of Beta Alpha Psi." Having estimated that a 5-page piece would be nearly two thirds as long as the booklet, he had deliberately kept the paper much shorter, with the result that it would consume less than 1 1/2 Newsletter pages. More importantly, "the entire theme" had been changed, "in the hope of making interesting reading without being too repetitious," an initiative welcomed by Professor Taylor.

The result was an analysis of the origin and development of Beta Alpha Psi in terms of four basic factors: "(1) favorable environment, (2) common interest, (3) mutual benefit, and (4) imaginative leadership." Several paragraphs were added on chartering and membership standards.

President Odmark added a very brief look ahead, within the context of further historical reference.

Odmark on "the Next 50 Years"

Odmark referred first to the formation early in the century of numerous collegiate business schools, and several major accounting or educational organizations besides the fraternity. He mentioned that Beta Alpha Psi chapters, 79 in number as of the publication date, had admitted some 38,000 members, including many well known accountants. The president observed that more than twice as many new units had been formed during the fraternity's second 25 years as over the first quarter century (ending during the war years).

Glancing forward, Odmark cited three major developments or issues that would be vitally important to the fraternity during at least the first phase of the next half century. He reported that during his term special committees had considered policy issues concerning (a) activity program reform, (b) the chartering of "branch campuses" of a university, and (c) increasing graduate-level enrollments in accounting. The first area was covered in the preceding chapter, and the others comprise the subjects of the following one.

Editor Taylor's foremost contribution was probably a full listing of the _charter memberships_ of the 82 chapters formed through 1968-69, inclusive of units that had been discontinued.

Listing of charter memberships for the chapter roster

Development of the information

A proposal that Andy Penz plan to list the first presidents and FVPs of each chapter had been dismissed due to the extensive research that would be required, with no assurance of reasonably full coverage in the end.

Charles Taylor's comparable project concerning membership was more realistic. Relevant information was available from an abundance of sources, including local charters, petitions (or supporting documentation), chapter directories, certificate orders, installation programs, roll card files, the 1939 national directory, and Newsletters. With an isolated exception in the first case, there is no evidence that the latter two sources were used.

Taylor naturally looked first for the desired information, in April 1969, toward Secretary-Treasurer Harvey Donley. Late in May, Donley submitted charter membership lists for 46 chapters, including already defunct Alpha Tau at Pittsburgh, citing "about 35" local groups for which the information was less readily available. No prewar unit was covered, and indeed only Alpha Delta at Pennsylvania (1949) was included among groups formed before 1953. Along with use of sources of several of the other kinds cited, photocopies had been made of charter records in thirty cases.

Immediately upon hearing from Donley, Taylor wrote the faculty vice-presidents of the 33 active chapters that, besides Alpha Theta on his own Mississippi campus, had not yet been covered. He asked them to inspect the actual charters to determine original student and faculty memberships, and the dates of installation. The editor was probably unaware that faculty participants had in the early days been designated "honorary" members, and seems to have disregarded the absence of dates on most of the documents already received. Although exact dates were provided for many of the remaining chapters, only calendar years of installation, as given in traditional Newsletter directories, would be published.

Sixteen FVPs, a chapter president, and a department secretary supplied the membership information before the editor's desired cutoff date of June 20, 10-15 of them based on inspection of charters. Four chapters responded

positively over the following week, in three cases not before Taylor had enlisted more help from the secretary-treasurer's office. His specific request had included Epsilon at Oregon State, whose response (not counted above) had identified only the group inducted upon reactivation in 1959; and Alpha Kappa at Ohio, whose advisor had utilized the 1951 petition in lieu of other evidence.

Because Harvey Donley was vacationing in Europe, the new search was conducted entirely by his secretary Becky Adams. Primarily from available directories and card files, she obtained initial membership listings (and dates) for the 17 chapters still in question, 14 of them formed before World War II. Although "it was quite a job," the work was finished remarkably fast. Except for coverage of the discontinued chapters Eta at Boston and Kappa at William and Mary (evidently involving a separate request), the information was sent Charles Taylor on July 2, probably within a week of the arrival of his inquiry. Attached to the Eta and Kappa lists, for good measure, was repeat coverage of Alpha Tau at Pitt.

The result of such cooperative effort was an eight-page Newsletter listing of charter members, 1919-69 from Alpha at Illinois to Gamma Xi at San Jose State. "Active" members (students) were distinguished from "faculty" participants, subject to occasional deviation for early chapters, but "honorary" members in the modern sense were not cited. Alpha Tau at Pittsburgh was incorrectly classified with Beta Nu at Tulane, as a currently "Inactive" chapter, rather than with Eta at Boston and Kappa at William and Mary, as one that had been "Discontinued."

Five listings were seriously in error.

Five basically flawed listings

Prior to the development of Alpha to Omega, the original memberships of Epsilon at Oregon State (1922) and Mu at New York (1926) were not known. Becky Adams had submitted a list of six Epsilon brothers initiated in 1923, along with a highy deviant 1922 entry, and the earliest listing found in Mu Chapter directories, dated 1927. Unlike other errors concerning prewar chapters, these citations were consistent with Hermann Miller's 1939 Directory.

In four other cases, the listings provided by the secretary-treasurer's office included both charter members and persons inducted later in the same calendar year. Local directory material provided for Beta at Oregon, Sigma at Wisconsin, Tau at Maryland, and Alpha Kappa at Ohio was classified only by year. The same error was avoided for Omicron only because the Ohio State group had conducted no further initiations during the installation year, 1929. Editor Taylor correctly cited the original Beta membership, based on authoritative documentation reported by the local president, but ironically rejected the correct Alpha Kappa listing supplied by the chapter in favor of the full-year list. The charter memberships for the Wisconsin, Maryland, and Ohio chapters are presented in appendix 2, supplementing the listings for Oregon State and NYU appearing in the first volume.

Finally, Harvey Donley's secretary identified a charter Eta Chapter brother named Queenin as R. J. "Oveenin," and failed to list three original Alpha members, including President Russell Morrison and (of all people) founder Hiram Scovill. Fortunately, the Illinois FVP had in late June provided a full listing for his chapter after reviewing the 1939 national directory.

Taylor made another excellent historical contribution concerning the

national leaders of the fraternity over its first fifty years.

Biographical sketches of national presidents, with photographs

In conjunction with a project discussed below, C. Aubrey Smith early in 1969 requested relatively recent photos from all living former presidents for the editor's use. He obtained at least five pictures, although S. M. Wedeberg's (as described later) was not suited to the intended use, and Thomas Burns of Omicron at Ohio State sent on another likeness of W. E. Dickerson.

Professor Taylor followed up on the request in late May, while asking former presidents to submit basic biographical data for publication. He contacted chapter sources, for these purposes, in regard to deceased leaders. The letters sent to Illinois, Washington, and Colorado produced charter membership listings in addition to the pictorial and biographical material on Alpha's Hiram Scovill and Charles Schlatter, Delta's William Cox and James McConahey, and Nu's Hazen Kendrick (three of whom were cited among original members). By clerical error, a parallel request on Kendrick was sent to the FVP at Rho Chapter, while an inquiry regarding Minnesota's H(arry) J. Ostlund was directed elsewhere.

From one source or another, the editor eventually obtained appropriate information and usable photographs for all 37 national presidents, through Vern Odmark. Many biographical writeups were received, including resumes, formal personnel sheets, informal career summaries, and (for Scovill, Schlatter, and Kendrick) local obituary notices or tributes. Also collected were Newsletter profiles, 1949-65, of a number of past or contemporary councilors. Although the various clippings used represented other physical copies, it seems pertinent that Harvey Donley had around June 1st forwarded three bound volumes of the periodical (1936-57).

From the material accumulated, Charles Taylor prepared individual write-ups on all fraternal presidents of the half century, ranging from a full column on Scovill to a short paragraph on Ostlund. The resultant feature item comprised ten pages of text and photos. Most of the pictures of living fraternal leaders were recent ones. Exceptions included those of Wilbert Karrenbrock, in particular; Leon Hay, who "prefer[red] to look like" he had in 1960; and perhaps Nolan Williams, who may have come up with "a suitable print of an early vintage."

The anniversary issue also covered the interchapter competition that had just concluded its nineteenth year.

Coverage of the activity program: Leading chapters since 1950

In the spring of 1969, Secretary-Treasurer Donley's office compiled for Taylor a complete listing of certificate-winning chapters within the rating or activity program, 1950-68. As covered in chapter 6, the number of units honored had been increased in 1958-59 from three to five, although exact or virtual "ties" had earlier twice led to the recognition of more than three chapters. The secretary-treasurer also supplied the names of the faculty advisors for all chapters listed.

The editor asked his junior colleague Norman R. Kaylor (a source as well of further assistance on the project) to develop a brief Newsletter report based on these historical data. In addition to the listings of the top three or five chapters annually (or a comparable group) and their advisors, were accompanied by a useful tabulation and brief descriptive commentary that were not affected by an alignment error in the listings for the two years 1957-59. Alpha Beta had finished third in 1957-58 under faculty advisor Joe Lane, and Alpha Theta and Theta had led the field the following year

LEON HAY, Ca. 1960, AS HE WISHED TO LOOK IN '69

PRESIDENT LEON E. HAY PRESENTS CHAPTER AWARD TO BETA OMICRON
FVP HOLLIS A. DIXON, 1968

under FVPs Charles Taylor and Robert Seiler.

The 21 chapters that had at least once finished among the top three positions in the annual competition were listed according to number of (a) 1st-place, (b) top two, and (c) top three finishes. Although it had not ranked among the first five chapters since 1962, Theta at Texas had easily outdistanced the competition overall, with nine wins, places, or shows. Kaylor noted that Theta's four first-place and four second-place finishes had featured seven different FVPs, one of whom (the editor) had been the only "winning" faculty advisor from two different chapters.

The leading groups from the fifties, in addition to Theta, were covered in chapter 6. The top unit of the early sixties was Beta Alpha at Indiana, primarily under the leadership of Leon Hay, with successive rankings of 2nd, 1st, 1st, and 3rd over the period 1960-64. Going beyond the 1968 cutoff for the Newsletter feature, similar success was enjoyed over the period 1966-70 by Beta Omicron at Arizona (two firsts, one fourth, and a fifth), and Beta Pi at North Texas State (each of the top three positions, and a fifth-place finish).

For the full decade, the leaders were perhaps Alpha Iota at Arkansas, with seven top-four finishes (though no firsts), and Alpha Rho at Baylor and Alpha Psi at West Virginia, each with six top-five rankings, including one first-place year. Another impressive chapter was Beta Xi at Miami, formed in 1961, which registered first-, third-, and fourth-place finishes. Future councilors listed as FVPs of these outstanding chapters were Hollis Dixon, Joyce Dean, Robert Maust, and Harold Royer.

Recognition for highly ranked chapters was increased during the fourth era, beginning with the dispatch of congraulatory letters in the fall of 1962

to the deans of the top ten chapters of the preceding year, and the most improved local units. Two years later $50 cash awards were approved for the top _15_ chapters, and at least 13 such prizes were conferred annually for the balance of the period. Ordinarily, 15 chapters (raised to 20 in 1971) would be so rewarded unless, as in 1969-70, there were a sharp break in the point totals a bit earlier. As already noted, the National Council in the last year of the decade conferred _plaques_ upon the top eight chapters, rather than the first-place group only.

Publication of the gold-colored anniversary _Newsletter_, 24 pages in length, appears to have cost the fraternity $1,150.54, nearly as much as the total periodical expenditure of the prior year, and more than half of the nearly $2,000 increase reported for the year beginning August 1, 1969. The Mississippi printer completed the issue before the historical booklet, in reverse order of submission, but perhaps not in time for the banquet.

Charles Taylor's excellent editorial contribution was achieved under personally trying conditions, at least in the early going. His wife Nelda was treated for a heart ailment in 1969, but apparently was well on the way to recovery by June.[11]

---

[11] _Note_: Correspondence, unless otherwise indicated, is from 1969. Becky Adams to Charles W. Taylor, July 2 (quoted), 10, with enclosures; James R. Bentley, Epsilon FVP, to Taylor, June 17; Yezdi Bhada, Alpha Kappa FVP, to Taylor, June 12, and 12 other chapter advisors, 3 student officers, and a departmental secretary (in each case not otherwise cited) to Taylor, June 2-26; Thomas J. Burns, Omicron FVP, to Taylor, July 1; James Wesley Deskins, Alpha FVP, to Taylor, June 26 (with enclosures), July 1; Thomas M. Dickerson to C. Aubrey Smith, January 18: W. E. Dickerson to Smith, January 20; Harvey E. Donley to A. J. Penz, February 14; H. E. Donley to A. J. Penz, February 14; [Donley], Secretary-Treasurer's Report, 1968-69, pp. 8-9; Donley to Taylor, April 28 (with enclosed activity program compilation), May 26 (with enclosed membership records), 30; Mary Friou, [secretary], accounting department at Texas, to Taylor, July 7; Grand Council Minutes, 1964. p. 5; Grand Council Minutes Book, 1958, p. [8], 1959, p. 4, 1962, p. 2; Leon E. Hay to Taylor, June 5, quoted; W. Bruce Johnson, Beta president, to Taylor, June 25, with enclosure; Norman R. Kaylor, "The Beta Alpha Psi Chapter

GOLDEN ANNIVERSARY EDITOR
CHARLES TAYLOR, Ca. 1969

The remaining feature in the fiftieth-anniversary Newsletter related to the keynote speaker at the commemorative banquet.

The Fiftieth-anniversary Banquet, August 1969

As incoming president of the fraternity, Vern Odmark had at the 1968 meeting reported on his banquet plans, beyond the distribution of the two special publications. One area cited was covered earlier in this chapter, namely, an invitation to other major organizations to send an official representative. Past, current, or designated future presidents would thus be recognized from the NAA, AAA, and AICPA, together with Professor William A. Paton (who had headed the second group, under its original identity, in 1922), while the president of the FEI would send regrets, along with

---

Activity Program, 1950-69," Newsletter 8 (50th anniv. ed., [1969]):2-3; Kaylor to Kathy Nitch, Rand McNally & Co., February 7 (response to her letter of January 30); Donald A. Lux, Xi FVP, to Taylor, June 3; [Herbert E. Miller], "Professor Wilbert Eugene Karrenbrock, PhD., C.P.A.," with photo, Newsletter 5 (November 1960):307; Hermann C. Miller, ed., Beta Alpha Psi Directory, s.v. "Alpha," "Beta," "Omicron," "Sigma," "Tau" chapters, "Eta Chapter: Queenan, R. J."; National Council Minutes, 1965-71, cash awards to chapters, 1968, p. 8 (quoted); Newsletter [2]-6 (1949-65), clippings (or the equivalent) on a number of councilors, including John T. Madden (May 1949, p. 9), Vern E. Odmark (Fall 1965, p. 256); Vern E. Odmark, "Beta Alpha Psi--the Next 50 Years," Newsletter 8 (50th anniv. ed.), pp. 1, 15 (quoted); Odmark to Taylor, September 28, 1968, with marginal notation imputed to Taylor; A. J. Penz to Donley, February 6; Penz, "The Origin and Growth of Beta Alpha Psi," Newsletter 8 (50th anniv. ed.), pp. 1 (quoted), 16; Penz to C. Aubrey Smith, February 14; Penz to Taylor, May 9, July 7, both quoted; Rebel Press & Office Supply, Oxford, Miss., to Beta Alpha Psi, statement, (September 1969), reporting invoice nos. 16591 ($1,150.54) and 16693; [Donald R. Rogers], Nu FVP, to [Taylor], n.d., reply (in its lower margin) to Taylor's letter of May 28, with enclosure; Julius Roller to Taylor, June 16, 25, 26; Sheldahl, Alpha to Omega, pp. 66-67, 139, 159-51, 827-28; John K. Simmons, Rho FVP, to Taylor, June 5; C. Aubrey Smith to Penz, January 7, sample letter to former presidents; Smith to Taylor, July 8; Williard E. Stone to Smith, January 16; [Charles W. Taylor], "Charter Members, Alpha to Gamma Xi," Newsletter 8 (50th anniv. ed.), pp. 17-24, quoting classifications of Eta, Kappa, Alpha Tau, Beta Nu; Taylor to James Wesley Deskin[s] and Donald R. Rogers, May 28, illustrative letters to FVPs; Taylor to Eric L. Kohler and Nolan E. Williams, May 28, illustrative letters to former presidents; Taylor to Penz, May 16, July 10; [Robert S. Wasley], Secretary-Treasurer's Report, 1969-70, pp. 7, [12] ("Financial Analysis," p. 2); S. M. Wedeberg to Smith, February 8; and Nolan E. Williams to Smith, February 23, quoted.

Secretary of Commerce (and prominent accountant) Maurice Stans.

Other plans that were carried out included the delivery by Andy Anderson of a brief report on recent "changes in the fraternity"; the provision of "[a]dequate photographic coverage"; and the distribution of a "past president's key" to former Beta Alpha Psi leaders not already having one. As the outgoing councilor, Anderson received a certificate of appreciation for his six years of service. At a minimum, the group picture taken of ex-councilors in attendance would have been sent to each retired national officer; Andy Penz is known to have also received two large photos of the presentation by Odmark of a plaque recognizing him as fraternal historian. As related in chapter 8, the pin bequeathed by Bill Dickerson to Bob Wasley had evidently been conferred at the anniversary banquet.

Although there were advance plans to report it to that journal, no identifiable reference to the Beta Alpha Psi observance would be found in The Accounting Review. In particular, an October news notice contributed by the host department at Notre Dame did not mention the event; and no reports appeared from Odmark's school, San Diego State, during the academic year 1969-70, or following summer.

Vern Odmark naturally followed through with advance plans to invite the living former national leaders of the fraternity to attend the landmark gathering. Ten retired councilors were duly present in South Bend on the evening of August 25, 1969, for the commemorative cocktail party and banquet. They unfortunately did not include an early leader who on Odmark's invitation had compiled an excellent body of anecdotal material for delivery to the assembled group. The highlight of the formal program was a keynote address, not mentioned in the 1968 planning notes, given by one of the official presentatives attending the affair.

Attendance by ten ex-councilors, from Woodbridge to Vincent

All incumbent members of the National Council, including President Odmark and his predecessors Anderson and Leon Hay, were present for the festivities at South Bend, as was incoming councilor Harold Royer. Among a grand total of "[a]pproximately" 102 persons, they were joined by 10 of the remaining 22 living ex-presidents, ranging in point of service from Fred Woodbridge (1932) to Vern Vincent (1965-66). The spouses of seven councilors were also present, including the wives of early third-era leaders Tom and Bill Dickerson, but (because the location was "not too attractive as a vacation spot for residents of Indiana") not Bobbeye Hay.

Woodbridge and Bill Dickerson had both been initiated by Delta at Washington in 1921. After two years in retirement, charter member Woodbridge had early in 1969 at age 80 been pressed back into regular service with a Los Angeles firm of employment consultants. Before being temporarily sidelined with prostrate surgery in early summer, he had been as "busy as the one-armed paper hanger with a spider running up his back."

Absentees included still earlier presidents Eric Kohler, from nearby Chicago, and A. C. Littleton, retired in Arizona. Fayette Elwell, who at 84 (before year's end) was at least a year older than Littleton, sent his regrets based on a scheduling conflict with the twenty-fifth annual School of Banking conducted at the University of Wisconsin. He had originated the program during the forties, and even long after retirement from the university did "not like to leave the 1400 students and some 100 staff and lecturers for even a day while the School [wa]s in session."

Somewhat similarly, W. E. Karrenbrock reported from Los Angeles that he had too many business problems to address to carry through with his

PRESIDENT VERN E. ODMARK PRESENTS AWARD TO HISTORIAN
A. J. PENZ, 1969

FORMER COUNCILORS ASSEMBLED AT
GOLDEN ANNIVERSARY BANQUET, 1969

From left, William E. Dickerson, A. J. Penz, Julius A. Roller, Gould L. Harris, Emerson O. Henke, Fred W. Woodbridge, Thomas M. Dickerson, Vern H. Vincent, Herbert E. Miller, and Nolan E. Williams.

original plans to attend the AAA and Beta Alpha Psi meetings with his son Rodger, a doctoral graduate in accountancy from Illinois. His letter to Charles Taylor related several points of interest concerning business education in Japan, "the most interesting" of the twenty-five countries he had visited "because of the many basic differences between our cultures."

Willard Stone and C. Rollin Niswonger were both abroad at the time of the fraternal celebration. Stone and his wife were in England, taking advantage of their only vacation opportunity of the year, while the Niswongers, who had already in 1969 traveled widely in the United States, had left for "an extended trip" to eastern and northern Africa just two days earlier.

Finally, another ex-president (serving two years before Karrenbrock) had returned from foreign travel on a timely basis, but in mid-August been forced by untimely events of his vacation to cancel a special contribution prepared for the anniversary program.

C. Aubrey Smith's forced cancellation of a speech rich in anecdotage

Early in the fall of 1968, Vern Odmark had invited 1937 president C. Aubrey Smith to speak at the commemorative banquet, representing the past leaders of Beta Alpha Psi. This initiative had displaced prior plans to include "[s]hort remarks by several past presidents" within the program. Smith's subsequent written request for anecdotal material, or pertinent comment, from the other 23 former presidents, Kohler through Hay, who were "still on terra firma" (or the 22 besides his career-long colleague John Arch White) was briefly described in chapter 8.

Andy Penz, who had of course sought basically the same kind of human-interest material for his historical booklet, related two of the stories found in chapter 7 as well as sharing some of his own response (and offering

to send the rest). Tom Dickerson and Williard Stone provided Smith with the excellent anecdotes that they had sent to Penz, and S. M. Wedeberg repeated the one about his snow-delayed installation trip to Kentucky. Having become nearly a full-time gardener and fisherman, Wedeberg submitted a backyard snapshot of himself holding a salmon that he had caught in the Pacific Ocean, although a more conventional likeness would be published.

Aubrey Smith also received from Fred Woodbridge (briefly a colleague at Texas in the '20s), Gould Harris, and Nolan Williams the anecdotal material already credited to them. Among points not covered in volume 1, Woodbridge recalled in his typewritten letter of more than three pages that W. E. Karrenbrock had in effect served as secretary-treasurer even before his election to the Grand Council, through relieving Charles F. Schlatter (heavily immersed in other university work) of most of the responsibilities of the office.

Finally, Smith's correspondence extended to the four most recent presidents, through Leon Hay. With an assist from Herb Miller, Wilton Anderson provided the story about his harrowing flight to Columbia, Missouri to install Gamma Theta. Vern Vincent recalled a Texas incident of thirty years earlier, "when the boys took along a couple of quarts of milk for [Theta member] Stanley Scott to live on at the combination picnic and beer party at the park." He also noted that Professor Smith had stated in a "farewell talk" to seniors in 1940 that he and his colleauges hoped to remember all former students who might visit the campus, but most certainly they "would never forget those graduates who were in Beta Alpha Psi."[12]

---

[12]Failing, despite special effort, to come up with anecdotes, Rollie Niswonger and Leon Hay contributed more serious observations. Niswonger cited the ritual and (very fundamental) constitutional revisions made in his day as important developments. Hay observed that Beta Alpha Psi had

For reasons that are not given, Aubrey Smith forwarded the accumulated material to Charles Taylor two weeks prior to departing with his wife Mary Louise, around July 22, for a "British Isles holiday." He may have thought that it could be utilized in completing the anniversary Newsletter. A card sent from Edinburgh on August 1 referred to visits to the Universities of Dublin and Edinburgh, and plans to go to Wales and England the next day. After returning home, however, Smith wrote that, regretfully, he would be unable to attend the anniversary banquet in Indiana. Both he and Mrs. Smith had become ill in Ireland; and, although he had recovered, she was not as yet prepared to take another trip. Secretary-Treasurer Harvey Donley's summary of the dinner gathering implies that no speech of the kind planned was made.

The main speaker on August 25, 1969, was a long-time Beta Alpha Psi member who had reached high national prominence in the accounting field.

Keynote address by Louis Kessler

President-elect Louis M. Kessler, Alpha '35, represented the American Institute of CPAs at the fiftieth-anniversary banquet. The Alexander Grant partner from New York also delivered the keynote address, "Professional Accounting: Frustration or Fraternity."

Kessler identified several problems facing the accounting profession in regard to (a) financial reporting, (b) student unrest and alienation, and (c) education and recruitment of minority-group members, particularly blacks; and indicated ways in which Beta Alpha Psi could meaningfully contribute to

---

"not yet achieved a very successful two-way communication system between local chapters and the National organization"; and that overall changes in attitude found among "both students and younger faculty members" had caused further problems. Leon E. Hay to C. Aubrey Smith, January 24, 1969, quoted; and C. Rollin Niswonger to Smith, July 22, 1969.

their resolution. He discussed the first area partially from the standpoint of his current membership on the standards-setting Accounting Principles Board. Newsletter issues contained a brief article on the speaker, two photographs of him, and the full text of his address.

Two years after taking his first accounting course, at Illinois, Louis Kessler had been hired as a teaching assistant by Hiram Scovill, and he had stayed on campus as a graduate student and faculty member until Pearl Harbor. He had entered service as a doctoral candidate lacking only a dissertation requirement that he was destined never to complete. As a practicing accountant, however, the AICPA representative had maintained close contact with the educational field, partially through chairing the institute's Educational Committee and Board of Examiners. As an advocate of the formation of "professional school[s]" of accountancy, he had very favorably impressed C. Aubrey Smith during an American Accounting Association roundtable discussion held at Texas in 1961. The next year he had joined the "Committee of Accounting Faculty Associates" at Smith's university, an appointive advisory group of business and professional leaders formed in 1959 with the support of acting dean John Arch White.

Rounding out the program at the anniversary dinner was the presentation of the usual awards to top chapters in the activity program. The first-place plaque went to Beta Omicron at Arizona. The National Council in 1969 issued six emblematic certificates, one more than usual, as sixth-ranked Alpha Psi at West Virginia had stood closer in point totals to the top position than to seventh place.[13]

---

[13]The Accounting Review 54 (October 1969), 55 (January, April, July, 1970), nonreference to 50th anniversary of Beta Alpha Psi (consulting in particular "News Notes," ed. Charles H. Griffin, "Association Notes," "Miscellaneous Association Notes"); Wilton [T. Anderson] to C. Aubrey Smith,

In Transition

On the eve of the fiftieth anniversary, two academic "environmental" issues had come to the fore to commend the formation of special advisory committees. They respectively brought under review the centerpiece of quality control regarding the chapter roster, and concerned in particular three weak chapters (two of them recently chartered) and a unit that had already failed. These issues are fitting subjects on which to conclude coverage of a reform-minded fraternal era.

March 28, 1969; Burns and Coffman, Accounting Hall of Fame, pp. 33, 63, 77; Thomas M. Dickerson to Smith, January 18, 1969; F. H. Elwell to Charles W. Taylor, June 25, 1969 (quoted), with enclosed 1955 capsule biography; Gould L. Harris to Smith, [July 1, 1969]; Hasselback, 1984 Directory, individual listing, s.v. "Karrenbrock, Ro[d]ger"; W. E. Karrenbrock to Taylor, June 28, 1969, quoted; Louis M. Kessler, "Professional Accounting: Frustration or Fraternity," Newsletter 8 (Winter 1970):1, 3, 7-10; Herbert E. Miller to Smith, February 25, 1969; Hermann C. Miller, ed., Beta Alpha Psi Directory, s.v. "Delta Chapter: Dickerson, William E.; Woodbridge, Frederick W."; National Council Minutes, 1968, pp. 8-9, 1969, pp. 11-12, quoting each page; C. Rollin Niswonger to Smith ("Aubrey"), July 22, 1969; Vern E. Odmark ("Vern O.") to Taylor ("Charlie"), October 23, 1968, appended to Taylor's letter of October 18; "Past Presidents of Beta Alpha Psi," Newsletter 6 (Fall 1965):320; A. J. Penz to A. C. Littleton, January 26, 1967; Penz to Smith, February 4 (or 5), 1969, with enclosure; Smith, Forty Acres, pp. 87 (quoted), 91, 101, 135 (quoted), 150-51; Smith to Penz (illustrative), January 7, 1969; Smith to Taylor, July 8 (quoted), August 1, 14, 1969; [Taylor], "Professional Accounting--Frustration or Fraternity," Newsletter 8 (50th anniv. ed. [1969]):1, 3, profiling Kessler; Taylor to Eric L. Kohler, May 28, 1969; Taylor to Smith, December 16, 1968; three commemorative photos addressed to Penz; [Robert S. Wasley], "Beta Omicron Wins First Place in Chapter Activity Program," Newsletter 8 (Fall 1969):3; S. M. Wedeberg to Smith, February 8, 1969, with enclosure; F. W. Woodbridge ("Fred") to C. Aubrey Smith ("Aubrey"), March 3, 1969, quoted; and Woodbridge to Taylor, [summer of 1969], with enclosed "Condensed Data Sheet."

CHAPTER 12

TWO MAJOR "ENVIRONMENTAL" ISSUES OF THE PERIOD: BRANCH CAMPUSES, AND GRADUATE-ORIENTED CHAPTERS

The two major issues emerging in the fourth era relative to academic environment were basically first noted early in the decade. An unfulfilled expectation of 1962 that a "branch campus" of a long-time chapter site would seek a charter raised the question of whether eligibility policies should be revised to permit consideration of such schools, which at the time did not meet formal requirements. The prospective magnitude of the issue led a committee of the late sixties to recommend abandonment of the "accreditation" rule, just as Leon Hay's chapter was beginning, on a sound basis, to induct students from outlying campuses of Indiana University. That standard survived a repeat challenge, in the early 1970s, as branch campuses began to meet the traditional quality-control requirement, and form chapters under the traditional policy.

The second area attracting attention was the increasing presence of "graduate" students within a number of chapters. Policy changes designed to correct pertinent membership imbalances at Beta Alpha, for example, were discussed in chapter 10. Still holding to the same scholastic requirements for both undergraduate and advanced students, the National Council in the late sixties sought to make the fraternal program more relevant to a relatively graduate-oriented environment. The reform of the activity program featuring the option of nonparticipation was accompanied by a limited experiment with a third kind of approach (undocumented) to chapter reporting. More importantly, four Beta Alpha Psi campuses, two of them newly admitted to the ranks,

eliminated or phased out their _under_graduate business programs during the fourth era, leading to generally unsatisfactory experience with _all_-graduate chapters.

Branch Campuses: The Question of Eligibility

Emergence of an Ill-defined Issue

The essential issue raised concerning branch campuses was the long-established requirement of membership in the American Association of Collegiate Schools of Business. As discussed in chapter 2, it had been a routine matter to inform interested parties from schools outside the AAcCSB that a petition could not be considered prior to professional accreditation.

At the annual meeting in 1962, however, it was noted that an application might be forthcoming from the University of Wisconsin at Milwaukee, a school founded only six years earlier, and not (as yet) constitutionally eligible for a chapter. The original faculty had included Charles T. Horngren, who had since moved to the University of Chicago, and had just published the first edition of his celebrated text _Cost Accounting: A Managerial Emphasis_. Rather than simply dismissing at once the possibility of favorable consideration, and directing the secretary-treasurer to contact the Milwaukee group accordingly, the Grand Council discussed the matter inconclusively. No decision was made "regarding the attitude to be taken toward such an application should it be submitted."

The Wisconsin branch apparently did not proceed to apply for a charter. The issue was discussed again in 1963, however, and once more no decisions were made. One viewpoint raised was cited in the minutes: "The extent of _autonomy_ present in the operation unit [branch business school] was suggested to be a primary consideration" (emphasis added).

The quoted passage seems to imply, first, that a program operating (more than nominally) under a central deanship, headquartered on the main campus, should not be chartered. Such a business school would not be considered for separate accreditation; and under a theory of "derivative" qualification through the main campus, discussed below, the point would be made that only one chapter could be formed per AAcCSB member.

The citation appears, however, to have a more interesting implication relative to an autonomous program. Since it would be less than noteworthy to state that a separately accredited branch would be eligible for a charter, the Grand Council of 1963 was apparently discussing the possibility of _waiving_ the AAcCSB requirement in certain cases.

By a "branch" the Council understood, primarily, a degree-granting school that was identified in relation to a "main-campus" university, normally a public institution. Thus Wisconsin at Milwaukee was a branch of the university whose main campus was at Madison, whereas the state college system in California was made up of coordinate institutions having equal status. The distinction ultimately breaks down, however, as illustrated in the state of Wisconsin itself.

Until 1971, the Dairy State maintained two separate systems of higher education through (at least) the four-year leval. Besides the aforementioned multi-campus university, which had in 1968 been extended to a third location ("Parkside"), there was a Wisconsin State University system, headed by a statewide chancellor, that was comprised of nine separate schools. In the terms in which the Grand Council had broached the issue, Wisconsin at Milwaukee was a "branch" campus while Wisconsin State at Oshkosh, for example, was not. Yet in 1971 the two systems _merged_ as the University of Wisconsin, in effect undermining any such distinction.

Another illustration of the difficulty of defining the branch campus issue is provided by the contrast between Illinois and Ohio in the structure of public higher education. Excluding the Community College Board, there are four separate systems in the first case, each headed by a central administrative office; and Northern Illinois, Eastern and Western Illinois (jointly), and the two campuses of Southern Illinois belong to three separate groups, each distinct from the University of Illinois. A main campus may be identified only in the latter two instances. In Ohio, however, all state universities belong to the same "system," including Ohio State, its four 4-year "branch" campuses, Ohio, Akron, Bowling Green State, Kent State, Miami, and Toledo.

The problem of drawing a proper boundary no doubt contributed to the eventual consideration of a fundamentally new evaluation program, not specifically associated with the branch campus issue. Narrowly conceived, the matter was not a pressing one for the fourth-era Council. Among unaccredited schools, Wisconsin State at Oshkosh and, for the second time, Wisconsin at Milwaukee expressed interest in joining the Beta Alpha Psi ranks during the respective years 1965-66 and 1966-67; Texas at El Paso made two inquiries in the latter part of the decade; and Southern Illinois at Edwardsville submitted one in its final year. Many state colleges of a regional nature contacted the fraternity, however, over a period in which several municipal or secondary state universities were chartered besides the various California campuses. As already noted, Gamma Kappa became the first clearcut "branch" chapter when the University of Omaha was reconstituted as the University of Nebraska, Omaha.

More generally, immense growth was underway in "state schools of the second rank." For example, between 1960 and 1972 the Wisconsin State/Wisconsin campus at Whitewater expanded from 1,559 students to approximately 8,200,

and Western Illinois at Macomb went from 2,462 to some 12,500. Vocation-oriented subjects like accounting were probably leading fields of study at many such schools.[1]

By 1968, the National Council was ready to appoint a committee to review and assess the matter of branch campuses in full. By then, President Leon Hay's home chapter at Indiana may have already begun an initiative that for a time would allow Beta Alpha to serve students at other campuses of an emerging state system of the classic kind.

Induction by Beta Alpha of Students from Indiana's Branch Campuses, Accredited "Derivatively"

Indiana University was founded at Bloomington in 1820. In the present day, it consists also of a junior college at Richmond, a number of two-year technical schools, and half a dozen four-year campuses located around the state. The latter institutions were established as junior colleges during the period 1917-62, at (in sequence) Fort Wayne, New Albany, Kokomo, Indianapolis, Gary, and South Bend. During the 1960s the schools at Fort Wayne and Indianapolis merged with Purdue University branches located in those

---

[1]"AACSB Accreditation Council" (general reference); Akey, ed., Encyclopedia of Associations, vol. 1, section 5, "Educational Organizations," s.v. "American Assembly of Collegiate Schools of Business"; Barron's Profiles, s.v. "Ohio: The Ohio State University," "Wisconsin: The University of Wisconsin System; University of Wisconsin/Parkside"; Grand Council Minutes Book, 1962, p. 2, 1963, p. 4, both quoted; Ann A. Groves, secretary to president of Northern Illinois University, to Author, March 5, 1986, with enclosed chart, "Structure of Public Higher Education in Illinois"; Andrew Hacker, "The Decline of Higher Learning," The New York Review of Books 33 (February 13, 1986):35, quoted; [Leon E. Hay], Secretary-Treasurer's Report, 1965-66, p. 2, 1966-67, p. 3; Paul S. Olscamp, president of Bowling Green State University, to Author, February 27, 1986; Secretaries' or Secretary-Treasurers' Reports, 1963-64 through 1969-70, inquiries concerning chapter formation; [Robert S. Wasley], Secretary-Treasurer's Report, 1969-70, p. 4; and Kathy Williams, "Charles T. Horngren: Management Accounting's Renaissance Man," Management Accounting 67 (January 1986):26-28.

cities to form institutions that belong to both systems, and are designated accordingly. In the first case, the union occurred on the creation of the Purdue unit.

The six branch universities all graduated their first senior classes between 1967 (South Bend and Gary) and 1970 (Indianapolis and Kokomo). Accounting had traditionally been one of the principal subjects taught at the predecessor two-year units. Leon Hay, who had joined the main-campus faculty three years before the founding of Beta Alpha in 1957, recalls that "a hell of an allegiance to Bloomington" had prevailed among the outlying sites throughout the period of his own experience.

In their early years as four-year schools, the business programs at the branch campuses were all centrally administered from Bloomington, leading to a concept that they were accredited derivatively, "through" the main campus. This position was consistent with present-day AACSB standards. The general policy is that a branch program should be included within an evaluation of a '"unit holding or seeking accreditation"' unless it:

a. falls '"outside the jurisdiction or participating control of the dean or administrative head"' of that unit;
b. is '"located beyond a reasonable commuting distance"' from the other school; and
c. confers a '"degree designation and transcript"' that are '"clearly differentiated"' from those identified with the main campus.

Beta Alpha Chapter accordingly began a practice of offering membership to second-semester seniors at the other campuses who met chapter eligibility requirements that were somewhat higher than national standards. Such an opportunity would be extended as soon as the school had achieved four-year status, subject to Hay's qualification that

> probably it took us a year or two to wake up to the fact that there were persons at [the branch sites] . . . who would have been eligible if they were attending the Bloomington campus.

The nearest new four-year school was at Indianapolis, some fifty miles away. In the 1970s, joint meetings were held from time to time, usually in Bloomington, between Beta Alpha and the accounting group located in the capital city. The other locations were too far away to permit such interaction.

This approach naturally prompts questions concerning the activity program, "attendance" requirements in particular. The National Council maintained strict standards in the latter area, for example counting members who were part-time students or, until 1968, even students who had changed from accounting to another major field. Leon Hay and his fellow councilors had agreed in 1967

> that if a chapter initiate[d] students from more than one campus[,] it must include all students in reports under the Chapter Activity Program, not merely students at the home campus . . . .

Nonetheless, according to Hay members from Indiana's outlying campuses were <u>not</u> counted in measuring attendance at Beta Alpha meetings, based on the impracticability of their participation.

Changed conditions have sharply reduced Indiana's experiment in multiple-campus membership within a single fraternal chapter. The business schools at Gary, South Bend, Fort Wayne, Kokomo, and New Albany are all individually administered. None of them was listed in 1984 within the ranks of AACSB-qualified programs. Bloomington and Indianapolis, however, share a joint "Core Campus" School of Business, having full responsibility for undergraduate studies in both cities. Many faculty members teach in both locations. Although the five other programs are autonomous, "[t]he School of Business cooperates with the regional campuses and provides them counsel and other cooperative efforts."

In the present day, then, Beta Alpha is strictly a two-campus chapter,

initiating students from Bloomington and Indianapolis. In addition, account ing clubs are active at both sites, at the regional Indiana-Purdue campus in Fort Wayne (whose business school retains the first identity), and perhap at other branches. Upon leaving the National Council in 1981, incidentally, former fraternal president James Pattillo joined the faculty at South Bend.

Purdue, finally, has its own "Calumet" campus in Hammond, representing the greater Chicago area. Because that school has conducted an independent business program since before Zeta Alpha was installed at West Lafayette in 1980, there has been no basis for any outreach by the chapter to the regiona institution. The lack of geographical proximity would have prevented a close association in any case.[2]

At the 1968 National Council meeting over which Leon Hay presided, the new councilor elected represented a university system similar, at the time, to Indiana's. It was only fitting, then, that he was asked to "study the matter of schools with multiple locations, with the assistance of such faculty vice-presidents as he m[ight] designate." Bob Wasley of Colorado duly formed a committee that would over the next year develop far-reaching proposals.

---

[2]AAA Road Atlas, pp. 38-39; "AACSB Accreditation Council"; Barron's Profiles, s.v. "Indiana: Indiana University; Purdue University/Calumet"; Milton R. Blood, AACSB Managing Director and Director of Accreditation, to Author, February 21, 1986, quoted; [Harvey E. Donley], "1967-68 Instructions for Activity Program," Newsletter 7 (Fall 1967):5, "1968-69 Instructions," Newsletter 8 (Fall 1968):6; Robert K. Eskew, Zeta Alpha FVP, to Author, February 13, 1986 (postmark); N. J. Greenberg, Director of Undergraduate Business Programs at Indiana-Purdue in Fort Wayne, to Author, March 28, 1986, response to inquiry of March 26; Bruce Harrah-Conforth, Indiana University Archives, to Author, February 17, 1986; Hasselback, 1984 Directory, individual listing, s.v. "Pattillo, James W."; Leon E. Hay to Author, interview, May 2, 1980 (quoted), January 7, 1986 (1st indented citation); John G. Helmkamp, accounting department chairman at Indiana, to Author, April 4, 1986; National Council Minutes, 1967, p. 2, 2nd citation; Straughn and Straughan, eds., Lovejoy's College Guide, s.v. "Indiana: Indiana University at South Bend; Indiana University-Purdue University at Fort Wayne"; and Jack R. Wentworth, business dean at Indiana, to Author, February 24, 1986, quoted.

Formation of the Wasley Committee, 1968-69, and Proposal of Fundamental Change

Background to committee composition

Besides the main campus at Boulder, the University of Colorado had since 1964 and 1965, respectively, maintained commuter branches in both Denver and Colorado Springs. Business work at all three sites was administered from Boulder. According to Harvey Donley, Nu Chapter was interested at the time in admitting accounting majors from the nearby Denver campus. Such a step was never taken, however, because of the need for ongoing professional activity on the part of Beta Alpha Psi students, granting that in terms of location (if not the nonresident nature of the Denver operation) a reasonable level of interaction would have been feasible. Due to its different objectives, the Colorado chapter of the honor society Beta Gamma Sigma did begin to elect members from the two branches. As of 1985, incidentally, the University of Colorado at Denver had established an independent business school.

Professor Wasley selected faculty advisors Alan F. Smith of Beta Alpha at Indiana and Donald Lux of Xi at Syracuse to assist him in the study. Smith, who had been in Bloomington for three years, had recently completed doctoral work at Colorado. Through ownership of Utica College (fifty miles away), the source of a 1968-69 chapter-formation inquiry, Syracuse University may have been one of the few private universities operating a branch unit. Professor Lux was probably asked to serve for a different reason, however, for problems raised by "evening enrollments" were also reviewed by the committee, a natural extension of the agenda in that many branch campuses were urban schools attracting many part-time students. Syracuse conducted an extensive "University College" program for evening students.

Although no details are available, Wasley's group met one or more times during the year 1968-69, given that a total cost of $498 was incurred. The 1969 minutes reported that two major conclusions had been reached.

Two major conclusions or recommendations

The committee probably only reinforced existing policy in one area, in declaring that (as expressed years later by the chairman):

> a school or college which was in another city from its parent had to be as completely free of its parent school as possible in terms of administration policy in order to install a chapter.

Under existing administrative arrangements, then, no basis was recognized for establishing separate chapters at the auxiliary campuses within Indiana or Colorado, for example.

Far more strikingly, Councilor Wasley and his associates proposed that Beta Alpha Psi seek to broaden its membership base, emphasizing "professional" aspects of the program, by discontinuing the AAcCSB accreditation requirement. Instead, the National Council would evaluate accounting departments by means, in part, of an appropriate questionnaire. It was felt that the traditional quality-control policy had severely limited the fraternal base, given that "the AA[c]CSB had accredited only a small fraction of the schools which taught accounting."

No action was taken in 1969 on the Wasley committee's far-reaching recommendation, beyond qualified endorsement of the questionnaire proposal. Wasley and incoming president Harvey Donley were asked to incorporate a relevant evaluative section within the material submitted to petitioning groups, but no such action was taken during the coming year. In 1971, finally, the National Council unanimously approved a "checklist" for use in the new site visitation process, and a related policy statement, drawn

up by Secretary-Treasurer Wasley.[3]

The AA[c]CSB issue would remain before Beta Alpha Psi for several years to come, until it was finally decided to retain unchanged the constitutional restriction adopted a generation earlier. In due course concern developed over a period of years that the accrediting body was tending to "downgrade" accounting studies had been alleviated, and a number of branch campuses were independently accredited.

Retention of the Accreditation Requirement Following Serious Reconsideration

Broader background of concern, going back to earlier education critiques

The large number of accounting majors not attending professionally accredited schools was only one reason for concern that the AAcCSB linkage might have outlived its usefulness to the fraternity. As related by Bob Wasley, during his tenure as a councilor there was "a strong feeling" within the governing body that the accrediting agency:

> was trying to downgrade the importance of accounting in the business curriculum by allowing [or encouraging] college administrations . . . to be prejudiced toward the teaching of accounting in many ways: (1) wages, (2) reducing the number of required accounting hours in . . . curricula, (3) dropping the name 'accounting' from the name of the school, etc.

---

[3]Akey, ed., Encyclopedia of Associations, vol. 1, section 5, "Educational Organizations," s.v. "American Assembly of Collegiate Schools of Business"; Barrons' Profiles, s.v. "Colorado: University of Colorado"; Dean of business school at Colorado (or staff), to Author, February 21, 1986; [Harvey E. Donley], Secretary-Treasurer's Report, 1968-69, pp. 5, 8, 21; Donley to Author, interview, May 2, 1980; Hasselback, 1984 Directory, individual listing, s.v. "Smith, Allan F."; "Local Chapter News," Newsletter 6 (Fall 1965):285; National Council Minutes, 1968, p. 4 (quoted), 1969, pp. 4 (quoted), 5, 9, 1970, p. 9, 1971, pp. 1 (quoted), 2; Straughn and Straughn, eds., Lovejoy's College Guide, s.v. "Colorado--Colorado, University of: Boulder, Denver," "New York: Utica College of Syracuse University"; Robert S. Wasley, Secretary-Treasurer's Report, 1969-70, p. 1, 1970-71, pp. 1-2; and Wasley to Author, January 10, 1986, quoted, including indented passage. In referring to the evening program at Syracuse, the author drew from personal teaching experience of a later date.

The third point may not have been widely pertinent. The undergraduate unit at New York University was still the School of Commerce, Finance, and Accounts, however, at the conclusion of the Mu Chapter alumni controversy in 1965, but had become the College of Business and Public Administration by the time of a visit by Robert Maust in 1971.

In terms of broader background, two studies of business education published in 1959, sponsored respectively by the Carnegie and Ford Foundations, had exerted substantial influence. Franklin C. Pierson and collaborators, and Robert A. Gordon and James E. Howell, had both held that "mediocrity and vocationalism permeated business schools"; business majors generally were of indifferent ability and motivation, although accounting students tended to outshine the others; and faculties lacked proper academic credentials.

Accounting educators generally accepted the later contention, as doctoral qualification soon became recognized as a basic faculty standard. They were troubled, however, by the strong emphasis placed by the Pierson and Gordon-Howell reports upon accounting as a managerial field as distinguished from a socially vital independent profession. Faculty members and practicing accountants alike were cool to the proposal that the traditional undergraduate emphasis on financial accounting and auditing be replaced with a managerial focus.

An important outgrowth of the reaction that emerged to the 1959 critiques was the preparation of the influential AICPA study Horizons for a Profession, identifying the essential "common body of knowledge" for entry-level public accountants. More pertinent to Beta Alpha Psi, however, were broader educational developments that appeared to reflect the influence of the Pierson and Gordon-Howell analyses. New curricular emphasis was placed on "planning, management, and quantitative analysis," and, as later illustrated in detail,

some business schools abandoned undergraduate instruction.

The former development, at any rate, was in keeping with the evolution of the accreditation association/assembly's curricular standards. It is not surprising, then, that the idea of discontinuing the accreditation requirement within Beta Alpha Psi did not end with the disbanding of the Wasley committee in 1969.

Review of the issue, 1971-73, leading to a reaffirmation of the rule

Prelimininary discussion

The AA(c)CSB issue was raised next in May 1971, during the first long-range planning committee meeting. Retired councilor Emerson Henke stated that the trend within the association was "to deemphasize the accounting curriculum." Since there were "good" accounting programs at nonaccredited schools, he proposed that it was time to consider granting charters to other institutions. President Charles Taylor recommended that the matter be pursued further.

No relevant policy changes were discussed at the 1971 annual meeting, however. Instead, the accrediting agency was discussed primarily in terms of possible Beta Alpha Psi membership in the association's recently formed "Assembly," open to nonaccredited schools, business firms, and governmental and professional organizations. Such an affiliation had succeeded a non-evaluative "associate" membership introduced in the sixties that was not comparable to prior associate status as discussed in chapter 2. A remarkable increase in participation at that level registered in the "watershed" year of 1968 had by 1971 led the association to undertake a change in corporate structure that within two years would yield the present-day AACSB.

In agreeing on the desirability of such an affiliation, the National

Council (prompted by a new AAcCSB report concerning interprofessional relations) expressed interest in any prospect that the other organization might be able to perform a "service role" for the fraternity. Dean Henke's later recommendation that Beta Alpha Psi request office space or services from the accreditation body was rejected, based on estimated costs and benefits. President Robert Wasley was asked to arrange for the aforementioned membership, nonetheless, at a nominal fee of twenty-five dollars. The affiliation (which has been maintained through the present day) would be delayed, however, until the year 1972-73.

At the regular meeting in 1971, Wasley had been instructed to invite AAcCSB president Kermit Hanson of the University of Washington to attend the long-range planning session scheduled for December. In lieu of meeting with the Council, and his Baylor counterpart Henke, Dean Hanson wrote in essence that his organization '"in no way s[ought] to diminish the role of accounting departments or the teaching of accounting"'.

The fraternal leadership was not readily convinced on the matter, however. They devoted much of their two-day December gathering to Emerson Henke's proposal that the National Council form an "assembly" made up of non-AAcCSB schools, regionally accredited, that were interested in establishing chapters. It was asserted that the Council could at once assist such schools in meeting appropriate standards for chartering, academic and otherwise, and see to it that "the status of accounting" were "preserve[d]" at those sites pursuing professional accreditation. For purposes of quality control, the Council would evaluate the accounting programs at such schools, but not other fields of instruction.

Past President Charles Taylor added that the Fraternity "should be willing to establish a chapter at any school which me[t] the Council's

standards," and felt that it could provide a distinct service by assessing the strengths and weaknesses of accounting departments. Harvey Donley provided a cuationary note in observing that official Beta Alpha Psi recognition might "merely lend prestige" to nonaccredited programs, rather than improving them.

A major consideration advanced was that only slightly more than a third of the estimated 426 colleges and universities offering majors in accounting were professionally accredited at one or both levels, undergraduate or graduate. Former councilor Henke asserted, in essence, that the fraternity "ha[d] to recognize where accountants [we]re being educated, which [wa]s not necessarily AA[c]CSB schools." In light, however, of the magnitude of the proposed evaluative task, the Council asked President Wasley to solicit opinion on the topic by submitting a questionnaire (approved by the full group) to past councilors, current faculty advisors, and other appropriate parties. The latter group might include business deans drawn from the accounting field.

Finally, Wasley was encouraged at the midterm meeting to advise American Accounting Association president Charles T. Zlatkovich, of Texas, of the fraternity's concern about accounting education, perhaps recommending that the next AAcCSB president be invited to address the 1972 AAA convention. As it happened, comparable arrangements were worked out based on an opportunity presented on the fraternal leader's home campus, and probably contributing to an abrupt abatement of support for a new policy.

Retreat by the Council

Bob Wasley conducted the survey as requested. The heart of the memorandum submitted for comment to all FVPs and past councilors was a statement of pros and cons regrading an independent evaluation program, reprinted as exhibit 27. Strong support for change was apparently not forthcoming, for

EXHIBIT 27

PROS AND CONS ON COUNCIL EVALUATION OF ACCOUNTING DEPARTMENTS: PRESIDENT WASLEY'S 1972 STATEMENT

Possible Arguments in Favor of Establishing Beta Alpha Psi Chapters at Schools Not Accredited by the AACSB.

1.) Approximately 55% of all accounting graduates come from such schools, but, due to the schools' lack of AACSB accreditation, their graduates are denied an opportunity for membership in the fraternity.

2.) The granting of a charter might assist in the development, or preservation and improvement, of a good accounting program at a non-AACSB-accredited school.

3.) This move would compel the fraternity to determine its own detailed criteria for the establishment of chapters. The result of this, hopefully, would be that chapters were established only at schools with strong accounting programs. The AACSB accreditation reviews the operation, faculty, and facilities of an entire school. It is not primarily centered on the accounting program.

4.) Beta Alpha Psi could, by expansion of its membership, encourage more capable students to enter the accounting profession.

5.) Perhaps someone other than the AACSB needs to spell out the recognized characteristics of a good accounting program. If the AAA and AACSB won't do it, Beta Alpha Psi might make the initial move.

Possible Arguments Against Establishing Beta Alpha Psi Chapters at Schools Not Accredited by the AACSB.

1.) It would reduce the status and prestige of the fraternity to discontinue the direct affiliation with AACSB-accredited schools.

2.) If the direct affiliation with AACSB is severed, there could be a flood of petitions for chapters which could easily overtax our chief administrative officer, the Secretary-Treasurer. This could precipitate a complete reorganization of the administrative structure of the fraternity.

3.) This would cause the fraternity to become, in some respects, the equivalent of an accreditation agency.

4.) It seems probable that many schools would seek affiliation with the fraternity primarily to enhance their own prestige--rather than because they accept its philosophy and objectives. Coordination and/or supervision of the program of the fraternity would virtually disappear. Membership would become (only) a mark of achievement--analogous, perhaps, to existing "honorary societies" in mathematics, chemistry, etc.

SOURCE: Robert S. Wasley to Faculty Vice-Presidents and past Council members, February 16, 1972, p. 3. Transcript, with minor punctuation changes.

the accreditation issue was not directly discussed at the 1972 annual meeting. It arose incidentally within a discussion of whether Beta Alpha Psi should be identified *explicitly* as an "honor society," so that local chapters could decide whether to conduct a professional program. Concern was expressed about reducing the professional dimension still further than had the activity program option, and it was suggested, without explanation, that a "depart[ure]" from the accreditation rule might move the fraternity unduly toward the honorary side.

On President Wasley's initiative, the president-elect of the accreditation agency was invited that year to address a luncheon or (presumably) other plenary session of the American Accounting Association. William H. Baughn, who had been the fraternal leader's dean at Colorado since 1964, gave a talk that was intended "to allay the fears of Beta Alpha Psi" and other parties troubled by academic trends. His reassurances were apparently well received by the National Council, for the issue that had dominated the midterm gathering a year earlier was not mentioned at the final long-range planning committee meeting, held in December 1972.

The modern challenge to the accreditation rule was concluded during Dean Baughn's term as 1973-74 president of the American "Assembly" of Collegiate Schools of Business. The only pertinent reference found in the 1973 annual minutes simply cited an agreement among the councilors that "branch chapters" could not be established, at non-AASCB schools, "due to the accreditation problem."

Finally, there was a division of opinion on the general issue within the "Special Committee" assembled in Chicago in the fall of 1973, under the leadership of Bob Maust, to evaluate the overall fraternal program. Among the five members, it appears that Maust and Tom Burns supported the traditional

restriction and that Herb Miller was critical of it. Ultimately, however, it was agreed that "as of" that time "the requirement of only AACSB schools for Beta Alpha Psi . . . was the only acceptable" policy. The important point was made that many institutions already accredited (estimated, only slightly on the high side, at 60-70) had not formed chapters, giving the fraternity ample opportunity for further expansion even from the base that already existed.

Although not mentioned, a notable feature of the accreditation list by that time was the presence of several "branch" campuses in the narrow sense, a trend whose continuation would lead to a growing list of Beta Alpha Psi chapters located at such schools.

Accreditation of "branch" campuses

The very year that the Wasley committee proposed that the fraternity sever its traditional relationship with the accrediting agency, on behalf initially of branch campuses of state universities, the first such schools aside from Nebraska at Omaha became accredited. Texas at Arlington, Missouri at Kansas City, and Louisiana State in New Orleans joined the AAcCSB ranks in 1969. A year later the Missouri campus at St. Louis entered the fold, along with the Wisconsin branches at Milwaukee and (as of the imminent merger with the Wisconsin State system) Oshkosh. Over the following dozen years the Wisconsin campuses in Whitewater, Eau Claire, and La Crosse would likewise earn business accreditation, along with Southern Illinois at Edwardsville.

Between 1971 and 1982, inclusive, Beta Alpha Psi chapters were formed at the LSU branch (now the University of New Orleans), Texas at Arlington, both Missouri schools, and Wisconsin at Whitewater and Eau Claire. Belatedly, in 1985, Eta Theta was installed at the Milwaukee institution concerning which the branch-campus issue had originally arisen a generation earlier.

During the seventies, both Alabama in Birmingham and Arkansas at Little Rock were in turn recognized by the AACSB, and chartered by Beta Alpha Psi. During the eighties, through 1985-86, Houston at Clear Lake City, North Carolina at both Greensboro and Charlotte, Texas at San Antonio, and Tennessee at Chattanooga established fraternal chapters.

In summary, the fraternity had spread to a number of branch universities without any need to depart in the least from its traditional standards.[4]

Besides branch campuses, the most seriously discussed environmental issue of the fourth era was the increased reliance in some cases upon graduate-student membership. As policy changes or other influences reversed such a trend in selected instances already cited, eligibility criteria that were not questioned at the time invited substantial graduate membership at many schools. Efforts made to facilitate the successful operation or more or less graduate-oriented chapters were closely related to the 1969 reform of the activity program. A broad mix of opinion expressed by former councilors

---

[4]"AACSB Accreditation Council"; AACSB Membership Directory, 1980-81 ([St. Louis: AACSB, 1980]), pp. 1, 89; Norton M. Bedford, review of Horizons for a Profession, by Robert H. Roy and James H. MacNeill, The Accounting Review 43 (January 1968):208-210; Milton R. Blood to Author, February 21, 1986; Thomas J. Burns to Author, interview, May 3, 1980; "Chapter Information," 1983-84 Annual Report, ed. Metcalf, pp. 31-38; Hollis A. Dixon, Long-Range Planning Committee Minutes, December 1972; Dixon, "National Chapter Meeting" (Minutes), 1973, p. 1; Dixon, Secretary-Treasurer's Report, 1972-73, pp. 8-9; Frederick G. Horn, Mu Chapter FVP, to Julius Roller, March 6, 1965 (letterhead); Nancy Harke, Beta Alpha Psi executive secretary, to Author, by telephone, September 19, 1986; Ely Kushel, Mu FVP, to Author, March 10, 1986 (letterhead); S. Mason, University of Wisconsin-Madison (Archives), to Author, April 1, 1986; Robert S. Maust, Long-Range Planning Committee Minutes, December 1971, pp. 1-2 (quoted), 3; Maust, Visitation Report--Mu, December 15, 1971; National Council Minutes, 1971, pp. 2, 3 (quoted), 1972, p. 2 (no. 4.1, quoted), 1973, p. 3 (no. 28.0, quoted), February 1974, p. 2 (nos. 3-3.1, quoted, 3.5); Previts and Merino, Accounting in America, pp. 283, 284 (quoted); Smith, Forty Acres, pp. 180-81; [David E. Tinius], "Chapter Installations," Beta Alpha Psi, The National Accounting Fraternity: 1985 Annual Report, ed. [Tinius, (National Council, 1985)], p. 18; James A. Viehland, Associate Director of AACSB, to Author (by telephone), February 7, 1985, quoted; Robert S. Wasley to Author, January 10, 1986, indented citation; Wasley, "What About Our Four-Year Accounting Major [?]," Newsletter 10 (Spring 1972):4; and Who's Who in America 43 (1984-85), s.v. "Baughn, William Hubert."

on the place of advanced students within Beta Alpha Psi is of particular interest in light of later restrictions placed on their admission.

Relatively Graduate-oriented Chapters

Background and Introduction

From the beginning Beta Alpha Psi had been an organization primarily for undergraduate students. Even with the postwar growth in advanced studies in business and accounting, the fraternity had retained the traditional focus while welcoming increasing numbers of graduate students into membership. Indeed, Alpha alumnus Leon Hay had inquired just prior to the formation of Beta Alpha at Indiana whether master's-degree candidates were eligible.

As was explained in chapter 10, however, Beta Alpha, Theta at Texas, and other chapters became predominantly graduate-oriented in membership, for a time, based on local admissions policies or practices. Through changes in the activity program associated with a special definition for "eligibility," any such trend was for the moment halted or reversed. Exceptions were based on misunderstanding of national standards (as at Gamma Epsilon at Toledo), an honor-society orientation, or other local conditions.

Related references from the 1969 minutes and following year's Newsletter point up, however, the clear prospect of disproportionately high graduate-level membership in many chapters. Incoming president Harvey Donley was asked to express in a forthcoming column the National Council's "interest . . . in making the chapter[s] available to graduate students" in accounting, "most, perhaps all," of whom would be eligible. In a "Letter" of Winter 1970 dealing in general terms with challenges and opportunities for the accounting profession during the new decade, Donley duly exhorted the local units to "mak[e] the fraternity available to all those who are eligible," adding:

> [P]lease do not overlook graduate students in accounting; almost all such students would seem to meet the constitutional requirements at least after one academic term on the campus.

Although the use of the expression "at least" (referred to later) is initially puzzling, the overall thrust of the statement is clear. In setting minimum academic requirements for eligibility, the constitution of the day made no distinction between degree levels. Yet graduate students as a group would have significantly higher grades than undergraduates; and indeed a grade average of no lower than B would commonly have been required for completing a graduate degree. Even given higher entry requirements than set by the national constitution, the eligibility of graduate-level accounting students would have tended to be a routine matter.

The experiment with an optional activity program that was launched in 1969 was responsive in part to a graduate-oriented environment, by encouraging greater flexibility in chapter operations. Concurrently, an effort was made to try out a third kind of reporting system, that might ultimately simplify competitive participation. Only a meager record exists of the limited endeavor that resulted from the work of a 1968-69 committee appointed to address the issues posed by large-scale graduate membership.

The Roller Committee of 1968-69, and a Subsequent Reporting Experiment

Recommendations of the committee

The committee was chaired by former councilor Julius Roller of Washington, who had returned to the faculty vice-presidency at Delta. He was assisted by faculty leaders Thomas Burns of Omicron at Ohio State and (for 1965-68) Samuel Frumer of Beta Alpha at Indiana. The three state universities sponsored large graduate programs, and significant numbers of students would in each case have stayed on to pursue advanced degrees. Frumer had been in

interim FVP at the beginning of the decade, while Leon Hay was on leave teaching in Guatamala, as Beta Alpha was moving toward predominantly graduate membership.

During the year the Roller committee held one or more meetings, expending $427. Four main recommendations were presented to the National Council. Three of them were "substantially embodied" in the new activity program: (a) elimination of the "competitive" element; (b) identification of "specific constitutional requirements" of operation; and (c) continued restriction of chartering to accounting groups having already functioned for two years, and mandatory participation in the activity program for the first two years.

Perhaps the most interesting proposal was (d) that a "new reporting program" be devised, "emphasiz[ing] annual plan and summary of performance." The Council decided to "experiment" with an alternative system based on the issuance of summary reports once or twice yearly, in place of the standard monthly submissions. Although from a timing standpoint they would be like the reports to be filed (initially) at year's end by nonparticipants in the activity program, in scope of coverage they would be more comparable to traditional ones.

The reinterpretation of the activity program as a chapter option thus facilitated matters, rather than complicating them. By not taking part in the points competition, an experimenting chapter would have maximum opportunity to develop meaningful new reporting approaches, while the national secretary-treasurer would not have to try to assign points under uncharted conditions not comparable to those of regular participating groups.

As discussed later, three chapters were by this point made up _entirely_ of graduate students, or moving toward that condition. Beta Nu at Tulane had taken official inactive status, however, while serious operating

weaknesses left both Gamma at Northwestern and Gamma Iota at UCLA ill suited for a reporting experiment. The chapters cited as potential contributors to this effort were instead Alpha at Illinois, Theta at Texas, Nu at Colorado, Beta Rho at Baylor, and Roller's and Burns' respective Delta and Omicron Chapters. Only the latter two groups accepted the invitation, however.

Very limited experimentation: Delta and Omicron, 1969-73

The only reference found in the 1970 minutes to a special reporting initiative, separate from the optional activity program, was an agenda item citing only the Ohio State chapter. Based on a 1971 reference noted presently, and the recollections of Delta's Fred Mueller, the Washington unit may be identified as a second experimenter.

During the two years 1969-71, Delta and Omicron reported only at the close of the chapter year. As indicated in chapter 10, the National Council voted in 1971 to require nonparticipants in the activity program, *including* "the University of Washington and Ohio State University," to report semi-annually. Two years later monthly reporting was reinstituted for all chapters, discarding any innovations that the two chapters might have generated. No specific information is available, unfortunately, on the very limited reporting experiment, probably implying that no particular contribution was recognized.

Interesting data do exist concerning compliance by Delta and Omicron with constitutional mandates, or the absence thereof. Over the period 1969-73 the following levels of activity were reported, where "M" designates meetings and "I" stands for initiations:

	1969-70		1970-71		1971-72		1972-73	
	M	I	M	I	M	I	M	I
Delta	6	2	12	1	22	2	27	3
Omicron	11	2	18	2	25	3	22	2.

These figures indicate a high level of chapter activity, except for Washington in the first year and Ohio State in the last one. Delta's total number of meetings in 1969-70 was constitutionally sufficient only through counting one of the initiations, in recognition that a single ceremony was required. With its tradition of weekly dinner meetings, the chapter may have met more often than reported during the first two years.

Omicron was seriously deficient in 1972-73, on any interpretation, and was in fact placed on probation for two years. As a result the Ohio State chapter resumed formal points competition a year before other "nonparticipating" groups.

Until 1973, the National Council had shown more concern about Delta, mainly due to its failure to file an audit report during the first two years. Again in 1972-73, a year of remarkable reported activity, no audit statement was received from Seattle. Although the chapter had complied with all requirements in the year just past, the Council had in 1972 sized it up as a group that had not "bothered with reports" despite having been "probably one of the most active chapters."

A pattern of somewhat cavalier reporting at Washington was attributed to a measure of frustration about having been unable to achieve the top rank in the interchapter competition, based primarily on attendance requirements. In 1959, however, the Grand Council had made a concession to Delta at a time that sixteen meetings were required for full credit under activity item 4, "Regular Meetings." Delta had been allowed to count each month the two

meetings at which attendance had been highest.[5]

Interviewing of former national presidents in 1980 (primarily), by which time relevant entry requirements had been strengthened considerably, revealed a broad range of opinion on the place of graduate students within Beta Alpha Psi.

A Broad Mix of Viewpoints on Graduate-level Participation, in a Day of More Restrictive Entry

Selected councilor interpretations

One of the most favorable interpretations was expressed by Fred Mueller. The basic educational role of the fraternity, in his judgement, is to supply experience and content that are not suited to the classroom, or for which there is inadequate time for formal coverage. Terminal master's candidates share the professional aspirations of undergraduate majors, and thus should benefit equally from Beta Alpha Psi involvement. Doctoral students preparing for academic careers stand through their participation to develop more ease with groups of people, and to become more aware of what students expect from faculty members.

Andy Anderson supported Mueller regarding master's candidates, because of their "professional" orientation, but (commenting in 1980) saw no particular fraternal role for doctoral students. Bob Wasley observed that M.B.A. students at Colorado were often "ardent advocates" of Beta Alpha Psi

---

[5]"Chapter News," Newsletter 5 (Fall 1961):454; Harvey E. Donley, "Letter from the President," Newsletter 8 (Winter 1970):2, indented citation; [Donley], Secretary-Treasurer's Report, 1967-68, p. 4, 1968-69, pp. 8-9, 21; Donley to Author, interview, May 2, 1980; Grand Council Minutes Book, 1959, p. 4; Leon E. Hay to Nolan E. Williams, October 22, 1957; Fred J. Mueller to Author, interview, November 27, 1979; National Council Minutes, 1968, pp. 10-11, 1969, pp. 4, 8 (both quoted), 9, 1970, agenda, 1971, pp. 2, 3 (quoted), 1972, p. 5 (quoted), 1973, p. 5; and Secretary-Treasurers' Reports, 1969-70 through 1972-73, coverage of audit report deficiencies and nonparticipating chapters.

participation, seeking local offices as a "tool" for job acquisition.

While finding some merit in Mueller's position, Andy Penz was somewhat skeptical because of the lack of time characteristic of graduate study. A similar reference was made by Tom Dickerson, although the late Western Reserve professor noted that some advanced students would already be experienced chapter members through election as juniors or seniors. Emerson Henke and Harold Royer were especially dubious that the fraternity was suited to graduate students at any level, although the latter retired councilor did not favor exempting even an all-graduate chapter from the activity program.

Harvey Donley remarked that graduate students were "usually" a problem within Beta Alpha Psi, but "sometimes" were chapter leaders. Perhaps based on scholarship factors, he recalled that in his day there had been some resentment from wholly undergraduate sources toward chapters that included advanced students. Vern Vincent felt that the fraternity was designed primarily for students who did not plan to pursue graduate work, although he presumably did not mean to imply that other accounting majors should take a less active role in the organization. He did not think that graduate members should serve as chapter officers.

Speaking from firsthand experience of activity program reform in the late 1970s, Jim Pattillo asserted that the modern framework was broad enough for "any" educational format, including a graduate-student chapter. Tom Burns, however, cited the academically elite graduate school of business as an exception. He saw no existent fraternal "model" for schools like Harvard, Chicago, and Stanford, commenting that "We need Harvard more than Harvard needs us." This interpretation recognizes a limitation in the "comprehensive" character of Beta Alpha Psi cited in the title of this study.

As related in chapter 16, Tom Burns would play a major role in the

development of the graduate-level "case" competition that was intended, in part, to reduce the "model" deficiency perceived. That limitation had been intensified by the abandonment, in the seventies, of the 1969 viewpoint that nearly 100% eligibility of graduate-level accounting students was desirable.

Much stricter eligibility requirements

In 1972, on former president Donley's motion, required accounting work had been extended beyond a year's course, and a requirement had been adopted that candidates '"[s]hall rank not lower than [the top] 35% of class within the University in general scholarship"'. The latter provision appears to have related undergraduate and graduate students to respective peer groups, and thus introduced a severe restriction on eligibility at the advanced level, but was decidedly ambiguous.

At a meeting of early 1975, Editor Doris Cook recommended that special coverage be developed for graduate-student eligibility. President Hollis Dixon voiced concern that some chapters might be admitting advanced students based on "undergraduate work done at schools which d[id] not qualify" for a charter, bringing to mind Harvey Donley's statement (in 1970) that graduates would commonly be eligible "at least" after one term. The National Council later in 1975 restricted induction to graduate students, concentrating in accounting, who after at least one semester or two quarters of relevant study (a) stood academically "within the top 35% of their graduate class" within the business school, and, on a 4.0-scale, (b) held at least a 3.5 average in accounting and a 3.25 average overall at the graduate level. The first provision would probably have often been more restrictive than the second one, even though the traditional B/B- (3.0 and 2.5) standard was

maintained for undergraduates.[6]

Fourth-era coverage is concluded by reference to four Beta Alpha Psi schools that elected during the 1960s to emulate the strictly graduate-level approach to business education found at Harvard, for example, by eliminating their undergraduate programs. Subsequent chapter developments did not bode well for the operation of exclusively graduate chapters.

Emergence of Exclusively Graduate Chapters at Four Beta Alpha Psi Schools

Historical Background on Wholly Graduate Programs

The most striking development concerning the level of students served within Beta Alpha Psi could not be altered through a change in fraternal policies. During the fourth era four chapters became strictly graduate-level units, or moved to the point of so becoming, because the undergraduate programs at their schools were phased out. Two of the four chapters involved were new ones of the period, and in one case the decision to abandon non-graduate work had preceded the installation. Three of the units were soon or eventually disbanded, two of them before the much more restrictive policy on graduate membership took effect. The fourth group benefited from later resumption of undergraduate studies.

A strictly graduate-level approach to business education was far from new. It was very much identified with a half-dozen elite private institutions: Stanford, Chicago, and Ivy League campuses Harvard, Dartmouth, Cornell, and Columbia. Four of these schools had been charter members (1916)

---

[6] Beta Alpha Psi, "National Bylaws," National Constitution and Bylaws (1977), article 4, sections 1, 2 (quoted); interviews with ex-councilors cited, besides Mueller and Royer, March, April, July, 1980; Fred J. Mueller to Author, interview, November 27, 1979, quoted; National Council Minutes, 1972, p. 8 (no. 18.2, quoted), August 1974, p. 8 (no. 7-m), February 1975, p. 2 (no. 5, quoted), May-June, 1975, p. 6; and Harold L. Royer to Author, September 12, 1985, interview equivalent.

of the AAcCSB, having been joined later by Stanford and Cornell.

Significantly, none of them was affiliated with Beta Alpha Psi. Two of the business schools had been approached during the fraternity's formative period, and one of them had later registered some degree of interest. Columbia, offering undergraduate business work until the early 1950s, had been contacted in 1919, a month after the formation of Alpha Chapter; and submitted an inquiry to the Grand Council a generation later, not long before wartime deactivation. In 1923 an unsuccessful effort had been made to promote the accounting organization at Darmouth's Amos Tuck School, which on its founding in 1900 had pioneered graduate study in business. Except for an inquiry from Cornell in 1969-70, there is no other record of contact between Beta Alpha Psi and any of these graduate business schools concerning the formation of a chapter.

In 1963, the American Association had for the first time classified members by academic level of accreditation, "undergraduate" or "graduate." The six schools just cited were among a dozen universities cited at the graduate level only. The other six institutions offered undergraduate degrees at the time, however. Rutgers and Carnegie-Mellon (then Carnegie Institute of Technology) did so under the administration of appropriate graduate divisions.

From Beta Alpha Psi ranks, Western Reserve was recognized at the advanced level only even though undergraduate programs had been offered long before the organization in 1952 of the School of Business. Cleveland College, a largely adult-education unit with which Tom Dickerson was identified, had opened a business school in 1926. B.A. degrees in business had been available to students at Adelbert (men's) and Flora Stone Mather (women's) Colleges by way primarily of the economics department of the

former division. Upon the federation in 1967 of Western Reserve and Case Institute of Technology, the School of Business was combined with its counterpart at Case to form the modern-day School of Management.

More interesting cases of solely graduate-level accreditation were those of Northwestern, Pittsburgh, and Tulane, the sites of Gamma, Alpha Tau and Beta Nu Chapters. The latter two schools were already in the process of eliminating their undergraduate programs in 1963, and a similar action would be taken at Northwestern soon thereafter. Finally, the University of California at Los Angeles initially enjoyed AAcCSB recognition at both levels, but would become a strictly graduate business institution not long after the chartering of Gamma Iota in 1967.[7]

The elimination of undergraduate work had been foreshadowed at Pittsburgh in the late 1950s, while at Northwestern the decision to become a graduate business school was made with dispatch in the mid-'60s.

Abandonment of Undergraduate Work at Two Pre-1960 Chapter Sites

Pittsburgh--Alpha Tau

The Grand Council had noted during the 1959 meeting that Pittsburgh was considering a change to purely graduate instruction in business (in the daytime), "using the case method of instruction." The expectation had been

---

[7] [Hazen W. Kendrick], "Dickerson Elected to Council," Newsletter [2] (March 1942):6; C. M. Kenebel, Graduate School of Industrial Administration at Carnegie-Mellon University, to Author, March 5, 1986; E. Lange, AACSB, to Author, March 4, 1986; Lovejoy, Lovejoy's College Guide, s.v. "Pennsylvania: Carnegie-Mellon University"; "News from the Chapters," Newsletter [1] (February 1936), p. [11]; Bob Psuik, Assistant University Archivist at Case Western Reserve University, to Author, February 16, March 10, 1986; R. E. Schlosser, Graduate School of Management at Rutgers University, to Author, March 11, 1986; Sheldahl, Alpha to Omega, pp. 16, 18, 127-29, 316, 318, 735, 740-42; and [Robert S. Wasley], Secretary-Treasurer's Report, 1969-70, p. 4.

that Alpha Tau "w[ould] have to be discontinued" in that event. No doubt a special point of concern was that, as noted in chapter 8 regarding Williard Stone's unusual visitation to Pitt earlier in the year after a long, cold, and bumpy night on the rails, the fraternal group was already a small one.

The decision to terminate day instruction in business was made in 1960, and the last B.B.A. class were graduated four years later. Although the B.S. degree continued to be offered to evening business students, the Grand Council understandably would not have wanted to rely strongly on a night-school program to sustain a chapter.

During the transition to a strictly advanced-level unit, the Council took a cautious and deliberate approach to the Pittsburgh situation. Councilor Vern Vincent from nearby West Virginia visited Alpha Tau during the year 1962-63, and reported on "the problems observed to exist" there at the next annual meeting. After no audit report or other evidence had been received the following year to indicate that the required number of chapter meetings had been held, Secretary-Treasurer Vincent was asked to work with Alpha Tau "on the problem of their continuity."

Vincent duly attended an initiation in March 1965. In his report for the year, he discussed the "marked decline of activity" that had occurred at Pittsburgh over the prior two years. No audit report had been received for three years, although one was in preparation (never to be filed) as of mid-August. The secretary-treasurer was "certain that far less than the minimum number of meetings" had taken place. He felt that Stanley Jablonski, who (unaccountably) had been the faculty vice-president since the installation of the chapter ten years earlier, "expect[ed] Alpha Tau to come to an early end."

Furthermore, Professor Vincent had found strong "resentment" by many

chapter alumni employed as professional accountants in Pittsburgh concerning "the decline in accounting under the new plan" at the university. They seemed actually to want the local group to fold. Based on the continuing failure to file an audit report for the preceding period, Vincent had not recognized the 1964-65 initiation, and had withheld membership certificates from the chapter. Such action by the secretary-treasurer had been approved by the Grand Council the previous summer.[8]

By 1965, Alpha Tau had fallen to last place, nationally, in the inter-chapter competition, and Vern Vincent reported to the other councilors that the "dearth of eligibles" created by the cessation of B.B.A. work had left "no good solution . . . in sight." Still, two "ranking" members of the accounting department "strongly desire[d]" that the chapter be continued, in the hope that its problems could somehow be resolved. The secretary-treasurer himself was inclined to be patient in light of a significant improvement that had occurred over the year just past at Beta Nu at Tulane, not yet all-graduate in composition.

In 1965-66, finally, the chapter hit rock bottom, having been "completely

---

[8] It was explained in chapter 10, note 11, that 1967-69 secretary-treasurer Harvey Donley did not recognize initiations until they had been properly accounted for. Under the policy adopted in 1964, an initiation would not be processed unless and until the prior year's audit report had been filed. The sanction was applicable only to the Pittsburgh ceremony of March 1965, which would have failed Donley's additional test as well. Otherwise, the 12-16 delinquences recorded annually, 1963-69 (prior to a large increase in 1969-70), were removed over the following year. Several chapters were delinquent in this area for three or more consecutive periods, up to 1970, including Alpha Omega at Fordham (five years) and Epsilon at Oregon State (four). Later, Secretary-Treasurer Hollis Dixon recognized current initiations at four of the five chapters that as of his reporting date in 1972 were two years behind in their audit reports; Alpha Omega, derelict for the seventh straight time, had not added members during the year. Hollis A. Dixon, Secretary-Treasurer's Report, 1971-72, pp. 5, 7-9; Grand Council Minutes, 1964, p. 4; Secretary-Treasurers' Reports, 1965-66 through 1970-71, p. 1 (to 1970), and listings of delinquent chapters; and [Vern H. Vincent], Secretary's Report, 1964-65, pp. 1, 3.

inactive." Professor Jablonski, who responded in place of the business dean to a letter from Secretary-Treasurer Leon Hay reporting Alpha Tau's delinquencies, indicated that he had retired in May 1966. Hay noted that, technically, there were no student members to conduct a program, since the last initiation had not been validated.

President Vincent's National Council voted in 1966 to place Alpha Tau on probation for six months. The local dean was informed that, to be restored to good standing, the group would have to:

a. Submit audit reports for the prior three years, prepared by a CPA who was not a chapter officer
b. Submit national initiation fees for the ceremony attended by Vincent in 1965
c. Indicate that a faculty member was willing to be the FVP, replacing the recently retired Jablonski, "and that a nucleus of students [was] eligible for initiation and desirous of active participation."

These conditions were not met by March 1, 1967, the closing date of the probation. Accordingly, a mail ballot was conducted concerning further disciplinary action. The Council voted to <u>revoke the charter</u>, making Alpha Tau the third chapter (following Eta at Boston University and Kappa at William and Mary) to be terminated, not counting the long-term deactivation of Epsilon at Oregon State. Some discussion later took place of repossessing the physical charter, but no such action had been taken by the summer of 1969.

Reflecting on the episode some years later, Professor Vincent felt that primarily through his influence the National Council had been too lenient with the Pittsburgh chapter. The implication was that disciplinary action should have been taken sooner. The circumstances had no fraternal precedent, however, and yet were arising concurrently at other chapter sites as well. Any leniency shown by Vincent and his colleagues thus seems fully understandable.

In 1980 Pittsburgh resumed full-time undergraduate programs in business,

by way of a dual-major option leading to a B.A. or B.S. degree from the College of Arts and Sciences. They were promptly sanctioned by the AACSB. A proposal for a new B.S. program was under review at the business school as of early 1986.[9]

Pitt was removed from the Beta Alpha Psi ranks just as a much older member of the roster was beginning to phase out its own undergraduate program.

Northwestern--Gamma

Except for an early first-place finish in the "rating" program (1952-53), Gamma at Northwestern had generally been a rather weak chapter, beset by familiar metropolitan-area problems. In addition, as explained in chapter 6, Gamma had functioned in the late fifties without appreciable faculty leadership, due to advisor Ambrose Reiter's political career. Virgil Boyd succeeded Reiter in 1961, subsequently serving briefly as the chief financial officer for the Northwestern business school before becoming the business dean at Loyola of Chicago in February 1966. Coincidentally, Beta Iota at Loyola stood in 1965-66 as the "most improved" fraternal chapter, based largely on the return of FVP Robert Meier following a semester's leave. Despite having compiled a 3.22 cummulative grade average during the spring of 1965, however, the chapter had rated only 30th among 70 full-year chapters in the "scholarship" category.

At Northwestern, Professor Reiter had returned as Gamma's faculty

---

[9]"AACSB Accreditation Council," s.v. "University of Pittsburgh"; [Harvey E. Donley], 1968-69 Secretary-Treasurer's Report, p. 1; Grand Council Minutes, 1964, p. 3, quoted; Grand Council Minutes Book, 1959, p. 3, 1963, p. 3, both quoted; [Leon E. Hay], Secretary-Treasurer's Report, 1965-66 pp. 1, 9, 23 (quoted), 1966-67, p. 1; National Council Minutes, 1964, p. 3 (quoted), 1965, pp. 1, 3 (quoted), 1966, pp. 3-4, 1967, p. 1; [Vern H. Vincent], Secretary's Report, 1963-64, p. 3, 1964-65, pp. 1, 3, 4 (quoted), 8; Vincent to Author, interview, July 21, 1980; and H. J. Zoffer, business dean at Pittsburgh, to Author, [January 1986].

vice-president in 1964. At the banquet the following spring, closing out (it is assumed) a year in which the chapter had apparently held fewer than the eight meetings required, Gamma honored its faculty leader:

> For his devoted service to both Beta Alpha Psi, and to his many students, Mr. Reiter was presented with an engraved briefcase . . . . For his added future enjoyment, students placed some ungraded papers inside his gift.

Under the administration of a new dean, the momentous decision was made during the following year to discontinue undergraduate business studies at Evanston. Both a faculty committee and a newly appointed business council representing leading Chicago firms recommended that such enrollment be concluded with the admission, in the fall of 1966, of the Class of 1970. Each group had concluded that Northwestern would be unable, within the foreseeable future, to support outstanding business schools at both levels. Ironically, accreditation conditions notwithstanding, graduate study had traditionally been the less distinguished part of the program.

The faculty committee were persuded, in part, by the Pierson and Gordon-Howell reports that a strong graduate school was essential to recognition as a national leader in business education, and felt that the research-oriented faculty essential to academic distinction would usually favor a graduate-level environment. The executives were impressed by a subcommittee survey of national trends in business higher education, inclusive of a recent tendency by "private" schools to deemphasize or abandon undergraduate programs in favor of advanced studies.

In May 1966 the full business faculty at Northwestern voted, two-to-one, to terminate bachelor's-degree work, day and evening alike. As undergraduate work was phased out over the next four years, pertinent daytime enrollment fell from 585 students to 78, and registration was closed altogether in 1971.

Because of the greater length of part-time degree programs, some business courses were offered in the evening until the mid-seventies.

After Gamma Chapter had surpassed only four other year-long local units in the 1965-66 interchapter competition, Secretary-Treasurer Leon Hay was asked to write Northwestern's accounting chairman concerning its "poor performance." The letter was intended to be positive in tone, however, through urging "a revitalization of the chapter to serve the needs of graduate students." A year later, Northwestern agreed to assign a junior faculty member to help Ambrose Reiter mold Gamma accordingly until his retirement, expected with the graduation of the last senior class.

Harvey Donley made no reference to such an assistant, however, in a visitation report of May 1968. New department chairman Thomas R. Prince had shown a very positive attitude toward the chapter, and seemed optimistic that it could move to purely graduate-level status in two years without a period of deactivation. Ten doctoral students in accounting were expected for the coming year, including Faculty Vice-President Edward J. Lusk from Beta Gamma at DePaul; and Northwestern was offering a two-year M.B.A. concentration in the field. A major point made by the secretary-treasurer during his visit was that Gamma vitally needed to induct graduate students as early in their programs as possible, an objective that was hindered by current entry requirements (eighteen completed quarter hours) and initiation practices (one ceremony per year).

For the year 1967-68 Gamma reported only four meetings, an initiation included, leaving Donley without "much hope for significant change." In 1969 he classified the Northwestern group as one of several that 'remain[ed] in the "problem" area[,] . . . show[ing] no significant change'. Cited also were Alpha at Illinois, Beta at Oregon, Pi at Case Western Reserve, and

Nu at Colorado, the home chapter for incoming secretary-treasurer Bob Wasley.

As might have been expected, finally, Gamma elected in 1969-70 not to take part in the activity program. More importantly, the only meeting reported was an initiation for which payment had not been made. The following year the chapter took formal "inactive" status, and it did not resume operations until May 1973. Unless one or more of the remaining part-time students were included, by then it was a purely graduate organization.

Gamma Chapter would operate for only seven more years before resuming inactive status in 1980-81. After three years of inactivity, and no signal from Evanston of any wish to resume operations, the National Council in 1983 revoked the charter of the group founded sixty-two years earlier.[10]

Two units established during the fourth era also soon terminated their undergraduate programs. Beta Nu at Tulane, served briefly by an advisor about to move to Northwestern, differed from Alpha Tau at Pitt in that undergraduate studies would be reinstated before the chapter had reached the point of no return. Gamma Iota at UCLA, however, would be terminated only six years after its founding.

---

[10]Hollis A. Dixon, Secretary-Treasurer's Report, 1972-73, p. 9; [Harvey E. Donley], Secretary-Treasurer's Report, 1967-68, pp. 6 (quoted), 7, 1968-69, p. 11 (quoted); Donley, Visitation Reports--Gamma, May 17, 1968, Beta Gamma, May 17, 1968; "Grand Chapter: Chapter Representatives," Newsletter 5 (April 1961):351, (Fall 1961):403, 6 (Spring 1964):73; Hasselback, 1984 Directory, individual listing, s.v. "Boyd, F. Virgil"; [Leon E. Hay], Secretary-Treasurer's Report, 1966-67, pp. 4 (quoted), 10, 13-14, 1966-67, p. 1; "Local Chapter News," Newsletter 6 (Fall 1965):264, indented citation; National Council Minutes, 1966, pp. 3, 5 (both quoted), August 1980, p. 4 (no. 8), June 1983, p. 5 (no. 13); Sedlak and Williamson, Evolution of Management Education, pp. 115-19; and Robert S. Wasley, Secretary-Treasurer's Report, 1969-70, pp. 6, 8, 1970-70, p. 1 (quoted).

Adoption of Strictly Graduate Missions at Two New Chapter Sites

Tulane--Beta Nu

Historical Background

Business studies at Tulane, 1914-58. Although the business school had been organized only two years earlier, Tulane University in New Orleans was counted among the charter members in 1916 of the American Association of College Schools of Business. Six years later Jay C. Van Kirk, one of the original members of Gamma Chapter, arrived as an accounting professor. He was a leading candidate for appointment to a Beta Alpha Psi expansion committee formed in 1923 that was finally composed of three Delta brothers and the faculty advisor to Eta at Boston. Alpha alumnus Paul C. Taylor, a charter member of the entire fraternity, joined the Tulane faculty in 1938, a few months before he and Van Kirk were guests at the installation of Phi Chapter at nearby Louisiana State.

There is no record that Tulane registered any interest in joining the fraternal roster, however, until the year 1950-51, when the first of three inquiries of the fifties was received from New Orleans. Beta Nu was finally installed there in May 1961, directly before the retirement of Professor Van Kirk after 39 years of service. Professor Taylor would remain on campus for three more years to complete 26 years on the faculty.

Two factors stand out in the long delay at Tulane in considering an affiliation with Beta Alpha Psi. First, by the eve of World War II the daytime business enrollment was still very low, although the growth from 28 students in 1917 to 262 twenty-three years later was substantial. Even in modern times evening enrollment had far exceeded daytime registration--by some 1,500 students to fewer than 500 in the fall of 1957.

Second, during its first quarter-century or more, <u>in particular</u>, the business school "did not emphasize specialization in a particular functional area within business." Instead, "students were encouraged to select elective courses from a variety of areas." From another viewpoint, however, the program was narrowly vocational, inasmuch as business majors, from early on, took virtually no work outside the college. Even English and foreign language requirements were covered by the business faculty, and given a distinctly commercial slant.

In 1940, under new dean Leslie Buchan, one of A. C. Littleton's first doctoral students at Illinois, Tulane began an M.B.A. program, and also took the first steps toward a more balanced undergraduate curriculum that within a decade would include nearly as much liberal arts work (inclusive of economics taught as a social science) as business study. Only a small master's program was conducted until 1957, when the thesis requirement was dropped, and second-year work became more standardized and rigorous.

A year later, the undergraduate curriculum was enhanced substantially, as a distinctly modernized accounting program emerged.

<u>An enriched undergraduate program, beginning in 1958</u>. In 1958 there was a substantial infusion of new requirements in economic theory, mathematics, and noneconomic behavioral science. Perhaps the strongest emphasis was upon quantitative methods and applications. During their freshman and sophomore years, business students took a foundational sequence of 12 semester hours from the mathematics department. As juniors and seniors, subsequently, they completed 12 additional credits of required quantitative work within the business school itself. Two advanced courses were intended to build upon elementary computer skills obtained in a required noncredit course. The computer was also used to facilitate management "gaming," a

major element of a required two-semester management seminar for seniors.

Electronic data processing systems were discussed in the only sophomore business course, introductory accounting, a year's course required of all business majors. The quantitative thrust of the accounting curriculum is pointed up within a 1964 writeup:

> [I]n Introduction to Financial and Managerial Accounting . . ., the logic of set theory has been used to introduce the concept of accounting classification, both for internal managerial uses and for financial statement presentation. Matrix format and techniques of manipulation . . . have been used in accounting to illustrate the transaction and its inherent property of duality (as distinquished from "double entry"). In this course and in Cost Accounting the calculus is used in discussions of breakeven analysis. Recently, concepts of linear algebra . . . have been introduced in the introductory and cost analysis courses with good results. Also, in Auditing the use of statistical sampling techniques is discussed in detail and probability theory is used in establishing likely magnitudes in, and relationships among, accounts.

The Tulane business program had moved far indeed from the narrow vocationalism of the early years. In one important respect, however, there had been continuity. Intensive specialization within a particular major field was still not permitted. In most fields only two or three "advanced" courses were offered. Even in accounting, a student could take no more than four one-semester courses beyond the introductory level, based on a managerial emphasis of the kind associated with the two 1959 educational critiques. Students interested in a "professional" career as independent accountants could be served only by an extra year's study leading to an M.B.A. in accounting.

It seems fair to say that by the time Beta Nu Chapter was installed, in 1961, Tulane had developed one of the nation's most "modern" undergraduate programs in business, one fully in accord with the philosophy of the Pierson and Gordon-Howell reports. Yet within two years the school had decided to phase out bachelor's-level work.

The decision to discontinue undergraduate work

In the fall of 1960, the School of Business Administration had begun a wide-ranging, and highly participative, study of program objectives in light of available resources. Following more than two years of committee and schoolwide faculty meetings, visitations, surveys, literature reviews, and other activities, the faculty voted "by a very substantial majority" to recommend that the B.B.A. degree be discontinued. The university's governing board acted accordingly the following April, and the last class was admitted in the fall of 1963. Except for three students graduating, belatedly, between 1968 and 1974, the last undergraduate degrees of the day were conferred in 1967.

Three reasons were given for the change to an all-graduate program at Tulane. First, the faculty had become increasingly convinced that, ideally, "professional" education for business management should be built on a strong base of "general" education. Granting that much breadth had been imported into Tulane's undergraduate curriculum, the judgement was made that a superior base for business study was (a) a liberal arts education that included work in mathematics, or (b) a modern-day engineering education whose liberal arts component was slanted toward the social sciences. Early experience with the upgraded M.B.A. program had reinforced this perception inasmuch as it had attracted many students who had majored as undergraduates in engineering, mathematics, or the physical sciences rather than business. The overall notion, as stated in a newspaper report of the school's decision, was that business administration should be placed "on a footing similar to . . . other professional fields, such as law and medicine," and thus be studied <u>after</u> the completion of a four-year degree.

Second, the faculty and administration at Tulane, like their counterparts at Northwestern, were very skeptical that university resources would support maintenance of a quality business program at both undergraduate and advanced levels. The enriched undergraduate program had imposed increased demands on faculty time, even aside from the development of new courses, because extensive "faculty-student consultation outside the classroom was needed."

Further, the modernized M.B.A. program that was still being upgraded had significantly added to the faculty workload, and otherwise demanded more resources. It had attracted "many more students" than the earlier one, and, as noted above, they were far more likely than before to have been nonbusiness majors, who needed a full year of foundational study before taking advanced work. Moreover, at the very time the new undergraduate curriculum was introduced, Tulane had begun planning for a doctoral program in business, emphasizing mathematics and computer applications, to prepare "better qualified teachers and research specialists." It would not be implemented until 1968, ten years after the subject had first been discussed.

Finally, the business school wished to initiate a part-time M.B.A. program comparable to the regular one (doing so in 1963); strengthen and expand professional development work for executives and educators; and develop an "international accounting program" suited, especially, to the close relationships existing between New Orleans and Latin America. As of 1964, month-long seminars had been conducted for Mexican executives, and the faculty were assembling a library collection, identifying research issues, and designing course work in international accounting.

Third, since redesigning the academic programs Tulane had been much more successful, from quantitative and qualitative standpoints alike, in

attracting M.B.A. than B.B.A. students. As graduate enrollment had steadily increased both in numbers and in recorded student qualifications, undergraduate degrees conferred had dropped by more than forty per cent (1956-62), and the overall academic caliber of business majors stayed "significantly below" that of their peers within other divisions of the university. Further, a nationwide survey conducted by the business school revealed that Tulane's recent experience at the bachelor's-degree level was very typical among, in particular, business programs "in private universities charging substantial tuition rates and having selective admission policies."

Although not an independent reason for eliminating undergraduate work, the Tulane business school recognized a special regional mission that extended as far back as its founding in 1914 as only the third such college in the South. Reorganized as the region's first strictly graduate school, it would be well-suited to develop "more highly trained leaders to guide the South's and the nation's business and industry through the ever-increasing complexities of a technological era." Similarly, amidst a national shortage of academically qualified business professors there was a particular dearth of opportunities for doctoral study in the South, inviting an entry into the market by an established university like Tulane.

Without questioning in any way the merits of the decision to abandon undergraduate work, it most certainly did not promise an auspicious setting for a Beta Alpha Psi chapter scarcely through its second year.

Fraternal implications: A chronically weak chapter in the '60s

Bleak prospects, overall, despite potential support. Except for one year, Beta Nu Chapter was consistently very weak through 1968, as measured by the point standings; and it finished the fourth era in the midst of a

prolonged deactivation. Since there was a senior class in residence as late as 1966-67, this record cannot be attributed simply to the cessation of undergraduate studies, although faculty commitment to the fraternal program may have been impaired by the transitional environment.

In any case, the long-term prospect was full membership reliance upon M.B.A. or doctoral candidates concentrating in accounting. The master's-level concentration was apparently not a strong emphasis within the school, and as pursued by undergraduate majors would normally require only a year of residence, allowing very limited time for fraternal involvement. The doctoral program was destined to yield only one accounting graduate before becoming dormant.

The best hope for Beta Nu lay in faculty and administrative support available for a significant accounting program within the new structure. Charter faculty advisor Peter A. Firmin was ironically a proponent of a "five-year" professional accounting program, a curriculum obviously not consistent with a strictly graduate format. The spring before the faculty had approved the new structure, Firmin had been a visiting professor at Pittsburgh, where the phaseout of the undergraduate program was already well underway.

A more junior member of the faculty was future National Advisory Forum member (and AAA president) Stephen A. Zeff, who had arrived in the fall of 1961, a few months after the installation. As mentioned in chapter 1, Zeff had been an officer of Nu Chapter at Colorado in the fifties. At the administrative level, Dean C. Jackson Grayson, who returned to New Orleans from a European assignment in 1964 to oversee the transition to exclusively graduate work, was a certified public accountant in Louisiana, although he was identified primarily with the management and production areas. Grayson

would later head the U.S. Price Commission during the 1971-73 experiment with wage-price controls.

The chapter record, 1961-70. In 1961-62, Tulane joined two of the other four schools chartered a year earlier among the five continuing chapter sites lowest ranked in the activity program. Records are unavailable for the following year, but the standings reported in 1964 listed Beta Nu ahead only of Beta at Oregon and Pi at Western Reserve, each earning zero points. Outgoing president Emerson Henke thus agreed, at the annual meeting, to keep in touch with Professor Firmin.

The faculty vice-presidency changed hands, however, in the fall of 1964, passing to a new doctoral graduate from a school, Illinois, not known for supporting the activity program. Under the faculty leadership of Arthur D. Karlin, a chapter that had begun with only four returning members posted impressive operating results over the year that followed. Beta Nu recorded easily the nation's largest improvement, moving from 63rd place with but 151 (of 6,000 available) points to 31st place with a very respectable 4,569 points.

The year 1964-65 would prove to be an aberration, however "Very sloppy reporting" returned the Tulane group to the depths in the next annual rankings, as it surpassed only the Pittsburgh chapter. Karlin was succeeded in 1966 by fellow Illinois doctoral alumnus Alfred Rappaport, who in Leon Hay's judgment proved to be "a very poor FVP" as Beta Nu finished last. Rappaport left for Northwestern at year's end, and, largely because the last senior class had just been graduated, no chapter members were slated to return in the fall.

After conferring with Peter Firmin, Hay concluded that Beta Nu

"deserve[d] one more year" to see if it "serve[d] any useful purpose." The chapter unfortunately fell still further, submitting no reports and, accordingly, earning no points. Secretary-Treasurer Donley recommended in his report that "the Council take definite action" concerning Tulane. Meanwhile, as the newly appointed dean Firmin formally requested that the local group be placed on "inactive" status for two years, based on constitutional article 13, section 12. The National Council took such action, for the first time on record, indicating that the situation would be reviewed a year later.

At the next annual meeting, in 1969, incoming president Harvey Donley was instructed to contact Dean Firman on the school's plans for the chapter. Charles Taylor followed up with a visitation to the New Orleans campus. Rather than sending plans for reactivation, however, Professor Stephen Zeff asked in 1970 that inactive status be continued for another year. The Council granted this request on the understanding that no further extension could be made.

Reactivation would be followed promptly by disciplinary action to which Beta Nu responded positively. The key to the survival of the chapter, however, was the restoration several years later of undergraduate studies.

Developments of the '70s--Probation, and resumption of undergraduate work

Prior to the 1971 meeting, 1967-68 faculty advisor James J. Linn notified Secretary-Treasurer Robert Wasley that the Tulane faculty wished to revive Beta Nu, but no action was taken until early 1972. Following only a minimum renewal of chapter operations, as only two meetings (an initiation included) were reported, and no audit report was filed, the Council voted in 1972 to place the Tulane group on probation for two years. While making

the action official on a fall visit, however, Professor Taylor was supposed to assess whether there were grounds for charter revocation.

Although no visit was made, the probation was duly imposed, requiring Beta Nu to participate in the activity program. As of the time of the midyear planning committee meeting of 1972-73, the chapter was complying with all reporting conditions. The need for a visitation was reaffirmed, for purposes of discussing local problems or questions, but none would take place in the spring, either. The Tulane group was remarkably active in the first probationary year, holding 25 meetings besides two initiations, and finishing 22nd among 51 participants in the interchapter competition. The chapter was apparently restored to good standing on schedule, following a somewhat less productive second year. Secretary-Treasurer Fred Mueller observed early in 1975 that Beta Nu, by then headed at the faculty level by Professor Zeff, "was doing much better than in the past."

In 1976, finally, Tulane resumed undergraduate instruction in business with the introduction of the bachelor of science in management degree. At the same time the doctoral program, which would ultimately produce a total of only thirteen degrees, was "inactivated," a status remaining unchanged as of the mid-eighties. The former action, at least, clearly enhanced prospects for a successful Beta Alpha Psi chapter. Although Beta Nu was not destined to become a nationally prominent group, it was the only one of the four chapters discussed in this section that remained in operation by the mid-eighties. During the year 1984-85 it was recognized as one of seven "significantly improved" local units.[11]

---

[11]Doris Horn Antin, Tulane University Archivist, to Author, March 5, 1986; Beta Alpha Psi National Constitution (1965), article 13, section 12; "A Brief Sketch of the Origins of the College of Commerce and Business Administration, Tulane University," [1957], p. 2, three-page typescript,

Beta Nu had been formed shortly before the local faculty voted to end undergraduate studies. Gamma Iota was installed at UCLA, however, after such a decision had already been made, in what is recognized as one of the major National Council misjudgments of the fourth era.

Gamma Iota at UCLA

The University of California at Los Angeles had applied for a charter in 1939, shortly after the arrival on campus of former Beta Alpha Psi president W. E. Karrenbrock, but action had been "deferred" with the effect,

---

Tulane University Archives; "College of Commerce and Business Administration: Degrees Conferred," January 26, 1966, updated through 1976, two-page typescript, Tulane Archives; Hollis A. Dixon, Long-Range Planning Committee Minutes, December 1972, p. 2 (no. 3.2); Dixon, Secretary-Treasurer's Report, 1971-72, pp. 5, 7, 1972-73, pp. 1, 4, 8; [Harvey E. Donley], Secretary-Treasurer's Report, 1967-68, pp. 6, 15 (both quoted), 13; "Final Point Accumulation under Chapter Activity Program - June 15, 1974," Newsletter 13 (Fall 1974):4; Peter A. Firmin, "The Five-Year Accounting Program--With Due and Deliberate Speed," The Accounting Review 34 (October 1959):591-602; "Grand Chapter: Chapter Representatives," Newsletter 5 (Fall 1961);403; Hasselback, 1984 Directory, individual listing, s.v. "Karlin, Arthur D.," "Rappaport, Alfred"; [Leon E. Hay], Secretary-Treasurer's Report, 1965-66, p. 10 (quoted), 1966-67, pp. 5 (quoted), 7; [Emerson O. Henke], "Congratulations," Newsletter 5 (Fall 1961):415; [Henke], Secretary-Treasurer's Report, 1961-62, p. 4; Richard Kelsey, Beta Nu FVP, to Author, January 7, February 9 (quoted), 1986; Robert A. Maust, Long-Range Planning Committee Minutes, December 1971, p. 4 (no. 9.5); Hermann C. Miller, ed., Beta Alpha Psi Directory, s.v. "Gamma Chapter: Van Kirk, J. C."; Fred J. Mueller, Secretary-Treasurer's Report, 1974-75, p. 8; "National Chapter Members," Newsletter 6 (Fall 1965):inside front cover; National Council Minutes, 1965, p. 3, 1968, p. 5 (quoted), 1969, p. 2, 1970, p. 6, 1972, p. 5 (no. 6.4), August 1973, pp. 1-3 (nos. 3.0-3.6), August 1974 (last two sources cited based on nonreference to Beta Nu's status); February 1975, p. 2 (no. 5, quoted); "New Tulane Program: A Vote for Progress," New Orleans Times Picayune, July 16, 1963, quoted, Tulane Archives; Clinton A. Phillips, Experience with Undergraduate Business Program: Tulane University School of Business (New Orleans: 1964), 38-page report provided by Tulane Archives, quoting pp. 4, 11 (indented citation), 13, 15, 21-22, 27, 35; Sheldahl, Alpha to Omega, pp. 18, 48, 69, 137, 159-60, 698; [David E. Tinius], "Outstanding Chapter Awards," 1984-85 Annual Report, ed. [Tinius], p. 5, quoted; L. L. Vance, ed., "News Notes," The Accounting Review 37 (April 1962):373; [Vern H. Vincent], Secretary's Report, 1963-64, p. 7, 1964-65, pp. 7-8, 10; Robert S. Wasley, Secretary-Treasurer's Report, 1969-70, p. 2, 1970-71, p. 1; and Who's Who in America 43 (1984-85), s.v. "Firmin, Peter Arthur, Jr.," "Grayson, Charles Jackson, Jr.," "Zeff, Stephen Addam."

ultimately, of rejection. Another inquiry, not followed by a petition, had been received in 1956-57. Ten years later, finally, a group from UCLA filed a successful application, and Editor Vern Odmark of nearby San Diego State installed Gamma Iota in May 1967. The Los Angeles school had admitted its last undergraduate class in business the preceding fall, a few months before the removal from the chapter roster of all-graduate Alpha Tau at Pittsburgh.

Years later, Leon Hay would recall that the National Council "intuitively knew it was wrong" to charter UCLA. He recalled that accounting club president Wayne Label and faculty advisor Corine Thompson, soon to become Corine Thompson Norgaard, had presented a petition that, formally, was flawless. Perhaps the Council was unduly influenced by the academic prestige of one of the nation's foremost public universities.

As noted earlier, Odmark seemed pleased with a visitation made to Gamma Iota late in 1967. In its first full year, the chapter finished 59th out of 78 continuing local units, and failed to file a timely audit report, but there was as yet no cause for alarm. For example, Gamma Theta, founded at Missouri the preceding spring, stood only one place ahead of the California group in the rankings.

It was the chapter's second year that raised severe concern. In 1968-69 Gamma Iota issued only one report, covering an initiation that "was not done right," and ranked dead last, nationally, with only 270 points. Somewhat questionably, the faculty vice-presidency had been passed to a newly arrived doctoral candidate from Harvard who would finish his degree requirements during the year, namely, John J. McDonough.

In his 1968-69 report Secretary-Treasurer Harvey Donley, remembered by Andy Anderson as having been "as hard as nails" as the activity program administrator, described the UCLA chapter as "hopeless." He added a

judgment that meshes well with Leon Hay's later assessment: "the [C]ouncil should admit that this was a mistake and revoke the charter."

At the subsequent Council meeting, outgoing president Vern Odmark was asked to write the UCLA accounting chairman regarding Gamma Iota's weak performance. Under its third FVP in three years, the group elected in 1969-70 not to participate in the points competition. Constitutional requirements were met in full, however, as the chapter conducted eight program meetings and two initiations, and submitted an audit report. The upswing in chapter fortunes was short-lived, however, probably because at the 1970 spring commencement degrees were awarded to the final undergraduate class in business.

At the 1972 annual meeting, Fred Mueller of Washington was asked to visit UCLA to determine whether Gamma Iota should be placed on probation, or should have its charter withdrawn. No visitation was conducted, but the chapter was placed on a year's "conditional" probation at the start of the academic year. During the fall semester, nine meetings and one initiation were reported, exceeding or matching full-year requirements. No reports were filed in the spring, however, leading Secretary-Treasurer Hollis Dixon to move at the 1973 meeting that the charter be revoked, and the symbolic document be returned. The motion was passed unanimously.

The following spring local professor Eric G. Flamholtz requested that Gamma Iota be reinstated. The National Council held fast to the position that only the successful conclusion of a new petition process could restore the Los Angeles school to the roster. A similar inquiry received from Flamholtz during the year 1974-75 brought forth the same response.

As of 1984, the business schools at UCLA, Northwestern, Stanford, Chicago, and the four Ivy-League institutions cited earlier were joined within

the AACSB ranks by only four other all-graduate units (excluding the separately accredited graduate schools at Virginia and NYU). Initially accredited, in business studies, between 1964 and 1972, the other universities were Rochester, offering undergraduate degrees over the period 1958-72; Duke and Vanderbilt; and Atlanta, a graduate institution cited in chapter one as a predominantly black school that had once expressed interest in the fraternity. It seems significant that, with the termination of Gamma Chapter in 1983, none of these dozen campuses held a Beta Alpha Psi charter.[12]

In Transition

The quarter century of significant growth, reform, and service constituting the third and fourth periods provided a fitting background for Beta Alpha Psi's fifth era. Over the 1970s themes of broadened participation and pluralism that had taken root earlier became dominant fraternal motifs, within an environment of activism and expansion found at levels not previously recorded.

---

[12] "AACSB Accreditation Council"; Wilton T. Anderson to Author, interview, March 20, 1980, quoted; John G. Baker, Graduate School of Management at Rochester, to Author, March 12, 1986; Hollis A. Dixon, Secretary-Treasurer's Report, 1972-73, p. 4, quoted; [Harvey E. Donley], Secretary-Treasurer's Report, 1967-68, p. 8, 1968-69, pp. 1, 11 (quoted), 16; exhibit 7 (chapter 2), UCLA reference; Grand Council Minutes Book, 1939, p. 5, quoted; Hasselback, <u>1984 Directory</u>, school listing, s.v. "Duke University," "Vanderbilt University," individual listing, s.v. "McDonough, John J."; [Leon E. Hay], Secretary-Treasurer's Report, 1966-67, pp. 2, 7; Hay to Author, interview, May 2, 1980, quoted; National Council minutes, 1969, p. 3, 1970, p. 6, 1973, p. 2, February 1974, p. 5 (no. 13), May 1974, p. 5 (no. 13), February 1975, p. 2 (no. 4); Vern E. Odmark, Visitation Report--Gamma Iota, December 4, 1967; Sheldahl, <u>Alpha to Omega</u>, pp. 734-35; Straughn and Straughan, eds., <u>Lovejoy's College Guide</u>, s.v. "Georgia: Atlanta University"; and [Robert S. Wasley], Secretary-Treasurer's Report, 1969-70, pp. 6-8.

Only advisor A. B. Carson, a former president of the American Accounting Association, had been present from the UCLA faculty for a 1970-71 visitation by new councilor Hollis A. Dixon to Gamma Iota. Dixon to Author, interview, March 22-23, 1980; Robert S. Wasley, Secretary-Treasurer's Report, 1970-71, pp. 2, 7; and Zeff, <u>American Accounting Association</u>, p. [95].

PART 3. THE ACTIVIST PARTICIPATION (or FIFTH) ERA, 1971-79

CHAPTER 13

PARTICIPATION AND PLURALISM IN FRATERNAL GOVERNANCE: RECONSTITUTION OF THE NATIONAL COUNCIL, AND CREATION OF THE NATIONAL ADVISORY FORUM

The 1970s brought marked expansion in Beta Alpha Psi participation by students, chapter officers, professional accountants, fraternal alumni (on a representative basis), and a National Council that at the outset added a second yearly meeting, and later instituted a third one. During the "Activist Participation Era," also, two women and one black person served on the Council.

The fraternal program was developed or expanded in one area after another. "Regional" and truly "national" meetings emerged; visitation became a vital part of the chartering process in a day of accelerated roster growth; a nationwide literary competition was resumed, after a thirty-year lapse, and steadily enhanced; outstanding accountants were honored at national and local levels; and the activity program was made significantly more responsive to the diversity in chapter environments. In light of such developments, financial administration of the fraternity required not only fee increases, from time to time, but also budgetary and fund-raising activities not previously undertaken.

Program development during the period, as covered largely in the next chapter, was generally related in one way or another to two fundamental changes in the national structure of Beta Alpha Psi. First, the governing body was reconstituted to a degree unknown since the adoption of the Grand

Council framework in 1927, as a faculty slot was added, a new structure of offices was established, a process of outside "election" of councilors was introduced, and two short-term nonfaculty positions were created. Second, Beta Alpha Psi reached out to the professional accounting community by creating an active supporting body known as the National Advisory Forum.

The era ended in 1979 with the opening of a national office for the fraternity, and the transfer of various administrative functions from the National Council to the Florida facility. That event climaxed a long process of institutional change that had been particularly visible over the preceding five years.

Major Changes in the National Council: Structure, Composition, and Member Election

At the beginning of the fifth era, in the fall of 1970, the National Council consisted of six male accounting professors serving six-year terms, inclusive of two years as secretary or editor, to which they had been elected by a prior Council without formal participation by outside parties. At its close in 1979, there were seven faculty slots, two of them held by women, and the annual vacancy was filled through election by a definitionally enlarged National Chapter; one office had been split into two separate positions, and each new faculty councilor was slated to spend three years of a seven-year term in one of three posts; and two nonacademic constituencies--professional accountants and fraternal alumni--were also represented.

The secretary-treasurership was the focal point in the numerical expansion approved in two stages, during the mid-seventies, in faculty positions, terms, and officerships.

Developments at the Faculty Level

Background: Perceptions and evidence, since the third era, of an overburdened secretary-treasurer

With the resumption of steady growth in the chapter roster and, more importantly, of monthly reporting by all local units, it is natural that concern resurfaced early in 1974 that the secretary-treasurship had become an overburdened office. This perception, and a proposed solution that the National Council was not as yet ready to adopt, went back at least to the early days of the "rating" program. By the fifth era, there was increasing need for paid clerical assistance, along with some skepticism that the office was being conducted as efficiently as in the past. An episode of 1974 provides interesting anecdotal evidence (only) of the remaining dimensions of a position that had already been simplified by Council reform of the sixties.

Discussion since 1953 of an "executive" secretaryship

Early in his term, the following observations were shared by one of Beta Alpha Psi's more prominent secretary-treasurers:

> Possibly we have come to the point where we have to think about a[n] . . . Executive Secretary with permanent headquarters rather than the rotating plan we are following now. When I took over last September so much work was dumped into my lap that I have not yet [three months later] completely caught up.

The writer was not new secretary-treasurer Fred Mueller in the late fall of 1973, when the roster of continuing chapters numbered 95 units. It was instead A. J. Penz twenty years earlier, in December 1953, when there were 33 local groups, and it was generally possible "to handle all current work in connection with chapters on a daily basis, that is, reply on the same day in which received." Directly in response to Penz's comments, former

councilor James McConahey remarked that he had felt "for some time" that the responsibilities of the post were "much too heavy for a full time accounting professor."

Andy Penz was teaching in an accounting department, at Alabama, that employed one secretary, and had almost no office equipment besides a single manual typewriter. Fortunately, the councilor was able to handle his own fraternal correspondence, on another such machine located in his office. He typed "beautifully," and indeed had taught both typing and shorthand early in his career. As department head in 1954-55, Penz engaged a student assistant to help with the Beta Alpha Psi work. Even though the student was paid by the fraternity, total clerical costs absorbed during the two years exceeded only slightly the lowest amount otherwise recorded, in the fifties, for a single period.

In 1956 the Grand Council discussed possible appointment of a salaried executive secretary. Three years later, as noted in chapter 9, the president's advisory committee of which A. J. Penz was the senior member recommended that such an initiative be taken, based on "at least" a five-year term. The idea was raised again in 1964, but the only relevant change made in the sixties was the creation of a separate editorship. The experiment begun in 1969 with an "optional" activity program somewhat reduced the routine workload for the time being.

Nonetheless, significant growth in student membership, and the prospect of major expansion of the roster, kept alive the option of appointing a paid executive secretary. During the second long-range planning conference, in December 1971, the National Council discussed the possibility of appointing a former councilor, presumably serving part time, to a five-year term. President Robert Wasley agreed to ask Julius Roller, who was less than four

years short of retirement from Washington, whether he favored such an approach and, if so, might be interested in taking the post himself.

In the next year's minutes, Roller was mentioned only as one of a number of persons who had nominated his colleague Fred Mueller for placement on the Council. His election in 1972 put Mueller in line to become secretary-treasurer a year later, by which time relevant clerical costs had well exceeded earlier levels.

Recently increasing costs for outside clerical assistance

Downward trend in the sixties. Secretary-treasurers had long depended in some measure on clerical assistance not supplied by their universities, and thus charged to the fraternity. Except for a $49 total submitted by Andy Penz in 1953-54, the lowest annual charge of the 1950s had been $248 (including a $50 audit fee), and the average cost over the final three years had closely approximated the $641 amount reported by John Arch White in 1950-51. During his term, 1957-59 secretary-treasurer Nolan Williams of Arkansas had administered Beta Alpha Psi business from a downtown office (not at rental cost to the Grand Council), sharing the services of a legal secretary. Several years earlier S. M. Wedeberg of Maryland had reduced fraternal expenditure on outside secretarial help by typing considerable correspondence himself, due to the scarce availability of stenographic services within the Washington, D. C. area.

Such costs generally were lower in the sixties, despite a substantial increase in the number of chapters. Indeed, Harvey Donley had reported no clerical costs during his secretary-treasurership, 1967-69, after Vern Vincent and Leon Hay had listed totals ranging from $261 to $741 over the prior three years. Donley's secretary Becky Adams, credited with developing

files needed for the golden anniversary Newsletter, had been paid in full by Bowling Green State University. Although donated stenographic help would have varied from one campus to another, clerical resources available had perhaps expanded even more than enrollments, overall, during the sixties.

The picture changed abruptly, however, just as secretary-treasurer duties were temporarily reduced by the altered activity program structure.

Sharply higher costs, generally, 1969-73. In passing the secreatry-treasurership to Bob Wasley in 1969, the National Council authorized him to hire clerical assistance as needed. In his first year, Wasley reported costs of $1,173, primarily for correspondence. The following year, 1970-71, the total was $1,621, an amount slightly exceeding Newsletter costs of the period.

Under Secretary-Treasurer Hollis Dixon, outside clerical cost reverted in 1971-72 to the zero level of a few years earlier. There is reason to believe, however, that Dixon relied more heavily upon an assistant than had his predecessors. His secretary Laura Blake was paid in full by the University of Arizona that first year, during which the Council officer had missed the midyear long-range planning conference after contracting valley fever. Robert Maust had indeed been designated as Dixon's replacement should he be unable to resume his official responsibilities.

Over the following year, 1972-73, the university was unable to pay the full cost of Blake's services. Accordingly, she received some $2,100 from the National Council, which expended an additional $78 in payroll taxes. She also attended the 1973 Council meeting in Quebec, at fraternal expense, due to an unusual situation that would leave the secretary-treasurer function entirely in her hands for a limited time. Both Dixon, the incoming president, and Fred Mueller, his successor in his prior post, were scheduled to be

abroad during the fall. Mueller, indeed, had interrupted a visiting professorship in Australia having begun in June to attend the meeting. Accordingly, the governing body authorized a $500 monthly salary for Laura Blake until the new secretary-treasurer could assume his duties following his return to Seattle sometime in November.

According to Harvey Donley, Blake "abruptly resigned" while Mueller was still on leave, marking a "dark day" for Beta Alpha Psi. There was no more than minimum disruption of the secretary-treasurer function, however. Available records reveal only that $2,857 was paid for clerical support over the fraternal year 1973-74.

In a 1980 interview, Donley in effect indicated a further reason for fifth-era reevaluation of the secretary-treasurership.

Possible skepticism concerning
recent performance levels

Professor Donley had stayed on the Council an extra year, in 1972-73, to replace Bob Wasley while the past president was away teaching in New Zealand and lecturing in Australia. He was later somewhat critical of Hollis Dixon's term as secretary-treasurer, evidently feeling that he had relied excessively upon the assistant. Near the midpoint of his second year in the office, at the final long-range planning committee, other councilors had "reminded" Dixon of four rather routine duties to be carried out over the remainder of the fraternal year; and he was instructed to conduct a nomination balloting for a new award, "Accountant of the Year," that for reasons not documented would not take place.

Dixon himself, in 1980, questioned his predecessor Wasley's administration of the Chapter Activity Program. These observations are reported, not to suggest that serious conflict existed, but as further evidence that

by the early seventies the position under discussion had taken on the complexion of a thankless burden.

Because of processing and fee-collection implications, it seems pertinent that there was remarkable growth in membership during this time despite, by later fifth-era standards, only modest installation activity. From 2,277 new members in 1969-70, all categories included, the total successively passed 3,000 and 3,700 the next two years before reaching 4,268 in 1972-73. The rise by 1,991 new initiates in just three years was the total number inducted in 1964-65, and slightly exceeded the following year's level.

Finally, an anecdotal reference concerning a belated transfer of files from Hollis Dixon to Fred Mueller may help dramatize the burdens of the job then held by the latter councilor.

Transfer of a half-ton of files in Reno, 1974

Although both President Dixon and Secretary-Treasurer Mueller had returned to active fraternal service before the first officially designated "winter" meeting was held in Las Vegas in February 1974, the full transfer of files did not occur until later in the year, in the same state. In September Dixon loaded up some one thousand pounds of files stored at his home into a rented U-Haul trailer, to be filled, on Mueller's recollection, with a load of hay for the return trip to Tucson; covered the materials as a protection against rain; and headed for Reno in his pickup truck to meet the Washington professor, who was driving his own pickup from Seattle.

The transfer was duly made in Reno, as the two men filled the secretary-treasurer's vehicle with the records that had been inessential, at any rate, to his conduct of the office the preceding year. To help fill up remaining space, they also packed "some booze." According to Fred Mueller, the two fraternal leaders took advantage of the occasion, at their hotel, to discuss

possible ways of making Beta Alpha Psi more visible within the accounting profession.

In 1971, a similar transfer had taken place in Boulder, Colorado, after Hollis Dixon had driven his truck there to receive the files from prior secretary-treasurer Bob Wasley. In light of the volume loaded three years later, it is noteworthy that Wasley had discarded considerable material that had routinely been passed on from one secretary-treasurer to the next one. Some years earlier, moreover, 1963-65 incumbent Vern Vincent had seen fit to reduce the inventory substantially from the some 1,200 pounds of records received from Emerson Henke. Finally, in passing the office to Joyce Dean in 1976 Fred Mueller would deliberately hold back important historical files later to prove critical in preparing Alpha to Omega and the present volume, based on his concern that they might be deemed expendable.

As such references imply, much of the half-ton of materials changing hands in Reno had been unrelated to Secretary-Treasurer Mueller's non-custodial responsibilities. Even so, the event provides a rich symbolic depiction of the magnitude of duties that in his case were shared by another member of the family. Joy Mueller compiled the minutes for at least four of the nine Council meetings held during her husband's term.

In the spring prior to the Reno episode, the National Council had taken an interim step toward reorganization that would within two years reassign a major area of service to another councilor.

Two-stage reorganization, 1974-76

Expanded terms, and a "directorship" office

At the winter meeting in February 1974, Hollis Dixon was critical of

the idea of appointing an executive secretary (a "permanent" secretary-treasurer), while endorsing the related idea of establishing "a permanent file location" for fraternal archives. Fred Mueller expressed concern that an officer serving as an employee of the National Council might in time "usurp" its "administrative duties."

At a more positive level, Dixon proposed that the secretary-treasurer and editor positions each be extended to a three-year term. Although scarcely responsive to the overload of the former office, such an approach promised greater efficiency in its administration through reduced turnover. In the absence of broader change, however, the president's suggestion would have required (a) the immediate officership of two of every three new councilors, and (b) the exclusion of the third one from a pre-presidential office. In the interests of maintaining an opportunity to begin national service with a year of general orientation, and avoiding reversion to an "off-year" membership carrying no specific duties for three years, the National Council accordingly adopted a broader reorganization at its "spring" meeting three months later.

Specifically, the terms of the secretary-treasurer and editor were extended to three years within the context of two additional changes. First, the Council was enlarged from six members to seven, and the existing six-year term was increased similarly. As a result, the two traditional non-presidential officers would be held during a councilor's second, third, and fourth years.

Second, a new post occupied during the same three years was created for the (otherwise) off-year member. The "special projects councilor," or "director of special projects," would provide leadership in identifying, implementing, and/or administering desirable programs not falling under

established officerships.

For purposes of transition to the new format, it would be necessary to add a year to the terms of all sitting councilors, and to have either Dixon or his designated successor Bob Maust serve two terms as president. By secret ballot, according to his recollection, Hollis Dixon was returned to the office for 1974-75. Maust was appointed interim director of special projects, a very logical assignment since he had turned over the editorship early in the year to new member Doris Cook to concentrate on a committee assignment mentioned below. Under the new setup, Cook would continue as editor until becoming president in 1977, and Fred Mueller would serve a third year as secretary-treasurer, through 1975-76. Past presidents Bob Wasley (otherwise set to retire in 1974) and Harold Royer would serve an extra year in that capacity. Finally, Tom Burns of Omicron at Ohio State was selected as the incoming councilor for 1974-75, and slated to succeed Maust as special projects councilor a year later.

After only one year, the National Council was restructured again by in effect downgrading the new post just created to a one-year directorship later assigned to new councilors; and, more importantly, creating a new three-year office by removing one major responsibility from the secretary-treasurership. To permit prompt implementation of the revised structure without disturbing the role already assigned to Professor Burns, two four-year appointments were required as ad hoc measures.

Establishment of a directorship of activities

At a meeting of February 1975, seventh-year councilor Robert Wasley made a motion "to remove the chapter activity program from the duties of the Secretary-Treasurer the year following 1975-76." After a second by Doris

Cook, the proposal was adopted. With the establishment of the new position of "director of chapter activities," the burdens of the secretary-treasurer had been significantly relieved. The planned delay for one year in filling this new post signified that Thomas Burns would assume his new three-year office in the fall of 1975, as originally planned. At the annual meeting, incoming councilor James Pattillo was duly selected to assume the chapter activities directorship a year later, in 1976.

The complication was of course that under the reorganization plan approved in 1974 the second-year councilor of 1976-77 would serve as secretary-treasurer. The solution adopted was to appoint the incoming councilor of 1976 to a four-year term as secretary-treasurer, beginning immediately. Since that approach left the editorship open in 1977, the new councilor appointed in that year was similarly brought in as *Newsletter* editor, for four years.

To break the cycle, when Tom Burns became president in 1978 his former position was supplanted by a one-year directorship of "regional meetings," an area that had grown so rapidly during his term that it had finally been added to his position title. A "committee" structure had by this point emerged within the National Council to deal with all manner of projects, and an advisory organization had become prominently involved in several areas. After being held first by Past President Doris Cook, the scaled-down directorship was for a time vested in the incoming faculty councilor.

As special projects director, Burns had in 1977-78 edited and published the first National Chapter telephone/address directory, and top papers from two years' manuscript contests; coordinated a new fund-raising program; chaired committees regarding the formation of alumni chapters and establishment of a central office; served on committees for the student manuscript

competition and a proposed new award; and designed a nomination form for the "alumni" post on the National Council. The Ohio State councilor had also made significant contributions during the year in regard to regional meetings.

The net result of the cited structural changes in the Council was a (faculty) membership of seven professors serving seven-year terms, made up of one year as regional meetings director; three years as secretary-treasurer, editor, or director of chapter activities; and one year each as president, (immediate) past president, and senior past president. Even more fundamental change, perhaps, had occurred in the method of electing councilors.

Election by National Chapter

At the annual meeting in 1973, Robert Maust was appointed to chair a special committee to be convened

> for the purpose of defining, studying and recommending to the Council the purposes and goals of Beta Alpha Psi and suggesting meaningful . . . activities for local chapters to become involved in that might aid them in obtaining the goals the committee has defined.

The other committee members were former president Herbert Miller; Faculty Vice-Presidents Thomas Burns of Omicron at Ohio State and James C. Caldwell of Beta Delta at Texas Tech; and Wayne Brown of Delta Chapter at Washington, not otherwise identified. The group's meeting in Chicago in the fall of 1973 was cited earlier regarding both the initiation ritual and the foremost chartering requirement (AACSB accreditation).

Councilor Maust's report on the committee session to the National Council, in February 1974, included notice that the group had opposed "the present . . . method of choosing members" for the governing body. That method was of course one of self-perpetuation, as each year's membership, ordinarily with special leadership by the president, selected the new councilor on a consensus basis.

Clearly the special committee had favored a more democratic or participative approach. Following a discussion that is not characterized in the minutes, the Council approved a motion submitted and seconded, respectively, by Bob Wasley and Harold Royer. It provided that, as of 1975, the new member each year would be selected from among three nominees by vote of the faculty vice-presidents. The nominations would be made by a committee composed of the three most recently retired Council members, working with a list of potential candidates drawn up by the current membership, and securing the consent of the nominees to serve if chosen. The National Council itself would vote only to break a tie for first place from an FVP canvas requiring at least 50% participation.

The actual electorate for the annual National Countil vacancy would be much larger than at first envisioned. Besides faculty advisors, it would include all other members of the "National Chapter," that is, (a) all living or former councilors; (b) all current Council members (inclusive, in the '80s, of "area" councilors); (c) the faculty vice-president of each chapter; and, by 1977, (d) the president, or another student representative, of each local unit.

The nominating committee was reconstituted in 1978 as the three senior councilors--the national president and his or her two immediate predecessors. After a basic change in Council structure, the committee was redefined as the three senior members of the "Board of Directors," namely, the past president (serving as chairperson), the president, and the "vice president" or, as of 1985, "president elect." The transfer of the nominating function from past to current members promised better acquaintance with the records of prospective candidates.

Six years after the adoption during his presidency of "democratic"

election, Hollis Dixon expressed mixed feelings. He felt that the continuity in outlook that was promoted by the traditional method had been undermined, but that on balance the change had been worthwhile. Harvey Donley, who had in 1975 and 1976 served on the first two nominating committees, similarly voiced some concern that the new method had jeopardized "solidarity." He observed in 1980 that for the first time he felt unqualified that year to vote in the election of the incoming councilor, due to unfamiliarity with the three nominees.

The last member elected by the traditional method was Tom Burns, in 1974. One of the major merits of the current process, in his view, is that it tends to elect the "best known" nominee, based on recognized achievement within accounting education. As more conventional points in its favor, the modern selection method favors the admission of "new blood" to the Council, is designed to bring a broad range of candidates into consideration, and from a faculty vice-presidential standpoint confers special legitimacy upon, and identification with, the councilor-elect.

Both the next-to-last member elected by the National Council, and the second one chosen by the National Chapter, represented a new element in national leadership, a generation after it had first appeared within the fraternal membership.

Election of women councilors: Doris Cook and Joyce Dean

Doris M. Cook, 1973

During the 1972 annual meeting in Salt Lake City, Senior Past President Harvey Donley recommended that his colleagues consider for the next National Council vacancy a former faculty advisor at Arkansas. After taking office midway through 1956-57, Doris Marie Cook had led Alpha Iota to nine consecutive

finishes among the top seven chapters in the activity program, including annual certificate-winning placements for the years 1958-65. She had stepped down in 1965 to begin doctoral work at Texas, on the encouragement of colleagues, and completed degree requirements three years later.

Just before temporarily leaving Beta Alpha Psi work, Cook had joined Donley, of Alpha Upsilon at Bowling Green State, on a committee headed by a Donald F. Pabst of Alpha Sigma at Cincinnati. The three faculty advisors had drafted a summary of basic fraternal information, including objectives, programs, awards, membership categories and standards, and organizational structures, that provided the basis for a circular published by the National Council in 1965 for "broad distribution," especially to candidates for membership.

Donley's recommendation was favorably received. By happenstance, the former president and his wife met Professor Cook a few days later at the Salt Lake City bus station as the three of them were waiting to begin a trip to the Grand Canyon, perhaps scheduled in connection with the American Accounting Association annual meeting. Cook joined the Donleys for four or five days of vacationing that included a mule trip; and during that time agreed to serve on the Council if she were to be invited.

Following favorable consideration at the midyear planning session, the invitation was duly extended the next year amidst strong agreement that the candidate was "very enthusiastic about Beta Alpha Psi." Doris Cook, who in the fifties had become the fraternity's first woman FVP, thus in 1973 became its first female councilor. Furthermore, she became Newsletter editor after the publication of the first issue of 1973-74, holding that position until her election as national president in 1977. Cook's editorship produced the first bound volume of the periodical (1974-77) prepared in twenty years.

As immediate past president in 1978-79, she edited a volume of student papers delivered at regional meetings as the first designated director, exclusively, of such conferences.

A particular highlight of Doris Cook's presidency was a winter meeting that she scheduled in Peurto Vallarta, Mexico. Two previous winter or spring meetings had been held in Mexico, and one on an island of the British West Indies. Reminiscing nostalgically about the 1978 setting some years later, first-year councilor Henry R. "Hank" Anderson, the new editor, remarked that an academic group who were largely donating their services perceived a rather exotic meeting place as a special reward. The next two winter meetings took place in Sarasota, Florida, in connection with the establishment there of a national office; and the incipient practice was abandoned after an early chairperson of the National Advisory Forum criticized the selection of locations like Puerto Vallarta from a financial stewardship standpoint. Based on scheduling by the American Accounting Association, the meeting of August 1979 took place in Hawaii.

President Cook's principal operating objectives in 1977-78 were to place the National Council on a sounder financial base, following a year of substantial deficit spending and a forecast of more of the same; to conduct Beta Alpha Psi affairs in a more orderly and businesslike way than in the past; and to proceed through an entire year without need to place a chapter on probation. As related in chapter 15, substantial improvement was made on the financial front during the year.

To reduce the "jam-session" atmosphere that she had found to prevail during Council meetings, Cook introduced an expanded committee structure; encouraged the advance circulation of motions, by mail; and sought a more careful organization of the annual meeting, so that things would be done

"on time." It is probably more than coincidental that her term brought with it the reappearance of agendas, last filed in 1970 by Secretary-Treasurer Robert Wasley, for the meetings. The three agendas reveal the existence of some 20 committees. At the beginning of his term, 1978-79 president Tom Burns appointed 18 such groups, two thirds of which were composed (at least mainly) of three or four councilors, and a subcommittee.

Only Alpha Omega at Fordham was placed on probation under Doris Cook's presidency, although at the 1978 meeting that concluded it ten other chapters were routinely designated for such action (which would be required in one case) if they failed to submit audit reports by mid-October. Cook had "kept after" Director of Activities Jim Pattillo to help the chapters meet their responsibilities, and given them timely information on where they stood; and she herself had sent memos to local groups from time to time.

The Fordham unit, bearing a tradition of delinquent reporting (chapter 12, note 8), was plagued by an indifferent faculty extensively involved in accounting practice. It was hoped that an Arthur Young & Company partner whose daughter was the incoming local president could be of some help in regard to the New York City chapter. Alpha Omega responded very well, gaining official recognition in 1979 as a "significantly improved" chapter.

As a pioneer, Doris Cook was perhaps inevitably a somewhat controversial fraternal leader. Several colleagues considered her unduly lenient with chapters, based for example on reported statements from her first two years that she would not tell Beta Alpha Psi units after a visitation that "they [we]re in bad shape" (an attribution from national minutes that she questioned); and, making specific reference to Gamma Iota at UCLA, that the National Council should not revoke charters. One councilor whose tenure

briefly overlapped with hers even asserted in an interview that neither Cook nor Arkansas's third-era president Nolan Williams had ever given a course grade of F; and that Williams had exerted undue influence over her Council service. In another case, a contemporary member who described himself as very supportive of Professor Cook is remembered by a third party as instead having been "relentless" in keeping her under pressure.

Probably no one would have contested the judgment of that "third party," however, that Doris Cook was completely dedicated throughout her seven years on the National Council to providing service to student members; and was totally free of any personal ambitions, or objectives, that might conflict with that purpose. In addition, she is seen as having smoothed the path for a second woman president, elected three years later.

Joyce Dean, 1976

So far as is known, the first woman to be recommended for a national appointment was Joyce Clare Dean of Alpha Rho at Baylor. Dean Emerson Henke suggested her as a worthy candidate during the long-range planning conference of December 1971, but she was passed over the next year in favor of Fred Mueller of Washington, who had ironically been instrumental in Delta's long delay in admitting women members. In 1976, however, Joyce Dean was elected by the National Chapter after having been nominated by three past presidents who had attended the aforementioned meeting--Bob Wasley, Harvey Donley, and Charles Taylor.

By 1976, Dean had established credentials in the activity program that were very comparable to Doris Cook's. Under her leadership, Alpha Rho had been an award-winning chapter eight out of ten years, and she had been recognized in 1971 as a member of the second group of recipients of the

Richard S. Claire Award.

During her first four years on the Council, Dean was the national secretary-treasurer. Under her leadership annual budgeting, undertaken in Fred Mueller's last year in the post, took hold within the governing body of the accounting fraternity. Although the 1976-80 secretary-treasurer had no responsibility for the activity program, her own experience implies that the position was still a demanding one.

Secretary-Treasurer Dean relied extensively on her secretary at Baylor. Evelyn Hupp accompanied her on a trip to Sarasota, Florida in the summer of 1979 to deliver the "permanent" fraternal files to a newly established national office, and set them up, and later assisted President James Pattillo at the 1980 national convention and attended a committee meeting at Richard Metcalf's request. On one occasion Dean told Editor Henry Anderson that she was "nothing," as a Beta Alpha Psi officer, without her secretary's help. In 1981 Anderson was particularly insistent that the National Council compensate Mrs. Hupp, at an hourly rate of $6.50, for more than a hundred hours of work done for President Dean in preparation for the August meeting. A divided Council approved the payment.

Overall, it appears that Joyce Dean had an easier time of it on the National Council than had Doris Cook, in no small measure because of her precedessor's dedicated perseverance. One matter obliquely referred to after she was recommended to the Council by Emerson Henke in 1971 would create some concern during her tenure. The introduction of the Baylor associate professor's name in December 1971 had prompted a discussion of whether Council service should be restricted to full professors.

The general question had been raised before, based on concern that the opportunity costs of holding national office in Beta Alpha Psi might

frequently hinder academic promotion. Of course a similar point could be made in regard to the faculty vice-presidency, frequently held by assistant professors. At any rate, the cited rationale for a restriction was not persuasive in the particular case.

First, in view of Dean Henke's support for Joyce Dean's consideration by the governing body, and his own earlier six-year term, fraternal service at the national level seemed certain to be favorably received at Baylor. Second, the primary obstacle to her promotion to full professor was independent of the demands of Beta Alpha Psi office, namely, her nonpossession of a doctoral degree. It seems reasonable to think that the real issue, in 1971, was whether a person should be elected who did not have terminal academic credentials.

In that regard, the issue was much more the "image" of the fraternity, in a day in which the AAA, the other major academic organization in American accounting, had established a strong research emphasis, than the career advancement of the prospective councilor. The group assembled in December 1971 may have been especially sensitive to that matter because first-year member Robert Maust was only a doctoral "candidate" (at Michigan). Although he was destined never to complete the degree, Maust achieved a full professorship at West Virginia, a school at which national leadership in Beta Alpha Psi was a much esteemed role, in 1977.

Although not included among sixteen "possible nominees" mentioned at President Maust's winter meeting, Joyce Dean was nominated for the National Council in 1975-76, based on her remarkable FVP record at Alpha Rho, and was of course elected by the National Chapter. Hank Anderson, elected in 1977, recalls, however, that there was always an undercurrent of reservation within the Council about her nondoctoral status, a viewpoint with which

he did not personally identify. It was presumably only through an editorial lapse that in his 1979-80 Annual Report President Jim Pattillo identified Dean, his successor, as a full professor holding a Ph.D. degree.[1]

Although Doris Cook had completed her seven-year term in 1980, President Dean had a female colleague on the 1980-81 National Council, due to one of two new slots that had been created in the mid-seventies to represent nonfaculty constituencies. Through coincidental happenstance, there was at the time a third nonacademic councilor.

---

[1]Henry R. Anderson to Author, interview (Greenville, S.C.), April 18, 1986, quoted; Beta Alpha Psi, The National Accounting Fraternity ([National Council, 1965]), leaflet; Beta Alpha Psi, "National Bylaws," National Constitution and Bylaws (1977), article 8, section 4, article 10, section 1, (1983), article 11, section 1 (quoted), article 12, section 2, (1985), article 12, section 1 (quoted), article 13, section 2; Thomas J. Burns to Joyce C. Dean, September 1, 1978, with enclosed listing of committee assignments; Burns to Author, interview, May 3, 1980, quoted; "Chapter News," Newsletter 4 (April 1957):400; Doris M. Cook, ed., Beta Alpha Psi Newsletter 13-15 (Fall 1974 - Spring 1977), bound; [Cook], "Dean and Gattis Elected to National Council, Royer Retires," Newsletter 15 (Fall 1976):2; Cook to Author, interview, March 20, 1980; Margaret Corriher, accounting secretary at Alabama since 1954, to Author (by telephone), May 22, 1986, quoted; [Joyce C. Dean], "Revised Budget for National Council for Year Ending June 30, 1978" [1977]; [Dean], Secretary-Treasurer's Report, 1977-78, p. [7]; Dean to Author, September 8, 1986; Hollis A. Dixon, Long-Range Planning Committee Minutes, December 1972, pp. 1-2, 5; Dixon, Secretary-Treasurer's Report, 1972-73, pp. 6, 8-9, [1]2-13; Dixon to Author, interview, March 22-23, 1980, quoted; [Harvey E. Donley], Secretary-Treasurer's Report, 1968-69, p. 20; Donley to Author, interview, May 2, 1980, quoted; "Grand Chapter: Chapter Representatives," Newsletter 4 (March 1954):131; Grand Council Minutes, 1964, p. 6; Grand Council Minutes Book, 1959, p. 4, quoted; Nancy Harke, Executive Secretary of Beta Alpha Psi, to Author, May 13, 1986; James R. Hasselback, comp., Prentice-Hall Accounting Faculty Directory, 1978-79 (Englewood Cliffs, N.J.: Prentice-Hall, 1979), school listing, s.v. "Fordham University"; Hasselback, 1984 Directory, individual listing, s.v. "Cook, Doris Marie," "Dean, Joyce Clare," "Maust, Robert S."; [Leon E. Hay], "National Council News," Newsletter 6 (Fall 1965):255; [W. B. Jencks], Secretary-Treasurer's Report, 1956-57, p. 8; Kaylor, "Chapter Activity Program, 1950-69," p. 2; James M. McConahey to A. J. Penz, December 19, 1953, quoted; Debbie Maletsky, administrative assistant to accounting department at Washington, to Author, May 9, 1986; Robert S. Maust, Long-Range Planning Committee Minutes, December 1971, pp. 1, 3, 5; Maust to Author, interview, July 14, 1980; [Herbert E. Miller], Secretary-Treasurer's Report, 1959-60, p. 1; [Fred J. Mueller], "Budget for National Council for Year Ending June 30, 1977" [1976]; Mueller, Secretary-Treasurer's Report, 1974-75, p. ; Mueller to Author, interview, November 27, 1979, by telephone, August 11, 1986 (second call); "National Council," 1979-80 Annual Report, ed. [Pattillo], p. 4; "National Council of Beta

Two Nonfaculty Councilorships--and Temporarily, by Happenstance, a Third One

The other woman member was Anne K. Robertson, a recent student member of Delta Gamma at South Florida who held a one-year appointment as a representative of Beta Alpha Psi "alumni." Existing since 1976, that post is discussed after covering one that had been established a year earlier to represent a new "professional" body within Beta Alpha Psi.

Two-year term for chairperson of the "National Advisory Forum," 1975

On the initiative of President Hollis Dixon, the fraternity in 1974 established the "National Advisory Forum," an advisory group composed primarily of leading professional accountants, from public, management, or governmental practice. Discussed in detail a bit later, this group was soon standardized at eighteen members serving three-year terms, plus a chairperson having (in that role) a two-year term.

During the formative year, 1974-75, it was decided that the chairperson should serve on the National Council, perhaps based in part on an earlier

---

Alpha Psi, 1977-1978," Beta Alpha Psi, The National Accounting Fraternity: Annual Report - 1978, ed. [Doris M. Cook, (National Council, 1978)], inside front cover; "National Council of Beta Alpha Psi: 1978-1979," 1978-79 Annual Report, ed. [Burns], inside front cover; National Council Minutes, 1965, p. 4, 1968, p. 1, 1970, agenda, 1972, pp. 1, 3, 1973, pp. 3-4 (2nd indented citation), February 1974, pp. 1, 4 (quoted), 5, May 1974, pp. 1, 5 (quoted), August 1974, p. 2 (quoted), February 1975, pp. 1, 2 (quoted), 4, 7, May-June, 1975, p. 12, August 1975, pp. 9 (quoted), 11, December 1975, pp. 1, 9-10, 11 (quoted), 12, August 1976, pp. 4, 8, January 1978, p. 1, August 1978, pp. 1-3, January, June, August, 1979, agendas, January 1979, pp. 1, 4-5, June 1979, pp. 2 (quoted), 5, August 1979, pp. 1-3, 12, August 1980, p. 1, August 1981, p. 5; Penz to McConahey, December 10, 1953, 1st indented citation; Penz, Secretary-Treasurer's Report, 1954-55, pp. 1-2; [Harold E. Royer], "Accounting Fraternity," Newsletter 10 (Spring 1972):1; [Royer], "Professor Maust Becomes National Councilor," Newsletter 10 (Fall 1971):6, quoted; Vern H. Vincent to Author, interview, July 21, 1980; [Robert S. Wasley], 1969-70 Secretary-Treasurer's Report, pp. 1, 10; Wasley to Author, interview, March 23, 1980; Wasley to Author, by telephone, late 1979 or early 1980 (date not recorded); S. M. Wedeberg, Secretary-Treasurer's Report, 1951-52, p. 2; and Nolan E. Williams to Author, interview, March 21, 1980. Also, Grand Council Minutes Book, 1956, p. 4; and Maust to Author, by telephone, June 10, 1986.

commitment to add an "alumni" representative to the governing body. During an informal session in April 1975, on the occasion of the installation of Delta Mu at Virginia as the one hundredth active chapter, the Council (minus Bob Wasley) agreed to appoint the first forum leader. At the spring meeting a few weeks later, this position was in effect reiterated, despite President Dixon's proposal that the choice be left to the advisory group itself. At the same time, a constitutional amendment was adopted by which the Advisory Forum would henceforth make the selection. As more clearly worded in the bylaws published in 1977,

> That member of the National Council who is the chairperson of the Beta Alpha Psi Advisory Forum shall be elected by a majority vote of the members of the Forum.

Dixon was instructed in May 1975 to ask two charter members if either of them would be willing to chair the forum. Three months later, he "proposed" that a third member, instead, be elected to the leadership post. Albert L. Cohen of Price Waterhouse & Co., in New York, was accordingly chosen to chair the National Advisory Forum, and serve on the National Council, for the two years 1975-77.

If the Council of the day were somewhat sensitive about academic image, Al Cohen would have been an especially attractive choice, as one of the very rare practicing accountants without a prior background in teaching (after graduate school) to hold a doctorate. The charter Alpha Eta member had finished the degree at Michigan in 1953, and published a research study on tax, finance, and accounting issues regarding long-term leases a year later.

Dr. Cohen's strong support for such participation, at his first National Council meeting, contributed to the decision to open the 1976 National Chapter meeting (more than nominally) to <u>student</u> representatives, marking a landmark change. In retrospect, however, perhaps his foremost influence as

a councilor lay in his determined advocacy of "pooled" funding of Beta Alpha Psi projects by accounting firms, corporations, and associations, in preference to the identification of specific programs with particular donors. Such an approach would later be adopted with the development of the "Associates" program covered in chapter 15. In broader terms, 1975-76 president Robert Maust felt that Cohen's respect for high ethical standards had often lifted the tone of Council deliberations during his two-year term.

The ink was scarcely dry on the National Constitution and Bylaws dated March 1 when the National Council assembled for the spring meeting of 1977. On the motion of Councilor Cohen, the as yet unapplied bylaw cited above was amended by replacing the last word, "Forum," with the term "Council." The governing body thereupon proceeded to elect Cohen's successor, by secret ballot, from among three persons nominated by the retiring chairperson. The candidates included Herb Miller, who would have become the first *ex*-councilor ever elected.

The choice fell instead, however, upon David H. Abramson, a student of Tom Burns' at Minnesota who had become managing partner in the Twin Cities office of Alexander Grant & Company. During his term, Councilor Abramson was particularly identified with the development of an external funding program, an effort in which he displayed excellent communication skills; and, according to Burns, with an ongoing "national directory" project that (as related in chapter 15) consumed a number of years.

Reference to the directory effort is an apt basis for introducing the second new National Council post, representing fraternal *alumni*.

One-year "alumni" councilorship, 1976

Background, 1974-76

One of several recommendations made in 1973 by Bob Maust's special committee on goals was the addition to the Council of "one student and one student alumni member."

Reaction in February 1974, at the first midyear meeting not designated a "long-term planning" conference, was generally favorable. Indeed, on the motion of Doris Cook the group voted to invite each of the "top chapters," within the activity program, to nominate one member to be considered for a new two-year slot. Although no explicit distinction was drawn between current membership and alumni status, it seemed to follow that by the start of such a term a nominee would ordinarily have been graduated.

At the annual meeting the following August, it was agreed that a student or alumni member should be added for the year 1976-77. On one day's notice, President Hollis Dixon asked Councilor Maust to develop and report to the National Chapter a "procedure . . . to get this member on the [C]ouncil." The following day, the special projects director reported to the assembled faculty vice-presidents that the "Outstanding Chapters" of the following year would be asked to nominate a recent alumnus (by implication) for consideration for appointment in 1976 to "a <u>one</u> year term as a voting member of the National Council" (emphasis added). The National Chapter minutes identified the new councilor as the "Alumni member," and indicated that the selection would be made by the Council.

The reference made to "Outstanding Chapters" would be clarified with the adoption the following year of a new structure for activity program

ratings. In 1975, the National Council recognized three levels of chapter distinction, namely, "Superior," "Excellent," and "Meritorious," a classification that would soon be reduced to the categories "Superior" and "Distinguished."

Identified as superior chapters in 1974-75 were Alpha Beta at Alabama, Alpha Epsilon at Southern Methodist, Alpha Phi at Temple, Beta Delta at Texas Tech, Beta Epsilon at Georgia, and Gamma Omega at California State, Long Beach. The faculty advisors at SMU and Georgia were future councilors Henry Anderson and Jack Kiger. Four of the six chapters responded to the invitation to nominate a recent alumnus. The first two alumni councilors were both associated with southeastern offices of the same accounting firm, and the third one also represented public accounting.

Alumni councilors, 1976-79: Three public accounting representatives

The first alumni councilor was T. Larry Gattis, a recent recipient of two degrees from Georgia who had been nominated by Beta Upsilon, based in part on his virtually straight-A average. Gattis, who (like his two immediate successors) had passed the CPA examination in one sitting, was a staff accountant for Price Waterhouse in Atlanta. According to Robert Maust, he was selected by Advisory Forum councilor Albert Cohen rather than through the prescribed vote, illustrating the potential ability of the professional representative (fully informed or not) to fill a National Council vacuum.

The second alumni representative was a staff accountant with Price Waterhouse in Birmingham who would soon open his own CPA practice. The election of Leroy Tanker, Alabama '76, was particularly noteworthy in adding a black member to the National Council. The Alpha Beta alumnus had in 1976 passed the CPA exam with the highest score recorded in Alabama, and the

CMA (Certificate in Management Accounting) examination with the third best mark attained nationwide.

Councilor Tanker gave special attention during his year to a minority scholarship program sponsored by the American Institute of CPAs, with Beta Alpha Psi participation, that had recently been in decline. Foreshadowing later developments, he also proposed that the alumni term be extended to two years (with increased fraternal travel), and soon be filled by a management or governmental accountant.

In 1978 the Price Waterhouse monopoly was ended, but the position (which had been expressly restricted to new alumni in their first year of employment) remained identified with a southern public accountant. The third alumni councilor was Mark A. McClure of Deloitte Haskins & Sells in Houston, the nominee of Theta at Texas, where he had earned two degrees with honors. During the year 1978-79, McClure addressed several regional and chapter meetings (and spent some time in Saudi Arabia) before serving as a panalist at the National Chapter gathering in Hawaii. As a student, he had in 1976 conducted the Southwest regional meeting held in San Antonio, and been a delegate to the first National Student Meeting, taking place in Atlanta.

As covered in chapter 15, the monopoly of public accounting within the alumni position was finally ended in 1979. Ironically, the incoming *president* was a practicing CPA who, uniquely among holders of the office, held no current academic affiliation, of any kind.

Councilor James Pattillo's non-academic affiliation, 1978-81

Although primarily identified as a practitioner, Eric Kohler had taught at Northwestern during his Beta Alpha Psi presidency, 1924-27. A quarter-century later, in 1952-53, President Charles Staehling had already reached

"emeritus" status at Berkeley. In 1979, however, James Pattillo was elected to head the fraternity while employed full time in public accounting. He had a year earlier left his post as Peat, Marwick, Mitchell & Co. professor at Notre Dame to join Crowe, Chizek, & Co. in South Bend as a manager. In response to this unusual situation, the National Council in 1979 amended the bylaws to restrict future "faculty" slots to persons holding "a full-time faculty appointment." Coincidentally, Jim Pattillo returned to teaching upon retiring from the Council in 1981.

It is noted in passing that a degree of resentment toward Beta Alpha Psi had reportedly developed at Notre Dame in reaction to an incident from Hollis Dixon's presidency. It seems that Dixon had at a National Chapter gathering openly criticized the local fraternal unit, Beta Sigma. It is not known whether any remaining effects of that episode had played a role in Pattillo's decision to leave the campus.[2]

---

[2] [Henry R. Anderson], "Anderson, Abramson and Tanker Join National Council, Dixon, Cohen and Gattis Retire," Newsletter 16 (Fall 1977):4; [Anderson], "Changes in the National Council for 1978," Newsletter 17 (Fall 1978):8; Beta Alpha Psi Annual Meeting: Honolulu, Hawaii, August 20-21, 1979, program leaflet, pp. [ii], 1; Beta Alpha Psi, "National Bylaws," National Constitution and Bylaws (1977), article 8, section 5, indented citation, (1983), article 10, section 3 (quoted); Burns and Coffman, Accounting Hall of Fame, p. 31; Thomas J. Burns to Author, interview, May 3, 1980; Albert H. Cohen to Author, May 12, 1986; [Doris M. Cook], "Dean and Gattis Elected . . .," Newsletter 15 (Fall 1976):2; [Cook], Newsletter 14 (Fall 1975):2, 3, 5 (2nd photo); [Cook], "Regional Meetings Increase," Newsletter 14 (Spring 1976):8; Harvey E. Donley to Author, interview, May 2, 1980; Hasselback, 1978-79 Directory, 1984 Directory, individual listings, s.v. "Pattillo, James W."; "Local Chapter News," Newsletter 4 (November 1952):17; Robert S. Maust to Author, interview, July 14, 1980; Fred J. Mueller, Secretary-Treasurer's Report, 1974-75, pp. 6-8; National Chapter minutes, August 1974, p. 1, quoted; National Council Minutes, February 1974, pp. 2, 4 (both quoted), August 1974, p. 4 (quoted), May-June, 1975, pp. 1-3, 8, August 1975, pp. 4, 8 (both quoted), December 1975, p. 4, April 1976, p. 7, June 1977, pp. 4 (quoted), 3, August 1977, pp. 4-5, January 1978, pp. 5, 7, June 1978, p. 5, August 1979, p. 6 (quoted), June 1980, p. [4]; "National Council of Beta Alpha Psi, 1977-78," "1977-79," as cited in note 1; Previts and Committe, comps., Index to Accounting Review, book review section, s.v. "Cohen, Albert H."; and [Charles W. Taylor], "Charter Members, Alpha to Gamma Xi," s.v. "Alpha Eta."

The advisory body providing one of the two councilorships for non-academic constituencies had been created by the fifth era's two-term president, following limited advance consultation with his colleagues.

The National Advisory Forum, Created in 1974

Hollis Dixon, who had earlier requested suggestions regarding a special meeting with professional accountants, announced the formation of the National Advisory Forum in August 1974. A preliminary meeting was held on that occasion, and over the next year the charter membership was filled out in preparation for a second gathering that would be followed by one of the fraternity's major social highlights. During Al Cohen's term as first chairperson of the forum, 1975-77, the National Council worked out further organizational and procedural points while defining a varied role for an advisory body that included very influential advocates of change in the structure of accounting education. Functions assumed by the new organization included the judging of a student literary competition having early roots within Beta Alpha Psi, and the administration of an external awards program originating the same year as the forum itself.

Origin in 1974, and Formative Development to August 1975

From germinal idea to formal organization and first meeting, 1974

Judging from the formal record, the concept of the advisory body formed in August 1974 had developed over the prior three months. At the first regular spring meeting, President Dixon had

> suggested a social hour and dinner . . . in New Orleans [site of the 1974 annual meeting] for members of public accounting firms, industry and government. The purpose of this meeting would be to permit the National Council to take a more dynamic role in education for the profession and to encourage support by the accounting profession of the local chapters . . ..

While giving full credit to Dixon for implementation, Fred Mueller stated several years later that he had proposed the idea of an advisory group to the president, as a means of bringing greater professional recognition to Beta Alpha Psi. Such a suggestion would necessarily have preceded the transfer of secretary-treasurer records in Reno, the setting identified by the Washington professor.

At the May meeting the other members were asked to propose names for invitation. The perennial issue of the proper balance between "honorary" and "professional" aspects of the fraternity was a topic suggested for discussion at the planned gathering.

Between May and August, 1974, Hollis Dixon contacted some 50 prominent accountants regarding the planned session in New Orleans, and on that basis expected 8-12 of them to be present for the occasion. At the annual meeting he not only reported on these developments, but in essence "announced" the formation of an "Advisory Forum." In 1980 the former leader said that he had "ramrodded" the concept through the National Council, although there is no evidence of opposition to it.

Dixon had wanted a turnout roughly within the range forecast, on the assumption that 10-12 participants would create a more productive discussion than, say, 30-40. In anticipation of the late-afternoon meeting scheduled with the professional accountants, the Council held a roundtable discussion on a Sunday morning to help forge "a solid front." The minutes contain a single-spaced page of twenty-five largely random observations, some of them linked remotely, if at all, to the topic at hand.

Bob Maust and Fred Mueller stated that Beta Alpha Psi's unique roles in, respectively, (a) being organized on the local campus, and (b) complementing formal study with other dimensions of professional preparation,

should be emphasized. Dixon felt that the guests should be assured that (c) their hosts were seeking ideas, that might enhance the fraternity's educational contribution, rather than money, and (d) Beta Alpha Psi was not fundamentally a "recruiting" instrument. A difference of opinion surfaced concerning the potential contribution to be made by outside speakers (an area in which forum members would provide an obvious resource) at local meetings.

In the afternoon, 15 persons turned up for the first meeting, in effect, of the National Advisory Forum. The assembled group recommended that "the chapters appoint a professional vice president from among the practicing accountants in the[ir] area" (emphasis added), an idea "strongly" endorsed by the National Council some months later. Otherwise, the only information available on the discussion is Dixon's contemporary observation that "[t]he ideas generated . . . were excellent." A listing in the fall of the first 14 appointees to the forum probably included all but one of the individuals present.

Appointment of the original 24 members, 1974-75

In announcing the first 14 members, President Dixon stated, despite his earlier preference for a smaller group, that additional appointments would be made to bring the forum to 25 persons. During the year 1974-75 he in fact appointed 10 additional members. Of course some allowance was appropriate for absenteeism at meetings, although the case of an original forum member who (as recalled by Bob Maust) never attended a session was an isolated one. The charter membership of the National Advisory Forum are listed in exhibit 28, identifying those who had presumably attended the New Orleans meeting.

EXHIBIT 28

CHARTER MEMBERS OF THE NATIONAL ADVISORY FORUM

Appointed in 1974 (nos. 1-14) or 1975 (15-24)

1. Donald Barr, Coopers & Lybrand, Dallas
2. Robert J. Canning, General Electric Company, Fairfield, Conn.
3. Albert H. Cohen, Price Waterhouse & Co. (now Price Waterhouse), New York
4. Leo Herbert, U.S. General Accounting Office, Washington D.C.[a]
5. Robert E. Knox, Touche Ross & Co., San Francisco
6. Leroy Layton, Main Lafrentz & Co. (KMG Main Hurdman), New York
7. Eldon C. Lewis, Elmer Fox & Co. (Grant Thornton), Denver
8. David Linowes, Laventhol, Krekstein, Horwath & Horwath (Laventhol & Horwath), New York
9. Robert W. Pivik, Haskins & Sells (Deloitte Haskins & Sells), New York
10. Claude W. Rodgers, Arthur Andersen & Co., Chicago
11. Robert E. Stevenson, Exxon Corporation, New York
12. Guy W. Trump, American Institute of Certified Public Accountants, New York
13. Frank T. Weston, Arthur Young & Company, New York
14. Singleton B. Wolfe, Internal Revenue Service, Washington, D.C.

15. David H. Abramson, Alexander Grant & Company (Grant Thornton), Minneapolis
16. Wayne J. Albers, Ernst & Ernst (Ernst & Whinney), Cleveland
17. James Bulloch, Institute of Management Accounting (Institute of Certified Management Accountants), Ann Arbor, Mich.
18. John C. Burton, Securities and Exchange Commission, Washington, D.C.
19. James Don Edwards, University of Georgia, Athens, Ga. (AAA representative)
20. William R. Gifford, Price Waterhouse & Co. (Price Waterhouse), New York
21. Charles R. Lees, Peat, Marwick, Mitchell & Co., New York
22. Herbert E. Miller, Arthur Andersen & Co., Chicago
23. Elmer M. Thierman, Peat, Marwick, Mitchell & Co., Tucson, Ariz.
24. Lorin H. Wilson, Haskins & Sells (Deloitte Haskins & Sells), New York

SOURCES: Lee Berton, "Peat-KMG Merger Will Form a Goliath," The Wall Street Journal, September 12, 1986, p. 6; David Brumbeloe, Chairman, Public Service & Information Committee, Georgia Society of Certified Public Accountants (GSCPA Committee), to Author, August 25, 1986; James Bulloch, ed., "Institute of Certified Management Accountants," Management Accounting 67 (June 1986):40; [Doris M. Cook], "Beta Alpha Psi Advisory Forum Meets," Newsletter 14 (Fall 1975):8; Hollis A. Dixon, "Message from the National President," Newsletter 13 (Fall 1974):8; "Firms," pp. 203-222, Georgia Society of Certified Public Accountants, Inc.: Membership Directory, 1986 . 1987 (Atlanta: GSCPA Committee, 1986), s.v. current names, with isolated exceptions, of accounting firms listed; [Robert S. Maust], "News in Brief," Newsletter 11 (Spring 1973):8; National Council Minutes, May-June, 1975, pp. 1-2; and Steve Samp, "Alumnus Heads Merger," The Sun, Winter 1985, p. 7.

[a]The next two GAO representatives died in office, Ellsworth H. Morse soon after his appointment in 1977, and Donald L. Scantlebury, of a heart attack, in 1981. [Fred J. Mueller], "National Advisory Forum," 1976-77 Annual Report, ed. [Mueller], p. 4; National Council Minutes, January 1978, p. 4; and [David E. Tinius], "News Notes," Newsletter 20 (Fall 1981):18.

In terms of current professional role, the 24 members included:

a. 16 CPA partners, all from national or international firms, 12 of them from the famous "Big 8" roster
b. Three (federal) governmental accountants
c. Two management accountants, from industry
d. Two executives of professional institutions
e. One professor.

Ten members were from New York, and another one came from a nearby town in Connecticut.

Considering that James Don Edwards was the only current accounting educator in the group, it is notable that seven other charter members held doctoral degrees. Guy Trump had been the business dean at Emory; John "Sandy" Burton had taught at Columbia, and would return there as dean; James Bulloch had been faculty vice-president to Alpha Eta at Michigan; and Herb Miller, who had spent most of his career at Michigan and Michigan State, would serve as the first director of the School of Accounting at Georgia. Eldon Lewis, the National Training Director for his firm, and first recipient of the "Distinguished Service Award" conferred by Nu at Colorado, had held "various administrative positions" at Wichita State, and been business dean at West Texas State. After retiring from the General Accounting Office, Leo Herbert joined the faculty at Virginia Tech in 1975, possibly by way of an interim appointment at Brigham Young; and Al Cohen became "Executive in Residence" at Tulane seven years later upon retirement from Price Waterhouse.

Hollis Dixon reported in the spring of 1975 that 19 of the 24 forum members expected to attend the first official meeting of the group in August, leading to a discussion of appropriate topics and format. The president cited five topics that could be presented in ten-minute talks by assigned councilors, after which (following a break) there would be a discussion, while Tom Burns (who was asked "to formulate a theme" for the meeting) favored

joint presentation and discussion. Dixon, who planned to submit several recent or current fraternal documents to forum members, proposed to issue the following "challenge" to the advisory group:

> You all know what we are doing. Where do our deficiencies exist; where can we as Beta Alpha Psi improve; what role should Beta Alpha Psi take in the professional education of the accountant?.

During the same meeting, Bob Maust observed that the length of initial terms on the Advisory Forum, and appropriate "on-going work" of the organization, needed to be addressed. The first topic, at least, was finally taken up at the 1975 annual meeting, just before the scheduled session with the forum, and a memorable social occasion.

Three Gatherings in Tucson, August 1975: The Annual Meeting, the Session with the Forum, and the Dixon Mexican Barbecue

Initial assignment of terms (later revised), and meeting with forum

As previously noted, Albert Cohen was selected at the annual meeting as the first chairperson of the National Advisory Forum. Assignments were also made to three-, two-, and one-year terms, commencing as of August 1975. The general assumption was that a full term would last three years. To allow for "staggered" terms by which vacancies would arise in 1976 and 1977, it was necessary to divide the initial membership terms into the three lengths. At the August meeting the three different terms were split up unevenly, as six persons were appointed for three years, eight for two years, and ten for a single year (1975-76).

At the next National Council meeting, however, the assignments were revised so that eight members each would be retiring in 1976, 1977, and 1978. In December 1975, full three-year terms were assigned to forum members Albers, Bulloch, Burton (who would leave early), Canning, Cohen, Pivik,

Rodgers, and Wolfe. Although listed for only a two-year term, David Abramson would actually serve until 1979 through his appointment as Cohen's successor as chairperson. Singleton Wolfe, incidentally, would join the faculty at Tennessee after retirement from the Internal Revenue Service, and be designated an Outstanding Faculty Vice-President in 1984-85 as the Alpha Lambda advisor.

The following format was laid out for the 1975 meeting with the forum:

1. A half-hour discussion of the general role of Beta Alpha Psi
2. A roundtable discussion of professional ethics, chaired by President Dixon
3. Coverage of ways in which the forum might function, with brief Council presentations on (a) the Newsletter, (b) the advisory group's view of the activity program (supportive?), (c) increasing the effectiveness of local chapters on campus, and (d) regional meetings.

At least 16 of the 24 forum appointees assembled for the Sunday afternoon session at Tucson. A Newsletter writeup cited only the first two topics, the first one in terms of "what Beta Alpha Psi can do to be more effective in educating the accountant." At the subsequent winter meeting, Councilors Thomas Burns (who had earlier questioned the warrant for such a summary) and Doris Cook agreed to attempt to develop a Newsletter article from the stenographic record of the discussion of the second topic. The result was a one-column item, "Ethics in Accounting Practice," appearing in the issue dated Spring 1976.

One suggestion made at the 1975 annual meeting was that in future years the National Council reserve an evening for social interaction with members of the Advisory Forum. A dinner hosted by the Council the following year in the revolving restaurant atop Atlanta's Peachtree Plaza Hotel, at seventy-two floors reputedly the world's tallest such facility, led to a regular function, hosted again by the governing body in 1978 and by the forum in '79. Socially, however, Hollis Dixon had set an example in 1975 that would be hard to match.

Hollis Dixon's barbecue

Local professor Dixon gave warm official welcomes at Tucson to persons attending the Beta Alpha Psi and/or American Accounting Association gatherings. For example, he had the greeting "Welcome to Beta Alpha Psi" placed on the marquee at Braniff Place, the headquarters for both groups. The highlight, however, was a barbecue at his home attended by 120-150 people on Sunday night, following the meeting with the National Advisory Forum, whose members had naturally been invited.

Dixon had started preparations on Friday morning, before the opening (at 9:00) of the first National Council Session, by digging a hole of 6 x 4 x 6 feet and starting the coals. At 6:00 that evening, he had placed a steer wrapped in cheesecloth in the pit, and added sauces. A sampling the next evening, after twenty-four hours of cooking, had revealed "magnificent" results. Mexican food, watermelon, and beverages completed the menu.

Late Sunday afternoon, the guests were bused to the Dixon home, where they were met by a five-piece mariachi band. A most festive evening followed. About half of the guests later wrote the host to thank his for the wonderful party.

One guest was American Accounting Association president R. Lee Brummet of North Carolina, who would recognize outgoing Beta Alpha Psi president Dixon at the forthcoming AAA banquet.[3] Brummet would shortly assume an official role within the fraternity as part of the continuing process of defining the National Advisory Forum.

---

[3] AAA Road Atlas, p. 22; [Henry R. Anderson], "Chapter News," Newsletter (Winter 1979):12, quoted; [Thomas J. Burns and Doris M. Cook], "Ethics in Accounting Practice," Newsletter 14 (Spring 1976):4; [Cook], "Beta Alpha Psi Advisory Forum Meets," Newsletter 14 (Fall 1975):8 (including photos), quoted; Hollis A. Dixon, "Message from the National President," Newsletter 13 (Fall 1974):8, quoted; Dixon to Author, interview, March 22-23, 1980, quoted; exhibit 29; Hasselback, 1978-79 Directory, school listing, s.v. "University

Developments Under Al Cohen's Leadership, 1975-77

Groping toward structural, pro-
eedural, and role definition

The structure, operating policy and procedure, and role of the advisory group were gradually identified during Al Cohen's two years of leadership, culminating in a policy statement discussed later. The chairperson's tenure and method of selection were set; membership was reduced, not initially by design; criteria on the composition of the group, by occupational or organizational affiliation, were established; a midyear gathering was approved; and various specific contributions that might be made by the members, individually or collectively, were identified.

The national bylaws of March 1977 stated that both regular members and the chairperson of the National Advisory Forum would serve for three years. If the latter position were to be filled by an experienced member, the total term in that instance would range from four to six years. At the spring meeting in 1977, however, the leadership post was reduced to two years, with the provision that it could be added in whole or part to the regular three-year term. David Abramson was duly elected chairperson near the close of his second (and otherwise last) year on the forum, and Albert Cohen stepped down to complete his own tenure, in 1977-78, as one of 18 other members.

The forum's size had been reduced by one member in 1976, with the

---

of Georgia," individual listing, s.v. "Bulloch, James," "Herbert, Leo"; Hasselback, 1984 Directory, school listing, s.v. "Tulane University" (quoted), individual listing, s.v. "Burton, John C."; Robert S. Maust to Author, interview, July 14, 1980 (quoted), September 28, 1985, by telephone; Fred J. Mueller to Author, interview, November 27, 1979; National Chapter Minutes, 1974, p. 2, quoted; National Council Minutes, May 1974, p. 1 (1st indented citation), August 1974, pp. 3, 8 (both quoted), May-June, 1975, pp. 1, 2 (quoted, including 2nd indented citation), August 1975, pp. 1, 9, December 1975, pp. 7a, 9, January 1978, p. 6, January 1979, p. 3; [David E. Tinius], "Outstanding Faculty Vice President Awards," 1984-85 Annual Report, ed. [Tinius], p. 3; [Robert S. Wasley], Secretary-Treasurer's Report, 1969-70, p. 7; Western Peachtree Plaza Hotel, Atlanta, to Author (by telephone), September 14, 1986; and Who's Who in America 35 (1968-69), s.v. "Trump, Guy Winston."

replacement of the eight retiring members by six new ones. Mary Lanigar of the Arthur Young office in San Francisco had declined an invitation to serve, and efforts to secure a member from the General Accounting office had failed. The first woman member was finally added the following year with the appointment of Sharon L. Donahue, Manager of Minority Recruiting for the AICPA, whose first year coincided with the term of black alumni councilor Leroy Tanker. Only four other members joined the forum in 1977, and Sandy Burton (slated to continue through 1977-78) had already resigned, leaving the advisory body at a newly prescribed membership level (19).

Past President Doris Cook was assigned in 1978 "to conduct [an] immediate search for a[nother] woman member" for the forum. The result was the appointment in 1979 of Madie Ivy of Peat, Marwick, Mitchell & Co. in New York. The following year Madlyn M. Harrell of Seidman & Seidman in Houston, the home of American Accounting Association representative Stephen Zeff, joined the advisory organization.

Councilor Cohen wished to keep the Advisory Forum from becoming slanted toward the recruitment of Beta Alpha Psi graduates. Substantial agreement was registered that members should ordinarily not be drawn from the "personnel" ranks of public accounting. There was no desire to suggest that Beta Alpha Psi was largely a placement vehicle, and had created the forum on that basis.

Al Cohen himself, however, helped arrange the appointment in 1978 of his partner Robert M. Maynard, National Director of Manpower for Price Waterhouse. Joining the advisory group the same year was Thomas J. Nessinger of Arthur Andersen, listed as the Firm Director of Recruiting when he succeeded David Abramson as chairperson in 1979. Charter members of the forum, or the next group of appointees, had included Robert W. Pivik, the

partner in charge of all areas of "human resources" for (Deloitte) Haskins & Sells; James A. Morgan, his counterpart at Peat Marwick; and William R. Gifford, a long-term National Director of Recruiting for Price Waterhouse.

In 1980 Bob Maynard, though describing himself as "not a recruiter," stated that it was difficult truly to "divorce" the placement angle from the fraternal role; and Bob Pivik remarked that he continued to make certain that his firm's personnel and recruiting policies took full advantage of the educational contribution made by Beta Alpha Psi. The latter characterization implied that the fraternity had gained enhanced professional recognition, not that a conflict of interest had existed.

An important operating development that emerged during Dr. Cohen's two-year term was a decision reached in June 1977 that the National Advisory Forum should ordinarily meet shortly before the midyear (or winter) Council meeting, as well as in the joint session of August. According to President Fred Mueller's Annual Report of 1976-77, a second meeting was conducted sometime that year. Early in 1981, Chairperson Tom Nessinger reported that there was no need for the forum to gather independently during the year then in progress.

Early discussion of the functions to be served by the National Advisory Forum was rather random in nature. In December 1975, for example, it was suggested that the forum or its individual members (as appropriate) might endeavor to promote campus recognition for faculty vice-presidents; develop policy positions on selected issues; contact deans and alumni members to help resolve Beta Alpha Psi problems identified at particular schools; and conduct "a summer program" of some kind. Bob Maust, Doris Cook, and Jim Pattillo were asked to develop an informative promotional brochure on Beta Alpha Psi that might be circulated to the forum membership as well as chapter

members and advisors, pledges, and other parties. As already noted, Cook had participated in a similar project during her FVP days. A new brochure on "Objectives," "Organization," and "Activities" was ultimately issued early in 1978.[4]

By then, a much clearer picture had emerged of the National Advisory Forum, as largely embodied in a 1977 document.

1977 policy statement on the forum

At the spring meeting in June 1977, President Fred Mueller submitted a list of items that should be included or covered in a "policy statement" on the forum, and asked Tom Burns, Hollis Dixon, and incoming chairperson David Abramson to draw up such a statement in time for the annual gathering two months later.

The product of that assignment is shown as exhibit 29 . Part 1 governed the functions of the forum at the levels of (a) the full organization, (b) sub-groups or committees, and (c) individual members. Part 2 concerned constitutional issues of size, sources, election of members, and election and duties of the chairperson. The role identified in context a by item 2-e is particular interesting in light of former president Dixon's earlier emphasis that the advisory body had not been created with fund raising in mind.

---

[4]Robert Maust, who early in 1977 was placed in charge of completing the brochure, credits the restatement made of fraternal objectives primarily to 1976-77 president Fred Mueller. The focus placed on "encourag[ing] and giv[ing] recognition to scholastic and professional excellence in . . . accounting" was very helpful to Maust, Mueller, and Tom Burns in speaking on behalf of the fraternity in the late seventies. _Beta Alpha Psi, The National Accounting Fraternity: Objectives, Organization, Activities_ ([National Council, 1978]), leaflet, quoting p. 1; Joyce C. Dean, "Minutes, Chapter Activity Program Committee," January 1977, p. 3; Robert S. Maust to Author, interview, July 14, 1980; and National Council Minutes, December 1975, p. 6, January 1978, p. 2.

THIRTEEN MEMBERS OF THE NATIONAL ADVISORY FORUM, 1976

Seated, from left, Robert J. Canning, Donald Barr, William R. Gifford, Herbert E. Miller, James A. Morgan. Standing, from left, James Bulloch, Paul L. Dillingham, Jr., Eldon C. Lewis, Leo Herbert, Albert H. Cohen (Chairperson), Robert E. Stevenson, and Claude W. Rodgers. All were charter members except Morgan, from Peat Marwick, and Dillingham, from Coca-Cola.

NATIONAL COUNCILS OF 1978 AND 1979,
ASSEMBELED DURING '78 CONVENTION

'rom left, Robert S. Maust, Jack E. Kiger, Leroy Tanker, Fred J. Mueller, Doris M. Cook, Mark A. McClure, Joyce C. Dean, James W. Pattillo, Henry R. Anderson, and David H. Abramson. Absent, Thomas J. Burns.

NATIONAL COUNCIL POLICY STATEMENT ON NATIONAL ADVISORY FORUM [1977]

Part I

1. The National Advisory Forum of Beta Alpha Psi, in cooperation with the National Council of Beta Alpha Psi, shall enhance membership in all Beta Alpha Psi chapters by:

   a. assisting in promoting the activities of all chapters.
   b. serving as an advisory group, at the call of the National Council President, reacting to policies referred to it by the National Council and recommending to the National Council, through its chairperson, policies the National Council should consider.

2. The National Advisory Forum of Beta Alpha Psi, shall as a whole:

   a. provide an assembly with whom the National Council President and members would consult and communicate annually (or semi-annually) on the accomplishments of the fraternity, the objectives not achieved, and any unresolved problems confronting the fraternity.
   b. review annually (or semi-annually) with the National Council President-elect and members specific objectives to be achieved in the forthcoming period.
   c. offer comments and suggestions for consideration by the National Council as a result of a. and b.
   d. make recommendations to the Council which arise from discussion within the Forum, and from sub-groups of the Forum organized to seek out and to analyze activities appropriate to Beta Alpha Psi.
   e. consider various ways in which the Forum may assist in funding activities of the Council and chapters.

3. Sub-groups of the National Advisory Forum shall be established and announced publicly by the National Council to:

   a. aid in accomplishing any of the forementioned activities of the Forum and the Council.
   b. select "Accountant of the Year" recipients from nominations forwarded through the National Council from the chapters.
   c. present workshops or panels on topics selected by the National Council at national and regional meetings.
   d. judge the annual student manuscript contest; the manuscripts are to be forwarded by the National Council Editor after preliminary screening.

4. Individual National Advisory Forum members are encouraged to:

   a. attend the National Chapter meeting, the plenary sessions of the National Student meeting, the annual banquet and the annual or (semi-annual) meetings of the Forum with the National Council.
   b. stress the importance of Beta Alpha Psi activities in particular when meeting with university personnel including those at

eligible universities without chapters.

c. determine and promote ways in which their organizations might fund Beta Alpha Psi national, regional and local activities.
d. assist in promoting Beta Alpha Psi activities within the member's own organization.
e. explore availability of films, displays, publications, presentations and similar materials on accounting related subjects that could be made available for Beta Alpha Psi use.
f. recommend speakers on a national basis who would be available for chapter special events.
g. as requested by the National Council, stimulate chapter activity within the National Forum member's area by serving as a resource person for chapters or with National Council members, participate in chapter visitations particularly at the weaker chapters.
h. attend Beta Alpha Psi regional conferences (where Forum members receive early notification as to dates and locations).
i. initiate contacts between the member's organization offices and local chapters and faculty vice-presidents.
j. explore possibilities of inviting faculty vice-presidents as faculty interns or as consultants to the member's organization.
k. attend local chapter meetings and encourage others in the member's organization to do so.

Part II

1. In addition to its chairperson the National Advisory Forum of Beta Alpha Psi shall consist of eighteen leaders of accounting thought and practice from public accounting, industry and government. Ten members shall represent the public accounting profession; six shall represent industry and government; and one each shall represent the American Accounting Association, the American Institute of Certified Public Accountants and the National Association of Accountants. There is not to be more than one member from the same organization.

2. The members of the National Advisory Forum shall be selected by the National Council for a three year term. Members shall be selected on the basis of: their interest in the Beta Alpha Psi fraternity, their stature in the professional community, and their willingness and capacity to serve.

3. The chairperson of the Forum shall be elected by the National Council after consultation with the two members of the National Council who will serve as president during the term of the chairperson. Three Forum members will be proposed for the post by the retiring chairperson from nominations received from Forum members.

4. The chairperson shall serve a two-year term and be a voting member of the National Council. The chairperson shall be the primary spokesperson for presenting views of the Forum to the National Council and to inform the Forum as to subjects being considered by the National Council.

Subgroups were identified concerning two relatively new award programs discussed presently. The National Council accepted a proposal by outgoing member Al Cohen that members of the selection committees not be announced in advance. It was assumed, also, that workshops and panel discussions on assigned topics would be presented by forum members at regional and national meetings.

Finally, individual members were encouraged to participate in Beta Alpha Psi activity in their particular localities, commonly at the chapter level, and to encourage participation by their employer organizations.

At the constitutional level, total membership had been set at 19, representing three different sources:

1. 10 members from public accounting
2. 6 from industry and government
3. 1 each from the AAA, the AICPA, and the NAA.

No accounting firm, company, agency, or other organization would have more than one representative--a restriction that was destined to be violated in 1985 when Sandra A. Suran moved from an Oregon practice bearing her surname to a partnership with Peat Marwick. Although perhaps no slots were considered officially "proprietary" to a given firm or company, all "Big 8" accounting points had to that point been continuously represented on the forum. The first "local" practitioner to be appointed, in 1977, was Edwin E. Merriman (Theta '32) of Lubbock, Texas, who in the sixties had joined golden anniversary speaker Louis Kessler on the Accounting Faculty Associates at Texas.

Three accounting associations were assigned permanent slots following possible consideration in that regard of the Financial Executives Institute and the General Accounting Office, a federal agency whose representation had by 1981 been cut short three times by retirement or death (exhibit 28). The

three pertinent members in 1977-78 were former AAA president Lee Brummet, appointed the preceding year; AICPA official Sharon Donahue; and James Bulloch from the NAA's Institute of Management Accounting, the administrator for the CMA Examination.

Donahue's immediate predecessor, and a forum colleague having special ties to the fraternity, were leaders in a notable dual educational movement of the day that Beta Alpha Psi supported at somewhat of a distance.

"Professional" accountancy programs and their "accreditation": Roles of two forum members and the Council

The kind of concern found in the National Council of the early 1970s that accounting was being submerged within modern business curricula had produced much support for the creation of distinctly "professional" accounting programs that could be independently "accredited." The American Institute of Certified Public Accountants was at the very forefront of this movement, which was identified especially with advocacy of a *five-year* curriculum. Two charter members of the Advisory Forum, serving until 1977, held major official positions in this regard. Guy Trump was the institute's Vice-President for Education, and Herbert Miller chaired its Board on Standards for Programs and Schools of Professional Accounting.

At the winter meeting of 1975-76, the National Council agreed that Beta Alpha Psi should take no official position on the administrative structure, content, or evaluation standards appropriate for professional accounting programs. For example, the accounting fraternity wished to stay clear of controversy considering the desirability of forming "schools" of accounting (or accountancy) that were at least partly independent of colleges of business administration.

Without retracting its neutrality on special issues, the governing body voted in the spring of 1976 to advise both Trump and Miller that Beta Alpha Psi was

> 'vitally interested in joining with the AICPA and other appropriate organizations in the discussion of the establishment and implementation of standards and the formulation of an accreditation process for professional programs of accounting'.

Secretary-Treasurer Fred Mueller wrote the two forum members in May to express Council interest in discussing the matter with them ("as a group or as individuals"), and neutrality on the question of whether "autonomous professional schools" should be developed. One of the letters may have represented a formality, in part, for Mueller and President Bob Maust had apparently already talked with Herb Miller, while visiting Arthur Andersen headquarters in Chicago on March 1 to discuss funding for the Richard S. Claire Award. Miller advised the fraternity, in any event, to try to become involved in the development of policy, nationally, relative to accounting programs and their accreditation.

Although Maust would as an ex-councilor speak (in effect) approvingly of that advice, the National Council chose basically to remain on the sidelines over the next few years, while the National Advisory Forum may have signaled widespread professional attitudes in the selections made for "Accountant of the Year" in education, 1977-79. The three men honored were directors of three of the earliest schools (identified in the third case as an "institute") of accounting or accountancy. They were Joseph A. Silvoso of Missouri; Herb Miller of, following his retirement from Arthur Andersen, Georgia; and K. Fred Skousen of Brigham Young, the second president of the Federation of Schools of Accountancy.

By the close of the decade, designated professional schools representing

varying levels of autonomy had been formed at several other well-established Beta Alpha Psi universities, including Alabama, Denver, Florida, Louisiana Tech, Mississippi, San Diego State, and Southern California. In broader terms, a plan was taking shape by which the AACSB (once headed by Guy Trump's brother Ross, as dean at Washington University) would accredit programs leading to bachelor's and master's degrees in accounting, or with a concentration therein.

During the year 1979-80, finally, Past President Thomas Burns (chairing a five-member committee formed to review pending arrangements) drafted a letter stating that Beta Alpha Psi supported the accreditation of accounting programs by the assembly. Approved by the National Council, it was sent early in 1980 by President James Pattillo to his AACSB counterpart Veron K. Zimmerman, a long-term accounting professor at Illinois who had coauthored an accounting theory book with A. C. Littleton. The fraternity saw no need, however, to take part in a public hearing conducted in Dallas in February concerning a variety of specific issues raised, or otherwise address such points.

The charter "Accounting Accreditation Committee" appointed for 1980-81 was headed by Fred Mueller's dean at Washington, Kermit Hanson, and included as members Lee Brummet and former fraternal president Wilton Anderson. The first group of programs accredited, in 1982, included more than one degree each offered on thirteen Beta Alpha Psi campuses, only five of them by expressly designated professional "schools."[5]

---

[5]AACSB Membership Directory, 1980-81, pp. 4, 20, 89; Beta Alpha Psi, "National Bylaws," National Constitution and Bylaws (1977), article 6, section 2, article 9, section 3; Thomas J. Burns to Joyce C. Dean, September 1, 1978, enclosed committee assignments, p. [2], quoted; [Doris M. Cook], "Manuscript Contest," 1977-78 Annual Report, ed. [Cook], p. [7]; exhibit 30; Hasselback, 1979-80 Directory, school listing, 1984 Directory, school

Two particularly well-defined roles for the National Advisory Forum concern awards programs honoring students and professional accountants (including educators), respectively, that originated during the fifth era, or on its eve.[6]

Selection Committees for Two Awards Programs

Manuscript Contest

Reinstatement, after thirty years, and early design, 1970-75

Chapter 11 of the first volume was devoted to a student manuscript

---

listing, individual listing, s.v. "Zimmerman, Vernon K."; Steve Hentz, "1980 Outstanding Alumnus Award: William R. Gifford," *The Sun* (Omicron newsletter, Ohio State), Winter 1980, p. 5; Robert S. Maust to Author, interview, July 14, 1980; Robert M. Maynard to Author, interview (Boston, Mass.), August 10, 1980, quoted; Herbert E. Miller to Author, interview, April 18, 1980; Hermann C. Miller, ed., *Beta Alpha Psi Directory*, s.v. "Theta Chapter: Merriman, Edwin E."; [Fred J. Mueller], "Manuscript Contest," *1976-77 Annual Report*, ed. [Mueller], p. 9; Mueller, Secretary-Treasurer's Report, 1975-76, p. 6; Mueller to Guy W. Trump, May 14, 1976, quoted; "National Advisory Forum," Annual Reports, 1975-76 through 1984-85, especially 1976-77, p. 4, 1978-79, pp. 21-23, 1979-80, pp. 6, 8-9, 1985, p. 33; National Chapter Awards Banquet, Honolulu, August 21, 1979, tape recording (presentation to K. Fred Skousen); National Council Minutes, December 1975, pp. 6 (quoted), 7, April 1976, pp. 3, 4 (quoted), August 1976, p. 3, June 1977, p. 3 (quoted), August 1977, pp. 1, 5, January 1980, p. 4; *Newsletter* 16-18 (Fall, 1977-79):1, "Accountant of the Year" writeups; [James W. Pattillo], "Beta Alpha Psi, . . . 1979-80: Objectives, National Office Functions . . ., [and] National Council Committees" [1978], 7-page Council document, p. 4; Robert W. Pivik to Author, interview (Boston), August 10, 1980, quoted; Previts and Committe, *Index to Accounting Review*, book reviews, s.v. "Zimmerman, Vernon K."; Smith, *Forty Acres*, p. 102; Gary White, Texas Tech University accounting area, to Author, June 10, 1986; and *Who's Who in America* 35 (1968-69), s.v. "Trump, Guy Winston," "Trump, Ross Myron."

[6] Forum members also served as judges for two contests begun in 1979, honoring chapters respectively for (1) "public interest" projects and (2) local newsletters. The program sponsored by Accountants for the Public Interest was discontinued after three years due to extremely low participation, as nine of the twelve projects submitted had come from the same chapter, three-time winner Gamma Eta at Akron. The newsletter contest, won once by Gamma Eta and twice by Delta Beta at California State, Fullerton, was likewise last held in 1980-81. "Beta Alpha Psi Chapter Newsletter Award" and "Public Interest Award" (or equivalent), *Annual Reports*, 1978-79 through 1980-81, pp. 9, 15, 15, respectively; and National Council Minutes, June 1978, p. 3, August 1978, p. 2, June 1979, p. 2, June 1980, p. [2], January 1981, p. 8, June 1981, p. 2.

contest conducted over the years 1929-40. Each chapter had been eligible to submit one student paper presented at a local meeting, and authors so nominated had received a copy of the Accountant's Handbook. The Grand Council had additionally awarded fifty dollars to the student adjudged to have written the top paper of the year.

A prompt outgrowth of the publication of student manuscripts in the Newsletter was a new manuscript competition, initially based on the articles printed during the year. Without any announcement in the prior year's minutes or in the periodical itself, it began in 1970, probably on the initiative of Editor Charles Taylor. At the National Chapter banquet that year, a commemorative plaque was presented to Warren Moorehead, a black member of Beta Phi at Sacramento State, for his article "Community Business Center Opens in Sacramento." He had traveled to the gathering as a guest of the Council, which in the years to come would continue to finance such trips for winning or (at least) first-place authors. Somewhat ironically, by 1972 Beta Phi Chapter would have no address for Moorehead, initiated only three years earlier.

The program was continued in 1971, when plaques were presented to two coauthors from Beta Upsilon at Georgia, an outcome not permitted by subsequent restriction of eligibility to manuscripts having a single author. The contest was substantially altered the following year. First, there was an announced topic, "Cost Benefit Analysis," in regard to social issues. Second, the Manuscript Contest was accordingly separated from Newsletter submissions, and from the relevant component of the activity program, although it would not be recognized in its own right within the points competition for another four years. Third, the winning essay would be published in the fraternal periodical after its selection. Finally, a cash prize was added, raised

following the 1971-72 contest from $50 to $100.

Through 1975 the winners were selected, subject to ratification by the National Council, by successive editors Taylor, Harold Royer, Robert Maust, and Doris Cook, or committees chaired thereby. Without the engagement of outside reviewers, some excellent talent was identified in the essay competition. From 1973 through 1975, the winning authors, and their assigned topics, were (a) Thomas L. Stober of Omicron at Ohio State, "Significance of Forecasts to Meaningful Financial Disclosure"; (b) Gary C. Biddle, also of Omicron, "Price-Level Accounting: Irrelevant or Conveniently Forgotten?"; and (c) Rick Antle of Chi at Oklahoma State, "Interperiod Income Tax Allocation: A Cost-Benefit Analysis." By the fall of 1985, the three authors, who had all competed as undergraduates, had taught respectively at Michigan; Chicago and Washington; and Chicago and Yale.

The National Advisory Forum entered the picture in 1976 as the program was significantly expended.

Expansion of the program, and entry of the Advisory Forum, 1976

In the competition of 1975-76, three cash prizes were awarded. After having made a single $100 award the preceding year, the National Council gave out checks respectively for $600, $400, and $200. Along with the plaque to the first-place entrant, certificates were presented to the top three contestants and to eight others cited for "honorable mention." The following year the three cash prizes were each raised by one fourth, and a $50 award was added for honorable mention status.

Another major change of 1976 concerned the judging of the competition. The 38 manuscripts received from 17 chapters were screened by a committee headed by Editor Doris Cook. The 10 entries considered strongest were then

turned over to a committee made up, apparently, of forum members John Burton, Robert Pivik, and (from Exxon Corporation) Robert E. Stevenson, who selected the first-, second-, and third-place papers. In each of the next two years, NAA representative James Bulloch served on a similar panel drawn from the forum. The screening committee chaired in 1977-78 by Editor Henry Anderson reviewed 74 manuscripts.

The following year Anderson, Past President Cook, and Councilor Jack Kiger selected the top 8 papers (from 96 submissions arriving from 54 chapters) for review by representatives of three major professional or scholarly journals. The initial plan was to engage one editor or associate editor each from The Accounting Review, The Journal of Accountancy, and The Journal of Accounting Research. The third post was filled instead by Bulloch's successor on the forum, Management Accounting publisher James D. Collier. The first- and third-place manuscripts of 1978-79, and the top-ranked paper of the preceding year, had come from Alpha Nu Chapter at Creighton. Twelve entries were designated for honorable mention in 1979, including seven not sent to the panelists.

The following year, finally, the selection of the top papers reverted to the National Advisory Forum. By then, however, two committees were needed, because (as discussed in chapter 15) the manuscript contest had been divided into "undergraduate" and "graduate" competitions. Specifications in each case included a maximum of 3,000 words, "including footnote material," as compared to earlier limits ranging from 8-12 double-spaced pages; and evaluation based both on content (65%) and presentation (35%).

Publication of leading manuscripts was notably expanded in the late seventies beyond the printing of the top-ranked paper in the fall Newsletter.

Expanded publication of papers

James Bulloch, one of the three judges the first two years, published the first-place papers of 1977, 1978, and 1979 (twice in excerpted form) in his column in the NAA periodical Management Accounting. In addition, the six finalists of the first two years, and the top eight papers of 1978-79, were edited and published by Tom Burns and Hank Anderson. In 1978 Burns brought out two volumes, covering the topics segmental reporting (1976-77) and replacement costing (1977-78), while Anderson issued a third volume of papers a year later, dealing with foreign currency translation from the standpoint of multinational corporations. In 1980, finally, Past President Burns published, in separate volumes, all award-winning entries from both manuscript contests.[7]

---

[7]Beta Alpha Psi, Beta Phi Chapter: Membership Directory, 1972 ([Sacramento, Cal.: Beta Phi Chapter, Sacramento State College, 1972]), "Alphabetical Listing," s.v. "Moorehead, Warren"; James Bulloch, ed., "Institute of Management Accounting," Management Accounting 59-61 (October 1977, February 1979, April 1980):65-68, 59-60, 54-55, respectively; Thomas J. Burns, ed., The Audit Committee: Its Impact on the Independent Auditor (National Council, [1980]), especially pp. v, vi (quoted); Burns, ed., Imputed Interest: Is it a Recognizable Cost? (National Council, [1980]), especially p. v, quoted; [Doris M. Cook], "Antle Receives 1975 Manuscript Award," Newsletter 14 (Fall 1975):3; [Cook], "Beta Alpha Psi Announces Manuscript Contest for 1975," Newsletter 13 (Fall 1974):7; [Cook], "Biddle Receives 1974 Manuscript Award," Newsletter 13 (Fall 1974):3; Cook to Author, May 19, 1986; Joyce C. Dean, Secretary-Treasurer's Report, 1977-78, p. [7]; Hasselback, 1984 Directory, individual listing, s.v. "Antle, Rick," "Biddle, Gary C.," "Stober, Thomas L."; James R. Hasselback, comp., Prentice-Hall Accounting Faculty Directory: 1986 (Englewood Cliffs: Prentice-Hall, 1986), individual listing, s.v. "Antle," "Biddle," "Stober," as above; "Manuscript Awards" or "Manuscript Contest," Annual Reports, 1975-76 through 1979-80; [Robert S. Maust], "Beta Alpha Psi Announces Manuscript Contest for 1973," ". . . 1974," Newsletter 11 (Fall 1972):8, 12 (Fall 1973):8; [Maust], "R. N. Gilbert Wins Manuscript Award," 11 (Fall 1972):1; [Maust], "Stober is 1973 Manuscript Winner," Newsletter 12 (Fall 1973):2; Warren Moorehead, "Community Business Service Center Opens in Sacramento," Newsletter 8 (Spring 1970):3; Fred J. Mueller, Secretary-Treasurer's Report, 1975-76, p. 3; National Council Minutes, 1971, p. 7, 1972, p. 11, 1973, p. 10, May-June, 1975, p. 12, August 1975, p. 5, December 1975, p. 7, August 1976, pp. 2, 5, January 1979, p. 3, June 1979, p. 4, August 1979, p. 8; [Harold L. Royer], "Harrington and McLendon Win Manuscript Award," Newsletter 10 (Fall 1971):3; [Royer], "More than 100 Beta

The Advisory Forum promptly became involved in a second honors program, in this case at a policymaking level as well as in the selection area. The first "Accountant of the Year," who would himself soon be appointed to the advisory body, had been honored at the same meeting (in 1974) during which the forum had first gathered. Related local programs included one of particular interest that was already well established by that point.

Accountant of the Year

Origination of the idea, 1971

The idea of honoring one or more outstanding professional accountants each year, from any sector of the field, is credited primarily to 1970-71 president Charles Taylor, who has in turn attributed the initial suggestion to one of his two immediate predecessors, Harvey Donley or Vern Odmark. The matter is first documented in the minutes of the long-range planning conference of May 1971. In a day of National Council concern "as to the future of accounting education in collegiate schools of business," one topic discussed was possible "Closer Affiliation" of Beta Alpha Psi with the American Accounting Association.

On association business, AAA president-elect Charles Zlatkovich of Texas was himself in Las Vegas, the meeting site, at the time. Some or all of the councilors and former members present called on him,

> suggest[ing] that Beta Alpha Psi make a presentation of <u>national honorees</u> at the AAA luncheon similar to what Beta Gamma Sigma does at the annual AACSB luncheon, thus making Beta Alpha Psi more a part of the AAA [emphasis added].

Since 1963 the honorary society Beta Gamma Sigma had conferred from three to

---

Alpha Psi delegates . . .," <u>Newsletter</u> 9 (Winter 1971):2; and Sheldahl, <u>Alpha to Omega</u>, pp. 550-51, 555-58.

nine "National Honoree" awards yearly upon outstanding business executives and educators, at a specially designated luncheon held during the accrediting agency's annual meeting. The leaders of the accounting fraternity had in mind an award that might be presented at one of the association's yearly noontime functions. Despite the reference made to "honorees," Professor Taylor is certain that there was no thought at the time of honoring more than one person annually.

Zlatkovich showed some interest in the suggestion, and invited the Council to submit a formal proposal for him to take to the December meeting of his executive committee.[8]

Development of a program, without AAA linkage, 1972-74

The response from the American Accounting Association, not received until after the fraternity's own midterm planning session of 1971-72, was affirmative but "not enthusiastic." It may be pertinent that the professional fraternity Alpha Kappa Psi had in some years presented its own award to outstanding accountants, established in 1952, at AAA functions; and that the association was considering the initiation of an annual award of its own to honor leading accounting educators. The Outstanding Educator Award was duly instituted by the other organization in 1973, when Wilton Anderson

---

[8]Zlatkovich, who would be honored in 1983 as the fraternity's Accountant of the Year for education, was not receptive to another idea brought forth--that Beta Alpha Psi be represented, by the national president, on the AAA executive committee. Early in 1980 Past President Thomas Burns suggested that the National Council consider seeking a slot on that body in terms of prospective funding for the association from granting student membership to new initiates: "[I]t could be pointed out that the Fraternity has some 8,000 new members yearly who could become 8,000 AAA members." The Council were not particularly enthusiastic about the idea, however, although an isolated reference to an association "request to sell associate memberships through Beta Alpha Psi" (heading format disregarded) appears in 1981 minutes. Thomas J. Burns to Author, interview, May 3, 1980; National Council Minutes, January 1980, p. 9, June 1981, p. 11 (both quoted), June 1983, p. 4; and Robert S. Wasley, Long-Range Planning Committee Minutes, May 1971, p. [2].

and Charles Horngren were honored as the charter recipients.

The American Accounting Association agreed to provide a setting for a Beta Alpha Psi presentation only if honorees would not be restricted to the fraternal membership. Nonetheless, at the 1972 annual meeting the National Council approved President Robert Wasley's motion to establish a "National Honorary Award" on the following basis:

1. Presentation at an AAA luncheon
2. Nomination by Beta Alpha Psi chapters
3. Selection of ten finalists, at most, by the Council
4. Selection of the winner by a committee composed of the national president, as chairman and secretary, and one "outstanding representative" each from (a) government, (b) industry, (c) teaching, and (d) public accounting.

A suitable plaque would be presented to the accountant (singular) selected each year.

It was agreed to introduce the award the next year, in 1973. Procedures were accordingly set forth, and potential members of a selection committee mentioned, at the midyear planning conference. The matter was not followed up, however, and at the 1973 annual meeting the National Council decided to abandon a linkage with the AAA, and to make the presentation at its own banquet, as of the following year. Although Guy Trump had conveyed his preliminary approval of such an arrangement to outgoing member Charles Taylor, the Council decided not to ask the American Institute of CPAs to host an awards ceremony.

As the (planned) retiring councilor, Bob Wasley was designated to supervise the first year's selection process. Secretary-Treasurer Fred Mueller reported on the matter at the 1974 spring meeting, however, by which point eight finalists had been identified for referral to an unidentified selection committee, from among nineteen nominees. The winner was the first of three successive professors (one of them also a long-time dean) to be

cited as the "(Outstanding) Accountant of the Year."

Honoring three academic leaders as
"Accountants of the Year," 1974-76

The committee chose Professor James Don Edwards of Georgia, a prominent textbook author, as the 1974 "Outstanding Accountant of the Year." With several members of his family present, he received a plaque at the annual banquet. The following year the designation was changed to "Accountant of the Year," and a framed collection of testimonial statements received on behalf of the nomination was added to the commemorative prize.

The first available statement of nomination criteria appeared in the *Newsletter* of Winter 1975. Requirements included (a) recognized national service to the field, (b) effect on "a great number of lives," (c) contribution to "the knowledge of the profession," (d) wide acceptance as an outstanding accountant, and (e) "currently active" status. The nomination statement itself was expected to document adequately the candidate's qualifications. Senior Past President Wasley, who would write the citation and present the plaques in 1975, had probably drafted the specifications, in refinement of criteria he had announced at the National Chapter meeting a few months earlier.

Nominees originally were not restricted to alumni, faculty, or honorary members of a chapter, or indeed to members of the fraternity. It was stated that "honorary" membership would be conferred upon an Accountant of the Year not already affiliated with Beta Alpha Psi. Since there was no provision for election on a national or at-large basis, arrangements would by implication be made for induction by a chapter selected by the accountant. The same policy would be adopted concerning members of the National Advisory Forum.

In regard to Accountants of the Year, at any rate, there would be no need to "arrange" for honorary induction. The winners of 1974-76 were already

members of Beta Alpha Psi, and their successors were required to be so. Don Edwards was an honorary member of Theta at Texas, and the next two recipients of the award were alumni members Paul Garner of Theta and (based on original "faculty" induction) Norton Bedford of Omicron at Ohio State.

The fraternity took a suitably broad interpretation of the eligibility requirement, "currently active" status in the case of the 1975 winner. Fifteen years after his retirement from Alabama in 1971, Dean Garner continued to maintain an active schedule that featured regular travel to accounting conferences throughout the world. Reference to selection in 1976 of Professor Bedford of Illinois, a leading scholar, brings to mind his dispute with the Grand Council a generation earlier concerning the activity program.

In view particularly of the separate requirement that candidates had "contributed to the knowledge of the profession," it is not surprising that the first three Accountants of the Year represented the academic field. On the initiative of the Advisory Forum councilor, the program was broadened beginning in 1976-77, and placed largely in the hands of the forum.

Restructuring in 1976-77: An expanded program conducted by the forum

In August 1976 Councilor Albert Cohen submitted a new plan by which chapters would nominate up to three persons from their own alumni, one each from public accounting, education, and business, industry, or government. "Honorary" members could be nominated by a chapter only if during attendance at the school prior to fraternal chartering they would have been eligible for Beta Alpha Psi induction by the national standards of the day. Three members of the Advisory Forum appointed by the chairperson would review the 100-word nominating statements, and supporting material, and select an

honoree (by implication) from each category.

Cohen's proposal was adopted, but certain strictures were relaxed by "implementing criteria and operating procedures" drawn up by Councilors Cook, Burns, Maust, and Mueller. In view of the difficulty of making a persuasive case more briefly, the size limit for nomination statements was raised immediately to 250 words, and soon to 500.

Also, nomination was opened to any honorary member of a chapter, so that a group recently formed could elect a prominent accountant not already affiliated with the fraternity, and then nominate the person for an Accountant of the Year award, even if he or she had never attended the school. As a geographically interesting case in point, Harvard professor emeritus Robert N. Anthony was the Accountant of the Year for education in 1985 as the (presumed) nominee of Delta Omega at Utah State, to which he had been admitted, before retirement, eight years earlier.

The three winners in 1977 were the aforementioned Joseph Silvoso of the University of Missouri, in education; Joseph B. Collinson, the president and chief executive officer of Textron Inc., in industry; and Richard T. Baker, the managing partner of Ernst & Ernst, in public accounting. Silvoso had obviously been eligible through (charter) "faculty" membership earned in Gamma Theta at Missouri in 1967 (not, as stated in the published citation, two years later). The other two men were both alumni of Omicron at Ohio State. Business executive Collinson was eligible based on prior identification, professionally, as an accountant. A photo of the three 1977 winners, standing with incoming president Doris Cook, was printed in Management Accounting.

The first "governmental" Accountant of the Year was honored in 1979, while a member of the National Advisory Forum. A(rthur) Clarence Sampson

had joined the Securities and Exchange Commission some eight years after his induction by Tau at Maryland in 1951, and recently succeeded John Burton as its chief accountant. The "public" accountant selected in '79 was likewise a forum member. After succeeding fellow Omicron alumnus Richard Baker at the helm of Ernst & Ernst, at age 42, Ray J. Groves had led the firm into expanded national and international practices under the new name Ernst & Whinney.

Through 1985, thirty men had received the fraternal Accountant of the Year award. The term "men" is used in a noncontroversial sense, for no female accountant had as yet been so honored by Beta Alpha Psi.

For the year 1978-79, only 22 nominations, from all categories, had been received from the 126 chapters operating throughout the period. In order to stimulate more participation, nominations were soon incorporated as a subcategory within the Chapter Activity Program. The partial results reported through 1979 absolve Omicron of any responsibility for the disappointing level of involvement registered. The Ohio State chapter had preceded the National Council in establishing an honoree program, and variations on the same theme would soon appear at other localities, with some encouragement (beyond the national program itself) from the governing body.

Chapter programs, particularly the Omicron alumnus award

In 1967 Omicron initiated an annual "Outstanding Alumnus Award" that was destined to become a fixture of the local program. Included among the twenty accountants honored through 1986 were national Accountants of the Year Norton Bedford, Richard Baker, and Ray Groves; Advisory Forum members Groves, William Gifford, Robert Maynard, Robert A. Kleckner of Alexander Grant (managing partner), and Eugene H. Flegm of General Motors; and, as

the first educator cited, Councilor Fred Mueller, a Delta alumnus who had transferred to Omicron as a graduate student at Ohio State in the fifties.

In 1973 the National Council voted to implement a plan approved a year earlier to introduce "Faculty Certificates of Merit," patterned after the scholarship certificates discussed in chapter 8, that local units could present to retiring FVPs, or other professors recognized for chapter service. More pertinently, a similar award was approved for purposes of "recognizing outstanding accountants in each chapter's area." Every chapter would be eligible to confer two certificates of each kind per year.

Production of "Meritorious Service Award" certificates, promptly defined in terms of contributions by an accountant to the particular chapter, was deferred pending the designation of the first national honoree in August 1974. The specific design was chosen by Secretary-Treasurer Fred Mueller, whose signature (according to original specifications) would have joined those of the local president, secretary, and faculty advisor on the certificate. Twenty-two certificates were ordered by chapters during the year following senior councilor Robert Wasley's announcement of the new award to the National Chapter in 1974.

The honor was not restricted to a chapter's own alumni or honorary members, or even (apparently) to persons affiliated with Beta Alpha Psi, although it seems unlikely that a credible candidate would have escaped induction at one level or the other. Early in 1977 a national committee briefly considered (but rejected) a proposal to charge five dollars per certificate ordered, suggesting that some chapters may have wished to confer more than the two awards authorized per year.

Finally, chapters have introduced "Accountant of the Year" programs patterned after the original or revised national awards. Epsilon Upsilon,

PRESIDENT HARVEY E. DONLEY PRESENTS FIRST MODERN-DAY MANUSCRIPT AWARD TO WARREN MOOREHEAD OF BETA PHI, 1970

A 1977 GATHERING OF ACCOUNTANTS OF THE YEAR AND OUTSTANDING OMICRON ALUMNI

From left, incoming president Doris Cook, Accountants of the Year Richard T. Baker (public practice), Joseph B. Collinson (industry), and Joseph A. Silvoso (education) and incoming president Fred Mueller. Baker and Collinson had earlier earned the Omicron Outstanding Alumnus award, and Mueller would later be so honored.

destined to qualify as a "Superior" chapter for six consecutive years (through 1985) following its installation at Emory in the last months of the fifth era, chose to honor one accountant yearly. Alpha Iota at Arkansas and Alpha Upsilon at Bowling Green State, the respective home chapters for Doris Cook and Harvey Donley (who in December 1982 presented his group's first education award), instead instituted separate honors for education, public accounting, and industry, business, or government. Both chapters limit the field to their own members, at some level, in keeping with a stated purpose of the national award--"to encourage chapters to honor" local "members in one or more of the three [professional] areas." Honorees affiliated with the local chapter would be logical candidates for national nomination. Arkansas in some years makes more than one award in a given category.

---

[9] "Accountant of the Year" or (as of 1978-79) "Accountant of the Year Awards," Annual Reports, 1976-77 through 1984-85; Alpha Kappa Psi Foundation: Devoted to Education and Research ([Indianapolis, Ind.: Alpha Kappa Psi Foundation, 1980]), leaflet, p. [2]; [Henry R. Anderson], "Chapter News," Newsletter 16 (Spring 1978):10; "Beta Alpha Psi Accountant of the Year Awards," Newsletter 15 (Winter 1977):9, 22 (Fall 1983):16, each quoted; "Beta Alpha Psi Outstanding Accountant of the Year Award," 13 (Winter 1975):8, quoted; Beta Gamma Sigma Directory, 1980-81 (St. Louis: Beta Gamma Sigma, [1980]), pp. 34-36, "National Honorees"; "Chapter/Member News," Management Accounting 59 (October 1977):69; [Doris M. Cook], "James Don Edwards: Outstanding Accountant of the Year," Newsletter 13 (Fall 1974):1; [Cook], "Norton M. Bedford: Accountant of the Year," Newsletter (Fall 1976):1; [Cook], "S. Paul Garner: Accountant of the Year," Newsletter (Fall 1975):1; Joyce C. Dean, Activity Program Committee Minutes, January 1977, p. 3; Hollis A. Dixon, Long-Range Planning Committee Minutes, December 1972, pp. 4-5; Dixon to Author, interview, March 22-23, 1980; Anthony Foti, "Outstanding Alumnus of 1984," The Sun (Omicron), Winter 1984, p. 3, with photo of '83 winner; Paul Garner to Author, January 9, 1986, enclosing Christmas letter sent (with Mrs. Garner) to friends worldwide, December 1985; Hasselback, 1984 Directory, individual listing, s.v. "Garner, S. Paul"; Leon E. Hay to Author, interview, May 2, 1980; Steve Hentz, "1980 Outstanding Alumus Award," as cited in note 7; Kevin Kagarise, "Outstanding Alumnus, 1985," The Sun, Winter 1985, p. 6; "Local Chapter News," Newsletter (3) (March 1952):24, 4 (November 1952):23; Robert S. Maust, Long-Range Planning Committee Minutes, December 1971, pp. 3, 6; Fred J. Mueller, Secretary-Treasurer's Report, 1974-75, p. 1; quoted; National Chapter Minutes, 1974, p. 1; National Council Minutes, 1972, pp. 6, 11 (quoted), 1973, pp. 8 (quoted) 13, February 1974, p. 7, May 1974, p. 1, August 1974, pp. 4, 9, February 1975, p. 3, May-June,

In Transition

The reconstitution of the National Council, and the creation of the National Advisory Forum, were highly pertinent to several leading program developments of the fifth era not as yet covered. They facilitated, or made possible, levels and modes of student involvement in Beta Alpha Psi, and pluralism in chapter activity, never previously approached.

1975, p. 10, August 1975, pp. 1-2, August 1976, pp. 3, 5 (quoted), August 1977, p. 1, August 1979, pp. 2-3; "National Council: 1978-79," 1978-79 Annual Report, ed. [Burns], inside front cover; "1984 Outstanding Accounting Educator Award," AAA Accounting Education News, November 1984, p. 1; "Purcell Receives Honor," Current Accounts, newsletter of Georgia Society of CPAs, May 1986, p. 7; Smith, Forty Acres, pp. 61, 67, 180-81; [Charles W. Taylor], "Charter Members, Alpha to Gamma Xi," s.v. "Gamma Theta"; Taylor to Author, interview, April 18, 1980, quoted; [David E. Tinius], "News Notes," Newsletter 20 (Winter 1982):11, 21 (Spring 1983):9, 22 (Fall 1983):19; James A. Viehland, Associate Director of AACSB, to Author, May 15, 1986; Robert S. Wasley, Long-Range Planning Committee Minutes, May 1971, pp. 1-2, quoted, including indented citation; and Nolan E. Williams to Author, interview, March 21, 1980. Also, Thomas J. Burns to Author, August 28, 1986; Doris M. Cook to Author, August 5, 1986; and "Outstanding Alumnus 1986," The Sun, Winter 1986, p. 11.

In the spring of 1980, Omega at Miami of Ohio for the first time designated its three national nominees as local Accountants of the Year. Professor Harold Q. Langenderfer of North Carolina and charter Advisory Forum member Wayne J. Albers of Ernst & Whinney also won national honors that year. Albers, another personnel-oriented member of Al Cohen's forum, had along with Herb Miller and Guy Trump been active in the areas of development and accreditation of professional degree programs in accounting. In 1982, Phi Chapter at Louisiana State would nominate all three national Accountants of the Year. "Accountant of the Year Awards," Annual Reports, 1979-80, ed. [Pattillo], p. 11, 1981-82, ed. [Henry R. Anderson], p. 12; exhibit 29; and [David E. Tinius], "Chapter News Notes," Newsletter 19 (Spring 1981):11.

CHAPTER 14

PARTICIPATION AND PLURALISM IN THE FRATERNAL PROGRAM: SITE VISITATION, INTERCHAPTER COMPETITION, AND DUAL INTERCHAPTER ASSEMPLY

Major areas of fourth-era reform, as covered respectively in chapters 11 and 10, included the chartering process and the activity program. Aside from the experimental recasting of the interchapter competition as an "option" in the last year of the period, the changes made in the sixties provided a base for more fundamental ones the following decade. The beginning of "site visitation" in 1970 marked a logical conclusion of a pronounced trend toward more methodical review of petitioning schools, although a remarkable surge in roster expansion in the late seventies may have raised legitimate questions of quality control. Equally significant changes in the reward structure and internal design of the activity program served in different ways to expand its coverage and relevance.

The manuscript competition and Accountant of the Year award were not the foremost new elements of the Beta Alpha Psi program as it developed in the 1970s. That distinction deservedly rests instead with two innovations in fraternal assembly, namely, the introduction of "regional" and "national" meetings of _student_, as well as faculty, representatives of the local chapters. The student seminar initiated by Omicron in 1969 provided an antecedent at both levels, having been expanded from an area to a national program four years before the first National Student Meeting was held. The new

meetings ended a half century of virtual exclusion of student members from fraternal participation beyond the local level.

Site Visitation

Origin and First Year, 1970-71

Except perhaps for the initiation of interim Council meetings, the sharpest dividing line between the fourth and fifth eras was drawn by the National Council in discussing new chapter approval in 1970. By then formal requirements included two years of active operation by the accounting club, featuring at least four student-led meetings each year. It was agreed, however, that compliance with formal rules (which had been flawless in the case of failing Gamma Iota at UCLA) did not indicate that a chapter would '"be capable of mounting a successful program"'. In particular, prospective campus support for Beta Alpha Psi would depend substantially on '"the attitude of faculty, department chairmen, dean[s], etc."'

Such matters had often been addressed during visitations to chapters already formed. Advance "[s]ite" visitation was accordingly approved, in 1970, as part of the chartering process. The first "sites" selected were Northern Illinois, whose petition was accepted during the meeting, subject to a satisfactory visit, and Rhode Island, whose application had the "tentative" approval of a Council majority.

During the year 1970-71, Past President Harvey Donley visited both campuses, and other members made trips to five other petitioning schools, leading to the installation in 1971 of the first seven chapters of the era. This flurry of roster expansion, following the virtual standstill of the late sixties, was another mark of transition. Gamma Pi FVP Henry Anderson had simply been instructed by department chairman Clarence G. Avery to start a

chapter at Northern Illinois. The ceremony establishing Gamma Epsilon at Rhode Island was the fifth and last one in the spring, suggesting that initial reservations about the level of local activity had not immediately been relieved.

The new practice of site visitation was pronounced a success during the long-term planning conference of May 1971. Retiring councilor Vern Odmark stated that an advance visit was "the most valuable" one "that could be made," and former president Emerson Henke added that it provided an opportunity to obtain a timely "feel for the campus." To assist visitation officers, Secretary-Treasurer Bob Wasley was asked to prepare "a paragraph of suggestions" for their use. The yield from this modest assignment was a twofold document that would define and direct the program for the foreseeable future, and by implication reveal potential pitfalls.

Wasley's Policy and Guideline Statements of 1971, and Implicit Pitfalls

Adoption of a twofold document emphasizing support for the FVP

At the 1971 annual meeting, incoming president Wasley presented a statement of site-visitation policy, and a procedural checklist for visitors based thereon, that were officially approved by the National Council. They are shown as exhibit 30. It was agreed that the practical guidelines developed could be applied to traditional, or "regular," visitations as well.

The most fundamental factor, according to Professor Wasley, was the degree of "commitment . . . to students and to the teaching and learning process" that existed within the department and college. Through interaction with the business dean, department chairman, prospective faculty advisor and other accounting instructors, and (to assess their "energy and enthusiasm")

EXHIBIT 30

ROBERT WASLEY'S 1971 STATEMENT ON SITE VISITATION

Part A. General Policy Objectives

A great deal more can be learned about the commitment of a school or college to students and to the teaching and learning process from a personal visit than can possibly be learned from reading answers to questions which were prepared and distributed to the school administrators.

To determine the degree of this commitment, the Dean of the School, the Chairman of the Department, the faculty of the department, and prospective members of the fraternity should all be visited with and questioned. The Dean and the Department Chairman should both be questioned concerning their attitude as well as the reward system in existence at the school in regard to a faculty member commiting his time to being a Faculty Vice President. An active Faculty Vice President is a basic key to a successful chapter, and if the attitudes and the reward system available to a faculty member are not conducive to his giving his time and talents to the chapter, the likelihood of his being willing to do so are not great.

Another important attitude to attempt to determine is the attitude of the faculty toward teaching and toward students. There are schools where faculties attach great importance to this and there are schools where they do not. The reasons for this goes back to the attitudes of the administrators and the reward system in existence.

Also of importance is the energy and enthusiasm of the existing student body who would be the eligible members of the fraternity.

All of the above are important ingredients to the long run success of a chapter.

EXHIBIT 30--Continued

Part B. Checklist for Site (or Regular) Visitation

Dean

1. What is the attitude of the Dean toward the professional aims of the fraternity?
2. Is the Dean willing to recognize that time spent with chapter is meritorious?
3. Is the Dean willing to facilitate the aims of our group in any way possible?

Faculty of Department

1. What is their attitude toward the professional aims of the fraternity?
2. Is working with the activities of the local chapter an important activity for a faculty member?
3. How important is the teaching function to the faculty?
4. In what regard is the position of FVP held by the faculty?
5. Can the faculty members be readily approached by the students?
6. How frequently do faculty members, other than FVP, attend chapter meetings?
7. What is the attitude of the department chairman toward the professional activities of the fraternity?
8. What is the attitude of the department chairman of his faculty participating in the activities of the fraternity?

Chapter Activities

1. How frequently does the chapter meet?
2. Does it have a well organized plan of operation suitable to the environment in which it is operating?
3. What is the average number of members of the chapter?
4. What is the average meeting attendance? (Percentage of membership)
5. What is the attitude of the student members toward the fraternity and what it stands for?

Accounting Student Body

1. What is the primary composition of the accounting student body? (Grad, Undergrad)
2. What is the approximate number of students eligible to become members of Beta Alpha Psi each year?

student petitioners, the visiting councilor would try to size up that commitment. The fraternity looked, particularly, for a dean and department head who would properly <u>reward</u> dedicated service by the faculty vice-president:

> An active Faculty Vice President is a basic key to a successful chapter, and if the attitudes and the reward system available to a faculty member are not conducive to his giving his time and talents to the chapter, the likelihood of his being willing to do so are not great.

The masculine gender used points up the rarity of women FVPs in 1970-71, a year in which there were only one or two such advisors besides Joyce Dean.

Alpha Rho likewise had a woman faculty advisor at the close of the fifth era eight years later, along with at least 17 of the other 131 local units in existence by that time. Reference to 1978-79 FVP data provides a useful backdrop for discussing appropriate modes of administrative support.

Modes of support for FVP service

Faculty advisors are drawn from all academic ranks, and a wide diversity of educational backgrounds and amounts of teaching experience. Exhibit 31 presents selected data from the fraternal year 1978-79 concerning position, academic degree (or candidacy), and length of service at the institution. It shows that half of the FVPs were assistant professors (fifty, comprising more than a third of the total group) or had a lower rank, ordinarily lecturer or instructor. Although assistant professors outnumbered any other group, associates were not far behind, and there were half as many full professors, a few of whom headed their departments. Half of the assistant professors had either received their doctorates during the prior four years, or were still doctoral candidates, <u>and</u> had taught at their current schools for less than four years.

One factor that may contribute to the frequent appointment of relatively

EXHIBIT 31

PROFILE OF 1978-79 FVPS: RANK, YEARS ON FACULTY, DEGREE STATUS, AND (AS APPLICABLE) YEARS HOLDING DOCTORATE

FVP Classifications[a]	Full Prof.	Associate Prof.	Assistant Prof.	Other Rank	TOTALS
Pre-1975 doctorate and appointment	18	19	3	1	41
Pre-1975 doctorate, later appointment	3	8	2	1	14
Post-1974 doctorate, earlier appointment		2	6	1	9
Post-1974 doctorate and appointment		1	18		19
"A.B.D.,"[b] pre-1975 appointment			1		1
A.B.D., post-1974 appointment			6	2	8
Non-doctoral status,[b] pre-1975 appointment	3	11	5	4	23
Non-doctoral status, post-1974 appointment		1	9	7	17
TOTALS	24	42	50	16	132

SOURCES: Bobbe M. Barnes, 1978-79 Theta FVP, to Author, July 17, 1986; Hasselback, 1978-79 Directory, individual and (in isolated cases) school listings; Ely Kushel, 1978-79 Mu FVP, to Author, July 8, 1986; and "The National Chapter: 1978-1979," 1978-79 Annual Report, ed. [Burns], pp. 1-2.

Two persons for whom Hasselback supplied only rank and appointment date, and who were not listed in his later volumes, were classified as non-doctoral FVPs, in the sense clarified in note b. There was at least one "adjunct" assistant professor. The presence of 25 non-doctoral advisors ranked lower than associate professor prompts the question of how often the fraternal post might be assigned to faculty members not on "tenure-track" appointments.

[a]The dividing line for date of receipt of a doctorate and of faculty appointment, between (1) 1974 and earlier and (2) 1975 and later, identifies faculty advisors having by the start of the fall term at least four years' possession of a doctorate and/or faculty service at the school.

[b]"A.B.D." denotes a doctoral candidate having completed "all but dissertation" requirements. The final two categories are understood to exclude such FVPs. All doctorates represented were Ph.D. or D.B.A. degrees.

inexperienced faculty members as chapter advisors is the greater involvement of other professors, by and large, in university committees and in off-campus professional organizations. Another one is the potential advantage of comparative youth in establishing non-classroom rapport with students, yielding in Doris Cook's judgment some "absolutely great" FVPs. Coverage of support or reward for service may be focused to a degree on "junior" faculty members.

An entry-level person is vitally concerned with qualifying within a reasonable time for promotion to the associate professor level (sometimes in two steps); and with earning academic tenure within the normal six-year "probationary" span. Yearly salary adjustments are important in themselves, and as an index of performance evaluation. Accordingly, a visitation officer would seek assurance that Beta Alpha Psi service would be favorably regarded by administrative officers in making decisions or recommendations on tenure, promotion, and salary.

As formulated by earlier councilor Williard Stone, the basic question is whether established criteria extend reasonable credit for organizational activity of that kind; and, if they do not, whether the school would be willing to make an exception on behalf of a Beta Alpha Psi advisor. At Stone's last Grand Council meeting, Secretary-Treasurer Herbert Miller was instructed (on his own motion) to send letters to the deans of the top ten schools in the 1959-60 activity program, "commenting about the contribution of the Faculty Vice-President." Earlier, Professor Stone himself had received no credit locally for his FVP service to Alpha Delta at Pennsylvania. The Wharton School of the 1950s "didn't give a damn" about such work, and appeared to regard it as "childish stuff."

A significant problem, as observed by fifth-era president Tom Burns,

is that the faculty vice-presidency falls outside of both (a) teaching and (b) research and publication. Even at teaching-oriented AACSB schools, the latter area had commonly moved in front of professional and campus "service" in the performance evaluation of professors. That development had been reinforced by the intensive research emphasis found within the American Accounting Association of the day, although both Burns and Leon Hay saw some evidence, by 1980, that a broader outlook on accounting education was reappearing with the AAA. Past President Burns commented at the time that FVP work was usually best recognized in the case of a leading teacher, by providing a base for enhancing his or her classroom work.

A major attraction of publication at an "emerging" campus is the visibility given to the institution. Within Beta Alpha Psi, Richard S. Claire had proposed the annual awards for outstanding FVPs

> because of his awareness of the fact that working with student professional organizations was frequently not included in the criteri[a] for promotion in faculty rank and salary increases.

Similarly, the initiatives taken by the National Council of the 1970s to promote fraternal recognition and prestige nationally were designed in good measure to boost the stock of faculty advisors locally, by making it more difficult for administrators to ignore Beta Alpha Psi. National Advisory Forum president David Abramson was instructed in 1979 to write "support letters" to the deans and (presumably) department heads of faculty advisors from "Superior" and "Distinguished" chapters.

As another dimension of support for faculty vice-presidents, certain <u>concessions</u> may be made by the department or college to facilitate their service. A reduced teaching load is a prime example. By granting such a concession to the FVP, while "riding herd" on his work with the chapter, the dean at Virginia Tech contributed to the excellent start made by Gamma Lambda

in the late sixties. Emerson Henke noted in 1980 that the Alpha Rho advisor at Baylor, although teaching a regular complement of courses, was excused from night classes to compensate for evening fraternal commitments. Another important kind of help is the assignment of part-time assistants to faculty leaders.

At Arizona, FVP Taylor W. Foster III led Beta Omicron to first place in the activity program rankings his first year on the job (and second on the faculty), 1972-73. He gave up the Beta Alpha Psi post upon completing his doctorate in 1974, having been informed by his administration that the fraternal service would not assist him in qualifying for promotion. Ironically, Foster's senior colleague Hollis Dixon was the national president at the time. Beta Omicron subsequently fell into steep decline under the leadership of a full professor, and was placed on probation during Dixon's last National Council meeting, after placing next-to-last in 1976-77 among all 107 chapters formed before February 1. The ex-councilor straightened things out in an interim stint as FVP before Taylor Foster returned to the leadership position in 1978, one year before he was promoted to associate professor. Based in part on the fraternal assignment, he received a three-hour teaching reduction during his second term.

Just prior to retiring from Florida in 1980, Williard Stone observed that some precedent had been established during his twenty years at the school for reducing the classroom work of the Upsilon faculty advisor. Jesse V. "Buddy" Boyles had won an Outstanding Faculty Vice President award the preceding year, but been "warned" by the school of accounting at Florida that he would not qualify for promotion or tenure unless he began to divert some of his abundant effort from Beta Alpha Psi work to publication activity. He had consequently stepped down as faculty advisor in 1979,

a few years before favorable promotion and tenure decisions would be made.

Another Richard S. Claire Award winner of 1978-79, already an associate professor, was the advisor to Gamma Beta at South Carolina. He left the university in the middle of the following year after having been denied tenure, in his final year of eligibility, despite for the third time enjoying the support of his college. One of his new colleagues in 1978, incidentally, had received Outstanding FVP honors a year earlier for service to Alpha Mu, only to leave Kentucky after six years to take a nontenured appointment.

The South Carolina case points up the problem raised for site visitation if tenure or promotion decisions are made, in substance rather than form, outside the faculty member's college. A similar complication is illustrated by the coverage of both areas at Syracuse by an elected independent committee within the business school. The lodging of such authority in a school of accounting would presumably tend to enhance prospects of receiving some recognition for Beta Alpha Psi service.

A supportive administration is of course no guarantee of high-quality, or even acceptable, FVP service. For example, the advisor to Mu at New York over the first half of the seventies apparently applied his significant teaching load reduction to a private consulting practice rather than to chapter activity. This reference points up one of the <u>limits</u> inherent within site visitation.

<u>Limitations of site visitation</u>

One problem was noted at the long-range planning session of December 1972, namely, the <u>transiency</u> of college or university personnel (not to mention students). The attitudes expressed by a dean, department head, and faculty group at best indicate the support available at the time of

chartering. Should those individuals leave the school soon thereafter, "a whole new set of attitudes m[ight] arise from their replacements."

Further, the depth, or even genuineness, of support expressed may be difficult to judge. Tom Burns has noted that at many "emerging" institutions of the '70s a Beta Alpha Psi chapter was sought in part as a mark of prestige. Without imputing any reflection against local faculty members or administrators, one may assume that a visitation could be somewhat "contrived" or "staged" to assure a favorable impression. For example, the councilor might not be permitted to talk with "just any" member of the accounting organization. Burns summed up his point, colorfully, by stating that at an emerging school a visitation was something like a "visit from the pope."

The other side of the coin, also noted by Professor Burns, is that an institution seeking to make a mark through Beta Alpha Psi chartering and chapter performance has a strong incentive to provide support to the faculty vice-president. Furthermore, the student body are likely to have fewer other extra-curricular involvements than their counterparts at, for example, Ohio State, many of whom would be involved in a variety of campus organizations.

Finally, even strong administrative support may not count for much in the absence of enthusiasm at lower levels. At New York University, Mu Chapter activity had fallen to such a low ebb by 1971 that the National Council decided to revoke the charter, unless there was "extenuating circumstances" not as yet known. When President Bob Wasley requested that the charter be shipped to him, at Colorado, the faculty advisor informed him that the university definitely wished to retain the chapter. Bob Maust was accordingly assigned to visit the Washington Square campus.

Several extenuating circumstances were discovered. The FVP had received

only a small part of the mail sent over the prior two years by Secretary-Treasurer Wasley, because it had been sent to another campus of the university. Further, it was confirmed that an initiation had been conducted the preceding fall, and duly reported, although somehow Mu had not received credit for it. Moreover, a recent change in curriculum structure had made it possible to initiate members during their junior year.

Most importantly, perhaps, Dean Abraham Gitlow expressed strong support for the chapter. He had already given the faculty advisor a course reduction of one third to do Beta Alpha Psi work. In the officer's presence, the dean told Maust that he would have him replaced as FVP if the National Council felt that he was performing inadequately. Earlier, according to "[s]everal faculty members," Gitlow had "stormed into the office of the chairman of the Accounting Department," who was lunching with his finance area counterpart, "and demanded to know why the situation had been permitted to deteriorate to the point" that charter revocation was being considered.

By the time of the visitation, in November 1971, Mu was maintaining an active schedule, involving reasonable faculty participation. A cautionary note disclosed was that the advisor did not know the names of the "enthusiastic" student officers, except the president. On balance, the visitation led Professor Maust to recommend probation, rather than charter revocation.

After the recommendation had been approved, the NYU unit failed to file a 1971-72 audit report. Terms of probation announced at the next annual meeting (a year before monthly reporting was resumed for all chapters) included two years' reporting under the activity program. Mu ranked 48th of 51 participating chapters in 1972-73, despite another visit by Bob Maust, but did well enough the next year to be removed from probation. The sanction was reimposed in 1975 after the New York group had dropped to the

bottom of the chapter roster, submitting (as the source of its 500 points) only the annual report. After operating under a new faculty leader for the first time in nine years, Mu was restored to good standing in 1976.[1]

By reference to eight visitations of the fifth era, a broad range of outcomes may be illustrated, ranging from unqualified approval of the petitioning school to effective termination of the application process.

---

[1] Henry R. Anderson to Author, interview, April 18, 1986; appendix 4; [Burns], ed., 1978-79 Annual Report, pp. 1-2 ("National Chapter"), 7 ("Outstanding" FVPs); Thomas J. Burns to Author, interview, May 3, 1980, quoted; "Chapter Activities," 1979-80 Annual Report, ed. [Pattillo], pp. 18-19; Doris M. Cook to Author, interview, March 20, 1980, quoted; Hollis A. Dixon, Long-Range Planning Committee Minutes, 1972, p. 3, quoted; Dixon, Secretary-Treasurer's Report, 1971-72, p. 5, 1972-73, pp. 4, 7-8; Dixon to Author, interview, March 22-23, 1980; exhibits 30 (quoted, including 1st indented citation), 31; Grand Council Minutes Book, 1960, p. 4; Hasselback, 1978-79 Directory, school listing, s.v. "University of Kentucky," "University of South Carolina," individual listing, s.v. "Foster, Taylor W. III," 1979-80 Directory, individual listing, s.v. "Foster III, Taylor W.," 1983 Directory, s.v. "Boyles, Jesse V."; James R. Hasselback, comp., Prentice-Hall Accounting Faculty Directory: 1980-81 (Englewood Cliffs, N.J.: Prentice-Hall, 1981), inidividual listing, s.v. "Boyles, Jesse V. (Buddy)"; Leon E. Hay to Author, interview, May 2, 1980; Emerson O. Henke to Author, interview, March 21, 1980; Robert S. Maust to Author, interview, July 14, 1980; Maust, Visitation Report--Mu, December 15, 1971, quoted; [Herbert E. Miller], Secretary-Treasurer's Report, 1960-61, p. 2; [Fred J. Mueller], "Outstanding Faculty Vice Presidents," 1976-77 Annual Report, ed. [Mueller], p. 6; Mueller, Secretary-Treasurer's Report, 1974-75, pp. 7-8, 10, 1975-76, p. 10; "The National Chapter: 1978-1979," 1978-79 Annual Report, ed. [Burns], p. 1; Ntional Council Minutes, 1970, pp. 8-10 (quoting p. 9), 1971, pp. 1-3 (quoting p. 2), 1972, p. 5, August 1975, p. 4, August 1976, p. 2, August 1977, p. 3, January 1978, p. 4, January 1979, p. 6 (quoted); "Results of 1976-77 Chapter Activity Program," 1976-77 Annual Report, ed. [Mueller], pp. 12-13; [Harold L. Royer], "Arthur Andersen & Co. Foundation Sponsors Richard S. Claire Awards to Outstanding Faculty Vice Presidents," Newsletter 10 (Fall 1971):1, 2nd indented citation; Williard E. Stone to Author, interview, April 18, 1980, quoted; Syracuse University and University of South Carolina sources, 1978-81, 1981-82 (author's year(s) of service on respective faculties), concerning promotion and tenure authority and, in latter case, related personnel matters; Vern H. Vincent to Author, interview, July 14, 1980, quoted; and Robert S. Wasley, Secretary-Treasurer's Report, 1969-70, p. 3, 1970-71, pp. 2-3, 6-7.

Selected Site Visitations: Seven Outcomes at Eight Schools

Pacific Lutheran, 1976: Unqualified approval

Fred Mueller traveled from Seattle to nearby Tacoma, Washington in March 1976 to visit Pacific Lutheran. The local accounting group had actually taken the initiative, by inviting him to attend a meeting. An unexplained delay in scheduling a site visitation had led to some concern at the school, so the secretary-treasurer had decided to expand his trip to the campus into such an inspection.

Mueller's day began with a meeting for more than half an hour with the university president, whom he had known as a professor of medicine at Washington. He was assured that the FVP would receive strong recognition at the "teaching university." Although more reserved in manner, the business dean likewise conveyed "full support," and the several faculty members with whom the visitor lunched were "enthusiastic."

Secretary-Treasurer Mueller was impressed most of all, however, by the "sincerity and enthusiasm" of the students, several of whom took him on a walking tour of "their university" after a thirty-minute talk. The formal meeting drew a large attendance on initiation night for the local chapter of the business fraternity Alpha Kappa Psi. The accounting club president had belonged to Beta Tau at Arizona State before transferring to Pacific Lutheran.

Mueller noted in his report that four of the students had already attended a Beta Alpha Psi regional meeting; the accounting group had scheduled joint meetings in the spring with Delta at Washington and Delta Eta at Seattle; and the students had offered, assuming the receipt of a charter, to host the next Northwest regional meeting. Having been installed by Fred

Mueller soon after he had "wholeheartedly" endorsed the formation of a chapter in Tacoma, Delta Rho would indeed serve as the 1977 regional host.

Texas Southern, 1975: Prompt, but reserved, approval

A milestone in Beta Alpha Psi history was the installation of Delta Xi in the fall of 1975 at predominantly black Texas Southern. The school's petition had been discussed at the winter meeting early that year. Secretary-Treasurer Mueller had reported that faculty vice-presidents from the area favored granting a charter to the Houston campus. Based on President Hollis Dixon's concern that the program might be too small to support "a viable chapter," the National Council had voted to defer action on the application pending visitation, rather than approving it subject to a satisfactory campus visit.

Dixon himself made the spring inspection, accompanied by Theta president Patti Smith from Texas. Although he had concluded that "the students w[ould] have a hard time having a good active chapter," the National Council accepted Doris Cook's motion at the 1975 spring meeting to form a chapter at Texas Southern. In November, installation officers Dixon and Fred Mueller observed "some possible problems" of a substantive nature (as distinguished from the questionable honorary inductions of Dean Luzine Bickham, Theta '57, and Dr. Joe J. Cramer, Beta Alpha at Indiana, '60). They confirmed, however, the existence of "much support from the community" for the new chapter.

James Pattillo was asked to visit Delta Xi in the spring of 1976, but for unrecorded reasons did not do so. In August the chapter was placed on probation for failure to file an audit report, an action taken (without the grant of a grace period) against each of the several chapters delinquent in that regard. Following, apparently, a spring visitation by Secretary-Treasurer

Joyce Dean, Texas Southern repeated the reporting violation in 1977, but received an extension due to the death during the year of FVP James Whitmire, and filed by early fall. Finally, the chapter was threatened with probation again in 1978 for failure to submit the year-end statement, but avoided the sanction by reporting within the grace period (to October 15) routinely granted that year.

Hawaii: Approval after a brief delay

Two years after reducing the role of formal criteria within the chartering process, the National Council began to be concerned that petitioners were supplying inadequate information on student-oriented activity. It was agreed in December 1972 that instructions sent to prospective applicants should be revised to emphasize the need for documentation in that area, and to provide examples of pertinent activities. In addition, a "model" application may have been drafted.

The following spring, President Harold Royer visited the main campus at Hawaii before a petition had been submitted, in conjunction with attending the AACSB convention in Honolulu. In August, having the completed application in hand, the Council responded very favorably to the visitation report without formally approving an installation. Instead, Royer agreed to ask the Hawaii group to conduct at least two "student-run programs" during the fall term, and send a schedule for the remainder of the year that included at least two more such programs. It was agreed that no further visitation was needed.

The petitioning group complied with these requirements, and Fred Mueller installed Delta Theta during the 1973-74 spring semester. A former visiting professor at Hawaii noted for his love of travel, Mueller had advised

President Hollis Dixon that he would be obliged to conduct the ceremony because the timing could not be accommodated to Dixon's schedule. The secretary-treasurer wanted to make a regular visitation to the campus a year later, but Dixon made the trip himself soon after the end of his second term. In the interim, the two men had collaborated in scheduling a winter National Council meeting in Matzalan, Mexico, located directly below the Tropic of Cancer on the country's inner west coast. President Dixon had prepared an analysis to show that such a setting was "cost justified."

Other new Beta Alpha Psi schools of 1973 and 1974 that were required to submit supplemental information on student programs or activities were Seattle, Washington State, and (prior to the site visitation) Montana. In the second case, the timing was unique as the Council in December 1972 voted to require a revised petition in the course of approving a charter. In addition, the critical issue in the visitation that led to the chartering of California State, Chico was whether there was sufficient student participation in the local program.

Georgia Southern and Middle Tennessee: Requirement of a second year of advance reporting

An evolving issue of the fifth era concerned the point at which an organized group should begin reporting "as if" it were a chapter. At a planning conference in December 1972, it was suggested that following the activity program _prior_ to petitioning was an "excellent guideline," but it is unclear whether the actual submission of reports was intended. Six years later, in January 1979, Director of Chapter Activities Jim Pattillo noted that reporting might start either (a) as soon as a group indicated an intent to petition; (b) when the application was made; (c) when the site visitation

occurred; or (d) when the chapter was finally installed. He was asked to review the matter, and submit a recommendation.

The following August, at the final meeting of the era, Pattillo's motion was adopted to require future petitioners "to report activities for [at least] one year, which may be[gin] before, . . . [as soon as], or after the petition is received." A "provisional" chapter concept had thus become accepted as a regular part of the chartering process, a generation after a two-year "pledge" period had been approved at the 1956 Grand Council meeting in an action that was promptly rescinded.

The decision made in 1979 may have been assisted by site visitations conducted earlier in the year at Middle Tennessee and Georgia Southern. Action had the previous June been deferred on petitions from the two schools, pending their operating for a year under the activity program. A similar position had been taken at that time regarding George Washington University, with the further requirement that the petition be revised.

At the beginning of 1979, visits were approved to the three campuses. The revised George Washington petition was subsequently approved by mail, and Epsilon Sigma was installed in the nation's capital prior to the spring meeting. Jack Kiger reported, however, that the site visitations at Middle Tennessee and Georgia Southern had been disappointing, and Jim Pattillo related that "the level of activity reporting" from those schools "had not been very satisfactory." The National Council consequently agreed to require a second year of activity reporting from the two regional institutions prior to reconsidering their applications. Zeta Gamma and Zeta Delta were finally installed at the respective campuses in the fall of 1980.

San Francisco: Reluctant rejection; acceptance following revisitation

The best indication of the importance placed by the National Council on reasonable assurance of sustained faculty leadership commitment was provided by the trip made by President Bob Maust early in 1976 to the University of San Francisco. The Jesuit school, which had over the period 1928-53 three times applied for or expressed interest in a Beta Alpha Psi chapter, had petitioned the preceding fall.

Maust recommended issuance of a charter based on highly favorable findings on nearly every point. As confirmed by National Advisory Forum member Robert E. Knox of Touche Ross, the university "had a long history of attempting to meet the needs of the accounting profession" in the area. Two undergraduate degree programs, one of them remarkably intensive, served the some two hundred accounting majors on campus.

The dean, a former business executive, pledged to recognize the substantial commitment that would be required of the faculty advisor "in promotion, salary and tenure evaluations." The job placement director reported that strong demand existed for the accounting graduates, many of whom took part in an internship program. A vice-president felt that a chapter would bring much "prestige" to the school. An enthusiastic student group was in place; and both the former dean and a member of the campus religious community "expressed strong support" for a chapter, and confidence in its success.

At the faculty level, prospective FVP David P. Weiner was "an extremely student-oriented person" who seemed likely to become "an outstanding" leader. There were only two other full-time accounting professors, however, one of whom was on leave due to illness, while two other regular faculty members

taught accounting part time. The well-respected department chairman indicated that he would assume the chapter post in the event of Dr. Weiner's departure, but President Maust wondered if his many professional, consulting, business, and writing commitments would leave much time for such service.

Despite the favorable recommendation made, the National Council in April 1976 rejected the San Francisco application, in view of questionable "ability to maintain an active chapter due to the small number of full-time accounting faculty." The rejection was registered "without prejudice" against repetitioning by a school that was seeking to expand its accounting faculty.

Following a new petition, Past President Fred Mueller visited San Francisco in November 1977. A recent doctoral graduate from Santa Clara had been added to the staff, evidently along with one other person. Mueller's recommendation that a charter be granted was approved at the subsequent winter meeting, and he and President Doris Cook installed Epsilon Iota in April 1978. Somewhat ironically, a preliminary petition (as defined presently) received from Santa Clara had prompted the judgement that the school "still ha[d] a long way to go" to justify a charter. San Francisco, incidentally, initiated 15 "honorary" members on the founding date, breaking the presumed single-meeting record of 13 such initiates set by Mu at New York in 1954 just before the Grand Council had placed limits on honorary induction.

Kansas: Rejection, as a practical matter, after approval of petition

In 1980, Past President Tom Burns commented rather casually that about the only "leading" undergraduate center of accounting studies not as yet affiliated with Beta Alpha Psi was the University of Oklahoma. He attributed

the absence of that school to "jealousy" on the part of senior professors concerning the status of a well-established accounting club.

Burns, whose first observation was probably not intended to be taken at face value, had overlooked another school from the same "Big 8" athletic conference--the University of Kansas. Three years after an application had seemed imminent, Secretary-Treasurer Joyce Dean had received a "preliminary" petition from Kansas that appeared to be "in good shape." As the first stage in the process, schools had since 1973 routinely submitted a draft petition for inspection and appraisal by the secretary-treasurer. At the meeting of January 1978, the National Council had accepted the consequent petition, and assigned Jim Pattillo to make a site visitation to the Lawrence campus. The only earlier reference to Kansas found in available records, incidentally, appeared in a 1930 Grand Council listing of nine possibly desirable chapter settings.

In June 1978, Pattillo reported that the Kansas faculty were "still fairly indifferent" (emphasis added), implying that faculty support had earlier been questioned, so that the Council would "not [further] pursue establishing a chapter . . . this year." The school's Beta Alpha Psi initiative would end at that point, and there is no record that a plan to contact Kansas again a year later was carried out. Disinterest in the fraternity may have been fostered by the absence within the local business school of a departmental structure, or a counterpart thereto. Epsilon Theta was installed at nearby Kansas State in April 1978, just three months after site visitations had been approved for both schools. Having filed a draft petition prior to its neighbor, Kansas had apparently not been prodded by Kansas State into applying for a charter.

Illinois at Chicago: Rejection at a most fundamental level

During the spring of 1973 President Harold Royer visited the Chicago campus of the University of Illinois. Based on his recommendation, the National Council in August agreed that the accounting organization at "Chicago Circle" was not acceptable, and would have to be reconstituted. Further, the new group would have to operate for two years before a new petition could be considered. Like Kansas, where the objection concerned an important element of environment rather than the organizational unit itself, Illinois at Chicago apparently did not pursue the matter further.[2]

The topic of site visitation leads naturally to broader reference to new chapter locations of the fifth era, a roster that resists general description in terms of "emerging" universities. As the pace of installation

---

[2] AAA Road Atlas, p. 134; appendix 4; Barron's Profiles, s.v. "Hawaii, University of Hawaii," "Kansas: Kansas State University, University of Kansas"; Thomas J. Burns to Author, interview, May 3, 1980, quoted; [Doris M. Cook], "New Chapters of Beta Alpha Psi," 1977-78 Annual Report, ed. [Cook], p. [4]; Joyce C. Dean, "Minutes, Chapter Activity Program Committee," January 1978, p. 3; [Dean], Secretary-Treasurer's Report, 1977-78, p. 2; Hollis A. Dixon, Long-Range Planning Committee Minutes, 1972, pp. 2, 3-4 (quoted); Dixon, Secretary-Treasurer's Report, 1972-73, pp. 4, 8; Dixon to Author, interview, March 22-23, 1980, quoted; exhibit 7 (chapter 2), s.v. "San Francisco"; Grand Council Minutes Book, 1956, p. 4, quoted; Hasselback, 1978-79 Directory, school listing, "University of Kansas," "University of San Francisco," individual listing, s.v. "Pitre, Richard"; [Robert S. Maust], "Fred J. Mueller is Elected to Council," Newsletter 11 (Fall 1972):1; [Maust], ed., 1975-76 Annual Report, pp. [4] ("Faculty Vice Presidents"), [8] ("New Chapters"); [Maust], "Royer Attends Hawaiian Meeting," Newsletter 11 (Spring 1973):2; Maust, Site Visitation Report--University of San Francisco, April 8, 1976, quoted; [Mueller], ed., 1976-77 Annual Report, pp. 11 ("Faculty Vice Presidents"), 17 ("Regional Meetings"); Fred J. Mueller, Secretary-Treasurer's Report, 1975-76, pp. 4, 13; Mueller, Site Visitation Report Pacific Lutheran University, March 11, 1976, quoted; National Chapter Minutes, 1974, p. 1; National Council Minutes, August 1973, pp. 3-4 (quoted), 5, February 1974, p. 4, August 1974, p. 10, February 1975, pp. 1, 6 (quoted), May-June, 1975, p. 11 (quoted), December 1975, p. 1 (quoted), April 1976, p. 3 (quoted), August 1976, p. 3, August 1977, pp. 3, 4 (quoted), January 1978, p. 3, June 1978, pp. 5, 6 (quoted), August 1978, p. 1, January 1979, pp. 2, 5, June 1979, p. 5 (quoted), January 1981, p. 1; and Sheldahl, Alpha to Omega, pp. 158, 729-31.

was stepped up in the latter part of the period, and interchapter contact became widespread, "regular" visitation was sharply reduced.

Selected Installation Patterns and Trends, and Decline in "Regular" Visitation

Numerous "land-grant" schools and/or primary state universities

The 78 chapters installed during the years 1970-84 are shown in appendix 3. Fifty-two units were formed in the fifth era, ending in August 1979, from Gamma Pi at Northern Illinois to Epsilon Phi at Wayne State. As illustrated by those two schools, three California State University sites, and several "branch" campuses of the kind discussed in chapter 12, a number of developing or emerging institutions were included.

It is noteworthy, however, that 18 campuses were "land-grant" schools and/or the principal public universities in their states, naturally varying somewhat in national prominence. No fewer than 14 land-grant institutions entered the Beta Alpha Psi fold:

1. Colorado State
2. Rhode Island
3. Wyoming
4. Washington State
5. Hawaii
6. Texas A&M
7. New Mexico State
8. Massachusetts
9. Nebraska-Lincoln
10. Delaware
11. Utah State
12. Kansas State
13. Connecticut
14. Auburn.

Charter FVP Cecilia Tierney of Delta Epsilon at Washington State, Xi '50, was identified in chapter 1 as having become one of the earliest female members of the fraternity while teaching at Syracuse. The formation at Nebraska of Delta Omicron, the "DO" chapter, permitted future councilor Richard Metcalf to take the faculty helm of a third Beta Alpha Psi group, following Alpha Pi at Iowa and Gamma Mu at Drake. The first advisor to Delta Omega at Utah State was Larzette G. Hale, a black woman who in 1980

won a Richard S. Claire Award, and was a finalist for election to the National Council. Chapters were formed also at Utah and Montana.

Outside the land-grant tradition, two of the nation's leading state universities were chartered during the era. Two fraternal elder statesmen joined all but one incumbent councilor at the 1975 installation of Delta Mu at Virginia as the hundredth active chapter. In fragile health at age 82, Eric Kohler made the trip from Chicago, and spoke at the banquet. A. J. Penz was already in the area as a visiting professor at Virginia Commonwealth, which would itself join the roster two years later.

A third special guest at Virginia was American Accounting Association president Lee Brummet of North Carolina. Three years later Epsilon Eta was installed at Advisory Forum member Brummet's own campus. The local faculty were "strongly oriented toward management accounting," a focus that, if traditional, might earlier have impeded campus consideration of a Beta Alpha Psi chapter.

Finally, the only "private" universities chartered during the period were Seattle, a Jesuit institution employing future councilor David E. Tinius; Hofstra, Pacific Lutheran, Drexel, and George Washington; and Emory, a prominent Methodist campus whose chapter advisor John R. "Casey" Jones, a long-time practitioner, would join Tinius as an Outstanding Faculty Vice President honoree. Drexel, the recipient of some state funding in Pennsylvania, is of particular interest as the site of a "co-op" program of alternating study and employment terms, attracting the participation in 1976 (the installation year) of some 80-90% of accounting majors; and as one of the first universities to require that all students have a computer.

Several months after the installation at Emory in 1979, the Atlanta school received from alumnus and retired Coca-Cola chairman Robert Woodruff

the largest recorded gift in the history of American higher education--three million shares of Coke stock valued at $102 million. Company operating executive Paul L. Dillingham, Jr. had served on the National Advisory Forum the preceding three years, and would be reappointed in 1981 and designated the new chairperson before withdrawing his name in the latter regard. Succeeding him on the forum in 1983 was Coca-Cola controller M. Douglas Ivester, soon to be appointed senior vice-president of finance, who would a year later become the advisory body's fourth chairperson.

Site visitation and installation activity reached a peak in 1977-78 as regular visitation was being scaled back.

Accelerated expansion, along with a decline in "regular" visitation

Although reducing the need for travel to a new chapter shortly after installation, site inspection was in no sense a replacement for traditional visitation as a communication and control device. Both in August 1972 and February 1974, it was agreed that all chapters should be visited at least every third year, "weak" units more often. Later in the second year a concentration on "problem" chapters was endorsed in the course of approving, in general terms, an ambitious schedule for 1974-75.

In 1975-76, there were 29 regular visitations, ranging from 2 by Director of Special Projects Thomas Burns (whose travel was always limited somewhat by arthritis) to 9 by Secretary-Treasurer Fred Mueller. Six site visitations, half of them by President Robert Maust, and a like number of installations, all of them at least in part by Mueller, were conducted.

Two years later, the comparative figures were much different. There were 9 site visitations and 10 regular ones, two of which (to Seattle University and his own Washington campus) did not require Fred Mueller to

leave town. There were also <u>11</u> installations, not counting 3 made over the three weeks leading up to the 1977 national meeting that complicated the timely completion of President Mueller's annual report.

This remarkable spurt of expansion was a matter of happenstance and opportunity only in part. It also reflected a prevailing attitude that strong growth would bolster the National Council's hand in dealing with uncooperative chapters. No unit could consider itself indispensable to a fraternity whose charters were so clearly in demand.

Fourth-era councilor Vern Vincent expressed concern in 1980, however, that a strong expansionary policy could lead to a relaxation of entry standards that would make effective future control all the more difficult. Non-specific references made by Hank Anderson to two installations that he had conducted lend some credence to such concern, as (at a broader level) do remarks made by Tom Burns that the activist "go-go" mentality that he had observed in his early Council years had impeded proper attention to long-term issues. It is noted that after 1978 roster expansion resumed a fairly moderate pace.

The cumulative effect over time of even a moderately growing chapter roster, combined with the demands of site visits and installations, would have required some reduction in regular visitation. The financial and, more importantly, human costs of maintaining business as usual would have been prohibitive. Fortunately, new circumstances emerging in the mid-seventies would render traditional visitation in most cases unnecessary. In particular, by providing for extensive chapter interaction and exposure to National Council members, <u>regional and national meetings</u> represented a major advance in fraternal communication.

Largely due to President Doris Cook's success the year before in

minimizing the need for probationary action, there were apparently no regular visitations in 1978-79. Cook had participated in all eleven installations of her term, after having installed chapters at South Alabama and Central Florida (then known as Florida Tech) just before taking office. In the spring of 1977, she had made site inspections to the two campuses on successive nights, and her suitcase had not arrived in Orlando until after the meeting at the Florida school. A similar delay occurred on a Sunday a year later regarding the installation of Eta Kappa at Appalachian State. Luckily, Boone, North Carolina was open for business that afternoon, so the local president, who "never saw a lady buy a dress so fast," could take her national counterpart to a clothing store. The pace of activity in 1977-78 is best illustrated by the fact that the following weekend Doris Cook installed chapters on successive nights in Connecticut, Texas, and Kentucky.[3]

---

[3] [Henry R. Anderson], "National Advisory Forum," 1981-82 Annual Report, ed. [Anderson], p. 7; [Anderson], "News Notes," Newsletter 20 (Fall 1981):18; appendix 3; Barron's Profiles, s.v. (omitting "University") "Kentucky, Murray State," "North Carolina, Appalachian State," "Pennsylvania, Drexel," "Texas, Stephen F. Austin State," "Washington, Seattle"; Brunner, Land-Grant Colleges, pp. 75-78; [Burns], ed., 1978-79 Annual Report, pp. 2 ("National Chapter"), 21 ("National Advisory Forum"), 26 ("Financial Report"); Thomas J. Burns to Author, interview, May 3, 1980, quoted; Burns and Coffman, Accounting Hall of Fame, p. 31; [Doris M. Cook], "100th Chapter Installed," Newsletter 14 (Fall 1975):9; Cook to Author, interview, March 20, 1980, quoted; [Joyce C. Dean], Secretary-Treasurer's Report, 1977-78, pp. [2-3]; Hollis A. Dixon, Secretary-Treasurer's Report, 1972-73, p. 5; Dixon to Author, interview, March 22-23, 1980; "Education: $102 Million Adds Life," Newsweek, November 26, 1979, p. 76; "Faculty Vice Presidents for 1976-77," 1976-77 Annual Report, ed. [Mueller], p. 11; Hasselback, 1984 Directory, individual listing, s.v. "Jones, John R.," "Tinius, David E."; John R. "Casey" Jones to Author, conversation (Boston, Mass.), August 9, 1980; Robert A. Maust, Site Visitation Report--Drexel University, March 9-10, 1976, quoting "co-op"; [Metcalf], ed., 1983-84 Annual Report, p. 23 ("National Advisory Forum"), [40] ("Former Advisory Forum Chairmen"); Fred J. Mueller, Installation Report--Delta Omicron ("DO"), February 27-28, 1976; Mueller, 1975-76 Secretary-Treasurer's Report, pp. 4-5; National Council Minutes, 1972, p. 4, February 1974, p. 1, August 1974, p. 2 (each quoted), February 1975, p. 1, January 1980, p. 3, June 1981, p. 7; June 1983, p. 3; [James W. Pattillo], "Outstanding Faculty V.P. Awards," 1979-80 Annual Report, ed. [Pattillo], p. 12;

As earlier indicated, the introduction of site visitation was a prime reason for recognizing the year 1970-71 as the beginning of a new fraternal era. Another major Beta Alpha Psi program, however, would have called for an earlier division between periods.

Development of the Activity Program During the Fifth Era

In 1969-70, as already covered in detail, participation in the Chapter Activity Program was for the first time an "option." A more enduring initiative of that year was the abandonment of special recognition for the "number 1" chapter in the points competition, in favor of equal recognition of a group of outstanding units. A committee approach to program planning had emerged by the time the first director of activities (distinct from the secretary-treasurer) assumed the position in 1976. Involving "maximum" and "minimum" point totals, respectively, the major policy developments of the fifth era were matters of intense deliberation by the full National Council, however. One of them, finally, related closely to a revised awards structure introduced (subject to further change) in 1975 that by the close of the period featured very substantial prizes for top chapters.

Restructuring the Awards Program on the Eve of the Fifth Era, Ending the "Number 1" Honor

As related in chapter 10, the year 1969-70 had marked the end of the practice of awarding a "traveling plaque" to the top-ranked chapter in the points competition. Instead, the top eight chapters had received plaques as "outstanding" units, without reference to their specific numerical ranks. This approach was continued during the next four years, although only seven

---

Robert F. Randall, "Lee Brummet, NAA President, 1979-80," Management Accounting 61 (July 1979):8, 9 (quoted); and [David E. Tinius], "Five Outstanding Faculty Vice Presidents Recognized," Newsletter 21 (Fall 1982):10. Also, A. J. Penz, "A Glimpse of the Life of a Retired Professor," May 20, 1985, pp. 5-7.

groups were honored in a year in which the first material break in point totals appeared between positions 7 and 8. From 15 to 20 units yearly, a particularly large number in view of the contemporary option of non-participation, were awarded cash prizes for their placement in the activity program, raised from $50 to $100 in 1973.

The abandonment of the "number 1" honor may have disappointed some of the emerging schools, recently accredited by the AACSB, that comprised much of the new chapter roster. For example, the several California State campuses, tending to have a blurred identity, might have welcomed an opportunity to establish singular identity nationally in the accounting field. Nonetheless, the abandonment of the first-place plaque award, after nineteen years, was a very logical development, beyond markedly increasing a chapter's opportunity to achieve high honors.

President Wilton Anderson had recommended during the year 1966-67 that a group of excellent chapters should be recognized each year, without drawing any distinction based on minor point differences. According to his recollection, he had met "unanimous resistance" from his colleagues. In any event, as president in 1969-70, following two years as a highly rigorous and conscientious administrator of the activity program, Harvey Donley had supported the change advocated by Anderson. The new approach adopted may have lent some incentive for participation in a newly optional points competition, as well as reducing controversy regarding the assignment of points during the year.

It was very difficult to believe that the points program was so logical in design and exacting in administration that slight differences were meaningful. Biases concerning scholarship and attendance provisions have been discussed in some detail. Further inequities, as noted by Tom Burns,

included provision in a "directory" year for just as many points (800 out of 6,000, or 6,800) for a directory covering one initiation by a newly installed unit as for one covering several decades of operation by a long-established group; and treatment of a major project like Omicron's pioneering student seminar at Ohio State, in 1969, on the same basis as a variety of strictly local activities. The former problem was removed through the abandonment of the directory element in 1971.

Another consideration was brought out in 1979 by Fred Mueller, who during the fifties had been a student and faculty officer of Delta at Washington, and a graduate member of Omicron. He recalled that "rumors" had been "rampant" in those formative years of the activity program that awards presented to top chapters at the annual banquet were often based on "fraudulent" reporting. Also, department chairman may have often urged their faculty simply to "sign in" at some point during a chapter meeting, to build up (beginning in 1954) special activities credit.[4]

Somewhat similarly, Vern Vincent suspected during his term as secretary-treasurer in the following decade that the faculty advisors to certain chapters were doing much of the monthly reporting, thus subverting the valuable learning objectives of the process. He observed in 1980 that basic accounting

---

[4]Fred Mueller was close during the 1950s not only to Julius Roller, the Delta FVP of his student days whom he succeeded in the post in '57, but also to prewar councilor Hermann Miller, who was a member of his dissertation committee at Ohio State before suffering a fatal heart attack in October 1955. Having in the judgment of the local faculty already taken '"as much accounting as anyone could ever need"' by the time he completed his M.A. degree at Washington in '54, Mueller at the doctoral level minored in the field, and majored in business finance. He attended his first Beta Alpha Psi national banquet at Colorado in 1959, although the event had occurred at Washington three years earlier, when he had returned as a faculty member. Grand Council Minutes Book, 1956, p. 6, 1957, pp. [5-6], 1958, p. [7], 1959, p. 5; Hasselback, 1984 Directory, individual listing, s.v. "Mueller, Fred J."; [W. B. Jencks], "In Memoriam," Newsletter 4 (November 1955):266; and Fred J. Mueller to Author, interview, November 27, 1979 (source of references in text), by telephone (first call), August 11, 1986, both quoted.

concepts of auditing, planning, and reporting provided an ideal base for high standards of chapter performance and documentation. Whatever its limitations, the activity program was "a wonderful thing," in guiding students toward making plans, and accomplishing them in an orderly way.

Only two "traveling plaques" had been made, the one retired by Theta at Texas in 1957 after heading the field for a third time in seven years, and the one used for the final dozen years of the first-place competition. In the first case, a plate commemorating Theta's special honor was inserted in the space freed by removal of two smaller plates (those unused) provided for recording the winning chapters, and appropriate rotation of others. The last group to display the award was Beta Omicron at Arizona, under advisor Hollis Dixon, in 1969-70. More than a year after the close of that period, at the midyear planning session of 1971-72, the National Council accepted a motion by Past President Charles Taylor that the plaque be redone to serve as a symbol of the fraternal presidency, to be passed from one holder of the office to the next. Harold Royer was later asked to make the appropriate redesign arrangements. In 1975, finally, Fred Mueller was appointed to arrange for the production of miniature plaques for former presidents interested in receiving a momento of that kind.

Spurred by opposition expressed by Robert Maust's committee on long-range goals, there was actually some consideration early in 1974 of abandoning the points competition. President Hollis Dixon proposed an alternative program that would have required year-end reporting for all chapters. Although it was decided at the spring meeting to continue the activity program, the National Council agreed to establish an "activity program review committee" chaired by the president. The original idea was to appoint three faculty advisors and two alumni members, representing both chapters generally

favorable toward the program (one in each group) and ones resistant to it. A larger committee soon formed from faculty ranks would shortly be reconstituted as a working unit of the Council.

Activity Program Committees, 1974-79

At the 1974 National Chapter meeting in New Orleans, Hollis Dixon "announced the formation of a Chapter Activity Program Review Committee to study the purposes, contents, and implementation" of the program. The group apparently did not meet until the following February, in the same city, when Dixon was joined by eight faculty advisors:

a. Outstanding Faculty Vice Presidents James N. Solano of Alpha Phi at Temple (1973-74); David R. Ganz of Gamma Psi at Missouri-St. Louis, James Morton of Alpha Beta at Alabama, and Mohamed E. Moustafa of Gamma Omega at California State, Long Beach (1974-75); and 1984-85 national president David Tinius of Delta Eta at Seattle (1976-77)

b. Charter "area" councilor (1981-82) Katherine M. Horstmann of Gamma Phi of Texas at Arlington

c. John Cumming of Rho at Minnesota and Jack B. Wollman of Beta Gamma at DePaul (which under the same FVP would be cited in December for having not as yet filed any reports, or otherwise communicated with the National Council, during the year 1975-76).

General agreement was registed that the fraternity "should be professional with an honorary philosophy"; chapter activity must accordingly be reported; and seven local meetings ought to be required each year.

The following year, Secretary-Treasurer Fred Mueller, President Bob Maust, and future activities director Jim Pattillo met as a committee to draft the Chapter Activity Program for 1976-77. As discussed below, their recommendations were significantly changed by the full National Council in a landmark revision of the program. In January 1977, Director of Chapter Activities Pattillo chaired a session attended by Mueller, Maust, two other faculty councilors, and alumni councilor Larry Gattis. Several changes in

point allocation were approved, visitations to a number of "poorly performing chapters" were assigned, and an earlier decision on "minimum points" for probationary units was ratified. Revised attendance provisions adopted in 1978 were probably based upon the recommendations of a committee that had met in Dallas the prior September.

Jim Pattillo's 1978-79 committee, recommending no major activity program changes, included Jack Kiger (his designated successor as director), Doris Cook, and FVPs Jesse Boyles of Upsilon at Florida and William L. Stephens of Delta Gamma at South Florida. Finally, the review group appointed by President Pattillo in 1979 included the fraternal administrator at the new national office in Florida, in keeping with the transfer of routine administration of the program to that facility.[5]

Two significant activity program changes of the fifth era were noted in chapter 10: elimination of the traditional scholarship element, and significant reduction (basically, to fifty per cent) in attendance requirements. The most fundamental and controversial alterations were, however, a restructuring that made the achievement of "maximum" points truly

---

[5]Wilton T. Anderson to Author, interview, March 20, 1980, quoted; Thomas J. Burns to Author, interview, May 3, 1980; Joyce C. Dean, "Minutes, Chapter Activity Program Committee," January 1977, pp. 1-3, quoting p. 3; Hollis A. Dixon, Secretary-Treasurer's Report, 1972-73, p. 8; Harvey E. Donley to Author, interview, May 2, 1980; exhibit 14 (chapter 6); Robert S. Maust, Long-Range Planning Committee Minutes, December 1971, p. 6; Maust to Author, interview, July 14, 1980; [Metcalf], ed., 1983-84 Annual Report, pp. 39 ("Prior Recipents of . . . [FVPs] Award"), [40] ("Former Area Councilors"); Fred J. Mueller to Author, interview, November 27, 1979, quoted; National Chapter Minutes, 1974, p. 1, quoted; National Council Minutes, 1969, pp. 5, 11, 1970, p. 3 (quoted), 1971, pp. 1, 7, 1972, pp. 6, 9, 1973, p. 9, February 1974, pp. 2-4, May 1974, pp. 2-4 (quoting p. 3), May-June, 1975, p. 5 (quoted), August 1975, p. 7, December 1975, p. 3, April 1976, p. 4, January 1978, p. 1, January 1979, p. 2, August 1979, p. 1; [James W. Pattillo], "Beta Alpha Psi, . . . 1979-80," as cited in chapter 13, note 5; [Charles W. Taylor], "Top 15 chapters Listed in '67-68 Activity Program," including photo and caption; and Vern H. Vincent to Author, interview, July 21, 1980, quoted.

accessible, and a policy decision on "minimum" point requirements.

The Two Most Fundamental Changes: Policy Concerning "Maximum" and "Minimum" Points

Adoption of a much more flexible program, 1976

At least since 1954, when a total of 1,600 itemized points had been made available for achieving the maximum 1,000 points allowed in the category "Special Activities," the activity program had provided for a measure of flexibility. During the sixties, as covered in chapter 10, the same differential between points "available" and "allowed" had been adopted for two categories, numbers 6, "Chapter Involvement in Campus or Community Activities" ("Community Activities") and 7, "Chapter Involvement in Professional and Fratern[al] Activities" ("Professional Activities"). These provisions were still in effect in 1973 when total points that could be earned were increased from 5,400 to 8,000. Although point allowances for categories 6 and 7 were increased from 1,000 to 1,900, it is unlikely that the fraternity's first "perfect" activity program score was earned in 1973-74 under more restrictive conditions.

At the spring meeting in 1976, Councilors Mueller, Maust, and Pattillo recommended major changes in the Chapter Activity Program that would increase total points allowed to 12,000. Following "heated discussion" of an "apparent increase in required activity," implications for "minimum performance standards," and alleged "inequities" based on chapter size, the National Council voted 4-3 to establish an itemized total of 12,000 points available while retaining 8,000 maximum points "allowable." The negative votes were cast by Fred Mueller, Jim Pattillo, and Harold Royer, while through abstention highly diplomatic president Bob Maust averted a deadlock that would

have defeated the motion. A subsequent vote, on which Fred Mueller abstained, produced the following three differences between points (a) available and (b) allowed:

1. Item 3, "Organizational Meeting & Professional Programs," 3,000 and 2,700
2. Item 4 (in new plan), Community Activities, 3,900 and 2,000
3. Item 5 (new plan), Professional Activities, 3,400 and 1,600.

A year later the figures for category 4 were changed to 4,450 and 2,200 points, through respective transfers of credit available and allowed from nos. 5 and 3.

This liberalization of the program made it more suited than ever before to the broad variety of Beta Alpha Psi environments, as (for example) even the relaxed "attendance" element soon qualified for a degree of trade-off under category 3. Although its most predictable effect was that a number of chapters began earning "maximum" points, the new flexibility also strengthened the case for binding standards of "minimum" performance for maintenance of good standing, a topic of fundamental controversy during the period 1975-77.

"Minimum" performance standards, and dispute on their proper status

Prior to the mid-seventies, the only established basis for placing chapters on probation was noncompliance with the constitutional requirements of holding at least one initiation and seven other meetings (reduced to six in 1974, apparently as yet without formal amendment) during the year, and submitting a year-end audit report. In February 1975, President Hollis Dixon suggested that further "minimum standards" of chapter performance might be asserted in the basic restatement of the constitution then underway. The idea, specifically, was that the achievement of a certain point total (or

percentage of total allowable points) would be required for a chapter to stay in good standing, or be restored to that position. Subsequent discussion implies that such an approach had been considered, and debated, previously by councilors of the day.

The proposition that minimum point standards were desirable was readily accepted by a National Council who had reinstituted full participation by all chapters in the activity program, and did not doubt the need for a clearer policy in dealing with "weak" units. The central issue was whether they should be stated at the constitutional level. There were essentially three alternatives:

a. Stating specific requirements in the constitution (inclusive, under the forthcoming structure, of bylaws)
b. Stating them in the Chapter Activity Program, and asserting in the constitution that such specifications would be enforced
c. Stating them in the Activity Program without making any such constitutional reference.

Although the minutes of 1975-77 draw no explicit distinction between approaches b and c, the principal issue was whether the first or second course should be taken, since the third one would not have justified taking disciplinary action against deficient chapters.

Two decisions were made in 1975. First, a minimum performance standard of 2,400 points, of the 8,000 allowed, was set for the year 1975-76. Although the constitutional revision was still in progress, the requirement was enforced as ten chapters were placed on probation for failure to achieve minimum points during a year by whose midpoint local groups had generally been reporting "increased activity."

Second, the Council at the spring meeting approved a resolution that

> an article be added [to constitutional bylaws] to set forth minimum standards for chapters to remain in good standing[,] including the procedures to be taken by the National Council if such standards are not maintained.

Based on a draft prepared by Bob Maust, a bylaw was adopted that probably specified the three-stage progression to 3,200 points (or 40% of the maximum total) cited below. Maust later stated that the minimum standards topic had been "beaten to death" during this time period, and that "a couple of walkouts" (probably signified by reference in the minutes to "heated discussion") had occurred based on strong differences of opinion.

The major argument presented for specifying minimum point requirements in the constitutional bylaws was that they would on that basis enjoy stronger authority, and thus greater enforceability, in part because they would be subject to less frequent revision. Bob Maust felt that a "professional" interpretation of Beta Alpha Psi called for highly authoritative standards. Secretary-Treasurer Fred Mueller, who had been asked by President Dixon to draft a proposal concerning minimum "acceptable" activity level, concurred, based on the need "to protect the reputation of the fraternity" on behalf of "the active participating chapters." Senior councilors Bob Wasley and Harold Royer also favored specific constitutional coverage, expressing frustration with the inability of the National Council during their years of service to develop a consistent policy in this area.

The leading argument against direct bylaw coverage of minimum performance standards was simply a denial that relatively long-term provisions were realistic for a highly changeable activity program. A more limited point was that a period of experimentation, at least, would be needed to identify proper standards. The basic structural changes made in 1976 seemed to support such concerns, and indeed the requirement of 2,400 points for 1976-77 was immediately questioned in light of the new flexibility of the activity program. A higher requirement had been adopted for chapters that were on probation, but was abandoned on grounds of inconsistency.

An early advocate of specific coverage through the Chapter Activity Program, backed by a general reference in constitutional bylaws, was Doris Cook. Besides inviting proper "flexibility," she felt that such an approach would be "more palatable to the chapters." Although Cook's influence was reduced by a perception that she was unduly reluctant to take disciplinary action, her position eventually prevailed, as was foreshadowed during the activity program committee meeting of January 1977. Director Jim Pattillo indicated on that occasion that he would ask the National Council the following month to rescind the bylaw on minimum point requirements, shifting coverage to the program instructions. That action was duly taken in time for the publication in March of the new constitution and bylaws.

Indeed, the bylaws specifically asserted only an audit report requirement, otherwise stating that to avoid probation chapters would have to conduct "a minimum acceptable level of activity" as defined by the annual activity program. Hence initiation and regular meeting requirements had been transferred to program specifications that required a two-thirds vote by the Council. It had been agreed, provisionally, that minimum points would remain at 2,400 for 1977-78, and be increased by 400 each of the next two years to reach a new standard of 3,200 points by 1979-80, based on a maximum of 8,000 points. The second increase was apparently postponed, however, until 1981-82. Delta Lambda at New Mexico State was removed from probation in 1980 after having fallen slightly short of 3,200 points, and attention was focused at the August meeting on audit report deficiencies rather than the failure of a dozen other chapters to reach the projected requirement. Based on the absence of an initiation, one of the three local units falling between 2,800 and 3,200 points in 1980-81 was placed on probation.

A new approach to recognition of outstanding chapters that was begun in 1975 would be strongly affected by the enhanced flexibility of the restructured activity program adopted a year later.

Chapter Awards Programs, 1975-79

At the meeting in August 1975, on the recommendation of Secretary-Treasurer Fred Mueller, the National Council abandoned the practice of making $100 cash awards to the top fifteen (or more) chapters. Instead, three categories were recognized: "Superior," "Excellent," and "Meritorious" chapters, receiving respective prizes of $150, $100, and $50. In 1975, the awards were made to chapters 1-6, 7-13, and 14-22 in the year's point standings. The commemorative plaque was continued for Superior chapters. Although the three cash prizes were new, the fraternity had by way of the plaques distinguished previously between two levels of recognition.

In 1977, the Council was unable to distinguish between chasses 2 and 3, and so recognized a group of 14 "distinguished performance," or "Distinguished," chapters, receiving $75 each, in addition to the 15 "Superior" ones. Under the new provisions by which 12,000 points were "available," 12 local groups had earned the maximum 8,000 points, five more than the previous historical total of full-credit chapters. When the number of units earning maximum points rose the next year to 23, the "Superior" rating was redefined to require such achievement, and in 1979 the "Distinguished" category was similarly identified with the interval 7,500 to 7,999 points, inclusive. Concern was expressed in 1979 that too many chapters were being honored, but no major changes in the interchapter competition were adopted.

The awards structure was changed dramatically in 1979, with the funding by the Peat, Marwick, Mitchell Foundation of two $500 scholarships for each

superior chapter--29 in number that year. The original plan also to provide two $250 scholarships for each distinguished unit was not enacted. Discontinuing the $150 and $75 awards, the National Council a year later instituted a $250 scholarship for distinguished chapters. Forty-one chapters qualified for the Peat Marwick prizes in 1980, and nine others for the Council award.

Prior to 1976-77, maximum point totals had been earned only seven times, all during the preceding three years. Beta Delta at Texas Tech was the first full-credit chapter, in 1973-74, and repeated the following two years. Gamma Omega at California State, Long Beach, assisted by joint operation with the local accounting club, achieved 8,000 points during the two years 1974-76, and Alpha Beta at Alabama and Beta Upsilon at Georgia (both very strong chapters throughout the decade) followed suit in 1975-76. All four of these chapters would continue to earn full credit through the close of the fifth era in 1979, being joined the last three years by Upsilon at Florida, Gamma Lambda at Virginia Tech, and Delta Beta at California State, Fullerton. Among ten units earning maximum points twice during the period 1976-79 were Delta at Washington and Alpha Eta at Arkansas, traditionally very active units that had been unable to reach the "number 1" position, and Gamma Beta at South Carolina, which barely missed 8,000 points in 1976-77.

The selection of "Outstanding Faculty Vice Presidents" in 1979 reflected an interesting result of the rapid expansion of maximum activity program scores. With so many chapters earning 8,000 points, it had become increasingly difficult to identify particularly worthy candidates for the award. On the motion of Editor Henry Anderson, it was agreed "that the Council [should] recognize the six highest ranked FVPs, according to their chapter records." That is, the six current faculty advisors not previously honored

who had the highest cumulative activity program records (based, ordinarily, on more than two years of service) were selected for the 1979 awards. Even that approach (disregarding any inherent limitations) might not always be workable in a day of regular achievement of "perfect" scores by many chapters.

The reference made to Henry Anderson, finally, brings to mind another annual chapter award. Beginning with Alpha Phi at Temple and Alpha Epsilon at Southern Methodist in 1973-74, one or more units received $100 in recognition as "significantly improved," or "most improved," chapters, based on activity program measurement. At SMU, first-year advisor Anderson had devised "a master plan to maximize points" for a group that had the preceding year violated one constitutional requirement and barely met two others; and in the mid-sixties pleaded '"Don't ever send that man again"' following a visit by Councilor Wilton Anderson. As NAA education director, Hank Anderson was particularly adept at arranging cooperative activities that secured points for both Alpha Epsilon and (in the Stevenson Trophy competition) the Dallas Chapter of the National Association of Accountants.

As of 1978, when "superior" chapter Omicron at Ohio State was selected, the "most" improved prize was limited to one group annually, while others were recognized as "significantly" improved. To broaden the field of honored chapters, it was decided the following year to confine both citations to units not qualifying for other awards.[6]

---

[6]Henry R. Anderson to Author, interview, April 18, 1986, quoted; Beta Alpha Psi, "National Bylaws," National Constitution and Bylaws (1977), article 15, sections 5 (quoted), 6; Beta Alpha Psi National Constitution (1971), article 13, section 6, article 14, section 5; "Chapter Activities," Annual Reports, 1979-80, ed. [Pattillo], 1980-81, ed. [Dean], pp. 18-23; Doris M. Cook to Author, interview, March 20, 1980; Joyce C. Dean, Chapter Activity Program Committee Minutes, January 1977, pp. 1-3; [Hollis A. Dixon], "Instructions for 1971-72 Chapter Activity Program," Newsletter 10 (Fall 1971):5-6; Dixon to Author, interview, March 22-23, 1980; "Final Point Accumulation under Chapter Activity Program - June 15, 1974," Newsletter 13

In terms of the dominant theme of participation, the foremost development of the fifth era was the emergence of extensive *student* involvement in the fraternity beyond the local chapter level, through the institution of student-oriented "regional" and "national" meetings.

Modern Fraternal Assembly: Regional and National

Regional Meetings, Beginning in 1974

Regionalism developed rapidly within Beta Alpha Psi from the modest base of FVP breakfasts begun in 1972-73 at regional meetings of the American Accounting Association. A full-fledged conference of Beta Alpha Psi chapters from Texas and at least two other states was held a year later, and within three years similar annual (or, in one case, semiannual) meetings were being conducted in eight regions spanning the nation. The National Council assisted and promoted the new program in a variety of ways as two additional regional groups were established.

Starting point: FVP breakfasts at regional AAA meetings

As noted in chapter 9, in lieu of taking a more formal approach to councilor communication with chapters on a geographical basis the National

---

(Fall 1974):4; [Leon E. Hay], Secretary-Treasurer's Report, 1965-66, p. 1; Hay to Author, interview, May 2, 1980, quoted; Robert S. Maust to Author, interview, July 14, 1980, quoted; Fred J. Mueller, Secretary-Treasurer's Report, 1975-76, pp. 1 (quoted), 13; National Chapter Minutes, 1973, p. 2; National Council Minutes, 1973, p. 12, May 1974, pp. 3-5 (quoting p. 4), August 1974, pp. 1-2, February 1975, pp. 3, 4 (quoted), May-June, 1975, pp. 2 (quoted), 9 (indented citation), August 1975, pp. 2-4 (quoted), December 1975, p. 3 (quoted), April 1976, pp. 4-5 (quoted), August 1976, p. 3, February 1977, p. 2, June 1977, p. 2 (quoted), June 1978, pp. 2-3, January 1979, p. 2, June 1979, pp. 2, 3 (quoted), August 1979, pp. 5-6, January 1980, p. 3, August 1980, pp. 3-4, August 1981, p. 3, August 1982, p. 4; "Outstanding Chapters," or comparable title, *Annual Reports*, 1976-77 through 1979-80; "Results of 1976-77 Chapter Activity Program," *1976-77 Annual Report*, ed. [Mueller], pp. 12-13; and Secretary-Treasurers' Reports, 1970-71 through 1975-76, omitting 1973-74, listing of activity program points.

Council agreed in 1971 that members should where possible attend "regional" meetings of the American Accounting Association, and host breakfasts for faculty vice-presidents in attendance. No specific assignments were made, however, until the following year, when five of the six councilors were asked to attend six of the seven regional AAA meetings.

There were six "regional group[s]," combining two that conducted a joint meeting, and a "state chapter" within the AAA of 1972-73:

1. Canada, or Canadian
2. Midwest
3. Northeast
4. Southeast
5. Southwest
6. West and Northwest
7. Ohio.

A year later, a Middle Atlantic region was created, and the West region was expanded through the absorption of the Northwest and a decision not to create an area group representing the "Great Plains." Some years later, the Canadian group, whose 1972-73 meeting had for obvious reasons been excluded from the Beta Alpha Psi assignments, was disbanded. The reference made to one individual state foreshadows difficulties experienced later in assigning borderline Ohio to a fraternal area.

Travel expense to the fraternity for this first phase of regionalism was only $209.45, as costs were generally covered by employer universities. The only nonparticipant was the plan's originator, Charles Taylor of Mississippi. Harvey Donley, serving an extra year while Bob Wasley was abroad, was originally assigned both the Ohio and Midwest gatherings, but would be replaced in the latter case by President Harold Royer of Miami of Florida. Royer's trip presumably also included his site visitation to Illinois at Chicago.

During a "buffet breakfast" in Amherst, Mass., Editor Bob Maust conducted a roundtable discussion that enabled representatives from several

accredited schools without chapters to inquire about Beta Alpha Psi chartering. Secretary-Treasurer Hollis Dixon was assisted by Alpha Rho advisor Joyce Dean, from Baylor, in arranging a breakfast for all FVPs, student officers, and other student members attending the Southwest Social Science Convention (inclusive of the American Accounting Association region) in Dallas.

At the spring meeting the following year, four councilors reported on 1973-74 faculty vice-presidential gatherings scheduled in conjunction with meetings of the association. Fred Mueller indicated that 23 persons had attended an "excellent" breakfast session sponsored by Coopers & Lybrand. Harold Royer and Past President Dixon spoke very favorably of respective meetings of the Southeast and Southwest regions. Bob Maust, however, had attracted few participants to a "very lonely" Northeast function.

Hollis Dixon's reference to a "debate" presented on chapter activities implies that he was covering a function that had extended well beyond an FVP breakfast, having been in fact the first full-scale Beta Alpha Psi regional gathering. Over the next two years, such meetings were established throughout the country as the fraternity developed a regional structure independent of the American Accounting Association.

Development of the regional structure, spring 1974 - spring 1976

The pioneering Southwest meeting of March 1974

Under the faculty leadership of Jim Caldwell, destined to win a Richard S. Claire award for the year, Beta Delta at Texas Tech organized a full-day program held on the campus of Southern Methodist, in Dallas, on March 20, 1974. The occasion marked only the most visible of a variety of

initiatives on which Caldwell and Alpha Epsilon advisor Hank Anderson collaborated for the mutual benefit of their chapters.

A writeup of the meeting shown as exhibit 32 indicates that, from out of state, Chi at Oklahoma State and Alpha Iota at Arkansas were represented. The need for a points program, the AACSB accreditation requirement, and long-range objectives were among several controversial topics discussed and debated.

The following August Professors Caldwell and Anderson, along with a student officer from Theta at Texas, reported on their meeting to the National Chapter. Commencing a new practice, the faculty leaders present were asked to assemble afterwards in regional groups, with designated councilors, to discuss problems encountered by their chapters, and possible arrangements for area meetings not coordinated with AAA schedules. Beta Alpha Psi conferences were subsequently held in several additional geographic areas in 1974-75.

Several meetings in 1974-75

By March 1975, when representatives from 12 chapters met in Houston for another Southwest meeting, groups had convened in the midwest, southeast, and northeast, and in Southern California. Another midwest meeting was only a month away, opening a regional tradition of assembling in the fall to discuss chapter issues (and plan the second meeting), and in the spring, in conjunction with the American Accounting Association, to cover accounting topics.

Gamma at Northwestern had hosted a two-day workshop for FVPs and officers from 13 chapters in the fall that had engaged the assistance of Councilors Tom Burns and Bob Maust. Along with Burns, more than seventy-five

EXHIBIT 32

REPORT ON THE FIRST BETA ALPHA PSI REGIONAL MEETING: THE SOUTHWEST, MARCH 1974

Southwest Regional Conference

by
Judy Feagin
Beta Delta Chapter
Texas Tech University

The first Southwest Regional Conference of Beta Alpha Psi was coordinated by the Beta Delta Chapter at Texas Tech University and held March 20, 1974, on the Southern Methodist University campus. The day was filled with numerous panel discussions which provided an exchange of ideas and presentation of problems facing individual chapters. The conference was highlighted by a luncheon with Dr. Hollis Dixon, National President of Beta Alpha Psi, as guest speaker.

The morning session was an officer workshop with panel members from Texas Tech and the University of Texas at Arlington. The participants outlined the duties of each of their officers as set forth in their chapter by-laws. This was followed by an explanation of how each chapters' executive committee coordinated chapter activities.

At the luncheon, Dr. Hollis Dixon discussed questions facing Beta Alpha Psi. He questioned the extent to which Beta Alpha Psi is an honorary, professional and social organization. He also talked about a change in the competitive point system.

Chapter activities was the topic for the first of three afternoon discussions. Panel members from Southern Methodist University, Baylor, and Texas Tech presented ideas for campus and community involvement. Some of the suggested projects were: setting up accounting systems for campus organizations, working with small businesses and community organizations, operating tax clinics in conjunction with the Internal Revenue, tutoring sessions for elementary accounting students, holding seminars for high school students to encourage them in the field of accounting, and organizing Accounting Emphasis Weeks.

Representatives from North Texas State, Oklahoma State and Texas Christian University discussed changes in the National Council, initiation ritual, and expansion of Beta Alpha Psi. Panel members from North Texas State expressed the viewpoint that there was a lack of input from chapters to the National Council. A proposal was made that chapters of the southwest region meet annually and submit ideas from the conference to the National Council. The initiation ritual was briefly described by Oklahoma State University. Most chapters agreed the present ritual was suitable with the exception of the oath taken by honorary members. Since Beta Alpha Psi is a National Organization, it should have a uniform initiation ritual.

Delegates representing Texas Christian University talked about the expansion of Beta Alpha Psi. They questioned the validity of requiring chapters to be formed only in universities accredited by AACSB. A suggestion was made that there be some criteria set for evaluating the standards of nonaccredited schools. This would allow chapters to be established if the objectives of the institution coincided with the objectives of Beta Alpha Psi. The need for organizing chapters in more accredited universities was also recognized.

The most controversial issue of the day was the panel on Competition vs. Non Competition. Presenting the arguments were the University of Arkansas, who participates in the national point system, and the University of Texas, who did not participate. There were many interesting reasons cited for their respective viewpoints. As an end to the discussion, it was indicated that there is a need for a new system of evaluation. The suggestion was made that separate measures be established for young chapters and the more mature chapters.

The last discussion of the day focused on long range objectives of Beta Alpha Psi.

Reprinted from Newsletter 13 (Winter 1975):7.

(mainly) student representatives from 26 schools in the region, a dozen of them not as yet chartered, had attended a meeting organized at Georgia by Beta Upsilon advisor Jack Kiger. Maust questioned whether the program featuring presentations by Charles Horngren, James Don Edwards, and Herbert Miller had been designed for "what we wanted," namely, "promoting solutions to problems of . . . chapters." A function hosted in Philadelphia by Alpha Phi at Temple had featured a debate on "the increasing role of the Securities and Exchange Commission," judged by representatives from the American Institute of CPAs and the Pennslyvania State society. President Hollis Dixon was an especially appropriate guest at the meeting at the state college in Long Beach sponsored by Gamma Omega, since the state of Arizona would promptly be added to the Southern California region.

The National Council agreed in August 1975 to provide financial support for each regional meeting that attracted at least five chapters, although a specific plan would not be settled upon for another year. On the same occasion, Jim Caldwell and Jack Kiger were appointed 1975-76 southwest and southeast "Regional Coordinators," and Tom Burns and Bob Maust reported on regional developments to the National Chapter. Burns' recommendation that the coming year's meetings address specific "Emerging Topics in Financial Reporting," possibly leading to publication of selected material, was belatedly endorsed in December. The rather different perspectives expressed by Burns and Maust would be harmonized as a general policy was developed.

A full-fledged regional structure emerged in 1975-76 with the scheduling of nine meetings in eight regions.

Nine meetings in eight
regions, 1975-76

New entrants included the Rocky Mountain, Northwest, and Northern

PARTICIPANTS IN THE FIRST SOUTH-EASTERN REGIONAL MEETING, 1975

From left, Herbert Miller, Charles T. Horngren, Accountant of the Year (1974) James Don Edwards, Regional Coordinator (1975-76) Jack E. Kiger, Councilor Thomas Burns, and student members Dennis Korner, John Murphy, and charter alumni councilor (1976-77) T. Larry Gattis.

California areas. The first two meetings were hosted by the Colorado and Washington campuses of Bob Wasley and Fred Mueller. The Midwest group again gathered twice. Newsletter writeups of the meetings at Penn State and, the following year, West Virginia (later absorbed by the Southeast area) referred to the "Eastern," rather than "Northeast(ern)," region.

Particularly in recognizing four western regions (beyond the southwest) rather than one, the fraternity had departed substantially from an AAA regional structure that was not consistent with patterns of chapter concentration. The "regional coordinator" post listed in the 1977 national bylaws had effectively already ended with the close of Caldwell's and Kiger's one-year terms, as the National Council was unable to find new coordinators. President Maust had implicitly questioned the need for such a position in stating, late in 1975, that host chapters should plan the regional meetings.

An important issue needing prompt attention was the nature of funding to be provided by the Council. It was addressed at an interim level late in 1975, and a more permanent one within a broad policy statement prepared by Special Projects Director Tom Burns the following fraternal year that helped shape further program development as the fifth era drew to a close.

Adoption of a policy statement, and further development of the program, 1977-79

Burns' 1977 policy statement

At the meeting of December 1975, it was decided that beginning in 1976-77 a "host" chapter would receive $100 plus $10 for each chapter attending. Each "participating" chapter (tentatively defined as involved in some way in the program) would be reimbursed for one car's mileage at a rate to be set after Alpha Psi at West Virginia had completed a pertinent study, for activity program credit.

On the recommendation of the chairman, a nondriver, Burns' regional meetings committee replaced the mileage approach to funding with a $100 payment to "each chapter sending representatives." It also called for an additional payment to the host chapter of $2 per student attending. The committee report approved in 1976 also recommended a threefold program structure divided equally among outside speakers (with discussion sessions), student presentations on "Emerging Issues in Accounting," and discussion of chapter operations.

Professor Burns subsequently drew up a much broader statement of National Council policy that was ratified at the meeting in August 1977. On the funding side, it changed the provision for host chapters to:

> $150 plus $10 for each chapter sending an official student delegate, plus $2 for each student representative attending all functions other than the official delegate . . . and $10 for each Faculty Vice President, National Advisory Forum member and National Council member attending.

Over the next two years the National Council would contribute more than $34,000 to support regional meetings, although President Burns would in 1979 express some concern (not shared by his colleagues) that an observed trend toward increased funding by host chapters might signal reduced National Council influence over the program.

The 1977 statement called for planning by a faculty councilor (the director of regional meetings), working with a regional planning committee made up of area FVPs and students from the host chapter. The recommended meeting format included:

a. One student paper presentation for each chapter, based on assigned themes
b. A "plenary panel discussion" moderated by students supplying prepared "guideline questions"
c. A banquet or luncheon with a keynote address given by a councilor, National Advisory Forum member, or other appropriate person
d. One or more sessions on chapter operations
e. Announcement of plans for the next meeting.

Each member of the Council was encouraged to attend and participate in at least the regional meeting(s) relating to his or her geographical area. It was anticipated that selected papers delivered at regional meetings would be edited for publication, as feasible. A broader publication effort would indeed be one of several highlights of program development over the next two years.

Selected highlights, 1977-79

At the meeting during which his policy statement was adopted, Burns commented that three regions had not as yet provided for the level of student involvement desired, namely, the Southeast and the two California areas. At the midyear meeting in January 1978, he reported that the former region was switching to "our type of format," but that by and large the regional committees were not doing much advance planning with him.

In 1978 a "New York (City)" region was created to serve Mu at NYU, Alpha Gamma at Baruch, Alpha Omega at Fordham, and Delta Pi at metropolitan Hofstra. The following year the Midwest area, stretching from Ohio (moved temporarily to the Northeast group in 1983) to Nebraska and North Dakota to Missouri, was divided into separate Midwest and Missouri Valley regions. Created to stimulate fraternal activity with America's largest urban environment, the New York region was disbanded in 1981 after holding only an organization session featuring nonstudent presentations, and a meeting in which the designated host chapter did not participate.[7]

---

[7] To facilitate a gathering in New York, Mu at NYU agreed to host the Northeast meeting of 1979-80, when (by coincidence) the faculty vice-president under whom the chapter had nearly been discontinued eight years earlier resumed the post. Delta Pi at Hofstra, the host for the earlier New York City conference, and National Council representative Tom Burns were obliged to step in at the last minute to arrange the meeting of April 1980 after Mu had defaulted on its commitment. Burns to Author, interview, May 3,

Sixty-one student papers presented on a series of "Current Issues in Accounting" at eight meetings of 1978-79 were published at the close of the year under the editorship of Past President Doris Cook. Approximately half of the papers were from the Southeast and Midwest groups, while only two each had been presented in Northern California and the Northeast. Attendance had ranged from 74 persons at the organizational meeting in New York, featuring nonstudent presentations, and 75 in Southern California to 227 at at Midwest meeting that had attracted nine members of the National Advisory Forum, presumably gathered in Chicago on other fraternal business. Professional and/or academic accountants had participated in all ten meetings (two in the Midwest), which collectively had involved 104 chapters and 13 petitioning groups.

At the 1979 National Chapter meeting, first-year forum member Robert Maynard of Price Waterhouse reported briefly on visits he had made during the year to three regional conferences. He was "very enthusiastic" about the interaction he had observed and been part of, and commented that the exposure to student attitudes and viewpoints afforded by the program stood to benefit the National Council and prospective employer firms alike.

On the same occasion, Outstanding FVP Konrad W. Kubin of Gamma Lambda at Virginia Tech displayed a banner that he had designed for the southeastern region, in adaptation from the pattern of the national banner. There was a round of laughter as he and the chapter's student representative unfurled it upside down, quickly reversing it, after which Director of Regional Meetings Doris Cook characterized 1978-79 as "a banner year in more ways than one." More importantly, the National Council had accepted Kubin's

---

1980; Doris M. Cook, "Regional Meetings," 1978-79 Annual Report, ed. [Burns], p. 19; and [Pattillo], ed., 1979-80 Annual Report, pp. 18-19 ("Chapter Activities"), 26 ("Regional Meetings").

proposal that such a symbol be prepared for each region for transfer from one host institution to another, and adopted his design. By August 1979, producers David and Lisa Penz had completed and sent out banners for the Southwest, Midwest, and Northeast as well as the Southeast; and orders had already been placed by the Rocky Mountain and Northwest regions. One chapter had asked permission to make its own banner, a request denied "in the interest of standardization."[8]

---

[8]Richard L. Allen, Alpha Psi, "Third Eastern Regional Meeting," Newsletter 15 (Spring 1977):1; "American Accounting Association: Committees . . .," 1971-72 through 1973-74, 1983-84, 1984-85, The Accounting Review 47 (January 1972):192, 48 (January 1973):1979 (quoted), 180, 49 (January 1974):186, 59 (January 1984):131, (January 1985):134, reference to AAA supplied in first two titles; Henry R. Anderson to Author, interview, April 18, 1986; [Anderson], "Six FVPs Honored as Outstanding for 1978-79," Newsletter 18 (Fall 1979):8; Mary Ann Andrews, Beta Theta, "Second Eastern Regional Meeting," Newsletter 14 (Spring 1976):1; Beta Alpha Psi, "National Bylaws," National Constitution and Bylaws (1977), article 12; [Thomas J. Burns], "The National Council of Beta Alpha Psi: Policy Statement on Interchapter and Regional Meetings of the Chapters," Newsletter 18 (Winter 1980):2, 3 (quoted), 8 (indented citation), printing of 4-page document of 1977; Doris M. Cook, ed., Current Issues in Accounting -- Student Papers, Presented at Regional Meetings [of] 1978-1979 (Sarasota, Florida: National Council of Beta Alpha Psi, 1979); [Cook], "Outstanding Faculty Vice Presidents and Chapters Honored," Newsletter 13 (Fall 1974):5; [Cook], "Regional Meetings," 1978-79 Annual Report, ed. [Burns], pp. 15-19; [Cook], "Regional Meetings Increase," Newsletter 14 (Spring 1976):8; Cook, report on regional meetings, National Chapter Meeting (Honolulu), August 21, 1979, quoted (tape recorded); Cook to Author, June 16, 1986; [Cook], writeups on 1974-75 or (in one case) 1975-76 regional meetings, Newsletter 13 (Winter 1975):6-7, (Spring 1975):3 (quoted), 14 (Fall 1975):9, (Winter 1976):2; Hollis A. Dixon, Long-Range Planning Committee Minutes, 1972, p. 4; Dixon, Secretary-Treasurer's Report, 1972-73, p. 13, quoted; exhibit 32; [Robert S. Maust], "News in Brief," Newsletter 11 (Spring 1973):8, quoted; Robert M. Maynard, invited remarks at National Chapter Meeting, August 21, 1979, quoted; National Chapter Minutes, 1974, p. 2; National Council Minutes, 1971, pp. 4-5, 1972, p. 7, 1973, p. 8, May 1974, pp. 1, 2 (quoted), August 1974, p. 2, February 1975, p. 2 (quoted), August 1975, pp. 5-6, 9 (quoting pp. 5, 9), December 1975, pp. 8-9 (quoted), April 1976, p. 1, August 1976, p. 4 ("Emerging Topics"), August 1977, pp. 2-3, January 1978, p. 1 (quoted); August 1979, p. 10 (quoted), June 1981, p. 7, August 1983, p. 7; "Regional Meetings," Annual Reports, 1975-76 through 1980-81 (excluding 1978-79); and Helen (Mrs. Robert S.) Wasley to Author, conversation (Denver, Colorado), March 23, 1980.

The 1979 gathering just mentioned was part of a particularly memorable national meeting, the fourth convention of a National Chapter fundamentally expanded (as implied by the reference to a student delegate) as an outgrowth of regional meetings.

Annual National Meeting

During the 1950s, in the early days of the function, "local" student officers were commonly invited to attend the Grand Chapter banquet, normally followed by a short business meeting. After a lapse of some years, this practice was resumed in 1970, and student participation in National Chapter activity was significantly greater the following two years. It receded somewhat as the meetings moved from university campuses to urban hotels, only to increase dramatically in 1976 with the beginning of the modern national meeting.

Student participation before 1970: Grand Chapter attendance by "local" officers in fifties

As covered in volume 1, in its first years as a national organization Beta Alpha Psi was governed as a confederation of chapters within which student representatives played a central role. With the adoption of the Grand Council structure in 1927, three years after the occurrence of a second national convention featuring major student participation, the fraternity became exclusively faculty-oriented beyond the local level. An event of eleven years later, however, would anticipate a development that would give rise to limited involvement of students in connection with the annual Council meeting.

During the 1938 American Accounting Association convention in Detroit, six faculty advisors and four former members of the Grand Council (or a

predecessor body) joined four councilors for a luncheon meeting to discuss the fraternal program, and similar arrangements were made a year later in Philadelphia. A dinner meeting conducted on a larger scale at Michigan in '49, when the AAA commenced gathering on campuses, marked the beginning of an annual Grand Council banquet. The following year's function took place in Cambridge, Mass.

Although Alpha Eta would be installed at Michigan a year and a half after the 1949 sessions, no local chapter existed in any of the three cases to help host the AAA meetings. In 1951, however, the association and the Grand Council met at Denver, the home of Alpha Zeta, which "had the privilege of assisting the faculty" with the AAA gathering. More to the point, chapter president Eugene E. Shoppell and (apparently interim) secretary M. L. Sanchez attended the banquet, along with 28 accounting professors. The three Denver teachers present were Faculty Vice-President Jerome J. Kesselman, erroneously cited in golden anniversary listings as a charter "Active" member; Chi alumnus (and 1985 Accounting Hall of Fame honoree) Oscar S. Gellein; and R. B. (Bruce) McCosh, who years later would delight Alpha Beta representative A. J. Penz of Alabama by introducing him to his Gamma Tau Chapter at Colorado State as the '"Grandfather of Beta Alpha Psi"'. In keeping with a practice followed with one exception until 1968, a business meeting was held after dinner. The two students observed a discussion of a variety of fraternal matters that no doubt consumed considerably more than the ten minutes that would be devoted to business after a 1966 dinner in Miami Beach.

Over the next seven years, 1952-58, there were three or (in one case) four students at all but one Grand Chapter banquet. The site in 1953 was the University of North Carolina, which was not a Beta Alpha Psi school, and was not located in the vicinity of one. At Illinois the following year, a student representative from host Alpha Chapter, President Harold Arnett, was

joined by two students from Gamma at Northwestern. Four student officers from Alpha Delta at Pennsylvania attended the dinner and separate business meeting held in Philadelphia in 1955.

As related in chapter 6, the Grand Council offered funding to the top three chapters in the 1956-57 interchapter competition to send a student delegate to the 1958 Grand Chapter banquet and meeting. Theta at Texas, Alpha Theta at Mississippi, and Sigma at Wisconsin all exercised the option to use the funding otherwise, namely, for scholarships.

From 1959 through 1969, students were apparently present at the Grand or National Chapter banquet (or, in the last two years, separate business meeting) only once. At Michigan State in 1962 one student from host Alpha Omicron was joined among the guests by two student members of Alpha Eta at nearby Michigan (assuming that the minutes are incorrect in referring instead to "Beta" Eta at San Diego State). The setting was outside the Beta Alpha Psi roster three times, although members of Lambda at California (which had made no advance banquet reservations), Chi at Oklahoma State, and Beta Xi at Miami of Florida might logically have been invited to the banquets that followed respective meetings at Stanford, Oklahoma, and a Miami Beach hotel. Indeed, Chi's Wilton Anderson was a member of the governing body that renamed itself the "National" Council in his home state in 1965.

The virtual disappearance of student representatives over the eleven years ending in 1969 may have been a matter purely of happenstance. At least half seriously, however, Herb Miller recalled in 1980 that the Grand Council of his day, 1958-63, would not have considered asking students to attend national meetings at which they might see faculty vice-presidents returning to their rooms at very late hours, in a state of reduced sobriety, and possibly with companions other than their wives. As far as students were concerned, he had probably forgotten about the aforementioned 1962

banquet on his own campus over which he had presided.

An anecdote supplied by Leon Hay gives an interesting behavioral picture of contemporary councilors themselves. In Bloomington, Indiana in 1964, incoming member Hay invited the Grand Council and (having advisory committee status) Miller over to his patio, a deck attached to the garage. There were not many takers when drinks were offered. Leon Hay recalls specifically that Herb Miller, Andy Anderson, and (perhaps) Emerson Henke were nondrinkers. President Henke was "a pretty good Christian gentleman" who was very kindly, "proper but not too tough," and "pretty much like a man from [Baptist-sponsored] Baylor should be." Hay's mother had incidentally questioned his joining an Indiana faculty that included pioneer sex-researcher Alfred Kinsey.

In 1970, the National Council reinstated the earlier practice of inviting students from the host chapter to National Chapter functions, and the following year student participation was stepped up.

A transitional period of student involvement, including two workshops, 1970-75

The University of Maryland hosted the AAA meetings of 1970. Five student members of Tau attended the National Chapter banquet, two of them were able to "participate" and share in the dialogue" at the business session, and one of them served as "personal aide" to President Harvey Donley.

The following year marked a significant breakthrough, as the four FVP workshop panelists were students. They were Randall Minix from Gamma Lambda at Virginia Tech, Charles Keller from Gamma Epsilon at Toledo, Adrian Ulatowki of Psi at Marquette, and William McLendon of Beta Upsilon at Georgia, corecipient of the year's manuscript award. Students from host chapter Alpha Mu at Kentucky were apparently also in attendance.

Hollis Dixon had recommended that students be invited to the workshop,

and someone had suggested that they serve as panelists, during the long-range planning conference in the spring. At that point three of the chapters to be represented on the program (destined to finish among the top five for the year) stood atop the 1970-71 point standings. Having been reimbursed for travel costs and "out of pocket expense" in Lexington, probably for two nights, the student participants would presumably have also attended the business meeting and banquet.

The FVP workshop the following year, at the University of Utah, featured a discussion of "Beta Alpha Psi in Retrospect" by alumni members of Gamma Alpha at Brigham Young, Nu at Colorado, and Delta at Washington. President Robert Wasley had also been authorized to invite the student officers from Bringham Young, located forty-five miles away. The National Council meeting and the banquet were held off campus, at Hotel Utah, in a kind of anticipation of an imminent environmental change cited below.

In October 1972, the first "National" Student Seminar was hosted by Omicron at Ohio State, under the faculty leadership of Thomas Burns. As indicated in chapter 10, the chapter had earlier sponsored "regional" seminars. The 1972 session on the use of "direct valuation" for several specific external and internal reporting purposes marked the first full-scale national student conference in Beta Alpha Psi annals. Forty chapters sent delegates, each of whom had been asked to bring a petition paper, to be included in published proceedings, supporting or opposing a particular application of the concept. The meeting was funded by Arthur Andersen; Lybrand, Ross Bros., & Montgomery (soon to become Coopers & Lybrand); and, in the amount of $500, the National Council.

The seminar was a regular annual event at Ohio State until 1979, when Gamma Pi from Northern Illinois hosted the eighth national gathering at

Arthur Andersen conference facilities in St. Charles, Illinois, attracting members from sixty-eight chapters. Founding Gamma Pi advisor Henry Anderson, on hand for at least the opening of the 1979 seminar, vividly recalls attending, as president, the event hosted two years later by Theta at Texas. He was struck by the "growth" that could be observed in just two days as outstanding students interacted with their "peers" across the country.

The American Accounting Association, and Beta Alpha Psi, met in August 1973 at Laval University (Université Laval) in Quebec. There is no evidence that students, other than the manuscript winners, participated that year or the following one. The AAA arrangements committee for the 1974 meeting in New Orleans was headed, however, by Beta Nu FVP Stephen Zeff of Tulane, and other members included Gamma Sigma advisor Mary Beeler of Louisiana State, New Orleans. The most noteworthy development in 1974 was the movement "off campus," in recognition that large hotels were better suited than universities to handling modern-day association attendance, reaching 1,452 that year not counting the many nonmembers (primarily spouses and children) on hand.

At Tucson in 1975, several members of Beta Omicron at Arizona assisted President Hollis Dixon with the memorable barbecue held at his home; and students were represented at the faculty vice-presidents' workshop. Although specific details are unavailable, by this point students and (presumably) faculty members from several petitioning universities, or prospective ones, had appeared at National Chapter meetings to underscore their interest in chapter formation. It is noted, in passing, that Delta Upsilon was installed at Northern Arizona two years after the fraternity had met in Tucson.

In 1976, finally, there was full-scale student participation in the meetings held in Atlanta, marking the beginning of the modern-day national

meeting.

Beginning of the modern national meeting--Atlanta, 1976

In November 1975, Fred Mueller visited Beta Mu at Georgia State, the designated host for the National Chapter the following summer. At his invitation, the chapter afterwards sent the secretary-treasurer a proposal that it be authorized to sponsor a "student" meeting in conjunction with the FVP gathering.

Presenting the Georgia State request at the winter meeting the following month, Mueller observed that Beta Alpha Psi was "student oriented" locally, but "solely faculty oriented" nationally, and that Atlanta would be a good location for attracting student attendance. Hollis Dixon was opposed to any prospect of diverting resources from the growing regional program, and Doris Cook favored "work[ing] into" a student grogram "gradually." Councilors Maust, Cohen, Royer, and Pattillo joined Professor Mueller in support of a student meeting. Bob Maust would later describe undergraduate participation as "a great experience." Al Cohen stated that "if it cost $50 to have one charged-up student going back to the chapter, he was in favor of spending" it.

With Dixon's lone dissent, the Council voted to make available $50 to each chapter for sending a student representative to the next National Chapter meeting and banquet. Fred Mueller was asked to contact Beta Mu regarding plans for a student program.

The resultant program was memorable not only because it brought a new group into the National Chapter. Thirty-eight official student delegates, and at least twenty other student members, attended the business meeting on August 23, 1976, and the banquet the next evening. Between those events,

the first National Student Meeting was held. Eminent accounting theorists R. J. Chambers of Sydney (in Australia) and Robert R. Sterling of Rice, the AAA's 1975-76 "Distinguished International Lecturers," addressed the assembled group in one of the best accounting programs Bob Maust had ever seen, and the highlight for Fred Mueller of the year's fraternal and association meetings. Afterwards, the host Georgia State chapter led workshops covering (a) motivation of members to participate in fraternal activities, and (b) contributions made by local units to professional education in accounting.

Coincidentally, the first Beta Alpha Psi "annual report" was distributed at the 1976 meetings. It had been prepared by President Maust and his wife Brenda after the fraternal leader had conferred in Seattle with Secretary-Treasurer Mueller on appropriate contents. The new reporting initiative was intended to help enhance fraternal visibility.

The handsome 1975-76 Annual Report included sixteen sections in as many letter-sized pages:

1. President's Report
2. Outstanding FVPs
3. Outstanding Chapters
4. Faculty Vice Presidents
5. Chapter Activity Program
6. New Chapters
7. Changes in National Council
8. Regional Meetings
9. AICPA-BAPsi Minority Scholarships
10. Accountant of the Year
11. Manuscript Contest
12. National Advisory Forum
13. Computerization of Membership Data
14. Past Presidents of National Council
15. Financial Section
16. General Information.

Photos accompanied items 3, 9, and 11, while no. 13 was a progress report on a national directory project. Pictures of the eight 1975-76 councilors and two incoming members appeared on a inside front cover, while a map depicting the locations of chapters appeared on its rear counterpart. Expanded to include new programs and activities, and more photos, yearly reports brought out by future presidents would be patterned substantially after the original one.

Banquet guests in 1976 included outgoing American Accounting Association President Wilton Anderson, his successor Charles Horngren, and incoming president-elect David Solomons. New fraternal leader Fred Mueller was recognized at the comparable association luncheon, as retiring president Hollis Dixon had been a year earlier. The registered AAA attendance, 1,776, was particularly appropriate for the nation's bicentennial year. As a particular irony in light of Anderson's long fraternal identification, the only negative feature of the meeting involved Beta Alpha Psi's relationship with the AAA.

First, the two-day program had coincided with the bulk of the association's own convention, a year after unidentified sources had complained to Dixon that the fraternity had "infring[ed]" somewhat on the AAA meeting at Tucson. Shortly after completing a two-year term as director of education, Leon Hay recalled in 1980 that his executive committee colleagues within the other organization had been concerned with "overlapping" and "impingement" from Beta Alpha Psi.

Second, the fraternity had booked a full floor at the Atlanta Hilton Hotel, leading the Hilton to turn away "special guests" for whom the American Accounting Association (meeting at the Hyatt Regency) had reserved space. Although it could have been viewed as a hotel blunder, this conflict also led to strained feelings.

The accommodations problem was avoided the following year in Portland, Oregon, as Beta Alpha Psi made "private arrangements" to solve a lodging shortage in connection with a student meeting attracting more than 70 representatives from 60 chapters. The scheduling conflict persisted through the meetings in Denver in 1978, however, although it had by then already been resolved for gatherings of the following year in a unique setting.

The 1979 meeting in Hawaii

Selection by the American Accounting Association of Waikiki Beach in Honolulu as its 1979 meeting site led the National Council to begin making pertinent plans two summers in advance. Due to their familiarity with Hawaii, and his slated retirement from the Council the following year, Fred Mueller and his wife Joy were in January 1978 placed in charge of planning the Beta Alpha Psi convention. It was already fully intented that the fraternity would conclude its program before the association's got underway, and past president Mueller was to announce a schedule suiting that objective a full year in advance. President Doris Cook had already related such a prospect to her AAA counterpart David Solomons, as the fraternity seems to have heeded (dual) fourth-era leader Herb Miller's advice to Mueller that it seek greater harmony with the other academic group. Due to the remote location, the fraternity for 1979, only, raised funding per FVP and official student representative from $100 (introduced for students two years earlier) to $200.

Joy Mueller had been "the most visibly active," since Lenore Miller, of several councilor wives from the fourth and fifth eras whose special interest in Beta Alpha Psi had led to a number of close family friendships within the governing body. Hollis Dixon states that she contributed much in his day to National Council morale, unity, and achievement. Directly before Dixon replaced Bob Wasley as secretary-treasurer, the Council had in 1971 expressed appreciation for Helen Wasley's support over the prior two years.

The 1979 meetings began on the island of Maui, where the National Council had assembled for business. That part of the program ended on a Sunday with the annual meeting with the National Advisory Forum. Presumably after

DELEGATES TO FIRST NATIONAL STUDENT MEETING, 1976, VISIT WITH SPEAKERS ROBERT R. STERLING (LEFT) AND R. J. CHAMBERS (RIGHT)

JOY MUELLER IN LIGHT-HEARTED CONVERSATION WITH
OMICRON STUDENT MEMBERS, 1979

a formal session at the Maui Surf Hotel, members of the two groups discussed Beta Alpha Psi matters while sipping drinks under the shade of palm trees, as they awaited the short trip to Honolulu for the national Chapter and student meetings. Several years later Hank Anderson recalled the occasion of being "locked on" the island together as the only time he had become really "close" to the Advisory Forum, whose members otherwise were subject to very tight schedules that left little time for informal visits.

The subsequent meetings at the Princess Kaiulani Hotel on Waikiki Beach attracted more than 200 students from a hundred chapters. The student program included panel sessions featuring three leading textbook authors; Herb Miller and AAA president Maurice Moonitz, at least, speaking on Beta Alpha Psi from an historical standpoint; and Vice Chairman Robert T. Sprouse discussing the Financial Accounting Standards Board. Moonitz and Sprouse had been faculty advisors to Lambda at Berkeley prior to their well-known collaboration of 1962 on the controversial _Accounting Research Study No. 3_ published, but not endorsed, by the American Institute of CPAs.

C. Aubrey Smith had been listed on the historical panel, but been unable to make the trip due to myocardial bypass surgery. Similarly listed in the official program but not the subsequent writeup was Robert K. Mautz, the former strong critic at Illinois of the activity program. Four years earlier in Tucson, numerous telephone calls intended for Mautz (mouts) had reached Robert Maust (mawst) instead, with the caller usually not waiting to find out if he or she had reached the right party, leading to the development of a "reasonably good friends[hip]" between the two accounting educators with similar names.

Opening with breakfast, the National Chapter meeting had become highly student oriented. Three hours of presentations and panels involving

councilors, forum members, and students were followed by regional planning sessions. Fred Mueller good-naturedly observed that he and Joy had built the hotel, arranged for the excellent weather and scenery, and otherwise provided the idyllic environment. The 1979 Beta Alpha Psi convention concluded with an evening banquet representing the sole overlap with the American Accounting Association meeting (disregarding forty-five minutes of one AAA business session). The association's special "Welcome to Hawaii" social function somewhat rankled Mueller, in light of the emphasis he had placed on removing any conflict between the two national meetings. A pivotal administrative linkage just underway between the two organizations signaled, however, the onset of a new fraternal era.[9]

---

[9]"AAA Committees," 1973-74, 1976-77 through 1979-80, The Accounting Review 49, 52-55 (January, 1974, 1977-80); "Accounting Hall of Fame," AAA Accounting Education News, March 1986, p. 13; [Henry R. Anderson], "Gamma Pi Chapter Hosts Eighth National Seminar," Newsletter 18 (Winter 1980):1; [Anderson], "Honolulu Hosts Fourth National Student Meeting," Newsletter 18 (Fall 1979):2; [Anderson], "Omicron Chapter Hosts Seventh National Student Seminar," Newsletter 17 (Winter 1979):1; [Anderson], "Second National Student Program Held," Newsletter 16 (Fall 1977):8; Anderson to Author, interview, April 18, 1986, quoted; Wilton T. Anderson to Author, interview, March 20, 1980, quoted; Barron's Profiles, s.v. "Utah, Brigham Young University"; Lee Berton, "News Feature: AAA's Portland Meeting Considers Key Issues Affecting the Profession," Journal of Accountancy 144 (October 1977):40,42; Beta Alpha Psi Annual Meeting: 1979, program, pp. 1-[3]; [Doris M. Cook], "Distinguished Guests at Annual Banquet," Newsletter 15 (Fall 1976):9; [Cook], "First National Student Program Held," Newsletter 15 (Fall 1976):8, quoted; [Joyce C. Dean], Secretary-Treasurer's Report, 1977-78, p. 1; Hollis A. Dixon, Secretary-Treasurer's Report, 1971-72, p. 1, 1972-73, pp. 2, 8; Dixon to Author, interview, March 22-23, 1980; Harvey E. Donley to Author, interview, May 2, 1980; "Grand Chapter: Chapter Representatives," Newsletter [3] (March 1951):3, 5, (April 1959):147; Grand Council Minutes, 1964, pp. 6-7; Grand Council Minutes Book, 1955, p. 5, 1956, p. 3, 1958, p. [4], 1962, p. 7 (reference to "Beta" Eta), 1952-63, listings of banquet participants; Leon E. Hay to Author, interview, May 2, 1980, quoted; "Local Chapter News," Newsletter [3] (May 1951):27, (November 1951):25; Robert S. Maust, Long-Range Planning Committee Minutes, December 1971, pp. 5-6; [Maust], ed., 1975-76 Annual Report; [Maust], "Omicron Hosts National Seminar," Newsletter 11 (Winter 1973):1; [Maust], "Quebec is Site of Annual Meeting," Newsletter 11 (Spring 1973):1; Maust to Author, interview, July 14, 1980 (quoted), by telephone, October 4, 1985 (quoted), and June 10, 1986; Herbert E. Miller

In Transition

A vital question from the fifth era that generally has not been addressed concerns how the National Council managed to pay for its remarkably expanded program. The principal innovation in that area was a product jointly of the fifth and sixth eras. Financial development highlighted by an external funding program represents one of three major themes identified for the concluding phase of this study, the partial era 1979-84, along with major national reorganization involving an element of paradox, and new programs for three major fraternal "constituencies."

---

to Author, interview, April 18, 1980; [Hermann C. Miller], "Meeting of Grand Chapter," Newsletter [2] (March 1939):5; Fred J. Mueller, invited remarks at National Chapter Meeting, August 21, 1979 (tape recorded); Mueller to Author, interview, November 27, 1979, quoted; National Council Minutes, 1965-69, National Chapter coverage, 1971, pp. 6-7, 9, August 1974, p. 1, December 1975, pp. 7-8 (quoted), 11, April 1976, p. 3, August 1976, p. 2, August 1977, p. 5, January 1978, pp. 2, 6-7, August 1978, p. 5, June 1979, p. 3, August 1979, p. 1, January 1982, p. 8; "News Report," Journal of Accountancy 138 (October 1974):7, 142 (October 1976):34; "Program Outline, 1979 Annual Meeting," Accounting Education News, 1979 Annual Meeting Issue (AAA), p. 1, quoted; [Harold L. Royer], "Toledo Jumps into Eight Point Lead in 1970-71 Chapter Activity Program," Newsletter 9 (Spring 1971):8; [Royer], "University of Utah Hosts National Council Convention," with accompanying inset, Newsletter 10 (Spring 1972):1; Sheldahl, Alpha to Omega, pp. 95, 98-106, 253-55; Michael A. Stein, Tau, "Tau Chapter Participates in the AAA Convention," Newsletter 9 (Fall 1970):1; [Charles W. Taylor], "Charter Members, Alpha to Gamma Xi," s.v. "Alpha Zeta, quoted; Robert S. Wasley, Long-Range Planning Committee Minutes, May 1971, p. 1; Wasley to A. J. Penz, May 31, 1972 (supplied by Penz); Wasley, Secretary-Treasurer's Report, 1970-71, pp. 6-7; [S. M. Wedeberg], "Grand Chapter News," Newsletter [3] (November 1951):4-6; [John Arch White], "Grand Chapter News," Newsletter [3] (November 1949):7, (November 1950):5; and Zeff, American Accounting Association, pp. 66-67. Also, Funk & Wagnalls, s.v. "Kinsey, Alfred Charles"; Grand Council Minutes Book, 1939, pp. 1, [7]; A. J. Penz to Author, February 15, 1984, quoted; and C. Aubrey Smith to Author, August 14, 1986 (postmark).

The idea of meeting each year, perhaps over dinner, with the faculty advisors "in attendance at the annual meeting of the" American Accounting Association was approved by the Grand Council in December 1930, eight years prior to the first recorded luncheon. The depressed economic conditions of the time presumably contributed to the delay. Grand Council Minutes Book, 1930, p. 3, quoted.

PART 4. THE DECENTRALIZED CONSOLIDATION (or SIXTH) ERA: THE FIRST FIVE YEARS, 1980-84

CHAPTER 15

EARLY YEARS OF "DECENTRALIZED CONSOLIDATION": A NATIONAL OFFICE, A TWO-LEVEL COUNCIL, AND MAJOR OUTSIDE FUNDING

As the fifth era drew to a close, a growing need and an opportunity converged for the National Council. Beta Alpha Psi had expanded in size and in scale of operations to the point that the establishment of a _central office_ to coordinate ongoing administration could not be deferred much longer. The opportunity was provided by the construction by the American Accounting Association in 1978 of an office building in Florida. Beginning in the spring of 1979, three AAA employees served the fraternity part time, in succession, until a full-time "national administrator" was hired midway through 1980.

The administrative "consolidation" made possible by the opening of a national office permitted reorganization that remade the existing Council as a "board of directors" featuring reduced faculty membership and tenure. At the very same time, the vital area of communication with local chapters was "decentralized," in part, through the creation of a new group of "area" councilors responsible for keeping the pulse of the fraternity on a regional basis.

The early years of the "Decentralized Consolidation Era" were consolidating in a second way. The board of directors solidified the much enlarged program inherited from the fifth era by recasting and expanding a major

fund-raising initiative of the late '70s. Also, as covered in the following (and final) chapter, the themes of participation and pluralism were enhanced through program innovations or refinements serving student members generally, graduate students, and alumni members. These developments were assisted by the substantial relief concerning routine operations afforded faculty councilors by the national office.

Principal Administrative Changes and Reforms

Establishment of a Central Office, with a Full-time Administrator

An "administrative liaison" with the AAA

Background, 1974-78

An abortive request of 1966-67 that the American Accounting Association conduct (for a fee) certain administrative functions for Beta Alpha Psi at its new offices in Evanston, Illinois was covered in chapter 9. Intermittent discussion over the period 1953-74 of the feasibility or desirability of establishing an executive secretaryship, and/or a central facility for file storage, was otherwise summarized in chapter 13.

During the year 1974-75, AAA president-elect Wilton Anderson proposed that the two organizations share offices and the services of a "permanent secretary." On that occasion, it was the fraternity that "declined" to pursue the matter, for the time being, without closing the door to reconsideration. It was felt that a councilor should handle the activity program, and that, not long after Fred Mueller had received half a ton of records, storage was not yet a problem.

In 1978, however, the association constructed an office building in Sarasota, Florida that increased available space by four fifths, and helped justify the addition of two full-time employees. Some months before the new office opened on December 1, Administrative Secretary Paul Gerhardt responded "favorabl[y]" to an inquiry made by Tom Burns on possible use of the facilities by Beta Alpha Psi. Also "receptive" to the idea were Anderson and, provided that acceptable arrangements could be made on fees and space utilization, President David Solomons.

At the August meeting in 1978, Burns reported that future (as executive director, 1982-85) AAA Advisory Forum representative Gerhardt had proposed an $8,000 yearly charge for an administrative linkage with the association, pending further clarification of fraternal needs. The National Council voted to meet the following winter in Sarasota to pursue the matter further. One issue raised was whether the transfer of functions to a "central office," if established, should occur all at once, as favored by Fred Mueller, or instead gradually, as preferred by incoming president Burns. Arrangements approved at the winter meeting would lead to a phased, but not lengthy, transition to the new setup.

Negotiation of arrangements and opening of office, in 1979

On January 4, 1979, President Thomas Burns, Secretary-Treasurer Joyce Dean, and Councilor Jack Kiger (scheduled to become chapter activities director in August) met with Paul Gerhardt at his new office in Sarasota. An agreement was reached, subject to approval by the full National Council and the association's executive committee, for the establishment of a Beta Alpha Psi national office at the American Accounting Association facility. The following day the Council unanimously approved the agreement, providing

for:

a. A fee of $8,000 plus applicable postage and (on a separate line) phone calls
b. The half-time services of Katherine A. Hayes, a recent Georgetown graduate who since September had coordinated AAA "special interest section activities," and was expected to be "a long-range employee"
c. Office space and, as needed, editor/proofreader services
d. Transfer virtually at once of secretary-treasurer clerical work; activity program administration in the fall; and Newsletter publication and distribution later on
e. Attendance by Hayes at all Council meetings, where she would keep notes of the proceedings, and coverage by the association of most of her expenses in Hawaii in August.

The preceding summer, retiring councilor Robert Maust had expressed concern that close affiliation with the AAA might jeopardize the fraternity's independent identity.[1] The individual phone line, and separate identification inside the building (and, as it would develop, outside as well), were intended to help minimize any such risk. The "administrative liaison agreement" was ratified by the association in late March.

---

[1]In an interview of late 1979, Fred Mueller stated that there had been some talk of reorganizing Beta Alpha Psi as a "section" of the American Accounting Association. Since 1976 seven subordinate organizations had been formed within the association based on disciplinary specialty (five cases), academic environment, or administrative role (identified, uniquely, as a "[g]roup"), and three more "sections" would be created in the early '80s. Katherine Hayes was just cited as coordinator of section activities. The administrative linkage established in 1979 might well have generated some thoughts of sectional status, although the absence of any reference within contemporary minutes implies that the matter was not seriously considered. Tom Burns felt that differences between the two groups in sources of national leadership would have prevented approval by the association in any case.

Former Beta Alpha Psi presidents who commented on the topic in 1980 interviews generally agreed with President Jim Pattillo that there was "no way" that the fraternity could become an AAA special interest group without losing the independence vital to its objectives. Andy Penz added the further objection that the association was already being "sectionalized to pieces," and (on a somewhat related point) Tom Burns noted the "structural" difference between "individual" association membership and "collective" fraternal affiliation, through a chapter. A dissenting favorable viewpoint on sectional status was expressed later by Harold Royer, whose belief that fraternal identity need not be jeopardized may have been based on Beta Alpha Psi's long independent existence. Among AAA sections, only the American Taxation Association, formed in 1974, had a prior identity. Thomas J. Burns

"Katie" Hayes was duly present at the June meeting of the National Council on Mackinac Island, in Michigan. Her designated responsibilities included ordering certificates and banners; receiving initiation reports; drawing up checks and vouchers to be forwarded for Secretary-Treasurer Joyce Dean's approval and signature; and, following a transfer of funds later in the summer, fraternal banking. Director of Chapter Activities James Pattillo explained that his successor would receive monthly reports on each chapter's progress so that he could investigate apparent problems.

Katherine Hayes abruptly resigned from the American Accounting Association staff shortly after the 1979 spring meeting, due to her husband's unexpected job transfer. Taking over as interim Beta Alpha Psi administrator in late June was Accounting Review production manager and copy editor Kenneth Matthews. A widely published author who had traveled extensively as a reporter for several years with The National Enquirer, Matthews was finishing a biography of circus promoter John Ringling. Sarasota had for a third of a century, beginning in 1929, been the winter home for the Ringling Brothers-Barnum and Bailey Circus, and was the site of the family mansion and a circus museum and hall of fame.

All permanent Beta Alpha Psi files held by Secretary-Treasurer Joyce Dean were shipped to Sarasota that summer, and set up at the new office by Dean and her secretary Evelyn Hupp. The secretary-treasurer arranged for

---

to Author, interview, May 3, 1980, quoted; Fred J. Mueller to Author, interview, November 27, 1979; James W. Pattillo to Author, interview, August 9, 1980, quoted; A. J. Penz to Author, interview, April 18, 1980, quoted; Harold E. Royer to Author, response to interview questionnaire, September 4, 1985, item V-B; and Stephen A. Zeff, "President's Message," AAA Accounting Education News, January 1986, pp. 3, 5, March 1986, pp. 1, 3 (quoted).

substantially complete series of national constitutions and financial reports, and 1978-79 National Council documents, to be transferred to the newly appointed fraternal historian on a visit to the office in August that would also yield files on Mu at New York and Alpha at Illinois underlying coverage in chapters 4 and 6.

At the August meeting in Hawaii, Ken Matthews showed photos of the AAA building revealing that Beta Alpha Psi had been identified on the outside. Later he pointed out to the faculty and chapter officers assembled for the National Chapter breakfast that a major purpose of the central office was to consolidate routine clerical duties under the national administrator, thus freeing time for councilors to address longer-range policy issues.

By this point all supplies relating to the activity program had been sent to Sarasota, and most chapters had already begun sending their activity reports to the new office. By an interesting coincidence, daily control of the program had been passed outside the National Council just as the consequences of that responsibility had been substantially expanded by the creation of the $1,000 scholarship awards for superior chapters. In his remarks to the National Chapter, Jack Kiger stressed that although the national administrator would be processing the reports, he would as director take full responsibility for activity program administration. He also reminded the audience that all reports should be submitted to central headquarters, and hinted that his patience in forwarding material sent him instead might wear thin after he had written a chapter on the matter three times.

Interim appointee Kenneth Matthews held the fraternal post only six more months, although his tenure would exceed those of his successor and predecessor combined. Before the next national meeting was convened, a

full-time national administrator was on board who would prove to be a "long-range employee."

Major developments, 1979-84

The first full year, capped by Nancy Harke's full-time appointment

Matthews resumed full-time service with the association in late February of 1980. At the winter meeting the prior month, he had distributed a written report on national office administration, and Professor Kiger had noted that through forwarding he was seeing a '"reasonable number"' of chapter activity reports, enabling him to keep current on the activity program. During his stint with the fraternity Ken Matthews had found a printer willing to supply membership certificates for $.99, at a time at which the National Council was paying $2.25. The current printer had consequently reduced the price to a dollar, yielding an immediate annual savings, in a day of some 8,000 new members a year, of around $10,000.

The third national administrator was Janice L. Gonzalez, also serving the American Accounting Association as its first meetings and convention director. After less than four months, however, she resigned in June to take a post with the local Chamber of Commerce. Her prospective replacement Nancy Harke, already on the job on a trial basis, was present when the National Council assembled in Sarasota in June for the spring meeting. After reviewing a report submitted by Gonzalez concerning "the volume of work currently processed through the National Office," the Council unanimously approved the appointment of a full-time administrator. Harke was duly hired before the 1980 annual convention, and was still in office six years later.

The transfer of administrative and certain publication functions would

be completed, and office facilities be substantially upgraded, during Nancy Harke's first three years as administrator.

Completion of the transfer of duties,
and upgrading of office facilities

Beginning with the 1980-81 winter issue, the Newsletter was printed in Florida and distributed from there. The year's president continued to arrange for publication of the annual report, as well as taking full responsibility for its preparation, until Dick Metcalf's report was printed in Sarasota in 1984. The original plans were to transfer some responsibility for Newsletter composition to the national administrator, consistent with formats laid out by the editor. Partly based on concern expressed at her final Council meeting by former editor Doris Cook, however, that idea was abandoned during her successor Henry Anderson's last year, 1980-81, in the role. While serving in turn as chairman, acting dean, and dean at California State, Fullerton, Anderson had regularly worked with a team of students in preparing for distribution by bundling thousands of copies in stacks of 50-100 each. After the transfer of the other function, he composed his last issue in a conference room filled with source materials.

Checkwriting authority and general bookkeeping duties were finally moved to Sarasota in 1982-83, more than two years after National Advisory Forum member Madie Ivy of Peat Marwick in New York had offered the assistance of her firm in making the bookkeeping transition. A long-term "national directory" project discussed later was assigned a permanent home in Florida the same year. In 1983 the national administrator assumed responsibility for handling registration and making hotel arrangements for the annual convention.

Until the AAA building was enlarged in 1981, Beta Alpha Psi shared a small office with an association employee. The addition yielded a separate office for the fraternity, and two years later, by which point the staff included two part-time assistants, much larger quarters were obtained at the opposite end of the building. The rental agreement provides also for some storage space elsewhere in the building, and the fraternity shares use of the association's mailroom and answering service. Nancy Harke was authorized in 1982 to expend up to $12,000 for an IBM microcomputer and appropriate software, and a Diablo printer was purchased within the same context.

In 1983 student members Charles Caldwell, Sarah LaMarche, and Joe Zeoli of Delta Gamma at South Florida, located some fifty miles to the north in Tampa, conducted an important study that documented national office procedures in detail for inclusion in a National Council policies and procedures manual. Accounting systems and managerial accounting professor Jerry D. Siebel was the faculty consultant for a project that was supported through payment for mileage to a maximum of $500.[2]

---

[2] [Henry R. Anderson], ed., 1981-82 Annual Report, pp. 2 ("National Council"), 9 ("National Advisory Forum"); Anderson to Author, interview, April 18, 1986; "Beta Alpha Psi News," p. 4 (quoted), "New AAA Office Building," p. 6, Accounting Education News, vol. 6, May 1979; [Thomas J. Burns], "New National Office," 1978-79 Annual Report, ed. [Burns], p. 24; Funk & Wagnalls, s.v. "Sarasota"; Paul L. Gerhardt to Author, July 14, 16, 1986; Nancy Harke to Author, July 8 (postmark), 11 (by telephone), 16, August 4, 1986; Hasselback, 1984 Directory, individual listing, s.v. "Siebel, Jerry D."; Jack E. Kiger, invited remarks at National Chapter Meeting, August 21, 1979 (tape recorded); [Jack E. Kiger], "National Office and Administration," Beta Alpha Psi, The National Accounting Fraternity: 1982 - 1983 Annual Report, ed. [Kiger, (Knoxville, Tenn.: Graffix, for National Council, 1983)], p. 21; Kenneth Matthews, report on national office, National Chapter Meeting, August 21, 1979; Matthews to Author, July 9, August 30 (conversation in Sarasota), 1979; [Metcalf], ed., 1983-84 Annual Report, title and contents page; National Council Minutes, February 1975, p. 1, June 1978, p. 4, August 1978, p. 3 (all quoted), January 1979, pp. 1 (quoted), 2,

AMERICAN ACCOUNTING ASSOCIATION AND BETA ALPHA PSI
HEADQUARTERS, IN SARASOTA (first fraternal office)

EXECUTIVE SECRETARY NANCY HARKE, AND THE THREE PRIOR NATIONAL ADMINISTRATORS

NANCY C. HARKE

KATHERINE A. HAYES

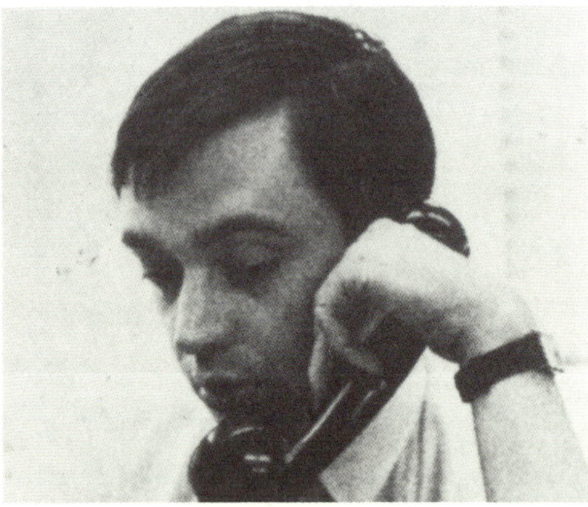

KENNETH MATTEWS

JANICE L. GONZALEZ

The national administrator or (as retitled in 1985) "[e]xecutive [s]ecretary" serves under the supervision of the national "director of administration." Reference to that office draws attention to the modern-day "Board of Directors," reflecting one of two basic structural revisions of the National Council originating in 1980 airport-related sessions that featured a councilor Anderson.

Twofold Restructuring of the National Council, Traced to Airport(-area) Meetings Featuring Respective Councilors Anderson

Tom Burns' 1980 call for fundamental change, striking a responsive chord

In January 1980, Past President Tom Burns proposed that the Council be expanded, and the faculty term be shortened. In response, the formation of a relevant "study group" was unanimously approved. Burns' recommendations, though mutually incompatible based on the long practice of defining the tenure in years by the number of members, recognized two hard facts. First, as remarked some weeks later by retired councilor Hollis Dixon, members generally were "drain[ed]" after seven years in office. Second, even the opening of the national office could not assure the National Council, as constituted, sufficient time adequately to handle ongoing fraternal operations, keep in touch with local chapters, and consider policy matters of the longer range.

In essence, then, the call was for structural change more basic than had occurred in the sixties, when a separate editorship and an additional

---

June 1979, p. 1, August 1979, p. 2, January 1980, pp. 2 (quoted), 3, 8, June 1980, p. [5, quoted], August 1980, p. 8, January 1981, p. 2, June 1981, p. 11, August 1981, p. 6, June 1982, pp. 5-6, August 1982, p. 6, January 1983, pp. 1-2, 6, June 1983, p. 6; and "Staff Changes," Accounting Education News 7 (May 1980):7.

slot had been created; or even the seventies, when comparable expansion of faculty membership had been accompanied by the addition of two short-term nonfaculty posts. At an airport hotel in Chicago, a committee headed by fourth-era councilor Wilton Anderson developed recommendations that yielded the National Council expansion sought by Tom Burns by way of a new kind of position having geographically defined responsibility. At the airport in Sarasota, a thoroughly ad hoc committee composed of Henry Anderson and two fellow councilors very quickly drafted a proposal leading to the desired reduction in length of the regular term. Because it embodied less drastic change, the latter redefinition of the existing Council as a fraternal "Board of Directors" is discussed first.

The "Board of Directors"--Reduced faculty membership and terms, conceived by a very ad hoc committee

In an interview of March 1980, senior councilor Doris Cook commented that it would not be enough to reduce the term from seven years to six, its length when she was appointed in 1973. A few months later the regular term was cut to five years, effective with the member elected in 1982.

The format had been developed in an unlikely setting. Following the 1980 spring meeting, Hank Anderson, Jack Kiger, and Dick Metcalf found themselves briefly stranded at the Sarasota airport awaiting delayed flights. The three most junior councilors of the day took advantage of the free time by working out a structure for a "board" consisting of five professors, plus the forum chairperson and alumni representative.

Supplied with pen or pencil and the back of an envelope, the "airport committee" developed in thirty minutes a format that would be adopted with changes only in detail. Anderson remarked later that it would have taken

six months to make such progress through regular operating procedure.

It was recognized, first, that the shift of various secretary-treasurer, activities program, and editor responsibilities to the national administrator had or would recast the three multi-year offices as in one degree or another "directorships." Hence the secretary-treasurer was renamed the Director of Administration, having supervisory authority over the administrator in Sarasota; and the editor, whose functions would change less than was then anticipated, was designated additionally as Director of Publications. The chapter activities post was already known as a directorship.

Second, the absence of any defined duties for the past presidents indicated a ready means of reducing faculty membership by two, and the term by two years. It was necessary only to reassign the directorship of regional meetings from the new councilor to the immediate past president, and assign the vacant three-year directorship each year to the incoming member. As a result, a faculty councilor would serve three years as director of administration, chapter activities, or publications; one year as president; and a final year as director of regional meetings.

The new design was implemented in 1981 through the retirement of Jim Pattillo, the sixth-year councilor, along with Tom Burns, and the nonappointment of a new academic member. Junior councilor David Tinius assumed the publications directorship vacated by new president Hank Anderson, and like all other transitional faculty councilors would serve (like Pattillo) for six years. Past President Joyce Dean completed her term as the director of regional meetings.

In light of the unavailability of his designated successor Paul Dillingham, forum chairperson Tom Nessinger agreed to remain in office through the transitional year 1981-82. In 1983 two significant changes were made at

the alumni level, generally in keeping with suggestions made during their terms by Councilors Leroy Tanker, 1977-78, and Andrew J. Rosman, 1981-82.

First, the alumni term was extended from one year to two. Second, another alumni councilor was added. Only the second-year, or "senior," representative enjoyed voting privileges, although according to initial plans a "junior" member would enter the board at the spring meeting (as did Debra Beck, then known as Debra B. Shanley, of Beta Pi at North Texas State in 1983), and begin voting the following winter. The senior representatives of 1983-85 served as the regional meeting director, a particularly unstable appointment that would be reassigned yet again in '85. By that point the junior/senior distinction had been abandoned, and both councilors were voting members.

A highlight of the alumni position during the earlier years of the sixth era was the conduct of a special project. Omicron alumnus Nicholas S. Ecos, a 1977 manuscripts honoree (third-place tie) as a junior who had been chapter president and held two professional internships at Ohio State, was in 1979-80 the first alumni representative from industry. In two years with highly diversified and decentralized Textron Inc., prior to entering the Harvard Business School in 1980, he worked on the internal audit staff and held a nine-month assignment with the chief financial officer.

Councilor Ecos conducted an innovative nationwide survey of corporations that identified at least a hundred firms that were definitely or potentially interested in participating in Beta Alpha Psi activities at the chapter level, a project that was probably extended in 1980-81 by Anne K. Robertson of Delta Gamma at South Florida. Ecos was also active as a link between student members and faculty councilors, serving in respective appearances at regional meetings as a formal speaker and "an active member of the

audience."

Discussed later is an important survey by 1981-82 representative Andrew J. Rosman concerning alumni participation in Beta Alpha Psi. Charter two-year alumni councilor James R. Greisch (gresh) from Alpha Nu at Creighton announced that for his "senior . . . project" in 1983-84 he would derive a preferred model for chapter reporting from an examination of current activity program files, and review chapter performance in light of fraternal objectives. Those plans were abandoned, however, upon his subsequent appointment as regional meetings director. Greisch's 1984-85 successor in the latter post, Debra Beck, had earlier reviewed and suggested changes in the national office manual drafted by the Delta Gamma students at South Florida, and been instructed to update it on certain points.

The "Board of Directors" title not only excellently described the new structure, but also distinguished the modern-day version of the "traditional" National Council from a new group of councilors, "area" representatives, formed on the recommendation of a more formal airport-related committee.

<u>Creation of "area" councilorships, on the recommendation of Wilton Anderson's 1980 study group</u>

As noted earlier, the National Council had agreed in January 1980 to appoint a study group concerning reorganization. Those plans led to a gathering that spring of former president Wilton Anderson and Councilors James Pattillo, Thomas Burns, Thomas Nessinger, and Joyce Dean at the Hilton Hotel serving Chicago's O'Hare Airport. Anderson, who chaired the group, later credited Secretary-Treasurer Dean with having "had the best grasp of all the issues involved," and recalled the meeting as follows:

> During the morning session each member expressed his or her views[,] which appeared to be widely divergent. As the discussion of the various

> views progressed, the differences became narrower and narrower. By lunch a consunsus appeared to be achievable. After lunch the members were able to agree on all points. Members were able to return to their homes on earlier than planned flights.

The standpoint that emerged called for "focus[ing] more responsibility in the various regions, because [the] National Council seemed rather remote from local chapters" (emphasis added). Specifically, Anderson's committee recommended that regional, or "area," representatives serving relatively short terms be added to the Council to take special responsibility for communication with the local units. With only minor modification, their entire proposal was approved at the August meeting. One issue initially in dispute, but resolved negatively at (it appears) the August session, was whether the new councilors would have voting privileges.

The approach developed split the National Council into an operating board of directors, as characterized above, and an advisory team of area members better situated to keep the pulse of the fraternity at regional and local levels. The result was to add a significant measure of decentralized control to the administrative centralism provided by the national office.

With regionalism already well established within Beta Alpha Psi, the 1980-81 Council, roughly speaking, combined adjacent regions in pairs to produce five areas comparable in chapter population. To be more exact, Areas 1-5 were defined as follows:

1. Northeast, New York City (in its last year of regional identity), and Ohio (still in the Midwest region)
2. Southeast
3. Midwest (minus Ohio) and Missouri Valley
4. Southern California-Arizona and Southwest
5. Northwest, Northern California-Nevada, and Rocky Mountain.

With Ohio's regional transfer in 1983, areas 1 and 3 became simply the Northeast, and the Midwest and Missouri Valley combined.

Each chapter in an area was assigned one vote in electing a councilor from a slate approved by the Board of Directors based on the recommendation of the three senior members. As with prospective board members, candidates would be contacted prior to formal nomination to confirm their availability to serve. In 1985 each chapter's voting strength was doubled to reflect its dual faculty and student National Chapter membership.

Responsibilities of area councilors were defined by a committee during the year before the first group took office.

Functions of area councilors

The committee made up of Henry Anderson, Jack Kiger, and David Tinius laid out six functions or duties at the 1981 spring meeting. The list had been slightly refined by August, when the following responsibilities were cited:

a. Coordination of, and attendance at, pertinent regional meetings
b. Availability to local chapters, as expressed through contacting each of them at least annually, and assisting those performing poorly
c. Monitoring of local "feelings" on National Council operations, and reporting of relevant concerns and ideas to appropriate board members
d. Service on manuscript contest committees, and on other committees as requested
e. Meeting with the board, as a group, during the annual convention.

Meeting with the Board of Directors during the 1981 annual gathering, the charter area councilors were brought up to date on the 1981-82 Beta Alpha Psi program. Two of them were assigned to the coordinating committee for the new "graduate case analysis competition," as discussed later. In 1983 the board agreed that area councilors should, as feasible, participate in site visitations to petitioning schools, only to decide the following winter that they should endeavor instead to visit new chapters during their first year of operation--thus reviving one component of "regular" visitation.

The area councilor role concerning regional meetings was reaffirmed and clarified in June 1984. It included managing and approving the selection of the "preliminary plan and topic" for each meeting in the area; and coordinating the preparation of reimbursement reports by host chapters, and reviewing and approving them for submission to the regional meetings director. Two months later, finally, the board decided to ask area councilors to meet with selected members the following January in Sarasota to discuss a number of topics. It was felt that

> it would be productive for the area councilors to have greater interaction with current national officers, see the National Office, talk to each other to gain cohesiveness, and to feel they are noticed, needed, and are able to get support.

President David Tinius reported very favorably at the 1984-85 winter meeting on the session with area councilors held on schedule a week earlier.

Two-year terms were set for area councilors, although to provide for staggered terms two of the original representatives were designated to serve a single year. These arrangements were changed somewhat before the 1982 elections, which in moving one charter area person to the other branch of the National Council led to the <u>appointment</u> of a councilor who, after election in his own right, would take a more independent course than desired.

Original area councilors, and a controversial replacement

The original area representatives were (1) Richard J. Murdock of Omicron at Ohio State, (2) Adolph A. "Ade" Neidermeyer of Alpha Psi at West Virginia, (3) Robert E. Bennett of Gamma Pi at Northern Illinois, (4) Katherine M. "Kaye" Horstmann from Gamma Phi of Texas at Arlington, and (5) E. Dee Hubbard of Gamma Alpha at Brigham Young. The first three new councilors had won the Outstanding Faculty Vice President Award, the second one in

1980-81.

The area 3 and 4 representatives were designated for retirement after one year, to permit a regular cycle of area elections. As it developed, Murdock was elected to the Board of Directors in 1982, requiring a special appointment for the completion of his unexpired term. Although a constitutional bylaw had been adopted prohibiting area councilors from serving consecutive terms, there was no restriction against moving directly from an area post to the governing board.

The replacement in the Northeast was Vincent P. Kopy of Gamma Eta at Akron, who was subsequently elected in 1983 to a full term. Kopy's service to Beta Alpha Psi went back much further than his tenure as faculty vice-president at Akron, 1977-82. He had held the same post at Western Reserve during the years 1962-65, preceding the federation with Case Institute. Pi Chapter's perennial problem of heavy reliance on part-time students had received attention from the Grand Council of that day. As noted in chapter 12, the evening-school environment was a secondary topic discussed by Robert Wasley's 1968-69 committee on branch-campus programs.

More revelantly in terms of his councilor appointment, Kopy had in 1980 earned Outstanding FVP recognition in the midst of complete domination by Gamma Eta of the three-year "public interest" award. As indicated in a chapter 13 note, the latter program had been discontinued in 1981 due to very limited participation.

In 1984, the Board of Directors noted certain problems concerning Professors Kopy's service that might warrant his resignation. He was cited specifically for (a) continued involvement in the activities of his local chapter; (b) "lobbying for Ohio regional status"; and (c) "severe" public

NATIONAL COUNCILS OF 1982 AND 1983, INCLUDING AREA COUNCILORS

Pictured above are (left to right) Front row: Andrew J. Rosman, Alumni Representative, 1981-82; Richard W. Metcalf, Director of Administration; Henry R. Anderson, Past National President; Joyce C. Dean, Past National President 1981-1982; E. Dee Hubbard, Area 5 Councilor; and Katherine M. Horstmann, Area 4 Councilor, 1981-1982. Second row: David E. Tinius, Director of Publications/Newsletter Editor; Richard J. Murdock, Director of Chapter Activities; William R. Welke, Area Councilor; Nancy Harke, National Administrator; Ulyesse J. LeGrange, Chairman, National Advisory Forum; Vincent P. Kopy, Area 1 Councilor, and Jack E. Kiger, National President. Third row: Robert E. Bennett, Area 3 Councilor, 1981-1982; H. Ronald Pitt, Area 4 Councilor; Thomas J. Nessinger, Chairman National Advisory Forum, 1980-1983; Adolph A. Neidermeyer, Area 2 Councilor, and James R. Greisch, Alumni Representative.

Correction - Nessinger served during the years 1979-82.

criticism of national fraternal policy. The first issue had been raised nine years earlier by an Ohio State colleague concerning Thomas Burns' relationship to Omicron during his first year on the National Council. It seems that Burns had not immediately resigned as chapter FVP upon his election to national office; and had continued throughout the year "to actively help" the local unit. He had satisfactorily explained that he had not at first been aware that a councilor was barred from FVP service; and had stepped down immediately upon being so advised, continuing to assist the chapter in support of his successor Richard Murdock, then still a doctoral candidate.

Regarding "regional status," Richard Metcalf had proposed shortly after Ohio's transfer to the Northeast in 1983 that a new "Ohio Valley" region be formed, but his motion had been defeated. Since the Ohio River flows nearly a thousand miles from Pittsburgh to the Mississippi, at Cairo, Illinois, forming the boundaries between West Virginia and Ohio and between three states and Kentucky, all or part of several states would have been involved.

Vincent Kopy was directly questioned on the matters of concern between the June and August meetings of 1984, and agreed to discontinue each of the activities objected to. He completed his regular term a year later, by which time the ten Ohio chapters had ironically been allowed to choose their region. Seven of them, including Gamma Eta at Akron, but not Omicron at Ohio State, had by January 1985 opted for Midwest classification. The full state continued to be classified with the Northeast for "area" purposes, evidently, as the regional relocation of his home chapter did not affect Kopy's councilorship, and one of the three candidates to succeed him was likewise from an Ohio chapter that had joined the Midwest region.

Coincidentally, an area councilor having a secondary Ohio connection

resigned in midterm in 1985, namely, area 2 representative Eugene Willis of Alpha at Illinois, a doctoral alumnus of Cincinnati. Also in 1985, retiring area 2 councilor Robert M. Brown of Gamma Lambda at Virginia Tech was appointed to a new one-year renewable post as "Councilor at Large." Constituting a free-standing directorship of regional meetings, that position marked the sixth different identity in eight years (counting the past president twice) for the regional coordinating post. The board had decided that it was unfair to impose such a responsibility on an alumni councilor, who as such was in the formative stages of a professional career.[3]

The scale of fraternal operations that developed during the seventies and early eighties required not only significant increases in rates (at least in terms of nominal dollars) for conventional internal sources of funding, but also the creation of major external sources. The first three

---

[3] [Henry R. Anderson], "Outstanding Faculty Vice Presidents for 1979-80," Newsletter 19 (Fall 1980):4; Anderson to Author, interview, April 18, 1986; Wilton T. Anderson to Author, July 5, 1986, quoted, including 1st indented citation; Beta Alpha Psi, "National Bylaws," National Constitution and Bylaws (1983), article 11, sections 1-4, 7-8, (1985), article 12, section 8; chapter 13, note 6; [Joyce C. Dean], "National Council," 1980-81 Annual Report, p. 6; Hollis A. Dixon to Author, interview, March 22-23, 1980, quoted; Nicholas S. Ecos, Industrial Survey Report: National Council of Beta Alpha Psi, August, 1980 ([National Council, 1980]), 9 pages; Ecos, remarks as National Chapter Meeting panelist, August 21, 1979 (tape recorded); Ecos to Author, interview (Boston, Mass.), August 10, 1980; Funk & Wagnalls, s.v. "Ohio [all capitals], river of the United States"; Grand Council Minutes Book, 1962, p. 4, 1963, p. 3; Hasselback, 1984 Directory, individual listing, s.v. "Horstmann, Kaye M.," "Willis, Eugene"; [Leon E. Hay], Secretary-Treasurer's Report, 1966, p. 9; National Council Minutes, August 1975, pp. 10 (quoted), 11, June 1978, p. 4, January 1980, p. 7 (quoted), June 1980, pp. [4], [10], August 1980, pp. 3, 6, January 1981, pp. 4-5, 12-13, June 1981, pp. 5-6, August 1981, pp. 1-2, June 1982, pp. 1-2, August 1982, pp. 2, 7, January 1983, pp. 9, 11 (quoted), June 1983, p. 6 (quoted), August 1983, p. 4, January 1984, p. 11, June 1984, pp. 1, 11, August 1984, pp. 3 (quoted), 8 (2nd indented citation), January 1985, pp. 1, 3, 6, 12-13 (quoted); Kirk Salisbury, "National Council Alumni Member: Nicholas S. Ecos," The Sun, Omicron newsletter, Winter 1980, p. 3; [Tinius], 1984-85 Annual Report, pp. 17 (". . . Regional Meetings"), 20-26 ("Chapter Information"), 30 ("National Council"); and [Vern H. Vincent], Secretary's Report, 1964-65, p. 8.

chairpersons of the National Advisory Forum played prominent leadership roles in the latter regard, and a number of accounting and business firms represented thereon were active participants.

Funding of the Modern-day Program

Initiation Fees, and Other Conventional Sources

Until outside funding became available, beyond Arthur Anderson's support for the annual faculty vice-president awards, initiation fees for student and honorary members represented the vast bulk of fraternal revenue. Omitting respective FVP provisions of $1,000 and $2,500, they provided $49,000 of 1973-74 revenues totaling $54,822, and $65,585 of the overall amount of $71,291 reported the following year. The difference was based largely on an increase of the fee from $10, a level reached through a one-third boost in 1971, to $12. The initiation charge was raised to $14 in 1978, and in one fell swoop, over the dissents of Hank Anderson and Jim Pattillo, to $20 three years later. Almost entirely due to the latter adjustment, initiation revenue rose slightly more than $50,000 in 1981-82, to a total of some $165,000, ten times the level recorded at the close of the fourth era a dozen years earlier. Yet under the markedly changed financial conditions of the day, that figure constituted barely more than half of overall revenues for the year.

Charter fees were raised from $100 to $250 in 1972, and reached three times that amount (for new petitioners) in 1980 after having been doubled five years earlier. The highest proceeds from this source were earned during the (fiscal) year 1977-78, when the remarkable total of fourteen installations yielded $7,000. Even that total did not cover current costs of site visitation and installation, although the deficit of less than five

per cent was lower than usual.

Interest income was generated during the seventies on a variety of investments. On August 1, 1973, for example, the fraternity had holdings of $20,000 each in federal national mortgage bonds and U.S. treasury bills, yielding 7.9 and 7.85%, respectively, and certificates of deposit paying 6.25%. Interest earnings had slightly topped $4,000 in the year recently ended. Such income was marginally higher two years later when maturing investments included United States treasury bills and notes and a time certificate of deposit, and some $78,000 in year-end holdings were split almost equally among bank-corporation bonds, a savings certificate, and a savings account. On the eve of the certificate's maturity in the summer of 1975, Secretary-Treasurer Fred Mueller placed $25,000 in ten-year bonds of a bank holding company in Washington, paying 4% higher at 9.5.

Just before the fifth era closed, Joyce Dean was authorized in June 1979 to invest "excess savings and cash" in "the ready-assets program of Merrill Lynch, Pierce, Fenner & Smith" in Waco, Texas (emphasis supplied). The secretary-treasurer immediately placed $75,000 in such a trust fund in a transaction that utilized proceeds from a savings certificate valued eleven months earlier at approximately $31,400, and reduced the ending cash balance to less than one third the beginning level of some $44,700. As of June 30, 1984, temporary cash investments totaled $81,040, more than three times the cash balance, and the $25,000 ten-year bond acquired in 1975 was still held by the fraternity. Interest revenue for the year just ended exceeded $8,000, compared with approximately $13,600 the preceding year and $5,400 in 1978-79.[4]

---

[4]Hollis A. Dixon, Secretary-Treasurer's Report, 1972-73, p. 13; "Financial Report," Annual Reports, 1978-79, pp. 26-27, 1981-82, p. 35,

The primary financial developments of the fifth and sixth eras, through 1984, concerned two significantly different external funding programs in which the National Advisory Forum played a prominent role. The first one involved identification of funding sources with individual "special projects," building on a notable precedent established in 1970.

External Funding Identifying Donors with Particular "Special Projects"

Background and early developments

When the National Advisory Forum was created in 1974, external funding within the fraternity was limited to the Outstanding Faculty Vice President Awards supported by the Arthur Andersen Foundation. During the 1973 annual meeting, Fred Mueller had volunteered to explore possible acquisition of "matching funds" from Big 8 accounting firms. Before contributions made by individual partners or staff employees could be "matched," however, they would have to be generated; and there was no ready way for the National Council to identify alumni members attached to the firms. There is no record of any yield from Mueller's proposed initiative.

Two years later, in August 1975, retiring president Hollis Dixon asserted that Beta Alpha Psi had reached its "highcrest of the past 15 years," and that programs already underway or planned could be "very expensive," to the tune for example of $10,000 a year for regional meetings (an estimate quickly to prove much too low). He recommended that the Council strive to maintain a year's costs as a "reserve," a goal that would not

---

1983-84, pp. 29-30; Fred J. Mueller, Secretary-Treasurer's Report, 1974-75, pp. 17-18, 1975-76, p. 21; National Council Minutes, 1970, p. 10, 1972, p. 8, May-June, 1975, p. 10, January 1978, pp. 5-6, June 1979, p. 1 (quoted), January 1980, p. 5, January 1981, pp. 5-6; and [Robert S. Wasley], Secretary-Treasurer's Report, 1969-70, p. [1]2, "Financial Analysis."

be feasible in the high-expenditure days that lay ahead. At the same meeting, Fred Mueller was asked to draft a statement of Beta Alpha Psi "financial philosophy," and Tom Burns proposed that "packages for funding" be submitted to the Advisory Forum.

The reference made to the forum signaled the onset of the first phase of developing a funding program, 1975-77, revolving around the issue of whether donor firms should be identified specifically with funded projects, a topic on which the forum's chairperson held strong views. A somewhat amusing prologue involved the only established funding program of the day, soon to become entangled within the debate.

The first phase, 1975-77: Controversy concerning specific identification with donor firms

Prologue--Inadvertant deviations in announcing 1974 and 1975 FVP awards

The origination in 1970 of the Richard S. Claire Award for Outstanding Faculty Vice Presidents was covered in Chapter 10. It was explained that both the National Council and the Arthur Andersen Foundation awarded plaques to honored professors, and that the outside party also provided a $500 cash prize, raised to $750 in 1977. The checks themselves were drawn on the fraternal account, as the foundation made an annual contribution to cover the sum total.

In 1974, the Council approved James Caldwell of Beta Delta at Texas Tech, Charles P. Skaggs of Alpha Psi at West Virginia, and Metwalli "Walli" Amer of Beta Phi at California State, Sacramento for the 1974 awards. In announcing the honorees at the National Chapter banquet in New Orleans three months later, President Hollis Dixon omitted Skaggs and, probably, one of the other designated winners, while citing both Jack Kiger of Beta Upsilon

at Georgia and James Solano of Alpha Phi at Temple as award recipients. The personalized National Council plaques available for presentation were naturally not suited, in full, for the announced winners.

Skaggs was ironically a close personal friend of Dixon's. He was also a colleague and former teacher of Councilor Bob Maust's. As the local FVP during the councilorship of another West Virginia colleague and former teacher, Vern Vincent, Maust had some years earlier drawn a mental blank when asked at another national banquet to identify his chapter. The embarrassment had been compounded by the presence of "Alpha Psi" within the fraternal name.

At a "confab" held directly after the 1974 banquet, the Council agreed that the Claire award should be presented to Kiger and Solano as well as all three faculty advisors originally designated. Bob Maust recalls running out of LePavillon Hotel to catch up with an "omitted" winner, and ask him to return for picture taking.

Hollis Dixon's "ad hoc" selections fortunately were very defensible. James Solano had led his chapter to recognition as one of the nation's two most improved units of 1973-74, and been tapped for the chapter activity program review committee that would meet in New Orleans the following winter. Jack Kiger had sustained the strong record of chapter performance at Georgia established by his eventual National Council successor Jan Williams, and after having organized the first Southeast regional program would in 1975 join Jim Caldwell as a regional coordinator. Furthermore, both Alpha Phi and Beta Upsilon had been counted among the eight outstanding chapters of 1973-74.

The next year, at home in Tucson, two-term president Dixon made an omission of a different kind in identifying the outstanding faculty advisors of 1975. At that banquet, he made no reference to Richard S. Claire, the Authur Andersen partner in whose memory the award had so appropriately been

named. As recalled by Tom Burns, current partner Herb Miller "went through the floor," so to speak, in reaction to the perceived slight to the deceased individual and the firm. Arthur Andersen forum representative Claude Rogers was "visibly upset," and made a point of expressing his concern afterwards to incoming president Bob Maust.[5]

From all indications, Dixon's failure to mention Mr. Claire had been no more deliberate than his deviations in announcing the award winners a year earlier. For example, the Newsletter writeup in the fall showed no change in the high level of visibility given the sponsoring organization and its late partner. By coincidence, however, the event foreshadowed a policy controversy that would be launched at a pivotal meeting of a few months later by the charter forum chairperson, and give rise to further concern on the part of the donor organization.

Raising of the issue, and deciding on first steps, December 1975

At the 1975-76 winter meeting, in late December, President Robert Maust reported two significant developments concerning outside funding of Beta Alpha Psi activities. First, National Advisory Forum member Robert Pivik had indicated that Haskins & Sells was ready to fund the student manuscript awards. Second, Advisory Forum member William Gifford had offered on behalf of the Price Waterhouse Foundation to supply $3,000 for publication of regional meetings' papers, perhaps after considering two other projects, including a new fraternal history; and his partner Albert Cohen had specified that the grant would be made anonymously, that is, "without recognition."

---

[5]The paragraph just concluded represents a composite of independent recollections expressed by two councilors, one of whom (Bob Maust) stated that at the 1975 ceremony the president had not mentioned donor Arthur Andersen. Thomas J. Burns to Author, interview, May 3, 1980, quoted (on Herbert Miller); and Robert S. Maust to Author, interview, July 14, 1980, by telephone, February 10, 1986 (quoted on Claude Rodgers).

Perhaps by happenstance, neither contribution would actually be made. In the latter case, regional papers would not appear in print until Doris Cook brought out the comprehensive 1979 volume mentioned in chapter 14, destined to be an isolated publication. It is nonetheless noteworthy that Gifford (or a staff member from the foundation) had been insistent that Price Waterhouse be publicly recognized for the planned donation, but in effect been overruled by forum chairperson Al Cohen. In keeping with the vital importance of the advisory body to any prospective fund-raising program, Councilor Cohen strongly influenced early discussion of the topic.

In his clear reluctance to seek professional or corporate funding for Beta Alpha Psi activities on any basis, Cohen was out of step with a national fraternity whose program was simply outgrowing internal sources of financing. His influence was reflected, however, in several unattributed points made at the meeting of late 1975. It was observed that it would be preferable "if firms' generosity were on a quieter basis"; that the National Council should consider "the ethical problem of having firms identified with specific [fraternal] programs"; and that "[p]erhaps endowments could be obtained from various donors and an announcement on the meeting program be made that some awards are underwritten." The most direct evidence that this advocacy of "pooled" funding took hold, at the time, lay in instructions given President Maust to contact Claude Rodgers to discuss how the Arthur Andersen FVP award could be accommodated within "a common funding pool for all awards."

Just over ten years later, Tulane executive-in-residence Albert Cohen explained his preference for a collective approach to external funding, forbidding specific identification of donors with projects, in terms of three arguments:

1. It promised "greater flexibility over time in allocating funds to projects"
2. It prevented competition among donors for the most '"glamorous"'

funding opportunities
3. It invited expansion of the donor group beyond firms able or willing to finance an activity in full.

The most important decision made 1975-76 winter meeting, relative to funding, was that a budget would be prepared for special projects, to be sent to potential donors with an explanation that the National Council would contribute at least one fourth of the amount. The budget developed the following summer would project higher internal funding. The current president and his designated successor had in the interim met with the aforementioned Arthur Andersen official in the course of forging an experimental compromise approach to donor identification for a structurally unique award.

The Arthur Andersen FVP award again: Forging a temporary policy compromise in 1976

On March 1, 1976, President Bob Maust and Secretary-Treasurer Fred Mueller met with Claude Rodgers at his office in Chicago. They had in all probability conferred on the matter earlier with Past President Hollis Dixon, who is known to have felt that the Arthur Andersen partner wished to maintain undue control over the FVP award funded by his firm. No record exists of the discussion that took place in Chicago slightly more than six months after Dixon had neglected to mention Richard Claire in presenting the 1975 awards. At the subsequent 1976 banquet in Atlanta, however, every effort was made to strike a precise balance or compromise between the viewpoints of Albert Cohen, who opposed specific donor identification, and the Arthur Andersen Foundation, which expected such recognition for the faculty advisor honor that it had largely created.

The approach taken was to draw a sharper distinction than had been made previously between the "Beta Alpha Psi Outstanding Faculty Vice President

Award" conferred by the National Council, and the "Richard S. Claire Award" presented by Arthur Andersen. The writeups in the initial Annual Report and, subsequently, the fall Newsletter implied that they were separate honors that as a matter of policy were given to the same individuals. In the former case, also, no reference was made to the $500 stipend, although the foundation was credited with funding the Claire award.

This attempted compromise was probably doomed to failure, in terms of satisfying the conflicting interests involved. It diminished specific donor identification with the program without removing it. The problem was that in doing so it risked some offense to the sponsor, through drawing an artificial distinction, without providing a model for future funded programs.

Specifically, the FVP honor was a unique case in that from the outset the Council had awarded a plaque at the annual banquet, prior to local presentation of another plaque, and the check, by an Arthur Andersen representative. There was no reason to expect other funded projects to have a dual structure of that (or a similar) kind. Even in the case in question the compromise implied an artificially firm distinction between what were really only different facets of one and the same program.

Without mentioning the subtle change being made that year, the National Council had during the August meeting discussed two alternatives to the "present procedure" of dual national and local presentation, on either of which both checks and plaques would be presented at the annual banquet. One of them would have retained the Arthur Andersen connection, in accented form, by conferring the "Richard S. Claire Award" at the banquet. The other one would have severed the linkage between the "Outstanding Faculty Vice President Award" and the accounting firm (or foundation), leaving it free on its own discretion to continue to honor the FVPs on their home campuses.

The first special-projects "budget" was adopted in 1976 on the premise that the faculty honor would be conferred on the latter basis, that is, independently of Arthur Andersen. Yet in actual fact the "present procedure" would be retained, stripped of the questionable effort just cited to straddle the fence on specific identification. In announcing the 1977 awards, the fraternity restored full recognition as sponsor to Arthur Andersen, and the following year the existence of a single honor with multiple dimensions was stated more clearly still.

The surface significance of this reinstatement of unequivocal association of donor and specific project was that other funding sources would expect similar identification. Such a preference (or condition) was actually expressed by potential donors from the beginning, however, resulting in early abandonment of the pooled approach favored by Al Cohen during the 1976-77 year of transition to a fund-raising program.

Adoption of a special-projects
budget in 1976, followed
by a transitional year

During the August meeting in 1976, President Maust, Secretary-Treasurer Mueller, forum chairperson Cohen, and incoming councilor Joyce Dean assembled for ninety minutes one afternoon to make a final review of a budget for 1976-77 that marked the start of annual budgeting by the National Council. In accordance with a decision reached the prior December, Fred Mueller had included a "Special Projects Budget." It called for Council contributions of <u>one-third</u> toward a total expenditure of $17,250, itemized as follows:

a.	FVP awards, including plaques	$2,200
b.	Regional meetings	9,500
c.	Manuscript awards	1,550
d.	FVP sessions at American Accounting Association regional meetings	1,500

e. History of Beta Alpha Psi 2,500 $17,250.[6]

In conjunction with approving this plan, the governing body adopted Albert Cohen's motion to "embark on a special funding program to finance special activities." As implied by the first item above, that program was intended to include the Outstanding Faculty Vice President Award, thereby severing its specific identification with Arthur Andersen. The reference made in the minutes to payment of the $500 awards "out of that fund" indicates clearly that a pooled concept of funding had been approved.

Preliminary inquiries, however, were not supportive. It was reported at the meeting of February 1977, without comment, that "[f]irms seem[ed] to be of the opinion that any continuous funding they might be willing to give . . . would be in the nature of specific projects" (emphasis added). The reference to "specific" rather than "special" projects tellingly indicates that potential donors expected to be identified with particular activities. Further confirming this interpretation is the fact that on the same occasion

---

[6] Item d indicates that, in the formative period of Beta Alpha Psi regionalism, official National Council representation at AAA meetings had not been abandoned. During the year just ended, 1975-76, four councilors had in groups of two or three appeared at three such gatherings. A year earlier Fred Mueller had reported that an expenditure of (on the readiest interpretation of unaudited data) $1,305 for attendance at four regional association meetings by from one to five members had permitted contact with FVPs that the local advisors had found beneficial. Fred J. Mueller, Secretary-Treasurer's Report, 1974-75, pp. 4, 17-19, 1975-76, p. 6.

The reference made (item e) to a history project was based on a plan adopted in December 1975, not to be carried through, to enlist Andy Penz to conduct "at least preliminary work" toward a more detailed document (by implication) than his golden-anniversary booklet. Reimbursement for expenses had been authorized, up to $2,000, for the development of either tape-recorded or written historical material. Fred Mueller later consented to work on a fraternal history, and as past president in 1977-78 was joined by Tom Burns in reviewing selected archival material. The two councilors were at the time seriously considering a collaborative project, although each of them credits the other one with having taken the principal initiative. Thomas J. Burns to Author, interview, May 3, 1980, July 8, 1986; Fred J. Mueller to Author, by telephone (1st call), August 11, 1986; and National Council Minutes, December 1975, p. 8 (quoted), August 1977, p. 5, August 1978, p. 4.

the National Council approved Claude Rodgers' proposal that the FVP stipends provided by Arthur Andersen be raised to $750, a development squarely opposed to the earlier plan to sever the linkage of the award with the traditional sponsor. For the balance of the year the Council largely marked time on the funding matter, although it was reported in June that the National Association of Accountants might be interested in supporting the manuscripts program.

In August 1977, finally, it was noted that the current prospect of continued deficit spending had arisen largely through inadequate provision for regional meetings and special projects. Incoming president Doris Cook accordingly proposed that the National Council proceed immediately with "solicitation of outside funding." Cook was immediately appointed to a funding committee to be headed by incoming forum chairperson David Abramson. Other members were Tom Burns, senior faculty councilor Bob Maust, and incoming member Hank Anderson. Visible progress would be made by the time the governing body assembled for the winter meeting.

Implementation and early growth of the funding program, 1977-81

Report of the Abramson committee, January 1978

Since the accounting and, perhaps, industrial firms represented on the National Advisory Forum were the most obvious prospective donors, David Abramson of Alexander Grant & Company in Minneapolis was the logical choice to head the funding committee. His principal colleague was his former Minnesota professor Tom Burns, the newly appointed department head at Ohio State. Burns not only was in his third year as special projects director, but had over a period of years obtained financial support from CPA and business sources for a variety of "freelance" academic and professional activities.

An excellent example was of course the Beta Alpha Psi student seminar that he had started on a regional basis in 1969, and later expanded to the national level.

The committee report presented by David Abramson at the 1977-78 winter meeting was ratified by the full National Council. To increase conventional funding by approximately $15,000 a year, the report recommended the aforementioned two-dollar increase in the initiation fee to $14. To permit fund-raising activity to be undertaken among fraternal alumni, it called for a special funding effort that would hasten completion of the "National Directory" project discussed in chapter 16.

To promote credibility with potential funding sources in general and members of the National Advisory Forum in particular, the Council was advised to expand its financial reports to include more detail and comparative data, and to demonstrate greater "budgetary control" over expenditure. The recent adoption of a formal budgetary process had of course in itself permitted one new kind of comparison; and the comparative financial statements found in 1977-78 files (summarized somewhat in the annual report) were more detailed than their 1975-76 counterparts.

One important step toward expenditure control had occurred on the eve of the deficit year 1976-77, with the approval of a presidential travel allowance, inclusive of attendance by a spouse at "special functions," for which the officer would have to account. Perhaps coincidentally, incoming president Fred Mueller and his wife Joy were avid travelers. Two years later, a travel claim for nearly $5,000 submitted belatedly by ex-councilor Hollis Dixon was paid in full following a review by President Doris Cook.

Besides the national directory, six other activities or programs were identified for "project funding" early in 1978, including full coverage of

the manuscript contest (an area in which Touche Ross had proposed a five-year program supplying approximately $4,000 annually) and national publications. The other funding targets cited were regional proceedings "on a joint basis," the National Chapter banquet, the anticipated history study, and an unexplained "supplemental dollar advance" concerning the Outstanding FVP program.

Tom Burns was asked to draft "a solicitation letter" for the several projects that would be cleared with the other councilors prior to being mailed. Positive response would not be long in coming.

Excellent response, acknowledged in the 1977-78 annual report

In June, Burns and David Abramson reported the receipt to date of $17,000, all of it relating to publication. All Big 8 firms, or their foundations, except Touche Ross had along with Alexander Grant and General Electric contributed $1,000 to a general publications fund totaling $9,000. The remaining funds were reported as deferred revenue because the expenditures would occur during the fiscal year commencing July 1. They included $2,000 from the Touche Ross Foundation for the year's annual report and $3,000 each from Deloitte Haskins & Sells and Ernst & Ernst for the coming year's *Newsletter* costs, to be acknowledged in each issue.

In addition, Arthur Young had agreed to provide $1,000 annually for "undesignated projects," which would be assigned to the National Chapter telephone directory; the Peat Marwick and Coopers & Lybrand foundations were considering support in turn of the national directory and "a small project" that would turn out to be the existing manuscript contest; and the National Association of Accountants was interested in sponsoring a new manuscript

program. By the time of the August meeting, another $8,000 had been received in project funding, including $1,000 from Alexander Grant ear-marked for the volume of regional papers that would be brought out the following year by Doris Cook.

A full-page acknowledgment of external funding, including the regular Arthur Andersen provision for honored faculty advisors, appeared in the annual report for 1977-78, and is shown as exhibit 33. Two limitations of the program as of that formative stage, both noted at the spring meeting, were reflected.

First, new funding covered only publication, or related literary, activities. Although Tom Burns stated in 1980 that still more publication was needed, his very statement pointed up the vital dependence of that area upon a strong nonliterary program. Second, only General Electric was cited from the corporate realm, its participation having probably been arranged through charter forum member Robert J. Canning. It had been resolved in June, then, that "more specific projects" should be identified for funding efforts, and that "[r]epresentatives of industry" should be approached.

Subject to one major exception in the first area, already covered in chapter 14, these limitations would not be overcome under the special-projects funding program as conducted over the following three years. The nine public accounting firms or foundations would indeed be the only continuing donors, disregarding a low-participation nonliterary activity ending after three years, although the levels of support raised through 1981 were vital to the ongoing Beta Alpha Psi program.

Funding over the years 1978-81: Consistency, and limitation

President Thomas Burns and Councilor David Abramson co-chaired a 1978-79

EXHIBIT 33

FUNDING ACKNOWLEDGMENT FROM 1977-78 Annual Report

Funding Program

An extensive funding program was undertaken during the year to finance some of the ongoing activities and special projects of Beta Alpha Psi. The National Council expresses sincere appreciation to the following Firms and Foundations for their generous contributions.

Outstanding Faculty Vice Presidents Awards - Arthur Andersen Foundation

The monetary awards to the Outstanding Faculty Vice Presidents selected each year have been funded by the Arthur Andersen Foundation since 1970. The recipients also receive the Richard S. Claire Award.

Student Paper Publication - Alexander Grant & Company

This annual publication will print selected student papers submitted at regional meetings and possibly some submitted to the national editor. Costs of printing and mailing this publication will be paid from funds contributed by Alexander Grant & Company.

Beta Alpha Psi Telephone Directory - Arthur Young & Company

Cost of printing and mailing the Beta Alpha Psi Telephone Directory for 1978-79 will be paid from funds contributed by Arthur Young & Company.

Manuscript Contest - Coopers & Lybrand Foundation

Monetary awards, plaques, and certificates for the winners of the 1979 manuscript contest will be funded by the Coopers & Lybrand Foundation.

Beta Alpha Psi Newletter - Deloitte Haskins & Sells
Ernst & Ernst

Cost of printing and mailing the three issues of the 1978-79 *Newsletter* will be paid from funds contributed by these two firms.

Beta Alpha Psi National Directory - Peat, Marwick, Mitchell Foundation

Computerization and printing of the first national membership directory of Beta Alpha Psi, planned for publication in 1979, will be funded by the Peat, Marwick, Mitchell Foundation.

Beta Alpha Psi Annual Report - Touche Ross Foundation

The cost of printing and mailing the 1978 *Annual Report* were paid from funds contributed by the Touche Ross Foundation.

General Publications Fund

Alexander Grant & Company
Arthur Andersen & Co.
Arthur Young & Company
Coopers & Lybrand Foundation
Deloitte Haskins & Sells
Ernst & Ernst Foundation
General Electric Company
Peat, Marwick, Mitchell & Co.
Price Waterhouse Foundation

Publication of the first Beta Alpha Psi Telephone Directory, 1977-78, listing all Chapters, National Advisory Forum members and National Council members, was paid from this fund. This fund was also used for other regular Beta Alpha Psi publications, including "Objectives, Organization, Activities," "Principles of Professional and Personal Conduct," and "New Member Initiation, Officers' Election and Installation."

Reprinted from 1977-78 Annual Report, ed. [Cook], p. [20].

funding committee also including Editor Henry Anderson and new councilor Jack Kiger. At the winter meeting, it was reported that earlier funding arrangements for the annual report ($2,500), telephone directory, and (at a reduced dollar level) Newsletter would be continued. Ernst & Whinney and Peat Marwick had funded the seventh national seminar (recorded in published proceedings) and the first New York City regional meeting through contributions that, as with Arthur Andersen's sponsorship of the next seminar at its own professional education center, had not been routed through the national fraternity.

Peat Marwick had also provided $2,500 toward the continuing directory project. Price Waterhouse was considering sponsorship of an activity not as yet defined. It was destined to be a graduate-level manuscript contest, an area in which the NAA had originally been interested, coordinate with an undergraduate competition supported by Coopers & Lybrand.

The funding highlight of 1979 was certainly the agreement reached with the Peat Marwick Foundation that provided $1,000 in scholarship funds for each "Superior" chapter in the activity program, a commitment in the amount of $29,000 the first year. Based on the closing date of June 30, that total would not appear in 1978-79 financial statements reporting $21,500 in "[p]ublication contributions," $9,000 of it deferred.

Approximately $27,000 was raised both in 1979-80 and the following year for publication-related activities. The donor base had not been enlarged, however, nor had the program moved into new areas, disregarding the small awards ($200 and an engraved plaque) conferred from 1979 through 1981 on Gamma Eta at Akron by Accountants for the Public Interest. For example, support had not been obtained for national office operations or for the first volume of the fraternal history, project areas for which a combined

total of $17,000 had been sought in 1979-80.[7]

Actually, it was already recognized by the winter meeting of that year that a new approach was needed to enlarge the scope, and base, of project funding, without jeopardizing established fraternal activities. Under the leadership of the forum chairperson of the day, the solution developed was to add a program suiting the first forum leader's values that would leave firms free, at their discretion, to continue prior specifically identified funding. The result was a highly successful "Associates" program that promptly yielded almost three times the proceeds of publications funding while leaving intact the two established nonliterary funding programs.

---

[7]Thomas J. Burns to Joyce C. Dean, September 1, 1978, enclosed list of committees, p. [2]; [Burns], ed., 1978-79 Annual Report, pp. 24 ("Funding Program"), 26 (from "Financial Report," quoted); Burns to Author, interview, May 3, 1980 (quoted), August 11, 1986; Albert R. Cohen to Author, May 12, 1986 (postmark), quoted; [Doris M. Cook], "Outstanding Faculty Vice Presidents" articles, Newsletter 13 (Fall 1974):5, 14 (Fall 1975):4, 15 (Fall 1976):4; [Dean], ed., 1980-81 Annual Report, pp. 5 ("Special Projects Funding"), 31 (from "Financial Report"); [Joyce C. Dean], Secretary-Treasurer's Report, 1977-78, p. 1, and "Detail Statement of Revenues, Expenditures and Changes in Fund Balance"; Hollis A. Dixon to Author, interview, March 22-23, 1980; exhibits 28, 33; Hasselback, 1984 Directory, individual listing, s.v. "Skaggs, Charles P."; Robert S. Maust to Author, interview, July 14, 1980, by telephone, February 10, 1986, both quoted; [Fred J. Mueller], "Changes in the National Council," 1976-77 Annual Report, ed. [Mueller], p. 3; Mueller, Secretary-Treasurer's Report, 1974-75, p. 1, 1975-76, pp. 1, 6; [Mueller], "Special Projects Budget, for Year Ending June 30, 1977," [1976]; National Council Minutes, 1973, p. 7, August 1975, p. 8, December 1975, pp. 7-8, August 1976, p. 8, February 1977, p. 3, August 1977, p. 4, January 1978, p. 5, June 1978, pp. 3-4 (all quoted), May 1974, pp. 5-6, August 1974, p. 1, June 1977, p. 2, August 1977, p. 7, January 1978, p. 6, August 1978, p. 4, January 1979, p. 3, June 1979, p. 4, August 1979, p. 5, June 1981, p. 7; "Outstanding Faculty Vice Presidents," Annual Reports, 1975-76, ed. [Maust], p. 2, 1976-77, ed. [Mueller], p. 6, 1977-78, ed. [Cook], p. [4]; [James W. Pattillo], "Beta Alpha Psi 1979 Public Interest Award," [1978], three-page typewritten announcement, p. 1; and [Pattillo], ed., 1979-80 Annual Report, pp. 5 ("Special Projects Funding"), 31 (from "Financial Report").

Substantial Broadening of Participation and Growth of Support: The "Associates" Program, 1981-84

Development of concept and origination of program, 1980-82

Having combined with David Abramson to spearhead the original funding effort, Thomas Burns would join with the forum chairperson's successor Thomas Nessinger to develop the second one. During the presidency of James Pattillo in 1979-80, Burns and Nessinger co-chaired a financial planning and funding committee that also included Secretary-Treasurer Joyce Dean and new councilor Richard Metcalf. Although he had retired from the Advisory Forum, Abramson was listed as a special consultant to a committee asked to "develop short- and long-run plans and [an] implementation program for funding sources & uses; . . . [and a] projects list for special funding."

Tom Burns gave a report for his group at the 1979-80 winter meeting, after Joyce Dean had reported on behalf of her budget and finances committee (whose other members were Councilors Nessinger and Metcalf) that the year's budget forecasts were holding up well. The past president stated that "the special projects" already identified should "continue to be funded by the nine firms," that is, the "Big 8" CPA partnerships plus Alexander Grant. He also proposed that the National Council "try to develop an _associates'_ program in which firms would make annual contributions according to a schedule based on . . . size" (emphasis added). Tom Nessinger added that such a schedule could be drafted once total financial needs had been determined.

These needs would be increased by the agreement reached at the same meeting to provide "some [Council] funding" for annual National Student Seminars. The more specific commitment made subsequently for one-half travel coverage for up to 60 delegates (initially) led to an expenditure of $7,644

in 1980-81. Three years later the cost incurred for a seminar in Omaha attracting 86 students was nearly triple that amount.

Throughout the year 1980-81, the National Council largely left the initiative in the funding area to the Advisory Forum as it focused on the reorganization discussed earlier. A motion was adopted in January 1981 to finance regional meetings in part from an "Associates Fund," once established, and as noted later an exploratory alumni fund-raising effort was approved. Five months later forum leader Nessinger was instructed to write selected accounting and business firms proposing "associate membership" in the sponsorship of Beta Alpha Psi activities. The schedule of required contributions, based on scale of operations and scope or "level" of professional accountant involvement therein, was as follows:

1.	International accounting firms	$6,000
2.	Regional (multistate) accounting firms	3,000
3.	Local (intrastate) accounting firms	1,000
4.	"Fortune 500" companies	3,000
5.	Other industrial firms	1,000.

The basic concept of associate funding was that members would receive collective recognition relative to each event or project so sponsored, and not otherwise be approached (at any organizational level) for support of national projects or regional meetings. Accounting firms already sponsoring specific programs would have the option of continuing to do so. Participation would not affect any support that an organization might wish to extend to local chapter activities.

At his last originally scheduled National Council meeting, Tom Nessinger reported in August 1981 that he had thus far sent 46 letters and obtained responses, and would promptly contact nonrespondents, again, and the full complement of Fortune 500 industrial firms. With his term extended to a

third year, the Arthur Andersen partner reported in January 1982 that all nine accounting firms participating in the current funding program had expressed interest in an associates program, as well as Seidman & Seidman. The latter reference recalls the important contribution made thirty years earlier by tax authority Jack Seidman as a member of the special Beta Alpha Psi chapter accounting and budget committee. Although there had been a second mailing, response from the corporate "500" had been "very slow," inviting a suggestion that a Newsletter issue or the latest annual report might be enclosed to stimulate greater interest.

Councilor Nessinger and his secretary Mary Honey were commended at the 1981-82 winter meeting for getting the new program underway. The fall Newsletter had already credited the coverage of printing and distribution costs to the Beta Alpha Psi Associates. The winter issue would additionally display a "logo" developed by the Arthur Andersen graphics department, and alphabetically list as members the ten CPA firms, Coca-Cola, Exxon, General Mills, Gulf Oil, and Nalco Chemical. By the close of the fraternal year, the Bendix Corporation had joined the fold as the only charter associate not represented on the Advisory Forum (counting incoming members).

The introductory writeup in the winter periodical issue implied that the associates program would supplant "publications" funding, while also covering many other costs. Cited as prime "Examples" of collective funding objects were the annual report, telephone directory, national directory, manuscript awards, and Newsletter; and regional meetings, the student seminar, the graduate case competition (just beginning), and the scholarship awards conferred on "distinguished" chapters. The obvious ommissions from the list were the annual faculty vice-president awards and the scholarships presented to "superior" chapters. Those programs would continue to be

funded specifically by the Arthur Andersen and Peat, Marwick, Mitchell foundations. The sponsor's special attached to the FVP honor has been amply documented, and the $1,000 awards to the top chapters represented a substantially larger commitment than all other previously funded activities combined, having the preceding year reached $44,000.

During the fiscal year 1981-82, a total of $78,000 was received through the new Associates system (plus a residual $7,000 through the supplanted program), approximately three times the amount of publications funding that had been generated the preceding year. This development coincided with a comparable dollar increase in aggregate initiation fees, based on the rise from $14 to $20, to yield a remarkable gain for the year of nearly $80,000, slightly more than doubling the fraternal "[f]und balance."

In August 1982, the National Council approved a policy statement drafted by David Tinius by which, in keeping with the national approach, measured recognition should be extended donors to <u>local</u> fraternal activities or events. Plans were announced to write the sixteen initial associates by mid-September to request continued funding, enclosing the new annual report with the letter. Outgoing councilor Thomas Nessinger planned to make several suggestions concerning expansion of the base to his successor Ulysse J. LeGrange of charter member Exxon, the 1980 Accountant of the Year from industry, including that each forum member invite five firms to join the ranks.

The extent of participation would only hold steady or rise minimally over the next two years, however, leading up to an increase in required support levels that promised needed significant expansion in revenue. Other pertinent developments included a regional version of associate funding and preventive avoidance of a behavioral problem.

Development of the program, 1982-84, including a regional spinoff and the averting of a behavioral problem

In 1982-83 and 1983-84 total Associate membership remained virtually constant, at 16, the original number, and 17. Annual receipts were $3,000 lower and higher, respectively, than the $78,000 of the first year. There were a few changes in the composition of the cast, as the IBM Corporation, Standard Oil of California, McGladrey Hendrickson & Co., and (in the latter year) KMG Main Hurdman joined the field. Although only the last member was represented on the Advisory Forum, the third one, a national accounting firm with seventy offices in eighteen states known by 1984 as McGladrey Hendrikson & Pullen, had through its office in Davenport, Iowa been the fraternal auditor since '81, and would supply one of the new forum members of 1985-86.

The Associates program brought with it a potential problem of a behavioral kind that the Council acted quickly to avert. International accounting firms or pertinent local offices frequently hosted cocktail parties, or other social functions where drinks were served, at the annual meeting of the American Accounting Association. With the new level of participation by such firms and major corporations in Beta Alpha Psi activities, it seemed only a matter of time until a cocktail hour would be scheduled in honor of Beta Alpha Psi students and faculty representatives attending the yearly convention.

In June 1983, accordingly, the National Council instructed President Jack Kiger to write "all members of the Associates, asking them to refrain from entertaining any students in New Orleans during the Annual Meeting." Although the letter went out on schedule, it was learned prior to the August gathering that Peat, Marwick, Mitchell & Co. was planning to conduct a party for Beta Alpha Psi students. Incoming president Richard Metcalf

had accordingly advised the firm that the Council would sever the scholarship funding agreement unless the affair were cancelled, as it was. As a special precautionary measure, board members contacted the fifteen other Associate forms just prior to the National Student Meeting to make sure that no parties had been scheduled.

A variation of the same issue having a different twist, if not outcome, arose during the August meeting in New Orleans. On behalf of his own Alpha Nu unit at Creighton, Alumni Councilor James Greisch sought permission to solicit public accounting support for a cocktail party that would accompany the forthcoming National Seminar to be hosted also by the University of Nebraska chapters at Omaha and Lincoln. The request was turned down, as a matter of policy, although the social function would be held, as an "ice-breaker."

Also at the meeting of August 1983, forum chairperson U. J. LeGrange proposed the creation of a "Regional Associates" system for support of regional meetings, subject to the same policy on recognition as governed the national program. His motion to establish a regional group, based on a minimum contribution of $150, was adopted. The governing policy was reiterated a year later:

> No individual firm should receive specific credit for funding or have more members present than allowed under the Associates Program [one, unless specified otherwise for a given function or activity funded], at any social, meal, or technical program (other than for speakers or forum members) of a Regional meeting. Meals or other social events planned and/or funded by a specific firm and scheduled at the location and time of a Regional meeting should not be described in any way as a Beta Alpha Psi function and should not draw students away from the Beta Alpha Psi sponsored activities.

It was agreed that associates at both levels, and regional host chapters, should be "reminded" of this policy.

An interesting implication of the associates program for the activities

of local chapters was brought out at the meeting of August 1984. Iota at Southern California had requested activity-program credit "for hosting a multiple[-]chapter program supported by outside funding." With one dissent and one absention, the National Council adopted Councilor Greisch's motion to deny such credit, under any category. Specific objections raised, and communicated to the chapter, included the absence of any convincing reasons to regard Iota as the initiator or sponsor of the function. At a broader level, the chapter had violated a Council requirement of advance notice concerning multichapter initiatives, intended "to promote the Fraternity's objectives but at the same time protect the integrity of the Associates Program and prevent competition with Regional Meetings."

Earlier in the year, Arthur Andersen & Co. had invited chapter officers to attend a "Beta Alpha Psi Workshop." Since the function was not fraternally sanctioned, President Dick Metcalf asked the firm's recruiting director Tom Nessinger to see to it that all references to Beta Alpha Psi were removed, as was done.

Finally, with a membership base that seemed unlikely to expand very much in the near future, and following a year that had produced a substantial operating deficit ($37,744, or 12.6% of revenues), the National Council in August 1984 increased the dues structure for the national associates program. The highest level, for international accounting firms, was raised to $8,000; the next one, for their regional counterparts and Fortune 500 companies, was increased to half that total; and the lowest rate, for other accounting and industrial firms, was set at $1,500. Membership actually increased in 1984-85, by one, as the eighteen associates contributed $112,500, a rise of $31,500.

The funding developments covered in this chapter point up, above all, the remarkable expansion in the Beta Alpha Psi program over the fifth and

sixth eras, through 1984. A useful overview of that growth is provided by exhibit 34, showing comparative operating statements from 1971-72, when Secretary-Treasurer Hollis Dixon had reported "Receipts" and "Disbursements," 1977-78, and 1983-84. The terminological progression from cash-based to accrual accounting was completed with the replacement in 1983 of "Expenditures" by "Expenses," a development invited by the acquisition for the central office of depreciable computer resources. On the revenue side, accrual of initiation fees, the largest item, continued to be impracticable; "associates" membership required current payment; and there was no real question of advance or deferred funding for scholarship or FVP awards.[8]

In Transition

The next chapter concludes this study by reference to several major program initiatives begun or advanced in the sixth era, serving respectively (a) student members in general, (b) graduate students, and (c) alumni members. They reveal a modern-day fraternity that clearly has a "comprehensive" reach, even where its grasp may have as yet fallen short.

---

[8] Annual Reports, 1979-80 through 1984-85, "Financial Report" (1st page, 2nd page also after 1980, 3rd page, 1982-83), 1981-82 through 1984-85, "The Beta Alpha Psi Associates Program," "National Advisory Forum"; Joyce C. Dean and Thomas J. Nessinger to Charles A. Kaiser, Jr. (managing partner of a New York City CPA firm), July 6, 1981, enclosed contribution schedule, quoted; "Honorary Members Initiated During the Past Year," Newsletter [3] (March 1952):9-10; National Council Minutes, January 1980, p. 4, January 1981, p. 7, June 1981, p. 9, January 1982, pp. 7-8, June 1983, p. 13, August 1983, p. 6, June 1984, p. 14, August 1981, pp. 3, 11 (indented citation) [all quoted], January 1980, p. 5, June 1980, p. 5, August 1980, p. [6], August 1981, p. 6, August 1982, pp. 3-4, August 1983, pp. 2-3, 7, August 1984, pp. 2, 6; Thomas J. Nessinger to Author, July 18, September 2, 1986; Newsletter 20 (Winter 1982):2, masthead, and listing of "The Beta Alpha Psi Associates"; [James W. Pattillo], "Beta Alpha Psi, 1979-80: Objectives, Functions, and Committees" (chapter 13, note 5), p. 4; Van Thompson, McGladrey Hendrickson & Pullen (forum member) to Author, August 28, 1986; [David E. Tinius], 'Beta Alpha Psi Establishes "Associates" Group', Newsletter 20 (Winter 1982):1, quoted; [Tinius], "National Advisory Forum," 1984-85 Annual Report, ed. [Tinius], p. 34; and [Tinius], "Twelfth National Student Seminar Held in Omaha," Newsletter 22 (Winter 1984):1, quoted. Also, Hollis A. Dixon, 1971-72 Secretary-Treasurer's Report, p. 10, quoted.

EXHIBIT 34

THREE NATIONAL COUNCIL OPERATING STATEMENTS FROM THE FIFTH AND SIXTH ERAS

NATIONAL COUNCIL OF BETA ALPHA PSI

STATEMENT OF REVENUES AND EXPENDITURES (CASH BASIS)

	Year Ended June 30, 1972	Eleven-Month Period Ended June 30, 1971
Revenues		
Initiation fees	36,339	26,582
Royalties on jewelry	632	282
Interest on investments	2,907	3,288
Charter fees	700	500
Duplicate certificates	108	40
Miscellaneous	230	226
Arthur Anderson Foundation proceeds	3,500	
TOTAL REVENUES	44,416	30,918
Expenditures		
National Council and National Chapter expense:		
Chapter visitations	3,848	3,368
National Chapter meetings	5,806	4,354
Secretary's honorarium	2,500	2,500
Arthur Anderson Foundation grants	3,500	
Insurance expense	198	303
Chapter installation	1,538	410
Faculty vice-president awards	21	300
Chapter awards	1,925	1,382
Charter printing	420	648
Corporation filing and registration	68	277
New programs expense		200
Editor honorary	500	1,000
	20,324	14,742
Local Chapter Expense		
News Letter	2,176	1,552
Membership certificates	8,743	3,672
Scholarship certificates		19
Chapter banners		370
Faculty vice-president workshop	484	300
	11,403	5,913
General Expense		
Clerical	452	1,675
Miscellaneous expense	2,644	60
Postage, printing, and stationery	1,838	2,500
Audit fee	75	75
Travel expense	345	740
Telephone	105	53
	5,459	5,103
TOTAL EXPENDITURES	37,186	25,758
EXCESS OF REVENUES OVER EXPENDITURES	7,230	5,160

EXHIBIT 34--Continued

Statement of Revenues and Expenditures and Changes in Fund Balance

NATIONAL COUNCIL OF BETA ALPHA PSI
Years ended June 30, 1978 and 1977

	1978	1977
Revenues:		
Initiation fees	$ 90,095	$ 82,313
Interest on investments	5,151	5,497
Outstanding faculty vice-president awards contributions	3,750	2,000
Membership insignia royalties	1,138	562
Publication contributions	9,000	
Charter fees	7,000	3,000
Other	2,204	384
	118,338	93,756
Expenditures by activity:		
National council:		
Annual, mid-year and spring meetings	11,310	12,655
Visitations to chapters	1,044	4,448
Special committee meetings	575	6,033
Chapter installations	7,339	3,341
National chapter:		
Annual banquet and student meeting	6,046	5,308
Faculty vice-president and student expense reimbursements	13,500	8,950
Local chapters:		
Membership certificates	17,550	18,015
Banners and miscellaneous	1,512	1,340
Performance awards	4,357	2,647
Directory	200	1,307
Administration:		
Supplies	285	755
Postage and telephone	2,533	2,978
Miscellaneous	960	1,750
Special projects:		
Faculty vice-president awards	3,750	2,277
Regional meetings	16,779	13,513
Manuscript awards	2,778	1,480
Omicron national seminar		1,000
Publications	12,414	6,710
Honoraria	9,750	11,750
	112,682	106,257
Excess (deficiency) of revenues over expenditures	5,656	(12,501)
Fund balance, at beginning of year	89,565	102,066
Fund balance, at end of year	$ 95,221	$ 89,565

EXHIBIT 34--Continued

National Council of Beta Alpha Psi
STATEMENTS OF REVENUE, EXPENSES AND CHANGES IN FUND BALANCE
Years Ended June 30, 1984 and 1983

	1984	1983
Revenues		
Initiation fees	$147.300	$162.560
Associates program contributions	81.000	75.000
Scholarship contributions	52.000	47.000
Outstanding faculty vice-president awards contributions	6.000	5.000
Charter fees	2.250	3.750
Membership insignia royalties	1.313	1.274
Interest on investments	8.032	13.617
Other	1.536	1.930
	$299.431	$310.131
Expenses, by activity:		
National Council:		
Annual, mid-year and spring meetings	$ 30.374	$ 27.327
Chapter installations and visitations	3.878	4.610
National Chapter:		
Annual banquet and student meeting	14.344	14.769
Faculty vice-president and student expense reimbursements	34.675	19.000
Local Chapter:		
Membership certificates	10.119	8.260
Banners and miscellaneous	1.596	483
Performance awards	5.694	5.358
Case competition awards	17.784	14.229
Administration:		
Supplies	1.915	1.088
Postage and telephone	7.206	9.790
Publications	4.348	3.725
Miscellaneous	6.022	5.730
Depreciation	2.461	1.173
Special Projects:		
Faculty vice-president awards	6.000	5.000
Regional meetings	39.985	37.466
Manuscript awards	9.709	11.013
Student seminar	22.376	14.812
Publications	23.629	25.435
Beta Alpha Psi History		8.069
Superior Chapter Scholarship Awards	52.000	47.000
Central office costs	42.060	31.688
Honoraria	1.000	1.000
	$337.175	$297.025
Revenue over (under) expenses	$ (37.744)	$ 13.106
Fund balance, beginning of year	171.779	158.673
Fund balance, end of year	$134.035	$171.779

Reprinted from Audited Financial Statements [for] National Council of Beta Alpha Psi, Tucson, Arizona: June 30, 1972, issued by Crable & Parsons, CPAs (Tucson, Ariz.), p. 5; "Financial Report," 1983-84 Annual Report, ed. [Metcalf], p. 29; and "Financial Section," 1977-78 Annual Report, ed. [Cook], p. [22].

CHAPTER 16

PROGRAM DEVELOPMENT OF THE SIXTH ERA, TO 1984: SERVICE TO STUDENT MEMBERS IN GENERAL, GRADUATE STUDENTS IN PARTICULAR, AND ALUMNI

An important student-centered consolidation of the sixth era is a framework developed in 1982 to integrate several prominent "scholarly" activities. Two of the five original elements of the Beta Alpha Psi "National Scholars" program were recent initiatives taken on behalf of _graduate_ students, namely, a spinoff from an established literary contest, and a far more ambitious project bringing "case analysis" to the fraternity. Recalling fourth-era developments covered in chapter 12, the latter program was intended both to appeal to chapters having significant graduate membership, and to attract interest in Beta Alpha Psi at universities offering only advanced degrees in business. Its cancellation following three years of low participation points up the most evident limitation in the overall fraternal program as of the close of this study.

Another recurrent topic area is _alumni_ membership, relative specifically to national directory development, and local and (possibly) national organization. Modern-day coverage of both matters extends back to the latter part of the fifth era. A computerized directory project begun in the mid-seventies finally became operational some years later after being scaled back, and transferred to the national office. The formation of alumni "chapters" at a few Beta Alpha Psi schools prompted the development of

National Council guidelines concerning their operation that were intended to protect the identification of former student members with their campus units, without unreasonably restricting organized alumni involvement. Other modes of continuing participation are also noted.

Beta Alpha Psi "National Scholars" Program: A Framework Covering Five Student Activities

By 1982, the fraternity was conducting two manuscript contests; a case analysis competition; a student seminar; and a program of regional meetings highlighted by student papers. Two areas each were restricted to undergraduate and graduate students, respectively, while members at either level were eligible to present regional papers.

As director of chapter activities for the period 1979-82, Jack Kiger identified these five activities as basically "scholarly" in nature, and on that basis came up with a plan to encourage participation in them that was implemented during his presidential year, 1982-83. First, participants were designated "National Scholars," and specific titles were conferred for the respective programs. The specific programs and titles were as follows:

a. Literary Scholars - Undergraduate Manuscript Contest
b. Research Scholars - Graduate Manuscript Contest
c. Case Scholars - Graduate Case Analysis Competition
d. Regional Meeting Scholars - Regional Meeting Paper Presentation
e. National Seminar Scholars - National Student Seminar (for undergraduates, although advanced students were not strictly excluded until 1984).

Second, chapters were encouraged <u>to invite</u> particular students or groups of students to be their national scholars in the several programs. Following his retirement from the National Council, Professor Kiger commented that the underlying premise of the scholars framework was that students chosen by their chapters to participate in such activities would have special incentive for excellent performance.

Third, according to Kiger emblematic certificates were designed for

campus presentation to scholars in each activity. His designs for the first and fourth programs listed were approved at the 1982-83 winter meeting, a year after student certificates had been cited in announcing the new third area. Finally, chapters were encouraged in other ways "to recognize in an appropriate forum" those members qualifying as national scholars, in keeping with the defining common element of the five activities:

> Those selected as scholars will be considered to have participated with a high level of scholarly qualify in the traditional sense of the word: knowledge and learning exhibiting accuracy, critical, that is to say, objective, analysis, and thoroughness.

The National Council approved this framework in time for announcement at the 1982 National Student Meeting. Initial plans were to publish a booklet annually containing pictures and biographical sketches of the year's national scholars; the winning papers in each manuscript contest; the outstanding regional meetings papers; and the case manuscripts. They were abandoned, however, in favor of a comprehensive listing of scholars, by chapter and activity, in the annual report.

In 1982-83, 98 of the 148 chapters operating throughout the year had at least one national scholar, and 19 had at least four. Omicron at Ohio State and Gamma Alpha at Brigham Young led the field with eleven scholars each. All five students from Zeta Mu at Southern Mississippi, in its first full year, were on the graduate case team (by necessity involving at least two or three students), and more than half the participants from six other local units were case scholars. Each chapter from Utah was well represented. Delta Omega at Utah State trailed Brigham Young by two, with nine scholars (one representing two categories), and Epsilon Xi at Utah had six participants.

No fewer than <u>eight</u> of the Utah State students, however, were entrants

in the undergraduate manuscript competition. In June 1984 it was decided to limit manuscript submissions, at each degree level, to three per chapter. Although there may have been some concern about an "imbalanced" local program, the principal consideration was entirely practical. Without such limits, the volume of submissions would impose increasingly unreasonable burdens upon the manuscript committees.

In the first listing of national scholars, in the year-end report of 1982-83, only the chapters having one or more participants were listed. In June 1984 a divided National Council narrowly rejected Jack Kiger's motion that chapters having no such members be omitted from that section of the report, and in both '84 and '85 the scholars' listing itself included all local units, whether or not they were represented in any of the activities covered. Under either approach, a conspicuous nonparticipant in the national scholars program throughout this time was Alpha at Illinois, suggesting that the fraternity's oldest chapter had not entirely abandoned its reluctance to conduct an active professional program.[1]

The scholars framework was introduced during the fourth and second years, respectively, of a graduate-level manuscript competition, and a unique program for advanced students.

---

[1]Henry R. Anderson to Author, interview, April 18, 1986; Beta Alpha Psi, [Graduate Schools Chapter Activity Program Committee, chaired by Thomas J. Burns], "Beta Alpha Psi National Case Analysis Competition for Graduate Students, for 1981-1982," [1981], p. 5; "Beta Alpha Psi National Scholars," Annual Reports, 1982-83, ed. [Kiger], pp. 3-7, 1983-84, ed. [Metcalf], pp. 4-8, 1984-85, ed. [Tinius], pp. 6-10; [Kiger], ed., 1982-83 Annual Report, pp. 20-28, even nos. ("New Chapter Installations," "Chapter Activities"); Jack E. Kiger to Author, July 15 (by telephone), 30, 1986; National Council Minutes, January 1983, p. 6, January 1984, p. 5, June 1984, p. 2; and [David E. Tinius], "Beta Alpha Psi Scholars Program Announced by the Board of Directors," Newsletter 21 (Fall 1982):15, indented citation; and [Tinius], "National Student Seminar," 1984-85 Annual Report, p. 14.

Two Programs for Graduate Students

As covered in chapter 12, the emergence of wholly graduate chapters, and of substantial graduate membership in other cases, had raised concern during the sixties about the relevance of the Beta Alpha Psi program to such environments. The experiment with optional participation in the activity program had been based in part on the perception that it was geared toward the needs and interests of undergraduate students.

Graduate membership receded from attention during the seventies, following the failure of the all-graduate chapters at Pittsburgh and UCLA (foreshadowing a similar outcome at Northwestern), and the resumption of bachelor's-degree work at Tulane. On the eve of the sixth era, however, the National Council announced a purely graduate-member program as a spinoff of a highly successful competition of the 1970s, and several months later work was begun on a more ambitious initiative to served advanced students.

Graduate Manuscript Contest

As related in the preceding chapter, the National Association of Accountants seemed prepared in 1978 to sponsor a manuscript competition for graduate-level Beta Alpha Psi students, but later abandoned the idea. The fraternity had accepted the NAA's plan to use its own panel of judges. There is no indication that the association had intended to limit coverage specifically to management accounting topics.

In August 1979, incoming president James Pattillo, who had conducted the discussions with NAA representatives, recommended that a separate graduate manuscript contest be established, governed by the same policies and procedures as the traditional competition, and providing for the same structure of awards. The existing program would be continued for undergraduate

members. Pattillo's motion was adopted, not so much to add a new fraternal dimension for advanced students as to remove the unfairness of pitting juniors and seniors against master's and even doctoral candidates in manuscript preparation. In 1978-79, for example, nine of the fifteen papers earning first, second, or third place or honorable mention from the predominantly undergraduate fraternity had been submitted by graduate students.

Arrangements were soon made for funding of the new program by the Price Waterhouse Foundation, joining its Coopers & Lybrand counterpart (from the other contest) within the manuscripts area. The agreement provided for publication of the leading papers, as identified in the two-stage evaluation by a National Council screening committee and a National Advisory Forum selection group. The first year, 1979-80, 24 papers were received from 18 chapters on the topic "Imputed Interest--Is it a Recognizable Cost?," and ten of them representing as many local units earned national recognition.

First prize went to Georgia doctoral student Sue H. McKinley of Beta Upsilon, an accounting information systems specialist who would join the faculty at Arizona State after graduation. Her forthcoming article on cash control, coauthored with chapter advisor John B. Barrack and another Georgia professor, had been honored nationally as the second best manuscript submitted in 1979-80 (July-June) to the monthly NAA magazine <u>Management Accounting</u>. Tom Burns, who had chaired both screening committees, brought out separate monographs made up of the ten award-winning graduate papers, and the top fifteen undergraduate manuscripts (selected from among 44 submissions from 44 chapters) on the topic "The Audit Committee: Its Impact on the Independent Auditor."[2]

---

[2]Henry R. Anderson, report on publications, National Chapter Meeting, August 21, 1979 (tape recorded); Thomas J. Burns, ed., <u>Imputed Interest</u>,

All manuscript funding was assumed by the Beta Alpha Psi Associates upon the formation of that system in 1981-82. Under the same financial sponsorship, a more costly and ambitious graduate-level program was introduced that year. The Graduate Cast Analysis Competition was destined to be a short-lived project, however, due to time demands made upon participants.

The Graduate Case Analysis Competition

Background and planning, January 1980 - August 1981

Leadership by Tom Burns

Beta Alpha Psi leaders of the fifth and sixth eras, through 1984, prominently associated with graduate education include James Pattillo and Richard Metcalf, through service as directors of graduate studies in business and accounting, respectively, at Louisiana State and Nebraska. The councilor most strongly identified, nationally, with advanced degree work in accounting was probably long-term Ohio State doctoral advisor Thomas Burns, who feels that he is better known in academic circles for his doctoral students who have gone on to teach at leading universities than for his Beta Alpha Psi activity. Examples include Paul A. Griffin of Stanford and California at Davis, Ph.D. '74, and the late Cornelius J. Casey, Jr. of Harvard and Dartmouth, Ph.D. '78. As of 1986, Burns had chaired 43 dissertation committees, in twenty-one years, including 5 for theses still in progress.

Burns stated in a 1980 interview that the fraternity needed a "model"

---

pp. iii-vi, 1, Audit Committee, pp. iii, v (chapter 13, note 7); Hasselback, 1984 Directory, individual listing, s.v. "McKinley, Sue H.'; Robert A. Leitch, John B. Barrack, and Sue H. McKinley, "Controlling Your Cash Resources," Management Accounting 62 (October 1980):58, credits; National Council Minutes, August 1978, pp. 4-5, January 1979, p. 3, August 1979, pp. 8-9; and [James W. Pattillo], "Beta Alpha Psi, 1979-80: Objectives, Functions, and Committees" (chapter 13, note 5), p. 3.

that would relate it to schools, especially elite private institutions, that like those mentioned offered only graduate degrees in business. The following month he suggested that the National Council appoint a task force "to consider developing a graduate chapter model which would [be] centered around a national competion." President James Pattillo accepted the proposal, and two months later asked the Ohio State professor to head a committee "to continue work" on a special program for graduate-oriented chapters. The approach developed by the group, whose other members were appointed by new president Joyce Dean, would be pertinent also to other chapters that included advanced students.

In January 1981, Tom Burns reported that a "[c]ase" had been drafted for potential coverage within a national competition among chapters having graduate membership. Leading textbook authors Charles Horngren of Stanford, Roman L. Weil of Chicago, and Clyde P. Stickney of Dartmouth had agreed to serve as judges or (perhaps) consultants the first year, if such a program were introduced, but no further reference is found to any participation on their part. Weil and Stickney were textbook collaborators with Chicago dean Sidney Davidson, who had been the keynote speaker at the 1978 convention in Denver.

In June the National Council approved the provision of $10,000 in prize awards for a 1981-82 graduate competition concerning the topic proposed by Burns, and the case was distributed at the August convention together with an announcement of the new program that included a full set of instructions.

Nature of the competition

The case analysis program was focused on "the broad economic, political and societal aspects of accounting" and professional practice, rather than strictly technical issues. Each year's case would involve a realistic and

timely issue confronting

> an accounting firm, the management of an enterprise in preparing external general[-]purpose financial statements or in its internal planning and control activities, a standard-setting body (including perhaps a governmental agency), or some other identifiable policy decision maker.

As an essential part of case analysis, reasoned recommendations were to be developed regarding the hypothetical (or, the first year, actual) case problem involved.

The case analysis competition was between <u>teams</u> of graduate students rather than individual members. Eligibility was defined liberally, so that a participant need have graduate status during only one academic term, need not be enrolled throughout the year, and might be a chapter "pledge" not as yet initiated. Each participating chapter would field one team in interchapter competition, consisting of as many as six to ten students. For a large graduate program, the possibility was raised of forming multiple teams that might first vie on the local campus for the right to represent the unit.

At each stage of competition identified below, case analysis required all active members of a team to participate in an oral presentation of one hour or less, making use of any appropriate visual aids. It was initially assumed that there would be only two or three active members at the final level of competition, which required advance submission of a comprehensive written statement, or "treatise," that might be supported by audiovisual materials. The actual range over the three years 1982-84 was apparently from two to five speakers in the final round, with half the teams having had three active members at that point. The principal limitation of case analysis was the absence of interaction between participating teams, as in a debate, or questioning by assembled judges.

Beyond a possible intra-chapter round, the case program was structured

in terms of competition at three successive levels. Teams within a particular fraternal region would compete at the year's regional meeting before a panel of judges made up, preferably, of a member of the National Advisory Forum (or a designated stand-in), the area councilor, and the FVP from a neutral chapter. Based on a scoring format laid out in advance, the top chapter from each region would be determined by the mean scores assessed by the panel.

Regional winners would move on to semifinal competition designed to eliminate all but two teams, but left partially undefined in the initial announcement. Competitions evaluated as on the regional level were held the first year at separate eastern and western sites, while subsequently *videotaped* presentations were reviewed at this stage.

The two finalists would then meet at the national convention in a face-off judged by invited authorities in the topic area, generally not drawn in practice (contrary to the original instructions) from the Advisory Forum, followed by announcement of the first-place team at the National Chapter banquet. Prizes awarded for use by the respective institutions, to benefit both departments and chapters, were $4,000 for first place, $2,500 for second place, and $500 for "honorable mention," a status accorded two chapters each of the first two years after a low level of regional activity had undercut its original identification with nonfinalist regional champions. Prize money proper in those two years, at $7,500, was one-fourth lower than the amount authorized in June 1981.

"[T]ravel" allowances were approved of $500 for nonhost semifinalists, and, inclusive of "housing and meals," a maximum of $1,500 for finalists. It had been announced at first that up to $250 would be provided in the former case, and travel costs would be paid for as many as six team members

attending the national finals.

At a symbolic level, all student participants in the competition begun a year before the National Scholars framework emerged received certificates, and the first- and second-place chapters earned a plaque. Members of those teams also received special letters of commendation.

The 1981-82 competition revolved around a case written by the principal architect of the program. Significantly lower participation than was expected fell slightly below the minimum level originally specified.

The competition of 1981-82

The first case: The "Uneasy" FASB/SEC relationship

The case prepared by Tom Burns was entitled "The Financial Accounting Standards Board and the Securities and Exchange Commission: An Uneasy Relationship." The primary theme was the delicate and even fragile base of private-sector determination of accounting principles that was inherent in the statutory authority vested in the SEC. Several notable instances were cited in which the commission had over the years overruled the board or a predecessor standards-setting body, or forced its hand on a particular issue. The most recent ones concerned accounting for oil and gas reserves and for the effects of changing prices. The written case opened with remarks by SEC chairman Harold M. Williams that referred to both areas, and closed (in the regular text) with a summation of the "working relationship" between the two organizations:

> . . . perhaps now the FASB recognizes that it cannot sustain positions that are directly contrary to SEC judgments[,] while maybe the SEC understands that if it overrules the FASB too regularly, FASB effectiveness will be destroyed. Currently both bodies seem to understand that they must communicate so as not to surprise each other. But the relationship between the two groups seems to be a fragile one.

Burns' typescript consisted of six pages of text, a short table drawn from a text he had coauthored, and nearly eleven pages of appendix material covering the operations of the respective bodies and pertinent points of historical background. An unusual feature of the case writeup was that no explicit decision question was posed. Supplementary instructions specified five topics that should be addressed, however, and indicated their relative weights in the judging:

1. Assessment of existing attitudes and policy interpretations concerning the FASB and SEC and their relationship, based on review of literature and current events, study of pertinent laws and regulations, and survey of "officials and other leaders" (15)
2. Testing attitudes of (a) accountants and (b) nonaccountants toward both groups and their roles in the economy (15)
3. Defining and evaluating the roles and responsibilities of the two bodies (30)
4. Assessing the effectiveness of the two groups and of accountants in meeting their responsibilities (20)
5. Recommending specific means of "promoting a more satisfactory interface between these bodies, society and accountants" (20).

The breadth of the assignment was most impressive. Of particular note was the expectation, in items 1 and 2, that the teams would conduct empirical research in developing their positions. Notable by its omission was any kind of reading list. Teams were expected to take the full initiative in obtaining relevant reading material.

As of the August meeting of 1981 the number of chapters considered necessary for a successful national competition had already signaled an interest, and in the coming weeks several more would declare their intentions to take part. In light of the demands implicit in the instructions, it is not surprising that several local units later withdrew, leaving only seven participants for the initial year's program.

Regional and semifinal competition, following a reduction to seven participating teams

The National Council had decided in June 1981 to cancel the scheduled inaugural case competition if fewer than eight chapters had by early fall registered their intent to enter teams. Exactly the required number of participants had tentatively been lined up by August, however, when Director of Chapter Activities Jack Kiger was fittingly appointed chairman of a committee to supervise a program that would award "[m]ajor point credit" to participants. The committee also included Richard Metcalf of Nebraska and Area Councilors Richard Murdock of Ohio State and Dee Hubbard of Brigham Young, each of whose local chapters were counted among the likely 1981-82 competitors. Retiring councilor Thomas Burns was appointed as an adjunct member.

In September Professor Kiger sent case materials to all faculty vice-presidents, and asked them to inform Nancy Harke within four weeks whether their chapters would be participating. Since the faculty "coach" for a team need not be the FVP, the reply form included a separate space for identifying the proper contact for further correspondence.

Kiger's survey of the National Chapter revealed a significantly altered cast of prospective entrants. Three of the eight chapters having earlier made a "tentative commitment" had withdrawn, namely, Alpha at Illinois, Beta Upsilon at Georgia, and Delta Omicron at Nebraska. Seven additional units had signed up, however, including the activity director's own Alpha Lambda at Tennessee.

By happenstance, the dozen chapters that had replied positively were almost evenly distributed among the Southeast, Midwest, Rocky Mountain, and Southern California/Arizona regions. To provide for an exact division of

three schools each, the southwest team from Beta Delta at Texas Tech was asked to join the Southern California regional competition. On November 19, 1981, Jack Kiger was able to announce that first-round competitions would be conducted at three regional meetings scheduled in February or at the end of January, and that (since the Utah chapter had already hosted the regional gathering) a special session would be scheduled for the competing Rocky Mountain teams.

Early in 1982, however, Epsilon Xi at Utah and Delta Omega at Utah State in turn withdrew from the case analysis competition, giving Gamma Alpha at Brigham Young a first-round "bye." Still further west, Iota at USC abandoned the activity prior to the Southern California/Arizona meeting, and with only Beta Eta at San Diego State and Beta Delta at distant Texas Tech remaining that regional matchup was also cancelled. The result was an equitable western semifinal competition among three chapters without prior regional participation.

One chapter each also dropped out of the Southeast and Midwest regional competitions before the respective meetings, namely, Upsilon at Florida and Epsilon Omega at Eastern Michigan. In the first round, accordingly, Omicron at Ohio State competed against Pi at Case Western Reserve, and Alpha Lambda at Tennessee went against Delta Gamma at South Florida. Pi and Alpha Lambda were selected the winning chapters.

The western and eastern semifinal rounds were held at the Western Regional AAA meeting in Anaheim, California, and the University of Tennessee. Prevailing at that level were Beta Delta of Texas Tech in the west, and Alpha Lambda at host Tennessee in the east.

The final round of the first graduate case analysis competition took place at the 1982 annual convention in San Diego.

Conclusion: Alpha Lambda vs.
Beta Delta in San Diego

There were interesting differences between the two finalist teams. Tennessee's consisted of nine members, five of whom were women. R. David Mautz, Jr. and Kay Poston Harmon were doctoral students. Mautz, who joined the faculty at Virginia Tech in 1985, reports that so far as he knows he is not related to retired professor Robert K. Mautz, but that in view of the rarity of the name he would not be surprised if there were a distant relationship. Kay Poston, as she is known professionally, taught at Drexel, in Philadelphia, before moving to the University of Missouri. Scheduled for publication late in 1986 by the sponsoring National Association of accountants was her coauthored study Quality Costs: Measurement Planning and Control.

The Texas Tech team was composed of four men and three women, all of whom were candidates for an M.S. degree in accounting. In the final round Alpha Lambda used four speakers, two of each gender, and Beta Delta three. Included were Mautz, Harmon (Poston), and, appearing with male colleagues on the other side, Julie Phelps. Having "played important roles in preparing" the final presentation, the remaining five members of the Tennessee team were present in San Diego. Two of the five other Texas Tech students also attended the convention.

The faculty advisor to Alpha Lambda was charter Advisory Forum member Singleton B. Wolfe. The coaches for the case analysis team were, however, Professors Norman E. Dittrich, Keith G. Stanga, and Jan R. Williams, the future councilor, who had earlier taught at Texas Tech. Beta Delta FVP Paul H. Munter was joined on the rival coaching staff by Professors Robert J. Koester, a leading authority on FASB/SEC conflict area oil and gas

accounting, and Ben B. Trotter.

In August 1981, the National Council had mentioned as potential judges for the final round FASB vice chairman Robert Sprouse, SEC chief accountant Clarence Sampson, and Southern California accounting dean and Peat Marwick professor Doyle Williams, president-elect of the Federation of Schools of Accounting. The panelists on hand a year later excellently matched the intended profile, although two specific identities had changed. Past forum member Sampson was joined by Paul A. Pacter and Joseph Silvoso. Pacter was the executive director of the Financial Accounting Foundation, whose stewardship, appointive, and "general oversight" duties concerning the FASB had been explained in Tom Burns' case writeup, while Silvoso, the Peat Marwick professor at Missouri, was the new president-elect of the cited federation.

The judges' decision in 1982 was not announced until the National Chapter awards banquet. At that time

> [t]he jumping up and down and hugging and whooping it up by the [winning] Texas Tech team at the announcement seemed to say it all about the quality and intensity of the first year of graduate case competition.

The two presentations had been videotaped for review, on a request basis, by other chapters.

Both Tennessee and Texas Tech would distinguish themselves in later case analysis competitions marked by somewhat different formats, but the overall extent of participation would be highly disappointing.

Developments of 1982-84

Area Councilor Dee Hubbard coordinated the second year's competition, covering the topic "Conformity of Tax to Financial Accounting." The case was prepared by a National Advisory Forum committee that included Madlyn Harrell of Seidman & Seidman. In a pattern reminiscent of the first year,

FINAL-ROUND PARTICIPANTS IN THE FIRST GRADUATE CASE ANALYSIS COMPETITION, 1982

Texas Tech University - left to right:
Richard Rogers, Julie Phelps, and Mike Shaub.

University of Tennessee - left to right:
Daryl P. Johnson, Kay P. Harmon, Margaret E. Gordon, and R. David Mautz.

Other team members were Brian Cope, Rhonda Ginsburg, Melinda Owen, and Michael Prindible, at Texas Tech; and Janet I. Baudry, Paul Cardwell, Pat Harrenburg, Celeste Patterson, and Glynn Riddle, at Tennessee.

at least 12 chapters, and possibly 15, declared their intent to field teams, but only 8 actually did so. Four of them competed at the Southeast regional meeting, and the winner was an Alpha Lambda group from Tennessee having no holdovers from the prior year.

Scattered geographically from New York to Utah, the other four entrants did not participate at the regional level, at least in competition. Instead, their teams and the Alpha Lambda group submitted <u>videotaped</u> presentations for appraisal by case coauthor Harrell, Alpha Beta at Alabama '64, and tax accounting professor Dennis J. Gaffney from Michigan State, the 1965-66 president of Psi at Marquette. The fraternity covered the expense of videotaping up to $150, thirty per cent of the maximum reimbursement that would have been made for travel costs. Through a misunderstanding, a higher claim was apparently submitted the subsequent fall by Epsilon Delta from Missouri at Kansas City, whose team had shared honorable mention status with the one representing Zeta Theta from the State University of New York (SUNY) at Buffalo.

The two finalists were Alpha Lamda, again, and Gamma Alpha at Brigham Young, coincidentally the chapters of President Jack Kiger and program coodinator Hubbard. The Tennessee group this time won the national competition, as judged by a forum member, a Texas Tech taxation chairholder who had been one of Tom Burns' first two doctoral students, and an FASB representative who had earlier been an Accountant of the Year in public accounting.

At a cost of $2,500, the National Council in 1983 <u>commissioned</u> Professor Frederick D. S. Choi of New York University, honored as an Outstanding FVP during his service to Delta Theta at Hawaii, to prepare a case in international accounting. Its descriptive title was "<u>SFAS</u> [Statement of Financial Accounting Standards] <u>No. 52</u> and the Funds Statement" (emphasis added).

Included, perhaps for the first time, was a brief reading list. It cited, besides SFASs No. 8 and (reprinted without appendices) 52, an FASB discussion memorandum, exposure draft, and concepts statement, and two articles from Management Accounting. Choi, whose research would in 1986 earn him the AAA's distinguished Wildman Medal, also provided several representative consolidated and subsidiary statements.

To stimulate more participation, President Richard Metcalf sent the 1983-84 materials in early fall to the business deans and accounting chairpersons or directors at all Beta Alpha Psi schools. In addition, Area Councilor William R. Welker of Western Michigan, as program coordinator, personally contacted thirty FVPs on the matter. Ultimately, 21 chapters signed up for the competition, two of them after the winter meeting of the board of directors, but only 13 or 14 of them actually followed through. For reasons not explained, Omicron at Ohio State, newly assigned to the region, and Zeta Theta of SUNY-Buffalo did not square off against one another at the Northeast regional meeting, but instead represented respectively the Midwest and Northeast in the semifinal round. In four other regions, there were competing teams, including five in the Southeast. In the latter instance at least the teams submitted videotapes for the judging. Two of them were selected as semifinalists.

Seven teams reached the second round, again approached through videotaped presentation. Frederick Choi and Columbia assistant professor Trevor Harris selected the groups from Beta Delta, at Texas Tech, and Zeta Theta as the finalists. The Texas team, composed of three out-of-state M.S. students specializing in oil and gas accounting, had designed a cash-basis format for reporting changes in financial position generated by foreign currency translation. The New York team won national honors in a confrontation

judged by a panel that included Washington professor Gerhard Meuller (muler), under whom both Choi (with whom he would share the Wildman Medal) and Harris had studied. Zeta Theta was the first chapter founded in the sixth era to reach the finals, and won top honors with the smallest active team, at two members, to compete at that level.

The third year had brought nearly as many entries as the first two combined. Still, in light of the special efforts made by President Metcalf and Councilor Welke to expand interest, and the engagement of a prominent scholar as casewriter, the level of participation seemed disappointing. Even before the total number of 1983-84 teams was determined, the National Council decided in January 1984 that the demands of the program upon student time and effort must be reduced. At the next three board meetings case analysis was scaled back successively from a costly national competition that was attracting only a relative handful of chapters within a fraternity located predominantly at schools offering graduate grograms in accounting to a defunct Beta Alpha Psi activity.

Review and ultimate cancellation of the program, January 1984 - January 1985

Low participation levels against a background of widespread graduate offerings in accounting

Over the three years ending in 1984, a total of 18 chapters (based on identification of 13 entrants in 1983-84) had fielded case analysis teams. Tennessee and Brigham Young had completed all three years, and Texas Tech, SUNY at Buffalo, South Florida, Ohio State, Alabama, and Missouri at Kansas City had each participated twice.

These figures seem especially low when set against a profile of graduate

degrees offered by Beta Alpha Psi schools with a major or concentration in accounting. Exhibit 35, based primarily on James R. Hasselback's 1984 Accounting Faculty Directory, reports that more than 90% of the 154 institutions comprising the fraternal roster at the start of the year 1983-84 conducted at least one graduate program in accounting. Among those 139 schools, more than 45% offered at least two different master's degrees; inclusive of doctoral work (found in 54 cases), nearly two thirds conducted two or more advanced degree programs; and more than a fourth offered at least three distinct graduate degrees in the field. The University of Alabama, home of Alpha Beta, numerically led the field with five listed programs. The comparative breadths of overall graduate curricula may of course not be properly reflected by the respective numbers of degree designations.

These figures markedly overstate, in any event, the potential level of case analysis participation (estimated by the board of directors in 1984 as realistically limited to the neighborhood of forty chapters). First, they do not distinquish between full-time graduate programs, and ones of an evening (or comparable part-time) nature whose students would ordinarily be unavailable for such fraternal activity. Second, a school offering one or more advanced degrees in the field, on a daytime basis, might in a given year have only a handful of graduate students in accounting, or even none at all. Third, as a related point, graduate programs that have become dormant, or that have not as yet become active, are no doubt occasionally reported to Hasselback. Fourth, the data may be biased upward for the M.B.A. (or a comparable gneeral business) degree, through its improper inclusion within reports from schools that do not offer an accounting concentration. Finally, only graduate students ranking scholastically within the top 35% of their classes are eligible for Beta Alpha Psi.

EXHIBIT 35

LISTINGS OF ACCOUNTING-ORIENTED GRADUATE DEGREES: A PROFILE OF BETA ALPHA PSI SCHOOLS, 1983-84

Number of Schools Listing Pertinent Degrees

M.S.	M.A.	M.B.A.	M. Ac. or M.P.A.[a]	M. Taxation, or equiv.[b]	M.A.S. or M.S.A.	Ph.D. or D.B.A.[c]	Other[b]
57	19	88	33	13	3	54	1

Number of Schools Listing Each Number of Graduate Programs

	No. of degrees 0	1	2	3	4	5
1. Excluding doctorate	15[d]	75	52	10	2	0
2. Including doctorate	15	48	56	30	4	1

SOURCES: "Chapter Activities," 1982-83 Annual Report, ed. [Kiger], pp. 22-28, listing of chapters; Hasselback, 1984 Directory, 1986 Directory (in isolated cases), school listings, Beta Alpha Psi locations; Texas Southern University: 1983-85 General Catalog, Bulletin (1983-84 Microfiche Catalogs, TX-60; also, San Diego: Career Guidance Foundation, College Catalog Collection on Microfiche, 1985-86 ed., TX-71), pp. 272, 274; David E. Tinius to Author, July 15, 1986 (postmark); University of Nevada, Reno: Catalog, 1985-86 ([Reno, Nev.: 1985; 1985-86 Microfiche Catalogs, NV-1), pp. 139, 144, 149; and items cited in notes b-d.

[a]Master of Accountancy (or Accounting), or Master of (or in) Professional Accounting. Perhaps the earliest M.P.A. program was introduced at Texas in 1948. The preposition "in" was selected over "of" as part of the degree title in recognition that "education alone could not suffice to make a person master of his profession." Smith, Forty Acres, p. 80, quoted.

[b]The designation "M.A.T." (punctuation supplied), listed for the same six schools in both Hasselback editions, commonly stands for the professional education degree Master of Arts in Teaching. Since within accounting the letter "T" often represents taxation, recent catalogs from the six universities were examined, with the result that only the program at Portland State was classified as an education degree (under the heading "Other"). Four of the degrees were identified with taxation, while the Syracuse listing was omitted, as apparently a defunct or inactive program. All references are to microfiche editions. California State University, Fullerton: 1985-87 Catalog ([Fullerton, Cal.]: 1985 (effective date, August 26, 1985); 1985-86 ed., CA-37), pp. 189, 233; Graduate Study, Syracuse University: Academic Catalog, 1984-86 (Syracuse, N.Y.: 1985; 1985-86 ed.,

NY-36), pp. 56, 116-18; Portland State University Bulletin, 1985-86: General Catalog Issue (Portland, Ore.: 1985; 1985-86 ed., OR-11), OR-11), p. 165; University of Cincinnati Bulletin, 1984-86: Division of Graduate Studies and Research (Cincinnati: 1983; 1984-85 ed., OH-2, pp. 47, 81; University of Denver Bulletin[/Application]: Graduate School of Business and Public Management, 1985-86 (Denver: 1985; 1985-86 ed., CO-11), pp. 3-12, especially p. 12; and Virginia Commonwealth University Graduate Bulletin, 1984-1986 (Richmond: 1984; 1985-86 ed., VA-16), pp. 3-4, 126, 182.

Even with the inclusion of four of the "M.A.T." schools, explicit taxation degrees were identified with only 13 of the 139 schools offering graduate programs in accounting. Many of the other institutions offered pertinent concentrations under broader titles, however, as indicated by an Ernst & Whinney listing, current as of 1982, of 71 campuses at which master's-level specialization in the tax field was available. [David E. Tinius], "Explosive Growth in Graduate Tax Education for Accountants Reported," Newsletter 22 (Winter 1984):9.

[c]Hasselback's data were modified in light of a 1983 survey of doctoral programs indicating that Texas A&M and Utah continued (as confirmed by their catalogs) to offer Ph.D. degrees with a concentration in accounting, and that Lehigh was no longer actively conducting work at that level. Bulletin of the University of Utah: General Catalog, 1985-86 (Salt Lake City: 1985; 1985-86 Microfiche Catalogs, UT-6, 7), p. 37; William F. Crum and Don E. Garner, "1983 Survey of Doctoral Programs in Accounting in the United States and Canada," The Accounting Review 60 (July 1985):519, 524; and Texas A&M University Graduate Catalog: Announcements for 1984-85 (College Station, Texas: 1984; 1984-85 Microfiche Catalogs, TX-11), p. 85.

[d]The tabulations include the M.B.A., M.S., and Ph.D. programs offered at New York University, even though Mu Chapter is confined to undergraduate students, in part because the two levels of study are "geographically separate." Ely Kushel, Mu Chapter FVP, to Author, March 10, 1986, quoted.

Granting all these points, the overall scope of involvement in a graduate-level activity launched with high hopes had been distinctly lower than anticipated; a number of chapters that might have been expected to be attracted had ignored the program; and there had been no movement at all toward extending Beta Alpha Psi to strictly graduate business schools, whatever their level of national distinction. In view of resources committed to the competition, and the need for accountability to the Beta Alpha Psi associates who were providing the funds, by 1984 it was time to reevaluate the activity.

A year-long process of decision

Introduced after the disappearance (in effect, granting that inactive Gamma at Northwestern would formally exist until 1983) of all-graduate chapters, the case analysis competition had been intended primarily to serve units that combined undergraduate membership with a significant group of advanced students. As stated in the preface to the case of that year, however, it continued in 1983-84 to be viewed as a "foundation for establishing chapters at universities that offer only graduate programs in accounting." President Jack Kiger, who required no special authorization in that regard, had suggested in January 1983 that "a group from prestige graduate schools [be invited to] listen to the Case Analysis Competition and attend the banquet" in August.

A year later, the Board of Directors ascribed the low level of involvement to "the very high demand of time necessitated by the complexity of the cases, the long lead time during which to prepare, and the intense competition." At the outset it had been noted that departments might approach the activity by way of a special, or regular, course. Only the highly successful

teams at Tennessee and Brigham Young were known, however, to have earned academic credit for participation (1982-84), suggesting that there was some reluctance to take Beta Alpha Psi activity seriously from a strictly "academic" standpoint.

Jack Kiger agreed, in January 1984, to draft a recommendation for revising the program so that it would "provide a backdrop for a good learning experience . . . in the context of a reasonable time/cost/benefit tradeoff." After noting that leading schools with "reasonably large" graduate professional programs such as Georgia, Illinois, Texas, and Southern Cal had declined to participate, Kiger proposed in June that the competition be reconstituted as a strictly regional activity. The scope of the case would be narrowed; a "limited bibliography" would be provided; the exact case would be distributed only a day in advance, a prospective restriction later relaxed slightly; teams would be limited to three members; and presentations would be confined to half an hour.

These fundamental revisions were immediately approved. Very surprisingly, the board at the same meeting authorized the provision of up to $26,000 in prize money for the scaled-down competition, an unexplained amount substantially higher than prior full annual costs of the program. The bulk of those costs would appear in the subsequent fiscal period due to the timing of the yearly finals. After expenditures of only $1,864 had been reported in 1981-82, the respective amounts $14,229 and $17,784 (including $2,500 for the case) had been and would be stated the following two periods, suggesting that travel provisions may have exceeded original limits.

Developments in August and January of that fiscal year would help reduce 1984-85 costs to $10,600, however. In the first instance, it was decided to eliminate cash prizes entirely. Engraved plaques would be awarded

regional winners and, with more than four or eight entrants, the first or first two runners-up. Emblematic paperweights, or comparable awards, would be presented to the members of those teams. Specific questions or approach would be varied somewhat among regions, to minimize the bias from any inter-regional communication, and host chapters (receiving $20 for each member of a team attending the banquet) would be largely responsible for providing judges. The general topic "Management Financial Performance Initiatives" had been set for the year, and an expenditure of up to $1,500 was approved for case development. Participating chapters would receive $50, plus mileage at a rate of $.25, toward coverage of their travel expenses.

The case analysis competition was one of the topics discussed with area councilors at the special meeting in January 1985. Southeast councilor Robert Brown from Virginia Tech had been designated the program coordinator. Although specific details of the gathering are not recorded, a week later the board of directors voted to cancel the redesigned activity, "for lack of interest and participation." The fraternity's experiment with a graduate "model" had thus ended after three years.

It is purely speculative whether the case program, supported by appropriate provisions for academic credit, would have helped preserve Beta Alpha Psi at earlier graduate-level units. In any event, the regional structure and external funding on which it rested had not existed when the graduate-chapter problem had appeared. Although perhaps merely coincidental, it was fitting that the motion to cancel the program had come from forum chairperson Douglas Ivestor, pointing up the accountability or stewardship dimension of the decision. The only conclusion warranted is that the short-lived case analysis competition had underscored the problems of adapting Beta Alpha Psi to a graduate constituency. Since students who had

participated had generally reported "a very positive experience," the decision to end the activity was made with particular reluctance.[3]

---

[3]"AACSB Accreditation Council"; "Accountant of the Year Awards," Annual Reports, 1980-81, ed. [Dean], p. 11, 1981-82, ed. [Henry R. Anderson], p. 12; [Anderson], ed., 1981-82 Annual Report, pp. 24, 28 ("Chapter Activities"), 31 ("Regional Meetings"); [Anderson], "Third National Student Program Held in Denver," Newsletter 17 (Fall 1978):2, material under photo; Donald F. Arnold, Sr., review of Financial Accounting: An Introduction to Concepts, Methods, and Uses, 3rd ed., by Davidson, Stickney, and Weil, The Accounting Review 48 (January 1983):183-84; Barron's Profiles, s.v. "California, University of Callifornia/Davis"; Beta Alpha Psi, "1981-82 Case Analysis Competition" (note 1), quoting pp. 1 (1st indented citation), 2, 4; "Beta Alpha Psi National Scholars," Annual Reports, 1982-83, ed. [Kiger], pp. 3-7, 1983-84, ed. [Metcalf], pp. 4-8; [Thomas J. Burns], "The Financial Accounting Standards Board and the Securities and Exchange Commission: An Uneasy Relationship," 1981-82 case, [1981], quoting p. 6 of text (2nd citation); Burns to Author, interview, May 3, 1980 (quoted), August 11, 1986; Frederick D. S. Choi, "SFAS No. 52 and the Funds Statement," contents, following page of credits and statement of purpose (quoted), of Beta Alpha Psi Graduate Student National Case Competition, 1983-1984 ([National Council], 1983); [Joyce C. Dean], "National Council," 1980-81 Annual Report, p. 3; exhibits 28, 35; "Financial Report," Annual Reports, 1982-83, p. 38, 1984-85, ed. [Tinius], p. 36; Laura Forrester, "Casey Dies," The Sun, Omicron newsletter, Winter 1985, p. 3; "Graduate Case Analysis Competition," Annual Reports, 1981-82, p. 11, 1982-83, p. 10, 1983-84, p. 26, quoting advance year's topic in 1st and 3rd cases; Hasselback, 1980-81 Directory, individual listing, s.v. "Casey Jr., Cornelius J.," "Griffin, Paul A.," "Horngren, Charles T.," "Stickney, Clyde P.," "Weil, Roman L.," 1983 Directory, school listing, s.v. "University of Missouri," 1984 Directory, school, s.v. "University of Alabama," "Univ. of California-Davis," individual, s.v. "Choi, Frederick D. S.," "Gaffney, Dennis J.," "Harmon, Kay P.," "Harris, Trevor S.," "Mueller, Gerhard G.," 1986 Directory, school, s.v. "University of Michigan," individual, s.v. "Mautz, R. David," "Poston, Kay"; Judith A. Hora, ed., Area of Accounting Annual Report, 1984 (Lubbock, Texas: Area of Accounting, Texas Tech University, [1985]), pp. 1 ("Accounting Faculty"), 4 ("Continuing Education"), 25 ("Beta Alpha Psi Competition"), 30 ("Masters Degrees"), shortened titles; Jack Kiger to Faculty Vice-Presidents, September 18 (quoted), with reply form, November 19 (including later handwritten notations), 1981; Kiger to Author, July 15, 1986, by telephone; "Local Chapter News," Newsletter 6 (Fall 1965):274; R. David Mautz, Jr., to Author, July 16, 1986, quoted; [Richard W. Metcalf], "Incoming Council Members," 1983-84 Annual Report, p. 19; [Fred J. Mueller], "Outstanding Faculty Vice Presidents," 1976-77 Annual Report, ed. [Mueller], p. 6; National Association of Accountants (NAA), Research Opportunities in Management Accounting (Montvale, N.J.: NAA, [1986]), p. 14; National Council Minutes, June 1980, p. 4, January 1981, p. 12, August 1981, p. 2, January 1982, p. 5, January 1983, p. 6, January 1984, p. 3, June 1984, p, 12, January 1985, p. 2 (all quoted), August 1980, p. 3, June 1981, p. 4, January 1982, p. 4, August 1982, p. 3, January 1983, pp. 2, 9, June 1983, p. 3, August 1983, p. 3, January 1984, p. 2, June 1984,

To conclude the study, the full-length coverage of alumni members provided in chapter 4 is updated by some thirty years in terms of two topic areas other than National Council representation. Alumni were the focus of a computerized national directory project originating in 1975 that after a series of twists and turns was at last defined in workable fashion eight years later; and also of a policy issue concerning the establishment of a new form of chapter that likewise arose prior to the sixth era.

Beta Alpha Psi Alumni

National Directory Project

Background to emergence of interest in 1974

A traditional theme within Beta Alpha Psi has been expressed in two different ways: (a) "Once a member, always a member"; and (b) "A member is a member wherever he [or she] is." This concept of lifetime affiliation invites continuing fraternal involvement of certain kinds after graduation, sometimes (as a matter of feasibility) within a different chapter. Shortly after retiring from the Council in 1979, Fred Mueller stated that such a viewpoint, championed by charter Advisory Forum leader Al Cohen and himself, had in modern times become somewhat eroded. Several years later Henry

---

pp. 11, 13, August 1984, pp. 6-8, January 1985, p. 1; "1986 Wildman Medal Award," AAA Accounting Education News, June 1986, pp. 10-11; 1969 Alpha Beta Chapter Directory (University, Ala.: Alpha Beta Chapter, [1969]), alphabetical listing, s.v. "Harrell, Mrs. Madlyn M."; Hugo Nurnburg, review of Financial Accounting: Concepts, Methods, and Uses, 3rd ed., by Davidson, Stickney, and Weil, The Accounting Review 48 (April 1983):466; Patrick L. Romano, ed., "NAA Research," Management Accounting 68 (July 1986):69; Author to Paul H. Munter, Texas Tech, July 27, and reply, August 6, 1986; [David E. Tinius], "Graduate Case Competition" articles, Newsletter 20 (Winter 1982):10, (Spring 1982):8, 21 (Fall 1982):12 (3rd indented citation), 22 (Fall 1983):12, (Winter 1984):7; and G[ary E.] White, accounting area director at Texas Tech, to Author, July 30, 1986. Also, [Thomas J. Burns], The Ohio State University: The Ph.D. Program in Accounting and Management Information Systems, 1986 ([Columbus: Academic Faculty of Accounting . . ., Ohio State University, 1985-86]), pp. 4-6; and Burns to Author, August 28, 1986.

Anderson commented, similarly, that students often "don't realize that they're members for life," and suggested that the fraternity should emphasize this theme to enhance their sense of the significance of Beta Alpha Psi membership.

A major reason for any erosion in this regard is surely the difficulty of maintaining reliable current records on alumni membership within a fraternity that had by Mueller's day become a very large organization, at national and (in many cases) local levels alike. The original national directory project conducted by Secretary-Treasurer Hermann Miller of Ohio State yielded a volume, in 1939, serving a body that had in twenty years initiated some 250 fewer students than the total of 3,538 reported by Hollis Dixon for the single year 1971-72, an annual level that would intself quickly seem very low. After the war, plans for an updated national project had foundered on high price quotations; and the substitute decentralized approach of having local chapters prepare their own directories, every third year, had soon become a fixture of the new activity program.

There is no evidence from the fifties or sixties of any dissatisfaction with this approach, or of any notion that additional alumni documentation was needed. Inevitably, however, some chapters developed better alumni records than others, and as serious work began on a national project in the seventies the inadequacy of many local files became apparent. A contributing factor may have been the elimination on the eve of "directory year" 1971-72 of directory updating from the activity program, as a matter of equity _and_ of desire not to identify it too closely with "participation" in a temporarily optional program.

Although the National Council continued to offer twenty-five cents per verified address, directories prepared in time for payment by June 30, 1972,

covered fewer than 7,000 of an historical roster (inclusive of deceased members) that had by then surpassed 50,000 men and women. Three years earlier more than 12,000 members had been listed. Another 4,700 verified addresses were accounted for during the fiscal year 1972-73, however, suggesting that the changed conditions had induced a more leisurely approach to directory preparation.

With the rise of electronic technology, the governing body in 1974 for the first time in a generation broached the possibility of developing a national directory. One of the oldest chapters soon came forth with a proposal that would fall short of its objectives, in practice, but still lead to a new method of initiation reporting as the first phase of a new project.

The Theta Chapter phase, 1975-77, yielding a new approach to initiation reporting

Discussion in August 1974 of *computerized* directory preparation "at the national level" may have been prompted by the arrival of the triennial directory year, and the imminent transfer to Secretary-Treasurer Fred Mueller of the massive files of membership records held by President Hollis Dixon. In any case, prior to the winter session Theta at Texas offered to conduct a "pilot project" involving adaptation of computer programs already used locally. Chapter advisor Allen H. Bizzell subsequently drew up a budget that was reviewed at the 1975 spring meeting.

Projected "high" costs, not recorded, brought forth a "consensus" that the formation of a "national alumni association" should be considered as a means of funding the project. Hollis Dixon, who urged his collegues to survey chapter attitudes concerning an association that would be linked closely to local chapters, suggested dues of five dollars, split equally

between the National Council and the alumni member's chapter. First-year councilor Thomas Burns was skeptical that a national directory would be worth the cost.

The alumni association idea was not mentioned again, suggesting that it had attracted no more grass-roots enthusiasm in 1975 than when it had been seriously considered twenty-one years earlier. Dixon's successor Robert Maust felt that the Theta Chapter proposal might offer a remedy to "a serious deficiency" in ability to identify, as such, members of Beta Alpha Psi. While in San Antonio in October to attend the annual convention of the American Institute of CPAs, Presidents Maust and Dixon met with Professor Bizzell and immediate Theta past president Patti Smith to discuss the project further. At the 1975-76 winter Council meeting, Maust was authorized to negotiate a contract with the Texas group subject to specified (but not reported) cost limits, and to develop documentation that he could present to potential sources of project funding. New councilor Albert Cohen, who at the same meeting registered his opposition to specifically identified funding, objected that the prospective cost was prohibitive.

Soon after the December meeting, Bob Maust commissioned Patti Smith "to design and test" a system to be implemented the following year, 1976-77. Prior to the spring meeting in April, Smith submitted a package of materials for distribution to the chapters, and such action was duly approved, along with an extra month's pay for the consultant if she were needed for further service. Flaws found in the input forms and updating procedures required additional work on Smith's part that led her to request still another month's pay. Noting that one additional payment had already been made, the National Council in August 1976 approved a final $500 payment contingent on receipt of a satisfactory printout showing the capabilities

of the computer programs.

Cost of this phase of the project is uncertain, as the financial reports combine it with payment for chapter directory material. The $1,307 amount reported for 1976-77 presumably included a second supplemental payment to the Theta alumna working on the computer programs, and may have included the prior one as well. Reported directory cost for 1975-76, at $3,279, was nearly as high as for the "directory" year preceding it, when $3,525 had been paid thirty-one chapters at a rate of $.30 per address. The former amount included unspecified costs, however, for directories submitted after June 1975.

At the meeting of August 1976, it was agreed that President Maust would "prepare a statement covering need for and benefits" of a national directory, in preparation for any questions that might be raised at the forthcoming National Chapter session. In his charter annual report, Maust had characterized the endeavor as follows:

> At the National Council level, the new system facilitates the transportation, maintenance, and storage of . . . membership records as well as providing a back-up file and simplifying the retrieval of information for special request . . .. At the local chapter level, the new system facilitates the up-dating of membership records as well as providing a camera-ready copy of membership data for the preparation of chapter directories.

This description implies that the system would include original membership data as filed on roll cards over the prior history of Beta Alpha Psi; similar data for all new initiations as reported; and periodically updated mailing addresses for fraternal alumni. In the first regard, the project promised to harmonize the viewpoints of, for example, Fred Mueller, who felt obliged as secretary-treasurer to maintain the fraternity's historical records, and his successor Joyce Dean, who saw no value in much of the archival material. Mueller recalls that the national files occupied half

of his two-car garage in Seattle, and that more than half of that storage was made up of roll cards. A system of the kind described by Bob Maust would permit retention of the card data without the physical cards.

During the spring of 1976 Secretary-Treasurer Mueller had shipped the Theta roll card files to Patti Smith for processing at Texas; and as incoming president he had planned to have all remaining card files keypunched at Washington, for transmittal to Austin. Those plans were derailed, however, by persistent shortcomings in Smith's program. The full set of roll cards were shipped to the newly created National Office in 1979.

One vital part of the system did become operational, on schedule, in 1976-77, namely, the keypunching at the local chapter level of all data on new initiates. Punched cards thus replaced traditional roll cards, although edited "Data Request Forms" completed by the new members as the records of original entry were submitted with them, initially to the activity program director for awarding points under program category 2. "In the unlikely event" that a chapter lacked keypunching capability, the handwritten (or typewritten) forms would suffice. The change occurred with the passing of the secretary-treasurer position from Fred Mueller, who had "nearly [gone] blind" trying to read some of the roll cards submitted, to Joyce Dean.

By the summer of 1977 the problems of extending the Theta system to a nationwide roster of chapters had otherwise not been resolved. At that time the project entered a new phase with the withdrawal of the Texas chapter from the picture. Over the next two years the secretary-treasurer, a national president, and a National Advisory Forum member and his firm would take leadership roles in an unsuccessful effort to overcome the programming limitations.

Direct Supervision by National Council, and project suspension, 1977-79

In July 1977, Allen Bizzell, Patti Smith, and others met on the Baylor campus with Secretary-Treasurer Joyce Dean and her secretary Evelyn Hupp to discuss adaptation of the national directory programs to the local Honeywell computer. That meeting in effect marked the end of Theta Chapter involvement.

The major developments over the following year were forum chairperson David Abramson's call for completion of the project "to facilitate alumni solicitation," and the emergence of potential funding of the project by Peat Marwick. Joyce Dean evidently received a nominal honorarium as "National Directory Coordinator." In August 1978, a tradition ended as Fred Mueller's motion to provide financial assistance for the updating of chapter directories was not even seconded.

On a more positive note, the Council accepted Jim Pattillo's motion to approach the directory matter through a committee. Incoming president and (in collaboration with Abramson) funding coordinator Tom Burns appointed himself as the chairman of a group also including Dean, Alumni Councilor Mark McClure, Peat Marwick forum representative James A. Morgan, "and hopefully Peat, Marwick, Mitchell personnel." The committee's assigned "charge" was "to make progress on [the] directory."

By January, Peat Marwick had provided $2,500 in cash support, although 1978-79 financial reports identify no revenue or expense for the directory project. Consultant "personnel" from the firm worked on the programs inherited from Theta Chapter in an effort to remove remaining "bugs."

Any progress made was very limited. In June 1979, it was reported that work on the project had been "suspended," and in August discussion of

the topic was "deferred." New president James Pattillo did not appoint a directory committee. Under his leadership, however, the National Council made new arrangements that advanced the project significantly over the next two years.

The Control Data phase, 1980-81

The only information provided in the winter minutes of 1979-80 was that work on the directory had been resumed. In a spring interview, Tom Burns reported that one of his former students at Minnesota was helping President Pattillo bring the project to completion. Advisory Forum member Gary E. Polaczyk was the controller at Control Data Corporation in Minneapolis.

Polaczyk's first task was to convert to magnetic tape the punched-card files recording initiations since 1976. Finding many processing errors (despite provision for correction at the national level), he sent all deviant cards to the national office in Sarasota, with error reports and instructions, to be forwarded to the chapters for correction. This stage of the process was announced to the National Chapter at the 1980 convention, along with plans for the national administrator to send each active chapter formed before 1976-77 a photocopy transcription of its entire file of roll cards, for keypunching according to instructions provided. The Control Data controller planned likewise to convert the earlier initiation files to tape, and had set a target of January 1981, just five months away, for a comprehensive printout of original initiation data.

The area of updating the files to provide current addresses and, presumably, employment data for living members, and to identify deceased ones, was finally mentioned during the 1980-81 winter meeting, when Past President Jim Pattillo was assigned to send appropriate instructions to the chapters.

A member of the accounting services staff at Control Data had reported a month earlier, however, that "many" chapter representatives were already working with alumni offices to develop such information, and indirectly implied that some of it had already been processed.

At the meeting of January 1981, it was reported that the correction of 1976-80 chapter initiation cards was moving slowly, and no reference was made to the processing of prior roll cards. Nonetheless, a "first run" of available information was still planned for later in the month, and a second one was slated for June. It was decided that Gary Polaczyk would send a full list of nonrespondent chapters to Pattillo, who would then telephone the local units. A motion was made and seconded that any chapters not providing the corrected data by June would forfeit eligibility for activity-program scholarship awards, but was withdrawn following discussion.

At the June meeting, finally, it was announced that the data collected would be "out of" Control Data as of July 1, 1981, and several options were discussed for continuing the project. In addition, a provision for the updating of mailing addresses was added to the activity program, ten years after the triennial-directory element had been withdrawn. Although no details are available concerning chapter response during the winter and spring, it is fair to conclude that the dimensions of the project, behavioral as well as technical, had outgrown the scope of an essentially volunteer contribution by a forum member. The total of slightly more than $800 in project cost reported for 1979-80 and 1980-81, more than two thirds of it for the former year, no doubt represented only a small fraction of regular commercial expense for comparable services.

During the following year the National Council reviewed corporate proposals for continuing the project, and approved a fund-raising effort in

that regard that would itself have been rather costly, in a final effort to sustain the original vision of a comprehensive computerized directory.

Review of corporate proposals in a final effort to preserve the original objectives, 1981-82

As of the close of the volunteer Control Data phase, the essential options open to the fraternity (beyond simply abondoning the protracted effort) were to support an expensive corporate project, or to reduce the scale of the enterprise to the point that it could be handled internally. At first only the former alternative was considered. One possibility cited in August 1981 was returning the project to Control Data, on a regular contractual basis, through its Tampa office (near Sarasota). Another data processing firm, Epsilon Data Management, made a presentation during the convention meeting with charter area councilors, and joined Independent Electronics Corporation in submitting recommendations that were reviewed at the 1981-82 winter session.

Substantial expense was clearly implied, because Advisory Forum chairperson Thomas Nessinger was authorized to spend up to $2,000 (or even more, on approval by President Henry Anderson) for a "professional fund raiser" on behalf of the project. Such an initiative would not be undertaken, however. Due to Hurricane Alberto, Nessinger and Richard Metcalf missed the meeting of June 1982 at Key West, Florida. More importantly, the forum leader and his National Council colleagues reached the conclusion that the comprehensive project "was too difficult to handle." The idea of a funded Beta Alpha Psi endeavor thus "died of its own weight."

The result was adoption of the second course mentioned above, a process that would yield a full-fledged national "roster" by the summer of 1984.

Concluding phase, 1983-84: Development of a membership "roster" filed at the National Office

The meeting of August 1982 marks a transitional point en route to a scaled-back, workable, and inexpensive project. It was announced to assembled chapter representatives that punched cards would no longer be needed in reporting initiations or updated information. The following January, the comprehensive project was finally abandoned, after eight years, with the approval of a motion by new faculty councilor Richard Murdock that a "National Membership Roster" (emphasis added) be compiled for maintenance at the national office in Sarasota. This computerized system would record the names, schools, and initiation dates of the historical membership, as supplied by the chapters.

Director of Chapter Activities Murdock developed the roster from a tape supplied by Control Data Corporation of all information earlier collected. He recorded the appropriate data on disks designed for use on the IBM computer in Sarasota. In June 1983 he was authorized to spend up to $1,000 for assistance in completing that task by summer's end.

Subsequent financial reports do not identify such an expenditure, and in any case (almost, in light of prior stages of the project, as if by destiny) Murdock's timetable would prove to be too optimistic. It was finally announced in August 1984, however, that a "floppy disk file" for the reported members of each chapter was in place at central headquarters, and that newly initiated members were routinely being recorded therein. The activities program was appropriately modified at that point to require chapters to "update the list of . . . member[s]" rather than alumni mailing

addresses.[4]

In keeping with the traditional concept of lifetime membership, alumni participation within Beta Alpha Psi activity is in no sense a recent development. Near the close of the fifth era, however, the topic of formal organization of alumni groups reappeared as a local initiative that attracted National Council attention at a policy level. Guidelines established for alumni "chapters" were reiterated during the sixth era as other interesting approaches to alumni involvement were also observed.

Local Alumni Chapters

Developments Prior to 1978

As related in chapter 4, alumni organizations were formed during the year 1950-51 relative to one of the oldest chapters, Theta at Texas, and

---

[4]Henry R. Anderson to Author, interview, April 18, 1986, quoted; Beta Alpha Psi, "1977-1978 Program for Chapter Activities," [1977], pp. 7 (quoted), 17-18; Thomas J. Burns to Joyce C. Dean, September 1, 1978, with enclosed list of committees, p. 1, quoted; Burns to Author, interview, May 3, 1980; Hollis A. Dixon, Secretary-Treasurer's Report, 1971-72, pp. 8-10, 1972-73, p. [12]; [Harvey E. Donley], "1968-69 Instructions for Activity Program," Newsletter 8 (Fall 1968):7; [Donley], Secretary-Treasurer's Report, 1968-69, p. 23; "Financial Reports," 2nd page, Annual Reports, 1975-76 through 1980-81, 1983-84; Grand Council Minutes Book, 1948, p. 1; Maureen McLaughlin, Control Data Corp., to Author, December 17, 1980, quoted; [Robert S. Maust], "Computerization of Membership Data," 1975-76 Annual Report, ed. [Maust], p. [11], quoted; Maust to Author, interview, July 14, 1980, quoted; Hermann C. Miller, ed., Beta Alpha Psi Directory, preface; Fred J. Mueller, Secretary-Treasurer's Report, 1974-75, p. 19, 1975-76, pp. 6, 21; Mueller to Author, interview, November 27, 1979 (source of quoted lifetime membership adages), by telephone, August 11, 1986 (quoted, 2nd conversation of date); National Council Minutes, August 1974, p. 2, February 1975, p. 2, May-June, 1975, p. 5, August 1976, p. 5, January 1978, p. 5, June 1978, p. 6, June 1979, p. 4, August 1979, p. 9, June 1980, p. 8, January 1981, p. 10, January 1982, p. 1, January 1983, p. 1, August 1984, p. 9 (all quoted), 1971, p. 7, May-June, 1975, pp. 3, 11, December 1975, pp. 3-4, April 1976, p. 6, August 1976, pp. 7-8, August 1977, p. 3, June 1978, p. 3, August 1978, p. 1, January 1979, p. 3, August 1979, p. [2], June 1980, pp. 5-6, August 1980, p. 6, August 1981, pp. 4-5, January 1982, p. 2, June 1982, p. 1, August 1982, p. 5, January 1983, p. 2, June 1983, pp. 1-2; Thomas J. Nessinger to Author, July 18, 1986, quoted; [James W. Pattillo], "Beta Alpha Psi, 1979-80: Objectives, Functions, and Committees," (chapter 13, note 5), pp. 2-7; [Pattillo], "National Advisory Forum," 1979-80 Annual Report, pp. 8-9; and Sheldahl, Alpha to Omega, pp. 181, 757-59.

one of the newest ones, Alpha Gamma at the City College of New York; and three years later a serious movement to form a national alumni body with chapters in major metropolitan areas foundered on lack of interest. When President Hollis Dixon suggested in 1975 that such a group might be formed for fund-raising purposes, he asked the other councilors to sample attitudes from the chapter level concerning a national alumni organization "closely tied" to the local units.

Although the matter was not pursued in depth at the time, Special Projects Councilor Bob Maust made an interesting comment on the kind of alumni chapter that had been considered in the fifties. He feared that "rural schools would loose [sic] contact with their own" alumni "if members were listed" by area of residence rather than by original chapter. Harvey Donley, who had served with Maust on the governing body for two years after having been instrumental in his 1971 appointment, stated later that the National Council had generally opposed "alumni chapters," on the basis that former student members should be encouraged to participate in their original units.

Motivated by outside developments, the Council in 1978, at Professor Maust's last meeting, adopted guidelines on the organization of alumni chapters.

Establishment of a policy in 1978, following an initiative at South Florida

The first modern-day alumni chapter appears to have been formed by alumni of Delta Gamma at South Florida. According to chapter sources, it was started in 1978, five years after the installation in Tampa. In January 1978, however, the Council discussed the "[f]ormation of alumni groups," and Tom Burns was appointed to chair a committee, also including Jim Pattillo

and Fred Mueller, to draft a "policy statement" on the matter. Following the deletion of a sentence relating alumni chapter formation to the directory project, and a minor change in word order, their statement was adopted at the August meeting.

It is not clear that a strictly isolated case at South Florida would have prompted such action, and the wording of the document implies that a few other alumni groups were being formed at the time. The National Council wished to be entirely neutral toward the creation of an alumni unit, while specifying the conditions under which it would have legitimate claim to the Beta Alpha Psi title.

The starting point was the idea that, with an unstated qualification for "faculty" members moving from one fraternal school to another, membership in a chapter was "permanent" in the absence of resignation or expulsion. An alumnus member would always be entitled to attend "any or all activities" of his or her chapter or (if more convenient) another unit. Also, all chapters were "[a]s a minimum" encouraged to select alumni of the year in each category within the national Accountant of the Year program.

A distinct alumni "chapter" was expected to meet several conditions:

1. Have the same Greek name as the existing chapter
2. Have a relationship to the overall fraternity, the National Council, and the National Chapter similar to the existing chapter's
3. Limit membership to student, faculty, and honorary members of the local chapter, except where it would be more convenient for a person with a different home chapter to affiliate with the alumni group
4. Conform to the national constitution and bylaws.

Although stated separately, item 4 was presumably a major part of the intent of the second requirement.

The major thrust of these formal constraints was to reduce the risk that an alumni organization would undermine a chapter's relationship to former student members, in particular, or otherwise conflict with its

program. The first rule was challenged, without success, by a South Florida group that wished to be known as "Alpha" alumni chapter, in recognition of its apparent status as the first such unit of modern times. Certainly the alternative approach to name identity would have invited confusion, and severed a vital bond with the regular local chapter.

In January 1979, the constitution and bylaws themselves were amended to incorporate the adopted guidelines, in essence, and require at least ten petitioners for the establishment of an alumni chapter. These provisions were later deleted from the governing documents, leaving National Council policy in the area less fundamental than before. This development probably did not occur until 1983, more than a year after the retirement of Jim Pattillo, recalled by Tom Burns as the member "most strongly in favor of alumni chapters."

By multiple irony, Pattillo had himself been the lone dissenter to the 1979 constitutional and bylaw amendments offered by his alumni committee colleague Doris Cook, although his prior committee associate Fred Mueller had assented only "with reservations." The onetime advisor to Iota at Southern California, in Los Angeles, favored provision for "metropolitan" chapters that would not be associated with any particular existing unit, but would serve all Beta Alpha Psi alumni living in a particular area. That approach, criticized earlier by Bob Maust, had been considered by the Grand Council and proposed by Mu Chapter at NYU respectively one and two generations earlier, in 1954 and 1930.

The alternative concept is found within the business honor society Beta Gamma Sigma. Indeed, as of 1980 alumni chapters were identified with "New England" and "Arizona," as well as New York City, Philadelphia, Atlanta, and southern Florida. Founded more than fifty years earlier, the New York

organization in 1986 had more than 1,400 members, and reported holding periodic luncheon or early evening meetings. Although Beta Gamma Sigma is more active at the local level than most honor societies, it still differs materially in that regard from a professional body such as Beta Alpha Psi. The prevailing opinion within the National Council has been that "metropolitan" chapters would too often deprive local chapters of alumni participation, of one kind or another, within their programs.

Although he was the principal draftsman of the 1978 policy statement, Thomas Burns was among the most skeptical councilors regarding the merits of alumni chapters. He "always opposed them," because he "could not foresee any need for them given [the] strength of the professional organizations" in public accounting, management accounting, internal auditing, financial administration, and so forth. A similar viewpoint has been expressed by Wilton Anderson and A. J. Penz. From this standpoint, if alumni wish to remain involved in Beta Alpha Psi, they should do so as an extension of their student participation, not through a separate organization.

A more positive viewpoint is taken by Henry Anderson, who views alumni units as a natural outgrowth of a period of "high vitality" within a chapter. The student members develop a strong camaraderie that they wish to maintain after graduation. From this perspective, an alumni chapter can add a dimension not ordinarily found within professional organizations having a much broader membership base relative to distinct areas of professional practice.

The alumni chapter issue faded from National Council attention after the actions taken in 1978 and at the beginning of '79. It came up again three years later through the interest of the alumni councilor, following an unproductive funding experiment that had been undertaken among alumni members.

Renewed interest early in the sixth era in alumni membership and organization

A 1981 fund-raising experiment

In January 1981, Past President James Pattillo suggested that a special fund-raising campaign be conducted among Beta Alpha Psi alumni. Proceeds would be split equally between the national treasury and, in proportion to the contributions made by their respective memberships, the source chapters. Henry Anderson's motion that nine local units be invited to participate at an experimental level carried with two dissents and an abstention, and later in the year as chairman of an "Experiment" committee he contacted fifteen chapters. Ten of them responded promptly, and (it appears) favorably, and a minimum request of $15 was set.

The 1981 initiative, which was not tied specifically to the directory project, was abandoned after only one round of requests. Due to relatively low total proceeds, the one-half share owing to participating chapters was divided equally among them, rather than on a proportional basis. As a rough estimate of the response level, if the increase of $609 in "[o]ther" revenue reported in 1981-82 was based on alumni contributions, each at the $15 minimum, then eighty-one persons (a rounded total) would have participated, an average of eight per chapter.

At the meeting at which the final reference was made to the fund-raising experiment, the topic of alumni chapters resurfaced as the appropriate councilor announced his planned special project for the year.

Alumni Councilor Rosman's 1982 survey

In the only recorded action on the chapter issue during the first two years of the sixth era, the National Council had in June 1981 approved the

adoption of a banner by an alumni group, consistent with general policy governing that symbol. The two alumni chapters for which such information has been obtained, Alpha Nu at Creighton and Delta Gamma at South Florida, did not adopt their own banners.

At the 1981-82 winter meeting, alumni representative Andrew Rosman from Delta Pi at Hofstra reported plans to survey the fraternal roster on the nature and extent of alumni-chapter formation and activity to date, and the existing level of interest in the topic. An accountant with Touche Ross on Long Island who had in Doris Cook's 1979 regional-meetings monograph advocated a social responsibility slant within financial reporting, Rosman would soon be viewing the reporting function as a member of the staff at the FASB. In 1985 he began doctoral study at North Carolina.

In May 1982, Andy Rosman sent a brief questionnaire on alumni chapters to 148 faculty vice-presidents. A covering letter that summarized his interpretation of the 1978 policy statement provided a much more explicit assertion of objectives (chapter assistance, professional/student interaction, and financial support to the national fraternity) than had appeared in the document itself. Four questions were raised:

a. Does your school have an alumni chapter, or plan to start one?
b. If there is a chapter, how large is it? What are its activities?
c. Would the formation of an alumni unit, if one does not exist, benefit your chapter and the national fraternity?
d. Should the National Council debate the matter, and develop (beyond past coverage) an official policy?.

Seventy-two responses were received. Only those from Alpha Nu at Creighton, Epsilon Delta at Missouri-Kansas City, and Epsilon Alpha at Portland State reported that alumni chapters were in place. Delta Gamma at South Florida was among the 76 nonrespondents. Delta Beta at Seattle, the home chapter of Newsletter editor David Tinius, indicated plans to start

a group in the fall, although as noted later a broader approach to organization of accounting alumni would instead be taken at the school, on a delayed basis. The Alpha Nu alumni unit, formed in 1981, was still functioning in 1986, by which point the pioneering Delta Gamma group had become defunct.

The responses are tabulated in exhibit 36, drawn from Rosman's report to the Council at the close of his one-year term. Only slightly more than three fifths of the 69 advisors whose chapters did not have such affiliates felt that alumni chapters would be desirable, although a higher proportion favored National Council review of the issue. The three chapters, two of them formed over the prior five years, that had already given rise to alumni chapters credited them with the following areas of activity on their behalf:

<u>Alpha Nu</u> - Sponsoring of scholarships, and involvement in professional meetings

<u>Epsilon Alpha</u> - Assistance in professional meetings and social activities; judging of speech and (probably in relation to national submissions) manuscripts contests

<u>Epsilon Delta</u> - Special events and fund raising.

Early in 1986, a chapter was formed by alumni of Eta Gamma at Central Florida, to conduct social functions and generate funds for the campus unit. School of accounting director Hank Anderson reported the following summer that the question of admitting alumni from other chapters who resided in the area had not as yet arisen, although they would probably be considered eligible.

Several interesting comments were obtained in the 1982 survey. Positively, it was suggested that alumni chapters could help sustain school ties; provide guidance to the National Council; and encourage alumni support for local chapter activities. Negatively, some FVPs felt that such groups were at best redundant; could conflict with chapter fund raising; and

EXHIBIT 36

GEOGRAPHICALLY CLASSIFIED SUMMARY OF RESPONSE TO ANDREW ROSMAN'S 1982 SURVEY ON ALUMNI CHAPTERS

A question[n]aire was mailed to 148 faculty vice-presidents during May 1982 seeking responses to the following questions:

1. Do you have an active Alumni Chapter or plans to begin one?
2. If you do have a Chapter, what are some of the activities which are participated in? How large is your membership?
3. If you do not have a Chapter, do you believe that its formation would be beneficial to your Chapter, and the National Fraternity?
4. Do you believe that the National Council should debate the issue and formally draft a policy statement?
5. Additional comments.

SUMMARY OF RESPONSES

	1			3			4		
	Yes	No	*	Yes	No	*	Yes	No	*
Northwest, Rocky Mountain, and Northern California	1	9	-	5	4	1	6	3	1
Midwest and Missouri Valley	2	21	-	12	7	4	16	3	4
Southwest and Southern California/Arizona	-	14	-	5	8	1	5	6	3
Southeast	-	15	-	11	4	-	9	5	1
Northeast	-	10	-	8	2	-	8	2	-
	3	69	-	41	25	6	44	19	9

*No reply to this question.

Excerpted from "National Council of Beta Alpha Psi: Report [or 'Study', page 1] on Alumni Chapters," by Andrew J. Rosman, August 1972, pp. 1, [5]. In tabulating replies to question 1, the reference made to "plans to begin" a chapter was clearly disregarded.

might compete in other ways with regular chapters, interfering in particular with alumni participation. Some opposition was registered to the level of national control exercised over the operation of alumni units, perhaps a factor in the elimination of constitutional coverage.

Three significantly different forms of nonchapter alumni organization may be illustrated in closing this section. Of the three chapters involved, two represent the same city, and two are single-letter groups founded before 1930.

Other modes of continuing alumni participation: Three examples

Delta Chapter Alumni Association, formed in preparation for a golden anniversary

Delta Chapter was founded at Washington in 1921. With a long tradition of active alumni support, around 200 past student members, on Fred Mueller's estimate, were counted among the some 350 persons attending the fiftieth-anniversary celebration in May 1971, some of them having traveled from other parts of the United States. That total would have represented one in seven of Delta's historical membership roster. In addition, current student members of the chapter were on hand, along with professional accountants, spouses, and other guests not affiliated with the chapter. Included among participating alumni were charter Delta brothers Fred W. Woodbridge, the early national president, and Kent W. Ratcliffe, a 1928 Washington graduate.

Much of the credit for the remarkable alumni representation belongs to the Delta Chapter Alumni Association, an unincorporated nonprofit association that had been formed, in the first instance, to plan and conduct the 1971 event. On a continuing basis, the association endowed a scholarship for "worthy members of the Chapter," in memory of charter member and fourth

national president William E. Cox. The scholarship program remained intact in 1986, fifteen years after the first award had been made.

A much more "active" alumni organization exists in relation to a much younger chapter based in Seattle.

"Accounting Alumni & Friends" at Seattle, largely involving leadership of Delta Eta alumni

An organization named the Accounting Alumni & Friends of Seattle University (AAFSU) was founded in the spring of 1985, primarily for purposes of "generating alumni support" for the accounting department "through social activities." According to 1984-85 national president David Tinius, his department is "careful to ask all past accounting majors" and its "friends in the profession" to join the organization.

AAFSU has a vital, although indirect, relationship to Delta Eta Chapter. The outgoing president of the undergraduate chapter joins the governing board of directors. The charter president of the alumni organization was 1983-84 Delta Eta president Therese Coad, a former piano teacher with two music degrees from Washington who had become interested in accounting while working for a family business. At Seattle, she completed "the undergraduate accounting coursework" while working on an M.B.A. degree conferred after she had joined the local office of Touche Ross & Co. Coad's immediate predecessor and successor in the chapter post were likewise first-year officers of the new Seattle group.

AAFSU hosts semiannual receptions, planned in large measure by "Beta Alpha Psi student liaisons"; publishes an annual newsletter, edited in 1986 (its first year) by a student member of the chapter who had a year earlier joined with a classmate to organize the first alumni gathering;

and assists in an established annual telephone campaign for the accounting program. "[A]s usual, several Arthur Andersen employees arrived a half-hour early" for the second reception, perhaps compensating for the fact that Advisory Forum leader Tom Nessinger had been <u>late</u> for the 1980 installation of Zeta Alpha at Purdue, "a terrible thing for an Arthur Andersen man" as observed by backup installation officer Tom Burns. The first issue of the periodical, tentatively named "Subsequent Events," included a reply form for "Project A.S.K. -- Alumni Sharing Knowledge," by which alumni and other sources could "serv[e] as personal career resources" to the accounting majors on campus.

Therese Coad and undergraduate organizers Madeline O'Rourke and Deborah Scott (one of only five 1986-87 student interns at the FASB) joined Seattle department head William L. Weis in an invited presentation on AAFSU at the 1985 Beta Alpha Psi convention in Reno, Nevada. Newsletter editor O'Rourke summed up her impressions as follows:

> Given the turnout and enthusiasm at our presentations . . ., we expect our model for establishing an alumni organization to be emulated by accounting programs around the country.

Somewhat more cautiously, David Tinius observed in 1986 that with an average Beta Alpha Psi membership of 25-30 students, around 60 graduates annually, and a "general egalitarian philosophy" regarding service, his department had found an appropriate vehicle to reach professional accountants "predisposed" to provide support.

Finally, a less formal approach to alumni activity facilitated by a strong national internship program is identified with Omicron at Ohio State.

Informal association in Houston (for example) of alumni of Omicron at Ohio State

<u>A Newsletter</u> notice of March 1932 reported that many Omicron brothers

were doing public accounting "field work" during the winter quarter, an early reference to one of the nation's foremost student internship programs. After some years in which Columbus itself was the site of the majority of the appointments, by the early eighties half or more of them were in other major cities throughout the nation. Twenty-three of the 58 interns of the 1985 winter term were Beta Alpha Psi students working in Chicago, Cincinnati, Cleveland, Dallas, Houston, New York, Phoenix, and San Jose.[5]

One such student was Susan Zeleznik, who was with Arthur Andersen in Houston. The Texas city had become the most popular out-of-town locale for interning Ohio State students, having a year earlier attracted half of the 32 majors not based in Columbus, including 10 Omicron officers. Like many other students, upon graduation Zeleznik was hired by the office in which she had worked during her senior year.

A note contributed by the new alumna to the chapter newsletter of Winter 1986 related highlights of extensive professional and social interaction that was taking place among the many Omicron student and alumni members, in particular, resident in Houston. During the football season, preceding the arrival of interns, chapter alumni had frequently gathered at Judith's Bar and Restaurant, along with other Ohio State graduates, "to cheer the

---

[5]Ohio State also conducts an "industrial accounting" internship program, in the summer, for rising seniors. Unlike the public accounting assignments, the availability of such opportunities is highly dependent on general economic conditions. Nicholas Ecos, the fourth alumni councilor, held appointments of both kinds before joining Textron in 1978. At least nine of the 1983-84 officers of Omicron Chapter had held industrial internships the prior summer, eight of them in Ohio. Four of those students worked for Deloitte Haskins & Sells in Houston during the winter quarter in '84, and another one (the chapter president) was with the Arthur Andersen office in that city. Nicholas S. Eços, remarks as National Chapter Meeting panelist, August 21, 1979 (tape recorded); Jim Sandry, "Industrial Accounting Internship Program," The Sun, Omicron newsletter, Winter 1984, p. 6; and Debbie Varrasso, "Public Accounting Intership Program," The Sun, Winter 1984, p. 6.

Buck[eye]s on," presumably in the context of radio or television coverage of the games. Other favorite activities including Sunday-evening cookouts. On a somewhat different level, Zeleznik added the following list of activities:

> Down here there are [a] few things that every Yankee has to try. One is kicker dancing with the locals (Texas two step), a second the rodeo in February and third the great chili cook-off! Believe me we've done it all!.[6]

---

[6]AAA Road Atlas, p. 77, s.v. "Melville"; Henry R. Anderson to Author, interview, April 18 (quoted), August 7, 1986; Wilton T. Anderson to Author, interview, March 20, 1980; appendix 3; Beta Alpha Psi, "National Bylaws," articles 18 (1977), 21 (1983), "National Constitution," article 5, section 1, National Constitution and Bylaws (1977, 1983); Beta Gamma Sigma Directory, 1980-81, pp. 9, 15, 23 (quoted); Thomas J. Burns to Author, interview, May 3, 1980, July 8, 1986, both quoted; [Burns (chairman), Fred J. Mueller, and James W. Pattillo, comprising draft committee], "Draft of Policy Statement on Alumni Chapters for the National Council of Beta Alpha Psi," [1978], one-page typescript, quoted; [Doris M. Cook and James W. Pattillo, representing Alumni Committee], "Proposed changes in National Constitution" and Proposed changes in National Bylaws," [1979], one-page typescript, addition of alumni-chapter coverage; Andrew Corbin, "Internships," The Sun, Winter 1985, p. 7; Harvey E. Donley to Author, interview, May 2, 1980; exhibit 36; "Financial Report," 1981-82 Annual Report, ed. [Henry R. Anderson], p. 35, quoted; "Former Beta Alpha Psi National Presidents," 1983-84 Annual Report, ed. [Metcalf], inside front cover; Hasselback, 1986 Directory, school listing, s.v. "University of Central Florida"; Robert S. Maust to Author, by telephone, June 10, 1986; Hermann C. Miller, ed., Beta Alpha Psi Directory, s.v. "Delta Chapter: Ratcliffe, Kent W."; Fred J. Mueller to Author, interview, November 27, 1979, by telephone (twice), August 11, 1986; Name This Newsletter, Accounting Alumni and Friends of Seattle University, 1 (Spring 1986):2 (1st indented citation), 10, 16 (both quoted), 3, 6-9, 11; National Council Minutes, May-June, 1975, p. 5, January 1978, p. 5, January 1979, p. 2 (each quoted), August 1978, p. 2, January 1981, pp. 5-6, June 1981, pp. 9, 12, August 1981, p. 5, January 1982, p. 7, June 1983, p. 1; "News from the Chapters," Newsletter [1] (March 1932):9, quoted; "Notes," Beta Gamma Sigma Newsletter, June 1986, p. 2; James W. ("Jim") Pattillo to Author, August 12, 1986; A. J. Penz to Author, interview, April 18, 1980 (isolated alumni-chapter remark); Thomas J. Purcell III, Alpha Nu FVP, to Author, July 7, 1986; Andrew J. Rosman, "National Council of Beta Alpha Psi: Report on Alumni Chapters," August 1972, 10-page documentation of survey; Rosman, "The Prime Objective of Financial Statements Should be to Provide Information on the Activities of the Enterprise Affecting Society," Current Issues in Accounting, ed. Cook (chapter 14, note 8), pp. 150-53; [Harold L. Royer], "Delta Chapter Celebrates 50th Anniversary," Newsletter 10 (Fall 1971):3, quoted; Sheldahl, Alpha to Omega, pp. 361-63; William L. Stephens, Delta Gamma FVP, to Author,

OMICRON ALUMNI SOCIALIZING IN HOUSTON, 1985-86
(Susan Zeleznik is standing third from right.)

On that note of extra-professional activity, extending beyond the cut-off year 1984, it is time to conclude this study of three Beta Alpha Psi eras and part of a fourth one.

In Conclusion

The title of this volume is in one respect ironic. Nearly forty years of organizational history marked by remarkable growth in chapter roster, student levels, national program, complexity of governance, financial resources, internal and external participation, and overall diversity are represented geographically by a passage from Omega at Miami of Ohio, one regional state university, to Zeta Omega at Ball State in Indiana, another such school. The two references serve a related unifying function, however, since an Omega team traveled some sixty-five miles, from Oxford to Muncie, to help install Zeta Omega in April 1984. In closing, mention may be made of the principal topics of chapter 1, again, and to the possibility raised in '84 of another dramatic kind of expansion of the Beta Alpha Psi community.

The Delta Eta and Omicron alumnae just cited are reminders of the prominence of women within the contemporary fraternity, one sign that data showing that in 1983 one per cent of the partners and principals within the nine largest CPA firms were female will soon seem archaic as well as inequitable. Developments of the sixth era just beyond the present scope of converage that highlight modern-day fraternal pluralism include the reinstatement in the fall of 1984 of Eta at Boston, more than fifty years after its expulsion due to predominantly Jewish membership; and the appointment to the

---

July 14, 1986; [David E. Tinius], "The National Council Report on Alumni Chapters," Newsletter 21 (Winter 1976):1, accompanying information on Andrew Rosman; Tinius to Author, July 8, August 13, 1986, both quoted; Debbie Varasso, "Public Accounting Internship Program," The Sun, Winter 1984, p. 6; and Susan Zeleznik, "Houston Happenings," The Sun, Winter 1986, p. 8, quoted, including 2nd indented citation.

National Advisory Forum a year later of President William Aiken of the National Association of Black Accountants. An active Minority Recruitment and Equal Opportunity program begun in 1969 by the American Institute of CPAs had by '82 helped increase the number of black certified public accountants in the United States approximately tenfold. In the earlier year, institute president Louis Kessler had reported at the Beta Alpha Psi golden anniversary banquet that there were only some 150 black CPAs nationwide.

At the very close of the period covered, the possibility was raised of creating an _international_ fraternity through forming a liaison of some kind with universities in Canada. Prior to the 1984 convention in Toronto, invitations were sent to "many" Canadian schools to join outgoing and incoming presidents Metcalf and Tinius, along with two other board members, for a breakfast discussion of Beta Alpha Psi. After guests from four campuses had registered "great enthusiasm" concerning possible linkage of their programs in some way with the fraternity, the board of directors were disappointed by the "very limited" interest shown during the year 1984-85 in attending functions at "border" chapters. President David Tinius reported plans in 1985 to approach the matter through a "more personal university to university program."

It is decidedly premature in any case to consider policy implications of _chapter formation_ in Canada. An obvious problem would be the accreditation, as of 1986, of only two Canadian universities by the American Assembly of Collegiate Schools of Business. The University of Alberta received undergraduate and graduate recognition in 1968 and 1973, respectively, while the University of Calgary obtained both forms of accreditation in 1985. The University of British Columbia qualified at both levels in 1969, but

voluntarily withdrew from the accreditation council five years later. In 1968 the National Council had mentioned the possibility of contacting "new Canadian member<u>s</u>" of the AAcCSB (emphasis added), apparently including schools that held a nonevaluative "associate" status of the day, but there is no record that such action occurred.

Perhaps the foremost challenge facing the Board of Directors as of 1984 was to preserve a tradition of intense commitment to student-centered service within a modern environment equally rich in resources and in potential behavioral obstacles to their most beneficial use. Charter member and local president Russell Morrison, Alpha at Illinois '19, was understandably "amazed to see the scope, nature and vitality of the educational activities" of 1983-84 as reflected in the annual report sent him by Thomas Nessinger, a partner from his last years (1967-70) with Arthur Andersen in Chicago. Referring, however, to "political" conflicts and private "agendas" that he had experienced (he felt) in national office, Henry Anderson, Gamma Theta '68 (twenty-two years after Missouri had made the first or second postwar inquiry about chapter formation), concluded in an interview that "We've lost something in this bigness." Earlier, in a comment casually made on one facet of contemporary fraternal structure, third-era councilor Nolan Williams, Chi at Oklahoma A. and M. '46, had from a much further distance suggested a somewhat similar perception.

On the same occasion, Williams had stated in 1980 that in many years of professional activity that included tenures on the AAA executive committee and the AICPA council, he had never elsewhere seen a group "so emotionally committed to service" as the members of the Grand Council. Some years earlier, he had written C. Aubrey Smith, Theta at Texas '25, that on joining the governing body he had been "amazed" to learn "the actual impact" that

Beta Alpha Psi "was having and had had on the professional status of the accountant," and that he "treasure[d]" his association with the fraternity more than his affiliation with any other student organization.[7] On the showing of this volume and the prior one, present-day fraternal leaders at local, regional, and national levels are stewards of a heritage that merits such tribute.[8]

---

[7] AAA Road Atlas, p. 36; [Henry R. Anderson], "National Council," 1981-82 Annual Report, ed. [Anderson], p. 2; Anderson to Author, interview, April 18, 1986, quoted; Barron's Profiles, s.v. "Indiana, Ball State University," "Ohio, Miami University"; Milton R. Blood, AACSB, to Author, February 21, 1986; exhibit 4; Louis M. Kessler, "Professional Accounting: Frustration or Fraternity," Newsletter 8 (Winter 1970):9; "Letters from Local Chapters," Newsletter [2] (November 1946):11; Russell [H.] Morrison to David E. Tinius, May 17, 1985, quoted; National Council Minutes, 1968, p. 3, June 1984, p. 13 (both quoted), August 1984, p. 9; "New Chapter Installations," 1983-84 Annual Report, ed. [Metcalf], p. 27; Laura Ray, "The Doors are Opening," The Sun, Winter 1986, p. 4; Sheldahl, Alpha to Omega, pp. [v] (reference to C. Aubrey Smith, based on Theta records), 70; David E. Tinius, "Minorities in Accounting," Newsletter 22 (Winter 1984):1-2, 9; [Tinius], ed., 1984-85 Annual Report, pp. 2 ("President's Report," quoted), 18 ("Chapter Installations"), 34 ("National Advisory Forum"); James A. Viehland, AACSB, to Author (by telephone), February 6, 1985, quoted; Nolan E. Williams to Author, interview, March 21, 1980, quoted; and Williams to C. Aubrey Smith, February 12, 1969 (Golden Anniversary Files), quoted.

[8] In the 1986 interview, Hank Anderson cited the educational careers of Herb Miller, Bob Wasley, Fred Mueller, and (by implication) Doris Cook as particular inspirations to him, commenting that he was "try[ing] to follow in their footsteps." He had served as a councilor with Mueller and Cook, beginning in 1977, more than six years after Secretary-Treasurer Wasley had joined charter FVP Anderson at Northern Illinois to install Gamma Pi. Henry R. Anderson to Author, interview, April 18, 1986; and Robert S. Wasley, Secretary-Treasurer's Report, 1970-71, p. 3.

Two developments of 1986 that came to the author's attention following completion of the text are relevant to the closing section. In May, accounting students from the University of Waterloo, in Ontario, visited Ohio State for a three-day weekend as guests of Omicron. Some of them may have taken part in the '86 "Casey Run," an annual charitable event honoring the memory of chapter alumnus Cornelius Casey, Jr., an avid jogger who suffered a fatal cardiac arrest, at age 34, during a regular five-mile outing in 1984. In August, Larzette Hale of Delta Omega at Utah State was honored as the Accountant of the Year in education, becoming the first black and the first female winner of the fraternity's highest honor. [Thomas J. Burns], The Ohio State University Accounting Hall of Fame and Alumni Breakfast, program brochure for 1986 annual gathering (held in New York, August 21), p. [11, inclusive of title page], quoted; Burns to Author, August 28, 1986; and Laura Forrester, "Casey Dies," The Sun, Winter 1985, pp. 3-4.

APPENDIX 1

QUESTIONNAIRE UNDERLYING INTERVIEWS WITH NATIONAL PRESIDENTS, 1980[a]

Cover Page

BETA ALPHA PSI HISTORY PROJECT: INTERVIEW QUESTIONNAIRE

(Revised Statement)

Use of the questionnaire is intended to lead to productive discussion of the experience and perspective of each subject, as a national president of Beta Alpha Psi. Granting all limitations of the questionnaire, it is hoped that it will facilitate identification of areas of particular relevance and interest in each case.

SECTIONS:

1. Major Highlights of Your Period of Service on the Council
2. Expansion of the Fraternity
3. Objectives of the Fraternity, and Their Pursuit
4. The Human Element in Beta Alpha Psi
5. Local Chapter References
6. Major Contemporary Challenges and Opportunities

1. MAJOR HIGHLIGHTS OF YOUR PERIOD OF SERVICE ON THE COUNCIL

I. Highlights of Your Council Presidency

A. When you became Council president, how did you perceive your office? What kind of "leadership style" seemed appropriate? In the course of your term, did your viewpoint in these areas change?

B. When you assumed the presidency, what issues or problems appeared to be the most significant, or urgent, ones facing the Council?

C. Please specify any important issues which arose, or were identified, during your term. How did you perceive and approach them, and how did they affect pursuit of the original objectives?

D. Did major controversy or division arise <u>within</u> the Council concerning the issues before it?

E. In the light of items B-D, what do you regard as the most important contributions of your term? The most important shortcomings?

F. If not already mentioned, please indicate any major developments during your term regarding Council operating procedures.

G. Please indicate any important area, not already discussed, which the deliberations of your Council in effect placed "on the agenda" for subsequent action.

II. Highlights of Your Full Period of Council Service

A. What were the major issues or problems facing the fraternity during your tenure, and how were they approached?

B. Was there significant controversy or conflict within the Council on these issues?

C. What do you regard as the primary achievements of the Council during this period? The primary shortcomings?

2. EXPANSION OF THE FRATERNITY

A. Briefly discuss major "external" or "environmental" factors relating to <u>expansion</u> of Beta Alpha Psi during your period of service, through both establishment of new chapters and growth of existing ones.

B. Briefly discuss establishment of new chapters during your period of service in terms both of Council policy (or policies) and actual developments, commenting specifically upon the following aspects:

1. Magnitude
2. Types of institutions

3. Geographical patterns
4. Evaluations of petitioners.

C. Was there any significant controversy or conflict within the Council in this area during your tenure?

D. While "site visitation" is now an established part of the evaluation process, financial constraints long forestalled extensive visitation. If you served during such a period of time, please indicate whether the Council felt materially hindered, on this basis, in evaluating petitioners.

E. While you were on the Council, was the attitude of departmental chairmen and deans towards the importance of service as a faculty vice president a significant factor in issuing charters? If so, was a verbal commitment required from them in this regard?

F. On occasion the Council has discussed the possibility of including schools <u>not</u> accredited by the AACSB (for example, in regard to evening programs or branch campuses). However, the traditional policy of excluding such institutions remains intact, pending implementation of a national system for accrediting accounting programs as such.

1. Was this issue a matter of significant concern during your tenure on the Council?
2. What is your own viewpoint on the matter? Please comment, in particular, upon the following positions:

   a. The AACSB requirement is essential, because the Council cannot realistically undertake "evaluation" of accounting programs
   b. The requirement is not essential, because the Council can appeal to established "market" indicators of program quality
   c. The requirement is not essential, because a Beta Alpha Psi chapter should be available to any institution showing strong faculty and student dedication to relevant extra-curricular activity.

G. Recently the Council amended the national constitution to provide for establishment of "alumni" chapters. Please comment upon the prospective importance of this development.

3. OBJECTIVES OF THE FRATERNITY AND THEIR PURSUIT

I. Introductory

A. During your period of service on the Council, was there strong consensus as to:

1. Proper objectives of Beta Alpha Psi?
2. Appropriate means of achieving those objectives?

B. Assuming that there was basic agreement upon objectives within the Council, what were the major obstacles encountered towards communicating this perception to the chapter level?

In your judgment, how successful were the efforts of the Council in this regard?

1. Professor Penz has remarked that new faculty vice presidents sometimes seem genuinely uncertain as to objectives of the society.
2. Did you find there to be a significant problem in this area? If so, how did the Council respond to it?

II. "Professional" vs. "Honorary" Orientation

A. How would you characterize the "professional" dimensions of Beta Alpha Psi?
Was this interpretation generally shared within the Council while you were a member?

B. There is substantial indication that "professional" aspects of the fraternity have generally been emphasized at the national level, from the earliest days. (Scholastic requirements, indeed, have been somewhat upgraded over the years). Yet several of the very early chapters have tended, over prolonged periods of time, to function according to an "honorary-society" concept. Do you find any historical significance in this paradox?

C. The National (Grand) Council has traditionally required respectable, but not superior, academic performance for membership. Many individual chapters have imposed scholastic requirements exceeding national ones.

Briefly discuss your own Council experience in regard to grade requirements, and then address the following questions:

1. Is it realistic in the present day to speak of an "honor" society, if a B (major field) or B- (overall) average is sufficient for membership? [b]
2. Do you favor raising academic requirements at the national level? (Allowance could be made for varying grading standards, by a uniform requirement that members rank in the top X% of their class.)
3. If so, do you think that chapter activities in general should be made available to nonmembers as well as members?

III. The Activity Program

A. The activity program has changed materially since its inception some thirty years ago. Briefly discuss major changes and controversies, if any, which occurred in this area during your service.

(If you served prior to adoption of the activity program, please discuss any controversy that you recall concerning introduction of such a competition.)

B. The "points competition" has from time to time been strongly criticized even by Council supporters of a professional orientation. Is there a realistic alternative to a points competition, in which all chapters must participate?

C. As a result of changes in the program, by which points lost in certain areas may be "made up" in others, numerous chapters have in recent years earned maximum point totals. This result could be interpreted as an indication either of high motivational effectiveness, or insufficient challenge. Please comment upon these perspectives.

D. Several patterns are reflected in results of the points competition over three decades. Please comment on any of the following tendencies or trends that you find interesting:

1. Strong performance by relatively young, or "emerging," institutions, such as several members of the California State University system
2. Strong performance by Southern universities
3. Weak performance (as implied in II-B) by some of the oldest chapters.

IV. Dealing with "Problem" Chapters

A. There is some impression that the Council has been extrememly lenient over the years in dealing with recurringly weak or deficient chapters. For example, only four charters have been withdrawn (at Boston University, William and Mary, Pittsburgh, and UCLA), and in the last three cases there was a prolonged period of complete inactivity.

1. Do you feel that the Council was unduly lenient during your own period of service?
2. Was there significant controversy on this matter within the Council?

B. Do you feel that the Council can as a general rule minimize incidence of "problem" chapters through timely meaningful communication with the local chapters?

1. Discuss constructive approaches taken while you were a Council member towards encouraging acceptable levels of chapter performance, giving any suggestions of your own on the matter.
2. If you served prior to the present era of extensive visitation, did the Council of your period of membership feel significantly hindered in assisting chapters towards improved performance, by the financial capacity of the fraternity?

C. Please comment on the notion that an active policy concerning expansion of the fraternity strengthens the Council's hand in dealing with problem chapters.

V. Relations with the American Accounting Association, and Other Organizations

A. Beta Alpha Psi and the AAA (or equivalent) have been closely associated almost from the start. For example, a number of persons have served as presidents of both groups; many other Councilors have served on the AAA

executive committee; and national meetings have long been held in conjunction with one another.

Nevertheless, there is an impression that in recent years, in particular, the relationship has been rather cool, although the sharing of headquarters in Sarasota suggests a reversal of the assumed trend.

1. Please discuss the relationship between the two groups during your period of national service with Beta Alpha Psi, indicating any specific points of friction.
2. If you have been active in the AAA at the national level, please comment on the matter from that perspective as well.

B. It has been suggested that Beta Alpha Psi might become a "section" of the AAA. Would it be possible for the fraternity to maintain its identity on such a basis?

C. Is the strong current emphasis by the AAA upon rigorous research a potential basis for estrangement from Beta Alpha Psi? If so, would it be realistic, and otherwise appropriate, for the Council to seek significantly closer association with nonacademic "professional" accounting organizations?

Please discuss any major efforts during your own tenure on the Council to cultivate a working relationship with other organizations.

VI. Other Topics

A. Graduate Students as Members

1. Was the role of graduate students as members of the fraternity an area of concern to the Council during your service?
2. Do you think that participation in Beta Alpha Psi can be highly meaningful in the case of masters candidates? Doctoral candidates? Can a predominantly undergraduate chapter realistically expect to serve such students effectively?
3. Chapters within exclusively "graduate" programs (at UCLA, Pittsburgh, Tulane, and Northwestern) have not fared well, in activity terms, and indeed two have been terminated. Would you favor allowing exclusively graduate chapters to remove themselves from the points competition?

B. Accounting Clubs or Societies

1. Is there a plausible role for an active "accounting club" at an institution having a Beta Alpha Psi chapter?
2. Should the National Council attempt to define the appropriate provinces of an accounting club and a Beta Alpha Psi chapter, where both are found at an istitution?
3. Under what circumstances, if any, would a school having an active, well-established accounting club be ill-advised to seek a Beta Alpha Psi charter?

C. Service to Beta Alpha Psi as a Basis for Academic Recognition and Reward

1. Do you feel that service as a faculty vice president is generally appreciated sufficiently by colleagues, department chairmen, and deans?
2. Based upon your own experience and observation, do you feel that service on the National Council, obviously a very demanding commitment, tends to be appreciated sufficiently within the academic community?

D. A prevailing problem is the relatively short time generally available for active membership in Beta Alpha Psi, particularly prior to a student's final term of undergraduate work. Please suggest potential means for reducing this problem.

4. THE HUMAN ELEMENT IN BETA ALPHA PSI

I. Selection of Councilors (Items A and B apply wholly and primarily, in turn, to Councilors who served prior to adoption, in the mid-1970s, of the present method of selection.)

A. While you were on the Council, did the retiring president generally exercise primary discretion in selecting new Council members? Was there general satisfaction within the Council concerning the method of selection?

B. During your tenure, what were the major factors governing selection of new Council members?

C. Having until then been purely an internal matter, the procedure of selecting new Councilors was changed fundamentally a few years ago, so that each faculty vacancy is now filled by vote of the National Chapter, from among three persons nominated by a committee of recently retired members.*

Please discuss this reform in terms of overall impact promised upon governance of Beta Alpha Psi.

II. Reminiscences of Leaders, Personalities, and Unofficial Events

A. Among your fellow Councilors, who stand out as particularly strong personalities, having had significant effect upon the direction of Beta Alpha Psi?

B. Please relate any amusing anecdotes or human-interest stories which come to mind relative to your Council service.

C. Please cite particularly memorable social events which occurred during your period of service.

D. Please provide any reminiscences you might have of Councilors who no longer are living.

5. LOCAL CHAPTER REFERENCES

A. Briefly indicate major highlights of your prior service as a faculty vice president, indicating particular aspects of that experience which had an important influence upon your activity as a Council member.

B. Please cite any interesting chapter traditions of which you are aware.

6. MAJOR CONTEMPORARY CHALLENGES AND OPPORTUNITIES

A. In your judgment, what is the likely impact upon Beta Alpha Psi of current developments regarding (1) accreditation of accounting programs in general, and (2) establishment of "schools of accountancy" in particular?

Please comment from the points of view of:

1. Appropriate and feasible fraternity involvement in policymaking in these areas
2. Major opportunities offered
3. Major challenges presented.

B. Please comment upon other current developments or events in the external environment which promise to have an important impact upon Beta Alpha Psi.

*The Alumni and National Advisory Forum representatives on the Council, who serve terms of one and three years, respectively, likewise are selected on essentially, or partially, a democratic basis.[c]

---

[a]Fred Mueller submitted to a full afternoon of questioning relative to Beta Alpha Psi in November 1979, prior to the development of a questionnaire. An instrument differing only in detail from this one was distributed in advance to the six former presidents interviewed in Texas, Arizona, and Colorado in March 1980. It was also sent to the five men interviewed in the Carolinas the following month, although the refinements were made prior to the approximately hour-long meetings themselves. The revised questionnaire was sent to all ten ex-presidents later interviewed (by some means) in 1980, 1985, or 1986, although not on a very timely basis to C. Aubrey Smith.

[b]As indicated in chapter 3, by 1983 an overall B average was required.

[c]Updated or (in the latter case) corrected coverage of alumni and forum representation on the National Council is provided in chapters 13 and 15.

APPENDIX 2

CHARTER MEMBERSHIPS OF THREE CHAPTERS

*Faculty status (still covered by "honorary" membership when Sigma and Tau were installed)

Sigma, University of Wisconsin, March 14, 1932

Arthur C. Andersen
Roy L. Banker
J(ohn) C. Gibson*[a]
Ray R. Gilson
Edward D. Gruber
Earl C. Hanson
Oliver J. Hanson
John J. Hyland
V. L. Jenkyn
Russell T. Johnson
Haydn R. Jones
Chancey E. Juday
Joseph D. Kane
Bernhard C. Lemke
Keith B. McKy
A. Donovan Mortimer
Paul J. Nebel
Leonard T. Nelson
Paul Neumann
Dayton F. Pauls
Maynard T. Reierson
Norman H. Schuette
Seraph F. Schaenzer
Harold L. Steinhoff
Robert W. Talpick
Earl A. Starks
Gordon Wagner

Tau, University of Maryland, May 18, 1936

John W. Bell
William E. Bell
William H. Brown*
Francis Cave
C. Wilbur Cissel*
H. Daniel Drake, Jr.
Frank P. Duggan
Ernest R. Eaton
Louis Ennis
Isadore Fischer
John G. Hart
Herbert S. Hyatt
Henry Kozloski
Harry Lynn
James Rintoul
Robert Thomas
Sydney Tymeson[b]

Alpha Kappa, Ohio University, January 12, 1952

Jane Baldwin
Ralph F. Beckert*
John E. Biddle
William H. Fenzel*
Royal D. Fritz
Robert E. Jackovich
Richard B. Keyse
Martin W. Luoma
John F. McCoy
Robert N. McDougall
James F. Minor
James B. Patton
E. E. Ray*
Warren H. Reininga*
James C. Ruggles
Eugene A. Sauder
Don L. Sneary
Doris M. Sponseller*
D. Macil Via*
William L. Waters
Richard B. Werner
Frank J. Wojkiewicz
Edgar J. Zorn.

SOURCES: [W. E. Karrenbrock], "Tau Chapter Installed," Newsletter [2]

(October 1936):4; "Local Chapter News," Newsletter [3] (March 1952):31; and [Charles F. Schlatter], "Sigma Chapter Installed," Newsletter [1] (May 1932):3.

[a]Gibson's colleague Fayette H. Elwell had been inducted on an honorary basis by Zeta at North Dakota in 1926. As a professor at another school, Wisconsin, he was an honorary member in the modern sense of the term. F. H. Elwell to Charles W. Taylor, enclosed biogrphical entry drawn from Who's Who in America (ca.) 28 (1954-55), s.v. "Elwell, Fayette Herbert" (Golden Anniversary Files); and Hermann C. Miller, ed., Beta Alpha Psi Directory, s.v. "Zeta Chapter: Elwell, Fayette H."

[b]The final name, shown as "Tymenson" in the 1936 source, has been spelled in accordance with local and national directory records. Becky Adams to Charles W. Taylor, July 2, 1969, Tau Chapter enclosure (Golden Anniversary); and Miller, Beta Alpha Psi Directory, s.v. "Tau Chapter: Tymeson, S. W."

Professor S. M. Wedeberg, an alumnus of Delta at Washington, was also listed by Karrenbrock as a charter member of Tau.

APPENDIX 3

CHAPTERS INSTALLED DURING THE FIFTH AND SIXTH ERAS, 1971-84

NO.	CHAPTER	SCHOOL	CHARTERED
84	Gamma Omicron	California State University, Fresno	
85	Gamma Pi	Northern Illinois University	1971
86	Gamma Rho	Western Michigan University	1971
87	Gamma Sigma	University of New Orleans	1971
88	Gamma Tau	Colorado State University	1971
89	Gamma Upsilon	University of Rhode Island	1971
90	Gamma Phi	University of Texas, Arlington	1971
91	Gamma Chi	Memphis State University	1971
92	Gamma Psi	University of Missouri-St. Louis	1972
93	Gamma Omega	California State University, Long Beach	1972
94	Delta Alpha	University of Wyoming	1972
95	Delta Beta	California State University, Fullerton	1972
96	Delta Gamma	University of South Florida	1972
97	Delta Epsilon	Washington State University	1973
98	Delta Zeta	California State University, Chico	1973
99	Delta Eta	Seattle University	1973
100	Delta Theta	University of Hawaii	1974
101	Delta Iota	Texas A & M University	1974
102	Delta Kappa	University Montana [Univ. 'of' Montana]	1974
103	Delta Lambda	New Mexico State University	1974
104	Delta Mu	University of Virginia	1975
105	Delta Nu	University of Massachusetts	1975
106	Delta Xi	Texas Southern University	1975
107	Delta Omicron	University of Nebraska-Lincoln	1976
108	Delta Pi	Hofstra University	1976
109	Delta Rho	Pacific Lutheran University	1976
110	Delta Sigma	Eastern Washington State College	1976
111	Delta Tau	Drexel University	1976
112	Delta Upsilon	Northern Arizona University	1977
113	Delta Phi	University of Delaware	1977
114	Delta Chi	University of Alabama-Birmingham	1977
115	Delta Psi	Cleveland State University	1977
116	Delta Omega	Utah State University	1977
117	Epsilon Alpha	Portland State University	1977
118	Epsilon Beta	University of South Alabama	1977
119	Epsilon Gamma	University of Central Florida	1977
120	Epsilon Delta	University of Missouri-Kansas City	1977
121	Epsilon Zeta	Virginia Commonwealth University	1977
122	Epsilon Eta	University of North Carolina, Chapel Hill	1978
123	Epsilon Theta	Kansas State University	1978

NO.	CHAPTER	SCHOOL	CHARTERED
124	Epsilon Iota	University of San Francisco	1978
125	Epsilon Kappa	Appalachian State University	1978
126	Epsilon Lambda	University of Connecticut	1978
127	Epsilon Mu	Stephen F. Austin State University	1978
128	Epsilon Nu	Murray State University	1978
129	Epsilon Xi	University of Utah	1978
130	Epsilon Omicron	Auburn University	1978
131	Epsilon Pi	University of Arkansas-Little Rock	1979
132	Epsilon Rho	University of Wisconsin-Whitewater	1979
133	Epsilon Sigma	George Washington University	1979
134	Epsilon Tau	Wichita State University	1979
135	Epsilon Upsilon	Emory University	1979
136	Epsilon Phi	Wayne State University	1979
137	Epsilon Chi	California State University, Northridge	1979
138	Epsilon Psi	California State University, Hayward	1979
139	Epsilon Omega	Eastern Michigan University	1980
140	Zeta Alpha	Purdue University	1980
141	Zeta Beta	Western Illinois University	1980
142	Zeta Gamma	Middle Tennessee State University	1980
143	Zeta Delta	Georgia Southern University	1980
144	Zeta Epsilon	East Texas State University	1981
145	Zeta Eta	Clarkson University	1981
146	Zeta Theta	State University New York-Buffalo	1981
147	Zeta Iota	University of Nevada, Reno	1981
148	Zeta Kappa	University of San Diego	1981
149	Zeta Lambda	Bradley University	1981
150	Zeta Mu	University of Southern Mississippi	1982
151	Zeta Nu	St. Louis University	1982
152	Zeta Xi	Seton Hall University	1982
153	Zeta Omicron	University of Wisconsin-Eau Claire	1982
154	Zeta Pi	Old Dominion University	1982
155	Zeta Rho	Clemson University	1983
156	Zeta Sigma	North Carolina A & T State University	1983
157	Zeta Tau	Lamar University	1983
158	Zeta Upsilon	University of Houston, Clear Lake	1983
159	Zeta Phi	Tennessee Tech University	1983
160	Zeta Chi	University of North Carolina-Greensboro	1984
161	Zeta Psi	Boise State University	1984
162	Zeta Omega	Ball State University	1984

Reprinted from "Chapter Information, 1983-84," 1983-84 Annual Report, ed. [Metcalf], pp. 35, 37.

APPENDIX 4

BETA ALPHA PSI NATIONAL PRESIDENTS, 1946-84

Third Era

1. James M. McConahey, 1941[a]-47
2. Hazen W. Kendrick, 1947-48
3. Thomas M. Dickerson, 1948-49
4. William E. Dickerson, 1949-50
5. Gould L. Harris, 1950-51
6. John Arch White, 1951-52
7. Charles C. Staehling, 1952-53
8. S. M. Wedeberg, 1953-54
9. J. C. Gibson, 1954-55
10. A. J. Penz, 1955-56
11. Wayne E. Shroyer, 1956-57
12. William B. Jencks, 1957-58
13. Williard E. Stone, 1958-59
14. Nolan E. Williams, 1959-60

Fourth Era

1. Robert H. Van Voorhis, 1960-61
2. Herbert E. Miller, 1961-62
3. C. Rollin Niswonger, 1962-63
4. Emerson O. Henke, 1963-64
5. Julius A. Roller, 1964-65
6. Vern H. Vincent, 1965-66

Fourth Era (continued)

7. Wilton T. Anderson, 1966-67
8. Leon E. Hay, 1967-68
9. Vern E. Odmark, 1968-69
10. Harvey E. Donley, 1969-70

Fifth Era

1. Charles W. Taylor, 1970-71
2. Robert S. Wasley, 1971-72
3. Harold E. Royer, 1972-73
4. Hollis A. Dixon, 1973-75
5. Robert S. Maust, 1975-76
6. Fred J. Mueller, 1976-77
7. Doris M. Cook, 1977-78
8. Thomas J. Burns, 1978-79

Sixth Era

1. James W. Pattillo, 1979-80
2. Joyce C. Dean, 1980-81
3. Henry R. Anderson, 1981-82
4. Jack E. Kiger, 1982-83
5. Richard W. Metcalf, 1983-84.

---

[a]Elected December 28, 1941. Grand Council Minutes Book, 1941, pp. 1, 4.

SELECTED BIBLIOGRAPHY

Accounting Education and Practice

AAA Accounting Education News, or Accounting Education News, May 1979 - June 1986. Selected issues.

Anderson, Wilton T. "Highlights of My Life and Career." Issues in Accounting Education, pp. 1-4. Edited by Richard J. Murdock. American Accounting Association, 1983.

Burns, Thomas J., and Coffman, Edward N. The Accounting Hall of Fame: Profiles of Thirty-six Members. [Columbus, Ohio]: College of Administrative Science, Ohio State University, 1976.

Carey, John L. The Rise of the Accounting Profession. 2 vols.: From Technician to Professional, 1896-1936; To Responsibility and Authority, 1937-1969. New York: American Institute of Certified Public Accountants, 1969, 1970.

Hasselback, James R., comp. Prentice-Hall Accounting Faculty Directory, 1978-79 through 1986 eds., omitting 1982 (or 1981-82), 1985. Englewood Cliffs, N.J.: Prentice-Hall, 1979-81, 1983, 1984, 1986.

McConahey, James M. "History of Beta Alpha Psi (The National Accounting Fraternity), from Organization to October 31, 1948, Inclusive." [1949, with annual supplements through January 1954, extending coverage through the fraternal year 1952-53]. 57-page typescript.

Miller, Herbert E. "A Synopsis." Issues in Accounting Education, pp. 5-8. Edited by Murdock.

Penz, A. J. 50 Years: Beta Alpha Psi, 1919 - 1969. [Oxford, Miss.: Printed by rebel Press & Supply Co., for] National Council of Beta Alpha Psi, 1969.

Previts, Gary John, and Merino, Barbara Dubis. A History of Accounting in America: An Historical Interpretation of the Cultural Significance of Accounting. New York: John Wiley & Sons, Ronald Press div., 1979.

Previts, Gary John, and Committe, Bruce, comps. An Index to the "Accounting Review," 1926-1978, and Proceedings of the AAUIA, 1917-1925. Sarasota, Fla.: American Accounting Association, 1980.

Sheldahl, Terry K. Beta Alpha Psi, from Alpha to Omega: Pursuing a Vision of Professional Education for Accountants, 1919-1945. Accountancy in Transition series. Edited by Richard P. Brief. New York and London: Garland Publishing, 1982.

Zeff, Stephen A. The American Accounting Association: Its First 50 Years. [Evanston, Ill.: American Accounting Association, 1966].

Beta Alpha Psi National Files[a]

Beta Alpha Psi Annual Meeting, 1979. Tape recordings of National Chapter Meeting and Awards Banquet. Honolulu, Hawaii, August 21, 1979.

Beta Alpha Psi Annual Report. 10 eds., 1975-76 through 1984-85. Editors, publication dates, and (except for 1983-84) printers not identified in the reports.

Anderson, Henry R., ed. 1981-82 report. Anaheim, Cal.: Orange County Lithgraph, for (as in all cases) National Council, 1982
Burns, Thomas J., ed. 1978-79. Grove City, Iowa: Baesman & Son Printing, 1979
Cook, Doris M., ed. 1977-78. Fayetteville, Ark.: University of Arkansas Printing Service, 1978
Dean, Joyce C., ed. 1980-81. Waco, Texas: Advertising and Marketing Associates, 1981
Kiger, Jack E., ed. 1982-83. Knoxville, Tenn.: Graffix, 1983
Maust, Robert S., ed. 1975-76. Fairmount, W. Va.: Fairmount Printing Co., 1976
Metcalf, Richard W., ed. 1983-84. Sarasota: Dolphin Printing, 1984
Mueller, Fred J., ed. 1976-77. Seattle: Continental Printing, 1977
Pattillo, James W., ed. 1979-80. Notre Dame, Ind.: Notre Dame Press, 1980
Tinius, David E., ed. 1984-85. Sarasota: Dolphin Printing, 1985.

Golden Anniversary Files, 1969. Developed, unless otherwise indicated, by Charles W. Taylor.

Charter membership files, 83 chapters
Newsletter 8 (50th anniv. ed.), ed. Taylor
Kaylor, Norman R., "The Beta Alpha Psi Chapter Activity Program, 1950-69," pp. 2-3
[Taylor, Charles W.], "Charter Members, Alpha to Gamma Xi," pp. 17-24
________ (likewise imputed), "Past Presidents of Beta Alpha Psi, 1919 - 1969," pp. 4-11, 14-15
Resumes and other biographical material collected from or regarding national presidents through Leon E. Hay (1967-68), including numerous clippings from Newsletter issues
Smith, C. Aubrey. Correspondence with fellow ex-councilors, initiated to secure anecdotal material (or fraternal commentary). Files contain preliminary letter to Smith from Charles Taylor, December 16, 1968, and three letters or notes from Smith to Taylor the following July and August; Smith's letter to A. J. Penz, January 7, 1969; responses from 17 former presidents; and undated reply by Smith to Fred W. Woodbridge's letter of March 3.

Grand Council Cashbook, 1931-49.

Grand Council Minutes, 1964. Unbound.

Grand Council Minutes Book, 1922-63. Complete except for minutes of 1932, available in unbound form, and 1934.

McConahey, James M. Correspondence, 1947-54. 72 letters by, to, or (in one case) about McConahey, 1 unrelated letter; 3 enclosures.

Miller, Hermann C. Beta Alpha Psi, The National Accounting Fraternity: Directory. [Columbus, Ohio: Grand Council of Beta Alpha Psi, 1939].

National Constitution; or National Constitution and Statutes; or National Constitution and Bylaws. Two basic structures; titles vary. [1921], [1922], [1924, draft], [1927, draft], 1929, [1936], 1938, 1947, 1949, 1951, 1953, 1956, 1958, 1965, 1971, 1977, 1983, 1985.

National Council Minutes, 1965 - January 1985. Unbound.

Newsletter [1]-22 (1931-84). Vols. 1 (most available issues) through 4, 1931-57, and 13-15 (combined), 1974-77, are bound. Suspended, 1943-46; missing issues, vols. 1, 5-6, 12. All titles include "Newsletter" or "News Letter."

Penz, A. J. Extensive correspondence relating to his Beta Alpha Psi history project, 1966-69. Includes regular communication with National Council, and correspondence with former councilors in 1967 similar to that conducted by C. Aubrey Smith two years later.

Policies File, 1947-53. 42 letters filed by secretary-treasurers.

Secretary-Treasurers' Reports, 1942-46 through 1977-78 (omitting 1973-74, 1976-77).

Visitation Report Files.

1950-60, reports of 102 visits
1960-68, reports of 38 visits (mainly from last two years), plus six related letters, memoranda, or notes.

Business Education or Terminology

AACSB Membership Directory, 1980-81. [St. Louis: American Assembly of Collegiate Schools of Business, 1980].

Beta Gamma Sigma Directory, 1980-81. St. Louis: Beta Gamma Sigma, [1980].

Dirksen, Charles J., and Lockley, Lawrence C. "Development of Collegiate Schools of Business and Activities of AA[c]CSB." The American Association of Collegiate Schools of Business: 1916-1966, pp. 1-18. By Dirksen, Lockley, E. T. Grether, Arthur Kroeger, Ossian MacKenzie, and John T. Wheeler. Homewood, Ill.: Richard D. Irwin, 1966.

"Members of the Accreditation Council." AACSB Membership Directory, 1984-85, pp. 16-24. [St. Louis: AACSB, 1984].

[Prentice-Hall] Encyclopedic Dictionary of Business. New York: Prentice-Hall, 1952.

Collegiate Education

[Barron's] Profiles of American Colleges. 14th ed. Woodbury, N.Y.: Barron's Educational Foundation, 1984.

Brunner, Henry S. *Land-Grant Colleges and Universities, 1862-1962.* Washington, D.C.: U.S. Government Printing Office, 1962.

College Catalog Collection on Microfiche. 1983-84, 1984-85, 1985-86 eds., microfiche. San Diego: Career Guidance Foundation, 1983-86.

The College Handbook, 1984-85. 22nd ed. New York: College Entrance Examination Board, 1984.

Lovejoy, Clarence E. *Lovejoy's College Guide.* 15th ed. [posthumous]. New York: Simon & Schuster, 1981.

Straughn, Charles, and Straughn, Barbarasue Lovejoy, eds. *Lovejoy's College Guide.* 16th ed. New York: Monarch Press, 1983.

Files Developed by Author, or on His Behalf[a]

Penz, A. J. Four fraternal essays of 1980, edited for presentation in chapter 7. Four other Penz essays, including three from 1985 not having fraternal themes, are identified on page 285 (text and note).

Penz, A. J., to Sheldahl, Terry K., and Sheldahl to Penz. Extensive relevant correspondence, occasional telephone communication, and a brief informal interview (Tuscaloosa, Ala., August 15, 1984), 1980-86.

Sheldahl, Terry K.

General fraternal correspondence (supplemented by telephone contact), extensive and varied, 1984-86.

Interviews, or the equivalent, with 22 former Beta Alpha Psi presidents, 1979-86, generally based on questionnaire presented as appendix 1.

Anderson, Henry R. Greenville, S.C., April 18, 1986
Anderson, Wilton T. San Antonio, Texas, March 20, 1980
Burns, Thomas J. Cleveland, Ohio, May 3, 1980
Cook, Doris M. San Antonio, March 20, 1980
Dickerson, Thomas M. Charlotte, N.C., April 19, 1980
Dixon, Hollis A. Tucson, Ariz., March 22-23, 1980
Donley, Harvey E. Cleveland, May 2, 1980
Hay, Leon E. Cleveland, May 2, 1980
Henke, Emerson O. San Antonio, March 21, 1980
Maust, Robert S. Morgantown, W. Va., July 14, 1980
Miller, Herbert E. Columbia, S.C., April 18, 1980
Mueller, Fred J. Columbus, Ohio, November 27, 1979
Odmark, Vern E. Letter, August 13, 1980
Pattillo, James W. Boston, Mass., August 9, 1980
Penz, A. J. Columbia, April 18, 1980

Royer, Harold L. Letter, September 4, 1985
Smith, C. Aubrey. Tape recording (two-part), sent June 1980[b]
Stone, Williard E. Columbia, April 18, 1980
Taylor, Charles W. Columbia, April 18, 1980
Vincent, Vern H. Edwardsville, Ill., July 21, 1980
Wasley, Robert S. Denver, Colo., March 23, 1980
Williams, Nolan E. San Antonio, March 21, 1980.

Interviews with National Advisory Forum member Robert M. Maynard, retired member Robert W. Pivik, and outgoing alumni councilor Nicholas S. Ecos. Boston, August 10, 1980.

Survey of black membership in Beta Alpha Psi, 1946-60, conducted in summer of 1985. Letter sent on July 25 to archivists at 20 of the 21 chapters reactivated after the war (Theta excluded, due to an independent source of information). Full, or 100%, response, July through September. Information requested was provided in one case by a faculty advisor, and in another one by former councilor S. M. Wedeberg.

General Reference Works

AAA Road Atlas: United States, Canada, [and] Mexico. 1985 ed. Falls Church, Va.: American Automobile Association, 1984.

Akey, Denise S., ed. Encyclopedia of Associations: 1985. 19th ed. 5 vols. Detroit: Gale Research Co., 1984. Vol. 1, National Organizations of the United States.

Funk & Wagnalls New Encyclopedia. [1981] ed., c1979. 27 vols.

Information Please Almanac, 1955. New York: Macmillan Co., 1954.

Statistical Abstract of the United States. 68th-71st, 73rd, 75th, 77th, 79th, 81st, 83rd eds. Washington, D.C.: U.S. Government Printing Office, 1947-50, 1952, 1954, 1956, 1958, 1960, 1962.

Who's Who in America 34 (1966-67), 35 (1968-69), 43 (1984-85).

The World Almanac and Book of Facts, 1985. New York: Newspaper Enterprises Association, 1984.

Local Chapter or University Sources

Alpha Chapter. Grand Council correspondence concerning chapter's resistance to activity program. 10 letters. 1953-54, 1958.

Alpha Mu Chapter of Beta Alpha Psi: Membership Directory, University of Kentucky. Lexington, Ky.: Alpha Mu, 1969.

[Burns, Thomas J.] The Ohio State University: The Ph.D. Program in Accounting, 1984, . . ., 1986. [Columbus: College of Administrative Science, Ohio State University, 1983, 1985-86].

Mu Chapter. Grand Council correspondence, and visitation reports, concerning control of chapter by alumni members. 16 letters, 3 reports. 1958-65.

Phillips, Clinton A. Experience with Undergraduate Business Program: Tulane University School of Business. New Orleans: 1964.

Previts, Gary John, ed. Programs in Accounting: The University of Alabama. 5th ed. [University, Ala.: Programs in Accounting and Information Systems, 1974].

Sedlak, Michael W., and Williamson, Harold E. The Evolution of Management Education: A History of the Northwestern University J. L. Kellogg School of Management, 1908-1983. Urbana, Ill.: University of Illinois Press, 1983.

Smith, C. Aubrey. Sixty Years of Accounting Education on the Forty Acres. Austin, Texas: University Stores, 1974.

The Sun. Omicron Chapter newsletter. Winter 1980, 1983, 1984, 1986.

Xi Chapter, Beta Alpha Psi: 1966 Directory, Syracuse University. [Syracuse, N.Y.: Xi Chapter, 1966].

---

[a]Disposition of many of the sources, following their shipment to the national office in Sarasota, will depend on developments concerning a plan to establish a Beta Alpha Psi collection within the University of Illinois Archives. Jan R. Williams, Director of Publications, to Author, February 26, 1985.

[b]Eventually returned to Professor Smith.

INDEX TO VOLUME 1, *Alpha to Omega*

The four categories and their principal subcategories are coded, by letters and numerals, for purposes of cross reference.

Index, Vol. 1

---

[a] In keeping with his leadership role in chapter formation, Dean Hatfield may have been a charter member of Lambda's, and indeed its first faculty advisor. The 1939 directory, however, gives no date for his initiation; national files as of 1969 listed only one original member with faculty status, Charles C. Staehling; and chapter records of that date did not include a listing of the charter brotherhood at California. Becky Adams to Charles W. Taylor, July 2, 1969, enclosure concerning Lambda, Pi, and Rho Chapters; Alan R. Cerf, Lambda FVP, to Taylor, June 18, 1969; and Sheldahl, <u>Alpha to Omega</u>, pp. 146-47. First two items drawn from Golden Anniversary Files.

INDEX TO VOLUME 2, Omega to Zeta Omega

Present-day institutional names are used, with three clearly indicated exceptions (based on textual references) among nonschool organizations.[a]

COLLEGES AND UNIVERSITIES

INDIVIDUALS

ORGANIZATIONS

---

[a]Basic sources used for precise names, respectively, of schools, public accounting firms, and industrial companies are "Education --American Colleges and Universities," World Almanac, 1985, pp. 215-31 (four-year schools), 231-42 (two-year); exhibit 28; and Moody's Industrial Manual: 1986 1, 2.

[b]Public accounting "foundations" are covered under the firm names.

Accounting Books Published by Garland

New Books

Ashton, Robert H., ed. *The Evolution of Behavioral Accounting Research: An Overview.* New York, 1984.

Ashton, Robert H., ed. *Some Early Contributions to the Study of Audit Judgment.* New York, 1984.

*Brief, Richard P., ed. *Corporate Financial Reporting and Analysis in the Early 1900s.* New York, 1986.

Brief, Richard P., ed. *Depreciation and Capital Maintenance.* New York, 1984.

*Brief, Richard P., ed. *Estimating the Economic Rate of Return from Accounting Data.* New York, 1986.

Brief, Richard P., ed. *Four Classics on the Theory of Double-Entry Bookkeeping.* New York, 1982.

*Chambers, R. J., and G. W. Dean, eds. *Chambers on Accounting.* New York, 1986.
Volume I: Accounting, Management and Finance.
Volume II: Accounting Practice and Education.
Volume III: Accounting Theory and Research.
Volume IV: Price Variation Accounting.
Volume V: Continuously Contemporary Accounting.

Clarke, F. L. *The Tangled Web of Price Variation Accounting: The Development of Ideas Underlying Professional Prescriptions in Six Countries.* New York, 1982.

Coopers & Lybrand. *The Early History of Coopers & Lybrand.* New York, 1984.

*Included in the Garland series Accounting Thought and Practice Through the Years.

*Craswell, Allen. *Audit Qualifications in Australia 1950 to 1979.* New York, 1986.

Dean, G. W., and M. C. Wells, eds. *The Case for Continuously Contemporary Accounting.* New York, 1984.

Dean, G. W., and M. C. Wells, eds. *Forerunners of Realizable Values Accounting in Financial Reporting.* New York, 1982.

Edey, Harold C. *Accounting Queries.* New York, 1982.

*Edwards, J. R., ed. *Legal Regulation of British Company Accounts 1836–1900.* New York, 1986.

*Edwards, J. R., ed. *Reporting Fixed Assets in Nineteenth-Century Company Accounts.* New York, 1986.

Edwards, J. R., ed. *Studies of Company Records: 1830–1974.* New York, 1984.

Fabricant, Solomon. *Studies in Social and Private Accounting.* New York, 1982.

Gaffikin, Michael, and Michael Aitken, eds. *The Development of Accounting Theory: Significant Contributors to Accounting Thought in the 20th Century.* New York, 1982.

Hawawini, Gabriel A., ed. *Bond Duration and Immunization: Early Developments and Recent Contributions.* New York, 1982.

Hawawini, Gabriel, and Pierre Michel, eds. *European Equity Markets: Risk, Return, and Efficiency.* New York, 1984.

*Hawawini, Gabriel, and Pierre A. Michel. *Mandatory Financial Information and Capital Market Equilibrium in Belgium.* New York, 1986.

*Hawkins, David F. *Corporate Financial Disclosure, 1900–1933: A Study of Management Inertia within a Rapidly Changing Environment.* New York, 1986.

*Johnson, H. Thomas. *A New Approach to Management Accounting History* New York, 1986.

*Kinney, William R., Jr., ed. *Fifty Years of Statistical Auditing.* New York, 1986.

Klemstine, Charles E., and Michael W. Maher. *Management Accounting Research: A Review and Annotated Bibliography.* New York, 1984.

*Lee, T. A., ed. *A Scottish Contribution to Accounting History.* New York, 1986.

*Lee, T. A. *Towards a Theory and Practice of Cash Flow Accounting.* New York, 1986.

Lee, Thomas A., ed. *Transactions of the Chartered Accountants Students' Societies of Edinburgh and Glasgow: A Selection of Writings, 1886–1958.* New York, 1984.

*McKinnon, Jill L. *The Historical Development and Operational Form of Corporate Reporting Regulation in Japan.* New York, 1986.

Nobes, Christopher, ed. *The Development of Double Entry: Selected Essays.* New York, 1984.

*Nobes, Christopher. *Issues in International Accounting.* New York, 1986.

*Parker, Lee D. *Developing Control Concepts in the 20th Century.* New York, 1986.

Parker, R. H. *Papers on Accounting History.* New York, 1984.

*Previts, Gary John, and Alfred R. Roberts, eds. *Federal Securities Law and Accounting 1933–1970; Selected Addresses.* New York, 1986.

*Reid, Jean Margo, ed. *Law and Accounting: Pre-1889 British Legal Cases.* New York, 1986.

Sheldahl, Terry K. *Beta Alpha Psi, from Alpha to Omega: Pursuing a Vision of Professional Education for Accountants, 1919–1945.* New York, 1982.

*Sheldahl, Terry K. *Beta Alpha Psi, from Omega to Zeta Omega: The Making of a Comprehensive Accounting Fraternity, 1946–1984.* New York, 1986.

Solomons, David. *Collected Papers on Accounting and Accounting Education. (in two volumes)* New York, 1984.

Sprague, Charles F. *The General Principles of the Science of Accounts and the Accountancy of Investment.* New York, 1984.

Stamp, Edward. *Selected Papers on Accounting, Auditing, and Professional Problems.* New York, 1984.

*Storrar, Colin, ed. *The Accountant's Magazine—An Anthology.* New York, 1986.

Tantral, Panadda. *Accounting Literature in Non-Accounting Journals: An Annotated Bibliography.* New York, 1984.

*Vangermeersch, Richard, ed. *The Contributions of Alexander Hamilton Church to Accounting and Management.* New York, 1986.

*Vangermeersch, Richard, ed. *Financial Accounting Milestones in the Annual Reports of United States Steel Corporation—The First Seven Decades.* New York, 1986.

Whitmore, John. *Factory Accounts.* New York, 1984.

Yamey, Basil S. *Further Essays on the History of Accounting.* New York, 1982.

Zeff, Stephen A., ed. *The Accounting Postulates and Principles Controversy of the 1960s.* New York, 1982.

Zeff, Stephen A., ed. *Accounting Principles Through the Years: The Views of Professional and Academic Leaders 1938–1954.* New York, 1982.

Zeff, Stephen A., and Maurice Moonitz, eds. *Sourcebook on Accounting Principles and Auditing Procedures: 1917–1953 (in two volumes).* New York, 1984.

Reprinted Titles

American Institute of Accountants. *Fiftieth Anniversary Celebration.* Chicago, 1937 (Garland reprint, 1982).

American Institute of Accountants. *Library Catalogue.* New York, 1919 (Garland reprint, 1982).

Arthur Andersen Company. *The First Fifty Years 1913–1963.* Chicago, 1963 (Garland reprint, 1984).

*Bevis, Herman W. *Corporate Financial Reporting in a Competitive Economy.* New York, 1965 (Garland reprint, 1986).

*Bonini, Charles P., Robert K. Jaedicke, and Harvey M. Wagner, eds. *Management Controls: New Directions in Basic Research.* New York, 1964 (Garland reprint, 1986).

Bray, F. Sewell. *Four Essays in Accounting Theory.* London, 1953. *Bound with* Institute of Chartered Accountants in England and Wales and the National Institute of Economic and Social Research. *Some Accounting Terms and Concepts.* Cambridge, 1951 (Garland reprint, 1982).

Brown, R. Gene, and Kenneth S. Johnston. *Paciolo on Accounting.* New York, 1963 (Garland reprint, 1984).

*Carey, John L., and William O. Doherty, eds. *Ethical Standards of the Accounting Profession.* New York, 1966 (Garland reprint, 1986).

Chambers, R. J. *Accounting in Disarray.* Melbourne, 1973 (Garland reprint, 1982).

Cooper, Ernest. *Fifty-seven Years in an Accountant's Office. See* Sir Russell Kettle.

Couchman, Charles B. *The Balance-Sheet.* New York, 1924 (Garland reprint, 1982).

Couper, Charles Tennant. *Report of the Trial . . . Against the Directors and Manager of the City of Glasgow Bank.* Edinburgh, 1879 (Garland reprint, 1984).

Cutforth, Arthur E. *Audits.* London, 1906 (Garland reprint, 1982).

Cutforth, Arthur E. *Methods of Amalgamation.* London, 1926 (Garland reprint, 1982).

Deinzer, Harvey T. *Development of Accounting Thought.* New York, 1965 (Garland reprint, 1984).

De Paula, F.R.M. *The Principles of Auditing.* London, 1915 (Garland reprint, 1984).

Dickerson, R. W. *Accountants and the Law of Negligence.* Toronto, 1966 (Garland reprint, 1982).

Dodson, James. *The Accountant, or, the Method of Bookkeeping Deduced from Clear Principles, and Illustrated by a Variety of Examples.* London, 1750 (Garland reprint, 1984).

Dyer, S. *A Common Sense Method of Double Entry Bookkeeping, on First Principles, as Suggested by De Morgan. Part I, Theoretical.* London, 1897 (Garland reprint, 1984).

*_The Fifth International Congress on Accounting, 1938 {Kongress-Archiv 1938 des V. Internationalen Prüfungs- und Treuhand-Kongresses}._ Berlin, 1938 (Garland reprint, 1986).

Finney, H. A. _Consolidated Statements._ New York, 1922 (Garland reprint, 1982).

Fisher, Irving. _The Rate of Interest._ New York, 1907 (Garland reprint, 1982).

Florence, P. Sargant. _Economics of Fatigue of Unrest and the Efficiency of Labour in English and American Industry._ London, 1923 (Garland reprint, 1984).

Fourth International Congress on Accounting 1933. London, 1933 (Garland reprint, 1982).

Foye, Arthur B. _Haskins & Sells: Our First Seventy-Five Years._ New York, 1970 (Garland reprint, 1984).

Garnsey, Sir Gilbert. _Holding Companies and Their Published Accounts._ London, 1923. _Bound with_ Sir Gilbert Garnsey. _Limitations of a Balance Sheet._ London, 1928 (Garland reprint, 1982).

Garrett, A. A. _The History of the Society of Incorporated Accountants, 1885–1957._ Oxford, 1961 (Garland reprint, 1984).

Gilman, Stephen. _Accounting Concepts of Profit._ New York, 1939 (Garland reprint, 1982).

*Gordon, William. _The Universal Accountant, and Complete Merchant . . ._ [Volume II]. Edinburgh, 1765 (Garland reprint, 1986).

*Green, Wilmer. _History and Survey of Accountancy._ Brooklyn, 1930 (Garland reprint, 1986).

Hamilton, Robert. _An Introduction to Merchandise, Parts IV and V (Italian Bookkeeping and Practical Bookkeeping)._ Edinburgh, 1788 (Garland reprint, 1982).

Hatton, Edward. _The Merchant's Magazine: or, Trades-man's Treasury._ London, 1695 (Garland reprint, 1982).

Hills, George S. _The Law of Accounting and Financial Statements._ Boston, 1957 (Garland reprint, 1982).

*A *History of Cooper Brothers & Co. 1854 to 1954*. London, 1954 (Garland reprint, 1986).

Hofstede, Geert. *The Game of Budget Control*. Assen, 1967 (Garland reprint, 1984).

Howitt, Sir Harold. *The History of The Institute of Chartered Accountants in England and Wales 1880–1965, and of Its Founder Accountancy Bodies 1870–1880*. London, 1966 (Garland reprint, 1984).

Institute of Chartered Accountants in England and Wales and The National Institute of Economic and Social Research. *Some Accounting Terms and Concepts*. *See* F. Sewell Bray.

Institute of Chartered Accountants of Scotland. *History of the Chartered Accountants of Scotland from the Earliest Times to 1954*. Edinburgh, 1954 (Garland reprint, 1984).

International Congress on Accounting 1929. New York, 1930 (Garland reprint, 1982).

*Jaedicke, Robert K., Yuji Ijiri, and Oswald Nielsen, eds. *Research in Accounting Measurement*. American Accounting Association, 1966 (Garland reprint, 1986).

Keats, Charles. *Magnificent Masquerade*. New York, 1964 (Garland reprint, 1982).

Kettle, Sir Russell. *Deloitte & Co. 1845–1956*. Oxford, 1958. *Bound with* Ernest Cooper. *Fifty-seven Years in an Accountant's Office*. London, 1921 (Garland reprint, 1982).

Kitchen, J., and R. H. Parker. *Accounting Thought and Education: Six English Pioneers*. London, 1980 (Garland reprint, 1984).

Lacey, Kenneth. *Profit Measurement and Price Changes*. London, 1952 (Garland reprint, 1982).

Lee, Chauncey. *The American Accomptant*. Lansingburgh, 1797 (Garland reprint, 1982).

Lee, T. A., and R. H. Parker. *The Evolution of Corporate Financial Reporting*. Middlesex, 1979 (Garland reprint, 1984).

*Malcolm, Alexander. *A Treatise of Book-Keeping, or, Merchants Accounts; In*

the Italian Method of Debtor and Creditor; Wherein the Fundamental Principles of That Curious and Approved Method Are Clearly and Fully Explained and Demonstrated . . . To Which Are Added, Instructions for Gentlemen of Land Estates, and Their Stewards or Factors: With Directions Also for Retailers, and Other More Private Persons. London, 1731 (Garland reprint, 1986).

*Meij, J. L., ed. *Depreciation and Replacement Policy.* Chicago, 1961 (Garland reprint, 1986).

Newlove, George Hills. *Consolidated Balance Sheets.* New York, 1926 (Garland reprint, 1982).

*North, Roger. *The Gentleman Accomptant; or, An Essay to Unfold the Mystery of Accompts; By Way of Debtor and Creditor, Commonly Called Merchants Accompts, and Applying the Same to the Concerns of the Nobility and Gentry of England.* London, 1714 (Garland reprint, 1986).

Pryce-Jones, Janet E., and R. H. Parker. *Accounting in Scotland: A Historical Bibliography.* Edinburgh, 1976 (Garland reprint, 1984).

Robinson, H. W. *A History of Accountants in Ireland.* Dublin, 1964 (Garland reprint, 1984).

Robson, T. B. *Consolidated and Other Group Accounts.* London, 1950 (Garland reprint, 1982).

Rorem, C. Rufus. *Accounting Method.* Chicago, 1928 (Garland reprint, 1982).

*Saliers, Earl A., ed. *Accountants' Handbook.* New York, 1923 (Garland reprint, 1986).

Samuel, Horace B. *Shareholder's Money.* London, 1933 (Garland reprint, 1982).

The Securities and Exchange Commission in the Matter of McKesson & Robbins, Inc. Report on Investigation. Washington, D.C., 1940 (Garland reprint, 1982).

The Securities and Exchange Commission in the Matter of McKesson & Robbins, Inc. Testimony of Expert Witnesses. Washington, D.C., 1939 (Garland reprint, 1982).

*Shaplen, Robert. *Kreuger: Genius and Swindler.* New York, 1960 (Garland reprint, 1986).

Singer, H. W. *Standardized Accountancy in Germany. (With a new appendix.) Cambridge, 1943 (Garland reprint, 1982).*

The Sixth International Congress on Accounting. London, 1952 (Garland reprint, 1984).

*Stewart, Jas. C. (with a new introductory note by T. A. Lee). *Pioneers of a Profession: Chartered Accountants to 1879.* Edinburgh, 1977 (Garland reprint, 1986).

Thompson, Wardbaugh. *The Accomptant's Oracle: or, Key to Science, Being a Compleat Practical System of Book-keeping.* York, 1777 (Garland reprint, 1984).

*Vatter, William J. *Managerial Accounting.* New York, 1950 (Garland reprint, 1986).

*Woolf, Arthur H. *A Short History of Accountants and Accountancy.* London, 1912 (Garland reprint, 1986).

Yamey, B. S., H. C. Edey, and Hugh W. Thomson. *Accounting in England and Scotland: 1543–1800.* London, 1963 (Garland reprint, 1982).

ACCOUNTING THOUGHT AND PRACTICE THROUGH THE YEARS

Edited by Richard P. Brief

A Garland Series